Global Issues
Politics, Economics, and Culture

Third Edition

Richard J. Payne

Illinois State University

Longman

Boston   Columbus   Indianapolis   New York   San Francisco   Upper Saddle River
Amsterdam   Cape Town   Dubai   London   Madrid   Milan   Munich   Paris   Montreal   Toronto
Delhi   Mexico City   São Paulo   Sydney   Hong Kong   Seoul   Singapore   Taipei   Tokyo

Acquisitions Editor: Vikram Mukhija
Associate Editor: Donna Garnier
Editorial Assistant: Toni Magyar
Marketing Manager: Lindsey Prudhomme
Production Manager: Renata Butera
Project Coordination, Text Design, and Electronic Page Makeup: Joseph Malcolm/
    GGS Higher Education Resources, PMG
Creative Art Director: Jayne Conte
Cover Designer: Mary Siener
Cover Illustration/Photo: Stocktrek / Corbis and Duncan Smith / Getty Image, Inc
Manufacturing Buyer: Renata Butera
Printer and Binder: Courier Stoughton
Cover Printer: Courier Stoughton

Library of Congress Cataloging-in-Publication Data
Payne, Richard J.
 Global issues : politics, economics, and culture / Richard J. Payne.—3rd ed.
    p. cm.
 Includes bibliographical references and index.
 ISBN-13: 978-0-205-77908-6 (alk. paper)
 ISBN-10: 0-205-77908-5 (alk. paper)
 1. Globalization—Textbooks. 2. World politics—Textbooks. I. Title.
 JZ1318.P39 2011
 303.48'2—dc22

                                           2009042330

1 2 3 4 5 6 7 8 9 10—CRS—13 12 11 10

Longman
is an imprint of

www.pearsonhighered.com

ISBN-13: 978-0-205-77908-6
ISBN-10:   0-205-77908-5

BRIEF CONTENTS

To Elaine Cook Graybill
and
Alyson Sue McMillen

DETAILED CONTENTS

PREFACE

The global financial crisis and economic recession of 2008–2009 vividly underscored how the realities of globalization affect our lives as well as the relative decline of the power of states to act unilaterally to solve major problems. These crises also rekindled debates about the negative and positive aspects of globalization and supported the thesis that great powers generally decline because of their own actions and internal weaknesses. America's global leadership and its capitalist system are challenged to a much greater extent by rising powers such as China, India, and Brazil. The financial crisis and economic recession have profoundly affected virtually all global issues—from human rights, migration, the promotion of democracy, and inequality to the environment, trade, crime, and infectious diseases.

Throughout history, pivotal events have significantly altered perspectives on, and approaches to, academic disciplines. Terrorist attacks on the United States reinforced the need for scholars, political leaders, policymakers, international organizations, nonstate actors, and individuals to focus even more on global issues in an age of increasing globalization. Globalization links the fates of countries, intergovernmental organizations, nonstate actors, and individuals to an unprecedented degree.

My decision to write this textbook was strongly influenced by the need for a comprehensive, accessible, and student-oriented introductory textbook for undergraduates that focuses specifically on global issues. This text concentrates on global issues that students around the world are passionate about because they are directly related to the forces of globalization that are integral components of their lives. The issues discussed in this book are both primary global concerns and those in which students have shown great interest. This book's pedagogical features are based on classroom experiences that demonstrate how to help students understand complex concepts, develop critical-thinking skills, and engage in problem-solving.

NEW TO THIS EDITION

The global financial crisis and the economic recession have profoundly affected global issues. Consequently, this edition includes a new chapter on the financial crisis. It also covers

- New developments such as the swine flu (H1N1) pandemic, the escalation of the drug war along the U.S.-Mexican border, piracy off the Somali coast, greater emphasis on inequality, and reverse migration.
- Emerging powers and emerging markets receive greater attention as power shifts among nations and regions.
- Given their lethality, assault weapons, land mines, and cluster bombs are included in the discussion on weapons proliferation.
- Greater emphasis has been given to ethnic conflicts, Russia's growing assertiveness, and efforts by the United States to improve relations with the Muslim world.

- All the chapters have been substantially revised and updated to reflect current developments, especially the impact on global issues such as the global financial crisis and economic recession.
- Based on feedback from reviewers of the second edition, some chapters have been shortened and reorganized and pedagogical features have been enhanced.

FEATURES

Global Issues: Politics, Economics, and Culture is based on ten philosophical components that are interwoven into each chapter and throughout this book in order to provide students with:

1. A clearer understanding of how the powerful forces of economic, financial, cultural, political, environmental, and military globalization are affecting governments, nonstate actors, and individuals.
2. A deeper awareness of the growing inability of governments, nonstate actors, and individuals to neatly compartmentalize problems within countries outside broader global developments.
3. An appreciation for the complexities of global problems and their interdependence.
4. A broader sense of the global issues and problems in developing countries.
5. An historical background to many global issues that enables students to see continuity and change in human experiences.
6. A deeper awareness of how globalization is profoundly challenging the state-centric emphasis that dominates international relations and world politics.
7. A foundation for more advanced courses on globalization and global affairs.
8. An understanding of basic concepts and theories and an ability to evaluate and apply them to real-life events and problems.
9. An ability to think critically, develop independent judgment, and sharpen intellectual curiosity and imagination.
10. A recognition of the power of individuals, including students, to have a positive impact on global problems.

The text is composed of fourteen chapters, each focusing on a specific topic and related subtopics. The global issues covered in this book are widely regarded to be of critical importance by both the global community and instructors. In addition to providing instructors with the flexibility to stimulate student participation, the range of issues allows sufficient time during a semester to cover each chapter and to incorporate various pedagogical approaches. Instructors will have enough time to review for exams, administer at least three exams, and allow students to present research papers and other projects. This book can be easily supplemented with subscriptions to publications such as the *New York Times*, the *Washington Post*, the *Wall Street Journal*, or *Foreign Affairs*, enabling students to obtain more current examples of the global issues discussed in these pages.

As a comprehensive introduction to global issues for students from different academic disciplines, *Global Issues* is written in a style that makes information very accessible. A more conversational writing style engages students, encourages them to relate what they read to global developments and their own lives, facilitates the development of analytical skills, and makes it easier for them to engage in discussions. Above all, it attempts to present a clear, straightforward discussion of interesting and important global issues without obscuring their complexity.

- **Chapter Introductions** The introduction provides a brief overview of the main points in the chapter, tells students what is covered, and provides examples of controversial issues included in the chapter to stimulate students' interest in the material.
- **Current Examples** Consistent with the decision to adopt an accessible writing style, I have included many brief and current examples of global issues throughout the book. These examples make global issues more immediately relevant for students and encourages them to develop a concrete understanding of specific problems.
- **Historical Background** Each chapter provides practical historical background information to give students an understanding of the issue's broader context.
- **Cross-Referenced Issues** Chapters are cross-referenced to help students see the interrelatedness and interdependence of global issues. For example, by reading Chapter 10, "Environmental Issues," students will explore the impact of economic globalization on the environment and culture as well as the relationships among environmental issues, global and domestic inequality, economic development, migration, cultural conflicts, and the spread of infectious diseases.
- **"You Decide" Boxes** These boxes encourage students to be active participants. They discuss controversial issues and then ask students to evaluate them and make a decision. They engage students in problem-solving activities, help them develop critical thinking skills, and encourage classroom discussions.
- **Maps and Photographs** Maps help to put issues in context and enable students to better grasp essential points discussed in the text. Carefully selected photographs portray specific developments and capture students' attention.
- **Tables** Tables throughout the book help students understand important points discussed in the text.
- **Boldfaced Key Terms and Definitions** These are designed to draw students' attention to definitions, concepts, key terms, and main points. Stressing their importance reinforces the point that they are the building blocks of the chapter.
- **Marginal Glossaries** Small boxes in the margins define key terms and give students a quick reference to important definitions and concepts.
- **End-of-Chapter Summaries** These provide a brief review of the chapter. They focus students' attention on major points and help them to improve their comprehension and retention of the information.
- **End-of-Chapter Questions and List of Key Terms** These questions and key terms are designed to improve students' retention of information, stimulate discussions in study groups, and help students prepare for exams.
- **Suggested Readings** A list of suggested readings is included at the end of each chapter to familiarize students with scholarly literature and to help them gain additional information.

- **Index** This listing allows students to quickly find key terms, concepts, names, and subjects discussed throughout the text. Many students find the index especially helpful when reviewing for exams.

SUPPLEMENTS

Longman is pleased to offer several resources to qualified adopters of *Global Issues* and their students that will make teaching and learning from this book even more effective and enjoyable. Several of the supplements for this book are available at the Instructor Resource Center (IRC), an online hub that allows instructors to quickly download book-specific supplements. Please visit the IRC welcome page at **www.pearsonhighered.com/irc** to register for access.

For Instructors

MyPoliSciKit Video Case Studies. Featuring video from major news sources and providing reporting and insight on recent world affairs, this DVD series helps instructors integrate current events into their courses by letting them use the clips as lecture launchers or discussion starters.

 Test Bank. This assessment resource includes multiple-choice, true-false, and essay questions for each chapter in this text. Available exclusively at the IRC an online hub that allows instructors to quickly download book-specific supplements. Please visit the IRC welcome page at www.pearsonhighered.com/irc to register for access.

For Students

MySearchLab. Need help with a paper? MySearchLab saves time and improves results by offering start-to-finish guidance on the research/writing process and full-text access to academic journals and periodicals. To learn more, please visit www.mysearchlab.com <http://www.mypoliscikit.com/> or contact your Pearson representative. To order MySearchLab with this book, use ISBN 0205719341.

 Longman Atlas of World Issues (0-321-22465-5). Introduced and selected by Robert J. Art of Brandeis University and excerpted from the acclaimed Penguin Atlas Series, the *Longman Atlas of World Issues* is designed to help students understand the geography and major issues facing the world today, such as terrorism, debt, and HIV/AIDS. These thematic, full-color maps examine forces shaping politics today at a global level. Explanatory information accompanies each map to help students better grasp the concepts being shown and how they affect our world today. Available at no additional charge when packaged with this book.

ACKNOWLEDGMENTS

I am deeply indebted to many students who made significant contributions to this collaborative and interdisciplinary project. Feedback from students in my Global Issues courses over the years has been invaluable and has contributed to making the book accessible to other students. I am also indebted to many research assistants, especially Yu Bo, Lara Saba, Brian Zednick, Janet Schultz, Natalie Mullen, Anthony DiMaggio, Nadejda Negroustoueva, Lindsay Barber, Meaghan Gass, Jake Owen, and Vanda Rajcan.

I am grateful to many colleagues who read the manuscript, made useful suggestions, and shared their insights. I would like to thank Michele Ganschow, Jamal Nassar, and Cherie Valentine of the Department of Politics and Government at Illinois State University; Laura Berk of the Department of Psychology at Illinois State University; Kelly Keogh of Normal Community High School; Carole J. Cosimano of the Illinois Humanities Council; Mikhail Alexseev of San Diego State University; Lindsey Back of Morehead State University; Eric Budd of Fitchburg State College; Brad T. Clark and M. Dawn King of Colorado State University; Mark E. Denham and Richard F. Weisfelder of the University of Toledo; Erich Frankland of Casper College; Mark Haas of Duquesne University; Barbara Hufker of Webster University; Mark Martinez of California State University at Bakersfield; Daniel McIntosh of Slippery Rock University; Anjana Mishra of Florida International University; Luis Antonio Payan of the University of Texas at El Paso; George Quester of the University of Maryland; Timothy Russell of the University of Memphis; Houman Sadri of the University of Central Florida; Tom Schrand of Philadelphia University; Mark Schroeder of the University of Kentucky; Boyka Stefanova of University of Texas–Austin; and Thomas J. Volgy of the University of Arizona.

I would also like to thank Michele Ganschow for her invaluable assistance, as well as Kay Stultz of Institutional Technology Service; and Eric Stano, Toni Magyar, Lindsey Prudhomme, and Vikram Mukhija at Pearson Longman. Above all, I am especially indebted to Jason C. F. Payne for helping me with the chapter on the global financial crisis and to Elaine Cook Graybill for her support, insights, and suggestions throughout the process of writing this book.

Richard J. Payne

Global Issues: Challenges of Globalization

INTRODUCTION

The ongoing violence in Iraq and Afghanistan, terrorism in Pakistan and India, the terrorist attacks on the United States on September 11, 2001, the global financial crisis and economic recession of 2008 and 2009, the emergence of swine flu (H1N1) as a pandemic in 2009, the escalation of drug wars along the U.S.-Mexico border, and rising pirate attacks emanating from the failed state of Somalia have a significant impact on how much of the world thinks about security and the ability of governments to protect individuals. A general sense of global insecurity underscores how easily national boundaries are crossed and the difficulty of distinguishing between external and internal threats in an age of globalization. Thomas Friedman in *The World Is Flat* discusses how globalization has transformed relations among nations and individuals. However, widespread economic problems have shaken confidence in globalization. Walden Bello, for example, articulates this development in his book *Deglobalization: Ideas for a New World Economy*.

Revolutions in technology, transportation, and communication and the different ways of thinking that characterize interdependence and globalization are exerting pressures on nation-states that strengthen them in some ways but weaken them in others. Globalization—especially economic, financial, cultural, and environmental globalization—has spawned debates around the world. These debates illustrate both the significant resistance to and the widespread acceptance of globalization. The financial and economic crises of 2008 and 2009 reinforced these concerns, as unemployment increased, as manufacturing in America, Europe, and Japan declined, and as the implications of outsourcing jobs to China, India, and elsewhere became more obvious. Although some aspects of globalization are embraced as positive, others are rejected as destructive to cultures, the environment, and political and economic institutions, especially in poorer countries.

This chapter illustrates the economic, political, and cultural aspects of globalization. Like all the chapters in this book, it demonstrates how politics, economics, and culture are intricately linked in an increasingly complex global society. It also examines the causes of globalization, various forms of globalization, periods of globalization, and the debates about globalization.

FROM INTERNATIONAL RELATIONS TO GLOBAL ISSUES

International Relations ■ The relations among the world's state governments and other actors

Peace of Westphalia ■ The treaty that concluded the Thirty Years' War in 1648

State ■ A legal and political unit that must be internationally recognized, be politically organized, and be a populated geographic area that has sovereignty

Sovereign ■ The ability of a state to be independent and free from the control of another state

Ideology ■ A system of values, beliefs, and ideas

Nation ■ A group of people who identify as a political community based on common territory, culture, and other similar bonds

International relations is essentially concerned with the interaction of states. Such interactions are almost as old as human societies, although the oldest states are traced back to China and Ethiopia. The modern state emerged in Western Europe in 1648, following the **Peace of Westphalia**, which ended thirty years of war among various groups of princes and between political leaders and the Catholic Church. International relations, international politics, and world politics, which are all closely related, focus on states as the main actors. States are often referred to as nations, and most students of international relations use the terms *states* and *nations* interchangeably. They also use the term *nation-state*. The terms *state* and *nation* are related, but they are not exactly the same. A **state** is essentially a political unit composed of people, a well-defined territory, and a set of governing institutions. It is regarded as **sovereign**. This means that it is recognized by other states as having the exclusive right to make its own domestic and foreign policies. In other words, it is an independent actor in world politics. The United States is composed of diverse populations and is based on primarily an **ideology**. All states have ideologies, or systems of values, beliefs, and ideas. A **nation** is generally defined as a group of people who have strong emotional, cultural, linguistic, religious, and historical ties. Despite these differences between states and nations, the two concepts have become linked in everyday usage, and many scholars and practitioners of international relations use the term **nation-state** to capture this linkage.[1]

International relations focuses on three main questions:

1. What are the contexts in which states operate, and how do these contexts shape or influence the decisions governments make?
2. What are the major objectives and interests of states in international politics, and what strategies do they employ to achieve them?
3. How are the choices made by states explained?[2]

At the heart of these questions is the concept of power. Power is defined as the ability to get others to do things they would not ordinarily do or to behave in ways they would prefer to avoid. Central to an understanding of international relations is the view that the interactions among countries are characterized by a struggle for power.[3] This emphasis on states as the dominant, almost exclusive, actors in world politics is referred to as the **state-centric model**.

All fields of study are concerned with theories. The general purpose of a **theory** is to describe, explain, and predict how humans behave or how things work in the real world under certain circumstances. A theory is generally defined as an orderly, logical, integrated set of ideas or statements about human behavior or things in our environment. All theories provide conceptual frameworks and simplify complex realities.

PLURALISM AND INTERDEPENDENCE

A theory marking the transition from traditional international relations to global issues is pluralism and interdependence. Although this approach views states as the most important actors in world politics, it takes **nonstate actors** (i.e., organizations that are not formally associated with governments) into consideration. Its main concern is with how human activities are intertwined and interconnected across national boundaries. It is increasingly clear that new and far-reaching forces of globalization are having such profound effects on the world that how we approach international relations must also be significantly transformed. James N. Rosenau and Mary Durfee have concluded that "daily occurrences of complex and uncertain developments in every region of the world are so pervasive as to cast doubt on the viability of the long-established ways in which international affairs have been conducted and analyzed."[4] The rapid proliferation of states as well as nonstate actors, revolutions in technology and communications, the growing sophistication and global views of many ordinary citizens, and the changing nature of conflicts are all contributing to the complex environments in which we live.[5] State failure and the inability of governments to effectively address a wide range of global issues reinforce this transformation of international relations.

The violence and threat of violence that accompanied the emergence of modern states led to the pervasive emphasis on military power as the highest priority of states. The fear of losing territory or being eliminated was very real. It is estimated that 95 percent of the state-units in Europe at the beginning of the sixteenth century have been destroyed or combined to make other countries.[6] The devastating effectiveness of military force and the development of nuclear weapons that threatened the extinction of most of the world made countries, especially the superpowers, extremely reluctant to use military force.

In addition to terrorism, there are other nontraditional threats to national security. Economic competition, the global financial crisis, population growth and migration, organized crime, drug trafficking, environmental problems, poverty, inequality, the globalization of diseases, piracy, and ethnic conflicts are among the threats to security. Recognition of these threats is strengthening the concept of human security in an increasingly global society. **Human security** is viewed as being linked to challenges that human beings face every day, most of which are not primarily related to military power. The concept of human security focuses on seven categories of threats.[7] They are

1. Economic security (an assured basic income)
2. Food security (access to an adequate supply of food)
3. Health security (access to basic health care)

Nation-State ■ Nations and states that have similar boundaries where the people identify with the nation and establish a state for themselves

State-Centric Model ■ The view that world politics is dominated almost exclusively by state actors

Theory ■ Predicts how humans behave or how things work in the real world under specific circumstances

Nonstate Actors ■ Organizations that are not formally associated with governments and play a crucial role in setting the international agenda

Human Security ■ A concept of security that deals with the everyday challenges humans face that don't involve military issues

4. Environmental security (access to clean water, clean air, etc.)
5. Personal security (safety from physical violence and threats)
6. Community security (safety from ethnic cleansing and genocide)
7. Political security (protection of basic human rights and freedoms)

Global Politics ■
Political issues and activities that have implications for most of the world

Global Norms ■
A set of basic values that are increasingly common to human societies

Global Issues ■
Encompass traditional international relations and worldwide politics

The growing complexity of our world is generally viewed as giving rise to a new period in international relations, or postinternational politics.[8] This transition is characterized by greater attention to interdependence and globalization, and a stronger emphasis on global politics in particular and global issues in general. **Global politics** refers to political issues and activities by states and nonstate actors that extend across national boundaries and that have implications for most of the world. But the concept of global politics inadequately portrays how economic, cultural, environmental, and demographic factors, among others, are creating a global society with **global norms** (i.e., a set of basic values that are increasingly common to human societies). This book focuses on **global issues**. Stressing global issues indicates a recognition of how globalization intertwines many aspects of human activities and how essential it is to adopt an interdisciplinary approach in order to understand our world and its impact on our daily lives.

THE GROWTH OF THE MODERN STATE

Humanism ■ A system of thought that centers on human beings and their values, capacities, and worth

Renaissance ■ The humanistic revival in Europe of classical art, architecture, literature, and learning

The state emerged over several centuries through struggles for power among institutions, groups, and individuals with military, economic, cultural, religious, and political interests. As we will see, the power of ideas played a pivotal role in the process. The spread of **humanism**—with its emphasis on the study of ancient Greek and Hebrew texts, which concentrated on the Bible—strengthened individualism and critical thinking. Humanism was accompanied by the **Renaissance**, which evolved in Italy in the fourteenth century and marked the transition from the Middle Ages to modern times. Like humanism, the Renaissance concentrated on the individual, self-consciousness, creativity, exploration, and science. The combination of ideas, technological developments, ambition, the quest for freedom, and the constant struggle for power radically altered accepted practices, institutions, and patterns of authority. Because the Catholic Church was the dominant institution in Western Europe following the decline and fall of the Roman Empire, it was inevitably the target of those advocating change. Challenges to the Catholic Church were strengthened by the development of technology, namely, the printing press. **Johann Gutenberg** (1397–1468) invented the printing press around 1436, just as the Chinese and Koreans had done earlier.

Johann Gutenberg ■
(1397–1468); German inventor of the printing press

As the Church's influence eroded, queens, princes, and kings in Europe attempted to enhance their own power by promoting national consciousness and territorial independence. They were assisted in their efforts to consolidate their secular authority within their territories by the Protestant Reformation. This does not mean that European royalty emerged with an antireligious character. In fact, a clear separation of church and state within European countries is still a subject of debate today. This religious transformation was gradual. The most outspoken critic of the Catholic Church was **Martin Luther** (1483–1546), a professor of

Martin Luther ■
(1483–1546); German theologian and Reformation leader

theology at the University of Wittenberg who had been motivated to act by the campaign for selling indulgences (i.e., pardons of temporal or secular punishment due to sin) in Germany.[9] European monarchs also formed alliances with merchants to weaken the Catholic Church and the Holy Roman Empire. Small political units made it extremely difficult to engage in profitable trade and other economic transactions beyond their limited boundaries. Larger, unified political systems were beneficial to businesses because of uniform regulations and fewer taxing jurisdictions, and the enhanced ability of larger areas to enforce the laws. These economic interests coincided with the various monarchs' desire to collect more taxes in order to acquire military technology and build larger armies.

Traveling through Europe, one notices that many towns are dominated by old castles. These castles symbolized not only military strength but also the political and economic independence of local barons. Refinement of cannons and the availability of gunpowder enabled Europe's kings and queens to effectively challenge barons and others and to consolidate their power over increasingly larger areas. Between 1400 and 1600, large numbers of the smaller political entities lost their independence.[10] An excellent example of how Europe's monarchs strengthened internal control as they tried to weaken the power of the Catholic Church is provided by England's King Henry VIII in 1534. Named Defender of the Faith in 1521 for his strong support of the Catholic Church, the king clashed with Rome when he decided to divorce his first wife, Catherine of Aragon, on the grounds that she could not produce a son. Instead of retreating after being excommunicated by the pope, King Henry VIII persuaded England's Parliament to make him Protector and Only Supreme Head of the Church and Clergy of England, thereby creating the Anglican Church. By taking control of England's Catholic Church and its assets, the king ignited the spark of English nationalism and increased his own economic, political, and religious power.

Religious, cultural, political, economic, and technological developments ultimately led to the outbreak of the Thirty Years' War in 1618. The German Protestant princes, who also fought each other, were allied with France, Sweden, Denmark, and England against the Holy Roman Empire, represented by the Hapsburgs of Spain and the Catholic princes. The Hapsburgs, also concerned about maintaining their own power, often clashed with each other.[11] The Thirty Years' War had devastating consequences for Germany. Two-thirds of the population perished and five-sixths of the villages in the empire were destroyed. Those who survived experienced great hardship.[12]

SOVEREIGNTY

Pressures for change that spread across Europe were accompanied by the formulation of new philosophies. The interaction of the power of ideas and change is demonstrated by **Jean Bodin** (1530–1596) and his major contribution to the modern idea of sovereignty. Bodin was a French social and political philosopher and lawyer. During the last half of the sixteenth century, France was experiencing severe disorder, caused primarily by conflicts between Roman Catholics and the **Huguenots** (i.e., French Protestants who were followers of John Calvin).

Jean Bodin ■
(1530–1596); French social and political philosopher and lawyer

Huguenots ■
French Protestants who were followers of John Calvin

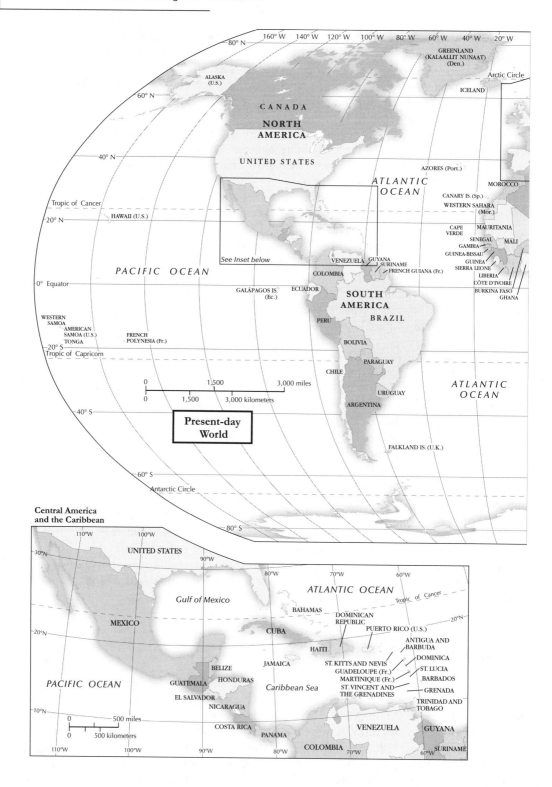

Present-day World

Central America and the Caribbean

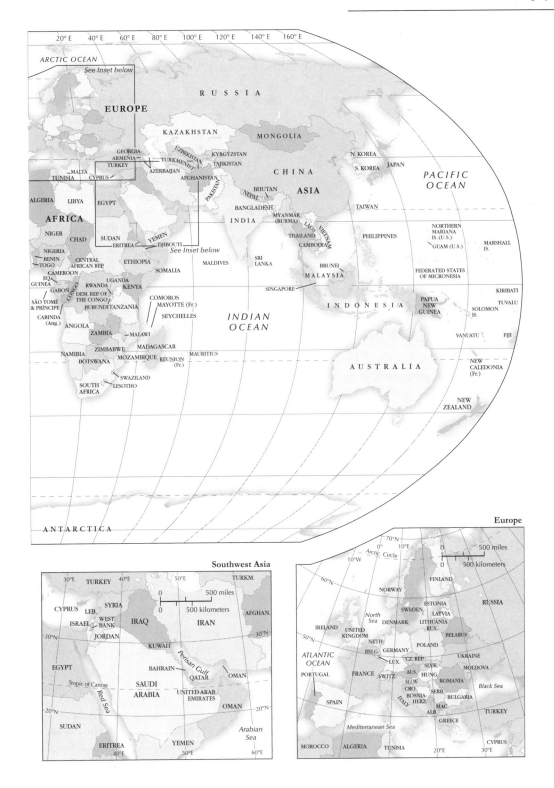

Southwest Asia

Europe

Bodin believed that order could be restored through a combination of greater religious tolerance and the establishment of a fully sovereign monarch. In his **Six Books on the Commonwealth** (or state), Bodin stressed that the state, represented by the king, was sovereign.

Universal Catholic laws that governed Europe were replaced by **international law**. Leaders and scholars realized that states also needed a system of rules and norms to govern their interaction and to establish order and predictability. This view was articulated by **Hugo Grotius** (1583–1645). Grotius was a Dutch lawyer, author, strong advocate of natural law, and is regarded as the father of international law. Grotius stressed that sovereign states were governed by natural law because they were composed of human beings who were ruled by nature and because it was in the interest of sovereign states to support an international legal system. A second component of the new international system was **diplomacy**. Diplomats, their possessions, and their embassies were regarded as extensions of sovereign states and accorded extraordinary legal protections. A third component of the system for maintaining international order was the balance of power, which attempted to prevent a state or group of states from becoming strong enough to dominate Europe. Finally, the new international system would rely on common cultural values and family connections to avoid disorder.[13]

There has always been a gap between the ideal of sovereignty and the actual realization of sovereignty. Sovereignty is used in at least four ways:

1. *International legal sovereignty*, which focuses on the recognition of a state's independence by other states and respect for its territorial boundaries.
2. *Westphalian sovereignty*, which focuses on the exclusion of other states from the affairs of the government that exists within a given territory.
3. *Internal or domestic sovereignty*, which refers to the rights of the government or formal organization of political authority within a state to exercise a monopoly of power over social, economic, political, and other activities within its borders.
4. *Interdependence sovereignty*, which reflects the realities of globalization. It is concerned with the ability of governments to control or regulate the flow of people, money, trade, environmental hazards, information, and ideas across national boundaries.[14]

The Decline of Sovereignty

Information and technological revolutions and the ease of international travel are contributing to the erosion of a state's control over its population as well as to the decline of citizens' identification with the state, two of the key components of sovereignty. Although most governments continue to exert significant influence over their domestic economies, many governments are perceived as "mere salesmen, promoting the fortunes of their own multinational corporations in the hope that this will provide a core prosperity that keeps everyone afloat."[15] The global financial crisis in 2008 and 2009 underscores this reality. The United States, Britain, and other countries implemented policy to diminish the negative economic consequences of problems emanating from subprime loans.

International Law ■ An international system of rules created to govern the interaction of states and to establish order

Hugo Grotius ■ (1583–1645); Dutch lawyer, author, strong advocate of natural law, and the father of international law

Diplomacy ■ The practice of conducting international relations

THE EUROPEAN UNION: REDEFINING SOVEREIGNTY

In 2001, the mark was replaced with the **euro**, the common currency of most countries of the European Union. Just as the dollar is a symbol of American power and independence, the mark symbolized German power and sovereignty. Compared with America, where sovereignty remains a powerful and positive idea, European states are voluntarily relinquishing some of their sovereignty to achieve political and economic objectives. European leaders redrew the map of Europe by extending the fifteen-member European Union eastward to include twelve additional countries, most of them former Communist bloc countries. This unprecedented European expansion created a new Europe that has a population of 491 million and the world's largest economy. The general view is that European countries are modifying their sovereignty on a scale not seen since the Emperor Charlemagne tried to unify Europe twelve hundred years ago.[16] However, the global economic crisis is undermining European unity as the twenty-seven countries turn their attention to their own domestic problems and adopt varying approaches to solve them.

Devastating wars, as we have seen, were instrumental in the growth of sovereignty and the rise of the modern state. But many Europeans began to believe that excessive sovereignty and nationalism were leading causes of wars that engulfed the continent and destroyed the most basic aspects of security and independence. This was especially the case in World War II. Statesmen such as **Jean Monnet** and **Robert Schuman** of France and **Paul Henri Spaak** of Belgium were visionaries who believed that a united Europe, in which traditional sovereignty would be redefined, was essential to preserving peace and security and preventing another European holocaust. The basic idea was that controlling coal and steel (materials essential for war) would ultimately result in the reconciliation of Europe. France and Germany, the two principal antagonists, would combine their coal and steel production. In 1957, France, Germany, Italy, Belgium, the Netherlands, and Luxembourg signed a treaty that led to the creation of the Coal and Steel Community, the first major European institution. The Europeans signed the **Treaty of Rome** in 1957, which established both the European Economic Community and the European Atomic Energy Community (EURATOM). Since then, in many areas of political and economic life, power has been gradually transferred from the state level to the European Union and its various institutions.[17] For example, the **European Court of Justice** has powers that are similar to those of the U.S. Supreme Court. It has weakened the sovereignty of states by declaring that the laws of the European Union are supreme in relation to the laws of individual states.

Euro ■ Common European currency established by the European Union

Jean Monnet ■ French statesman and distinguished economist

Robert Schuman ■ French prime minister after World War II who proposed the Schuman plan for pooling the coal and steel resources of West Europe

Paul Henri Spaak ■ Foreign minister of Belgium who was elected first president of the General Assembly of the United Nations

Treaty of Rome ■ Established the European Economic Community as an economic alliance

European Court of Justice ■ A judicial arm of the European Union, based in Luxembourg

THE RISE OF NONSTATE ACTORS

Nonstate actors, or **nongovernmental organizations (NGOs)**, are not formally associated with states or the authority structures of states, although they often cooperate with the government to achieve their goals. Transnational NGOs operate across national boundaries and have achieved significant influence in world affairs. Their rapid proliferation, from around two hundred in 1909 to more than twenty-six thousand today, and their wide range of activities have led many observers to conclude that their emergence is almost as important as the rise of the nation-state.

NGOs ■ Organizations that are not part of a government

There are several types of NGOs. These include

Economic organizations, such as transnational corporations;

Advocacy organizations, such as Greenpeace and Amnesty International;

Service organizations, such as the International Red Cross and Doctors Without Borders;

Transnational terrorist organizations that seek to undermine governments; and

Transnational criminal organizations that focus on profiting from illegal activities.

With the exception of terrorist and criminal NGOs, nonstate actors have played *four main roles* that are generally accepted by states and international governmental institutions:

1. *Setting Agendas:* NGOs often force national policymakers to include certain issues on their agendas.
2. *Negotiating Outcomes:* NGOs work with governments and business groups to solve global problems.
3. *Conferring Legitimacy:* Organizations, such as the World Bank, and transnational corporations derive legitimacy from the support or approval of various NGOs.
4. *Making Solutions Work:* Many governments and intergovernmental organizations rely on NGOs to implement their decisions in areas such as humanitarian relief and economic development.[18] Two of the oldest and most significant nonstate actors are the Catholic Church and transnational corporations.

The Catholic Church

On the streets outside the Palazzo Montecitorio, where the lower house of Italy's Parliament meets, crowds gathered to participate in an historic event on November 14, 2002. Pope John Paul II was scheduled to address eight hundred lawmakers and national leaders, including Prime Minister Silvio Berlusconi. Given the fact that Italy is predominantly Catholic, you are probably wondering why such an address would be significant. The pope's speech marked the first time a head of the Catholic Church had ever made an appearance in the Italian Parliament.[19] Much of Italy, unlike the rest of Europe, continued to be ruled by popes until the middle of the nineteenth century. In 1871, Italy was largely free of control by the papal authorities, and popes were deprived of almost all their land. A compromise between the Vatican and the Italian government was reached in 1929, when the **Lateran Treaty,** negotiated with **Benito Mussolini,** the Italian dictator and leader of the fascist movement, was signed. The Italian government recognized Vatican City as fully sovereign and independent, and the Vatican recognized the Italian government.

The Vatican has voiced strong opinions on social, economic, political, and military issues, especially under the leadership of Pope John Paul II. For many years the Catholic Church strongly opposed communism and reached out to Catholics in Poland and other communist bloc countries in an effort to

Lateran Treaty ■
A compromise between the Vatican and the Italian government

Benito Mussolini ■
Italian fascist dictator and prime minister from 1922 to 1943

Pope Addressing
Italy's Parliament.

(Enrico Oliverio-Pool/
Getty Images)

undermine communist rule. Pope John Paul II, a native of Poland, played a major role in the fall of communism in Eastern Europe. But the pope also criticized the West for its extreme materialism and individualism, as well as for its tolerance of poverty and inequality in the developing countries. The Catholic Church condemned the proliferation of nuclear weapons in the United States, Russia, and other countries and opposed America's military action against Iraq.

Transnational Corporations

A **multinational corporation** (MNC) is generally defined as a national company that has many foreign subsidiaries. These subsidiaries are basically self-contained, making what they sell in a particular country, buying their supplies from that country, and employing that country's citizens. **Transnational corporations** are structurally different from MNCs. A transnational corporation is organized as a global entity. Although selling, servicing, public relations, and legal matters are local, planning, research, finance, pricing, marketing, and management are conducted with the world market in mind.[20] Companies were instrumental in the conquest and settlement of North America, India, Southern Africa, and elsewhere. The **British East India Company** was in effect the government of British-controlled areas of India for a long time. The **Dutch West India Company** was granted a charter that allowed it to make agreements and alliances with leaders of conquered areas, to construct fortifications, to appoint and discharge governors, to raise armies, to provide administrative services, and to maintain order.[21]

MNC ■ A company that operates in more than one country and depends on interdependence for the operation of its enterprise

Transnational Corporations ■ Organizations with a global outlook and operations

British East India Company ■ Established under a royal charter of Queen Elizabeth I for the purposes of spice trading; it launched British rule of India

Dutch West India Company ■ Trading and colonizing company, chartered by the States-General of the Dutch republic in 1621 and organized in 1623

Multinational Companies and Patriotism

Although many of you think of the Caribbean islands as sunny places that provide a refuge from winter, many corporations have long regarded Bermuda, the Cayman Islands, the Bahamas, and elsewhere as tax havens, places of refuge from the U.S. Internal Revenue Service. Compared with many Caribbean islands, the United States is not an especially friendly tax environment. But under U.S. tax law, a company can have its headquarters in the Cayman Islands without having any operations or management there. Prior to September 11, 2001, President George W. Bush pressured the thirty members of the Organization for Economic Cooperation and Development (OECD) to end their opposition to such offshore tax havens. But when Stanley Works of Connecticut proposed to reincorporate in Bermuda in February 2002, it ran into strong opposition. Many Americans regarded the practice of moving to Bermuda and elsewhere to avoid taxes as unpatriotic. Their opposition grew as global trade and jobs became central issues in the 2008 and 2009 economic depression.

However, the financial and economic crisis underscored how globalization has complicated the operations of global companies. In fact, there are numerous tax shelters in many states in America, such as Delaware. Many companies that remain in the United States have used legal devices to avoid paying taxes. However, the economic recession has spawned both economic nationalism and protectionism. Outsourcing of manufacturing jobs in North America and Europe has become a very emotional issue.

1. Do you consider it unpatriotic for companies to move their headquarters overseas to avoid paying taxes?

2. Will the financial and economic crisis result in permanent job losses in America?

Source: Jonathan Weisman, "A Question of Patriotism," *The Washington Post National Weekly Edition,* 2–8 September 2002, 19. ■

INTERDEPENDENCE AND GLOBALIZATION

Interdependence ■
A political and economic situation in which two states are simultaneously dependent on each other for their well-being

Human societies have always been characterized by varying degrees of interdependence. **Interdependence** in world affairs, as it is in private life, involves mutual dependence and cooperation. This means that what happens in one place usually has consequences elsewhere. A war in Iraq, for example, drives up the price of gas at your neighborhood gas station. Countries rely on each other for raw materials, security, trade, and environmental protection. Their fates are intertwined, and they share a sense of mutual vulnerability, although some states are clearly more vulnerable than others in some areas. At the heart of the concept of interdependence is reciprocity.[22]

Globalization ■
The integration of markets, politics, values, and environmental concerns across borders

Globalization refers to shrinking distances among the continents, a wider geographic sense of vulnerability, and a worldwide interconnectedness of important aspects of human life, including religion, migration, war, finance, trade, diseases, drugs, and music. Globalization implies a significant and obvious blurring of distinctions between the internal and external affairs of countries and the weakening of differences among countries. Some countries, and groups within countries, are more entangled in the networks of globalization than others. Although globalization is generally regarded as the Americanization of the world, America itself was, and continues to be, profoundly shaped by the forces of globalization.[23]

CAUSES OF GLOBALIZATION

The process of globalization has been occurring for a long time, and, like most changes, it has been marked by advances and retreats, by hope and disappointment. But it marches on. The causes of globalization are inseparable from the human desire to explore, to gain greater physical and economic security, to be creative and curious, and to move from one place to another. When some of our ancestors left Africa, they began the process of globalization. But migration, like other causes of globalization, did not occur without the assistance of some basic forms of technology. The movement of large numbers of people from one part of the world to another over a relatively short time was facilitated by improvements in transportation. Canal building, the development of navigational equipment (such as the compass), the ability to construct stable oceangoing vessels, and the development and improvement of railways helped to speed up migration. Improved transportation also made it easier to conduct trade over long distances and to colonize new areas. Together with revolutions in communications, transportation plays a crucial role in shrinking distances and in creating greater interdependence.

Advances in military and medical technologies have also driven globalization. Military technology, as we have seen, allowed states to consolidate power internally and subsequently to challenge other states for power and dominance. The ability to mount a cannon on a ship gave a country a decisive advantage over its opponents and also allowed the countries possessing them to expand commerce and to acquire territories. The spread of empires is inseparable from innovations in military power. Perhaps nothing reminds us more about our interdependence than nuclear weapons and other weapons of mass destruction. Our security is still greatly determined by the ability of nuclear powers to preserve the strategic balance and to prevent the use of nuclear weapons. Our sensitivity to how military weapons link our fates was heightened during the **Cold War** (i.e., the competition between the United States and the Soviet Union that occurred after World War II). We have entered into an age of uncertainty heralded in by the use of both conventional and unconventional weapons by terrorist organizations. Medical technology has assisted globalization, and its inability to successfully control infectious diseases, such as AIDS, increases our sense of vulnerability in a global society.

As Table 1.1 indicates, commerce and finance provided the foundation for many of these advances. A major cause of globalization is **financial market expansion**. The availability of finance encouraged more economic interactions, innovation, entrepreneurship, and the development of new technologies. As Chapter 7 demonstrates, the global financial crisis affects nearly all aspects of globalization. New technologies made it easier to conduct trade, migrate, conquer territories, and resist diseases. These new technologies have now spread around the world, speeding up innovation and strengthening competition. Michael Pettis argues that globalization takes place largely because investors are willing to take risks.[24]

Global communications have been facilitated by the spread of the English language around the world during an earlier period of globalization. America's dominant technological, economic, military, and cultural position in the world helps to reinforce the centrality of English in all aspects of global life. The communications revolution is regarded as the major cause of globalization because it directly affects economic, financial, military, cultural, environmental, and criminal globalization.

Cold War ■ The hostile relations between the two superpowers, the United States and the Soviet Union, from 1945 to 1990

Financial Market Expansion ■ The global expansion of national markets

TABLE 1.1

PERIODS OF MONETARY EXPANSION AND GLOBALIZATION

Period	New Technologies and Commercial Applications
1807–1844	Extensive canal building, railway boom, steam power used in manufacturing, improved machine tool design, invention of McCormick's reaper, commercial gas-lighting, and development of the telegraph
1851–1873	Advances in mining, railways and shipping, and rapid growth of corporations
1881–1914	Increased productivity in Europe and the United States, improvements in steel production and heavy chemical manufacturing, first power station, spread of electricity, development of the internal combustion engine, and developments in canning and refrigeration
1922–1930	Commercialization of automobiles and aircraft, spread of artificial fibers and plastics, new electrical appliances invented, and telephone ownership grows
1960–1973	Development and application of transistor technology, advances in commercial flying and shipping, and the spread of telecommunications and software
1985–Present	Rapid growth in computer memory and information processing, advances in biotechnology and medical technologies, and commercial use of the Internet

Source: Michael Pettis, "Will Globalization Go Bankrupt?" *Foreign Policy*, No. 126 (September/October 2001), 56–57.

FORMS OF GLOBALIZATION

Among the most important forms of globalization are (1) economic and trade globalization, (2) financial globalization, (3) political globalization, (4) military globalization, (5) cultural globalization, (6) environmental globalization, and (7) criminal globalization. Although we will discuss each of these forms separately, they cannot be neatly separated from each other in the real world.

Economic Globalization

Economic Globalization ■ Free trade, open markets, and competition in the world economy

Economic globalization may be defined as the intercontinental exchange of products, services, and labor. This form of globalization has a long history and has intensified with the emergence of new technologies and their diffusion to major parts of the world. MNCs have been instrumental in globalization of both production and distribution networks. Consumers worldwide use similar products made by the same corporations. Buying an American brand or any other national brand is complicated by the nature of economic globalization. Economies around the world develop greater capability to produce and export goods as they obtain capital, technology, and access to distribution networks. As trade increases, competition intensifies, leading to lower prices and the elimination of companies that cannot effectively compete in the global market. Global competition and the shrinking of space combine to divide the world into areas that specialize in making products that require low-skilled labor.[25]

Economic globalization also includes the movement of people and the exchange of ideas. The most innovative companies encourage the formation of **global teams** that operate across national borders. Multinationals usually have training camps that help to create a common corporate culture. Engineers from India, Japan, Germany, Australia, and elsewhere who work for Hewlett-Packard, for example, work with their American counterparts in Los Gatos, California. Increasingly, leaders of several major U.S. corporations are from other countries. For example, Citigroup is headed by Vikram S. Pandit of India; Chevron's chief executive is David O'Reilly, a native of Ireland; and Texaco is led by Indra K. Nooyi of India. Economic globalization has also stimulated the development of **global cities**, such as New York, London, Tokyo, Shanghai, Hong Kong, Milan, Sidney, Zurich, and Chicago. Companies put their headquarters in major cities to take advantage of the services of lawyers, accountants, consultants, and advertising firms.

Global Teams ■
Groups of employees who work across national borders in MNCs

Global Cities ■
Major financial cities where companies place their headquarters

Financial Globalization

Terrorist attacks on the World Trade Center and the Pentagon on September 11, 2001, sent shock waves through financial markets worldwide, painfully demonstrating direct linkages among American, European, Asian, and Latin American economies. The financial world reacted in a synchronized manner, with each market that opened the day following the attacks falling precipitously in the first few minutes. A flood of sell orders inundated the Tokyo Stock Exchange, delaying the opening and pushing the benchmark Nikkei index down 6 percent. All of the major stock markets declined dramatically in the week after the terrorist attacks, as Figure 1.1 shows.

Financial problems spread across the world almost instantaneously, reflecting how revolutions in telecommunications and computers have linked financial institutions. The financial crisis of 2008 and 2009 reflected this reality. America borrowed 80 percent of the world's surplus savings in 2008.[27]

Four basic developments drive financial globalization, leading to the expansion and deepening of global finance. The first is the *consolidation of financial institutions* in most countries. Local banks were, until about two decades ago, largely locally owned and operated. The second development is the *globalization of operations*, which is evident everywhere as banking conglomerates extend their reach by forming strategic alliances with similar institutions in different countries. The third development is the emergence of *new technologies* that are familiar to all of us. Money moves across national boundaries at the touch of a button. The fourth development is the *universalization of banking*. Growing competition in financial markets, the increasing irrelevance of national borders, and the increasingly complex relationships among businesses have contributed to a blurring of bank and nonbank financial services.[28]

Other forms of globalization have strengthened financial globalization. When the British Empire stretched across much of the world,

STOCK INDEXES	PERCENT CHANGE
Britain	- 2.7%
S. and P. 500	**- 4.9**
Canada	- 5.9
Argentina	- 6.8
Nasdaq	**- 6.8**
Dow Jones ind. avg.	**- 7.1**
Spain	- 7.6
Japan	- 7.7
France	- 8.5
New Zealand	- 8.8
Australia	- 9.0
Germany	- 9.3
Hong Kong	-10.5
Brazil	-11.6
Italy	-11.9
South Korea	-13.3
Mexico	-14.7
Singapore	-14.8
Thailand	-18.1

FIGURE 1.1

Financial Market Response to Terrorists' Attack on September 11, 2001

Source: The New York Times, 18 September 2001, C3

**Bretton Woods
System** ■ A post-
World War II arrange-
ment for managing
the world economy;
its main components
are the World Bank
and the International
Monetary Fund

World Bank ■ A
UN agency that deals
with monetary aid
transfers to develop-
ing nations, usually
via a loan program
varying from nation
to nation

IMF ■ Established
in 1944 to prevent
countries from
defaulting on their
loans and to make
financing available

Eurodollar ■ The
process of European
banks accepting
dollars and not
changing them into
national currency

OPEC ■ Formed by
major oil-producing
nations in response
to the control of the
world oil market
by seven major oil
companies

**Political Globaliza-
tion** ■ The prolifer-
ation of international
and regional organi-
zations composed of
states and the
spread of nonstate
political actors

**Multilateral Institu-
tions** ■ Organiza-
tions composed of
many states pursuing
common objectives

the British pound became the strongest and most desirable currency. As British power receded, America rose to international prominence and the U.S. dollar became the leading global currency. In 1944, the United States, Britain, and other countries held a conference at Bretton Woods, New Hampshire, to determine the international financial order. The conference established the **Bretton Woods System,** which required the currencies of other countries to have an exchange rate fixed to the dollar, with the dollar fixed in terms of gold at $35 an ounce. This arrangement gave the United States significant influence over the international money supply. The global financial crisis of 2008 and 2009 challenged this system by weakening the United States and strengthening China.

The Bretton Woods System set up the **World Bank** (also known as the International Bank for Reconstruction and Development) to help stimulate Europe's economic recovery after the devastation of World War II. It also created the **International Monetary Fund (IMF)** to implement the rules of the international financial system and to help countries experiencing short-term balance-of-payment and liquidity problems. IMF loans, which now go primarily to developing countries, are given with certain conditions attached (e.g., reducing government spending, eliminating trade barriers, cutting social subsidies, devaluing currencies, and removing artificial barriers to foreign investment). As Europe recovered, and as the Soviet Union and other countries deposited their dollar holdings in West European banks, European banks receiving deposits in dollars simply kept them instead of changing them into the national currencies. The practice resulted in the growth of **Eurodollar** funds. Large U.S. budget deficits—caused partly by the Vietnam War, domestic inflation, and the practice of many American companies of depositing their foreign currency earnings in European banks—weakened the U.S. dollar and strengthened the Eurodollar. These developments eventually contributed to the collapse of the Bretton Woods System. On August 15, 1971, President Richard M. Nixon decided that the dollar was no longer to be freely convertible into gold, thereby ending fixed exchange rates. Furthermore, large financial surpluses accumulated by oil-exporting countries as a result of the quadrupling of oil prices by the **Organization of Petroleum Exporting Countries (OPEC)** in 1973 increased the liquidity of international banks. These financial institutions had approximately $50 billion to recycle through the world economy.[29] These developments provided the foundation for the current wave of financial globalization.

Political Globalization

Political globalization is characterized by the acceptance of states, the relative power of states, the proliferation of international and regional organizations composed of states, and the spread of nonstate political actors. The competition that dominated relations between the United States and the Soviet Union during the Cold War is an example of political globalization. The behavior of these superpowers had global implications, including the threat of a global nuclear holocaust. Most of the emphasis on political globalization is concentrated on the spread of **multilateral institutions**. These are organizations composed of many states pursuing common objectives and include international intergovernmental organizations (IGOs), such as the United Nations, the European Union, the Organization of American States, and the British Commonwealth.

Politics is both local and global. Many policies that were once considered to be primarily of local or national concern are now global, which suggests the strengthening of **policy interdependence**. In other words, national policies of one country are intertwined with those of other countries, and many national problems can be solved only through global cooperation. States form **international regimes** to cope with problems generated by complex interdependence. Regimes are essentially institutions designed to regulate the behavior of their members. The basic goal is to establish orderly and predictable interactions to secure the interests of those participating in these international institutions. At the heart of most international regimes is the concept of **global governance**, which refers to collective actions taken to establish international institutions and norms to deal with national and global issues.[30]

Policy Interdependence ■ National policies of one country are intertwined with those of other countries

International Regimes ■ International institutions designed to regulate the behavior of their members

Global Governance ■ Collective actions taken to establish international institutions and norms to deal with national and global issues

Military Globalization ■ Networks of military force that operate internationally

Military Globalization

Human societies have generally relied on the use of force to achieve certain objectives. The rise of great powers, the spread of civilizations, the age of imperialism, the dominance of one nation over others, and the rise of the nation-state itself, as we have seen, were inseparable from the application of military force. In a very real sense, military globalization is an integral part of other forms of globalization. **Military globalization** is characterized by extensive as well as intensive networks of military force. This includes both the actual use of force and threats to use violence. The most obvious example of military globalization is the nuclear age and the proliferation of weapons of mass destruction. The balance of terror created by nuclear weapons threatens the future not only of the countries that have them but also of all human existence on the earth. *Military globalization is demonstrated by several developments in modern history*. These include

1. The *competition among European powers and territorial expansion* that resulted in the colonization of Asia, Africa, and the Americas;
2. The emergence *of international alliances and international security regimes*, such as the Concert of Europe and the North Atlantic Treaty Organization (NATO);
3. The *proliferation of weapons and military technologies worldwide*; and
4. The creation of global institutions to deal with military issues, such as the nuclear nonproliferation regime.[31]

Cultural Globalization

Looking at the shelves in the local grocery store, one is likely to find more salsa than ketchup. Indian curry dishes have replaced fish and chips as Britain's most popular fast food. Management meetings at big banks such as Deutsche Bank in Germany and Credit Suisse in Switzerland are routinely conducted in English. Airbus, the European aircraft manufacturer, uses English as its official language. In fact, from Asia to Europe, English is the dominant language of business, entertainment, and finance. These examples show that societies are increasingly linked culturally and socially.

As we will discuss in Chapter 2, the transregional and transcontinental flow of cultural influences usually accompanies the expansion of economic and military power. In other words, **cultural globalization**—which involves the exchange of food, music, people, products, ideas, and technology across national boundaries—has very deep roots. Few people in Europe stop to think that potatoes came from South America, and few Americans realize that their cattle came from Europe and their corn came from Mexico. The spread of ideas, technology, and products from China and other parts of Asia through the Middle East to Western Europe profoundly influenced the development of Western civilization. Imagine America without Christianity. Christianity, like Islam, originated in the Middle East and later spread across the world. Although cultural globalization is often equated with Americanization, it is a very complex development.[32]

Sports, which have generally been associated with nationalism, are one of the most obvious and emotional aspects of cultural globalization. World Cup soccer (football), watched by billions of people around the world, demonstrates the global passion for sport. Demonstrations against the 2008 Olympic Games in China due to China's human rights violations, its support for Sudan's policies in Darfur, and its actions against protesters in Tibet also underscore the nature of cultural globalization. The globalization of sports has been accompanied by the development and enforcement of rules for athletes around the world.

Cultural Globalization ■ The spread of one culture across national borders

Environmental Globalization

Visitors to Boston generally observe that extremely valuable land in the center of the city has been preserved as a public park. The Boston Common was originally used by the city's residents as a place where their cattle could graze. When discussing the environment, it is useful to think of our planet as a common. We are all affected by what happens to it, and the problems can be solved only through the cooperation of the global community. **Environmental globalization** focuses on the interdependence among countries in relation to problems such as global warming, the spread of infectious diseases, air and water pollution, deforestation, the loss of biodiversity, and threats to endangered species. Environmental globalization refers to the impact that environmental problems in one part of the world have on distant places.

Environmental Globalization ■ The interdependence of countries to work together to solve environmental problems

Criminal Globalization

Terrorist attacks in the United States on September 11, 2001, represented an extreme form of criminal globalization and diminished the attention given to less dramatic but almost equally dangerous transnational criminal activities. The terrorists used the instruments of globalization to achieve their objectives. Criminal globalization is the intercontinental spread of global crime and its impact on governments and individuals. As Chapter 12 shows, criminal globalization includes transborder crimes, such as drug trafficking, money laundering, prostitution, alien smuggling, arms trafficking, piracy, and counterfeiting. National boundaries have never been effective barriers to the conduct of transnational crimes. As globalization has expanded, criminal organizations have deepened and widened their activities. Furthermore, globalization has imposed on governments certain burdens, such as smaller public budgets, decentralization, privatization, deregulation, and an open environment that is more conducive to criminal globalization.[33]

PERIODS OF GLOBALIZATION

Because globalization is a process that advances and retreats, that is more intense at some points than at others, it is artificial to divide it into distinct periods. However, for discussion, we can identify *five waves of globalization* in the constant sea of change that defines human experience.

The *first wave of globalization* is as old as human civilization. For more than five thousand years human beings from different places have interacted, mostly through trade, migration, and conquest. Globalization was occurring long before the language of globalization came into existence.[34]

The *second wave of globalization* is closely associated with the Western European conquest of Asia, Latin America, and Africa and the spread of capitalism to these areas. This wave of globalization continues to influence developments within and among societies today. **Dependency** theorists view this period of globalization as being profoundly influential on global politics and trade.

The *third wave of globalization*, which began around 1870 and declined around 1914, was marked by breakthroughs in technological development, the global production of primary commodities as well as manufactured products, and mass migration. Less-expensive transportation costs, the switch from sails to steam power, the development of railways, the availability of capital, and the reduction of trade barriers combined to fuel global economic growth. Vast areas of land in North America, Argentina, Australia, and elsewhere were cultivated, and agricultural products were exported. The production of primary products led to the demand for labor. In addition to the Africans and others who were already providing labor, about 60 million Europeans migrated to North America and Australia to work on farms. Argentina, Australia, New Zealand, and the United States became some of the richest countries in the world by exporting primary commodities and importing people, institutions, capital, and manufactured products.[35] This explosion of global activities was followed by a retreat into nationalism from 1914 to 1945. World War I was followed by the Great Depression and a wave of protectionism, led by the United States. America attempted to protect its economy by enacting the **Smoot-Hawley Tariff Act** in 1930, a move that led to retaliation abroad. Between 1929 and 1933, U.S. imports fell by 30 percent and exports fell by almost 40 percent.[36]

The *fourth wave of globalization*, from 1945 to 1980, was spurred by the retreat of nationalism and protectionism and the strengthening of internationalism and global cooperation, led by the United States. The removal of trade barriers was selective, but institutions—such as the World Bank, the IMF, and the General Agreement on Tariffs and Trade (GATT)—were formed to encourage global trade and development. Many developing countries, relying on the

Dependency ■ Belief that industrialized countries benefit from the present capitalist economic system at the expense of poor countries

Smoot-Hawley Tariff Act ■ Act that brought the U.S. tariff to the highest protective level in the history of the United States exports of primary commodities, continued to be marginalized and disadvantaged in the global economy. This period of globalization was characterized by both cooperation and conflict. Efforts to encourage nations to work together in the United Nations were weakened by the rivalry between the United States and the Soviet Union. Although the economic aspects of globalization are usually emphasized, the most important form of globalization during this period was military globalization, dominated by the constant threat of a nuclear war between the superpowers.

The *fifth wave of globalization*, which is the current period, is characterized by unprecedented interdependence among nations and the explosive growth of powerful nonstate actors.

RESISTANCE TO GLOBALIZATION

Overall, many countries, groups, and individuals who resist globalization do so because they equate it with westernization in general and Americanization in particular. Many see such problems as global inequality and conflict as direct results of globalization. However, much resistance to globalization comes from France and the United States, two countries that play a pivotal role in the process of globalization.

France's opposition to globalization is strongly linked to its desire to retain control over its borders and to preserve its culture. Although France has been instrumental in creating European organizations that clearly diminish national sovereignty, it also sees a weakening of sovereignty as a factor that facilitates the invasion of France by immigrants, most of whom are Muslims from North Africa. **Jean-Marie Le Pen**, the leader of France's National Front Party, views these immigrants as threats to his country's economy, culture, and national identity. France also resists globalization because it perceives it as an Anglo-Saxon threat to the French cultural model, which is portrayed as a "high-brow" culture of philosophers, fine dining, and intellectual films. Globalization is equated with the "low-brow" uniformity of American culture—fast food, bad clothing, and, even worse, sitcoms.[37] Globalization is also seen as promoting American individualism. France, on the other hand, values a strong centralized government that can provide essential benefits for the people as a whole. The election of Nicolas Sarkozy as France's president in 2007 and the election of Barack Obama as America's president in 2008 moderated friction between the two countries.

Jean-Marie Le Pen ■ Leader of France's far-right National Front Party

Consider America's resistance to globalization. On several fronts, Americans are increasingly embracing a view of sovereignty that rejects participation in a number of international regimes dealing with the environment, war crimes, land mines, arms control, and human rights. Even as President George W. Bush reiterated his confidence in the United Nations, he treated the organization as largely irrelevant to the achievement of America's objectives in the Persian Gulf, the Middle East, and elsewhere. Many American intellectuals and policymakers defend American institutions from the encroachment of international institutions.[38] At a more general level, many regard globalization as a threat to their jobs, wages, and culture.

DEBATING GLOBALIZATION

Throughout this chapter, globalization has been discussed as a fact, as reality. However, there is disagreement about the extent to which globalization exists. The *three dominant positions* in this debate are assumed by (1) the hyperglobalizers and transformationalists, (2) the weak globalizers, and (3) the skeptics and rejectionists. The *hyperglobalizers and transformationalists* see profound changes in the international system, such as the erosion of sovereignty and the weakening of nation-states, a borderless economy that integrates people everywhere in the global marketplace, and the emergence of new forms of social and economic organizations that challenge traditional states. Contemporary patterns of globalization are viewed as being unprecedented. The *weak globalizers*, while acknowledging that there are many important changes in the international system, argue that this increased internationalization is not altering the world to the extent claimed by the hyperglobalizers and transformationalists. States remain sovereign, and people around the world, while living in the "global village," continue to jealously guard their own huts. Culture, nationalism, and geography continue to divide us. Finally, the *skeptics and rejectionists* basically argue that globalization is largely a myth that disguises the reality of the existence of powerful sovereign states and major economic divisions in the world. National governments remain in control of their domestic economies as well as the regulation of international economic activities. National governments determine the nature of global interactions. Inequality continues to fuel nationalism, and, instead of cultural homogenization, the world is dividing into cultures that remain suspicious of each other.[39]

At another level is the debate about the nature and impact of globalization and whether it is temporary or reversible. The 2008–2009 financial and economic crises reinvigorated this discussion. Some groups see globalization as homogenization, whereas others view it as promoting diversity and greater tolerance of differences. Many nonstate actors view globalization as conducive to their efforts to improve social conditions, protect the environment, and promote democracy. By removing restraints on people's movement, globalization is perceived as instrumental in giving to the individual the power to choose. People are free to shape their identities, pursue an education anywhere in the world, and upgrade their standard of living.[40] On the other side, critics of globalization focus on how cultural homogenization imposes Western values on others and destroys their traditions, religious beliefs, identities, and sense of community and belonging. Many believe that globalization is a threat to national sovereignty and autonomy. Environmentalists, for example, believe that globalization contributes to environmental degradation, and labor unions and students contend that globalization lowers wages, creates greater inequality, and allows rich countries to maintain their dominant position in relation to poor countries.

SUMMARY AND REVIEW

This chapter discussed the foundations of international relations and provided a general view of how interdependence and the forces of globalization are creating serious challenges to governments as the almost exclusive major actors in world politics. It examined how technological, economic, social, political, and philosophical developments in Europe contributed to the rise of the modern state, the concept of sovereignty, the system of relations among states, and the decline of the Catholic Church as the dominant political and cultural institution in Europe. It illustrated how political, economic, and cultural forces contributed to the rise of the modern nation-state and how they continue to be integral components of contemporary globalization. We looked at interdependence and globalization. Just as interdependence plays a role in our private lives (e.g., most of us do not grow the food we eat), it also plays a role in world affairs. Globalization creates more obvious and extensive webs of interdependence. The causes of globalization can range from social issues (e.g., migration) to techno-logical advances (e.g., in fields such as communication and transportation) to economic issues (e.g., market expansion). The major forms of globalization are (1) economic and trade, (2) financial, (3) political, (4) military, (5) cultural, (6) environmental, and (7) criminal. Finally, we discussed the five historical waves of globalization and the current debate that exists between groups that have resisted it and those that have been more accepting of it.

KEY TERMS

international relations 2
Peace of Westphalia 2
state 2
sovereign 2
ideology 2
nation 2
nation-state 3
state-centric model 3
theory 3
nonstate actors 3
human security 3
global politics 4
global norms 4
global issues 4
humanism 4
Renaissance 4
Johann Gutenberg 4
Martin Luther 4
Jean Bodin 5
Huguenots 5
international law 8
Hugo Grotius 8
diplomacy 8
euro 9

Jean Monnet 9
Robert Schuman 9
Paul Henri Spaak 9
Treaty of Rome 9
European Court of
    Justice 9
nongovernmental
    organizations (NGOs) 9
Lateran Treaty 10
Benito Mussolini 10
multinational corporation
    (MNC) 11
transnational
    corporations 11
British East India
    Company 11
Dutch West India
    Company 11
interdependence 12
globalization 12
Cold War 13
financial market
    expansion 13
economic globalization 14

global teams 15
global cities 15
Bretton Woods System 16
World Bank 16
International Monetary
    Fund (IMF) 16
Eurodollar 16
Organization of Petroleum
    Exporting Countries
    (OPEC) 16
political globalization 16
multilateral
    institutions 16
policy interdependence 17
international regimes 17
global governance 17
military globalization 17
cultural globalization 18
environmental
    globalization 18
dependency 19
Smoot-Hawley Tariff
    Act 19
Jean-Marie Le Pen 20

DISCUSSION QUESTIONS

1. What roles do nonstate actors play in international relations?
2. This chapter discusses the five waves of globalization and provides examples of global-ization for each time period. What are some additional examples of globalization within some of these periods?

3. "Interdependence is the foundation of society." What does this mean? How does it relate to the concept of globalization?
4. What are some of the advances in technology that have contributed to globalization? What are some of the new problems we face because of these advances?
5. What are some of the arguments made against globalization? Do you agree or disagree with any of these arguments? Explain.

SUGGESTED READINGS

Campbell, Kurt, ed. *Climatic Cataclysm.* Washington, DC: Brookings Institution Press, 2008.
Cohen, Daniel. *Globalization and Its Enemies.* Cambridge, MA: MIT Press, 2006.
Friedman, Thomas. *The World Is Flat.* New York: Farrar Straus and Giroux, 2005.
Lawrence, Robert. *Blue-Collar Blues: Is Trade to Blame for Rising U.S. Income Inequality?* Washington, DC: Peterson Institute, 2008.
Levinson, Marc. **"Freight Pain: The Rise and Fall of Globalization,"** *Foreign Affairs* 87, No. 6 (November/December 2008): 133–140.

END NOTES

1. Richard J. Payne and Jamal R. Nassar, *Politics and Culture in the Developing World* (New York: Longman, 2003), 8–9.
2. K. J. Holsti, *International Politics: A Framework for Analysis* (Upper Saddle River, NJ: Prentice Hall, 1995), xi.
3. Hans Morgenthau, *Politics Among Nations* (New York: Knoff, 1948), 23.
4. James N. Rosenau and Mary Durfee, *Thinking Theory Thoroughly* (Boulder, CO: Westview Press, 2000), 48.
5. James N. Rosenau, *Along the Domestic-Foreign Frontier: Exploring Governance in a Turbulent World* (Cambridge: Cambridge University Press, 1997), 58–60.
6. Richard Rosencrance, "Trade and Power," in *Conflict After the Cold War*, ed. Richard K. Betts (New York: Longman, 2002), 281.
7. Steve Lonergan, "Human Security, Environmental Security, and Sustainable Development," in *Environment and Security*, eds. Miriam R. Lowi and Brian R. Shaw (New York: St. Martin's Press, 2000), 70; and C. Ford Runge and Benjamin Senauer, "How Biofuels Could Starve the Poor," *Foreign Affairs*. 86, No. 3 (May/June 2007), 41–44.
8. Rosenau and Durfee, *Thinking Theory Thoroughly*, 47; and Katie Zezima, "Brown Urges Global Push to Solve Global Problems," *New York Times*, 19 April 2008, A5.
9. Charles W. Kegley and Gregory A. Raymond, *Exorcising the Ghosts of Westphalia* (Upper Saddle River, NJ: Prentice Hall, 2002), 30.
10. James Lee Ray, *Global Politics* (Boston: Houghton Mifflin, 1998), 165.
11. Richard Cavendish, "The Treaty of Westphalia," *History Today* 48 (November 1998), 50–52.
12. Carlton Hayes, *A Political and Social History of Modern Europe* (New York: Macmillan, 1921), 231.
13. Geoffrey Stern, *The Structure of International Society* (London: Printer, 2000), 78.
14. Stephen D. Krasner, *Sovereignty* (Princeton, NJ: Princeton University Press, 1999), 4.
15. William Greider, *One World, Ready or Not: The Manic Logic of Global Capitalism* (New York: Simon and Schuster, 1997), 24.
16. Steven Erlanger, "Economic Crisis Pits Europe Against Its Parts," *New York Times*, 9 June 2009, A1.
17. Solange Villas, "The Path to Unity," in *Europe in the New Century*, ed. Robert J. Guttman (Boulder, CO: Lynne Rienner, 2001), 17.

18. P. J. Simmons, "Learning to Live with NGOs," *Foreign Policy*, No. 112 (Fall 1998), 84–87.

19. Frank Bruni, "John Paul Makes First Papal Address to Italy's Parliament," *New York Times*, 15 November 2002, A3.

20. Peter Drucker, "The Global Economy and the Nation-State," *Foreign Affairs* 79, No. 5 (September/October 1997), 8.

21. Marina Ottaway, "Reluctant Missionaries," *Foreign Policy*, No. 125 (July/August 2001), 45.

22. Robert O. Keohane and Joseph S. Nye, *Power and Interdependence* (Boston: Little, Brown and Company, 1977).

23. David Held et al., *Global Transformations* (Stanford: Stanford University Press, 1999), 28; and James H. Mittelman, *The Globalization Syndrome* (Princeton, NJ: Princeton University Press, 2000), 15.

24. Michael Pettis, "Will Globalization Go Bankrupt?" *Foreign Policy*, No. 126 (September/October 2001), 55.

25. Held et al., *Global Transformations*, 186.

26. Louis Story, "Seeking Leaders, U.S. Companies Think Globally," *New York Times*, 12 December 2007, A1.

27. Fareed Zakaria, "The Future of American Power," *Foreign Affairs* 87, No. 3 (May/June 2008), 30.

28. Thomas Balion and Angel Ubide, "The New World of Banking," *Finance and Development* 37, No. 2 (June 2000), 41.

29. Held et al., *Global Transformations*, 202; and Bern Steil, "The End of National Currency," *Foreign Affairs* 86, No. 3 (May/June 2007), 83.

30. Raimo Vayrynen, "Norms, Compliance, and Enforcement in Global Governance," in *Globalization and Global Governance*, ed. Raimo Vayrynen (Lanham, MD: Romman and Littlefield, 1999), 25.

31. Held et al., *Global Transformations*, 88; Robert F. Durant, *The Greening of U.S. Military* (Washington, DC: Georgetown University Press, 2007); and Wolfgang K. H. Panofsky, "Nuclear Insecurity," *Foreign Affairs* 86, No. 5 (September/October 2007), 109–110.

32. Robert O. Keohane and Joseph S. Nye, "Globalization," *Foreign Policy*, No. 118 (Spring 2000), 107.

33. Toby Miller et al., *Globalization and Sport* (London: Sage Publications, 2001), 11–12.

34. Moises Naim, "The Five Wars of Globalization," *Foreign Policy*, No. 134 (January–February 2003), 30.

35. Mittelman, *The Globalization Syndrome*, 18.

36. Paul Collier and David Dollar, *Globalization, Growth, and Poverty* (New York: Oxford University Press, 2002), 25.

37. Collier and Dollar, *Globalization, Growth, and Poverty*, 27.

38. Kishore Mahbubani, "The Case Against the West," *Foreign Affairs* 87, No. 3 (May/June 2008), 111.

39. Peter J. Spiro, "The New Sovereigntists," *Foreign Affairs* 79, No. 6 (November/December 2000), 9.

40. R. J. Barry Jones, *The World Turned Upside Down?* (Manchester: Manchester University Press, 2000), 11; Held et al., *Global Transformations*, 5; John Micklethwait and Adrian Wooldridge, *A Future Perfect: The Essentials of Globalization* (New York: Crown Publishers, 2000), xxvi; and Kenneth F. Scheve and Matthew J. Slaughter, "A New Deal for Globalization," *Foreign Affairs* 86, No. 4 (July/August 2007), 34–35.

The Struggle for Primacy in a Global Society

INTRODUCTION

Throughout history great powers—such as Rome, Spain, and Britain—have gone through growth and decline, through competition and internal weakness. **Power transition theory**, which is an offshoot of Cycle theories, stresses that the distribution-of-power changes in countries will rise and fall. Dominant countries are often referred to as great powers, hegemonies, superpowers, or states that enjoy primacy in the international system. Often, these terms are used interchangeably. They generally refer to the ability of a country or a small group of countries to have extraordinary influence over the behavior of the other states.[1] These dominant countries have economic, military, political, technological, and cultural resources that enable them to influence developments in distant places and to persuade or coerce other countries to do or to refrain from doing certain things.

A country enjoying international primacy, or hegemony, is generally regarded as having diverse interests. It affects many countries' behavior on a wide range of issues without having to significantly change its own behavior. When there are several hegemons, dominant states, or great powers, the international system is defined as being **multipolar**. An example is the international system that existed before World War II, when the United States, Britain, France, Germany, Japan, Italy, and the Soviet Union were considered great powers. Following World War II, there were clearly two dominant countries: the United States and the Soviet Union. The new structure was **bipolar**. The disintegration of the Soviet Union created a **unipolar** world, dominated by the United States. In his essay, "Why We Will Soon Miss the Cold War," John J. Mearsheimer argues that the Cold War provided a degree of order in a world characterized by anarchy. The end of the Cold War, he argues, engenders greater anarchy in international relations.

Implicit in the discussion of great powers is the existence of a hierarchical system of power and that positions often change within this hierarchy. In theory, the leading country, or **hegemon**, can single-handedly control the actions of other powerful countries.

The United States is often perceived as a hegemon. A dominant country exercises significant power, has few potential rivals, and leads an international system that benefits other powerful countries. Below the dominant countries are great powers, which help to maintain the international system. Then there are regional powers. But most countries are at the bottom of the pyramid of power.[2] Although the hegemon, or dominant power, can make decisions unilaterally and be dismissive of other countries, the strongest nation needs the cooperation of others. The concept of hegemony was developed by **Antonio Gramsci** (1891–1937), a leading Marxist theoretician and a founder of the Italian Communist Party, to describe relations, classes, and social groups within countries. Gramsci focused on how the ruling class legitimized its power; that is, how that class managed to get others to accept the existing order because they view the ruling class as having moral authority.[3] This moral authority is an essential component of the hegemon's economic, military, and political power.

This chapter examines the nature of power, factors that influence the rise and fall of nations, and the strategies countries use to maintain their dominant position. As we discuss these ideas, we will examine the rise and fall of Western Europe (including Britain) and the Soviet Union. The United States will be of special interest in our discussion.

Power Transition Theory ■ Stresses that the distribution-of-power changes in countries will rise and fall

Multipolar ■ The international system that includes several hegemons, dominant states, or great powers

Bipolar ■ The international system that includes two hegemons, dominant states, or great powers

Unipolar ■ The international system that has only one hegemon, dominant state, or great power

Hegemon ■ The leading country in an international system

POWER AND LEADERSHIP

Central to the rise and fall of dominant nations is the concept of power. Despite human preoccupation with power, measuring power is difficult. Because power is essentially a psychological relationship, there are numerous reasons for the failure of even great nations to exercise it effectively. **Power** is generally understood as the ability to get others—individuals, groups, or nations—to behave in ways that they would ordinarily try to avoid. *Power capabilities* are usually determined by economic strength, military strength, and political effectiveness. *Elements of power* include a country's geographic area and location, its population, and its natural resources. Other elements of power are intelligence capabilities, the quality of national leadership, the level of educational and technological achievement, the openness of the political system, the character of the people, transportation and communication capabilities, ideology, and a country's culture (generally referred to as "soft power").[4]

Economic power is often seen as the foundation of military and political power. It is measured in terms of the **gross national product (GNP)** or the **gross domestic product (GDP)**. The GNP measures the total market value of all goods and services produced by resources supplied by the residents and businesses of a particular country, regardless of where those residents and businesses are located. The GDP measures the total market value of all goods and services produced within a country. Military power is often the most visible and impressive manifestation of national power. Great powers generally have large, healthy, and relatively well-educated populations, which enable them to build large and technologically sophisticated militaries.[5] As we will discuss, a major challenge for great powers is to maintain a balance between economic strength and military might. Too much emphasis on the military often weakens the economy, and ultimately the military itself.

A nation's strength goes beyond simply possessing the various resources that are sources of power. Countries, like individuals, must be skilled at converting these resources into effective influence. **Power conversion** is defined as the capacity to change potential power, as measured by available resources, into realized power, which is determined by the changed behavior of others.[6] Knowing what resources to use, when, and how will also affect the exercise of power. Certain factors—such as globalization, domestic support for policies, and the willingness of citizens to support activities associated with international primacy—must also be considered. Globalization not only links states, but also constrains them. It restrains even powerful nations from using force unilaterally in many cases, partly because of the high costs and unintended negative consequences for themselves and their allies.

An important component of power is leadership. In fact, leadership is about power. Leadership is the ability to persuade others to behave in certain ways, to shape their interest, and to influence their thinking. Leadership implies a capability to get others to cooperate to achieve particular objectives.[7] At the foundation of leadership is the ability to get others to follow. It is impossible to be an effective hegemon without followers. Leadership can be structural, institutional, or situational. **Structural leadership** is derived largely from the control of economic resources, military power, technology, and other sources of power that enable a small group of countries to shape the international system. Structural leadership is often augmented by **institutional leadership**: that is, the ability to determine the rules, principles, procedures, and practices that guide the behavior of members of the global community. Institutions provide order and predictability and allow the dominant power to exercise control. Finally, **situational leadership** is primarily the ability to seize opportunities to build or reorient the global system, apart from the distribution of power and the building of institutions. Often, this kind of leadership is associated with a specific individual.[8]

THE RISE AND FALL OF GREAT POWERS

States generally expand because of *threats* and *opportunities* in their international system. States fear power vacuums because rival states are likely to take advantage of them if they fail to act. Weaker states tend to gravitate toward a rising power and to move away from a declining power.[9] Failure to demonstrate strength causes a bandwagoning effect, which benefits the rising power. These dynamics strongly influence states to expand to protect their interests and security. **Population pressures** influence the rise of great powers. Population growth puts pressure on available domestic resources. To address this problem, countries that are capable of expanding will venture across oceans or land boundaries to obtain raw materials, markets for their products, and living space for their people. Such expansion is usually accomplished through military force, which depends on a strong economic base. **Uneven economic growth** enables some countries to enhance their power while other countries decline.

Antonio Gramsci ■ (1891–1937); leading Marxist theoretician and a founder of the Italian Communist Party

Power ■ The ability to get others—individuals, groups, or nations—to behave in ways that they ordinarily would not

GNP ■ Measures the total market value of all goods and services produced by resources supplied by residents and businesses of a particular country, regardless of where the residents and businesses are located

GDP ■ Measures the total market value of all goods and services produced within a country

Power Conversion ■ The capacity to change potential power, as measured by available resources, into realized power, which is determined by the changed behavior of others

Structural Leadership ■ The possession of economic resources, military power, technology, and other sources of power that enable a small group of countries to shape the international system

Institutional Leadership ■ The ability to determine the rules, principles, procedures, and practices that guide the behavior of members of the global community

Situational Leadership ■ The ability to seize opportunities to build or reorient the global system, apart from the distribution of power and the building of institutions

Population pressures ■ The pressure on resources that leads countries to expand beyond their boundaries

Uneven Economic Growth ■ A factor that enables some countries to enhance their power while that of other countries declines

Hubris ■ A term used to stress the dangers of excessive pride and arrogance

Lippmann Gap ■ The disparity between the global ambitions of countries and their resources to fulfill those ambitions

Imperial Overstretch ■ The disparity between the global ambitions of countries and their resources to fulfill those ambitions

Urbanization has usually been associated with freedom and innovation. Urban areas attract diverse groups of people with differing ideas. They also improve the wealth-generating, administrative, and political capabilities of a rising power. The efficient functioning of great cities depends on a commitment to tolerance, freedom, and trust. These characteristics, in turn, attract more talent, wealth, innovation, and technology to cities. Trust, for example, is essential for commercial transactions as well as for mundane, routine interactions. Cities such as London and Amsterdam attracted refugees from religious intolerance and persecution. During the seventeenth-century religious wars, Protestants and Jews migrated to Amsterdam and other Dutch cities that were more tolerant of religious diversity. Repression and persecution in France after the French Revolution, for example, forced many French citizens—especially those who were young, educated, and had entrepreneurial skills—to seek refuge in a much freer England.[10]

Geography is another factor that influences the rise and fall of great powers. Britain, Russia, and the United States have benefited from their geographic location and, in the case of Russia and the United States, their continental-size territory. None of these countries is located in the middle of warring states, and they usually refrained from getting involved in other nations' conflicts until it was to their advantage to do so. They could fight in other countries and avoid destroying their own. Their geography also enabled them to concentrate resources on internal consolidation, which ultimately increased their power vis-à-vis other states. Equally important, their separation by water and expanses of land made it more difficult for countries to invade them.

War, which played a crucial role in making states, has been a major factor in the rise and fall of great powers. It usually increased the power of some nations at the detriment of others. Even when countries emerged victorious from war, some were so weakened that the countries that had avoided major damage rose to the top. An example is Britain after World War II: It experienced declining power as America's global dominance grew. Historically, war has been instrumental in strengthening patriotism and nationalism. Historically, Britain went to war against France and Spain to engender cohesion among England, Scotland, Wales, and Ireland.

Many great powers decline because of **hubris** (i.e., excessive pride) and imperial arrogance. They tend to overestimate their power and expand their military power so much that they ultimately erode their economic base. In other words, believing that their power is virtually limitless, they allow a gap to grow between their global ambitions and the resources they have to fulfill those ambitions. This disparity is referred to as the **Lippmann Gap** because Walter Lippmann clearly articulated the problem as early as 1943; Paul Kennedy, writing in the late 1980s, referred to this problem as **imperial overstretch**.[11] Taking resources away from domestic programs for military activities abroad often leads to the unraveling of domestic political cohesion. It may even force allies to find ways to balance against the power of the dominant state in order to protect their own interests and security. For example, even as the United States increased spending on the wars in Iraq and Afghanistan, the country faced rising budget deficits, a financial crisis related to subprime mortgages, and growing concerns about the viability of the Social Security program, national health insurance, and rising costs for Medicare. America's vulnerability was highlighted by the worst economic recession it had endured in seventy-five years.

STRATEGIES FOR MAINTAINING POWER

Leading powers, facing challenges from rising countries, adopt several strategies to preserve their position in the international system. *Democratic enlargement* is a prominent strategy in this effort. Potential challengers are restrained when they internalize the values, beliefs, and norms articulated by the dominant power. The United States, for example, has emphasized spreading democracy. But the dissemination of values and beliefs by great powers does not guarantee indefinite control, a reality that Britain had to face as India and other colonies demanded for themselves the rights enjoyed by people in Britain, including the right to self-government. Great powers also *build institutions to legitimize their control.* They articulate concepts of an international normative order, concepts that involve principles of order and change within the international system as well as normative claims about the role of the leading power within that order.[12] The Dutch used this approach in the seventeenth century, the British in the eighteenth and nineteenth centuries, and it is currently being used by the United States.

Another strategy used to prevent rising powers from creating disorder in the international system is *offshore balancing.* Following Napoleon's final defeat in 1815, European powers created the **Concert of Europe** to maintain stability by preserving a relatively equal distribution of power among them. The main goal was to prevent one country from gaining so much power that it would dominate the others. The balance of power relied on the willingness of a group of powerful countries to cooperate militarily, if necessary, against a rising hegemon. *Balancing*—which basically means opposing the stronger or more threatening side in a conflict—can be achieved through efforts by individual states to strengthen themselves and by building alliances to preserve the balance of power.[13] Closely related to balancing is the strategy of **containment**, which attempts to prevent ambitious powers from expanding and destroying order and balance in the international system. When the Soviet Union marched through Eastern Europe and subjugated the countries there, the United States and its European allies responded by implementing a policy of containment.

Binding and *engagement* are also important state responses to rising powers. The European Union (EU), as we have seen, has its origins in efforts by France and other countries after World War II to avoid the nightmare of another war in Europe by forming economic and political alliances with Germany, which had initiated the conflict. *Binding* aims at controlling the behavior of the rising or threatening country by embedding it into bilateral or multilateral alliances. By making the rising state a member of the alliance, dominant countries allow it to participate in decisions and to contribute to building the institutions that maintain the status quo. Binding makes it more difficult for the rising state to take unilateral actions that could weaken leading powers. West Germany and East Germany, belonging to the North Atlantic Treaty Organization (NATO) and the Warsaw Pact, respectively, are examples of countries that were included in alliances to prevent them from creating problems for the leading countries in each alliance. Many Europeans perceive the continuation and expansion of NATO in the absence of the Soviet threat as part of America's binding strategy. *Engagement* attempts to minimize conflict with a rising power and to strengthen those aspects of its behavior that are consistent with the status quo and the interests of the great powers.[14] Eventually

Concert of Europe ■ Created by European powers to prevent one country from gaining so much power that it would dominate the others

Containment ■ A strategy that attempts to prevent ambitious powers from expanding and destroying order and balance in the international system the rising power will have too great a stake in preserving the international order to challenge it. Finally, a hegemon could resort to *preventive war* to preserve its position in the international system. However, wars against major powers in a nuclear age and in an era of increasing globalization are almost unthinkable because of their devastating consequences for the world, including the hegemon.

America

America's decision to launch a preemptive war against Iraq in March 2003 without broad international support and with significant domestic opposition to war demonstrated its power to ignore world opinion. Its awesome military power was evident in its "shock and awe" campaign against Iraq. However, although there was strong disagreement about America's decision to engage in a preemptive war, there was global consensus about America's military predominance. By 2008 it was increasingly clear that the war in Iraq had weakened American power and that ways should be found to remove American troops from Iraq. More than 81 percent of Americans believed that their country was on the wrong track. The strength of the U.S. military is unprecedented in the history of great powers. The United States accounts for roughly half of global defense spending. America spends more on its military than the next twenty powers combined and three times as much on military research and development as the next six powers combined. America's economic might is also undisputed. With less than 6 percent of the world's population, the United States produces almost a third of the world's GDP. Culturally, intellectually, scientifically, and politically America dominates the global system.

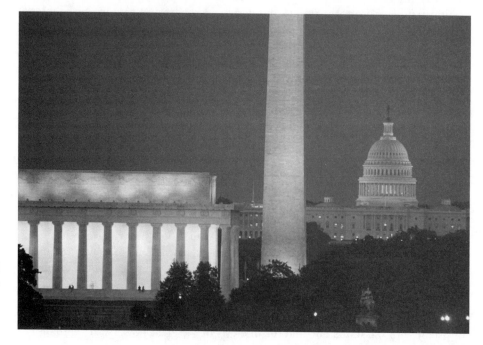

Lincoln Memorial, Washington Monument, and Capitol Building.

America's emergence as the most powerful country in history was a complex and relatively gradual process. The United States, like previous civilizations, borrowed heavily from others and built on foundations created by others. America, in many ways, was a continuation of British society in the New World. The Pilgrims who arrived in 1620 on the *Mayflower* at Plymouth in Massachusetts were English people who brought English values and institutions with them. The United States utilized strategies very similar to those used by other great powers to achieve its dominant position. It also benefited from the protection of the Pacific and Atlantic Oceans and unthreatening neighbors on its borders. The expansion of the United States occurred over land through the acquisition of Native American territories. Similar to other great powers, America relied heavily on military force to expand and consolidate its power. Believing in the concept of **manifest destiny**, it eventually expanded its territory from the Atlantic to the Pacific. The **Mexican-American War** (1846–1848) resulted in America's acquisition of two-fifths of Mexico's territory, including California and the present American Southwest, in the Treaty of Guadalupe-Hidalgo, which ended the conflict. However, the issue of slavery divided the United States into two warring factions, leading to the bloodiest war in American history. Even so, the American Civil War removed a serious obstacle to the United States' rise as a great power. In essence, the Civil War forged a common American culture and internal unification.[15]

Internal stability enabled the United States to concentrate on building its economy and broadening its interests. The Civil War produced advancements in American military organization and technologies. However, after the war the United States demobilized the army, scrapped over half its warships, and allowed the rest to rot. The government declined to remain ahead of other countries in construction of iron-clad steamships.[16] As a continental-size power, the United States remained largely preoccupied with domestic and regional affairs. Furthermore, America believed that it could be "a City on a Hill" and an example to other nations, albeit from a distance and without getting entangled in their problems. This proclivity toward isolationism has always been an essential component of American foreign policy. But isolationism also emanated from the reality that until the late 1880s America was far behind great powers such as Britain, France, Germany, Austria-Hungary, Russia, and Italy. In fact, when the Sultan of Turkey decided to reduce expenses in 1880, he closed Turkey's diplomatic missions in Sweden, Belgium, the Netherlands, and the United States.[17] Yet America's vast territory, abundant natural resources, spirit of freedom and innovation, ability to attract immigrants and investments, institutional stability, and cultural values contributed to its phenomenal growth in the 1880s. The United States became a leading producer of agricultural products, coal, iron and steel. Its banking and manufacturing sectors surpassed those of the major countries. By 1890 the United States had decided to strengthen its navy to be competitive with European navies. This development was fueled partly by America's imperial ambitions, evidenced by its conquest of the Philippines, Puerto Rico, and Guam and its increased influence in Cuba and Hawaii as a consequence of its victory in the **Spanish American War** in 1898. By ending Spain's declining position in the Americas and the Pacific, the United States established itself as the hegemon of the Western Hemisphere,

Manifest Destiny ■ Jingoistic tenet that the U.S. expansion is reinforced through God's will

Mexican-American War ■ The war between Mexico and the United States (1846–1848) that resulted in the U.S. acquisition of two-fifths of Mexico's territory, including California and the present American Southwest

Spanish American War ■ The war between Spain and the United States (1898)

Monroe Doctrine ■
The statement of
U.S. policy made by
President James
Monroe in 1823 that
resulted in dimin-
ished European
involvement in the
Americas

League of Nations ■
International alliance
created in 1920 to
promote international
peace and security

Pearl Harbor ■
Bombed by Japanese
submarines and
carrier-based planes
in 1941

thereby achieving the objective of the **Monroe Doctrine** of 1823, namely, diminishing European involvement in the Americas.

Reluctantly, America began abandoning its policy of isolationism during World
War I in response to dangers of war in Europe and indiscriminate German subma-
rine warfare. President Woodrow Wilson accelerated the construction of military
weapons and warships, drafted young men, and trained them to fight. World War I
stimulated a rapid growth in the foreign-policy establishment and brought out a
strong American commitment to free trade, the promotion of democracy, support
for national self-determination, and an emphasis on international cooperation to
achieve world peace through organizations such as the **League of Nations**. American power was applied to protect its growing interests abroad. The United States'
rise to global prominence meant that it could no longer avoid entanglement in
European affairs, a reality made clearer by World War II. President Franklin D.
Roosevelt, even before Japan bombed the American fleet at **Pearl Harbor** on
December 7, 1941, expressed an urgent need to strengthen the military. He created
the U.S. Air Force in 1939 and a two-ocean navy in 1940. The military draft was
reinstated, military cooperation with Britain was enhanced, and military assistance
was extended to Britain, the Soviet Union, and China. America's entry into World
War II unleashed unprecedented military growth. By the end of the war, the United
States was indisputably the dominant global power. But the Soviet Union, especially
after it acquired intercontinental nuclear weapons, also gained superpower status.
As Table 2.1 shows, the major European powers and Japan, destroyed by war,
declined. Figure 2.1 demonstrates the global reach of America's military power.

America's hegemony or primacy rests not only on its dominant power but
also on its ability to legitimize that power by making it acceptable to potential
challengers in particular and members of the global community in general. Cooperation, integration, and multilateralism became cornerstones of the American-led
postwar order. Certain institutions—such as the United Nations, the World Bank,
the International Monetary Fund, and the General Agreement on Tariffs and
Trade—benefited most countries and induced them to accept American leadership. Institutionalization and increasing globalization meant that the United

TABLE 2.1

GREAT POWERS FROM 1495 TO PRESENT

Period	Great Powers
1495–1521	France, England, Austrian Hapsburgs, Spain, Ottoman Empire, Portugal
1604–1618	France, England, Austria, Spain, Ottoman Empire, Holland, Sweden
1648–1702	France, England, Austrian Hapsburgs, Spain, Ottoman Empire, Holland, Sweden
1713–1792	France, Great Britain, Austrian Hapsburgs, Spain, Sweden, Russia, Prussia
1815–1914	France, Great Britain, Austria-Hungary, Russia, Prussia/Germany, Italy, United States, Japan
1919–1939	France, Great Britain, Soviet Union, Germany, Italy, United States, Japan
1945–1989	Soviet Union, United States
1989–Present	United States

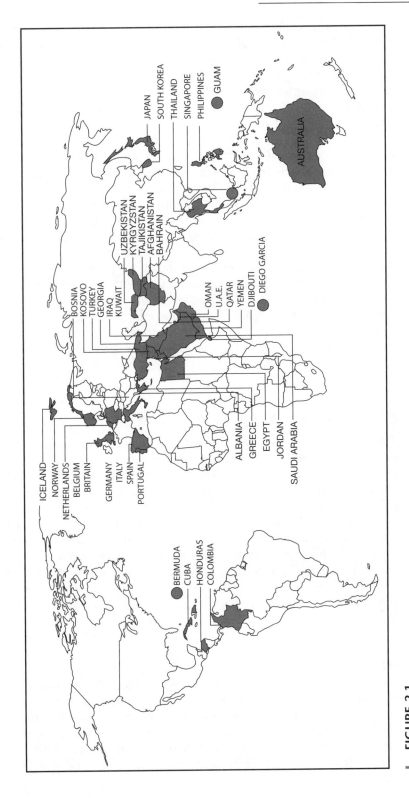

FIGURE 2.1
Location of U.S. Military Forces

Public Goods ■
Collective benefits, such as security, stability, open markets, and economic opportunities

States and other countries would be constrained to varying degrees and would embrace multilateralism and cooperation instead of unilateralism. As the global leader, America would play a major role in providing collective benefits or **public goods** (i.e., services such as security, stability, open markets, and economic opportunities). By doing so, the United States would minimize the possibility of envy and resentment that could escalate into the fear and loathing that spawn hostile alliances designed to balance power.[18]

In the Gulf War against Iraq in 1991, the United States' use of very sophisticated weapons stunned many countries and prompted them to upgrade their own military technologies. Ten years later, the war in Afghanistan was fought with even more advanced weapons. For example, American commandos using binoculars with laser range finders could spot distant enemy targets and relay the coordinates to satellite telephones or laptop computers in U.S. warplanes. Bombs weighing 2,000 pounds and guided by lasers and global positioning systems that improved their precision were dropped on targets in Afghanistan. Bombs weighing 4,700 pounds were used against Baghdad in the 2003 war. New technologies allowed American forces to detect heat, magnetic fields, and vibrations through as much as 100 feet of solid rock, and thermobaric weapons could be used to penetrate rock and concrete to destroy underground targets.[19] The Predator, an unmanned reconnaissance and surveillance plane that is controlled by a ground team from a remote location, can be equipped with Hellfire missiles to strike targets.

CHALLENGERS TO AMERICAN HEGEMONY

The U.S. military superiority, combined with what many countries viewed as unilateralism, deepened fissures between America and other countries, such as France, Germany, Russia, and China. Instead of being perceived as promoting the global welfare, American foreign policy was increasingly seen as being preoccupied with narrowly defined American interests. Instead of consulting, Washington was perceived to be issuing demands and ultimatums. America's preference for a unipolar system and American global hegemony threatened other great powers, most of which favored a multipolar system. The growing consensus in 2008 among foreign policy experts, political leaders, and others was that America's unipolar moment was over.[20] Even before the schisms caused by debates on Iraq, American power was being challenged. This section discusses the principal challengers to American power.

Japan

Throughout the 1980s and during the early 1990s, scholars, political leaders, and most of the business sector were preoccupied with Japan as an economic juggernaut. At the heart of their concerns was a growing realization that American hegemony was being challenged by a country that had been defeated by the United States in World War II. The U.S. occupation of Japan after the war enabled Japan to acquire American technology, organizational skills, political institutions and values, and to access American markets. Now America was looking at Japan's success as an indicator of its own failures. The strong religious tradition that permeates American thinking and foreign policy reinforced the perception of the United States as an exceptional country that was exempt from the logic of historical forces faced by the other great powers. The fact that Japan had achieved such unprecedented economic power in just twenty-five years and was widely viewed as the model for the world shook Americans' confidence in their belief that the United States was destined to be the global redeemer. This doubt was reinforced by the failures in Vietnam, declining trust in political institutions after the Watergate crisis, and a prolonged economic recession.[21]

Japan's extraordinary rise as an economic power is the result of several complex factors. *First*, Japan already had an industrial infrastructure and a well-educated, talented, and cohesive population. *Second*, Japan took advantage of America's military involvement in Korea and Vietnam by supplying trucks and other defense-related products to the United States. These wars stimulated Japanese exports, strengthening companies such as Toyota. *Third*, in addition to reducing government defense spending, Japan concentrated on encouraging high levels of personal savings. The availability of money at low interest rates enabled companies to borrow for investment both at home and abroad. *Fourth*, Japan created the **Ministry of International Trade and Industry (MITI)** to promote the country's industrial expansion and technological development and exports, thereby giving the government a direct role in the economy and helping Japanese companies to be more globally competitive.[22] *Fifth*, Japanese companies built modern industrial plants that were far more efficient than plants in other industrialized countries. *Sixth*, the Japanese developed flexible production strategies that allowed them to develop products tailored for specific markets. *Finally*, the Japanese implemented the *just-in-time* system to minimize accumulating large inventories of components and products required in manufacturing.

> **MITI** ■ Created by the Japanese to promote Japan's industrial expansion, technological development, and exports

Despite Japan's economic superpower status, its ability to emerge as a hegemonic power is hindered by serious drawbacks. Compared with America, whose values are generally regarded as universally applicable, Japan is generally perceived as not having an **ideology** (i.e., set of beliefs and principles) that is widely relevant beyond Japan. More importantly, Japanese exceptionalism stresses that the uniqueness of Japanese culture is genetically based. In other words, **Japanese exceptionalism** embodies homogeneity, insularity, and the exclusion of others who are not genetically and culturally Japanese. Furthermore, Japan's expansion in the 1930s and 1940s has engendered deep suspicions, among other Asians in particular, about Japan's intentions. Japan's actions in World War II have essentially limited its ability to gain the legitimacy required to emerge as a great power. Widespread protests in China in 2005 against Japan for its refusal to acknowledge its atrocities in World War II and China's determination to prevent Japan from gaining a permanent seat on the UN Security Council underscore the challenge facing Japan. David Rapkin argues that within Japan and externally, Japan is generally considered deficient in the universal norms, values, beliefs, and principles that could form the foundation of world order.[23] Most countries do not expect Japan to exercise global leadership beyond the economic sphere. Japanese power remains largely unidimensional, even though it has the technological ability to develop

> **Ideology** ■ Set of beliefs and principles
>
> **Japanese Exceptionalism** ■ Embodies homogeneity, insularity, and the exclusion of others who are not genetically and culturally Japanese

nuclear weapons and to strengthen its military. Because Japan depends heavily on international trade and investment, it is highly vulnerable to pressures by powerful countries, such as the United States, France, and Britain. A major beneficiary of globalization, Japan is also restrained by interdependence. Japan's small territory and lack of vital natural resources put it at a disadvantage in competition with large and resource-rich countries, such as the United States, China, and Russia, especially in a nuclear age and in a world in which acquiring territory forcefully is unacceptable.[24]

Finally, Japan's economy, once viewed as a juggernaut, has been steadily declining. Japan's aging population and its restrictive immigration policies combine to weaken its competitiveness. Moreover, the Japanese model has been successfully adopted by Taiwan, South Korea, China, and other countries. These countries manufacture many products that Japan exports for less without compromising quality. China's competitiveness, low wages, and huge potential market influenced many Japanese companies to invest in China in order to avoid Japan's high labor costs. Japan is also exporting technology, engineering, business, and organizational skills to China, which will help China to more effectively challenge Japan economically. Japan is viewed as having too many vulnerabilities and limitations to successfully challenge America's dominance. Furthermore, Japan's concerns about the emergence of China as a dominant power influence it to increase its cooperation with the United States and India.

China

China has been one of the world's leading powers for at least four thousand years. China was once far superior to Western Europe in virtually every human endeavor. These historical achievements reinforce China's self-perception as a great power. China's many contributions to human civilization, its population of more than 1.3 billion, its rapid economic growth, and the spread of its culture across continents combine to strengthen its view that it is entitled to play a major role in world affairs. Just as an individual's identity helps to influence his or her perception of his or her role in the world, a nation's identity is crucial in its determination of its global status. China's identity is that of a great power.[25] China has traditionally emphasized protecting its borders, fostering domestic integration and stability, and reducing regional threats.

But China is now widely viewed as a major challenger to America's dominance of the global system. An example of America's fear of a rising China was its strong opposition in 2005 to efforts by CNOOC, the Chinese government-owned oil company, to buy Unocal, an American oil company. China has established strong economic ties with oil-producing countries in Latin America, the Middle East, and Africa. As the United States became preoccupied with wars in Iraq and Afghanistan, fighting global terrorism, and preventing nuclear proliferation in Iran and Korea, China strengthened its navy and increased its defense spending.[26]

China's economic growth has been spectacular since it implemented far-reaching economic reforms and improved relations with the United States in the 1970s. The economy has consistently grown by around 10 percent a year, even during periods when the American economy experienced recession. Even when most of the industrialized world experienced a severe economic recession due to the financial crisis in 2009, China's economic growth was roughly 7.2 percent. China's economic growth was spurred by deliberate and often draconian policies to reduce population growth, by the adoption of the free market, by increased privatization of the economy, by promotion of entrepreneurship, and by the efforts to attract foreign investments through the creation of special enterprise zones.

Companies from around the world established subsidiaries in China to take advantage of low production costs as well as the growing Chinese market. Despite strained relations with Taiwan, which China claims to be part of its territory, many Taiwanese engineers and high-technology companies have moved to China to take advantage of business opportunities. China's own engineering and technological schools and universities are producing experts in information technology. China's goal is to replace India as the world's second largest producer of software, after the United States.[27] Such advantages in technology improve China's economic competitiveness as well as its military capabilities. Faced with declining exports due to the global recession in 2009, China focused on increasing domestic investing and consumer spending.

Although largely preoccupied with regional security, especially the significant U.S. military presence in the area, China developed nuclear weapons as a deterrent to threats from the Soviet Union and the United States. In addition to acquiring advanced Russian military technology, China is making a concerted effort to build a new generation of nuclear-powered submarines that can launch intercontinental nuclear missiles. It is also modernizing its air force and reorganizing its army to enable it to be a "mobile and technologically competent force able to fight limited wars under high-technology conditions." Describing China as a "peer competitor" and concerned about its rapid military growth, U.S. Defense Secretary Robert Gates met with China's President Hu Jintao in November 2007 in China to discuss relations between the two countries.[28]

China is building alliances with Russia, symbolized by the **Treaty of Friendship and Cooperation** of July 2001, to challenge the American framework for international security. It is also increasing economic ties with India through an agreement reached in 2005 to resolve the border dispute between the two countries. In July 2006 they reopened the Nathu La Pass, which was closed for forty-four years, to facilitate trade. With a third of the world's population, the alliance between China and India has the potential to significantly impact global affairs. The United States attempted to strengthen its ties with India in 2006 with the signing of a nuclear agreement. India's decision in 2008 to invest $500 million in development projects in Africa and to strengthen trade relations underscores India's willingness to compete with China. Growing perceptions of America's unilateralism and its willingness to use its military might reinforce China's determination to balance American power, especially in Asia. However, China is also careful not to jeopardize its strong economic links with the United States or its rapid economic development by allocating an overwhelming share of its resources to expanding its military.

As we have seen, financial and economic power is widely regarded as the foundation of global political power. Countries whose economies suffer severe declines

Treaty of Friendship and Cooperation ■ Chinese-Russian alliance designed to challenge the U.S. framework for international security often experience a diminution of power. America's wars in Iraq and Afghanistan, the rapid decline of its manufacturing sector, huge budget deficits, and its reliance on borrowing from China and other countries to fund its expenditures have contributed to the relative increase in China's power. The financial crisis exposed America's vulnerabilities and raised serious questions about America's capitalism. China clearly perceives itself as the leading rising global power. Although China is unlikely to directly confront the United States for global leadership, its financial and economic strength has influenced it to demand greater recognition and influence in global affairs. China's rise, in contrast to America's decline, is also fueling Chinese nationalism and changing America's relationship with China.

The European Union

Although Europe's major powers were devastated by World War II, the vision of a united Europe gained greater impetus due to the perception that only European political and economic cooperation could diminish the outbreak of other such destructive wars on the continent. Attempts at European unification can be traced back to the Roman Empire. Charlemagne, Napoleon Bonaparte, Adolf Hitler, and others relied on force to achieve their vision of a united Europe. Despite deep religious, political, and cultural schisms in Europe, the idea of a "United States of Europe" persisted. The success of the European unification was strongly supported by America, which implemented the **Marshall Plan** in June 1947 to rebuild the devastated economies of Western countries. Furthermore, the United States played a pivotal role in the formation of *NATO* in April 1949 to prevent the expansion of the Soviet Union beyond Central and Eastern Europe. Europe's success in avoiding war and achieving economic and political integration has enabled it not only to emerge as a united continent but also to be perceived as a serious challenger to American hegemony.

Marshall Plan ■
Post-World War II plan to rebuild the devastated economies of Europe

European unification heightened U.S. concern about the construction of a "fortress Europe" that would exclude American products and ultimately rise as a superpower to challenge the United States. Several developments helped to strengthen the perception that Europe and America are growing apart and becoming competitors. *First*, the end of the Cold War diminished European military and psychological dependence on the United States and influenced the United States to shift its attention from Europe in order to deal with domestic problems and emerging global threats. *Second*, Europeans are becoming more conscious of their European identity and more willing to differentiate themselves from Americans. *Third*, there are fundamental differences about the concept of power on each side of the Atlantic. Whereas the United States embraces an almost Westphalian concept of sovereignty and unilateralism, Europeans strongly support relinquishing important aspects of their sovereignty to achieve political, economic, monetary, and military unification, and they embrace multilateralism. *Fourth*, America's unprecedented power influenced it to reject cooperation and consultation with Europeans on important issues, especially under George W. Bush. *Finally*, Americans and Europeans have divergent positions on major issues, including the use of military power, the power of the International Criminal Court, the role of the United Nations, the environment, the treatment of terrorist

TABLE 2.2

DIVERGING U.S. AND EUROPEAN POSITIONS

Issue	U.S. Position	European Position
International Criminal Court	Opposed	Ratified
Kyoto Protocol	Opposed	Ratified
Comprehensive Test Ban Treaty	Opposed	Ratified
Land Mines Ban	Opposed	Signed
Biodiversity Treaty	Opposed	Approved
Anti-Ballistic Missile Treaty	Unilaterally withdrew	Preferred a multilateral decision
U.S. National Missile Defense	Strongly supports	Skeptical
Treaty Limiting Small Arms Exports	Opposed	Supports
Death Penalty	Exists in 38 states	Does not exist in Europe
Israeli-Palestinian Conflict	Strongly supports Israel	More supportive of Palestinians
Invasion of Iraq	Initiated/led	Generally strongly opposed
U.S. Farm Bill	Signed by Bush, May 13, 2002	Opposed
U.S. Quotas on Steel	Implemented by Bush	Opposed

suspects, and the death penalty. Arguments supporting the view that the EU will become a superpower and challenge the United States focus on the continent's economic strength and the desire of many countries to be included in the EU. Europe is widely seen as having the potential to become the dominant global economic power within two or three decades.[29]

Europe's economic power and technological and scientific achievements could enable it to develop stronger military capabilities. Both Britain and France possess nuclear weapons and advanced weapons systems. European political and economic integration is influencing the leading countries to coordinate the building and purchasing of military weapons. Instead of continuing to rely on the United States for the most technologically advanced weapons, the Europeans are making their own and competing more vigorously with American defense companies.[30]

Nonstate Actors

When faced with overwhelming power, represented by the giant Goliath, the Israelites employed a boy, David, with a slingshot to counteract that power. In Jonathan Swift's *Gulliver's Travels*, the Lilliputians are able to restrain the giant through cooperation. These stories illustrate the paradox of being a superpower. Instead of engaging a country that possesses overwhelming power with conventional weapons, the weak usually confront the strong in unorthodox ways. This strategy of counteracting the dominant power of a hegemon is called **asymmetrical warfare**. It enables the weaker side to gain military advantages and level the playing field to some extent by using comparatively unsophisticated weapons and strategies.

Asymmetrical Warfare ■ Strategy of counteracting the dominant power of a hegemon through unorthodox ways

Almost 98 percent of Americans view terrorist organizations as the most potent nonstate challengers to American dominance. Their ability to effectively utilize asymmetrical power has been facilitated by globalization. The United States has many interests around the world, which generate resentments that can escalate into violence. For example, in 1983, a suicide bomber drove a truck loaded with explosives into a U.S. Marine barracks in Beirut, Lebanon, killing 241 Americans. In 1996, a truck bomb destroyed part of the Khobar Towers housing complex near Dhahran, Saudi Arabia, killing 19 American soldiers. The following year American embassies in Kenya and Tanzania were bombed, killing 224 people, including 12 Americans. In 2000, a major military symbol, the USS *Cole*, a destroyer, was badly damaged by suicide bombers in Aden, Yemen.[31] Finally, the openness of American society has allowed terrorist organizations to operate without being easily detected, even with the increased security measures implemented after the devastating terrorist attacks in New York and Washington, DC, on September 11, 2001. Despite its superior military forces, America found itself bogged down in a war against insurgents in Iraq armed with roadside bombs and suicide bombers. Even as most Americans called for bringing American troops home as soon as possible in 2008, no clear plans were offered for how America could withdraw from Iraq without creating serious problems for itself, Iraq, and the region.

Domestic Challenges to American Hegemony

As the Pentagon prepared a postwar plan in early 2003 for a short-term military occupation of Iraq, followed by an indefinite period of a U.S.-run civil administration that would determine the form and time frame of an eventual resumption of Iraqi control, Americans appeared to be ambivalent about their country's new role as an occupying power. By 2007, almost 70 percent of Americans opposed the war in Iraq. By late 2009, a majority of Americans viewed the war in Afghanistan unfavorably. The financial crisis, related to subprime loans and high oil prices, pushed the United States into a severe economic recession in 2008 and 2009. Our discussion of previous empires has shown that empires decline not only because of challenges from rising powers, but also because of decisions made by their leaders and general attitudes and beliefs of ordinary citizens. In other words, empires are usually their own worst enemy. More important than what others do to them is what they often do to themselves that ultimately hastens their fall.

Following the disintegration of the Soviet Union, the United States enjoyed a unipolar moment. American ideals and values were widely regarded as models for the world. America launched a war against terrorism, invaded Iraq and Afghanistan, and embarked on a global mission to promote democracy and economic liberalization. The collapse of the financial system created by the United States and the accompanying global economic recession eroded global confidence in America's leadership. As we will discuss in Chapter 7, America's access to easy credit and its failure to effectively regulate the financial system covered up many fundamental weaknesses. The manufacturing sector declined and many of its high school graduates were unprepared to compete effectively in a global economy. In many ways, America's policies contributed to its relative decline.[32]

Responding to Asymmetrical Power

Focusing primarily on nations as the principal challengers to U.S. power, American leaders have concentrated on constructing even more technologically advanced weapons. The terrorist attacks on the United States in Lebanon, Saudi Arabia, Kenya, Tanzania, Yemen, and America itself show that despite possessing the most powerful military in the world, the country is vulnerable to attacks by nonstate actors. Despite its use of overwhelming military force in Iraq and its reliance on the military in Afghanistan and Pakistan, the United States has not achieved a decisive victory over nonstate actors that rely on relatively unsophisticated military technology.

In 2009, America's power was challenged by groups of Somali pirates who demanded huge sums of money as ransom for the ships they captured. The world's greatest military power seemed unable to eliminate the pirates. Faced with the reality of the effective use of asymmetrical power, there is a growing awareness by American leaders that traditional approaches to dealing with threats from nations are not very effective against terrorists and pirates.

1. Does the growing perception of American weakness encourage nonstate actors to attack it?
2. What should the U.S. government do to diminish these threats? ■

Public opinion polls consistently show that Americans have a definite lack of sustained interest in the rest of the world and in foreign relations. This attitude was especially prevalent prior to the terrorist attacks in 2001. A majority of Americans, ranging from 55 to 66 percent, believed that what happened in Western Europe, Asia, and even Canada and Mexico had little impact on their lives. This reality influenced Samuel P. Huntington, an astute observer of American international and domestic affairs, to conclude that "however much foreign policy elites may ignore or deplore it, the United States lacks the domestic political base to create a unipolar world."[33] Public opinion polls taken after the terrorist attacks showed an increased interest in global issues among Americans but ambivalence toward America's hegemony. Although 52 percent of Americans believed the United States should remain the only superpower, compared with 14 percent of Europeans who held this view, 62 percent of Americans rejected the idea that their country has the responsibility to be the world's police force.[34] This deeply rooted view was reflected in the growing opposition in 2007 to America's long involvement in the war in Iraq.

Most Americans support a volunteer army, one composed of people who generally come from less-privileged economic backgrounds. The country as a whole has demonstrated a low tolerance for combat fatalities and long-term military involvement in dangerous regions. Charles William Maynes observed that empires need to have either **Hessians** (i.e., mercenary soldiers from the region of Hesse in Germany) or citizens who, like the Romans, are anxious to go to war in distant places. America has neither.[35] Moreover, Americans, increasingly more affluent and better educated, are having smaller families and are unwilling to encourage their sons and daughters to join the military. Despite strong public support for the war against terrorism and short-term conflicts, Americans remain primarily concerned with economic issues and the implications of economic globalization. They have constantly viewed economic rather than military power as

Hessians ■ Mercenary soldiers from Hesse region in Germany the more important determinant of global dominance, thus their preoccupation with Japan's economic success during the 1980s and early 1990s. The financial crisis, high oil prices, and increasing unemployment in 2008 and 2009 reinforced Americans' focus on the centrality of economic power as the most critical measure of a country's strength.[36]

Will the United States Remain the Dominant Power?

As American troops marched across Iraq and its planes and ships bombed Baghdad to effectuate what the Pentagon called "shock and awe," the rest of the world watched the most awesome military force the world has ever known unilaterally impose its will on another country. America clearly demonstrated that it is a hegemon with a preponderance of power. On the other hand, some scholars, such as Paul Kennedy, caution that overwhelming power often leads a country to engage in imperial overstretch or to expand its interests and obligations to such a great degree that it overburdens its resource base and is unable to defend all of its interests simultaneously.[37] America's difficulties in Iraq made this obvious by 2008. Another concern was America's emphasis on unilateralism. Stanley Hoffmann, a leading scholar of international relations, argued that there is nothing more dangerous for a hyperpower than the temptation of unilateralism. It may well believe that the constraints of international agreements and organizations are not necessary. But those constraints provide for better opportunities for leadership than does the arrogant demonstration of contempt for the behavior of other states.[38] The danger for the United States, it is argued, is that its unprecedented power is likely to influence it to become insensitive to other nations' fear and interests. Great powers often succumb to hubris. This hubris often leads the dominant nation to believe that it is a benevolent hegemon and that it is immunized from a backlash against its preponderance by the attractiveness of its ideology and culture. But because states are competitive and worry about the predominant country's capabilities, they are likely to coalesce against what they perceive to be a threat.[39]

Many scholars argue that discussions of America's decline are routine and wrong and that the country is likely to remain the dominant power for the foreseeable future. Samuel P. Huntington, for example, identified *five waves of declinism* that turned out to be wrong. The *first wave* occurred with the launch of *Sputnik* by the Soviets in 1957. The *second wave* was at the end of the 1960s, when the United States and the Soviet Union were perceived to be losing to rising economic powers, such as Japan and Western Europe. The *third wave* came with the oil embargo by the **Organization of Petroleum Exporting Countries (OPEC)** in 1973. The *fourth wave* was marked by America's defeat in Vietnam, the Watergate crisis that undermined public confidence in U.S. government and institutions, and the upsurge in Soviet-Cuban expansion in Angola, Afghanistan, Nicaragua, Ethiopia, and Mozambique. Finally, the *fifth wave* came in the late 1980s as a result of growing U.S. trade and budget deficits and Japan's economic might.[40] All of these waves subsided, leaving the United States as a dominant power.

Huntington and Joseph S. Nye contend that the United States will remain the dominant power. Huntington states that the ultimate test of a great power is its

OPEC ■ Group of oil-exporting states that collaborate to elevate their export power ability to renew itself, and that the United States meets this test to a far greater extent than past or present great powers. The *forces of renewal* are competition, mobility, and immigration. Furthermore, America's strength is multidimensional, meaning that it is based on military might, economic power, technological capabilities, cultural appeal, political leadership and influence in international institutions, an abundance of natural resources, and social cohesion and political stability at home.[41] Nye argues that the American problem is different from that of Britain, which faced challenges from a rising Germany and the United States itself. Instead, the United States will remain the dominant power but will have to cope with unprecedented problems of globalization that cannot be solved unilaterally.[42]

Advocates of American dominance or primacy stress that rising powers are the greatest threat to international security. China and countries in Europe are viewed as the major challengers to American leadership. Advocates of primacy believe that American supremacy must be maintained by politically, economically, and military outdistancing any challenger.[43] Advocates of primacy argue that force should be used sparingly and strategically in defense of concrete American interests. They also recognize the need to prevent the proliferation of weapons of mass destruction because of the direct threats they pose to American primacy.[44] However, the global financial crisis and the severe economic recession of 2008–2009 have profoundly altered the global distribution of power.

SUMMARY AND REVIEW

This chapter examined the rise and fall of great powers and the essential role of politics, economics, and culture in that process. Countries with strong economies and well-managed political systems are able to spread their culture globally and to exercise power over other states. A state, or in some cases a small group of states, that has extraordinary influence over the behavior of other states is said to have international primacy. States that enjoy international primacy are generally said to have diverse interests. When several great powers are in the international system, it is defined as being multipolar. During the Cold War, when the United States and the Soviet Union were superpowers, the system was bipolar. Today, the United States remains the world's only superpower, which makes the current system unipolar.

States and groups of states become powerful and lose their power for many reasons. War is one major factor. Although investing in military power can help turn a state into a great power, it can also lead to its fall as a great nation. Many great powers decline because of hubris, or excessive pride, and imperial arrogance. These nations tend to overestimate their power and expand their military power so much that they ultimately erode their economic base. We discussed some challenges to the U.S. status as the world's lone great power. Some of these challenges come from nations that are quickly advancing economically, such as Japan and China. A second challenge to American hegemony is the consolidation of power in Europe under one EU. Finally, we discussed the challenge to American power from nonstate actors, such as terrorist organizations, that try to undermine the strength of great nations.

KEY TERMS

power transition theory 26
multipolar 26
bipolar 26
unipolar 26
hegemon 26
Antonio Gramsci 27
power 27
gross national product
  (GNP) 27
gross domestic product
  (GDP) 27
power conversion 27
structural leadership 27
institutional leadership 28
situational leadership 28

population pressures 28
uneven economic
  growth 28
hubris 28
Lippmann Gap 28
imperial overstretch 28
Concert of Europe 29
containment 29
manifest destiny 31
Mexican-American War 31
Spanish American War 31
Monroe Doctrine 32
League of Nations 32
Pearl Harbor 32
public goods 34

Ministry of International
  Trade and Industry
  (MITI) 35
ideology 35
Japanese exceptionalism 35
Treaty of Friendship and
  Cooperation 37
Marshall Plan 38
asymmetrical warfare 39
Hessians 41
Organization of Petroleum
  Exporting Countries
  (OPEC) 42

DISCUSSION QUESTIONS

1. Economic power and military power are often discussed as the two most important factors that make up a great power. What are some other elements of power? How might they contribute to a nation's rise to superpower status?
2. What are the three types of leadership? Provide some examples of how the United States and past world powers have exercised these types of leadership.
3. What are some strategies for maintaining power and preventing rising powers from creating disorder in the international system? Provide some examples of countries that have used some of these strategies.
4. What are some current examples of challenges to American hegemony? What are the strongest challenges the United States faces to maintain its status as a great power? Explain.

SUGGESTED READINGS

Bark, Dennis. *Americans and Europeans*. Stanford: Hoover Institution Press, 2007.
Dunlop, John B. *The Rise of Russia and the Fall of the Soviet Empire*. Princeton, NJ: Princeton University Press, 1993.
Hodgson, Godfrey. *The Myth of American Exceptionalism*. New Haven: Yale University Press, 2009.
Khanna, Parag. *The Second World*. New York: Random House, 2008.
Panzer, Michael J. *When Giants Fall*. New York: Wiley, 2009.
Shirk, Susan. *China: Fragile Superpower*. New York: Oxford University Press, 2007.
Zakaria, Fareed. *"The Future of American Power,"* *Foreign Affairs* 87, No. 3 (May/June 2008): 18–44.

END NOTES

1. Samuel P. Huntington, "Why International Primacy Matters," *International Security* 17, No. 4 (Spring 1993), 68.
2. Ronald L. Tammen et al., *Power Transitions* (New York: Seven Bridges Press, 2000), 6.

3. Alan W. Cafruny, "A Gramscian Concept of Declining Hegemony," in *World Leadership and Hegemony*, ed. David R. Rapkin (Boulder, CO: Lynne Rienner, 1990), 103.

4. Joseph S. Nye, *Bound to Lead: The Changing Nature of American Power* (New York: Basic Books, 1990), 32.

5. John J. Mearsheimer, *The Tragedy of Great Power Politics* (New York: W. W. Norton, 2001), 61.

6. Nye, *Bound to Lead*, 27.

7. G. John Ikenberry, "The Future of International Leadership," *Political Science Quarterly* III (Fall 1996), 388.

8. Ikenberry, "The Future of International Leadership," 389.

9. Randall Schweller, "Managing the Rise of Great Powers," in *Engaging China,* eds. Alistair Johnston and Robert Ross (London: Routledge, 1999), 2.

10. Torbjorn L. Knutsen, *The Rise and Fall of World Orders* (Manchester: Manchester University Press, 1999), 24.

11. Walter Lippmann, *U.S. Foreign Policy* (London: Hanish Hamilton, 1943), 5; and Paul Kennedy, *The Rise and Fall of Great Powers* (New York: Vintage Books, 1987), xvi.

12. G. John Ikenberry and Charles Kupchan, "The Legitimation of Hegemonic Power," in *World Leadership and Hegemony*, 49.

13. Schweller, "Managing the Rise of Great Powers," in *Engaging China,* 9.

14. Schweller, "Managing the Rise of Great Powers," in *Engaging China,* 14.

15. Knutsen, *The Rise and Fall of World Orders,* 175.

16. Ernest R. May, *Imperial Democracy: The Emergence of America as a Great Power* (Chicago: Imprint Publications, 1991), 7.

17. May, *Imperial Democracy,* 3.

18. Josef Joffe, "How America Does It," *Foreign Affairs* 76, No. 5 (September/October 1997), 27; and G. John Ikenberry, "Institutions, Strategic Restraint, and the Persistence of American Postwar Order," *International Security* 23, No. 3 (Winter 1998–99), 71.

19. Andrew C. Revkin, "U.S. Making Weapons to Blast Underground Hide-Outs," *New York Times*, 3 December 2001, B4.

20. Samuel P. Huntington, "The Lonely Superpower," *Foreign Affairs* 78, No. 2 (March/April 1999), 37; and Richard N. Haass, "The Age of Nonpolarity," *Foreign Affairs* 87, No. 3 (May/June 2008), 44.

21. Hugh De Santis, *Beyond Progress* (Chicago: University of Chicago Press, 1996), 33.

22. David S. Landes, *The Wealth and Poverty of Nations* (New York: W. W. Norton, 1998), 474.

23. David Rapkin, "Japan and World Leadership," in *World Leadership,* 199.

24. Michael M. May, "Japan as a Superpower?" *International Security* 18, No. 3 (Winter 1993/94), 183.

25. Gilbert Royman, "China's Quest for Great Power Identity," *Orbis* 43, No. 3 (Winter 1993/94), 183.

26. G. John Ikenberry, "The Rise of China and the Future of the West," *Foreign Affairs* 87, No. 1 (January/February 2008), 26.

27. Saritha Rai, "Chinese Race to Supplant India in Software," *New York Times,* 5 January 2002, B1.

28. Thom Shanker, "Gates Questions China on Military Growth," *New York Times*, 6 November 2007, A5.

29. Andrew Reding, "EU in Position to Be the Next Superpower," *Chicago Tribune*, 6 January 2002, Sect. 1, 19; and C. Fred Bergsten, "America and Europe: A Clash of the Titans," *Foreign Affairs* 78, No. 2 (March/April 1999), 20.

30. Philip H. Gordon, "Their Own Army? Making European Defense Work," *Foreign Affairs* 79, No. 4 (July/August 2000), 12; and Roger Cohen, "Europe's Shifting Role Poses Challenge to U.S.," *New York Times,* 11 February 2001, A1.

31. Michael R. Gordon, "Superpower Suddenly Finds Itself Threatened by Sophisticated Terrorists," *New York Times,* 14 October 2000, A9.

32. Thomas Friedman, "Swimming Without a Suit," *New York Times,* 22 April 2009, A23.

33. Huntington, "The Lonely Superpower," 40.

34. Michael J. Panzner, *When Giants Fall* (New York: Wiley, 2009), 5.

35. Charles William Maynes, "The Perils of (and for) an Imperial America," *Foreign Policy,* No. 111 (Summer 1998), 42.

36. Peter S. Goodman, "A Fresh Look at the Apostle of Free Markets," *New York Times,* 13 April 2008, A3.

37. Kennedy, *The Rise and Fall of Great Powers,* 515.

38. Stanley Hoffmann, "Clash of Globalizations," *Foreign Affairs* 81, No. 4 (July/August 2002), 113.

39. Fareed Zakaria, "The Future of American Power," *Foreign Affairs* 87, No. 3 (May/June 2008), 19.

40. Samuel P. Huntington, "The U.S.-Decline or Renewal?" *Foreign Affairs* 67, No. 2 (Winter 1988/89), 94–95.

41. Huntington, "The U.S.-Decline or Renewal?" 90–91.

42. Nye, *Bound to Lead,* 21.

43. Barry R. Posen and Andrew L. Ross, "Competing Visions for U.S. Grand Strategy," in *America's Strategic Choices,* eds. Michael E. Brown et al. (Cambridge, MA: The MIT Press, 2000), 30.

44. Posen and Ross, "Competing Visions," 39.

Human Rights

INTRODUCTION

Each culture or society has a moral sense, a set of feelings and beliefs about what is right and wrong. Cultural values in Asia, Africa, and the Middle East, for example, often create tensions with the West about human rights. Although cultural values differ significantly from one society to another, our common humanity has equipped us with many shared ideas about how human beings should treat each other. However, as this chapter shows, many societies, including the United States, engage in practices that others condemn as violations of human rights. In general, there is global agreement that human beings, simply because we exist, are entitled to at least three types of rights. One is **civil rights,** which include personal liberties, such as freedom of speech, religion, and thought; the right to own property; and the right to equal treatment under the laws. Second is **political rights**, including the right to vote, to voice political opinions, and to participate in the political process. Third is **social rights**, including the right to be secure from violence and other physical danger, the right to a decent standard of living, and the right to health care and education. Societies differ in terms of which rights they emphasize.

As a society that originated from a revolution, the United States often stresses rights and deemphasizes responsibilities. But rights do not exist apart from duties and responsibilities. A right is a claim that individuals may expect others to respect. When individuals claim the right to free speech, they are in essence saying that others are obligated to respect their right to speak freely. Their assertion of a right clearly implies that others have responsibilities. **Positive rights** require others to behave in a certain way. These include the right to a certain level of economic well-being, health, education, and cultural amenities. **Negative rights** include rights or claims of individuals and groups against governments and other institutions. Freedom of speech, of religion, of the press, and the right to a fair trial are examples of negative rights. *Four types of human rights claims* that dominate global politics are

1. Accusations that governments are abusing individuals;
2. Demands by ethnic, racial, and religious communities for autonomy or independence;
3. Claims in what is generally regarded as private life, including rights and obligations within families, and the demands for equality by minority groups with unconventional lifestyles; and
4. Demands by governments for protection against powerful governments and nonstate actors, as well as the right to economic development.[1]

This chapter discusses human rights as an integral component of the political, economic, and cultural forces of globalization. We will examine historical and philosophical foundations undergirding the development of human rights as a central component of modern civilizations. The issues involved in implementing human rights are essential to any discussion of securing freedom. Economic and political sanctions are often used to achieve compliance with human rights commitments. However, those societies that suffer from economic hardship generally experience widespread human rights violations. Haiti, Darfur, the Congo, and Cuba are obvious examples. In extreme cases, countries support humanitarian intervention to terminate violations of human rights. One of the most significant developments is the emphasis on women's human rights. All societies, to varying degrees, confer on women an inferior status that makes them vulnerable to discrimination and abuse. In this chapter, we will look closely at issues such as forced marriages, honor killings, and rape as a weapon of war. Closely related to women's rights is the contemporary debate on human rights in Islamic countries. In fighting terrorism, many governments violate human rights, which we will also discuss. Finally, we will briefly examine the death penalty issue, slavery, and the treatment of gays and lesbians.

Civil Rights ■
Personal liberties, such as freedom of speech, thought, and religion

Political Rights ■
Right to vote, voice political opinions, and participate in the political process

Social Rights ■
Right to health care, education, and other social benefits

Positive Rights ■
Rights a government/society is supposed to provide

GLOBALIZATION AND HUMAN RIGHTS

The different waves of globalization we discussed in Chapter 1 were accompanied by both positive and negative consequences for human rights. While some people benefited from global change, others paid an extremely high price for progress. The rise of the modern state in Western Europe and the European expansion into the Americas, Asia, and Africa increased both freedom and oppression. The modern state provided increased security, but often it also became a cold instrument for systematically abusing human rights. In fact, it was due to violence against Jews, gypsies, gays and lesbians, communists, religious groups, and others in Nazi Germany, which culminated in the **Holocaust**, that human rights became so prominent in global affairs.

The current wave of globalization has undoubtedly enhanced the observance of human rights. Telecommunications, trade, migration, travel, the weakening of national boundaries, the decline of **Westphalian** sovereignty, and growing interdependence have strengthened a commitment to human rights. Information is now relayed instantaneously, which helps to limit governments' ability to engage in secrecy and brutality. China, for example, uses telecommunications technologies to control its population, but many Chinese also use these technologies to diminish the government's ability to limit their freedom. Because their interests are intertwined with those of leading global actors, countries must consider the costs and benefits of decisions concerning their treatment of citizens. For example, China risks jeopardizing trade with the United States if it engages in gross violations of human rights. In March 2001, China decided to ratify the International Convention on Economic, Social, and Cultural Rights, partly because it was competing to host the 2008 Olympics.[2] This decision demonstrates how sports, which are a component of cultural globalization, often pressure governments to comply with global humanitarian values. China's actions in Tibet and its close ties to Sudan, which many saw as China's violations and disregard for human rights, engendered global demonstrations in 2008 against China's hosting of the Olympic Games. However, other aspects of globalization contribute to abuses of human rights. For example, many human rights activists argue that America's war against drugs in Colombia has contributed to widespread brutality by Colombia's armed forces and right-wing militias. Many of the victims belong to the Embera Indian group. It is estimated that twenty-seven indigenous groups risk being eliminated.[3] America's war on terrorism is also widely perceived as endangering human rights. Many terrorist suspects were tortured.

The horrors of the Holocaust and World War II marked a turning point in the struggle to obtain global respect for human rights. Equally important was the rise of the United States to global power and its competition with the Soviet Union for the hearts and minds of people around the world, especially in the developing countries. This period of globalization radically transformed the perception that domestic affairs could be automatically separated from international politics. A deeper awareness of the indivisibility of humanity and of our problems weakened the idea that governments are essentially free to treat their citizens as they wish. America's self-definition as a redeemer nation and a positive force made human rights a central global issue. The superpower struggle led to the signing of international agreements that protected both civil and political rights (strongly advocated by the United States) and social and economic rights (endorsed by the Soviet Union). To these were added the right of minority groups to equal treatment and a cultural identity; humanitarian treatment of civilians in internal conflicts; and the right to economic development, security, and a healthy environment. In addition to the influence of the United States and the Soviet Union, several other factors contributed to the expansion of and commitment to the human rights agenda:

1. The *creation of global institutions* to protect human rights.
2. A growing acceptance of the interdependence and indivisibility of rights. Violations of rights in one country have implications for people in other countries.
3. An *emphasis on promoting democracy*. The idea that democracy is essential to peaceful international relations became a central part of U.S. foreign policy.
4. The view that *respect for human rights facilitated market-based economic development.*[4]
5. *The effectiveness of nonstate actors.*

Negative Rights ■ Rights a government may not infringe upon

Holocaust ■ Mass murder of millions of Jews driven by ethnic and religious hate and discrimination

Westphalian ■ Concept of state sovereignty developed over 350 years ago

Nongovernmental Organizations and Human Rights

Because many governments violate human rights, responsibility for protecting individual freedoms was taken up by numerous nonstate actors at the local, national, and global levels. As citizens became more politically sophisticated, they challenged the assumption that governments are free to act without the consent of the governed. Increasingly, the legitimacy of governments came to depend on their citizens' opinions, as well as on those of members of the global community. Human rights organizations directly challenged the assumption that sovereignty allows governments to abuse internationally recognized human rights. Partly due to frustrations with other governments' bureaucratic approaches and often counterproductive measures to protect human rights, transnational groups now take direct action to prevent violations of basic rights. Amnesty International, one of the best-known human rights nongovernmental organizations (NGOs), was founded in London in 1961 by a group of writers and lawyers. It publishes reports on human rights problems in countries worldwide. It also encourages its global membership to participate in letter-writing campaigns to seek the release of **prisoners of conscience**; that is, individuals who are imprisoned because governments disapprove of their political, religious, social, or other beliefs. Many governments are sensitive to negative publicity and may face global economic and political pressures.

Prisoners of Conscience ■ Individuals imprisoned because of their political, religious, or social beliefs

Global Companies and Human Rights

Human rights activists are increasingly pressuring global companies to make the promotion and observation of human rights a centerpiece of their corporate strategy. Google's operations in China and its willingness to cooperate with the government raised questions about links between business and respect for human rights. Many students and activists around the world have made issues such as child labor and sweatshops integral components of human rights debates. Working conditions in India, Bangladesh, China, and in countries in Africa and Latin America are routinely condemned and efforts are made to improve them. Now we are seeing greater emphasis placed on **corporate social responsibility**, which includes safeguarding the fundamental rights and freedoms of individuals. Companies are expected to secure human rights in countries where governments routinely violate them. To some extent, the companies' new role reflects the growing power of nonstate actors vis-à-vis nation-states. It also demonstrates the power of NGOs in a global society. The most powerful companies with global recognition are also the most vulnerable to pressure from human rights NGOs and the global media. Although public awareness of human rights abuses does not automatically influence consumers to reject high-quality, brand-name products that are reasonably priced, many companies believe that supporting human rights is good for business. Increasingly, global companies are regarded as powerful instruments in the pursuit of human rights.[5]

Corporate Social Responsibility ■ Corporate initiatives aimed at achieving social justice

How much companies observe and promote human rights depends to some extent on their strategies and what they produce. Corporations that pursue a **market-building strategy** are distinguished from those that adopt a **cost-minimizing strategy**. Market-building companies are less likely to abuse human rights than cost-minimizing firms, which are more short-term oriented and more vulnerable to the

Market-Building Strategy ■ Seeks profit by building up markets rather than assaulting worker rights pressures of globalization to increase profits at the expense of employees' human rights. Market-building strategies involve making significant investments that are unlikely to produce immediate profits. Equally important, companies pursuing such strategies tend to have a greater commitment to the people and the country in which they operate.[6] What a company produces will also affect its human rights record. For example, many petroleum companies operate in countries that disregard human rights. When you think of the Middle East, you generally focus on its petroleum resources without realizing that few of the region's governments are strong supporters of human rights. Similarly, several African states that have huge deposits of petroleum have poor human rights records. Because petroleum companies have global operations, they are vulnerable to pressure from human rights NGOs. An example is Shell's experience in Nigeria. Operating in the delta region of Nigeria since 1937, Shell was accused by human rights groups of participating in government's oppression of the **Ogonis** and the execution in 1995 of **Ken Saro-Wiwa,** the Ogoni's leader, and others in the **movement for the survival of the Ogoni People** (**MOSOP**). Stung by global criticism and worried about its bottom line, Shell added the Universal Declaration of Human Rights (UDHR) to its business principles in 1997. It also consults with human rights activists, distributes a human rights guide to its managers, and trains them to deal with human rights issues.[7] However, conditions remain difficult for the Ogonis and violent clashes with Shell escalated in 2009.

DEVELOPMENT OF HUMAN RIGHTS

Inventors of Western democracy, the Greeks profoundly believed that humans have natural fundamental rights and freedoms, although these rights were not enjoyed by women and slaves in Greek society. Humans have always had a moral sense and have practiced, to varying degrees, rights embraced by the Greeks. But the Greeks clearly articulated and systematically practiced rights such as *isogoria* (equal freedom of speech) and *isonomia* (equality before the law). Greek philosophers, known as **Stoics**, developed the idea that rights enjoyed by Greeks were **universal rights**, freedoms that humans everywhere were entitled to simply because humans exist. These rights emanated from a law that was higher and more permanent than civil law—a universal law that was equated with the laws of gods. These laws were natural laws, which embodied elementary principles of justice that rational human beings could understand. Greek philosophy, like many other Greek inventions, was adopted by the Romans. Roman Stoics were primarily lawyers who attempted to implement the ideas of Greek philosophers in an expanding Roman Empire that encompassed diverse peoples. Marcus Tullius Cicero, Lucius Annaeus Seneca, and Marcus Aurelius were some of the leading Roman Stoics. **Cicero** (106–43 B.C.), the most prominent lawyer and philosopher of the Roman Empire, wrote that "true law is right reason in agreement with nature; it is of universal application, unchanging and everlasting."[8] This *natural law concept* was consistent with Rome's universal or cosmopolitan perception of humanity. Like other Greek and Roman institutions and ideas, Stoic philosophy profoundly shaped European societies. John Locke in England, Hugo Grotius in Holland, and Immanuel Kant in Germany were influenced by the Stoics.

Cost-Minimizing Strategy ■ Increases profits at the employees' expense

Ogonis ■ Ethnic group residing in the Nigerian Delta

Ken Saro-Wiwa ■ Executed in 1995 by the Nigerian government for involvement in the Ogoni movement

MOSOP ■ Indigenous movement aimed at protecting the Ogoni people

Stoics ■ Ancient Greek and Roman philosophers

Universal Rights ■ Freedoms to which all humans are automatically entitled

Cicero ■ The leading Stoic and Rome's greatest lawyer and orator

Social Contract Theories and Human Rights

A major step toward widespread acceptance and practice of natural rights, which are closely associated with universal human rights, was the significant recognition by England's kings, barons, and others that citizens were entitled to exercise basic freedoms without interference from their leaders and that such leaders' powers were limited by law and a sense of justice and fairness. The signing of the **Magna Carta** in 1215 was followed by England's King Edward III's acceptance in 1354 of the concept of **due process of law**, which means that a person cannot be deprived of life, liberty, or property without a fair trial based on fair procedures and rules. Another important step toward consolidating human rights was the decision of King Charles I of England, in his Petition of Rights in 1628, to guarantee the right of **habeas corpus**; that is, the right of a person to be brought before a judge or a court to determine whether or not he or she should be imprisoned. The right to habeas corpus became a central issue in America's treatment of prisoners suspected of terrorism.

Natural rights theories flourished during a period of revolutions, beginning with the English Revolution of 1688, then the American Revolution of 1776, and the French Revolution of 1789. These revolutions stressed that individuals' freedoms were natural and that governments could not violate them. Restrictions on governments emerged from various historical experiences, but more directly from social contract theories. *Thomas Hobbes*, an English philosopher, justified the absolute power of monarchs by arguing that in the state of nature, before governments existed, life was unbearably violent and insecure. The creation of a powerful state or ruler, which he called **Leviathan**, to provide security in exchange for obedience was a social contract. *John Locke*, another English philosopher, argued in his *Second Treatise on Government* (1690) that the state of nature was governed by natural law. People were relatively secure and free and could acquire property. From Locke's perspective, the social contract between citizens and government protected these natural rights. In sharp contrast with the obedience advocated by Hobbes, Locke believed that people had the right to overthrow governments that failed to honor freedoms promised in the social contract. Nowhere are Locke's ideas expressed more forcefully than in the American Declaration of Independence.

Another advocate of the social contract was the French philosopher *Jean-Jacques Rousseau*. He was convinced that civilization corrupts human beings, who are naturally good. Nonetheless, he stressed in the **social contract** that through their total and equal subordination to the government, which is based on and functions according to the *general will* of all its citizens, humans could regain some of their natural goodness and freedoms. However, Rousseau ended up supporting a social contract that subordinates individual freedoms to the tyranny of the majority. His philosophy justified the government's absolute power over citizens.[9] The French Revolution, despite its embrace of human rights in the Declaration of the Rights of Man and of Citizens (1789), soon degenerated into the **Reign of Terror**, a period that became a hallmark of the systematic, pervasive, and extreme abuse of human rights by the French government. *Immanuel Kant* developed the idea that human rights are directly linked to an inviolable obligation that we have to ourselves and to others. Kant believed that these obligations are universal, binding on all of us no matter where we live, thereby underscoring the concept of the indivisibility of humanity and universal nature of human

Magna Carta ■ The first written legal protections for the British people

Due Process of Law ■ Protection of individual life, liberty, and property through a fair trial system

Habeas Corpus ■ The right to be brought before a judge or court to determine guilt or innocence

Leviathan ■ A powerful state or ruler

Second Treatise on Government ■ By John Locke; addressed the state of nature and natural law

Social Contract ■ Government sovereignty over its people in exchange for protecting individual rights

Reign of Terror ■ Terrorism committed by the French government after the French Revolution rights. The most profound of these obligations is the *categorical imperative*; that is, the absolute obligation that each of us should always treat humanity never simply as a means but always at the same time as an end.[10]

Utilitarianism, Libertarianism, and Marxism

Jeremy Bentham, James Mill, and John Stuart Mill were among those who developed the theory of **utilitarianism**, directly challenging the idea that human beings have natural rights. The utilitarians, led by Jeremy Bentham, believed that individuals determine what is good for them and what they want. Conversely, they avoid the things that cause them pain. In his ***Principles of Morals and Legislation*** (1789), Bentham used his training as an Oxford-educated lawyer to develop a scientific analysis of morals and legislation. His theory of utilitarianism held that the greatest happiness of the largest number of people is the fundamental and self-evident principle of morality. In a nutshell, Bentham and the other utilitarians argued that self-interests are generally harmonious with the general welfare. The state should be designed to enable individuals to achieve their objectives. Through the careful balancing of individual interests, individual rights arise and are protected. From the utilitarians' perspective, rights are derived from laws. Individual rights, according to the utilitarians, are neither natural nor unalienable, and they cannot be allowed to frustrate the principle and practice of the greatest happiness for the greatest number.

But John Stuart Mill—a utilitarian advocate and the son of James Mill, a leading utilitarian—questioned major assumptions of utilitarianism. He stressed that the government, representing the majority, can brutally suppress the rights of individuals. This fear of the tyranny of the majority is what motivated Jefferson and others to insist on the inclusion of the **Bill of Rights** in the U.S. Constitution to protect individuals who disagree with the majority. In other words, John Stuart Mill believed that focusing on the greatest happiness for the greatest number could easily result in the suppression of speech, religion, private morality, artistic endeavors, and nonconformist behavior that were not acceptable to the majority. Mill articulated his philosophy in ***On Liberty*** (1859). He argued that one could justify interfering with an individual's liberty only to prevent that person from harming others, an assumption that must be proven by government authorities. Mill believed that individual freedoms, such as freedom of speech, benefited society as a whole by providing different viewpoints that could expose problems in the positions held by the majority. The rights of women, for example, were championed by Mill, partly because of the influence of his wife, Harriet Taylor.

Another challenge to prevailing perspectives on human rights came from socialist philosophers, such as *Saint Simon* and *Karl Marx*. Marx, the most famous socialist, believed that the history of society is essentially a history of class struggle. Capitalists, while producing unprecedented profits for the few, created high levels of unemployment, subsistence wages, and successively more serious economic crises. Marx and Saint Simon argued that traditional human rights were largely irrelevant to the majority who lived in poverty. They advocated that governments should develop policies that give people economic and social rights. Their perspective was embraced by the former Soviet Union, China, Cuba, and many other communist countries.

Utilitarianism ■ Theory contradicting the idea that humans have natural rights

Principles of Morals and Legislation ■ Bentham's scientific analysis of morals and legislation

Bill of Rights ■ Constitutional protections of individual political rights

On Liberty ■ Stated that an individual's civil liberties can be violated only to protect others' rights

Legal Positivism and Human Rights

Closely related to utilitarianism are the positivistic theories and conservatism. Some conservatives, such as Edmund Burke, strongly opposed natural rights theories and Rousseau's views on the social contract and the general will. Strongly influenced by the Reign of Terror that followed the French Revolution, Burke believed that individuals derived whatever rights they have from tradition and concrete laws, not from abstract philosophical theories of natural laws.[11] What distinguished the **legal positivists** from the utilitarians was the extent to which the former insisted on the absolute supremacy of laws and courts in determining rights. After World War I, the legal positivists became more extremist, arguing that law was what courts upheld and that justice was the correct enforcement of the law. Yet those bound to honor specific laws had to have given their consent. In many ways, the legal positivists embraced Hobbes's view that law was essentially the command of the sovereign. Legal positivism was taken to its logical and devastatingly destructive conclusion in Germany under the Nazis. When **Adolf Hitler** came to power in Germany, he made the courts subservient to him and used them as a tool of legal positivism to an extent unparalleled by even the most ardent proponents of legal positivism. Hitler enacted laws suppressing freedom of speech, as well as laws requiring children to spy on their parents and Germans to spy on each other. Individuals could be imprisoned and executed without public trials. Ultimately, laws were enacted that authorized the Jewish Holocaust.[12] The attack on the U.S. Holocaust Memorial Museum in June 2009 by an American Neo-Nazi and white racial supremacist, James von Brunn, reminded the world of continuing threats to human rights.

Globalization of Human Rights: The Universal Declaration of Human Rights

Concerns about human rights occurred largely within the context of domestic politics. An overriding emphasis on state sovereignty, which included a preoccupation with independence and control over citizens' lives, prevented broader applications of human rights philosophies from emerging. But increasing globalization—especially European colonization of the Americas and the enslavement of Africans and others—engendered greater global attention to human rights issues that transcended national boundaries. The horrors of slavery shocked people in Europe and the Americas and led to an antislavery campaign in the nineteenth century. Leading countries generally supported abolishing the slave trade at the Congress of Vienna in 1815, seven years after the United States had ceased importing enslaved Africans as required by the U.S. Constitution. *The First Anti-Slavery Convention* was held in London in 1840 by the **Anti-Slavery Society**, the oldest global human rights NGO. Wars also helped to globalize human rights. Horrified by the death and suffering of soldiers at the battle of Solferino in Italy in 1859, *Jean Henry Dunant*, a Swiss citizen, decided to publicize what he saw and to "humanize" war. These efforts resulted in the creation of the International Committee of the Red Cross in 1863, followed by the approval of the First Geneva Convention in 1864. The convention was designed to humanize war by making rules for the treatment of wounded and sick soldiers and sailors, prisoners of war, and medical personnel.

World War I led to the creation of the League of Nations in 1919, which made protecting inhabitants of dependent territories and the trafficking in children and women international human rights issues.[13] The covenant of the League of Nations also made the protection and treatment of workers an international human rights concern. But it wasn't until the global catastrophe of World War II that human rights became a dominant global issue.

Nazi Germany's brutal march across Europe and the rise of the United States as the leading global power under the leadership of President Franklin Delano Roosevelt combined to give the impetus to making human rights global. America's self-perception as a nation with a universal message facilitated this development. Addressing Congress in January 1941, President Roosevelt committed the United States to securing **four freedoms** for the world: freedom of speech and expression, freedom of religion, freedom from economic hardship, and freedom from fear. Achieving these freedoms became the centerpiece of the *Atlantic Declaration* made by President Roosevelt and Britain's Prime Minister Winston Churchill in August 1941. The allies met in Washington, DC, under the auspices of the American Law Institute to draft a declaration or bill of international human rights.[14] These developments laid the foundation for including human rights in the charter of the United Nations (UN) when it was founded in 1945 in San Francisco. The UN Charter provided for the formation of the Human Rights Commission, with the major responsibility for drafting global human rights standards. The final result of these efforts was the adoption by the UN General Assembly of the Universal Declaration of Human Rights (UDHR) **UDHR** in 1948. *Eleanor Roosevelt* played a crucial role in this accomplishment. She was largely responsible for promoting the use of the term *human rights* instead of the traditional emphasis on the rights of man, which actually meant just that. It is also important to point out that the Convention on the Prevention and Punishment of the Crime of Genocide (the Genocide Convention), a direct response to the Holocaust, was adopted by the UN General Assembly the day before it adopted the UDHR. Although the world was united in its determination to promote human rights, differences between the United States and the Soviet Union later led to the adoption in 1966 of two separate international covenants: the **International Covenant on Civil and Political Rights (ICCPR)**, which stressed negative rights and was favored by the United States, and the **International Covenant on Economic, Social, and Cultural Rights (ICESCR)**, which focused on positive rights and was favored by the Soviet Union.

The UDHR helped to unleash global demands for national self-determination by stating that all peoples have this right. Defining "a people" would become more complex than imagined. Countries in Africa, Asia, and the Caribbean succeeded in getting the UN General Assembly to adopt the International Convention on the Elimination of All Forms of Racial Discrimination in 1965. The global human rights agenda expanded to include the Convention on the Elimination of All Forms of Discrimination Against Women (1981), the Convention on the Rights of the Child (1990), the Convention Concerning Indigenous and Tribal Peoples in Independent Countries (1991), and the International Convention on the Protection of the Rights of All Migrant Workers and Members of Their Families (1991). Human rights issues often became entangled in political disputes between the

Four Freedoms ▪ Freedoms espoused by Roosevelt that are necessary for a just society

UDHR ▪ Universal rights entitled to all humankind

ICCPR ▪ Stressed the protection of negative political and civil rights from government infringement

ICESCR ▪ Stressed the protection and promotion of positive economic, cultural, and social rights that government should provide its people

United States and the Soviet Union during the Cold War. The end of this confrontation in the late 1980s renewed global interest in enforcing human rights. However, countries in the developing world are often in conflict with the United States about punishing countries such as Libya, Cuba, Zimbabwe, Saudi Arabia, Pakistan, and Egypt for human rights violations.

PHILOSOPHICAL CONTROVERSIES OVER HUMAN RIGHTS

The question on justice or torture in Saudi Arabia raises a fundamental philosophical controversy over human rights, one that persists and grows as societies feel increasingly threatened by the realities of cultural globalization. Other such controversies involve (1) the relationship between individuals and the communities in which they live, (2) the relationship between rights and obligations, (3) the prioritizing of rights and responsibilities, and (4) the absolute or conditional quality of various human rights.[15]

Universalism Versus Cultural Relativism

As we have seen, Greek and Roman Stoics articulated the view that people have natural rights no matter where they live. This idea was more clearly developed by Locke, Jefferson, and others and has become the dominant view of human rights. But even in societies that stress universal human rights, cultural factors often complicate these theories. The United States, for example, simultaneously embraced natural rights and slavery. In other words, countries

Cultural Relativism ■ Idea that culture determines the degree of human rights protections in each country

modify their support of universal rights by practicing **cultural relativism.** Often, leaders and ordinary citizens do not recognize their own biases in this regard. Proponents of cultural relativism believe that rights enjoyed by individuals are determined by each country's specific cultural and historical experiences. Consequently, what is acceptable behavior in one country could be a violation of human rights in another. Amputating limbs in Saudi Arabia, for example, is viewed in that society as reasonable punishment. Americans reject that punishment as barbaric. On the other hand, America's support of the death penalty is widely regarded in Europe as barbaric. Conservatives and traditionalists in virtually all societies strongly support national cultural relativism. Often, cultural relativism sustains power relations in a society and draws artificial distinctions between societies, instead of emphasizing common values across cultures and the cross-fertilization among cultures. One version of cultural relativism that was popular when Japan was viewed as a rising

Confucianism ■ Stresses obedience to authority and the importance of collective identities

superpower was **Confucianism.** Some argued that Asians were successful because their cultures embrace the Confucianism values of obedience to authority and intense allegiance to groups and stress collective identities over individual identities. Based on this perspective, the assumption was that universalism was essentially Western and largely incompatible with Asian values.[16] This treatment of Asian values as monolithic has since been widely rejected as being overly simplistic.

YOU DECIDE

Justice or Torture in Saudi Arabia?

Shari'a law, the Islamic legal code that governs Saudi Arabia, allows amputations of limbs for theft and floggings for certain sexual offenses and for drinking alcohol. For example, in 2007, a young woman and her former boyfriend she was with in a car were kidnapped and gang-raped. She was sentenced by the court to be given ninety lashes. After her lawyer appealed, her sentence was increased to two hundred lashes. Her sentence was later overturned by King Abdullah. Shari'a also allows murderers, rapists, and drug dealers to be executed. For most Saudis, cutting off a person's hand is acceptable because although that action harms the criminal, it protects society. However, the 1987 Convention Against Torture, signed by Saudi Arabia, outlaws floggings and amputations. The Saudis argue that Shari'a takes precedence over international agreements.

Are the Saudis justified in following their religious beliefs even if those beliefs violate human rights? Are their actions justice or torture? ■

Individuals and Communities

Complicating discussions of human rights are varying perspectives on the relationship between the individual and the community to which she or he belongs. In societies strongly influenced by Buddhism, Hinduism, or Confucianism, individualism is discouraged and community solidarity is a virtue. The individual is inseparable from the community and enjoys certain benefits from belonging to the community. However, the danger of denying individual rights is that the least powerful in these societies are often brutally suppressed by elites. Many authoritarian governments have justified violating human rights by stressing the need to promote the common good over individual rights and democratic values. However, individualism in the United States is often regarded as contributing to human rights violations, especially in relation to positive rights.

Relationship Between Rights and Obligations

Earlier in this chapter we discussed the connection between rights and responsibilities or obligations. The basic argument is that rights are simply corresponding obligations. In other words, failing to act to prevent human rights violations is in itself a violation of human rights. This argument assumes that we are capable of doing something either to prevent such violations or to mitigate their severity. The idea that we are responsible for what happens to others goes back to the idea that we have a moral responsibility for both acts of omission and acts of commission.

Prioritizing Human Rights

As American and British troops entered Baghdad in April 2003, many Americans and Iraqis celebrated the destruction of Saddam Hussein's regime and the idea of restoring fundamental freedoms to the Iraqis. But as chaos and violence escalated, many people worldwide, including the Iraqis, emphasized the urgency of providing electricity, medical supplies, petroleum, and basic services. Above all, the

Iraqis wanted security, food, and clean water. This situation demonstrates the philosophical controversy over prioritizing human rights. Freedom of religion, speech, assembly, and the press are often elevated above other concerns in the United States. But many other societies place a much higher priority on satisfying basic economic needs. Difficult economic conditions often contribute to violations of human rights. For example, the financial crisis and economic recession led to increased violence against the Roma (also known as Gypsies) in Hungary and elsewhere in Europe.

Absolutism Versus Consequentialism

Finally, there is the debate about whether we should be willing to compromise on upholding human rights under certain circumstances. Some human rights advocates believe that some rights are absolute; that is, they can never be violated. On the other hand, many of these same advocates would agree that some rights are sometimes limited because exercising them under specific circumstances could endanger the rights of others. The torture of terrorist suspects by the United States and the ongoing debate about their entitlement to basic human rights illustrate how easily human rights violations can be justified in the name of national security.

HUMAN RIGHTS REGIMES

UNCHR ■ Commission responsible for monitoring human rights on a global level

Regimes, as defined in Chapter 1, are institutions, rules, and regulations governing particular types of behavior and interactions. *Human rights regimes* consist of global, regional, national, and local institutions and rules designed to protect human rights, as well as the activities of numerous nonstate human rights organizations and grassroots campaigns. The **UN Commission on Human Rights (UNCHR)** is charged with the responsibility of monitoring human rights globally and for informing the UN Security Council of human rights violations. Previously, we also noted that nations and NGOs, especially after World War I and World War II, succeeded in developing international laws concerning the treatment of national minorities and laborers. These are all components of the global human rights regimes. In this section we will examine regional human rights regimes, focusing on those in Europe. The main institutions dealing with human rights in Europe are the European Commission for Human Rights, the European Court of Justice, and the Organization for Security and Cooperation in Europe (OSCE). Latin America, Africa, and other regions have essentially adopted Europe's regime.[17]

Council of Europe ■ Created in 1949 to promote democracy and human rights

Meeting in The Hague in 1948, European representatives laid the foundations for establishing the **Council of Europe** in 1949 to promote democracy and protect human rights. Recent events in Europe propelled the states belonging to the council to sign the *European Convention for the Protection of Human Rights and Fundamental Freedoms* in 1950. This agreement focused on safeguarding civil and political rights. The European Social Charter, signed in 1961, dealt with economic and social rights.[18] Continuing abuses of human rights in Europe, especially in countries under Soviet domination, influenced German Chancellor *Willy Brandt* to promote dialogue across ideological divisions. These efforts led to the adoption of the Helsinki Final Act in 1975 and the creation of the OSCE. The **Helsinki Final Act** provided for the dissemination of the agreement and information about it within countries that originated it. This allowed people in Eastern Europe and the Soviet Union to learn more about human rights initiatives and sparked debate within the communist countries. Combined internal and external pressure influenced Soviet leader Mikhail Gorbachev to adopt policies conducive to the exercise of both civil and political rights and economic and social rights.[19] Eventually, the Soviet domination of Eastern Europe collapsed in 1989 and the Soviet Union disintegrated in 1991. Nevertheless, human rights violations remain a serious issue in many parts of Europe.

Latin Americans have adopted many features of the European human rights regime but have been less successful in implementing human rights protections. The two most important agreements that established the **Inter-American regime** are the charter of the Organization of American States (OAS) and the American Human Rights Convention. Like Europeans, Latin Americans have a human rights commission (the Inter-American Commission on Human Rights) and a court (the Inter-American Court of Human Rights). However, unlike Europeans, who are willing to relinquish some of their sovereignty, Latin Americans cling so tightly to theirs that they impede the effectiveness of the human rights regime.

Helsinki Final Act ■ Created to implement civil and political rights throughout Europe and the Soviet Union

Inter-American Regime ■ Attempt to establish regional protections for human rights in Latin America

ENFORCING HUMAN RIGHTS GLOBALLY

Although much of the responsibility for enforcing human rights is placed on global institutions, governments, and various NGOs, we as individuals have the ultimate obligation for protecting human rights. Crimes against humanity are generally seen as crimes against all of us, a viewpoint supported by the widespread acceptance of the universal nature of human rights. Yet, as individuals, our effectiveness to combat major human rights violations, especially when they occur in distant countries and are carried out by governments, is limited. Consequently, government institutions and various organizations that represent individuals are regarded as bearing most of the responsibility for implementing human rights. The extent to which various global actors and individuals are morally obligated to take action depends on three factors: (1) the nature of the relationship with the rights being violated, (2) the degree of effectiveness, and (3) capacity. The nature of the *relationship* involves issues such as geographic, economic, cultural, or political ties and the depth and duration of those connections. Countries closest to where human rights abuses are taking place are generally expected to act to prevent them, although geographic proximity in an age of globalization is declining in importance. More stress is placed on the *degree of effectiveness* and *capacity*. These three factors are integral to the concept of a *fair allocation of responsibility*.[20] Generally, there are two approaches to implementing human rights. One is the soft systems of implementation, which concentrate primarily on conducting inquiries, exposing human rights violations, empowering the victims, and finding ways to damage the violating state's reputation. The other is the *hard, or coercive, enforcement measures*, which include making interventions, setting up international tribunals to prosecute violators, and establishing a permanent international criminal court (ICC).[21]

Sanctions

Sanctions ■ Punishments or penalties imposed on one or more states by another state, group of states, or the global community

Sanctions are punishments or penalties imposed by one state, a group of states, or the global community on another state or group of states in order to gain compliance with widely accepted global standards of behavior. Because political, economic, and military-strategic considerations affect decisions to impose sanctions, there are usually inconsistencies in how sanctions are imposed. For example, allies often escape sanctions even though their behavior is similar to that of the states being sanctioned. In Darfur and Myanmar (Burma), economic interests of China, India, and other countries have undermined sanctions. The complexity of the factors involved in imposing sanctions results in much controversy about using them to force a country to comply with global rules for protecting and promoting human rights. Sanctions can be nonviolent or violent; most are nonviolent. Nonviolent sanctions include economic, diplomatic, political, and cultural measures. **Economic sanctions**, the most prevalent, often limit trade, reduce access to international investments and financing, and freeze or confiscate bank deposits of both countries and individuals. **Diplomatic and political sanctions** include actions that aim at embarrassing a government and its leaders and reducing its interactions with the global community. **Cultural sanctions** usually try to reduce or stop cultural exchanges, tourism, educational ties, and sporting activities with the target country.[22] Often, sanctions not only fail to change the government's practices, but turn out to have devastating consequences for innocent civilians. For example, U.S. sanctions against Cuba, strengthened by the Bush administration in 2004 and reinforced in 2007, were widely perceived as being counterproductive as well as harmful to ordinary Cubans. Cuba's leader, Fidel Castro, relinquished power in 2008 because of his poor health, not because of U.S. sanctions. Recognizing this reality, the United States lifted some of the sanctions in 2009.

Economic Sanctions ■ Designed to limit or freeze a state's trade, investments, or financing

Diplomatic and Political Sanctions ■ Designed to isolate and embarrass a state on a political level

Cultural Sanctions ■ Seek to limit cultural exchanges, tourism, sports, and other interactions with a sanctioned state

Unilateral Sanctions ■ Sanctions imposed by only one country

Sanctions can be imposed unilaterally or multilaterally. **Unilateral sanctions,** imposed by one country, were used more often than multilateral sanctions and by several countries before the end of the Cold War. Since 1990, however, the use of **multilateral sanctions** has increased as the ideological conflicts that penalized the UN and other international organizations ended. Increased international cooperation has also encouraged using sanctions as an alternative to military force. At the same time, however, the spread of globalization, which engenders global cooperation, complicates efforts to impose sanctions that are ultimately successful.[23] In an interdependent world, one country's loss due to sanctions can easily become another country's loss as well. In other words, sanctions aimed at an enemy often damage a friend. The United States, the dominant global power, uses sanctions far more often than any other country, and it often influences other countries to do the same. Domestic factors often have significant influence on America's reliance on sanctions. The inherent competition and conflict between Congress and the president, built into the system of separation of powers, often motivates Congress and the president to act quickly in response to growing domestic pressures.[24]

Multilateral Sanctions ■ Sanctions imposed by more than one country

Although some sanctions have achieved their objectives, such as those applied against the apartheid regime in South Africa, the consensus is that they are usually ineffective. *Sanctions fail for several reasons.* One reason is that nationalism, present in all countries, spawns a rally-round-the-flag effect. Another is that globalization makes it extremely difficult to effectively isolate a state economically.

Third, sanctions may enable repressive governments to use external threats to justify cracking down on domestic opponents and to avoid responsibility for deteriorating economic, health, and social conditions. Fourth, sanctions are costly to countries that impose them. Over time, domestic pressures build to support removing sanctions against the targeted country. Finally, sanctions reduce the availability of resources in the target state, thereby strengthening its power to allocate scarce resources strategically to maintain support for its policies.[25]

Humanitarian Intervention

In extreme cases, when human rights violations shock human conscience, **humanitarian intervention** is regarded as a collective global responsibility. Humanitarian intervention usually involves deploying military forces to prevent or stop a country or group from engaging in gross violations of human rights.[26] It also includes efforts to provide humanitarian relief, to evacuate individuals, and to separate and monitor forces involved in conflicts. Humanitarian interventions fall into two basic categories: consensual and imposed. **Consensual interventions** are agreed to by those in control of a country or region. There is little need for military force. Uniformed forces are involved primarily because they have essential skills and technical capabilities that facilitate rescue operations or the provision of humanitarian supplies. **Imposed interventions** are conducted in a far more hostile environment and often against the wishes of governments or armed groups. Significant military force is required to reduce hostilities, protect civilians, and protect individuals who are delivering humanitarian assistance.[27]

Closely related to humanitarian intervention are peacekeeping and peacemaking operations. **Peacekeeping**, provided by Chapter 6 of the UN Charter, occurs within a consensual type of intervention. It involves largely impartial monitors and observers who are unarmed or lightly armed. They are generally required to monitor a separation of forces, verify and monitor troop withdrawals, provide some security, and supervise elections. Force is used as a last resort and only for self-defense.[28] **Peacemaking**, on the other hand, involves military forces that are heavily armed, well trained, and prepared to fight. But peacemaking is a far more circumscribed activity compared with standard military operations. Peacemaking occurs in situations in which most of the forces involved are friendly. The basic objective of peacemaking is to reduce the fighting and to restore or create an environment that will enable peacekeeping forces to function effectively.[29] Increasingly, humanitarian interventions involve a mixture of peacekeeping and peacemaking operations.

Responding to Genocide

In 1948, the UN adopted the Genocide Convention, which defines **genocide** as the intent to destroy, in whole or in part, a national, ethnic, racial, or religious group. Whole populations have been displaced or destroyed as others expanded their control over areas, usually through military force. Such behavior was largely justified in terms of progress and civilization. Often, only a small minority was concerned with the crime of genocide. Convinced that human beings were divided into different races and that some races were inherently superior to others,

Humanitarian Intervention ■ The use of military force to protect human rights

Consensual Interventions ■ Interventions agreed upon by all states involved in the conflict

Imposed Interventions ■ Interventions conducted against the wishes of the occupied state/territory

Peacekeeping ■ Intervention involving impartial monitors and lightly armed observers

Peacemaking ■ Intervention by heavily armed military forces

Genocide ■ Systematic mass murder of an ethnic, religious, or national group based on discriminatory preconceptions

Europeans expanded their rule to Asia, the Americas, and Africa. In the process, they destroyed many indigenous peoples. The genocide committed by Nazi Germany marked a turning point in the human rights debate, as we have seen. The victorious allies united against such crimes and punished those most directly involved in carrying them out. However, genocide continued and is still going on. For example, between 1975 and 1979, the **Khmer Rouge** in Cambodia killed more than a million people. Another million people died in Rwanda's genocide. Genocide was part of the conflict in the former Yugoslavia. Sudan's actions in Darfur were declared to be genocide in 2004. However, the global community, especially the UN, continued in 2009 to debate what actions should be taken against Sudan. Many countries refrain from declaring atrocities to be genocide partly because the Genocide Convention requires them to act to prevent and punish genocide. Despite daily reports of gross violations of human rights in Darfur, the global community has largely been indifferent to the problem.

A big step toward holding individuals and governments responsible for gross violations of human rights, including genocide, came at the end of World War I. Britain and France attempted to punish Germany for violating the neutrality of Belgium and Luxembourg by destroying their cities and creating large numbers of refugees and for using poison gas. The *Commission on the Responsibility of the Authors of War and the Enforcement of Penalties* was established at the Paris Peace Conference in 1919. Its main objective was to prosecute those accused of committing war crimes and crimes against humanity, including government leaders. France and Britain strongly supported prosecuting leaders, whereas the United States, Italy, and Japan opposed such trials, principally on the grounds that such actions would violate sovereignty.[30]

After World War II, however, the United States changed its position. It played the leading role in setting up the **Nuremberg Tribunal** to prosecute Nazi war crimes and the *Tokyo Tribunal* to prosecute crimes committed by Japan. Britain had also changed its position: Instead of trying the Nazis, Prime Minister Winston Churchill advocated shooting Nazi war criminals on sight. The United States, under Harry S. Truman's leadership, persuaded the allies to try the Nazis. The **London Agreement**—signed in 1945 by the United States, Britain, France, and the Soviet Union—provided for the creation of an international military tribunal for war criminals. This led to the establishment of the Nuremberg Tribunal, which focused on prosecuting high-level German officials. The tribunal held *individuals* responsible for (1) *crimes against peace*, which included planning, initiating, and launching a war of aggression; (2) **war crimes**, such as murder, abuse, and the destruction of private property and residential areas; and (3) **crimes against humanity**, including murder, enslavement, extermination, and deportation. The *Genocide Convention*, adopted by the UN Geneva Assembly in 1948, was a direct outgrowth of the Nuremberg Tribunal.[31]

Similar to Nazi Germany, Japan committed numerous atrocities, including the murder of prisoners, the extermination of civilians, sexual slavery, forced labor, and the use of humans in deadly medical experiments. Following America's defeat in the Philippines, Japan forced U.S. and Filipino troops to participate in the gruesome *Bataan Death March*, which resulted in the deaths of around ten thousand Filipino troops and six hundred American troops. Japan also committed

Khmer Rouge ■ Communist government of Cambodia that slaughtered over a million people in its rural pacification programs

Nuremberg Tribunal ■ Created after World War II to punish Nazi aggression and genocide

London Agreement ■ Created an international war tribunal after World War II

War Crimes ■ Include murder, the destruction of public property, and other abuses

Crimes Against Humanity ■ Inhuman acts committed against civilians by states and individuals crimes against Chinese civilians and soldiers. Even today, many Chinese continue to be suspicious of Japan. They talk about the indiscriminate bombings on Shanghai and other cities. But they are especially emotional when they recall the *Rape of Nanking*. Japanese soldiers, in October 1937, randomly raped, murdered, and executed Chinese civilians. Estimates of those killed range from forty-two thousand to one hundred thousand. On July 26, 1945, the United States, China, Britain, and the Soviet Union issued the **Potsdam Declaration**, stating their decision to prosecute Japanese war criminals. *U.S. General Douglas MacArthur*, the Supreme Commander for the Allied Powers in Japan, acting under the authority of the United States, established the *International Military Tribunal for the Far East* (Tokyo Tribunal) to try individuals for crimes against peace. Because the United States was primarily responsible for defeating Japan, Americans unilaterally created the Tokyo Tribunal.[32]

The Nuremberg and Tokyo Tribunals set the precedent for prosecuting war criminals in the former Yugoslavia and Rwanda. The disintegration of Yugoslavia in the 1990s and escalating conflicts among the Serbs, Croats, and Muslims culminated in widespread atrocities. Although all three ethnic groups committed war crimes and crimes against humanity, the dominant Serbs were clearly the most responsible for atrocities that included summary executions, torture, raping women as a weapon of war, mass internments, deportation and displacement of civilians, the inhumane treatment of prisoners, and the indiscriminate shelling of cities and villages. More than 7,000 unarmed Muslim men and boys were systematically executed near the Bosnian town of **Srebrenica** in July 1995. Roughly 740,000 ethnic Albanians were forcibly deported from Kosovo in 1999, and hundreds of Albanians disappeared or were murdered. The UN Security Council responded by establishing the *International Criminal Tribunal for the Former Yugoslavia* on May 25, 1993.[33] Based in The Hague, in the Netherlands, the tribunal indicted leading Serbians, including Serbian President **Slobodan Milosevic**, Radovan Karadzic, General Ratko Mladic, and Radislav Krstic for committing war crimes. Similarly, ethnic conflicts, primarily between **Hutu extremists** and Tutsis and moderate Hutus, in 1993 and 1994, stunned the world. Hutus systematically killed and raped. Almost 1 million people were slaughtered. Genocide in Rwanda led to the creation of the *International Tribunal for the Prosecution of Persons Responsible for Genocide in Rwanda (the Rwanda Tribunal)*. Ethnic conflicts and the accompanying atrocities have influenced the global community to establish the **ICC** as a permanent institution to prosecute those accused of war crimes and genocide.

The International Criminal Court

On April 11, 2002—more than fifty years after the victorious allies in World War II proposed the creation of a permanent international court to prosecute war criminals and others who engage in gross violations of human rights—the **ICC** was created. The **International Court of Justice (ICJ)**, or World Court, based in The Hague, had been created in 1945 to adjudicate disputes between states. Individuals, however, came before tribunals established on an *ad hoc basis* to try specific crimes against humanity. Examples are the Nuremberg and Tokyo Tribunals and the tribunals for Yugoslavia and Rwanda.[34]

Potsdam Declaration ■ Announced the prosecution of Japanese war criminals after World War II

Srebrenica ■ Bosnian town where over seven thousand unarmed Muslims were executed in 1995

Slobodan Milosevic ■ Former Serbian president prosecuted for war crimes

Hutu Extremists ■ Responsible for the genocide committed against over a million Rwandans in the early 1990s

ICC ■ Created to try and punish individuals responsible for crimes against humanity

ICJ ■ World Court created to adjudicate disputes between states

The globalization of human rights laid the foundation of new thinking about bringing violators of human rights to justice, regardless of where they committed their crimes. The world, less preoccupied by ideological rivalries, turned its attention to issues ordinary people confront daily, including widespread atrocities. Small countries, unable to unilaterally deal with crimes against humanity, stressed the need to create a permanent ICC. At the request of Trinidad and Tobago and several other Caribbean and Latin American countries, the UN General Assembly asked the International Law Commission to return to the work it had started in 1948 to create an ICC.[35] Drawbacks of the country-by-country approach to prosecuting war crimes, genocide, and crimes against humanity had become increasingly obvious. The *two major drawbacks* were (1) it was expensive and time-consuming to create new tribunals and (2) securing the unanimous consent of the five permanent members of the UN Security Council (the United States, Britain, France, Russia, and China) was very difficult. More than 160 countries and numerous NGOs, many of which worked closely with smaller states, gathered in Rome in 1998 to create a tribunal with universal jurisdiction.[36] The United States, which had initially signed the agreement under the Clinton administration, later renounced its involvement in creating the court under the Bush administration.

WOMEN AND HUMAN RIGHTS

Images of Brazil, especially of sophisticated cities like Rio de Janeiro, portray women as enjoying equal rights and personal freedoms. But images can be deceptive. It took the Brazilian Congress twenty-six years to change the country's legal code to make women equal to men under the law. The new code, adopted in 2001, outlaws a provision that had allowed a husband to annul a marriage if he discovered that his wife was not a virgin when they were married. It also eliminates laws that allowed Brazilian fathers to have unrestricted legal rights to make decisions for their family.[37] Although women are clearly not a monolithic group and do not face the same restrictions across all societies, even where laws support hierarchical patriarchy, the global community embraces the view that most women face violations of their rights. Women's rights are widely regarded as a category of human rights that deserve special attention.

Human rights for women are directly and strongly influenced by how women perceive themselves and how others perceive them. Perceptions help to determine our role in society. Roles can be defined as expectations regarding the skills, rights, and responsibilities of individuals. Women's roles are closely connected to their lower status (compared with men) in virtually all societies, including those in the industrialized world, a reality that complicates discussions of human rights regarding women. **Status** refers to one's position in the social, economic, and political hierarchy. The struggle for women's rights is as old as the struggle for human rights in general. Some people have always advocated equal treatment of men and women. International organizations composed primarily of women led the struggle for suffrage and various social policies. Women were instrumental in getting protections for women written into the UN Charter and in the establishment of the UN Commission on the Status of Women. Increased emphasis was

Status ■ Refers to one's social, economic, or political position in society placed on women's rights as human rights in the 1970s. The UN Fund for Women was created by the UN General Assembly to support women in grassroots organizations. In 1981, the UN Convention on the Elimination of All Forms of Discrimination Against Women was adopted, thereby reaffirming the view that women's rights should receive special attention within broader discussions of human rights. The Women's Conference in Beijing in 1995 and the UN Forum of Women in New York in 2000, among others, underscore a growing global consensus on women's rights.

Sexual Violence: Rape as a Weapon of War

Many young women worldwide are easily seduced by promises of job opportunities and a chance to better their lives in places far from home. Lena, a beautiful Russian woman, was told by a friendly, middle-aged woman that her own daughter had migrated to another country, was very happy, and was able to send remittances to her family. The older woman told Lena that she could help her migrate to Greece, where she would work as a domestic servant. When Lena arrived in Greece, her employers seized her passport, beat her, and forced her into prostitution.[38] Sexual violence against women has always been an integral part of most societies. Trafficking in women and children (i.e., buying and selling women as sex slaves) was outlawed at the global level by the *Convention for the Suppression of the Traffic in Persons and of the Exploitation of the Prostitution of Others* in 1949. Carol Bellamy, executive director of the UN International Children's Relief Fund, stated that "millions of children are bought and sold like fresh produce, commodities in a global sex industry steeped in greed and unspeakable cruelty."[39] During her tour of Africa in 2009, U.S. Secretary of State Hilary Clinton strongly supported measures to reduce sexual violence. Millions of women and children are victims of sexual violence within their own societies and millions more are trafficked across national borders. Globalization has facilitated sex trafficking. Networks of trafficking transport women from Asia, Russia, Latin America, Africa, and elsewhere to Western Europe, the United States, Canada, Japan, Australia, and the Middle East, where women and children are bought and sold as sex slaves. Sex tourism, especially in Southern Asia, is an important component of the sexual exploitation of women and children.[40] These abuses of human rights are extremely difficult to eliminate because poverty, tradition, and entrenched global criminal networks perpetuate them.

Sexual violence against women is often built into the legal system as well as the social structure of many countries. Men routinely kill women to protect the family honor or their own. In Jordan, Pakistan, Iraq, and other Islamic countries, honor killing, though illegal, is sustained by tradition and religion. Rape is often treated as a crime against the family, an approach that makes the woman who was raped guilty of dishonoring her family. Only in 1996 did Italy change its laws to emphasize that rape is a crime against the woman as opposed to being an offense against her family. Italy also recently abolished laws that enabled a rapist to avoid punishment by agreeing to marry the woman he had raped. Another example of how tradition, religion, and the law perpetuate sexual violence against women is the case of Zafran Bibi in Pakistan. While Zafran's husband was in prison, his brother raped her repeatedly. When she gave birth to a daughter, she was charged with adultery and sentenced to death by stoning. No charges were brought against her brother-in-law because, under Islamic laws in Pakistan, rape can be proved only with the testimony of four male witnesses. Domestic and global pressure persuaded General Pervez Musharraf, Pakistan's president, to force the court to overturn Zafran's death sentence.[41]

Rape has generally been considered part of war. The emergence of rape during conflicts as a direct human rights issue reflects the growth of humanitarian international law as well as the willingness of women, especially the victims, to demand justice. For example, Koreans who were used as "comfort women" and subjected to sexual slavery by the Japanese military during World War II demanded justice from the Japanese government. These experiences fueled protests in China and Korea against Japan in 2005. Rape as a weapon of war is receiving increased attention partly because of the frequency of such atrocities in numerous civil wars and ethnic conflicts worldwide. Sexual enslavement is often used as an instrument of **ethnic cleansing**. Sexual violence is used to humiliate and destroy families and communities, to terrorize members of a particular ethnic group, and to force people to flee an area. For example, the use of rape caused many Chinese to flee to Indonesia during the ethnic conflicts in 1998. The Hutus raped and deliberately infected Tutsi women with AIDS as part of their genocidal campaign in Rwanda. Serb troops raped more than twenty thousand Muslim women in the former Yugoslavia as part of their ethnic-cleansing campaign.[42] Rape of girls and women in the Democratic Republic of the Congo escalated in 2005 as that country's ethnic warfare continued to rage. Rape as a weapon of war continued in 2009 as violence remained widespread in the Congo. These atrocities helped to firmly establish global recognition of rape as a crime against humanity and as a war crime. Zoran Vukovic, Dragoljub Kunarac, and Radomir Kovac (Bosnian Serbs) were found guilty of such crimes by the Tribunal for Yugoslavia in The Hague in 2001. Genocidal rape is recognized as a crime against humanity by the ICC.

Ethnic Cleansing ■
Violence based on race, ethnicity, sex, religion, or other social issues

ISLAM AND HUMAN RIGHTS

Negative stereotypes of Muslims and Islam are so prevalent and so profound in most Western societies that even isolated cases of human rights violations are perceived as reflections of a profound inability of Islamic countries to respect human rights. Such images are reinforced by extremists in Saudi Arabia, Afghanistan under the Taliban, Iran, and Northern Nigeria, for example. The general lack of a clear separation of religion and government and the dominance of Shari'a law as the foundation for legal codes in Islamic countries convey the impression of traditional societies that are fossilized, changing very little since the Prophet Muhammad (570–632 A.D.) founded the religion. But compared with Western societies, Islamic countries are far more repressive and disrespectful of fundamental rights and freedoms. Saudi Arabia—Muhammad's birthplace and keeper of Islam's holiest places, Mecca and Medina, that are sacred to Muslims worldwide—is perhaps the most repressive Islamic society. But Islam's spread made it a global religion

Shirin Ebadi—
Nobel Peace
Prize Winner.

(Francois Mori/AP/
Wide World Photos)

long before the emergence of Western Europe as a dominant power and the subsequent spread of Christianity. Consequently, Islam is diverse and complex, reflecting how very different cultures interpret and practice the religion. The decentralization of Islam undermines efforts to portray the Islamic world, especially regarding human rights, as monolithic. It is also useful to distinguish the policies of governments from the aspirations of ordinary citizens to enjoy basic freedoms.

Although Islamic cultures are composed of numerous beliefs and values that promote humanitarianism and respect for some forms of human rights, the religion emphasizes the priority of the Islamic community over the individual. Under the Koran, the ruler and the ruled are equal before God. However, unlike in Britain, for example, where limitations on the monarch were formalized into contracts, such as the Magna Carta, most Islamic countries did not develop formal institutions to restrain leaders and define their powers and responsibilities or to make them accountable to the people. This enabled rulers to interpret the Koran in ways that served their own interests. The Western belief that each individual has natural rights stood in sharp contrast to the Islamic belief that the community mattered most and that God's law did not permit individuals to think for themselves. Justice, in Islam, is derived from obedience to God's commands as expressed in the Koran. In effect, challenging political authorities is tantamount to challenging the supremacy of religious thinking.[43] Even so, Islam has been challenged by forces within Muslim societies. In 2003, Shirin Ebadi won the Nobel Peace Prize for her efforts to promote human rights in Iran. Viewed as a threat by the Iranian government, her own rights continued to be routinely violated, especially in 2008 as Iran faced increased external pressure to refrain from acquiring nuclear weapons and to implement democratic reforms.

The best example of a Muslim society that rejected the fusion of politics and religion and embraced freedoms prevalent in Western societies is Turkey. As the Ottoman Empire contracted and finally fragmented, and after Turkey's defeat in World War I, it was clear that to modernize Turkey wide-ranging reforms had to be implemented. Mustafa Kemal Ataturk, founder of the modern Turkish state in 1923, deliberately and systematically dismantled much of the old system, abolishing Islamic control and secularizing the country. Secular movements are deeply rooted in the Islamic world, despite their relative lack of success in countries like Saudi Arabia.

Throughout the Islamic world, clashes occur between the conservatives who stress communitarianism and cultural relativism and the reformers who focus on the universality of human rights and their country's participation in organizations that promote and strengthen fundamental rights and freedoms worldwide. This confrontation highlights the reality that there are many different interpretations of Islam, especially in relation to individual freedom. While cultural relativists and traditionalists argue that global human rights are inapplicable to Islamic societies, many Muslims are aware that governments often use Islam to justify abusing them, especially those who threaten their power. Women suffer most from violations of human rights in Islamic societies. Ironically, the U.S. invasion and occupation of Iraq contributed to the strengthening of religious groups and the erosion of human rights for women. Although women comprised nearly a third of the Iraqi Parliament that was elected in 2005, women's rights have steadily diminished. By 2008, Iraq was widely regarded as a violator of women's rights. But even as Islamic religious leaders and institutions endeavor to maintain the subordinate status of women and their unequal treatment, secular forces also operate to challenge traditional ideas and behavior. In many Islamic societies, women occupy significant professional and political positions, including head of state.

FIGHTING TERRORISM AND PROTECTING HUMAN RIGHTS

Democratic societies confronted with terrorism face an enduring dilemma, namely, how to provide security for the country while avoiding taking measures that violate the fundamental rights and freedoms that define democratic states and distinguish them from nondemocratic regimes. Believing that short-term restrictions on civil and political rights are essential to combat terrorism, many governments find themselves on a slippery slope that leads to more durable infringements on democratic freedoms. Britain, for example, responded in the early 1970s to Northern Ireland's Troubles, as the conflicts between the Protestants and Catholics are called, with increased arrests, essentially arbitrary detentions, increased surveillance capabilities, the creation of a special court to prosecute terrorist suspects, approval of inhumane treatment of prisoners, and excessive military force. Apart from having the unintended consequence of inflaming passions and escalating terrorism, British actions were scrutinized and severely criticized by the global community and within Britain itself. The European Court of Human Rights ruled against Britain in several cases, contending that it had violated the European Convention on Human Rights.[44] Following the terrorist attacks in London in 2005, Britain adopted several policies that were perceived as threats to human rights.

Catastrophic terrorist attacks in the United States in 2001 influenced **Alan Dershowitz**, a Harvard University law professor and a leading criminal defense lawyer, to argue in favor of using nonlethal torture in extreme cases and of issuing torture warrants by judges.[45] Dershowitz posed the "ticking bomb" scenario. Imagine that you are a government official and you know that a bomb capable of killing thousands of people is about to be used by terrorists. You are almost certain that a suspect knows where the bomb is and believe that by torturing the suspect you can extract crucial information to save lives. Would you torture or support this suspect's torturing under these circumstances? Democratic societies routinely condemn other societies that torture people. No country, not even an authoritarian regime, openly admits to torturing its citizens. Some argue that legalization of torture in the United States would encourage its wider use and seriously erode democratic principles that are the country's foundations. Furthermore, the effectiveness of torturing individuals in the long- and short-term is highly debatable. Those who are tortured obviously attempt to avoid being tortured. *Mary Robinson*, former head of the UN Commission for Human Rights, criticized the United States for eroding civil liberties at home and human rights globally after it was attacked. Like many others, Robinson cited measures used by the United States in its war on terrorism to illustrate her point.[46]

In the war against terrorism, the United States significantly altered its policy on human rights abroad. Prisoners taken during the war in Afghanistan were subject to "stress and duress" techniques, including sleep deprivation, physical abuse, hooding, waterboarding (simulated drowning), and being forced to hold awkward positions for long periods of time. Many prisoners held at the U.S. military base in Guantanamo Bay in Cuba were denied access to lawyers and their families. Some prisoners were transferred to countries that are not only strategically located but also known to violate human rights, including Pakistan and Uzbekistan. Widespread abuse of prisoners held at **Abu Ghraib** in Iraq was vividly demonstrated by numerous photographs and videotapes that shocked the world in 2004 and undermined American credibility in promoting human rights, especially in the Islamic world. Some prisoners were killed, tortured, or suffered from inhumane treatment and degradation. U.S. Army dogs were used to abuse Iraqi prisoners. Support of torture by the Bush administration created a serious debate on the issue in the United States. Many human rights NGOs also drew attention to how other countries were justifying what are generally regarded as violations of human security. For example, India pushed the Prevention of Terrorism Ordinance to detain terrorist suspects for up to ninety days without a trial. China suddenly began to call the **Uighurs** (i.e., an ethnic separatist group that had been fighting the government for many years) terrorists. The Russians also called

Alan Dershowitz ■ Argued for the use of nonlethal torture to gather information from terrorists

Abu Ghraib ■ U.S.-run prison in Iraq infamous for abuse committed against Iraqi war detainees

Uighurs ■ An ethnic separatist group labeled a terrorist group by the Chinese government their conflict with the ethnic Chechens a war against terrorism. In November 2007, General Pervez Musharraf, the dictator of Pakistan and America's close ally in the war against terrorism, declared martial law, suspended the Constitution, and abolished the Supreme Court. America's emphasis on the war against terrorism raised concerns about balancing national security concerns against a strong commitment to upholding human rights. Musharraf's violations of human rights contributed to his loss of political power and the success of his political opponents in the election of 2008.

THE DEATH PENALTY AND HUMAN RIGHTS

There is a growing consensus that the death penalty violates the most fundamental human right: the right to life. Several countries have outlawed the execution of teenagers. In Yemen, often criticized for violating human rights, the government abolished the death penalty for individuals under eighteen years. Only Saudi Arabia, Iran, Nigeria, and Pakistan allow teenagers to be executed. The United States executed teenagers until 2005, when the U.S. Supreme Court outlawed the practice. After briefly suspending executions in 2007 and early 2008, the U.S. Supreme Court reinstated executions by lethal injections in 2008. Japan, which typically executes five or six prisoners each year, has been criticized by Amnesty International and other groups for its secretive and sometimes sudden executions. Many prisoners are told of their execution only moments before they are hanged.[47] Europeans are generally shocked by Americans' strong endorsement of the death penalty and will not extradite anyone to America if they face the death penalty. European societies abolished the death penalty in the latter half of the twentieth century, mostly in the early 1960s.

SUMMARY AND REVIEW

The promotion of universal human rights worldwide has become an increasingly contentious topic. This chapter examined how the progression and promotion of human rights have occurred within the broader political, economic, and cultural aspects of globalization. The concept of human rights has been significantly strengthened in recent history, especially with the growth of multilateral human rights NGOs, such as Amnesty International and Human Rights Watch, and international human rights-based institutions, such as the ICC and the UNCHR. Protecting human rights is no longer seen as an exclusively national issue, but one of global magnitude and scope. We examined the importance of and distinctions among civil, political, and social rights, as well as the distinction between positive and negative human rights. We also identified factors that have contributed to the expansion of human rights globally, including the globalization of human rights through the creation and strengthening of international institutions, the growing acceptance of interdependence among states, the international proliferation of democracy, the strengthening of human rights through economic development and corporate globalization, and the increasing effectiveness of nonstate actors dedicated to promoting human rights.

KEY TERMS

DISCUSSION QUESTIONS

1. Can you explain the differences between relativistic and universal human rights? How are they different in their scope and normative assumptions?
2. What are the differences between positive and negative human rights? How are positive and negative human rights related to the ICCPR and the ICESCR?
3. Are sanctions an effective weapon for promoting human rights? If so, how are they effective? If not, how do they hurt human rights?
4. What is ethnic cleansing? How was it used in Rwanda and Yugoslavia?

SUGGESTED READINGS

Alston, Philip. *Non-State Actors and Human Rights*. New York: Oxford University Press, 2005.

Greenberg, Karen, ed. *The Torture Debate in America*. Cambridge: Cambridge University Press, 2006.

Hopgood, Stephen. *Keepers of the Flame: Understanding Amnesty International*. Ithaca, NY: Cornell University Press, 2006.

Hunter, Shireen, and Huma Malik, eds. *Modernization, Democracy, and Islam*. Westport, CT: Praeger, 2005.

Lockwood, Bert. *Women's Rights*. Baltimore: The Johns Hopkins University Press, 2006.

Schwab, Klaus. "Global Corporate Citizenship," *Foreign Affairs* 87, No. 1 (January/February 2008): 107–118.

Straus, Scott. "Darfur and the Genocide Debate," *Foreign Affairs* 84, No. 1 (January/February 2005): 123–133.

END NOTES

1. Seyom Brown, *Human Rights in World Politics* (New York: Longman, 2000), 22.
2. Elizabeth Rosenthal, "China Ratifies Major U.N. Rights Accord," *New York Times*, 1 March 2001, A9.
3. Simon Romero, "Wider Drug War Threatens Colombian Indians," *New York Times*, 22 April 2009, A1.
4. Andrew Hurrell, "Power, Principles, and Prudence," in *Human Rights in Global Politics*, eds. Tim Dunne and Nicholas J. Wheeler (Cambridge: Cambridge University Press, 1999), 279.
5. Debora L. Spar, "The Spotlight and the Bottom Line," *Foreign Affairs* 77, No. 2 (March/April 1998), 12; and Klaus Schwab, "Global Corporate Citizenship," *Foreign Affairs* 87, No. 1 (January/February 2008), 107–108.
6. Michael A. Santoro, *Profits and Principles: Global Capitalism and Human Rights in China* (Ithaca, NY: Cornell University Press, 2000), 29.
7. Laurent Belsie, "Companies Operating Abroad Pay Closer Attention to Human Rights," *Christian Science Monitor*, 3 April 2000, 11.
8. Marcus Tullius Cicero, *De Re Publica*, translated by Clinton Walker Keyes (Cambridge, MA: Harvard University Press, 1943), 385.
9. Maurice Cranston, "Are There Any Human Rights?" *Daedalus* 112, No. 4 (Fall 1983), 2; Brown, *Human Rights*, 56; and Micheline Ishay, *The History of Human Rights* (Berkeley: University of California Press, 2008).
10. Brown, *Human Rights*, 59.
11. Edmund Burke, *Reflections on the Revolution in France* (New York: Holt, Rinehart and Winston, 1959), 37.
12. Cranston, "Are There Any Human Rights?" 5.
13. Yves Beigbeder, *Judging War Criminals* (New York: St. Martin's Press, 1999), 18.
14. Asbjorn Eide, "The Historical Significance of the Universal Declaration," *International Social Science Journal* 50, No. 4 (December 1998), 478.
15. Brown, *Human Rights*, 7.
16. Ken Booth, "Three Tyrannies," in *Human Rights in Global Politics*, 37; and Neil A. Englehart, "Rights and Culture in the Asian Values Argument," *Human Rights Quarterly* 22 (2000), 549.
17. Brown, *Human Rights*, 7; and Englehart, "Rights and Culture," 568.
18. Lammy Betten and Nicholas Grief, *EU Law and Human Rights* (New York: Longman, 1998), 27.
19. Eide, "Historical Significance of the Universal Declaration," 495.
20. Santoro, *Profits and Principles*, 155.
21. Hurrell, "Power, Principles, and Prudence," 283.
22. Margaret P. Doxey, *International Sanctions in Contemporary Perspective* (New York: St. Martin's Press, 1996), 14; and Gary Clyde Hufbauer et al., *Economic Sanctions Reconsidered* (Washington, DC: Peterson Institute, 2007).
23. David Cortright and George Lopez, "Economic Sanctions in Contemporary Global Relations," in *Economic Sanctions*, eds. David Cortright and George Lopez (Boulder, CO: Westview Press, 1995), 5.

24. Center for Strategic International Studies, *Altering U.S. Sanctions Policy* (Washington, DC: CSIS Press, 1999), 5.

25. Daniel W. Drezner, *The Sanctions Paradox* (Cambridge: Cambridge University Press, 1999), 62.

26. Stephen A. Garrett, *Doing Good and Doing Well* (Westport, CT: Praeger, 1999), 4; and Taylor B. Seybolt, *Humanitarian Military Intervention* (New York: Oxford University Press, 2007).

27. Richard N. Haass, *Intervention* (Washington, DC: Brookings Institution Press, 1999), 62.

28. Haass, *Intervention*, 57.

29. Haass, *Intervention*, 59.

30. Beigbeder, *Judging War Criminals*, 28.

31. Beigbeder, *Judging War Criminals*, 34.

32. Beigbeder, *Judging War Criminals*, 55.

33. Theodor Meron, "Answering for War Crimes," *Foreign Affairs* 76, No. 1 (January/February 1997), 2.

34. Barbara Crossette, "War Crimes Tribunal Becomes Reality, Without U.S. Role," *New York Times*, 12 April 2002, A3.

35. David Wippman, "Can an International Criminal Court Prevent and Punish Genocide?" in *Protection Against Genocide*, ed. Neal Riemer (Westport, CT: Praeger, 2000), 89.

36. Alton Frye, *Toward an International Criminal Court?* (New York: Council on Foreign Relations, 1999), 22.

37. Larry Rohter, "Brazil Passes Equal Rights for Its Women," *New York Times*, 19 August 2001, A9.

38. Fred Weir, "Russia Battles Its Sex Trade," *Christian Science Monitor*, 16 May 2001, 1.

39. "Slavery in West Africa," *Economist*, 1 November 2008, 57.

40. Andrea Marie Bertone, "Sexual Trafficking in Women," *Gender Issues* 18, No. 1 (Winter 2000), 5.

41. Seth Mydans, "Sentenced to Death, Rape Victim Is Freed by Pakistani Court," *New York Times*, 6 June 2002, A4.

42. Seth Mydans, "Sexual Violence as a Tool of War," *New York Times*, 1 March 2001, A1; Marlise Simons, "Bosnian War Trial Focuses on Sex Crimes," *New York Times*, 18 February 2001, A4; and Minh T. Vo, "Ending Rape as a Weapon of War," *Christian Science Monitor*, 25 April 2000, 6.

43. Ann Elizabeth Mayer, *Islam and Human Rights* (Boulder, CO: Westview Press, 1999), 49.

44. Laura K. Donohue, "A Lesson from the British," *Washington Post National Weekly Edition*, 14–20 April 2003, 22.

45. "Is Torture Ever Justified?" *Economist*, 11 January 2003, 9.

46. Julia Preston, "Departing Rights Commissioner Faults U.S.," *New York Times*, 12 September 2002, B22.

47. Howard W. French, "Secrecy of Japan's Executions Is Criticized as Unduly Cruel," *New York Times*, 30 June 2002, A1; and Charles Lane, "A View to a Kill," *Foreign Policy* 148 (May/June 2005), 36.

CHAPTER

4

Promoting Democracy

INTRODUCTION

Many ancient societies throughout the world attempted to apply democratic principles to make decisions about war and peace, migration, the allocation of scarce resources, and how to govern themselves. Democracy is therefore inseparable from politics, economics, and culture, as this chapter shows. Democracy as a form of government is always evolving, is always incomplete, and is most accurately described as a work in progress. The United States as a democratic society wrestled with the issue of slavery and was torn apart by a bloody civil war. It also faced severe economic crises, struggles for gender equality, and the challenges of racial equality and integration. The incomplete nature of democracy inevitably leads to the emergence of new issues, new challenges, efforts to undermine democracy, and attempts to consolidate democracy.

Globalization has been, and remains, a potent force in the spread of democratic values and practices. The growth of the British Empire was accompanied by the spread of democracy to India, the English-speaking Caribbean, the United States, and Canada. America's rise as a superpower further consolidated the globalization of democracy, despite its embrace of some repressive regimes during the Cold War. But America's struggle against the Soviet Union ultimately helped to strengthen the emergence of democracy in Eastern Europe and in Russia itself. The "orange revolution" in Ukraine in 2004, during which millions of Ukrainians peacefully demonstrated against fraudulent elections and in support of opposition leader Viktor Yushchenko, was strongly supported by the United States. Globalization also contributes to weakening the power of centralized government and helps to empower citizens by fostering economic prosperity, the acquisition of private property, and increased access to information. But globalization is also widely perceived as undermining democracy by weakening governments' control over many issues, thereby diminishing the effectiveness of citizen participation in the democratic process. Increasingly, at the global level, organizations that are not representative of the people are making decisions that have profound and global consequences for ordinary people.

This chapter examines factors that contribute to the growth and maintenance of democratic societies. We will analyze the roles of global civil society and of the United States in facilitating and encouraging transitions to democracy, paying special attention to America's decision to impose democracy through military intervention and by occupying Iraq. Transitions to democracy in America and Russia are also discussed. Finally, we will discuss how globalization is leading to greater global governance and spawning demands for more democracy at the global level.

DEMOCRACY

Democracy has been practiced by many societies throughout the world, especially by small communities. The ancient world understood the importance of obtaining the consent of powerful individuals and groups to achieve various objectives. The word **democracy** is derived from the Greek words **demos** (meaning people, or populace) and kratia or kratis (meaning rule). A basic definition of democracy is rule by the people. Determining who the people are has always been a central challenge for democracy. Women, slaves, non-Greeks, and other individuals were not considered to be among the people who could participate in the political process. Democracy in ancient Greece was a form of **direct self-government,** meaning that people voted directly on issues that affected them. With the exception of some small New England towns that hold town meetings, direct democracy is not practiced in the United States. Modern democratic societies practice **indirect, or representative, democracy**. Citizens elect representatives who vote for them and safeguard their interests. In the U.S. system of democracy, for example, **James Madison** strongly advocated the adoption of a system of checks and balances and the separation of legislative, executive, and judicial powers to prevent the abuse of power, to protect the rights of the minority, and to ensure the maintenance of democratic practices.

Two questions that often arise are, who will govern and how will the interests of various groups and segments of the population be protected and advanced? There are two dominant approaches to dealing with these questions. The first emphasizes that the majority of the people decide who will govern and who will benefit. Government by the people is synonymous with majority rule. This approach, practiced globally, is the **majoritarian model** of democracy. The second approach, also widely practiced, embraces the concept of majority rule but attempts to include as many of the people as possible in the decision-making process. The underlying objectives are to enlarge the size of the majority and to obtain widespread support for government policies. This approach is called the **consensus model** of democracy. In countries with significant political and ethnic divisions, the consensus model—characterized by inclusiveness, bargaining, and compromise—is widely adopted. The majoritarian model of democracy relies on a plurality of votes in single-member districts. It embraces the **winner-take-all system,** which means that the candidate who receives the most votes, not necessarily a majority, wins. The consensus model,

Democracy ■ Government that reflects the will of the people

Demos ■ Greek word for people

Direct Self-Government ■ Direct participation in the democratic process

Indirect/ Representative Democracy ■ Democracy run through indirect means, such as elections and representatives

James Madison ■ Founding father advocating checks and balances and separation of powers

Majoritarian Model ■ Government by the people on a global scale

Consensus Model ■ Focuses on achieving widespread support for government policies

Winner-Take-All System ■ System by which the candidate with the most votes wins

Proportional Representation ■ Political and electoral system under which both majorities and minorities are represented

Liberal Democracy ■ Defined by limitations on power of government and protections of civil liberties

Illiberal Democracies ■ Societies that fail to fully protect basic freedoms and human rights

Constitutional Liberalism ■ Government committed to ensuring individual rights and freedoms through constitutional protections

Constitution ■ Framework of laws designed to designate specific powers and responsibilities to governmental institutions

Rule of Law ■ Mandatory adherence to state laws

Legitimacy ■ Power to govern based on popular consent

Presidential Democracy ■ Democracy that elects a president to the executive level of government

Parliamentary Democracy ■ Governing system with no separation of powers

on the other hand, uses a system of **proportional representation** in which both majorities and minorities are represented, because seats in elective bodies are determined by the proportion or percentage of votes received. Smaller parties are generally more successful in this system because they have a better chance of getting enough votes to gain representation in government. The majoritarian model, by contrast, requires the winner to get just a plurality of votes, which leaves large numbers of voters unrepresented.[1] But neither the majoritarian nor the consensus model of democracy guarantees the functioning of **liberal democracy**, which is defined by limitations on the power of elected officials, freedom of speech, freedom of the press, the right to peacefully assemble, protection of private property, freedom of religion, protection of the rights of unpopular minorities, and respect for the rule of law. Although free elections are often equated with democracy in many parts of the world, societies that do not restrain power and protect basic freedoms and human rights are not fully democratic. Such societies are often referred to as **illiberal democracies**.

Fully developed democracies are characterized by **constitutional liberalism**; that is, a commitment to protecting individuals' rights, freedoms, and dignity from abuse by the government, institutions, society as a whole, and other individuals. Constitutional liberalism goes beyond simply having a constitution. The basis for constitutional liberalism can be found in many societies, the most prominent being the Magna Carta of 1215, the English Bill of Rights of 1688, the American Declaration of Independence, and the American Constitution. The Helsinki Final Act of 1975—which focused on basic human rights such as freedom of speech, freedom of religion, and freedom of assembly—represents a continuation of the tradition of constitutional liberalism.[2]

A **constitution** is defined as the fundamental framework or basic law of a country. A constitution assigns powers and responsibilities to government institutions, indicates how decision makers are to be selected, defines the scope of government authority, establishes the nature of the relationship between the people and their government, and has provisions for making political leaders accountable to the people. A constitution in a democratic society not only creates and distributes power, but also limits power. Central to democratic constitutions is the concept of the **rule of law**, which means that no person is above the law, that individuals are treated equally under the law, that basic freedoms are protected, and that the administration of justice is impartial. To secure rights and to facilitate the proper functioning of democracy, the people must believe that their government is legitimate. **Legitimacy** is the power to govern based on the consent of the majority of the people.

Most democratic societies have either a presidential or a parliamentary form of democracy. The United States is the best example of the **presidential democracy**. Partly in response to problems in the British parliamentary form of democracy, the framers of the U.S. Constitution decided to have a clear separation of executive, legislative, and judicial powers and to provide for a system of checks and balances among these distinct branches of government. The presidential form of democracy, particularly the American system, makes conflict inevitable. The **parliamentary democracy** is most strongly associated with Britain. Unlike the presidential system, there is no clear separation of powers in the parliamentary system. The prime minister—the chief executive—is an elected member of parliament who is chosen by the majority party in parliament for the leadership position. Consequently, there is generally very little conflict between the majority in parliament and the prime minister. On the other hand, the prime minister, unlike the president, can be forced from office by a vote of no confidence in parliament. Whereas the president is clearly at the top of the administrative hierarchy, the prime minister has a more collegial relationship with the cabinet.[3] The British model, often referred to as the Westminster model, is found in many former British colonies.

Political Participation and Democracy

Political participation entails communicating with elected officials and others in government—expressing viewpoints and demanding certain actions or public policies from the government. Vehicles for political participation include political parties, interest groups, and a free press. Political participation can be either conventional or unconventional. **Conventional participation** includes voting, running for office, assisting with political campaigns, writing to elected officials, writing letters to newspapers about particular issues, and joining an interest group to influence public policies. **Unconventional participation** includes protests, mass demonstrations, civil disobedience, and sometimes even acts of violence.

Political parties are coalitions of interests whose primary goal is to run the government by winning competitive elections. Some political parties represent narrow interests, and sometimes focus on just a single issue, but political parties that are successful usually appeal to a wide range of interests and attempt to win a majority of the votes. In some societies, minor parties form coalitions with each other or with a major party to exert greater influence on public policy and to gain more control over the government. The functioning of the **loyal opposition** is important in democratic societies. It means that the party out of power criticizes the ruling majority and suggests alternative programs and policies.

Interest groups, like political parties, are critical players in established democracies and in countries that are becoming democratic. An **interest group,** or a pressure group, is composed of individuals who share common concerns and who believe that the most effective way to achieve their objectives is to organize and engage in political activities that exert pressure on government decision makers.

Interest groups are an essential component of **civil society.** Civil society—a concept that originated with Greek philosophers who were concerned with building democratic societies—refers to the networks of social relations and institutions that exist and act independently of government institutions. Civil society is generally seen as encompassing the wide range of settings that bring individuals together to exchange ideas; discuss issues; and organize to achieve social, political, and economic objectives.[4] Individuals, groups, and organizations that operate across national boundaries and are linked together by common interests comprise what is referred to as **global civil society.**[5]

Women's Political Participation and Democracy

Although women in Kuwait gained the right to vote and run for office in 2005, it was not until 2009 that four women won seats in Kuwait's Parliament. In the vast majority of political systems, women's participation in politics is influenced to a

Conventional Participation ■ Traditional political activities, such as voting

Unconventional Participation ■ Engaging in less acceptable political activities, such as protesting

Political Parties ■ Competitive political groups that seek to win government positions and offices

Loyal Opposition ■ Antagonistic party in electoral politics that accepts the legitimacy of the ruling majority

Interest Group ■ Organization of individuals with common interests who attempt to influence public policy

Civil Society ■ Networks of social relations and structures that exist independently of the government

Global Civil Society ■ Individuals and organizations that operate across national borders large extent by their societies' perceptions of women, their roles, their status, and levels of economic development in the various countries. Another major barrier to women's involvement in politics is the widespread perception among both men and women that politics is a male activity. Najma Chowdhury and Barbara J. Nelson refer to this tendency as the "maleness of politics." They argue that politics has always been closely connected to the traditional fatherly connotation of patriarchy and to fraternalism, which essentially exclude women from political activities and power.[6] *Three main arguments are articulated in favor of increased participation of women in the democratic process*: (1) equity and democratic justice, (2) representation of women's interests, and (3) developing and making the maximum use of available human resources.[7] The *equity and democratic justice* argument rests on the widely accepted view that gender equality and fully including women in political life are prerequisites for democracy. Failure to remove impediments to women's political participation undermines the legitimacy of democratic governments and erodes public confidence in the democratic process. The *representation of women's interests* argument focuses on divergent interests between men and women and the need for women to protect and promote their interests themselves by becoming directly involved in the political system. Finally, the *using-all-available-talent* argument stresses the pragmatism of allowing women to contribute to all aspects of development, including the growth of democratic institutions and processes.

Women's political participation is increasing in mature democracies as well as in countries that are transitioning to democracy. This development is due primarily to three factors. *First*, globalization has facilitated the emergence of global networks that heighten women's political awareness and enable them to mobilize politically at local, national, and global levels. *Second*, removing barriers to women's political participation, making deliberate efforts to recruit women into politics and modifying electoral systems have contributed to women's inclusion in political life. *Finally*, the proliferation of women in legislative and executive positions was facilitated by the termination of the Cold War. As traditional security issues receded and domestic challenges became a priority, women effectively articulated their ability to provide leadership.[8]

Factors Conducive to Democracy

One of the most significant developments in global affairs at the beginning of the twenty-first century was the U.S. decision to launch a preemptive war against Iraq, partly to overthrow the Saddam Hussein regime and to establish democracy not only in Iraq but also throughout the Middle East. Many observers concluded that the cultural values associated with Islam were almost insurmountable impediments to transitions to democracy in the majority of Muslim countries. At the heart of this debate is the assumption that **culture** (i.e., a set of values, beliefs, and attitudes) is one of the most important prerequisites for the growth of democracy. Cultures that foster democracy are generally characterized by toleration for divergent viewpoints and practices, compromise, and a willingness to accept the policies voted on by the majority of citizens.

Cultural factors help to explain the existence of democratic governments in the English-speaking Caribbean as well as transitions to democracy in Botswana

Culture ■ A set of values, beliefs, and attitudes

TABLE 4.1

WOMEN IN NATIONAL PARLIAMENTS (LOWER OR SINGLE HOUSE)

Rank	Country	Election Year	No. of Seats (Total)	No. of Women	% of Women
1	Rwanda	2008	80	45	56.3
2	Sweden	2006	349	164	47.0
3	South Africa	2009	400	174	43.5
4	Cuba	2008	614	265	43.2
5	Iceland	2009	63	27	42.9
6	Finland	2007	200	83	41.5
7	Netherlands	2006	150	62	41.3
8	Argentina	2007	255	102	40.0
9	Denmark	2007	179	68	38.0
10	Angola	2008	220	82	37.3
11	Costa Rica	2006	57	21	36.8
12	Spain	2008	350	127	36.3
13	Norway	2005	169	61	36.1
14	Belgium	2007	150	53	35.3
15	Mozambique	2004	250	87	34.8
72	**United States**	**2008**	**435**	**73**	**16.8**

Source: "Women in Parliaments: World Classification," *Inter-Parliamentary Union*, May 2009.

and Nigeria. The British brought many of their democratic institutions and values with them to their colonies in the Caribbean and implemented a process of decolonization aimed at deliberately preparing the new countries for democratic government. The **Westminster model** (i.e., the British model of government) had been practiced to a limited degree from as early as 1639, when the House of Assembly in Barbados was created, making it the third oldest legislative body in the Western Hemisphere, preceded only by Bermuda's legislature and Virginia's House of Burgesses.[9] British rule helped to create a culture that emphasized the rule of law. Democratic competition was embraced, and attempts were made to use government as an instrument for promoting social welfare and economic equality.[10]

Botswana and Nigeria also demonstrate that culture plays a significant role in determining democratic transitions. Botswana is a stable democracy, due in part to its political culture of toleration for freedom of expression, community consensus, and a tradition of peacefully resolving conflicts. Similarly, the political culture of Nigeria frustrated efforts by successive military regimes to gain legitimacy and institutionalize authoritarian rule. Despite ongoing political turbulence, Nigerians' strong commitment to political and personal liberty played a decisive role in persuading military regimes to promise a transition to civilian rule and democratic government.[11] Despite many broken promises, Nigeria periodically experienced democratic rule and is now consolidating its democratic transition.

Westminster Model ■ British model of government dating back to as early as 1639

The *global or regional environment* is widely perceived as playing a crucial role in either facilitating or impeding the growth of democracy. As we will see, the ideological rivalry between the East and the West essentially diminished the opportunities for countries under Soviet domination to embrace democracy. On the other hand, Spain and Portugal became democratic partly because economic, political, and cultural forces in Western Europe undermined support for authoritarian rule in those countries. The global environment in the aftermath of the terrorist attacks in the United States in 2001 enabled many governments to take advantage of the war against terrorism declared by the United States. Fighting terrorism was elevated to the primary preoccupation of the dominant power in the global system. This development not only relegated promoting democracy to a secondary priority but, more significantly, provided an opportunity for many governments to portray opposition to their policies as terrorism, thereby undermining democratic movements and individuals committed to effectuating democratic transitions. As we mentioned, Pakistan's experience with martial law in 2007 is an obvious example.

Economic Development ■ Sometimes defined as greater economic growth and integration throughout the world

Another major factor that is conducive to democracy is **economic development**. As countries achieve greater economic prosperity, integration into global markets, exposure to democratic values, higher literacy rates and increased access to education, increased urbanization, and increased knowledge of other cultures through the global media and tourism, they tend to be more receptive to democracy. The forces of development bring people from diverse backgrounds together, encourage them to cooperate and compromise, and challenge as well as reinforce traditional beliefs that inhibit or support the development of democracy. This does not mean that poor countries cannot be democracies or that all countries that have achieved economic prosperity are democratic. India, for example, is the world's largest democracy despite a history of widespread poverty.

Middle Class ■ Class in capitalist society between the lower and upper classes

Finally, the emergence of a strong **middle class** is perceived as an important factor conducive to the growth of democracy and is closely related to economic development. Increased national wealth generally expands the middle class, which many people believe is essential to the acquisition and maintenance of democratic values. People who are middle class have greater economic security, are generally less dependent on governments, tend to participate in politics to protect their interests and to hold government accountable, are unwilling to allow governments to violate their rights, and have greater confidence in their abilities to govern themselves.

Promoting Democracy

When Nawabzada Nasrullah Khan was a young man, he was intrigued with the activities of Mohandas K. Gandhi, Jawaharlal Nehru, Ali Jinnah, and others who led independence movements against British control in India. Conflicts between Hindus and Muslims gave impetus to the creation of Pakistan in 1947 under the leadership of Ali Jinnah as a separate state for Muslims. India has become the world's largest democracy, and Pakistan has been ruled mainly by military dictators and authoritarian civilian rulers. Living in Pakistan, Khan saw that decolonization there was not replaced by democracy.

He spent more than fifty years working to promote a secular Western-style democracy that reflected indigenous influences, including respect for a moderate version of Islamic law. When General Mohammad Ayub Khan, Pakistan's army commander, seized power in a coup in 1958, Nawabzada Khan fought for the restoration of civilian rule by forming the **Democratic Action Committee**, the first of many opposition alliances. The fact that Pakistan continued to be ruled by a military ruler, General Pervez Musharraf, when Khan died in 2003, demonstrates how difficult promoting democracy can be in some societies.[12] Amid increasing violence, Pakistan continues to struggle to achieve democracy.

Democratic Action Committee ■ First oppositional alliance formed to oppose military rule in Pakistan

The disintegration of the Soviet Union removed a significant obstacle to creating and strengthening democratic practices globally. Although the United States had formed alliances with undemocratic governments during the Cold War, it became the primary proponent of exporting democracy when that conflict ended. Many Western governments made the promotion of democracy a prerequisite for assistance. In 2002, representatives from more than half of the world's countries met in Warsaw, Poland, to exchange ideas on how to create a global community of democracies. They signed the **Warsaw Declaration**, which committed them to promoting democracy in countries lacking it and strengthening democracy in countries that were building it. This development and other actions clearly underscored a growing global consensus that promoting democracy is a global priority.[13]

Warsaw Declaration ■ Global declaration made after the fall of the Soviet Union aiming at the proliferation of global democracy

Global Civil Society and the Promotion of Democracy

Global civil society transcends national boundaries. It consists of organizations and individuals who attempt to influence politics both within countries and globally.[14] Economic, cultural, political, educational, technological, and other networks combine to constitute global civil society. These nonstate voluntary associations blur distinctions between domestic and global political activities. Many cooperate with grassroots activists to effectuate democratic change. Increasingly, they are uniting to maximize their impact on governments. For example, **CIVICUS** consists of more than five hundred nongovernmental organizations (NGOs). The World Forum for Democracy, the National Endowment for Democracy (NED), and Transparency International also bring together many NGOs, a development reflecting the realities of globalization. Global civil society provides basic civic education, organizes and funds political parties and interest groups, assists with writing constitutions, observes and mediates elections, and lends credibility to the process of democratization among other activities. One of the most outspoken proponents of building global civil society and promoting democracy is former U.S. President Jimmy Carter.

CIVICUS ■ Organization of over five hundred NGOs

Jimmy Carter made strengthening human rights and democracy a central component of America's foreign policy while he was president. He championed these causes with even greater passion, energy, and commitment after leaving office. He has monitored elections around the world and has served as an interlocutor in international crises involving the United States in, for example, Haiti and North Korea. He was also the first U.S. president since Calvin Coolidge (1928) to visit Cuba. In 1982, he founded the **Carter Center**, which is affiliated with Emory University in Atlanta, Georgia, to assist in conflict resolution and global development and to promote democracy globally. In 2002, Carter visited Cuba, and addressing the nation in Spanish on Cuba's only television network, he called on Fidel Castro

Carter Center ■ Created to assist in global conflict resolution, development, and the promotion of democracy

Fidel Castro Steps Down as President of Cuba.

(Marcelino Vasquez Hernandez/AFP/Getty Images)

Varela Project ■
Cuban grassroots campaign demanding democratic reforms in Cuba

and his government to implement democratic practices. Carter contacted leading Cuban dissidents, such as Oswaldo Payá and Elizardo Sánchez, who launched the **Varela Project.** That prodemocracy grassroots campaign collected more than eleven thousand signatures supporting demands for the Cuban National Assembly to hold a referendum on democratic reforms. The Varela Project was named in honor of Felix Varela, a Cuban-born priest who opposed slavery and spent three decades in New York as an advocate of the poor until his death in 1853. Castro's illness in 2006 sparked renewed discussions about transitions to democracy in Cuba under new leadership. Although Castro's decision to relinquish power to his brother Raul Castro in 2008 contributed to some minor economic and political reforms, Cuba's transition to democracy remains elusive. However, changes in U.S. policy toward Cuba, including easing restraints on travel by Cuban-Americans to Cuba in 2009, offer hope for a transition to democracy.[15]

Private foundations, as well as foundations connected to governments, are components of civil society involved in building democracy. Foundations not only control significant financial resources, but also have experience working with other parts of civil society. Examples of such foundations are the NED, the Adenauer Foundation, the Ebert Foundation, the Ford Foundation, and the Seidel Stiftung Foundation. George Soros and his foundations played a prominent role in assisting democratization projects in Central Europe. Soros decided to provide resources quickly and to involve people at the local levels in the decision-making process.[16]

The Promotion of Democracy by the United States

Throughout its history, America has vacillated between splendid isolation, believing that it was a beacon on a hill providing light and direction to less fortunate societies, and military intervention to enforce its version of democracy in other countries. From its inception, the United States equated its perception of morality with universal ideals and often mobilized its vast resources to implement its socially constructed reality elsewhere. President **Woodrow Wilson** articulated America's involvement in World War I as a mission for democracy, as a struggle to secure the rights of individuals and for self-determination in small countries, and as a fight to make the world free. American attempts to promote democracy are inextricably linked to an entrenched **ideology** (i.e., set of beliefs that are often impervious to objective reality and verifiable facts). An ideological approach invariably oversimplifies reality by ignoring or downplaying obvious historical and contemporary contradictory developments.

The ideological polarization and military tensions that characterized the East-West struggle had many direct consequences for democratization. As Steven W. Hook observed, "The actual conduct of U.S. foreign policy reflected a **consequential ethic** that regarded anticommunism as a moral end in itself, one that superseded the means by which the outcome was achieved."[17] In the Cold War context, the United States believed that preventing the spread of communism justified both abandoning support for democratic principles and forming alliances with undemocratic governments in Africa, Asia, the Middle East, and Latin America. For example, the United States allied itself with Iran under Shah Mohammed Reza Pahlavi (1953–1979) and successive authoritarian governments in Saudi Arabia. A pragmatic reason given for building democracy is that democracies do not fight one another. However, as we discussed in Chapters 1 and 2, countries protect their interests against real or perceived threats. Consequently, democracies will fight each other to safeguard their interests. Athens and Syracuse, Rome and Carthage, England and Holland, Britain and South Africa, Britain and the United States, and the American Civil War itself are examples of democracies fighting each other.[18]

Despite its longstanding commitment to building democracy abroad, the United States continues to confront several obstacles, including the following:

1. *Inadequate Resources:* In most cases, the United States does not allocate enough financial assistance to build the political institutions, economic and social environment, and civil society essential for promoting democracy.
2. *Lack of Domestic Consensus:* Although in theory most Americans support promoting democracy in foreign countries, democratization in practice has generally failed to engender a lasting commitment, partly because of an overriding preoccupation with domestic concerns.
3. *Conflicting Policy Objectives:* Promoting democracy must often compete with other conflicting national interests.
4. *Limitations of the U.S. Democratic Model:* Each society has its own historical, social, and economic realities, which mitigate the usefulness of the American model of democracy.[19]

Pressure on countries to adopt market economies, which included the privatization of state-owned economic activities, was widely regarded as an essential

Woodrow Wilson ■ Idealist U.S. president who articulated the U.S. role throughout the world as one of a leader in democracy and self-determination

Ideology ■ A system of beliefs and values that influence one's activities and behavior

Consequential Ethic ■ Ethical system that prioritizes the end result of political actions

SEED Act ■
Designed to promote
economic liberaliza-
tion, privatization,
and democratic
reforms worldwide

step toward democratization. The U.S. government enacted the **Support for Eastern European Democracy (SEED) Act** in 2001 to promote economic liberalization
and privatization as well as democratic reforms. Foreign financial assistance—
provided through the NED and the U.S. Agency for International Development
(USAID)—was used to conduct free and fair elections, draft constitutions, establish independent judicial systems, train police forces, and reduce, if not eliminate,
competition in government. Financial assistance was also used to build the forces
of civil society. Despite these efforts, much of the money that was allocated for
building democracy was spent on aid consultants (many of them Americans) for
salaries, cost-of-living allowances, and a support staff in Washington, DC.[20]

Imposing Democracy by Force in Iraq

The United States remains a fervent disciple of *Thomas Paine*, who believed that
Americans have it in their power to begin the world all over again. Revolutionary
values and ideals are at the foundation of America's predilection to impose democracy by force. But strong democratic barriers also prevent the United States from
intervening in other countries without clear and direct threats to its national security interests. Although humanitarian crises and ruthless dictators influence the
United States to intervene, the size and power of the country involved is a factor in
such decisions. At the heart of the debate is whether democracy can be successfully
imposed by force. In addition to America's historical experiences, its unsurpassed
economic and military power influences many of its leaders to believe that they can
reshape the world in America's image. A different view is articulated by Dimitri K.
Simes, who argues that "it is condescending to claim that America has the right to
impose democracy on other nations and cultures. From the Roman Empire to the
British Empire, civilization brought on the tips of swords and bayonets has never
inspired lasting gratitude. Why should precision weapons be any more effective?"[21]

America's decision to invade Iraq in March 2003 raised many questions
about the efficacy of using military force to effectuate democratic change. Following a swift and successful American military campaign against Iraq, U.S. forces
captured Baghdad on April 9, 2003. Saddam Hussein's tyrannical rule ended, and
thousands of Iraqis greeted American troops, while other Iraqis looted government property and destroyed symbols of the old regime, especially the ubiquitous
statues of Hussein. Optimism about regime change and spreading democracy not
only in Iraq but throughout the Middle East was bolstered by the easy U.S. military victory, significant Iraqi support for the invasion, and the fact that Iraq contains large oil reserves, is comparatively secular and westernized, and has a
well-educated population. Table 4.2 shows U.S. efforts to impose democracy.

L. Paul Bremer III ■
Senior U.S. civilian
administrator in Iraq

**Coalition Provi-
sional Authority** ■
Retained responsibil-
ity for stabilizing
Iraq and helping the
country transition
from interim rule to
upcoming elections

President Bush appointed **L. Paul Bremer III** as the senior civilian administrator
in Iraq. As head of the **Coalition Provisional Authority**, Bremer faced the daunting
responsibility of stabilizing Iraq, rebuilding the country's economy and infrastructure, and imposing democracy. Iraq's ethnic and religious divisions complicated the
task. It was a major challenge to create political and economic institutions and
processes acceptable to the vast majority of Sunnis and Shiites, Arabs and Kurds,
religious fundamentalists and secularists, and men and women. Despite widespread
violence, elections for seats in a national assembly to draft Iraq's new constitution

TABLE 4.2

U.S. Efforts to Impose Democracy

Years	Country	Multilateral or Unilateral	Democracy Achieved?
2003–present	Iraq	Multilateral	?
2001–present	Afghanistan	Multilateral	?
1994	Haiti	Multilateral	No
1989	Panama	Unilateral	Yes
1983	Grenada	Multilateral	Yes
1970–73	Cambodia	Unilateral	No
1965–73	South Vietnam	Unilateral	No
1965–66	Dominican Republic	Unilateral	No
1945–52	Japan	Multilateral	Yes
1944–49	West Germany	Multilateral	Yes
1944–47	Italy	Multilateral	Yes
1924–25	Dominican Republic	Unilateral	No
1916–24	Cuba	Unilateral	No
1917–22	Haiti	Unilateral	No
1915–19	Mexico	Unilateral	No
1914	Nicaragua	Unilateral	No
1909–27	Nicaragua	Unilateral	No
1909	Cuba	Unilateral	No
1906–09	Honduras	Unilateral	No

Source: Minxim Pei and Sara Kasper, "Reconsider the U.S. Success Rate Before Forcing Democracy Again," *Christian Science Monitor*, 15 January 2003, 8.

were held on January 30, 2005. In December 2005, elections were held for the 275 parliamentary seats and to form a government. These elections were viewed by the U.S. government as evidence of Iraq's transition to democracy and as the beginning of democratic change throughout the Middle East. By 2006 it was obvious that U.S. efforts to promote democracy had failed and that the Middle East faced continuing violence and instability. Due partly to the global recession in 2009, American leaders were more preoccupied with withdrawing U.S. troops from Iraq than with promoting democracy. Ongoing wars in both Iraq and Afghanistan influenced the United States to focus instead on achieving greater political stability and reducing violence.

TRANSITIONS TO DEMOCRACY

In 1795, the philosopher Immanuel Kant, in his book, *Idea for a Universal History*, articulated the view that democratic government was destined to replace all other forms of government. The idea that progress was inevitable extended to beliefs about democracy. Despite history's cruel lessons, there was general optimism about a future characterized by justice, logic, and peace. But the auspicious beginnings of the twentieth century were destroyed by grave developments that threatened civilization and the survival of the human race. As Arthur Schlesinger Jr. put it, "Democracy, striding confidently into the 1900s, found itself almost at once on the defensive. The Great War shattered old structures of security and unleashed angry revolutions against democracy. Bolshevism in Russia, fascism in Italy, Nazism in Germany, militarism in Japan all despised, denounced, and, wherever they could, destroyed individual rights and the processes of self-government."[22] The Great Depression further eroded confidence in democracy's ability to engender prosperity for the majority of citizens. This economic devastation was quickly followed by World War II, in which antidemocratic forces triumphantly trampled democratic societies and forced Britain, the United States, and their allies to make unprecedented sacrifices to protect lives and liberties globally. It is estimated that by 1941 only twelve democracies had survived worldwide.[23] In his 1989 essay, "The End of History," Francis Fukuyama boldly asserted that with the end of the Cold War, democracy would inevitably spread to all countries. But the promise of liberal democracy encountered the harsh realities of antidemocratic forces.

Democratization (i.e., a transition to democracy) is a process of changing from an authoritarian or totalitarian system of government to a democratic government that is widely regarded by the population and the global community as legitimate and permanent. A *democratic transition* involves the negotiation and acceptance of democratic rules and procedures; the building or restructuring of political, social, and economic institutions; and the channeling of political competition along democratic lines.[24] An essential component of this transition is deciding on a new constitution that reflects political, religious, cultural, and economic realities within the society and its regional environment.

Liberalization ■
Traditionally equated with the implementation of Western concepts of liberal republicanism

Democratic transitions usually begin with **liberalization**. Liberalization includes implementing changes, such as imposing fewer restrictions on the freedom of the press and speech, recognizing the right of workers to unionize, moving away from arbitrarily arresting citizens, having greater respect for the rule of law, releasing political prisoners, and increasing tolerance for political opposition. *Democratization* includes liberalization but is a much broader concept. Democratization involves the right of citizens to compete in elections in order to gain control of the government and to determine the public policy agenda. But elections alone are not sufficient to bring about democratization. What is known as the **electoralist**

Electoralist Fallacy ■
The idea that elections are enough to foster democracy

fallacy (i.e., the view that free elections are a sufficient condition for democracy) is found in many societies transitioning to democracy. Even though nondemocratic leaders relinquish direct control of the government, they continue to exercise so much power that the democratically elected government is widely perceived as politically impotent.[25] Juan J. Linz and Alfred Stepan argue that a democratic transition is complete when there is a widespread agreement on how to elect a government; when the government has the authority to make decisions for the country; and when there is a legal separation of executive, legislature, and judicial powers.[26]

There must be a general societal consensus that no alternative to democracy exists before the transition to democracy occurs.[27] Democracies must deliver tangible benefits to demonstrate their superiority over nondemocratic systems. They must improve economic opportunities, maintain order, and provide an enhanced quality of life for their citizens in order to obtain legitimacy or acceptance by the people. A full transition to democracy is accomplished when basic democratic rights and freedoms are an integral component of life and when the overwhelming majority of the citizens, despite problems in society, believe that democracy is better than its alternatives.

Many military regimes in Africa, Asia, and Latin America implemented **managed transitions** to democracy. These regimes try to control the process of change to protect their own interests, to ensure social stability, and to minimize concessions to those advocating political transformation. In managed transitions, the military often establishes a timetable for the restoration or creation of democratic rule and determines the process of democratic elections.[28] These managed transitions usually occur in response to widespread national unrest and severe economic crises.

Managed Transitions ■ Attempt to create stable transitions of change throughout society

Consolidating democracy is a long-term process that involves behavioral, attitudinal, and institutional transformations. Behaviorally, a democratic regime is consolidated when there is widespread popular acceptance of the idea that governments should not be changed by force. Attitudinally, a democratic regime is consolidated when a strong majority of the population believes that democratic institutions and procedures are most appropriate for their society. Institutionally, a democratic regime is consolidated when society as a whole, including the government, believes that certain laws, procedures, and institutions must be used to govern society.[29] Conditions must exist that are conducive for the development and proper functioning of civil society. Specific arrangements must be made for groups and individuals to compete fairly and openly for political power. Society must respect and uphold the rule of law, and an impartial and independent judiciary must be regarded as the ultimate authority. Finally, there must be an institutionalized economic society or a significant degree of market autonomy and the right of individuals to own property.[30]

Waves of democratization have occurred since the eighteenth century and continue today. Samuel P. Huntington defines *a wave of democratization* as a group of transitions from nondemocratic to democratic regimes that happen within a specific period of time and that outnumber transitions away from democracy.[31] *Three* distinct waves of democratization can be identified in modern history. The *first wave* began with the American and French Revolutions and included parts of the British Empire (e.g., Canada, Australia, and New Zealand) and several small European countries (e.g., Switzerland). The *second wave* grew out of the retreat of democracy and the rise of Nazism, fascism, and totalitarianism in Europe and militarism in Japan. When these antidemocratic forces were defeated in World War II, democracy experienced a renewal or rebirth. Allied occupation of West Germany, Austria, Italy, and Japan led to the democratization of these former aggressive states. The *third wave* began with Portugal in 1974 and lasted until the late 1990s.[32] Because this wave was so expansive, we can subdivide it into *three distinct pathways to democracy* taken by various countries. The *first pathway* involved a movement away from military rule toward democracy in Greece, Spain, Portugal, Brazil, Argentina, and Chile. The *second pathway* toward democracy is characterized by a movement away from authoritarian regimes governed by a single dominant party. Examples are Taiwan, the Philippines, and South Africa.

The *third pathway* toward democracy began in countries that had been dominated by communism and a communist oligarchy. Countries in Central and Eastern Europe and the former Soviet Union are the leading examples of this pathway.[33]

Latin America

Between 1978 and 1993, fifteen countries in Latin America transitioned from dictatorship and totalitarianism to democracy. Several factors contributed to these developments. *First*, given the historical and cultural relationships between Latin America and Spain and Portugal, the end of the Francisco Franco regime in Spain and the Antonio de Oliveira Salazar regime in Portugal inspired democratic movements in Latin America. *Second*, economic difficulties, symbolized by the debt crisis, further eroded the legitimacy of nondemocratic governments, many of which justified their rule on the basis of the ability to develop the economy. *Third*, military conflicts in Nicaragua, El Salvador, Panama, and Argentina undermined dictatorships in those countries. The government in Argentina, for example, was weakened not only by economic problems but also by its defeat in the Falklands (Malvinas) by Britain. *Fourth*, the inability of governments to deal with the effects of natural disasters in countries such as Nicaragua and Bolivia contributed to their downfall. *Fifth*, some governments were pressured to democratize by sanctions, imposed primarily by the United States. *Sixth*, the demise of communism in the Soviet Union and Eastern Europe further weakened the credibility of dictatorships globally. *Finally*, the United States changed its approach to Latin America, becoming more reluctant to support dictators who were allies. These changes reinforced pressures within various Latin American countries for democracy.[34]

Chile, traditionally a stable democracy, is an example of a country in which democracy was replaced by authoritarian rule. In 1973, **Salvador Allende**, Chile's first democratically elected Marxist president, was overthrown and killed by General **Augusto Pinochet**, with the support of the United States. Pinochet and the military ruled Chile until the restoration of democracy in 1990. Domestic and international pressures, significant economic development under Pinochet, and the expansion of the middle class eventually influenced Pinochet to hold free and fair elections, which he lost. Although Pinochet continued to play an influential role in the government and the military, Chile had returned to its democratic roots. Despite progress toward democracy, many Latin American societies are confronted with numerous problems that weaken the democratic process. Many ordinary citizens are not convinced that democracy can improve their lives.[35] For example, violent protests against economic and political conditions in Ecuador forced President Lucio Gutierrez from office in 2005. Democracy in Honduras was undermined in 2009 when President **Manuel Zelaya** was ousted in a coup and replaced by **Roberto Micheletti**.

Russia

Emerging as a superpower after World War II, the Soviet Union embarked on an expansionist foreign policy and directly competed with the United States and its allies to promote communism as the dominant ideology and way of life. Domestically, the **Communist Party of the Soviet Union (CPSU)** exercised complete

Salvador Allende ■ Chilean Marxist who became president

Augusto Pinochet ■ General responsible for the military overthrow of Allende

Manuel Zelaya ■ President of Honduras elected in 2005 and ousted in June 2009 military coup

Roberto Micheletti ■ Interim president of Honduras sworn in after 2009 military coup that removed Manuel Zelaya

CPSU ■ Political party that exercised total economic, political, and cultural control over Soviet life control over the economy, politics, culture, and every aspect of Soviet life. Centrally planned economic activities excluded private enterprise and free markets. The government's control of the economy impeded the country's economic development and created many hardships for the population. Competition with the United States forced the Soviet Union to allocate a large proportion of its increasingly scarce resources to clients in the Third World and to military activities. Faced with a widening gap in living standards between themselves and the West, particularly the United States, Soviet citizens began to view global confrontation and the resources it required as undermining their own economic and social security. They began to turn their attention to domestic problems. As Marshall Brement observed, it was difficult to convince the Soviet public that events in distant places were more important than their own basic needs and interests. Only the most conservative ideologues within the leadership failed to grasp that the Soviet system was in crisis and that a radical shake-up was desperately needed.[36]

Mikhail Gorbachev, who was selected by the Communist Party in 1985 to lead the Soviet Union, inherited a stagnating economy and a deteriorating social and political system. Mounting Soviet casualties in Afghanistan, which the Soviets had invaded in 1979, further demonstrated the seriousness of the challenges confronting the Soviet Union. Gorbachev equated Soviet involvement in Afghanistan with America's failure in Vietnam and decided to stanch the "bleeding wound" by withdrawing Soviet forces from Afghanistan. These problems influenced Gorbachev to adopt radical economic reforms and political liberalization in an effort to strengthen the Soviet Union. His program of *perestroika* (i.e., restructuring of the Soviet economy) challenged the idea of a centrally planned economy and advocated implementing a more open economy that stressed greater local autonomy, economic incentives, and market forces. Another reform was the program of *glasnost* (i.e., openness), which challenged the Communist Party's assumption that it had a monopoly on truth. Instead, Gorbachev strongly supported more freedom of speech and freedom of the press, believing that truth emerges through the exchange of ideas, discussions, and debates. Finally, Gorbachev advocated a program of **demokratizatsiya** (i.e., democratization), a central component of which would be respect for the rule of law and the free and open election of government officials.

But Gorbachev's reforms, instead of strengthening the Soviet system, destroyed it. The Soviet Union disintegrated as the various republics declared their independence from Russia and communism itself fell. Hardliners were replaced by reformers, the military and the KGB (secret police) were reformed, and many Communist Party activities were abolished. When supporters of the old regime attempted to overthrow Gorbachev in 1991, Russians demonstrated against them in Moscow, helping to guarantee the failure of the coup. Although Gorbachev resigned as president in December 1991 when the Soviet Union was officially disbanded, he had been awarded the Nobel Peace Prize in 1990 for both his domestic and foreign policy reforms.

Boris Yeltsin, the former Communist Party chief in Moscow, was elected to replace Gorbachev in Russia's first free presidential election. Opposition to change continued to frustrate efforts by Yeltsin to reform Russia. Yeltsin responded by disbanding the parliament, which was dominated by communist conservatives who opposed change. His decision to schedule new elections and to create a

Mikhail Gorbachev ■
Leader who inherited the economic, political, and social problems during the final days of the declining Soviet Union

Demokratizatsiya ■
Program of democratization implemented by Gorbachev

Boris Yeltsin ■
Former Communist Party chief who was elected president of Russia

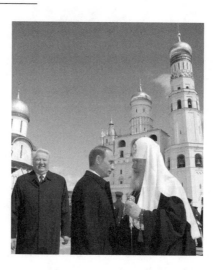

Yeltsin and Putin
at Inauguration.

(REUTERS/Itar Tass)

constitutional assembly to draft a new constitution, to be approved by the voters, prompted an armed revolt against the government, which was suppressed by the army. In 1995, Russia held its first fully constitutional parliamentary elections since the 1917 Bolshevik Revolution. Yeltsin was reelected president in 1996.[37] Despite ongoing problems with transitioning to democracy, Vladimir Putin, a former KGB agent, was appointed by Yeltsin to be his prime minister and acting president in January 2000; he was elected president later that year. During his inauguration, Putin held a red, leather-bound copy of the Russian Constitution and took an oath to "respect and guard the human and civil rights" of Russia. This event marked the first democratic transfer of executive power in Russia's 1,100-year history.[38]

Despite significant steps toward democracy, Russia remains at a crossroads, often leaning more toward authoritarianism than democracy. During her first visit to Russia in 2005 as U.S. Secretary of State, Condoleezza Rice emphasized that Russia should move closer toward democratic ideals, such as the rule of law and an independent news media.[39] Putin used the threat of terrorism to justify his retreat from democracy. By 2006, it was obvious that democracy in Russia, especially at the national level, had eroded. Rice's visit in 2007 underscored not only Russia's movement away from democracy but also a growing willingness to confront the United States. Although Dmitri A. Medvedev was elected as Russia's president in 2008, Putin, who became prime minister, retained significant power. That election did not advance democracy in Russia.

In August 2008, Russian troops and tanks occupied the pro-Russian enclaves of South Ossetia and Abkhazia (considered by Georgia to be parts of its territory) and moved into Georgia itself. Beyond the territorial dispute with Georgia, Russia believed that it had been humiliated by the United States following the disintegration of the Soviet Union. Western European countries expanded the European Union into former Soviet territories, and the United States continued to expand North Atlantic Treaty Organization (NATO) eastward, despite the end of the Cold War. Furthermore, arguing that it needed to counteract the threat of nuclear weapons from Iran (which does not have nuclear weapons), the United States proposed building a missile defense system in Poland. In 2009, America abandoned this project. Determined to end its humiliation and the growing global perception of it as an insignificant power, Russia has become more assertive. Using its vast revenues from oil and natural gas, Russia has pressured Western European countries and its neighbors to be more conciliatory toward it. Russia has expanded its naval presence in the Mediterranean and is exploring the Arctic for oil, gas, and minerals. In defiance of the United States, Canada, Western Europe, and other countries, Russia planted its flag on the bottom of the Arctic Ocean beneath the North Pole. Global warming is melting the ice, thereby making the area accessible to exploration and exploitation. Although the United States protested loudly, it was too preoccupied in Iraq and Afghanistan to confront a great power, along with China, India, and Brazil in an increasingly multipolar world.[40]

Islam and Democracy in the Middle East

Americans' perception of the Middle East as predominantly undemocratic and their association of Islam with oppression emanated partly from the objective reality that most countries in the region are not democratic and partly from their negative experiences with the Arab oil embargo of 1973–1974; the Iranian Revolution in 1979, led by the **Ayatollah Khomeini**, in which American diplomats were held hostage at the American Embassy compound in Tehran for more than a year; and the terrorist attacks in the United States in 2001 by Islamic extremists. While most scholars do not believe that democracy is incompatible with Islam, the general perception is that Islamic societies are inherently undemocratic. Furthermore, there is a general tendency, especially in the United States, to think that all Muslims are the same. Islamists are obviously not a monolithic group, just as Christians and Jews are not monolithic. Islamists are conservative, radical, moderate, authoritarian, and democratic. Countries in which Islam is practiced have their own particular cultural practices and beliefs that differentiate them from each other and moderate religious influences on political life.

Ayatollah Khomeini ■ Leader of the Iranian Revolution and of the Iranian state

Just as there are democratic values in Christian thought, there are democratic values in Islamic thought. As Graham E. Fuller put it, "Democratic values are latent in Islamic thought if one wants to look for them."[41] The interpretation of the Christian holy book, the Bible, is often arbitrary and subject to debate. The prophet **Mohammad** (570–632 A.D.), the founder of Islam, called for **shura** (i.e., consultation between the ruler and the ruled), which, as we discussed earlier, is the essence of democracy. The concept of limited government, a cornerstone of democracy, is central to Islam. Both the rulers and the ruled are, according to Islamic teachings on the state, subject to God's law. This means that not even the most powerful leaders are above the law. But unlike Christianity, which stresses that we should give to "Caesar what is Caesar's and to God what is God's," Islam makes no distinction between the secular and the sacred or between state and mosque. Despite difficulties inherent in using the **Koran** as the foundation of laws for Muslims, the authoritarian governments in the Middle East are less a product of strict adherence to Islamic teachings than they are creations of modernization and the universal human struggle for power.

Mohammad ■ (570–632); founder of Islam

Shura ■ Concept of consultation between the ruler and the ruled

Koran ■ Muslim holy book

Instead of viewing Islam as the primary obstacle to democratization, many citizens in the Middle East perceive U.S. policies that support authoritarian regimes

YOU DECIDE

Oil and Democracy

In a speech before the National Endowment for Democracy in November 2003, President George W. Bush attempted to change American and global perceptions of U.S. occupation of Iraq by stressing that the fall of Saddam Hussein was a "watershed event in the global democratic revolution." Pointing out that "sixty years of Western nations excusing and accommodating the lack of freedom in the Middle East did nothing to make Americans safe," President Bush concluded that "stability cannot be purchased at the expense of liberty." This speech underscored the concern of many advocates for democratic change in the Middle East that U.S. preoccupation with ensuring the flow of petroleum from the Middle East strengthened authoritarian governments in the region. At the heart of the lack of democracy in the Middle East, some argue, is the abundance of oil. The dependence of both exporting and importing countries on petroleum is seen as subverting democracy more than anything else. Countries with oil can flourish without having to provide the freedoms essential for developing human resources. Oil concentrates wealth in the state, enabling politicians, bureaucrats, and business people to gain and abuse power and for corruption to grow.

1. How in your view is oil a significant impediment to democratic transitions in the Middle East?
2. How does America's dependence on foreign oil affect transitions to democracy?
3. Can you think of oil-producing countries that become democratic? Why are these countries different?

Sources: Thomas L. Friedman, "The First Law of Petropolitics," *Foreign Policy*, No. 154 (May/June 2006), 31; and Tina Rosenberg, "The Perils of Petrocracy," *New York Times Magazine*, 4 November 2007, 44. ■

Mohammad Khatami ■ Iranian president who has advocated moderate reforms

as the most serious impediment to democracy.[42] Students in Iran, Egypt, and elsewhere in the Middle East routinely demonstrate against fundamentalist Islamic regimes and authoritarian governments and for democracy. In Iran, for example, students were instrumental in getting **Mohammad Khatami**, a moderate who advocated democratic changes, elected president. But powerful conservative clerics and their supporters prevented him from carrying out meaningful reforms. Many Iranian students have spearheaded protests against religious leaders. They want the same freedoms that they know exist in the West because of their access to television, the Internet, and other aspects of globalization. Students also strongly supported Mir Hossein Moussavi in the presidential election in June 2009 because they perceived him as being more supoportive of democracy than President Mahmoud Ahmadinejad.[43] Most governments in the Muslim world respond to demands for democracy by creating a veneer of freedom, allowing token opposition parties to function, and stressing the need for economic development. But effective opposition movements—whether they advocate democracy, Islam, or socialism—are perceived as threats to the power and privileges of ruling elites.[44]

Economic Globalization ■ Predominantly known as the spread of market values, institutions, and trade across state lines

GLOBAL GOVERNANCE AND DEMOCRACY

Globalization is often viewed as depriving democratically elected governments of their ability to determine public policies or to regulate the consequences of global decisions on the people who elected them. The gap between democracy at the national and global levels is most apparent in the area of **economic globalization.**

There is a widespread fear, especially within developed societies, that the global economy is undermining democracy by shifting power from elected national governments to faceless and often secretive global bureaucracies.[45] In most cases citizens cannot use their votes to hold global institutions accountable, despite the fact that many global organizations were created and are controlled by nation-states. For example, many Europeans believe that the Council of the European Union—composed of presidents, prime ministers, and cabinet ministers who meet regularly to approve various public policies—has essentially diminished the power of elected parliaments to make economic decisions. This loss of power, the relative inability of governments and citizens to influence decisions by global institutions, is generally referred to as a **democratic deficit**.

Democratic Deficit ■ Loss of citizen and government power in challenging the agendas of global institutions

International Regimes

Controversy surrounding the issue of a democratic deficit is a direct outgrowth of the proliferation of international regimes and global institutions as integral components of globalization. **International regimes** are basically institutions governing the behavior or actions of governmental as well as nongovernmental actors that are involved in specific activities. Regimes are characterized by complex interdependence and consist of rules, regulations, norms, and legal agreements that govern the behavior of those belonging to them.[46] Because regimes reflect power in the international system, the dominant actors or groups of actors often shape their organization, its functioning, and its policies. For example, although most countries are members of the World Trade Organization (WTO) and have a vote, actual decision making occurs in the **green room**, which is the small group meeting convened by the director-general and strongly influenced by the United States, the European Union, Canada, and Japan.[47]

International Regimes ■ International institutions that govern the behavior of governmental and nongovernmental actors

The proliferation and increasing complexity of international regimes combine to create a global governance system. **Global governance** is defined as "the formal institutions and organizations through which the rules governing world order are made and sustained as well as those organizations and pressure groups—from MNCs, transnational social movements to the plethora of nongovernmental organizations—which pursue goals and objectives that have a bearing on transnational rule and authority systems."[48] Global governance is based on cooperation as opposed to unilateralism. Coordination of actions occurs through governmental as well as NGOs.

Green Room ■ Small group meetings convened by the WTO director-general and strongly influenced by the United States, the European Union, Canada, and Japan

At the heart of global governance is the concept of global civil society, discussed earlier in this chapter. Global civil society is defined as a "decentralized network of autonomous social institutions that represent citizens and organized interests and engage in cooperative actions to achieve broad goals."[49] Just as the growth of civil society is essential to transitions to and consolidation of democracy within countries, global civil society plays a crucial role in promoting democracy at the global level. Global governance also reflects a growing awareness of the need to supply more global public goods as a consequence of increased globalization. *Global public goods* are characterized by nonrivalry in consumption and nonexcludability, as well as by the universal benefits they bestow on the majority of humanity.[50] They include global financial stability, environmental protection, basic human security, and the nonproliferation of weapons of mass destruction.

Global Governance ■ The institutions and structures that combine to govern many aspects of state policies, especially concerning international relations

Making Global Institutions More Democratic

Perceptions of a democratic deficit in global institutions and global governance have stimulated discussions about possible reforms to make the global system more accountable, transparent, and responsible to those affected by it. The global financial crisis of 2008–2009 strengthened demands for change. The *first suggestion* for the democratization of global institutions is changing the formulation and implementation of rules and procedures. This requires rethinking how interests are represented at the global level. Joseph S. Nye suggests that people could pressure their own governments to send representatives to meetings of global institutions, such as the WTO, to safeguard their interests; that legislators could hold hearings before or after meetings of global organizations; and that legislators themselves could become national delegates to various organizations.[51] A *second suggestion* is to make changes in the formal representation in global institutions, especially in relation to developing countries. The way seats and votes are allocated in many global organizations places developing countries at a disadvantage in terms of influence on decision making. Countries that contribute more financially tend to determine global public policies. For example, decisions of the World Bank and the International Monetary Fund (IMF) are largely shaped by the United States and Western European countries. The global financial crisis of 2008–2009 helped increase the power of China, India, Brazil, and other developing countries. A *third suggestion* is to expand representation in them to include citizens' representatives, in addition to government representatives and bureaucrats. This means including civil society actors. A *fourth suggestion* is to increase transparency in global organizations. Just as interest groups and a free press play important roles in creating transparency in politics within countries, they can function in a similar manner globally. Transparency is crucial to accountability and requires access to both deliberations of global institutions and relevant information. Transparency can also be achieved through regular monitoring and evaluation of the operations and effectiveness of global organizations.[52] A *final suggestion* is to enforce judicial-style accountability. This form of accountability is designed to ensure that organizations act within their powers. Specific actions or decisions are examined and attention is drawn to violations of operating rules and procedures. Judicial-style accountability is exemplified by the World Bank's Inspection Panel (created in 1993 to deal with loans) and the Compliance Adviser/Ombudsman Office (established in 1999 to deal with the work of the International Finance Corporation and Multilateral Investment Guarantee Agency). The Inspection Panel investigates complaints from groups able to demonstrate that (1) they live in an area or represent people who live in an area that could be negatively affected by a World Bank project, (2) they have suffered from the World Bank's failure to adhere to its policies and procedures, and (3) their concerns were not resolved to their satisfaction by the World Bank's management.[53]

SUMMARY AND REVIEW

This chapter focused on the spread of democracy at the global level. It shows how politics, economics, and culture are inextricably linked to the promotion of democracy on one hand and are shaped by democracy on the other. Democracy is defined as government that reflects the will of the people. There is much diversity among the different forms of democracy throughout the world, and many divergent paths toward democratization exist. Competitive elections—where various political parties representing various political interests effectively and fairly compete—are vital in such a democratic system. Civil society and global civil society play an important role in the democratization process, as the individuals and groups involved exert pressure on autocratic regimes to initiate democratic reforms. This chapter reviewed the many global waves of democratization. The waves of democratization were split into (1) the American and French Revolutions, (2) World War II and the defeat of Nazism and fascism, and (3) the explosion of democratization from the 1970s to the 1990s throughout Africa, Asia, Europe, the former Soviet Republics, and Latin America. Specific countries were examined from each of these regions, as we saw how democratization proliferated in Nicaragua, Chile, Russia, Portugal, and Spain.

Although democracy has not been universally accepted by all leaders throughout all nation-states, the strengthening of global civil society—as well as the rising expectations of those long deprived of democracy—have been driving factors in the growth of democratic developments and accountability in government. Democracy has increasingly becoming globalized, as many throughout the world continue to fight for universal human rights and for the establishment and consolidation of democratic government. With the success of the various waves of democratization, countries worldwide have been able to demand democratic reforms from their governments.

KEY TERMS

democracy 75
demos 75
direct self-government 75
indirect/representative democracy 75
James Madison 75
majoritarian model 75
consensus model 75
winner-take-all system 75
proportional representation 76
liberal democracy 76
illiberal democracies 76
constitutional liberalism 76
constitution 76
rule of law 76
legitimacy 76
presidential democracy 76
parliamentary democracy 76
conventional participation 77

unconventional participation 77
political parties 77
loyal opposition 77
interest group 77
civil society 77
global civil society 77
culture 78
Westminster model 79
economic development 80
middle class 80
Democratic Action Committee 81
Warsaw Declaration 81
CIVICUS 81
Carter Center 81
Varela Project 82
Woodrow Wilson 83
ideology 83
consequential ethic 83
Support for Eastern European Democracy (SEED) Act 84
L. Paul Bremer III 84

Coalition Provisional Authority 84
liberalization 86
electoralist fallacy 86
managed transitions 87
Salvador Allende 88
Augusto Pinochet 88
Manuel Zelaya 88
Roberto Micheletti 88
Communist Party of the Soviet Union (CPSU) 88
Mikhail Gorbachev 89
demokratizatsiya 89
Boris Yeltsin 89
Ayatollah Khomeini 91
Mohammad 91
shura 91
Koran 91
Mohammad Khatami 92
economic globalization 92
democratic deficit 93
international regimes 93
green room 93
global governance 93

DISCUSSION QUESTIONS

1. How would you define democracy? What are some of the basic elements that are needed for democracy to flourish?
2. Are there any pitfalls in trying to impose democracy, as in Iraq, by force? Can force be used to impose democracy, or are the two concepts incompatible?
3. Can you name some ways that would help the United States better promote democracy throughout the world today?
4. Name some ways in which global institutions have undermined democratic developments in individual nation-states.

SUGGESTED READINGS

Goldman, Marshall. *Retrostate: Putin, Power, and the New Russia.* New York: Oxford University Press, 2008.

Goldman, Merle. *From Comrade to Citizen: The Struggle for Political Rights in China.* Cambridge, MA: Harvard University Press, 2006.

Inglehart, Ronald, and Christian Welzel. "How Development Leads to Democracy," *Foreign Affairs* 88, No. 2 (March/April 2009): 33–48.

Wittes, Tamara. *Freedom's Unsteady March: America's Role in Building Arab Democracy.* Washington, DC: Brookings Institution Press, 2008.

Zakaria, Fareed. *The Future of Freedom: The Rise of Illiberal Democracy at Home and Abroad.* New York: W. W. Norton, 2003.

END NOTES

1. Arend Lijphart, *Patterns of Democracy* (New Haven, CT: Yale University Press, 1999).
2. Fareed Zakaria, "The Rise of Illiberal Democracy," *Foreign Affairs* 76, No. 6 (November/December 1997), 26.
3. Lijphart, *Patterns of Democracy*, 105.
4. Craig Warkentin, *Reshaping World Politics* (Lanham, MD: Rowman and Littlefield, 2001), 1; and Thomas Carothers, "Civil Society," *Foreign Policy*, No. 117 (Winter 1999/2000), 18.
5. Warkentin, *Reshaping World Politics*, 36–37.
6. Najma Chowdhury and Barbara J. Nelson, "Redefining Politics: Patterns of Women's Political Engagement from a Global Perspective," in *Women and Politics Worldwide*, eds. Barbara J. Nelson and Najma Chowdhury (New Haven, CT: Yale University Press, 1994), 16; and Robert F. Worth, "First Women Win Seats in Kuwait Parliament," *New York Times*, 18 May 2009, A4.
7. Ruth Henig and Simon Henig, *Women and Political Power* (London: Routledge, 2001), 104.
8. Jane S. Jaquette, "Women in Power: From Tokenism to Critical Mass," *Foreign Policy*, No. 108 (Fall 1997), 27; and Swanee Hunt, "Let Women Rule," *Foreign Affairs* 86, No. 3 (May/June 2007), 109–111.
9. Richard J. Payne, *Opportunities and Dangers of Soviet-Cuban Expansion* (Albany: State University of New York Press, 1998), 125.
10. Jorge I. Dominguez, *Democratic Politics in Latin America and the Caribbean* (Baltimore: Johns Hopkins University Press, 1998), 26; and Enrique Krauze, "Furthering Democracy in Mexico," *Foreign Affairs* 85, No. 1 (January/February 2006), 54.

11. Larry Diamond et al., "Introduction: Comparing Experiences with Democracy," in *Politics in Developing Countries*, eds. Larry Diamond et al. (Boulder, CO: Lynne Rienner, 1990), 18; and Staffan Lindberg, *Democracy and Elections in Africa* (Baltimore: Johns Hopkins University Press, 2006).

12. David Rohde, "In One Man's Life, a Glimpse of Democracy's Agony," *New York Times*, 5 October 2003, A5.

13. Peter J. Schraeder, "Promoting an International Community of Democracies," in *Exporting Democracy*, ed. Peter J. Schraeder (Boulder, CO: Lynne Rienner, 2002), 1; and Larry Diamond, "Globalization of Democracy," in *The Globalization Reader*, eds. Frank J. Lechner and John Boli (Oxford: Blackwell, 2000), 247.

14. Paul Wapner, "Politics Beyond the State," *World Politics* 47, No. 3 (April 1995), 313.

15. Sheryl Gay Stolberg and Damien Cave, "Loosening Cuba Restrictions, Obama Leaves the Door Ajar for More," *New York Times*, 14 April 2009, A5.

16. Kevin F. F. Quigley, *For Democracy's Sake: Foundations and Democracy Assistance in Central Europe* (Washington, DC: Woodrow Wilson Center Press, 1999), 2.

17. Steven W. Hook, "Inconsistent U.S. Efforts to Promote Democracy Abroad," in *Exporting Democracy*, 111; and Thomas Carothers, "The Backlash Against Democracy Promotion," *Foreign Affairs* 85, No. 2 (March/April 2006), 55–56.

18. Dimitri K. Simes, "America's Imperial Dilemma," *Foreign Affairs* 82, No. 6 (November/December 2003), 98.

19. Hook, "Inconsistent U.S. Efforts," in *Exporting Democracy*, 125.

20. Michael Dobbs, "Overseas Aid: Big Business at Home," *Washington Post National Weekly Edition*, 12–18 February 2001, 10.

21. Simes, "America's Imperial Dilemma," 97.

22. Arthur Schlesinger Jr., "Has Democracy a Future?" *Foreign Affairs* 76, No. 5 (September/October 1997), 3–4.

23. Schlesinger, "Has Democracy a Future?" 4.

24. Geoffrey Pridham, et al., "The International Dimension of Democratization," in *Building Democracy*, eds. Geoffrey Pridham et al. (London: Leicester University Press, 1997), 2.

25. Juan J. Linz and Alfred Stepan, *Problems of Democratic Transitions and Consolidation* (Baltimore: Johns Hopkins University Press, 1996), 4.

26. Linz and Stepan, *Problems of Democratic Transitions*, 3.

27. George Sorenson, *Democracy and Democratization* (Boulder, CO: Westview Press, 1998), 39.

28. Michael Bratton and Nicolas van de Walle, *Democratic Experiments in Africa* (Cambridge: Cambridge University Press, 1997), 239.

29. Linz and Stepan, *Problems of Democratic Transitions*, 6.

30. Linz and Stepan, *Problems of Democratic Transitions*, 7–11.

31. Samuel P. Huntington, *The Third Wave: Democratization in the Late Twentieth Century* (Norman: University of Oklahoma Press, 1993), 15.

32. Huntington, *The Third Wave*, 27.

33. James F. Hollifield and Calvin Jilson, "Introduction," in *Pathways to Democracy: The Political Economy of Democratic Transitions*, eds. James F. Hollifield and Calvin Jilson (New York: Routledge, 2000), 10.

34. Robert K. Shaeffer, *Power to the People: Democratization Around the World* (Boulder, CO: Westview Press, 1997), 124.

35. Peter Hakim, "Is Latin America Doomed to Failure?" *Foreign Policy*, No. 117 (Winter 1999/2000), 107; Peter Smith, *Democracy in Latin America* (New York: Oxford University Press, 2005); and Luis Rubio and Jeffrey Davidow, "Mexico Disputed Election," *Foreign Affairs* 85, No. 5 (September/October 2006), 75.

36. Marshall Brement, "Reaching Out to Moscow," *Foreign Policy*, No. 80 (Fall 1990), 58.
37. J. William Derleth, *The Transitions in Central and Eastern European Politics* (Upper Saddle River, NJ: Prentice Hall, 2000), 43.
38. Michael Wines, "Putin Is Made Russia's President," *New York Times*, 8 May 2000, A1; and Lilia Shevtsova, *Putin's Russia* (Washington, DC: Carnegie Endowment, 2005).
39. Alex Rodriguez, "Rice Offers Democratic Pitch During Visit with Russians," *Chicago Tribune*, 21 April 2005, Sect. 1, 4; Steven Fish, *Democracy Derailed in Russia* (Cambridge: Cambridge University Press, 2005), 1; Dmitri Trenin, "Russia Leaves the West," *Foreign Affairs* 85, No. 4 (July/August 2006), 87; and Marshall I. Goldman, *Retrostate: Putin, Power, and the New Russia* (New York: Oxford University Press, 2008).
40. Ellen Barry, "Russia Steps Up Its Push Into Georgia," *New York Times*, 12 August 2008, A1.
41. Graham E. Fuller, "The Future of Political Islam," *Foreign Affairs* 81, No. 2 (March/April 2002), 52; and Isobel Coleman, "Woman, Islam, and the New Iraq," *Foreign Affairs* 85, No. 1 (January/February 2006), 24.
42. Fuller, "The Future of Political Islam," 57.
43. Nazila Fathi, "Iran's Students Step Up Reform Drive," *New York Times*, 7 July 2002, A6; and Robert F. Worth and Nazila Fathi, "Both Sides Claim Victory in Iran Presidential Vote," *New York Times*, 13 June 2009, A1.
44. John L. Esposito and John O. Voll, *Islam and Democracy* (New York: Oxford University Press, 1996), 20; and Zeyno Baran, "The Battle Within Islam: Fighting the War of Ideas," *Foreign Affairs* 84, No. 6 (November/December 2005), 68–77.
45. R. C. Longworth, "Resisting Globalization's Democratic Deficit," *Chicago Tribune*, 15 October 2000, Sect. 2, 1.
46. Marian A. L. Miller, *The Third World in Global Environmental Politics* (Buckingham, UK: Open University Press, 1995), 53.
47. United Nations Development Program, *Human Development Report 2002* (New York: Oxford University Press, 2002), 118.
48. David Held et al., *Global Transformations* (Stanford, CA: Stanford University Press, 1999), 50.
49. Norman J. Vig, "Introduction," in *The Global Environment*, eds. Norman J. Vig and Regina S. Axelrod (Washington, DC: Congressional Quarterly Press, 1999), 5.
50. Inge Kaul et al., *Global Public Goods* (New York: Oxford University Press, 1999), 3.
51. Joseph S. Nye, "Globalization's Democratic Deficit," *Foreign Affairs* 80, No. 4 (July/August 2001), 5; Barbara Crossette, "How to Defuse the Bolton Bomb," *Foreign Policy*, No. 155 (July/August 2006), 68; and Colin Bradford and Johannes F. Linn, *Global Governance Reform* (Washington, DC: Brookings Institution Press, 2007).
52. UN Development Program, *Human Development Report 2002*, 115.
53. UN Development Program, *Human Development Report 2002*, 116; and Jessica Einhorn, "Reforming the World Bank," *Foreign Affairs* 85, No. 1 (January/February 2006), 21–22.

Global Terrorism

INTRODUCTION

Think about how the escalation of global terrorism affects our daily lives. This global problem is now virtually inseparable from personal concerns. Even traveling by plane from one city to another within the United States and Canada, which was once largely uneventful, has become much more complicated and stressful due to increased airport security. National and global institutions have also been profoundly affected by this problem. The U.S. Department of Homeland Security was created in 2003 as a direct response to the terrorist attacks in September 2001. It brought together twenty-two government agencies with 180,000 workers, making it the largest government reorganization in forty years. Domestic security has been strengthened, especially around bridges, water supplies, government offices, nuclear power plants, scientific laboratories, food supplies, and industrial factories. As we will discuss, political, economic, and cultural components of globalization are intertwined with various aspects of global terrorism.

This chapter emphasizes the growing importance of **asymmetrical power** in global affairs. When relatively weak groups use low-tech tools to inflict significant damage on very powerful countries that have the most advanced military technologies, they are using asymmetrical power. Moises Naim argues that terrorism has destroyed the idea that technology can make the American homeland impregnable.[1] The dominant and largely unchallenged view in the United States prior to the terrorist attacks on September 11, 2001, was that nonstate threats to national security were relatively unimportant. In 2000, Condoleezza Rice, who became President George W. Bush's National Security Adviser and later the U.S. Secretary of State, clearly and forcefully articulated the *foreign policy priorities* of the United States:

1. To ensure that America's military could deter war, project power, and fight in defense of its interest;
2. To promote economic growth and political openness;
3. To renew strong and intimate relationships with allies;

4. To focus U.S. energies on comprehensive relationships with the big powers, particularly Russia and China; and

5. To deal decisively with the threat of rogue regimes and hostile powers, which is increasingly taking the forms of the potential for terrorism and the development of weapons of mass destruction.[2]

In a speech at Kansas State University in November 2007, U.S. Secretary of Defense Robert M. Gates stressed nonstate threats to U.S. national security. While states are generally impeded by national boundaries, their nonstate adversaries routinely disregard national borders. Naim contends that if nation-states have benefited from globalization, criminal networks have benefited even more.[3] This chapter discusses difficulties involved in defining terrorism; factors conducive to the rise of terrorism; and goals, strategies, and weapons of terrorist groups. After examining specific cases of terrorism, we will discuss various responses to terrorism and the dilemmas democracies face in attempting to eliminate or reduce this threat. This chapter shows that taking a multifaceted and a global approach is essential to diminishing the problem of terrorism.

Asymmetrical Power ■ Form of conflict in which weaker groups or forces can inflict significant damage against more powerful states or forces

Reign of Terror ■ Terrorism committed by the French government during the French Revolution

Edmund Burke ■ British philosopher who strongly criticized the French Reign of Terror

DEFINING TERRORISM

Many actions have been called terrorism: From the violence of the French Revolution to the refusal of the National Education Association (NEA) to support federal policies. Proudly proclaiming their commitment to liberty, equality, and fraternity, the architects of the French Revolution instituted a **Reign of Terror** (1793–1794) to preserve the radical changes. Headed by Maximilian Robespierre, the Committee of Public Safety embraced terrorism in its effort to rule France during a period that was regarded as a national emergency. The French zeal for the *Terror*, the period of widespread violence, public executions, and intimidation of civilians, was strongly rejected by **Edmund Burke**, the British conservative philosopher who regarded French terrorists as hellhounds. In February 2004, U.S. Secretary of Education Rod Paige called the NEA, the country's largest teachers union, a terrorist organization because it opposed radical changes in federal education policies adopted by the Bush administration.[4] These two examples represent extreme definitions of terrorism. Although there is no universally accepted definition of terrorism, the standard view that one person's terrorist is another person's freedom fighter fails to distinguish among the various kinds and levels of terrorism and fails to acknowledge that freedom fighters' actions are not necessarily justified by their objectives. What is clear is that terrorism is a contentious issue that becomes hopelessly muddled by political and military considerations.

As American troops, tanks, and planes fought insurgents in the besieged city of Falluja in Iraq in early April 2004, opponents of the U.S. occupation kidnapped several foreign civilians and threatened to execute them. A group calling itself the Mujahedeen Brigades appeared on al-Jazeera television with three blindfolded Japanese civilians and threatened to kill them if Japan did not withdraw its 550 troops from Iraq within three days.[5] The horror the captives felt, evident from their screams, was made more palpable by guns pointed at them and knives

YOU DECIDE

Defining Terrorism

Martha Crenshaw, a leading expert on terrorism, argues that defining terrorism is difficult because terrorism is a social construction, which is relative to time and place. Because acts of terrorism generally occur within a political context, terrorism is essentially a political label. As such, this label reflects the struggle for power and the preferred approaches to solving the problem. Social construction helps to frame consciousness and to influence how behavior is perceived. Terrorism as a label is essentially subjective and judgmental. What Crenshaw is stressing is the politics of language: the struggle to define terms, and consequently to control behavior. Calling adversaries terrorists, in her view, is a way of depicting them as fanatic and irrational. Doing so forecloses the possibility of compromise, draws attention to the real or imagined threat to security, and promotes solidarity among the threatened. In other words, terrorism is not a neutral descriptive term, and those who define terrorism are usually not neutral parties.

1. How would you arrive at an objective definition of terrorism?
2. Discuss how Crenshaw's definition differs from your own definition of terrorism. Has Crenshaw's definition changed your ideas about terrorism?

Source: Martha Crenshaw, "Thoughts on Relating Terrorism to Historical Contexts," in *Terrorism in Context*, ed. Martha Crenshaw (University Park: Penn State University Press, 1995), 9–10. ■

and swords held to their throats. Many of the hostages were later beheaded. This example illustrates the nature of terrorism. *All acts of terrorism are designed to create fear*, to cause people to tremble. Our example of the hostages in Iraq points to another element of terrorism: communication with an audience that is far from the scene of violence. By using the most advanced technologies of global communication, terrorists seek to frighten people in distant places in order to exert pressure on governments. *Terrorism is essentially a form of psychological warfare*. Unlike most conventional wars, terrorism lasts for generations, as we will see in our discussions of the Irish Republican Army (IRA), the Basques in Spain, and the Palestinians. Terrorism is also *indiscriminate*. Most terrorist activities aim to create uncertainty and general fear by communicating that anyone can be a target.[6] In many ways, terrorism is closely associated with ideology. This is clearly the case with al-Qaeda: It is less an organization than an ideology that inspires groups and people worldwide to engage in terrorist acts.

Wars of liberation throughout history have generally been accompanied by actions that were defined as terrorism by those in favor of maintaining the status quo. Distinguishing terrorism from guerrilla warfare and insurgency is often challenging. **Guerrilla warfare**, which means little war, is the use of selective violence against military targets. But when societies experience extensive violence, distinctions between guerrilla warfare and terrorism tend to blur. Following the 2001 attacks in the United States, many governments applied the label of terrorism to very old conflicts of their own that were previously regarded as insurgencies. For example, China annexed what is now Xinjiang in 1759. The inhabitants, known as **Uighurs**, practice Sufi Islam and speak a Turkic language. They resisted China's rule and launched their first uprising in 1865. The disintegration of the Soviet Union in 1991 and the independence gained by some Muslim communities in Central Asia inspired the Uighurs to renew their struggle to establish a separate state. But China

Guerrilla Warfare ■ Use of selective violence against military targets by insurgency forces

Uighurs ■ Ethnic group that rebelled against China's annexation of Xinjiang in 1759

YOU DECIDE

The Difference Between War and Terrorism

In the documentary film, *The Fog of War*, former U.S. Secretary of Defense Robert McNamara discussed eleven lessons of war, using his experiences with World War II, the Cuban missile crisis, and the Vietnam War to illustrate his points. He talked about the extensive damage caused by the firebombing of Japanese cities by the United States. From his perspective, firebombing and dropping atomic bombs on Hiroshima and Nagasaki were meant to terrorize the Japanese people. Creating terror among civilians is an integral and inseparable component of war. Think of the widespread destruction caused by wars. In both Iraq and Afghanistan wars have caused widespread destruction and incalculable human suffering. Both adults and children have been severely traumatized and are routinely victims of violence by the terrorists as well as by U.S., Iraqi, Afghan, and Pakistani military forces. Millions of refugees have fled war zones. The fear experienced by ordinary civilians in wars is, in reality, indistinguishable from fear caused by roadside bombs, suicide bombers, and random mass killing.

1. What is the difference between war and terrorism?
2. Do you think that the use of force can ever be justified? If so, under what circumstances and at what costs? ■

was quick to label the Uighurs as terrorists after the global developments in 2001.[7] This raises the question: Who gets to define terrorism and why? Complicating definitions of terrorism is the general acceptance of war as a legitimate instrument of governments. Paul Wilkinson argues that "terrorist campaigns inherently involve deliberate attacks on civilian targets and are therefore analogous to war crimes."[8] But who decides which military actions are war crimes?

FACTORS CONDUCIVE TO TERRORISM

Examining the factors that make terrorism a useful tool to accomplish certain objectives is essential to any pragmatic effort to eliminate or diminish terrorist threats. As we try to identify the dominant cause, we will see that terrorism has, in fact, many interrelated causes.

Poverty is widely perceived as the root of terrorism. Following the 2001 terrorist attacks in the United States, a consensus supported the view that poverty is a major cause of terrorism. Poverty is closely linked to economic and political isolation, feelings of hopelessness, violations of human rights, and the lack of democracy, which all provide a fertile breeding ground for terrorism. In Pakistan, students enroll in religious seminaries, called **madrassas**. Supported by Muslim charities worldwide—especially those in Saudi Arabia—they feed, shelter, clothe, and educate students from poverty-stricken families. In addition to receiving training in the Koran, these students are indoctrinated to hate the West, especially the United States. Many terrorists graduate from madrassas.[9] However, terrorists who attacked the United States, Spain, and Britain were not poor. Many of them came from the middle class.

Globalization is a major factor in global terrorism. In many ways, terrorism is a product of resistance to change brought about by cultural, economic, political,

Madrassas ■
Religious seminaries supported by Muslim charities worldwide

military, and even environmental globalization. Individuals in distant places communicate instantaneously and are able to coordinate their activities on a global scale. Global transportation enables them to move easily from one country to another. Global cities provide an environment in which it is easy for people to be anonymous.

Legitimate grievances and the failure of governments to adequately address these problems often foment terrorism. In fact, most terrorist organizations trace their origins to political, religious, social, economic, and ethnic problems that were ignored, downplayed, or dismissed by those in power and by society in general. Why did the African National Congress (ANC) in South Africa, the Palestine Liberation Organization (PLO), and the IRA become terrorist organizations? Specific grievances motivated individuals to form these groups and to use terrorism to achieve their objectives. *Violence by governments* also causes terrorism. Governments routinely abuse their monopoly on legitimate violence regarding specific minority groups or majority groups that lack significant political, economic, and social power. The efficacy of official violence influences individuals and groups that want to change their circumstances to resort to violence.

Humiliation is another factor conducive to the use of terrorism. Terrorism, which was not a problem in Iraq before the U.S. invasion, became widespread. Many Iraqis felt humiliated by intrusive American searches, by being occupied, and by being mistreated. Thomas L. Friedman, an influential journalist with the *New York Times*, stated: "If I've learned one thing covering world affairs, it is this: The single most under-appreciated force in international relations is humiliation."[10]

The lack of democracy, and widespread and systematic violations of human rights contribute to the rise of terrorism. The 2001 terrorist attacks in the United States drew attention to Saudi Arabia and Egypt, countries to which most of the terrorists belonged. Egypt and Saudi Arabia are authoritarian societies in which there is no free press, no freedom of expression, and no free elections. Dissent is not tolerated, individuals are routinely tortured, and fair trials are rare. Dissidents, such as Osama bin Laden (from Saudi Arabia) and Mohammed Atta (the Egyptian-born leader of the 2001 terrorist attacks), were unable to express dissent at home, so they went to Afghanistan to organize al-Qaeda, a global terrorist network.[11]

Foreign policies contribute to terrorism. Roman occupation of Israel generated strong resistance by the Jews, and some Jews adopted terrorism in a futile effort to end Roman oppression. European expansion and colonization laid the foundation for the emergence of national liberation movements that used terrorism to achieve independence. Throughout the Cold War, the United States and the Soviet Union ignored the terrorism that was used by the side they supported, preferring instead to see the terrorists as freedom fighters. Many foreign policy and terrorism analysts view U.S. foreign policies in the Middle East—especially those involving the Palestinian-Israeli conflict, Saudi Arabia, and Egypt—as being conducive to terrorism. For example, Osama bin Laden strongly opposed the stationing of American troops in Saudi Arabia during the 1991 Gulf War. The U.S. policies are widely seen in the Middle East and elsewhere as contributing to the oppression of the Palestinians by Israel.[12] Finally, *failed states provide an environment conducive to terrorism.* Failed states generally abuse human rights; are undemocratic; are intolerant of ethnic, political, and religious diversity; and have weak economies. State failure is often accompanied by an increase in bureaucratic corruption and cooperation among government officials and criminals. In essence, state authority and civil society are severely undermined, and many regions within a country are lawless.[13] The most obvious example of how state failure breeds terrorism is al-Qaeda in Afghanistan. Ravaged by the Soviet Union invasion and years of war, the poverty-stricken country became a base for Islamic extremists and holy warriors. Under the leadership of the **Taliban** (i.e., a group of extreme Islamic fundamentalists), Afghanistan provided bin Laden with an ideal environment in which terrorism could grow and from which terrorist activities could be organized. By the end of 2006 Iraq was increasingly perceived as a failed state and the breeding ground of terrorists.

Taliban ■ Former government of Afghanistan that repressed its people and supported al-Qaeda

GOALS, STRATEGIES, AND WEAPONS OF TERRORISM

The goals, strategies, and weapons of terrorism vary from group to group and from one period of history to another. *The goals of terrorism* include

1. *Social and Political Justice:*   Terrorism has been used to achieve concrete political and social changes, including overthrowing repressive regimes.
2. *Self-determination:*   Many terrorist organizations emerged as part of the struggle to gain national independence.
3. *Racial Superiority:*   Many white supremacist groups attempt to preserve racial segregation and social, economic, and political power based on skin color.
4. *Foreign Policies:*   Terrorism is often used to influence governments to take or refrain from taking certain actions. In April 2004, bin Laden offered to stop terrorist attacks against European countries that ended military actions in Muslim countries. That offer was clearly designed to influence European policies toward Iraq.[14]
5. *Publicity:*   A central goal of most terrorist groups is to draw public attention to their cause.
6. *Demoralized Governments:*   By making governments appear weak and incompetent, terrorists believe they can undermine their legitimacy and policies.[15]

Terrorist organizations adopt several *strategies* to achieve their objectives. *Creating a climate of fear and insecurity*, partly to undermine people's confidence in their government, is an integral component of terrorists' strategies. But terrorism also depends on *cultivating popular support*. Terrorists are generally effective when they operate in an environment that enables them to hide, obtain resources (including weapons), gather information about government operations and plans, and communicate with each other. However, telecommunications and computer technologies have reduced the need for popular support as a component of strategy. Terrorists rely on **virtual networks**, a style of organization that is essentially leaderless and is facilitated by the Internet. American right-wing extremists developed this strategy to counteract the effectiveness of U.S. law enforcement agencies.[16]

Virtual Networks ■ A style of organization that is essentially leaderless and facilitated by the Internet

Some terrorist groups *reject the terrorist label* in order to gain greater legitimacy or acceptance in society. Governments, on the other hand, refuse to confer any kind of legitimacy on terrorist groups and reject defining terrorism as warfare.[17]

These terrorist groups are likely to select government targets, including embassies, military personnel and bases, and government officials. In Colombia, for example, terrorist groups launched a campaign of assassinations to get the attention of the government and its supporters. Judges, prosecutors, and elected officials were the main targets. This strategy attempts to undermine assumptions that government policies can ensure personal safety.[18] *Selective kidnappings* are also used by terrorists to achieve their goals. By taking government officials, soldiers, businesspeople, and prominent citizens hostage, the terrorists force the government to either take military action against them or bargain with them. Terrorists in Iraq adopted this strategy.

Weapons used by terrorists vary according to their goals, available technology, and resources at their disposal. Sarin gas, anthrax, and various poisons have been used in Japan and the United States. Motor vehicles packed with ammonium nitrate and fuel oil were used as bombs in Oklahoma City in 1995 and in Bali, Indonesia, in 2002. Suicide bombers are lethal weapons in many parts of the world, including Israel, Saudi Arabia, Afghanistan, and Iraq. The use of airliners fully loaded with fuel as missiles to destroy the World Trade Center and damage the Pentagon focused global attention on a new terrorist weapon. As terrorists use the Internet to spread their message and organize their activities, there is growing awareness of cyberspace warfare as a weapon in the terrorists' arsenal.[19] Although few terrorists are capable of using weapons of mass destruction on a large scale, terrorist attacks in the United States in 2001 and the subsequent U.S. invasion of Iraq in 2003 put the issue of chemical and biological weapons in the possession of terrorists on the global agenda.[20]

FINANCING TERRORISM

Much emphasis has been placed on determining how terrorism is financed and on finding ways to disrupt, if not eliminate, financial support for terrorism. However, compared with conventional military activities, terrorism is relatively low-cost and very effective. Consider the attacks on the World Trade Center and the Pentagon. The terrorists involved lived middle-class lifestyles, took flying lessons, traveled around the country, and bought first-class tickets on the planes they hijacked. The cost of these activities relative to the damage the terrorists caused using American planes to bomb American buildings is almost insignificant. Bombings in Spain in 2004 and in Britain in 2005 also show that terrorists do not have to be well financed to launch destructive attacks. Many terrorist cells are self-supporting, and many terrorists do not engage in financial activities that immediately draw attention. This makes it extremely difficult for governments to gather financial information. Furthermore, many terrorists use **hawalas** (i.e., an informal system of transferring money that is based primarily on trust and interpersonal relations). Developed in India before the arrival of Western banking, hawalas frustrate efforts to trace money because they leave no electronic and virtually no paper trail.[21]

Contributions from individuals and groups are a major source of money for terrorism. In the case of al-Qaeda, bin Laden used his considerable wealth to finance global terrorism. Many individuals make charitable contributions to

Hawalas ■ Informal system of transferring money based primarily on trust and interpersonal relations organizations that are principally concerned with assisting the poor. However, some of this money is also used to support terrorism. *Governments finance terrorism*, both directly and inadvertently. The most obvious way is by sponsoring their activities. For many years, Libya's leader, **Muammar Qaddafi**, openly financed and trained terrorist groups in the Middle East and Africa. In 2004, Qaddafi was embraced by Europe and the United States for his decision to fight terrorism and to compensate relatives of victims who were killed in the bombing of a Pan Am jet over Lockerbie, Scotland, in 1988. Libyan intelligence agents were blamed for that bombing. Libya eventually accepted responsibility and paid $2.7 billion to the families of the victims.[22] Governments, especially Saudi Arabia, provide substantial financial resources to charities and organizations that are indirectly linked to terrorism.

Diamonds, oil, and other natural resources provide revenues for terrorism. Terrorists often prefer diamonds because they are easily transported, easily hidden, and easily converted into cash. Failed states in Africa often provide opportunities for rebel groups to cooperate with terrorist groups. One of the best examples is Sierra Leone in West Africa. Sierra Leone has some of the richest diamond fields in the world. It has also been plagued by political instability. The diamond trade helped to fund both Sierra Leone's civil wars and al-Qaeda. Senior members of Sierra Leone's **Revolutionary United Front (RUF)**, a rebel group that challenged the government and engaged in horrific acts of violence and terrorism, took diamonds, often wrapped in rags, across the border into Liberia and exchanged them for cash from al-Qaeda and **Hezbollah**, a Shiite terrorist group in Lebanon. With the cooperation of corrupt customs and immigration officials, the diamonds, which were bought at below-market prices, were then taken to Europe by terrorist organizations and sold at much higher prices.[23] These diamonds are widely known as *conflict diamonds* because of their inextricable links with brutal civil wars and terrorism.

Criminal activities are a major source of funding for terrorism. Terrorists are often involved in armed robbery, credit card fraud, identity theft, kidnapping, extortion, and other crimes. In the Philippines, for example, the terrorist group **Abu Sayyaf** routinely kidnaps people, including tourists, to finance its activities. The **Tamil Tigers** in Sri Lanka controlled and operated boats that smuggled contraband in the Indian Ocean region before they were defeated in 2009. Often, terrorist groups coerce civilians into paying protection money, sometimes called a revolutionary tax. The IRA is a group that used this method to finance terrorism. Other groups, such as the Taliban in Afghanistan, use money obtained from the sale of illegal drugs.

THE COSTS OF TERRORISM

Costs associated with terrorism are so widespread, complex, and intangible that they are virtually impossible to measure. Daily, individuals, families, governments, companies, and nonstate actors worldwide bear the costs of terrorism to varying degrees. Time, money, and other resources are diverted from other global problems. Migration, trade, travel, and interpersonal relations are

Muammar Qaddafi ■ Libyan leader accused of financing and training terrorist groups in the Middle East and Africa

RUF ■ Rebel group that challenged the government of Sierra Leone through acts of violence and terrorism

Hezbollah ■ Shiite terrorist group based in Lebanon

Abu Sayyaf ■ Terrorist group in the Philippines that regularly kidnaps people to finance its activities

Tamil Tigers ■ Group in Sri Lanka that smuggles contraband in the Indian Ocean region affected. In September 2001, a very small group of individuals, nineteen of them, caused incalculable damage to the United States as well as the global community. Almost three thousand people from roughly fifty countries were killed. It is generally believed that the financial crisis and the global recession in 2008–2009 were caused in part by policies adopted by the Bush administration to fight global terrorism, including wars in Afghanistan and Iraq. Domestic terrorists, using anthrax, also damaged U.S. government offices, businesses, and individuals.

Costs to Individuals

Individuals usually suffer the most from terrorist acts in terms of loss of lives and social, psychological, and physical problems. Many citizens are made ill by fear and a sudden loss of personal freedom. They restrict their activities, limit their travel, and often distrust their neighbors, thereby weakening community bonds and support. For example, the 2001 attacks undermined trust between most non-Muslim Americans and Muslims in general, especially Arabs. Seven years later, almost any major violent act in New York as well as in other parts of the United States is initially evaluated as terrorism. Relations between non-Muslim Americans and Muslims remain problematic. President Barack Obama, as will be discussed in Chapter 14, made a concerted effort to improve relations with the Muslim world during visits to Turkey, Saudi Arabia, and Egypt in 2009.

Economic Costs

Calculating the economic costs of terrorism and the responses to it is virtually impossible because they are so complex and far-reaching. For example, after the 2001 attacks, airlines suffered major financial losses and continue to feel the impact of terrorism. It is estimated that the global airline industry lost $18 billion in 2001 and $13 billion in 2002 following the attacks. Combined, these losses were more than the total profit of all the airlines since 1945.[24] High oil prices and continuing fears about terrorism continued to create severe financial problems, including bankruptcy for some airlines in 2008.

Costs to Governments

Governments generally increase resources to fight terrorism and to provide their citizens with a heightened sense of security. For example, as you prepare to board an airline, the costs become obvious. There are more security guards, bags are carefully checked, and individuals are often searched. While airlines pay some of these costs, the U.S. federal government is primarily responsible for airport security. The federal, state, and local governments in the United States also spend money to guard bridges, nuclear power plants, train stations, and so on. The most obvious costs are associated with military actions against terrorists. The invasion of Afghanistan to destroy al-Qaeda and the Taliban, as well as the invasion, occupation, and rebuilding of Iraq, has cost hundreds of billions of dollars and many lives.

Foreign Policy Costs

Several times following the 2001 attacks, the United States closed its embassies in Saudi Arabia and elsewhere. These shutdowns meant that America was paying a price for not being able to conduct normal diplomatic relations.[25] Furthermore, heightened security for embassies creates additional expenses.

Costs to Democracy

People who are afraid, as Thomas Hobbes observed, are willing to turn to all-powerful rulers who promise to provide security. But part of the price for that security is less freedom. In a climate of fear, governments often justify violating individuals' rights on the grounds of national security.[26] Torturing terrorist suspects and denying them the fundamental right to habeas corpus continued to be debated in the United States.

Domestic Terrorism ■ Occurs within borders of a state

Nationalist Terrorism ■ Occurs as a result of struggles for independence

Religious Terrorism ■ Occurs as a result of religious extremism

State Terrorism ■ Government repression targeted against civilians

Global Terrorism ■ Partly a result of increased globalization

KINDS OF TERRORISM

Although the types of terrorism tend to overlap, they vary in their implications and affect us in different ways. For example, the indiscriminate nature of global terrorism contrasts sharply with domestic terrorism aimed at specific groups or governments. In this section, we will discuss *five kinds of terrorism*:

1. *Domestic terrorism* occurs within the borders of a particular country and is associated with extremist groups.
2. *Nationalist terrorism* is closely associated with struggles for political autonomy and independence.
3. *Religious terrorism* grows out of extreme fundamentalist religious groups that believe that God is on their side and that their violence is divinely inspired and approved.
4. *State terrorism* is a cold, calculated, efficient, and extremely destructive form of terrorism, partly because of the overwhelming power at the disposal of governments.
5. *Global terrorism* is partly an outgrowth of the forces of globalization, which enable the different kinds of terrorism to spread worldwide.

Domestic Terrorism

In June 2009 a doctor who performed abortions in Kansas was killed in a church by a gunman who opposed abortion. Later in June a white supremacist and neo-Nazi attacked the U.S. Holocaust Memorial Museum, killing a security guard. On April 19, 1995, Americans watched with incredulity as bloodied bodies were pulled from the federal building in Oklahoma City. Most Americans quickly blamed Middle Eastern terrorists for the Oklahoma City bombing, which killed 168 people. But the leader of this terrorist act was Timothy McVeigh, an American and a decorated Gulf War veteran. Domestic terrorism has existed in the United States and other countries for hundreds of years. Unlike most countries, where terrorist activities have been carried out primarily against governments, terrorism in America has been used mostly against racial, ethnic, or religious minorities. American terrorists are predominantly right-wing extremists who embrace white supremacist, anti-Jewish, antiforeign, and antigovernment philosophies based on a religious doctrine known as *Christian identity*. This doctrine essentially holds that white people are chosen by God, whereas Jews, Americans with African ancestry, Asians, and other racial minorities are "mud people." These terrorists generally believe that the U.S. government is dominated by Jews and is an occupying power and that the United States should not participate in the United Nations and other international organizations. Based on these beliefs, they have formed heavily armed militias, strongly oppose gun control, and refuse to pay taxes.[27] Domestic terrorist groups include the National Alliance, the Ku Klux Klan, the Aryan Nation, Posse Comitatus, and the Confederate Hammerskins. Many American terrorists subscribe to the theory of leaderless resistance, which means that small groups of terrorists operate essentially independent of a hierarchical organization.

Domestic terrorism has long been a significant problem in several European countries. Throughout the 1970s and 1980s, the **Red Brigades**, an Italian terrorist group, launched a campaign of bombings and assassinations of government officials. The terrorist act that received the most attention was the kidnapping and murder of former Prime Minister Aldo Moro by the Red Brigades in 1978. The widely published photograph of Moro's body slumped in the back seat of an abandoned car in Rome shocked many Italians.[28] Although most Red Brigades fled to France shortly after this terrorist act, in 2003 it was estimated that 140 members were still active in Italy. Germany, France, and Greece have also been plagued by domestic terrorism. In Greece, for example, the Marxist-Leninist terrorist group Revolutionary Organization 17 November (or **November 17**) has been involved in terrorist activities since 1975. November 17 took its name from the date of a student protest in 1973 that was violently crushed by Greece's military government. Embracing strong anti-American and anti-imperialist views, November 17 is believed to have killed several American and British citizens.[29] Many of the terrorist groups in Germany hold white supremacist, anti-Jewish, and antiforeigner views that are similar to those of their American counterparts. Bombings of trains in Spain in 2004 and in Britain in 2005 by Muslims, many of whom were born in these countries, underscored growing concerns about domestic terrorism.

Latin America has spawned many domestic terrorist organizations. Growing violence and terrorist activities by groups such as the *Montoneros* and the *Ejercitos Revolucionares del Pueblo* were met with extreme violence from right-wing groups and the Peronist regime. Argentina's military dictatorship launched what became known as the **dirty war**, in which thousands of people disappeared or were killed. Sendero Luminoso (**Shining Path**) in Peru and the **Revolutionary Armed Forces of Colombia (FARC)** are other examples of domestic terrorist groups in Latin America. Shining Path was formed by university students and professors who subscribed to the philosophy of *Mao Zedong (Mao Tse-Tung)*. They sought to weaken the government's authority by inspiring Indians and others to rebel. Violence by Shining Path and the Peruvian government resulted in more than thirty thousand deaths. Many Asian countries also face constant

Red Brigades ■ An Italian terrorist group that attacked government officials

November 17 ■ Marxist-Leninist group that committed terrorist acts in Greece

Dirty War ■ Terrorist campaign by the Argentine military dictatorship directed against those critical of their government

Shining Path ■ Peruvian terrorist group

FARC ■ Colombian Marxist guerrilla group practicing terrorism against civilians and government officials threats from domestic terrorists. For example, in 2006, an Islamic group, Lashkar-e-Taiba, bombed trains in Mumbai, India, killing roughly 135 people and wounding another 800. Such bombings occur routinely.

Nationalist Terrorism

Many nationalist groups attempted to achieve nonviolent political change but were often brutally suppressed by governments. Often, nationalist terrorism is accompanied by peaceful, legitimate political activities designed to achieve autonomy, political freedom and equality, or independence. Nationalist groups are routinely labeled terrorists by the governments they oppose and labeled national liberation movements or freedom fighters by their supporters, including other governments. In this section, we will discuss nationalist terrorism in the Middle East (focusing on the Palestinian-Israeli conflict), Northern Ireland, and Spain.

THE MIDDLE EAST   The Palestinian-Israeli conflict stands out as the most prominent contemporary example of nationalist terrorism. This conflict has plunged the Middle East into four major wars and fuels ongoing violence in the region. Failure to resolve this conflict has global implications, largely because of the world's dependence on petroleum imports from the Middle East. Furthermore, global terrorists, such as al-Qaeda, use this conflict to justify their activities and to recruit members throughout the Islamic world. The spiritual and emotional components of this conflict, combined with the sufferings of both Jews and Palestinians, make any discussion of it highly controversial and often subjective. In many ways, the pain and humiliation of both Jews and Palestinians often prevent both sides from empathizing with each other and reaching mutually beneficial solutions to their problems. Instead, both sides have been locked in an increasingly deadly embrace from which neither side is capable of extricating itself. To a large extent, the Palestinian-Israeli conflict is an outgrowth of virulent anti-Jewish practices in Europe that culminated in the **Holocaust**.

Holocaust ■ Mass murder of millions of Jews driven by ethnic and religious hate and discrimination

Nationalist terrorism, one could argue, began when Jews attempted to end Roman occupation of Israel by killing Roman soldiers and officials. The modern period of nationalist terrorism has its origin in the British efforts to establish a national homeland for Jews in Palestine under the Balfour Declaration. Palestine was controlled by the Ottoman Turks. However, after the Ottoman Empire disintegrated following Turkey's defeat in World War I, Palestine became a British mandate under the League of Nations in 1922. Britain's responsibility was to prepare Palestinians for independence. The persecution of Jews in Europe, especially in Nazi Germany, complicated the situation in Palestine and set the stage for conflict. Led by **Menachem Begin**, who later became Israel's prime minister and a winner of the Nobel Peace Prize, some Jews formed a terrorist organization, known as the **Irgun**, to drive the British out of Palestine and to establish a Jewish state. The Irgun and other groups created a climate of fear in Palestine that ultimately undermined the public's confidence in Britain's ability to maintain order and to protect civilians. The most significant terrorist act against the British was the 1946 bombing of the *King David Hotel* in Jerusalem, the headquarters of British military forces in Palestine. Ninety-one persons were killed and forty-five others were

Menachem Begin ■ Leader of the Jewish terrorist organization the Irgun, committed to Israeli independence

Irgun ■ Jewish terrorist group committed to driving the British out of Palestine injured.[30] This act was condemned by many Jews and Jewish organizations. The division of Palestine into a Jewish and a Palestinian state by the United Nations in 1947 ended Jewish terrorism but set the stage for Palestinian terrorism.

The creation of Israel was accompanied by a large Palestinian refugee problem, discussed in Chapter 10. Palestinian terrorists began to organize in the refugee camps and to form small groups of **fedayeen** (i.e., commandos). With military and financial assistance from Egypt's leader, **Gamel Abdel Nasser,** they began to conduct hit-and-run attacks inside Israel. Palestinian terrorism escalated following the defeat of Arab armies that had attempted to regain Palestinian land in the **Six-Day War** with Israel in June 1967. Instead of pushing Israel out, the conflict left Israel with the Sinai, the West Bank, Gaza, Jerusalem, and the Golan Heights. Palestinian terrorists, concluding that they could achieve their objectives only by attacking Israel and Jews, initiated a violent wave of bombings, hijacking airlines, and killing civilians. In 1968, the *Popular Front for the Liberation of Palestine*—one of the groups belonging to the umbrella Palestinian terrorist group the **PLO,** led by Yasser Arafat and his Fatah movement—hijacked an Israeli El Al commercial flight and held the passengers and crew hostage. Israel was forced to negotiate with the terrorists to secure their release.[31] One of the most serious terrorist attacks was launched by the **Black September Organization** (part of the PLO) in 1972 during which eleven Israeli athletes were seized and killed at the Olympic Games in Munich. This terrorist attack, together with the hijacking of airplanes, drew international attention to Palestinian nationalism and laid the foundation for increasing violence.

Despite numerous efforts to achieve a diplomatic settlement to the Palestinian-Israeli conflict, violence escalated. Israeli occupation of Palestinian areas and many counterterrorist activities contributed to the demise of many attempts to reach a peace agreement. Feeling abandoned by Arab states, Palestinians initiated a popular uprising, or **intifada,** in the late 1980s. During the second intifada, which began in September 2000, the Palestinian-Israeli conflict became even more violent as Palestinian terrorists from groups such as Hamas, Islamic Jihad, Fatah, and the Popular Front for the Liberation of Palestine decided to conduct devastating suicide bombings against innocent civilians and the government in Israel.[32] There were more than fifty suicide bombings in 2002, the height of this new wave of terrorism, which killed and wounded hundreds of Israelis. To prevent these attacks, Israel constructed a barrier or wall, much of which was built in disputed territory. From the Palestinian perspective, the barrier was essentially designed to seize their territory and make their lives even more difficult. In April 2004, Israel, under the leadership of Ariel Sharon, escalated its attacks on Palestinian terrorist leaders, killing Sheikh Ahmed Yasin, the founder of Hamas, and Abdel Aziz Rantisi, who replaced Yasin as the leader of Hamas, with rockets launched from helicopters. Kidnappings of Israeli soldiers by Hamas and Hezbollah in July 2006 led to Israel's invasion of Lebanon and the escalation of violence in the Palestinian territories. Conflict between Palestinians, especially those in Gaza, and Israelis continued in 2008 and 2009. As is usually the case in nationalist terrorism, both sides are accused of conducting terrorist activities.

NORTHERN IRELAND Terrorism in Northern Ireland (also known as Ulster) was rooted in Ireland's resistance to English control, exploitation, and widespread

Fedayeen ■ Small groups of Palestinian commandos

Gamel Abdel Nasser ■ Egyptian leader popular for his resistance to Israel

Six-Day War ■ 1967 war in which Israel seized the Sinai, the West Bank, Gaza, Jerusalem, and the Golan Heights

PLO ■ Once considered a terrorist organization, committed to fighting Israel and its occupation of the West Bank and Gaza

Black September Organization ■ Part of the PLO responsible for some of the most serious terrorist attacks

Intifada ■ Collective Palestinian resistance to Israel's occupation of the West Bank and Gaza violence that began in the twelfth century. Catholic Ireland, colonized by Protestants from Scotland and England, became engulfed in religious wars that characterized Europe for much of its recent history. Nationalist terrorism in Northern Ireland was essentially a struggle by Catholics to end Protestant political, economic, and social domination. Following numerous attempts to solve the "Irish problem," the Anglo-Irish Treaty was signed in 1921. It divided Ireland into the Republic of Ireland (an independent country) and Northern Ireland (which remained part of Britain). While the Republic of Ireland is predominantly Catholic, Northern Ireland has a Protestant majority. Catholics on both sides of this artificial border refused to accept the division of Ireland and maintained a strong sense of nationalism. Catholics in Northern Ireland, known as Republicans, remained committed to ending the British presence and reunifying the two parts of Ireland. The Protestants, known as **Loyalists,** or **Unionists,** were determined to retain Northern Ireland's ties with Britain and to perpetuate their economic and political power. Both Catholics and Protestants used terrorism to achieve their respective objectives.

**Loyalists/
Unionists** ■
Protestants committed to retaining Northern Ireland's ties with Britain

Although terrorism in Northern Ireland was deeply rooted in Ireland's long struggle to resist British domination, the contemporary problems began in 1922 when the Unionist government implemented the Special Powers Act to suppress opposition to its control. The **IRA,** founded by Michael Collins and composed of rebel units that had launched the **Easter Rebellion** in 1916 against British rule, became the military wing. **Sinn Fein,** a political party that represented Catholics in Ireland, was widely regarded as the political wing of the terrorist movement. Opposed to the division of Ireland and committed to reunifying it, the IRA engaged in terrorism in both the Republic of Ireland and Northern Ireland and was outlawed by the governments of both places. Terrorist attacks against the British in Northern Ireland continued, escalating between 1956 and 1962.[33] However, many Catholics in Northern Ireland were strongly influenced by the nonviolent Civil Rights movement in the United States under the leadership of *Dr. Martin Luther King*, a development that weakened the militant IRA. But the use of excessive violence against Catholic Civil Rights marchers and demonstrators in 1968 by the Royal Ulster Constabulary (RUC) and growing anti-Catholic hatred—inspired to a large degree by *Reverend Ian Paisley*, leader of the hard-line Protestant Democratic Unionists—rejuvenated the IRA and laid the foundation for terrorism that plagued Northern Ireland, London, and elsewhere in Britain. The IRA, widely perceived as ineffective in protecting Catholics, was challenged by the even more militant **Provisional IRA (PIRA)**, which was formed in 1970. As is often the case in conflicts, the most extreme groups gain the most support. Catholics in Northern Ireland rallied around the PIRA.[34] Protestants formed their own terrorist groups.

IRA ■ Rebel forces opposed to Britain's presence in Northern Ireland

Easter Rebellion ■ IRA rebellion against British rule

Sinn Fein ■ Catholic party in Ireland regarded as a terrorist threat to Britain

PIRA ■ Militant outgrowth of IRA

Similar to the Palestinians and Israelis, Catholics and Protestants seemed hopelessly locked in a cycle of deadly violence. Both the Republic of Ireland and Britain are strong democracies. Britain's use of violence against the IRA was checked by democratic processes and strong support for peacefully resolving the conflict. Close political, economic, and cultural links between Britain and Ireland also helped. Equally important was support among Irish-Americans for a negotiated settlement, despite the fact that the IRA received significant economic and military assistance from some of them. Another important factor was the growing unification of Europe and the declining nationalism that accompanied the process.

The activities of the IRA were receiving less and less public support. Furthermore, European integration brought many economic opportunities, recognition, and responsibilities to Ireland, which influenced it to reduce its support for the IRA.

A major step toward ending sectarian violence was the 1985 **Anglo-Irish Agreement**, which gave Ireland increased responsibilities in Northern Ireland and provided greater security for the Unionists by requiring an electoral majority to change Northern Ireland's political status. The major breakthrough came with the signing of the **Good Friday Agreement** in 1998. U.S. President Bill Clinton, British Prime Minister Tony Blair, Irish Prime Minister Bertie Ahern, Gerry Adams (head of Sinn Fein), and David Trimble (head of the Ulster Unionists) cooperated to achieve this agreement. While Britain will control Northern Ireland as long as that is the wish of the majority, Ireland is more involved in the affairs of Northern Ireland. Ireland had to terminate its territorial claim on Northern Ireland in exchange for an institutionalized voice in its government.[35] Sinn Fein and the IRA were persuaded to support the Good Friday Agreement by President Clinton and by British promises to reduce its troop presence in Northern Ireland and to support reforms of the police force to enable more Catholics to join. The 2001 terrorist attacks in the United States reinforced the peace process in Northern Ireland as many Americans pressured the IRA to abandon terrorism and disarm. For the first time, Sinn Fein supported disarming the IRA. The Independent Monitoring Commission was established to disarm it. Although this international panel concluded in April 2004 that Northern Irish paramilitaries continued to carry out violent attacks and were engaged in various criminal activities, the destruction of weapons, ammunition, and explosives underscored progress toward disarmament and ending terrorism in Northern Ireland. In 2005, the IRA renounced the armed struggle and committed itself to peaceful change. By 2006 terrorism in Northern Ireland ceased. However, sporadic violence continued. For example, in March 2009, two British soldiers were killed by a leading Irish nationalist and a member of the Real IRA, a splinter group of the IRA.[36]

Anglo-Irish Agreement ■ Gave Ireland increased responsibilities in Northern Ireland in exchange for security for the Unionists

Good Friday Agreement ■ Compromise that gave Britain control over Northern Ireland and the Irish a voice in government

SPAIN   In sharp contrast with nationalist terrorism in the Middle East and Northern Ireland, Basque separatists in Spain attracted relatively little attention beyond Europe. However, massive bombings of trains in Madrid in early 2004—in which ninety-one people died and seventeen hundred were wounded—focused the spotlight on Basque terrorism, despite the fact that terrorists linked to al-Qaeda were responsible for the bombings. The 2.5 million Basques, who are concentrated in mountainous northern Spain on the Bay of Biscay and across the border into Southern France, are one of the most ancient peoples in Europe. They speak a distinct language, Euskera, and have their own culture. Basques resisted Roman occupiers to maintain their independence. Spanish rulers, unable to exercise effective control over the Basque region and other parts of Spain, recognized the political, cultural, and economic autonomy of the Basques as early as the Middle Ages. This independence laid the foundation for the emergence of the **Basque Homeland and Freedom (ETA)**. Figure 5.1 shows the Basque region of Spain.

Determined to maintain their autonomy, the Basques participated in Spain's larger political and military struggle in the nineteenth century against the centralization of power in Madrid. Having joined the losing side in these conflicts,

ETA ■ Basque separatist movement operating in Spain

FIGURE 5.1
Basque Region of Spain

the Basques lost their autonomy and believed that their sense of identity was threatened. Between 1842 and 1868, the Basque provinces of Vizcaya and Guipuzcoa experienced rapid industrialization, urbanization, and significant population growth. While many Basques, especially the growing middle class and business leaders, strongly supported integrating the Basque region into Spain, resistance to these changes grew among the working class and others who wanted to preserve the status quo.[37] Prior to the Spanish Civil War (1936–1939), the government recognized the political and cultural autonomy of the Basque region. In return, Basques supported the government against insurgents led by Generalissimo **Francisco Franco**. Once again on the losing side in Spain's bloody struggle, the Basques were regarded as traitors by Franco, who centralized political power and abolished Basque autonomy. Any effort to maintain a separate Basque identity was severely repressed. Franco's authoritarianism, discussed in Chapter 4, fueled radicalization among the Basques. In 1959, a coalition of extremist youth groups separated from the more moderate Basque Nationalist Party to form ETA. Their principal objectives were achieving Basque independence from Spain and restoring Basque culture and language. ETA embraced a strategy of armed struggle against the Franco regime in 1962,[38] but refrained from engaging in major acts of terrorism until 1968.

Following Franco's death in 1975 and Spain's transition to democracy, the Basques regained a significant degree of autonomy. They gained control over the police force, schools, and social welfare agencies. ETA continued to demand independence for the Basque region. But only about 30 percent of the Basques believed that independence was a viable option for them, compared with 60 percent who claimed both Spanish and Basque identities and preferred to maintain the status

Francisco Franco ■ Former dictator of Spain who repressed Basque separatists quo.[39] In fact, ETA's political wing, Euskal Herritarrok, is relatively weak and has never received more than 18 percent of the Basques' votes. These realities influenced Euskal Herritarrok to work out an agreement in 1998 with more moderate Basque nationalist parties. Known as the **Lizarra Agreement**, it committed ETA to a cease-fire and the moderates to achieving independence through the democratic process.[40]

Intransigence and political maneuvering by the government under Prime Minister Jose Maria Aznar and ETA contributed to the demise of the cease-fire in December 1999. The government continued to maintain its hard-line policy toward ETA during the cease-fire, refusing to negotiate with it, ignoring its demands to bring ETA prisoners from the Canary Islands so that their relatives could visit them, and continuing to arrest and detain suspected ETA members. ETA became impatient with peace initiatives and escalated its terrorist activities. In a major departure from its practice of primarily targeting government officials, police officers, and members of the military, ETA became more indiscriminate in its use of violence, targeting anyone who opposed its demands for an independent Basque state.[41] Following the 2001 terrorist attacks on the United States, Aznar equated ETA with al-Qaeda and intensified Spain's fight against the Basque separatists. However, when Aznar quickly blamed the 2004 train bombings on ETA instead of al-Qaeda (the real terrorists), he lost the election that was held shortly thereafter, partly because the vast majority of Spaniards blamed his strong support for the U.S.-led invasion of Iraq for contributing to an escalation of terrorism in Europe. But the massive bombing in Madrid, Spain's consolidation of democracy and its integration into the European Union, and the sharp decline of terrorism in Northern Ireland weakened the public support for Basque terrorism and prompted the new government, led by Prime Minister Jose Luis Rodriguez Zapatero, to aggressively pursue Basque terrorists. The arrests of many of ETA's leaders in 2004 and 2005 significantly weakened the terrorist group. In 2006, ETA announced a permanent cease-fire, thereby ending its campaign of terrorism. But in June 2007, ETA renounced the cease-fire and continued to engage in violent activities in 2008. In April 2009, French officials arrested Jurdan Martitegi Lizaso, the leader and military chief of ETA.[42]

Lizarra Agreement ■ Committed the ETA to a cease-fire in its struggle for independence

Religious Terrorism

Throughout history, religion has been used to justify committing acts of extreme cruelty and violence against human beings. Religious terrorism, especially that of al-Qaeda and other Islamic extremists, is widely perceived to be the most dangerous kind of terrorism, one that results in more destructive acts of indiscriminate violence. There are *four basic reasons for the extreme violence of religious terrorism*:

1. Violence is believed to be a sacramental act or divine duty in accordance with theology;
2. Religious terrorists view large-scale and indiscriminate violence as necessary for achieving their goals;
3. Religious terrorists do not feel constrained by public opinion or a need to gain popular support because they are engaged in a total war; and
4. Religious terrorists generally believe that modifying the system is insufficient; they seek fundamental changes in the existing order.[43]

NOTES OF RELIGIOUS TERRORISTS WHO ATTACKED AMERICA

The Last Night

1. Read al-Tauba (a book of the Koran) and what God has prepared for the believers and the everlasting life for the martyrs.
2. Spend the night praying for victory and to smooth our affairs and that we will not be uncovered.
3. Cleanse your heart and purify it from impurities and forget anything related to this world for the time of play is past and the time of truth has come, for we have wasted much of our lives, shouldn't we spend those remaining hours in offering repentance and obedience?
4. You should be content for there are only a few moments before the beginning of happy life and eternal paradise with all righteous and martyrs.
5. Bring yourself, your suitcase, your clothes, the knife, your equipment, your identification, your passport, and all your papers.
6. Tighten your clothes well around your bodies, for this is what the righteous ones did

before the battle and make sure your shoes are not ill fitting, and that your socks do not hang out of your shoes.

7. When you board the plane and before you step in, read your prayer and repeat the same prayers we mentioned before, when you take your seat. Read this verse from the Koran: "When you meet a group, be steadfast and remember God, you will be triumphant."
8. Apply the rules of prisoners of war. Take them prisoner and kill them as God said. No Prophet can have prisoners of war. . . .
9. Open your chest welcoming death in the path of God and utter your prayer seconds before you go to your target. Let your last words be, "There is no God but God and Mohammad is His messenger." Then, God willing, you will be in heavens.

Source: Excerpts from a document released by the Federal Bureau of Investigation (FBI) and reprinted in *New York Times,* 29 September 2001, B3. ∎

Aum Supreme Truth ∎ Japanese terrorist group fighting against the Japanese government

In the shadow of Mount Fuji, members of the Japanese terrorist group **Aum Supreme Truth** developed and practiced to implement their deadly attacks on innocent Japanese in 1995 under the watchful eyes of *Shiva*, the Hindu god of destruction and rebirth. If you have visited Tokyo, you know how crowded the trains are that converge on Kasumigaseki, the center of power in Japan. Imagine the death and injury an attack on the subway system would cause. This is precisely why Aum Supreme Truth selected it to launch a preemptive attack on the Japanese government to implement its mission of world domination. Armed with bags containing a chemical solution that was about 30 percent *sarin gas* (i.e., a colorless, odorless, and deadly gas invented by the Nazis), the terrorists boarded the trains, determined to inflict catastrophic damage. Twelve people were killed and more than fifty-five hundred were injured in the sarin gas attack.[44]

In the heart of America, terrorist groups also believe that they are on a mission from God to destroy the U.S. government, create a racially pure society for whites only, and redeem the United States. The white supremacist Christian Identity movement and the Ku Klux Klan, among others, base their terrorist acts on

Jihad ∎ Translated as "holy war" when described by Islamic terrorist groups

Christianity. Their leaders often call themselves ministers. Muslim extremists also justify launching **jihads** (i.e., holy wars) on the basis of their religion. Many Islamic terrorists, including al-Qaeda, draw on medieval religious authorities to argue that killing innocents or even fellow Muslims is permitted if it serves the cause of jihad against the West.[45] Some Islamic terrorist organizations are closely tied to specific political and military developments in the Middle East. However, a common influence on the emergence of Islamic terrorism was the Iranian Islamic revolution, led by Ayatollah Khomeini, which overthrew the shah in 1979.[46]

State Terrorism

Our definition of terrorism as the use of violence to coerce or intimidate and to generally create widespread fear among the population clearly covers many states, both historically and now. Governments have relied on torture, both physical and psychological, as their ultimate instrument of terror to control the population. Nazi Germany, Stalinist Russia, Iraq under Saddam Hussein, China, North Korea, Argentina, Chile, Guatemala, Uganda, and many other countries have used terrorism, especially torture, to repress the population and stifle dissent.[47]

Three levels of internal state terrorism are

1. *Intimidation:*   The state uses its overwhelming power to discourage opposition and dissent, usually through excessive force by the police and paramilitary organizations.
2. *Coerced Conversion:*   This involves forcing the population to completely change its behavior, usually occurs after a revolution. The Soviet Union, China, and Iran are examples.
3. *Genocide:*   This is the deliberate and systematic killing of an ethnic, religious, economic, intellectual, or any other group of people. Nazi Germany, Stalinist Russia, Cambodia under Pol Pot and his Khmer Rouge party, Uganda under Idi Amin, Bosnia, Sudan, and Rwanda are examples of internal state genocide.[48]

States also use terrorism against other states or nationalist groups to secure foreign policy objectives. A distinction is often made between *state-sponsored terrorism* and *state-supported terrorism*. Both types of state terrorism are usually clandestine. In state-sponsored terrorism, states are more directly involved in the terrorist activities of the groups they support. States act through client groups and proxies. Sometimes they send terrorists to assassinate dissidents and opposition leaders who live abroad. In state-supported terrorism, states have less influence over the terrorist group.[49]

Global Terrorism

Global terrorism encompasses activities by domestic, nationalist, religious, and state terrorists. It is characterized by its significant implications for a large number of major countries, nonstate actors, and individuals on several continents. Global terrorism is facilitated by various aspects of globalization. Terrorists take advantage of porous borders and their ability to blend into almost any major city in most parts of the world. Following al-Qaeda's 2001 attacks in the United States, it became increasingly obvious that global terrorists belonged to **sleeper cells**. Reminiscent of the Cold War, during which the Soviet Union relied heavily on sleeper agents to spy on the United States, global terrorists become part of

Sleeper Cells ■
Groups of terrorists who live what appear to be normal lives until instructed to commit terrorist attacks

a particular society, live what appear to be normal lives, and participate in terror-ist activities against that society when instructed to do so. Sleeper terrorist cells have been found in the United States, Britain, Spain, Germany, Turkey, Belgium, Indonesia, Singapore, Malaysia, Italy, Pakistan, Morocco, the Philippines, and elsewhere. The Internet, inexpensive transportation, and the global media con-tribute to global cooperation among terrorists.[50]

Mujahedeen ■
Group of Islamic holy warriors fighting the Soviet occupation of Afghanistan

Global terrorism is most often identified with Osama bin Laden and al-Qaeda. Al-Qaeda made a strong commitment to jihad as its principal objective. This struggle began in Afghanistan. Bin Laden and other holy warriors (or **mujahedeen**) were trained and supported by America's Central Intelligence Agency (CIA) to resist Soviet occupation of Afghanistan. However, this struggle evolved into a global jihad against the West, particularly the United States. By focusing on the United States as the country primarily responsible for creating problems for Muslims and as the common enemy of Muslims everywhere, leaders of al-Qaeda and other Islamic terrorist groups recruit and unite Islamic terrorists worldwide. Al-Qaeda evolved into an organization that is loosely hierarchical and very decentralized. Al-Qaeda, the organization, is based on an ideology articu-lated by Abdullah Azzam in 1987, which called for *Al-qaeda al-sulbah* (i.e., a vanguard of the strong). He envisioned Sunni Muslim radical activists who, through independent actions, would mobilize the *umma* (i.e., a global community of believers) to act against oppressors. The word *qaeda* is generally understood by Islamic militants as a precept or a method, as opposed to an organization. *Al-Qaedism* is essentially a worldview. The terrorist groups in Iraq, led by Abu al-Zarqawi, acted independently of al-Qaeda led by bin Laden.[51]

Global terrorism is directed primarily against the United States and its close allies. There are several *reasons why America is the target*:

1. The United States is the dominant global power. From the Roman Empire to the United States, leading countries have been targets.
2. America is widely regarded as the leader of globalization. Groups opposed to globalization target the United States.
3. Close ties between the United States and repressive governments—such as Saudi Arabia, Egypt, and Pakistan—motivate terrorists to attack it.
4. Many American foreign policies are regarded by terrorists as hostile to Muslims.[52]

RESPONDING TO TERRORISM

The complexity of terrorism requires employing a wide variety of instruments to combat it. In addition to military, traditional law enforcement, and intelligence responses, there is growing support for the view that increased attention must also be given to the underlying causes of terrorism. The importance of global coopera-tion as a component of any counterterrorism policy became increasingly obvious in the wake of al-Qaeda's attacks on the United States and other countries.

The most prevalent response to terrorism is the use of force, both domesti-cally and internationally. Britain in Northern Ireland, Israel in the Palestinian

Prime Minister Tony Blair of Britain and Colonel Muammar Qaddafi of Libya. A combination of military action, economic sanctions, political isolation, and diplomatic and economic incentives contributed to Qaddafi's decision to renounce terrorism and to join global efforts to combat it.

(Stefan Rousseau/ Empics)

territories, and the United States globally have relied on force, to varying degrees, to eliminate terrorism. Following the attacks on the United States, military action was taken in October 2001 against the Taliban regime and al-Qaeda in Afghanistan, a decision that was widely supported. President George W. Bush declared "war against terrorism" and stressed that America was engaged in a war of indefinite duration against a nonstate enemy that had no territory. As stated in the National Security Strategy of the United States, the priority of the United States was to disrupt and destroy terrorist organizations of global reach and attack their leadership; command, control, and communications; material support; and finances.[53] Global support of military action was underscored by the response of the North Atlantic Treaty Organization (NATO). A day following the attacks on the United States, NATO's secretary general, **Lord Robertson**, promised military assistance for America's campaign against terrorism. For the first time, NATO invoked the mutual defense clause in its treaty, which states that "any armed attack against allies in Europe or North America shall be considered an attack against them all."[54] America's invasion and occupation of Iraq in early 2003 was also designed, in part, to fight terrorism. Although there was no evidence linking the Iraqi leader Saddam Hussein to al-Qaeda, President Bush asserted that Hussein was involved in global terrorism.

Lord Robertson ■ NATO's secretary general who offered military assistance for America's fight against terrorism

   An essential aspect of combating terrorism is gathering intelligence and using it. The purpose of acquiring information and analyzing it is to learn about impending threats and to develop strategies to counteract them. Many U.S. agencies are involved in gathering intelligence related to terrorism and other threats to national security. Governments worldwide also engage in similar activities. There are essentially *four ways to acquire intelligence*: (1) take aerial and satellite photographs and conduct general photo reconnaissance; (2) use a wide variety of listening devices to record conversations, intercept radio and other signals, and monitor computer activities; (3) use spies and informants; and (4) collaborate with intelligence agencies from other countries and nonstate organizations. The first two ways are referred to as *technical intelligence* methods and the last two are called *human intelligence* methods.

Terrorists and their supporters have access to technology and can counteract the effectiveness of technology. They may know satellite overflight schedules and how to use sophisticated encryption technologies. They also know not to use cell phones. In April 2002, terrorism investigators in Europe intercepted a cell phone call that lasted less than a minute, during which not a word was said. Suspecting that the call was a signal between terrorists, the investigators followed the trail first to one terror suspect, then to others, and eventually to terrorist cells on three continents. What linked them was a computer chip that carried prepaid minutes and allowed phones to be used globally. Authorities monitored the conversations, arrested several suspected al-Qaeda members, and prevented attacks on Saudi Arabia and Indonesia. But terrorists adjusted their strategies. They abandoned cell phones, preferring instead to use e-mail, Internet phone calls, and hand-delivered messages.[55] Although technical intelligence is essential, the United States has relied too heavily on it and has allowed its human intelligence capabilities to deteriorate, partly by neglecting to learn foreign languages and about foreign cultures. Many terrorism experts believe that *human intelligence* is the most critical ingredient for rooting out terrorist groups because the essence of the terrorist threat is the capacity to conspire.[56]

Richard A. Clarke ■
Former chief antiter-
rorism adviser under
the Clinton and Bush
administrations

Simply acquiring information is insufficient to counteract terrorism. That information must be utilized and ways of thinking about threats to national security must be critically examined. **Richard A. Clarke**, chief of counterterrorism in both the Clinton and Bush administrations, argued in his book, *Against All Enemies*, that the Bush administration essentially ignored the threat from al-Qaeda prior to the attacks on September 11, 2001. A major impediment to using intelligence effectively was inadequate communication between the FBI and the CIA. In an increasingly global society, distinctions between internal and external are becoming less relevant. In light of this reality, experts stressed the need to remove the barriers that divide domestic and foreign intelligence gathering.[57] Threats from global terrorism have influenced governments to strengthen their domestic security and to pay closer attention to how globalization and global terrorism intertwine. For example, water is the major link that countries have to the global economy. Almost all exports and imports are carried by ships. It is estimated that 95 percent of what comes into and goes out of America is by ships. Consequently, the global community, led by the United States, adopted a global code that requires the world's ships and ports to create counterterrorism systems, such as computers, communications gear, surveillance cameras, and security patrols. Ships that do not meet these standards or that have visited ports that do not meet these standards can be turned away from American waters.[58] Countering terrorism in this way could seriously undermine global trade. A major domestic step toward protecting the United States against terrorism was the creation of the *Department of Homeland Security*. Its functions include controlling immigration and U.S. borders, monitoring foreign students, enhancing airport security, inspecting foreign ports, examining cargo containers, and cooperating with state and local governments to prevent terrorist attacks.

FIGHTING TERRORISM AND PROTECTING DEMOCRACY

During the U.S. invasion of Afghanistan in 2001, approximately 650 persons were arrested, transported to the U.S. naval base at **Guantanamo Bay** in Cuba, and imprisoned by the U.S. military without access to lawyers or visits from family members. In 2004, the U.S. Supreme Court ruled against President Bush and strongly supported an individual's right to due process of law. In April 2009, the U.S. Justice Department released classified memos describing harsh interrogation techniques, including torture, used by the CIA against terrorist suspects. Many of these techniques were used by Communist China. One prisoner was waterboarded 183 times. The United States, a leading advocate of individual rights, prosecuted some Japanese interrogators at the War Crimes trials in Tokyo after World War II for waterboarding and other techniques.[59]

Immediately following the terrorist attacks in September 2001, the U.S. Congress enacted the **USA Patriot Act** to protect the country from terrorist attacks. This law gave the federal government the power to conduct wiretaps, monitor books borrowed from libraries, demand access to financial records, and employ a wide range of investigative tools against people suspected of terrorism.[60] All of these cases raise fundamental questions about finding a balance between fighting terrorism and protecting democracy within the United States.

Guantanamo Bay ▪
U.S. naval base where enemy prisoners of war are being held

USA Patriot Act ▪
Controversial initiative passed by the Bush administration to fight terrorist threats

SUMMARY AND REVIEW

This chapter addressed the problem of global terrorism. Since the September 2001 attacks in the United States, the assumption that superior state military power ensures a high degree of national security has been seriously challenged. Specifically, we have seen a rise in what has become known as asymmetrical warfare, in which smaller, weaker groups—such as al-Qaeda—can inflict significant harm and damage against more powerful states, such as the United States. Increased globalization has created a global environment more conducive to international terrorism. Increased global migration, the growth of global cities, relatively inexpensive global and regional travel options, revolutions in communication technologies, and the explosion in global trade have all helped to create an environment in which global terrorism has gained prominence.

In this chapter, we discussed the difficulties involved in accurately defining terrorism. As acts of terrorism incite emotional responses, it becomes increasingly difficult to agree on an objective definition of terrorism. Terrorist acts are designed to achieve specific, concrete goals. Often terrorists commit acts of violence against civilians in order to create fear and confusion. Terrorist acts are usually intended to be indiscriminate, in order to arouse a more fearful response from a population that does not know which public targets may be attacked next. In effect, terrorists are waging a form of psychological warfare against civilian populations. Another goal of terrorist acts is to humiliate governments, as we see in the example of Iraqi terrorists opposed to the U.S. presence in Iraq who have decided to target humanitarian aid workers in Iraq. In addition to the goals of terrorists, we also addressed the reasons and motivations for committing terrorist acts. We also discussed various forms of terrorism, including domestic terrorism, nationalist terrorism, religious terrorism, state terrorism, and global terrorism. Following the forms of terrorism, we examined some of the methods of financing terrorism, as well as various responses to terrorist acts.

KEY TERMS

asymmetrical power 100
Reign of Terror 100
Edmund Burke 100
guerrilla warfare 101
Uighurs 101
madrassas 102
Taliban 104
virtual networks 104
hawalas 105
Muammar Qaddafi 106
Revolutionary United Front
   (RUF) 106
Hezbollah 106
Abu Sayyaf 106
Tamil Tigers 106
domestic terrorism 108
nationalist terrorism 108
religious terrorism 108
state terrorism 108
global terrorism 108

Red Brigades 109
November 17 109
dirty war 109
Shining Path 109
Revolutionary Armed
   Forces of Colombia
   (FARC) 109
Holocaust 110
Menachem Begin 110
Irgun 110
fedayeen 111
Gamel Abdel
   Nasser 111
Six-Day War 111
PLO 111
Black September
   Organization 111
intifada 111
Loyalists/Unionists 112
IRA 112

Easter Rebellion 112
Sinn Fein 112
Provisional IRA
   (PIRA) 112
Anglo-Irish
   Agreement 113
Good Friday
   Agreement 113
Basque Homeland and
   Freedom (ETA) 113
Francisco Franco 114
Lizarra Agreement 115
Aum Supreme Truth 116
jihad 116
sleeper cells 117
mujahedeen 118
Lord Robertson 119
Richard A. Clarke 120
Guantanamo Bay 121
USA Patriot Act 121

DISCUSSION QUESTIONS

1. What is asymmetrical power? How does it relate to the war on terror?
2. Do you believe one can objectively define terrorism, or will such attempts always result in subjective, relative definitions?
3. What are some of the goals that drive terrorism discussed in this chapter?
4. What are the four reasons for the extreme violence of religious terrorism addressed in this chapter?

SUGGESTED READINGS

Ackerman, Bruce. *Before the Next Attack: Preserving Civil Liberties in an Age of Terrorism.* New Haven, CT: Yale University Press, 2006.
Hewitt, Christopher. *Political Violence and Terror in Modern America.* Westport, CT: Praeger, 2005.
Kean, Thomas, and Lee Hamilton. *The 911 Report.* New York: St. Martin's Press, 2004.
Richardson, Louise. *What Terrorists Want: Understanding the Enemy, Containing the Threat.* New York: Random House, 2006.
Sageman, Marc. *Leaderless Jihad.* Philadelphia: University of Pennsylvania Press, 2008.
Warde, Ibrahim. *The Price of Fear.* Berkeley: University of California Press, 2007.

END NOTES

1. Moises Naim, "Collateral Damage," *Foreign Policy* 127 (November/December 2001), 108.
2. Condoleezza Rice, "Promoting the National Interest," *Foreign Affairs* 79, No. 1 (January/February 2000), 46–47.
3. Philip H. Gordon, "Can the War on Terror Be Won?" *Foreign Affairs* 86, No. 6 (November/December 2007), 53–54.
4. "Education Chief Calls Teachers Union Terrorist Group," *Chicago Tribune*, 24 February 2004, Sect. 1, 5.
5. Steven Simon, "The Price of the Surge," *Foreign Affairs* 87, No. 3 (May/June 2008), 57.
6. Peter Chalk, *West European Terrorism and Counter-Terrorism* (New York: St. Martin's Press, 1996), 12.
7. Chien-peng Chung, "China's War on Terror," *Foreign Affairs* 81, No. 4 (July/August 2002), 8–9.
8. Paul Wilkinson, *Terrorism Versus Democracy* (London: Frank Cass, 2000), 1.
9. Paul Blustein, "A Cradle of Terrorism," *Washington Post National Weekly Edition*, 25–31 March 2002, 8; and Robert W. Hefner and Muhammad Zaman, *Schooling Islam* (Princeton, NJ: Princeton University Press, 2007).
10. Thomas L. Friedman, "The Humiliation Factor," *New York Times*, 9 November 2003, Sect. 4, 11.
11. Geneive Abdo, "Why Egypt Produces Extremists," *Christian Science Monitor*, 12 October 2001, 11.
12. James Bennet, "Sharon Coup: U.S. Go-Ahead," *New York Times*, 15 April 2004, A1.
13. Chester A. Crocker, "Engaging Failing States," *Foreign Affairs* 82, No. 5 (September/October 2003), 34.
14. Richard Bernstein, "Tape, Probably bin Laden's Offers 'Truce' to Europe," *New York Times*, 16 April 2004, A3.
15. Martha Crenshaw, "The Causes of Terrorism," in *The New Global Terrorism*, ed. Charles W. Kegley (Upper Saddle River, NJ: Prentice Hall, 2002), 97.
16. Jessica Stern, "The Protean Enemy," *Foreign Affairs* 82, No. 4 (July/August 2003), 33.
17. Martha Crenshaw, "Thoughts on Relating Terrorism to Historical Contexts," in *Terrorism in Context*, ed. Martha Crenshaw (University Park: Penn State University Press, 1995), 11.
18. Philip B. Heymann, *Terrorism and America* (Cambridge, MA: MIT Press, 1998), 11.
19. Ian O. Lesser et al., *Countering the New Terrorism* (Santa Monica, CA: Rand, 1999), 41.
20. Jessica Stern, *The Ultimate Terrorists* (Cambridge, MA: Harvard University Press, 1999), 8–10.
21. Jeanne K. Giralda and Harold A. Trinkunas, eds., *Terrorism Financing and State Responses* (Stanford, CA: Stanford University Press, 2007).
22. Patrick E. Tyler, "Blair Visits Qaddafi, Ending Libya's Long Estrangement," *New York Times*, 26 March 2004, A3.
23. Douglas Farah, "Diamonds Tainted by Terror," *Washington Post National Weekly Edition*, 12–18 November 2001, 15; and Augustus Richard Norton, *Hezbollah* (Princeton, NJ: Princeton University Press, 2007).
24. "Airline Losses Hit $14 Billion Worldwide," *Chicago Tribune*, 7 January 2003, Sect. 3, 3.
25. Paul R. Pillar, *Terrorism and U.S. Foreign Policy* (Washington, DC: Brookings Institution Press, 2001), 27.
26. Stanley Hoffmann, "Clash of Globalizations," *Foreign Affairs* 81, No. 4 (July/August 2002), 113.

27. Tore Bjorgo, "Introduction," in *Terror from the Extreme Right*, ed. Tore Bjorgo (London: Frank Cass, 1995), 4; and David Stout, "Security Guard Is Killed in Shooting at Holocaust Museum in Washington," *New York Times*, 11 June 2009, A15.

28. "Italian Policeman Is Killed in Gunfight with Terror Suspects," *New York Times*, 3 March 2003, A3.

29. Frank Bruni and Anthee Carassana, "Greece to Begin Trial Involving Long-Elusive Terror Group," *New York Times*, 3 March 2003, A3.

30. Bruce Hoffman, *Inside Terrorism* (London: Victor Gollancz, 1998), 51.

31. Hoffman, *Inside Terrorism*, 68.

32. Gal Luft, "The Palestinian H-Bomb," *Foreign Affairs* 81, No. 4 (July/August 2002), 2.

33. Wilkinson, *Terrorism Versus Democracy*, 31.

34. Wilkinson, *Terrorism Versus Democracy*, 31.

35. Jonathan Stevenson, "Peace in Northern Ireland: Why Now?" *Foreign Policy* 112 (Fall 1998), 41–46.

36. Brian Lavery, "Northern Ireland: Party Linked to IRA," *New York Times*, 21 April 2004, A6; and "Arrest in Killing of British Soldiers," *New York Times*, 22 March 2009, A9.

37. Goldie Shabad and Francisco Ramo, "Political Violence in a Democratic State: Basque Terrorism in Spain," in *Terrorism in Context*, 411.

38. Shabad and Ramo, "Political Violence," in *Terrorism in Context*, 411.

39. Susanne Daley, "Fear Spreads as Spanish and Basque Blood Flows," *New York Times*, 11 August 2000, A3.

40. Ray Moseley, "Divides Run Deep and Long in Spain's Basque Conflict," *Chicago Tribune*, 10 September 2000, Sect. 1, 3.

41. Carlta Vitzthum, "Basque Separatists Escalate Terrorism," *Wall Street Journal*, 4 December 2000, A20.

42. Dale Fuchs, "Huge Basque Arsenal Found in Southwestern France," *New York Times*, 5 April 2004, A3; Alberto Letona, "Basque ETA Offers Spain a Total Truce," *Chicago Tribune*, 23 March 2006, Sect. 1, 1; and Victoria Burnett, "Spain Hails Arrest of Man Seen as Separatists' Leader," *New York Times*, 20 April 2009, A11.

43. Hoffman, *Inside Terrorism*, 94–95; and Tony Blair, "A Battle for Global Values," *Foreign Affairs* 86, No. 1 (January/February 2007), 79–80.

44. David E. Kaplan and Andrew Marshall, *The Cult at the End of the World* (New York: Crown Publishers, 1996), 1.

45. Robert Worth, "The Deep Intellectual Roots of Islamic Terror," *New York Times*, 13 October 2001, A13.

46. Wilkinson, *Terrorism Versus Democracy*, 34.

47. Wilkinson, *Terrorism Versus Democracy*, 43.

48. Cindy C. Combs, *Terrorism in the Twenty-First Century* (Upper Saddle River, NJ: Prentice Hall, 2002), 67.

49. Combs, *Terrorism*, 73.

50. David E. Kaplan and Lucian Kim, "Nazism's New Global Threat," *U.S. News and World Report*, 25 September 2000, 34.

51. Karen DeYoung and Michael Dobbs, "The Architect of a New Global Terrorism," *Washington Post National Weekly Edition*, 24–30 September 2001, 20; and Jason Burke, "Al Qaeda," *Foreign Policy* 142 (May/June 2004), 18.

52. Pillar, *Terrorism and U.S. Foreign Policy*, 61.

53. George W. Bush, "The National Security Strategy of the United States," *New York Times*, 20 September 2002, A10; and David Cortright and George A. Lopez, eds., *Uniting Against Terror* (Cambridge, MA: MIT Press, 2007).

54. Suzanne Daley, "NATO Quickly Gives the U.S. All the Help That It Asked," *New York Times*, 5 October 2001, B6.

55. Don Van Natta and Desmond Butler, "How Tiny Swiss Cellphone Chips Helped Track Global Terror Web," *New York Times*, 4 March 2004, A1; and Bruce Riedel, "Al Qaeda Strikes Back," *Foreign Affairs* 86, No. 3 (May/June 2007), 24.

56. Richard K. Betts, "Fixing Intelligence," *Foreign Affairs* 81, No. 1 (January/February 2002), 46; and Elaine Sciolino and Stephen Castle, "European Officials Agree on Framework for Outlawing Online Terror Recruiting," *New York Times*, 19 April 2008, A8.

57. John Deutch and Jeffrey H. Smith, "Smarter Intelligence," *Foreign Policy* 128 (January/February 2002), 64–69; and Mike McConnell, "Overhauling Intelligence," *Foreign Affairs* 86, No. 4 (July/August 2007), 49–50.

58. Tim Weiner, "U.S. Law Puts Honduran Port on Notice," *New York Times*, 24 March 2004, A6.

59. Kenneth Roth, "After Guantánomo," *Foreign Affairs* 87, No. 3 (May/June 2008), 9–11; and Mark Mazzetti and Scott Shane, "Memos Spell Out Brutal CIA Mode of Interrogation," *New York Times*, 17 April 2009, A1.

60. Darius Rejali, *Torture and Democracy* (Princeton, NJ: Princeton University Press, 2007).

CHAPTER

6

Weapons Proliferation

INTRODUCTION

Inextricably linked to wars is the proliferation of weapons. Throughout history, human beings have used weapons deliberately designed to inflict maximum damage on their enemies. Ancient warriors regarded the catapult as the ultimate weapon of mass destruction. It was the sturdy springboard that hurled flaming missiles, diseased corpses, lethal arrows, and various projectiles over castle walls and into enemy territory.[1] The invention of gunpowder and the cannon marked another improvement in weapons of mass destruction. Biological weapons, and the terror they create, were also used during the American Revolutionary War by the British to prevent the colonies from gaining independence. **Smallpox**, which killed around 130,000 North Americans, was deliberately spread by British forces. General George Washington, aware that the British had infected Native Americans who threatened Fort Pitt, instructed the U.S. Postal Service to dip letters from Boston in vinegar to kill any germs. Smallpox devastated the Colonies because most people had not developed immunity to the disease. Furthermore, dislocations during the war facilitated the spread of smallpox. Armies going through towns, populations migrating to escape conflict, and demobilized soldiers became effective transmitters of the disease.[2] During the American Civil War, Dr. Luke Blackburn, a Southern sympathizer, arrived in Bermuda, which was being devastated by a yellow fever epidemic, claiming to be a specialist on the disease. Dr. Blackburn secretly collected victims' clothing, blankets, sheets, and poultices and put them into three trunks to be shipped to Canada and then to New York. His objective was to initiate a yellow fever epidemic in Northern cities. The plot was eventually discovered by spies loyal to the United States.[3] Diseases as weapons of mass destruction have a long history.

National defense has been the largely unquestioned dominant priority of governments throughout the world, and the development and deployment of weapons of mass destruction have been routinely justified on the grounds of national security. Competition among nations engenders arms races that directly contribute to the global proliferation of the most destructive weapons. As the frontiers of military technology advance, states attempt to maintain or enhance their relative position in the hierarchies of regional and global power.[4] However, as we pointed out in Chapter 2, the struggle for primacy among nations is complicated by the forces of globalization. Although weapons of mass destruction have long been a leading global issue, global terrorism has heightened concerns about the proliferation of nuclear, biological, and chemical weapons. However, this chapter shows that while such weapons are potentially catastrophic, small arms and light weapons are actually being used today as weapons of mass destruction. The chapter concludes with a discussion of missile defense schemes and broader nonproliferation efforts.

THE PROLIFERATION OF WEAPONS

Competition for power among groups and nation-states essentially guaranteed advancements in military technology and the spread of new and more destructive weapons. A basic problem with efforts to reduce the proliferation of weapons is that individuals and countries embrace the **Hobbesian worldview,** which places the constant struggle for power and dominance at the center of international relations. Many countries, especially the dominant powers, champion promoting nonproliferation regimes, but they generally remain committed to protecting their own national security interests primarily by developing even more deadly weapons and transferring more destructive weapons to their allies. Countries such as the United States, Russia, France, China, and Britain often resist global efforts to restrain their weapons sales. Nonproliferation efforts are undermined by the globalization of weapons production and trade. Modern nonproliferation efforts have generally

Smallpox ■ Disease that killed approximately 130,000 North Americans during the Revolutionary War; deliberately spread by British forces

Hobbesian Worldview ■ Places the constant struggle for power and dominance at the center of international relations

Genghis Khan ■ Thirteenth-century warrior

YOU DECIDE

Are Human Beings Destined to Make War?

Concerns about weapons of mass destruction raise serious questions about human behavior in relation to conflict. Despite an emphasis on peacefully resolving conflicts, we continue to engage in warfare. Militarism and round-robin carnage characterize human relations in many parts of the world. Common chimpanzees, which share about 98 percent of their genes with humans, routinely fight to exterminate their opponents. So many males have died in conflict that the sex ratio among adult chimpanzees is one male for two females. Plato's belief that only the dead have seen the end of war is supported by the constancy of conflict throughout human history. Archaeologists and anthropologists have found evidence of militarism in roughly 95 percent of the cultures they

examined. Wars have generally been glorified and countries willingly allocate huge proportions of scarce resources, especially people, to fight them. Warriors have generally been leaders and the most desirable mates. Rape has long been an instrument of war. Geneticists have concluded that **Genghis Khan,** the thirteenth-century warrior, fathered so many offspring as he conquered Asia that roughly 16 million men could be his descendants.

1. Are human beings genetically destined to fight?
2. Can you think of some nonviolent societies?
3. How can individuals contribute to nonviolent approaches to settle disputes?

Source: Natalie Angier, "Is War Our Biological Destiny?" *New York Times*, 11 November 2003, D1. ■

concentrated on weapons of mass destruction, principally nuclear, chemical, and biological weapons.

Although nuclear, chemical, and biological weapons pose catastrophic threats to global security, small arms and light weapons are now instrumental in mass destruction in many countries around the world. Roughly 300,000 to 500,000 people are killed every year by small arms and light weapons globally.[5] Small arms and light weapons, many of them supplied by France, were used in the Rwandan genocide. Although the United States, Russia, and China are the dominant manufacturers and exporters of small arms and light weapons, it is estimated that one thousand companies in ninety-eight countries produce such weapons and that there are 380 million civilian owners of these weapons worldwide. In practical terms, distinguishing small arms from light weapons is not very useful. As we mentioned earlier, machetes and other crude weapons are used to kill people in conflict around the world. In 1997, the United Nations, realizing the futility of trying to formulate precise definitions of small arms and light weapons, simply described them collectively as weapons that can be carried by an individual or transported in light trucks. These weapons include handguns, assault rifles, machine guns, grenade launchers, mortars, and shoulder-fired missiles. Throughout the world, the Automat Kalashnikov (AK-47) is the favorite light weapon of governments, rebel groups, criminals, and terrorists. Designed by Mikhail Kalashnikov in the Soviet Union in 1947 for the Soviet military, the AK-47 has many advantages over the Israeli-made Uzi and the U.S.-made M-16. It is relatively inexpensive, widely available, has only nine moving parts, weighs roughly 10 pounds, has a range of more than one thousand yards, and fires thirty rounds in just three seconds.

Confronted with escalating violence along the U.S.-Mexico border, U.S. Secretary of State Hillary Rodham Clinton stressed during her visit to Mexico in March 2009 that America's inability to stop U.S. weapons from being smuggled into Mexico fueled the violence. When President Barack Obama visited Mexico a month later, he was reminded by Mexico's President Felipe Calderón that roughly 90 percent of the weapons seized in Mexico come from the United States. A U.S. ban on assault rifles expired in 2004, thereby enabling the virtually unrestricted sale of lethal weapons. The basic argument advanced by the U.S. National Rifle Association and opponents to laws regulating the sale and ownership of guns rests on America's belief that the Second Amendment to the U.S. Constitution guarantees individuals the right to keep and bear arms. In addition to roughly 78,000 gun dealers nationwide, individuals are also permitted to sell assault rifles. Many of the military-style rifles used in Mexico are sold by dealers in Texas, Arizona, and New Mexico.[6]

Although *land mines* and *cluster bombs* are often overlooked in discussions on weapons proliferation, like assault rifles, they cause widespread suffering even after wars have ended. Thousands of innocent civilians are killed each year by these weapons. In fact, both weapons are deliberately deployed to inflict maximum physical damage and psychological terror. Millions of land mines have been laid in approximately sixty-two countries. Advances in technology have made land mines cheaper to produce but harder and more expensive to find and remove. Global opposition to land mines culminated in the 1997 Ottawa Treaty

Gun and Ammo Shop Displaying Fire Arms.

Michael Stravato / The New York Times / Redux Pictures

that banned land mines. However, major countries, including the United States, rejected banning these weapons. Although roughly 111 countries agreed to ban the use of cluster bombs, which are fired from aircraft and artillery and contain hundreds of bomblets that remain lethal long after the conflict, the United States, Israel, China, Russia, India, Brazil, Pakistan, and other military powers have not agreed to ban them. Cluster bombs were used by the United States and Britain during the 2003 invasion of Iraq and by Israel in its conflict with Lebanon in 2006.[7]

There are several distinguishing characteristics that make small arms and light weapons attractive.[8] These include

1. *Low Cost:* These weapons are relatively inexpensive to produce because of economies of scale and their relatively low level of technological sophistication.
2. *Easy Availability:* As we mentioned earlier, there are one thousand companies in ninety-eight countries producing them.
3. *Lethality:* These deadly weapons provide sufficient firepower to enable their users to effectively engage military forces and law enforcement agents.
4. *Simplicity and Durability:* They often require little training to be used effectively, are easy to maintain, and are very reliable under difficult environmental conditions.
5. *Portability and Concealability:* As you have seen many times, terrorists, rebel groups, criminals, and others are able to hide these weapons until they decide to use them.
6. *Dual Usage:* Small arms and light weapons in many countries are available to both military and police forces and ordinary civilians.

Small arms and light weapons are transferred in four basic ways: (1) governments transferring weapons to other governments, (2) government-sanctioned commercial sales, (3) covert deliveries by governments or private firms with the assistance of governments, and (4) illicit sales.[9]

Discussions of the nonproliferation of weapons also generally ignore transfers of **conventional weapons,** such as heavy artillery, missiles, tanks, aircraft, ships, submarines, and armored vehicles. Like small arms and light weapons, conventional weapons are widely regarded as acceptable for use in conflicts and are responsible for mass destruction in many countries. Given the lethality of both conventional weapons and small arms and light weapons and their routine use in conflicts, separating them from potentially catastrophic nuclear, chemical, and biological weapons is largely a matter of semantics.

Conventional Weapons ■ Regular weapons used in military conflict, including heavy artillery, missiles, tanks, aircraft, ships, submarines, and armored vehicles

Reasons for the Proliferation of Weapons

In this section we will briefly summarize the *strategic, economic, and political motivations for proliferation.* These include

1. *Superpower Rivalry During the Cold War:* Geopolitical considerations influenced the United States and the Soviet Union to transfer weapons to their respective allies. For example, both the North Atlantic Treaty Organization (NATO) and the Warsaw Pact justified the proliferation of weapons in terms of collective self-defense.

2. *Military Burden-Sharing:* Reluctant to engage in direct military confrontation, both superpowers provided weapons, technical assistance, and arms production technologies to their allies so that they could defend themselves. An example of this was the **Nixon Doctrine,** which supported weapons transfers to Japan, South Korea, Taiwan, and other Asian countries.[10]

3. *Regional Balance of Power:* Arms sales are often defended on the grounds that such transfers contribute to regional stability and diminish the likelihood of war.

4. *Political, Military, and Economic Influence:* Given the dependence of the United States on petroleum supplies from the Middle East in general and Saudi Arabia in particular, arms transfers are instrumental not only in bolstering these countries' security but also in enabling the United States to gain and maintain access to these countries' political, military, and economic elites.

5. *Economies of Scale:* Many countries export weapons to obtain resources to finance the development and production of more advanced weapons.

6. *Self-reliance:* Many countries develop their own weapons to preserve or enhance their independence.

7. *Economic Factors:* Much of the global weapons trade is motivated by financial considerations.

8. *Ethnic Conflicts:* Ethnic conflicts generate demand for weapons transfers.

9. *Authoritarian Regimes:* Governments that rule without the consent of the people generally rely on military force to exercise control.

10. *Global Criminal Activities:* Terrorism, drug trafficking, smuggling, money laundering, and other criminal activities stimulate demand for weapons.

11. *Cultural Values:* Beliefs in using force to resolve conflicts and the right of individuals to own weapons contribute to the proliferation of weapons.

Military Burden-Sharing ■ When superpowers provide weapons, technical assistance, and arms production technologies to their allies, they can defend themselves

Nixon Doctrine ■ Approach announced by U.S. President Nixon in 1969 shifting more responsibility to allies to contribute to their own defense

THE PROLIFERATION OF NUCLEAR WEAPONS

As the brutal war raged across the Pacific between the United States and Japan, scientists at the Los Alamos laboratory in New Mexico were developing the first atomic bomb. By July 16, 1945, the bomb was successfully tested near Alamogordo, New Mexico. The destructive power of this weapon, clearly recognized by its creators, became a reality when the American B-29 bomber, the Enola Gay, piloted by **Colonel Paul Tibbets**, dropped the first atomic bomb, nicknamed Little Boy, on Hiroshima, Japan, around 8:16 A.M. on August 6, 1945. A blinding flash of white light was followed by a huge fireball of several million degrees centigrade that vaporized people and buildings. Radioactive "black rain" and fires left roughly 130,000 people dead or injured and 70,000 buildings (out of a total of 76,000) destroyed or severely damaged. Three days later, a much more powerful atomic bomb, nicknamed Fat Man, was dropped on Nagasaki, Japan, killing or injuring around 100,000 people.[11] The nuclear age revolutionized warfare. These weapons of mass destruction could literally destroy our planet. America's nuclear monopoly was challenged by the Soviet Union, which developed its own atomic weapon in 1949. Britain became a nuclear power in 1952, followed by France in 1960 and China in 1964.

The nuclear age was accompanied by the emerging Cold War, a reality that underscored the dangers of nuclear proliferation. The Soviet Union began building long-range bombers that could reach the United States. Concerned about the **bomber gap** between the two superpowers, America escalated its own military build-up. It successfully tested a new and more powerful weapon, the hydrogen bomb (also known as a thermonuclear bomb), only to be followed by the Soviet Union nine months later (in 1953). Taking advantage of captured German technology on rocketry and German scientists, the Soviets began mass production of medium-range ballistic missiles in 1955. In 1957, the Soviet Union shocked the world in general and the United States in particular with the launching of **Sputnik**, the world's first artificial satellite. Using the same rocket engines that shot Sputnik into orbit, the Soviets fired an intercontinental missile over a range of five thousand miles,[12] clearly demonstrating the Soviet Union's ability to strike the United States with nuclear weapons. The United States, determined to close the missile gap and to prevent the Soviet Union from gaining nuclear superiority, developed a wide range of nuclear weapons. This nuclear arms race created what Britain's Prime Minister Winston Churchill called a **mutual balance of terror**. Neither the United States nor the Soviet Union could launch nuclear weapons against the other without suffering catastrophic consequences itself. The awesome destructiveness of nuclear weapons actually deterred countries from using them. The concept of **mutual assured destruction (MAD)** emanated from the reality that a nuclear exchange between the superpowers would be suicidal. It is estimated that there are 30,000 nuclear weapons in the world and that there is enough highly enriched uranium and plutonium to create 240,000 more.[13]

In addition to providing security through deterrence, nuclear weapons are also perceived as enhancing a country's global status, strengthening its sovereignty, and enabling it to intimidate other countries. A major concern about nuclear proliferation is that the larger the group of countries possessing them the more likely it is that some countries will deliberately or accidentally start

Colonel Paul Tibbets ■ Pilot of the Enola Gay, the airplane that dropped the first atomic bomb on Hiroshima, Japan

Bomber Gap ■ During the Cold War, the Soviet Union began building long-range bombers that could reach the United States; the United States did not yet have this capability

Sputnik ■ The world's first artificial satellite created by the Soviet Union

Mutual Balance of Terror ■ Situation during the Cold War nuclear arms race in which neither the United States nor the Soviet Union could launch nuclear weapons against the other without suffering catastrophic consequences itself

MAD ■ The reality that a nuclear exchange between the superpowers would be suicidal a nuclear war. A hallmark of the Cold War was the restraint exercised by the superpowers. They emphasized deterrence and the development of a system of command and control. By contrast, nuclear powers such as India and Pakistan have not implemented institutional safeguards to prevent accidental nuclear war. Furthermore, unlike the United States and the Soviet Union, which were allies in two world wars, India and Pakistan have engaged in military conflicts since their creation in 1947. In the following section, we will briefly discuss examples of nuclear proliferation.

China and Japan

America's use of nuclear weapons against Japan and the subsequent nuclear arms race between the United States and the Soviet Union influenced China to develop its own nuclear weapons to deter nuclear attacks and to inflict unacceptable damage on the enemy. China's policy of **minimum deterrence** called for potential retaliatory strikes against large value targets, such as major cities. Unlike global powers, such as the United States and the Soviet Union, China perceived itself more as a regional power that had to develop sufficient nuclear power to be taken seriously by the major countries. Most of its nuclear weapons are short- and medium-range that are suitable for use in Eurasia. However, China has developed a smaller number of intercontinental nuclear weapons that are capable of hitting targets in the United States. It accepted international restraints on its nuclear weapons activity in 1996 by signing the **Comprehensive Test Ban Treaty**, which limits the right of countries to conduct nuclear weapons tests.

Minimum Deterrence ■ Calls for potential retaliatory strikes against large value targets

However, several factors have contributed to China's decision to become a more robust nuclear power. As we saw in our discussion of the rise and fall of great powers in Chapter 2, economic success often fuels military growth and changes how countries perceive their position in the global system relative to that of dominant powers. China's rapid economic growth is undoubtedly influencing it to acquire greater military power. From the perspective of **power transition theory**, discussed in Chapter 2, China is likely to challenge the United States for global leadership. Another factor contributing to China's modernization of its nuclear weapons is the nuclear capability of both the United States and Russia. China would like to have an effective nuclear deterrence against both countries, especially in light of America's efforts to build a missile defense system that would lessen its own vulnerability to nuclear attacks while leaving other countries vulnerable to nuclear attacks. An important component of China's concerns is the United States' strong support for Taiwan. These concerns were diminished following the election of a more pro-China government in Taiwan in 2008. Furthermore, China's reassessment of its nuclear capabilities is influenced by the emergence of India and Pakistan, neighboring countries, as nuclear powers.[14]

Comprehensive Test Ban Treaty ■ Treaty that limits the right of countries to conduct nuclear weapons tests

Power Transition Theory ■ Stresses that the distribution-of-power changes in countries will rise and fall

Although Japan, the only country against which nuclear bombs were used, does not have nuclear weapons, nuclear proliferation in Asia, among other factors, has heightened concerns about Japan's rise as a nuclear power. Influenced by the bombing of Hiroshima and Nagasaki and forced demilitarization by the United States as the occupying power, Japan adopted a policy of pacifism, which rejected owning, producing, or allowing nuclear weapons to be placed on its territory. In fact, the Japanese Constitution, written by the United States during the occupation (1945–1952), prohibits Japan from having an army and from using military force to resolve disputes. However, Japan's emergence as a global economic and technological power has enabled it to acquire the ability to produce nuclear weapons. Japan, which relies heavily on nuclear energy, has enough plutonium and uranium to construct thousands of nuclear weapons. Japan's space program enables it to rapidly convert its rockets into missile launchers. North Korea's decision to test a ballistic missile that flew over Japan in 1998, China's rising military power, the nuclearization of India and Pakistan, and growing doubts among Japanese leaders about America's commitment to Japan's security have all contributed to increased public support in Japan for developing nuclear weapons.[15]

India and Pakistan

Although India's disputes with Pakistan played a pivotal role in its development of nuclear weapons, to understand the emergence of the second nuclear age in Asia we need to briefly examine India's perception of its position in contemporary global society. As we discussed in Chapter 1, an earlier period of globalization that was marked by European expansion into Asia, the Americas, and Africa heralded what many developing countries, including India, perceived as an unequal distribution of power. The acquisition of nuclear weapons by Asian countries represents a direct challenge to the world order constructed by Europeans. It is widely believed that both India and China, with combined populations representing a third of humanity and rapidly growing economies, are rising powers that view military strength as an essential component of global power. Based on their historical as well as contemporary experience, these countries have concluded that military might enables Europeans and Americans to shape the global economic, cultural, and political system. When the Portuguese, led by **Vasco da Gama**, arrived in India in 1498, Indians began their long experience of colonization by Europeans who had superior military technology. India's status as a nuclear power marks what has been called a post-Vasco da Gama era.[16]

Vasco da Gama ■ Portuguese explorer who arrived in India in 1498

Fueled by nationalism and a determination to reject the virtual nuclear weapons monopoly enjoyed by the five permanent members of the UN Security Council, India believes nuclear nonproliferation is not in its national interest. From India's perspective, the nuclear Non-Proliferation Treaty (NPT), the Comprehensive Test Ban Treaty, and other similar agreements are not really about nuclear disarmament. Instead, they are designed to ratify the nuclear status quo.[17] Shortly after gaining independence in 1947, India's first Prime Minister, **Jawaharlal Nehru**, advocated ending all nuclear testing. In 1962, China and India briefly fought each other over a disputed border. As we mentioned earlier, China became a nuclear power in 1964, a development that influenced India to focus on becoming a nuclear power. Although India declared its continued commitment to nuclear disarmament, it refused to sign the nuclear NPT. By 1974, the world learned that India had conducted its first nuclear test.

Jawaharlal Nehru ■ India's first prime minister; advocated ending all nuclear testing

Pakistan, a country formed in opposition to India, was clearly worried by its rival's nuclear capabilities and was determined to counteract India's power by

India's Agni
Missile.

Treaty of Almelo ■
International agree-
ment that led to the
establishment of the
Urenco in 1971 in
the Netherlands

developing nuclear weapons. As we will discuss in Chapter 11, global migration contributes to the globalization of scientific knowledge. In an effort to develop their own enriched uranium for their nuclear power industry and lessen their dependence on the United States, several European countries—Britain, Germany, and the Netherlands—concluded the **Treaty of Almelo** in 1970. This agreement led to the establishment of the Uranium Enrichment Company (Urenco) in 1971 in the Netherlands. Dr. Abdul Qadeer Khan, a Pakistani scientist, was employed as a metallurgist by Physics Dynamic Research Laboratory, a subcontractor working with Urenco. Khan had access to top-secret information. Following India's nuclear test, Khan stole the blueprints of the world's best centrifuges, hollow metal tubes that spin very fast to enrich natural uranium into bomb fuel, and returned to Pakistan to develop a nuclear bomb.[18] Known as the "father" of Pakistan's bomb, Khan admitted helping Iran, North Korea, and Libya obtain centrifuge parts, thereby contributing to nuclear proliferation. Pakistan's nuclear weapons program was aided by China and essentially condoned by the United States. In 1998, the world faced the dawn of the second nuclear age as India, followed shortly by Pakistan, detonated nuclear bombs in underground tests. Both countries remain committed to building more sophisticated nuclear weapons. By June 2004, India and Pakistan retreated from their belligerent positions, which had brought them to the brink of war in January 2002, and held talks on ways to diminish the possibility of an outbreak of a nuclear war between them. Significant steps were taken in 2005 to reduce tensions, including cricket matches, bilateral talks, and encouraging transportation links between parts of Kashmir controlled by the two countries. However, the imposition of martial law in Pakistan in November 2007 by General Pervez Musharraf and growing political unrest in the country raised global concerns about the security of Pakistan's nuclear weapons and the dangers posed by terrorists' access to them and to nuclear material. Furthermore, increased nuclear cooperation between the United States and India was not reassuring to Pakistan.

The Middle East

The proliferation of nuclear weapons as well as efforts to obtain nuclear weapons in the Middle East cannot be separated from the Arab-Israeli conflict. The emotional component of this ongoing dispute often clouds a clear, objective analysis of nuclear weapons in the region. President George Bush's decision to launch a preemptive invasion of Iraq to destroy its weapons of mass destruction (which were not found) and growing concerns about terrorist organizations being able to obtain nuclear weapons heightened awareness of efforts of Iran and Libya to acquire nuclear weapons and refocused attention on Israel as a nuclear power. Israel, under the leadership of Prime Minister David Ben-Gurion in 1952, built its nuclear arsenal preemptively but also sought to counter the conventional military power of the neighboring Arab states that threatened to destroy it.[19] In other words, nuclear weapons are viewed by Israel as a deterrent. Although Israel is widely recognized as a significant nuclear power, with roughly two hundred nuclear weapons, it has not ratified the nuclear **NPT**, which allows the International Atomic Energy Agency (IAEA) of the United Nations to monitor nuclear weapons activities. Israel, India, and Pakistan have not committed themselves to pursuing negotiations to end the nuclear arms race or to move toward nuclear disarmament because of their refusal to ratify the NPT. Unlike India and Pakistan, which are declared nuclear powers, Israel, under its policy of nuclear ambiguity, does not confirm or deny its nuclear capacity. Israel confirmed this position during a visit to that country in June 2004 by Mohamed ElBaradei, the director of the IAEA, as part of a larger effort to move toward a nuclear-free Middle East. However, Mordechai Vanunu, an Israeli nuclear technician who worked on Israel's nuclear weapons, revealed the extent of Israel's nuclear arsenal in 1986 when he provided photographs and details of Israel's reactor near the town of Dimona to the *Sunday Times of London*. Lured by a female agent of **Mossad**, Israel's spy agency, to travel from London to meet her in Italy, Vanunu was kidnapped by the Mossad, transported to Israel, and held in solitary confinement for most of the eighteen years he was imprisoned. Following his release from prison in April 2004, Israeli officials continued to be fearful that Vanunu would disclose new details of Israel's nuclear program and draw attention to it.[20] In April 2008, Ben-Ami Kadish, an American, admitted that he had leaked between fifty and a hundred secret U.S. government documents on nuclear arms, missiles, and fighter jets to the Israeli government during the early 1980s.

As we have seen so far, nuclear proliferation is often fueled by fear of countries that already have nuclear weapons or have the technological capability to produce them. Jonathan Schell pointed out that "every nuclear arsenal is linked to every other nuclear arsenal in the world by powerful ties of terror and response."[21] Iraq, Iran, and Libya have attempted to acquire nuclear weapons, partly due to the security dynamics of the Middle East, just as India developed nuclear weapons out of concerns about China's military power. Iranian officials, for example, justify their efforts to secure nuclear weapons on the grounds that Israel, India, and Pakistan have the nuclear bomb. Iraq's quest for nuclear weapons was effectively ended by the U.S.-led invasion and occupation, and Libya decided to abandon its nuclear aspirations in late 2003, partly to end its isolation from the global community and to avoid possible U.S. military action, especially in the wake of America's

NPT ■ International treaty allowing the IAEA of the United Nations to monitor global nuclear weapons activities

Mossad ■ Israeli spy agency

preemptive war against Iraq. Iran, while allowing the IAEA to conduct limited inspections of its nuclear facilities, in accordance with the NPT, remained committed to pursuing nuclear technology for peaceful purposes. In December 2007, American intelligence agencies concluded that Iran had halted its nuclear weapons program as early as 2003, contrary to assertions made by the Bush administration. However, Iran's ability to produce its own enriched uranium was generally perceived as enabling it to become a nuclear power around 2015.[22] Furthermore, Russia's involvement in building nuclear facilities in Iran and Iran's ability to purchase weapons designs, technical knowledge, and sophisticated technology on the global market strengthened its capacity to produce nuclear weapons. Given the U.S. invasion of Iraq, which did not have nuclear weapons, and America's negotiations with North Korea, which has nuclear weapons, Iran views nuclear weapons as a deterrence to U.S. military action. Facing a threat of sanctions by the United States in early 2006 and again in late 2007, Iran stressed that its nuclear program was for peaceful purposes. Iran refused to suspend its uranium enrichment activities, despite threats from the United States. At the same time, Iran continued to cooperate, selectively, with the IAEA. In March 2008, the UN Security Council reinforced efforts to prevent Iran from acquiring fuel for nuclear weapons by imposing sanctions that allow inspections of cargo to and from Iran and the monitoring of Iranian financial institutions.

North Korea

Hermit Kingdom ■
Label given to North Korea due to its largely self-imposed isolation from the global community

Kim Jong Il ■
Current leader of North Korea

As the United States prepared to invade Iraq to destroy that county's weapons of mass destruction (which were not found), North Korea stated that it actually had nuclear weapons, demanded that the United States sign a nonaggression agreement with it, and threatened to use its nuclear weapons if attacked by the United States. Widely known as the **Hermit Kingdom** because of its largely self-imposed isolation from the global community, North Korea emphasizes building a strong military to protect its interests. As we mentioned earlier, North Korea test-fired a ballistic missile over Japan in 1998, clearly demonstrating its ability to launch a military strike against that country. Furthermore, North Korea remains a communist state and, despite improved relations with neighboring South Korea, continues to concentrate its military power along the demilitarized zone (DMZ) that divides the Korean peninsula. Despite North Korea's admission that it is a nuclear power, the United States refrained from attacking it. In light of America's decision to invade and occupy Iraq, North Korea's leader **Kim Jong Il** stressed his country's nuclear capability to deter the United States from taking military action against it. North Korea, with close ties to China, has long been regarded as having nuclear ambitions. It has also played a significant role in weapons proliferation by providing ballistic missile technology and missiles to Iraq, Iran, Pakistan, Libya, Syria, and Yemen. North Korea has also received nuclear technology from Pakistan.

North Korea's determination to produce nuclear weapons created a crisis with the United States in 1993–1994. American officials considered the option of bombing North Korea's nuclear facilities but decided that the consequences of doing so would be catastrophic for both North Korea and South Korea. Instead of taking military action, the United States negotiated an agreement with

North Korea in 1994 that required North Korea to cease operating its plutonium reprocessing plant. In exchange, the United States and its allies agreed to put two light-water reactors in North Korea and to provide enough heavy fuel oil to compensate for lost energy from its nuclear production power plants while these reactors were being constructed.[23] In January 2003, North Korea restarted its nuclear power plants, terminated inspections by the IAEA, and asked the inspectors to leave the country. North Korea's production of plutonium for nuclear bombs and its rejection of the nuclear NPT occurred at the height of America's global efforts to prevent the proliferation of weapons of mass destruction. Partly due to pressure from China, Japan, Russia, and South Korea, the United States decided to negotiate with North Korea to resolve the conflict over nuclear weapons. By 2004 a proposed solution was formulated. In exchange for dismantling its plutonium and uranium weapons programs, permitting international inspectors to examine suspected nuclear sites, and dismantling and shipping its nuclear technology out of the country (as we saw in the case of Libya), the United States, China, Japan, Russia, and South Korea would supply North Korea with heavy fuel oil, retrain the scientists involved in nuclear weapons programs, and lift economic sanctions and the United States would agree not to invade the country.[24] It was widely believed that North Korea continued to pursue its nuclear program in early 2005 as efforts to negotiate a solution to the conflict failed. However, in September 2005, North Korea agreed to dismantle its nuclear program and to comply with the NPT. In exchange, the United States and the other countries agreed to provide energy assistance to and promote economic cooperation with North Korea. The United States also agreed to refrain from attacking North Korea and to normalize relations. However, negotiations were unsuccessful until February 2007, when North Korea agreed to dismantle its main nuclear reactor at Yongbyon and to allow the return of IAEA inspectors. Despite North Korea's decision to test-fire short-range missiles off its western coasts in March 2008, negotiations continued between North Korea and the United States. However, these negotiations ended in 2009 and tensions between the United States and North Korea escalated after North Korea conducted a nuclear test and test-fired three short-range missiles.

AMERICA'S NUCLEAR RESPONSE TO NUCLEAR PROLIFERATION

As the war against terrorism intensified and as countries such as India, Pakistan, North Korea, Iran, Iraq, and Libya demonstrated an interest in strengthening their nuclear capabilities or acquiring nuclear weapons, the United States increased its efforts to prevent the proliferation of weapons of mass destruction. Simultaneously, however, the Bush administration sent Congress its **Nuclear Posture Review**, in which it advocated a revitalized nuclear weapons complex capable of designing, developing, manufacturing, and certifying new nuclear warheads in response to emerging global threats. In sharp contrast to the traditional reluctance to advocate actually using nuclear weapons, the United States embraced the unprecedented view that nuclear warheads could be used preemptively against potential or actual adversaries. Specifically, the Pentagon regarded

Nuclear Posture Review ■ Bush administration document that advocated a revitalized nuclear weapons complex capable of designing, developing, manufacturing, and certifying new nuclear warheads in response to emerging global threats

Robust Nuclear Earth Penetrator ■ Nuclear weapon capable of hitting reinforced concrete underground bunkers; used as an effective deterrent against the development of weapons of mass destruction by countries as well as terrorist groups

the development of the **Robust Nuclear Earth Penetrator**, a nuclear weapon capable of hitting reinforced concrete bunkers as deep as 40 feet underground, as an effective deterrent against the development of weapons of mass destruction by countries as well as terrorist groups. Such a response to nuclear weapons proliferation is widely perceived as fundamentally undermining global efforts to prevent other countries from acquiring nuclear weapons to deter an attack by America. Furthermore, critics of America's nuclear response believe that using any type of nuclear weapon "will breach the firewall between conventional and nuclear war and pose a new threat to world security."[25]

While the United States pressures countries regarded as having hostile military intentions not to develop nuclear weapons, it has pursued an essentially selective policy, ignoring allies such as Israel, Pakistan, and India that possess nuclear weapons. Furthermore, the United States' current nuclear posture remains basically as it was during the Cold War. The United States seems oblivious to the fact that its unwillingness to significantly reduce the size of its own nuclear arsenal in light of the new strategic environment engendered by the end of military competition with the Soviet Union creates insecurity among vulnerable states. American nuclear weapons are managed by the National Nuclear Security Administration of the Department of Energy. Although the United States strongly opposed nuclear weapons programs in Iran, it allocated roughly $6.6 billion in 2005 to modernize the production infrastructure.[26] Robert S. McNamara, a former U.S. Secretary of Defense, argues that keeping such large numbers of weapons and maintaining them on hair-trigger alert are potent signs that the United States is not seriously working toward the elimination of its arsenal and raises troubling questions as to why any other state should restrain its nuclear ambitions.[27] This perception was challenged by President Barack Obama's agreement with President Dmitri A. Medvedev in July 2009 to reduce U.S. and Russian nuclear arsenals by at least one-quarter. The nuclear agreement signed by President Bush and Prime Minister Singh in March 2006 allowing India to obtain nuclear reactors, fuel, and expertise from the United States in exchange for the supervision of India's civilian nuclear reactors by the IAEA underscores problems with America's approach to nuclear nonproliferation. India, which has not signed the NPT, continues to operate its unsupervised military nuclear program.

CHEMICAL AND BIOLOGICAL WEAPONS

Chemical Weapons ■ Weapons that are dispersed as a gas, vapor, liquid, or aerosol or are absorbed; generally classified based on their effects

Although chemical and biological weapons are often referred to as though they are indistinguishable, in this section we will discuss them separately. **Chemical weapons** are extremely toxic and can be dispersed as a gas, vapor, liquid, or aerosol or absorbed onto a fine talcum-like powder to create "dusty" agents.[28] Chemical weapons are generally classified based on their effects. Categories include

1. *Checking agents*, which destroy lung tissue, such as chlorine phosgene;
2. *Blood agents*, which interfere with cellular respiration and include toxins such as hydrogen cyanide;

3. *Blister agents*, such as mustard gas, which cause severe burns to the skin and lungs; and

4. *Nerve agents*, such as sarin gas, that disrupt nerve impulse transmission and cause death by respiratory paralysis.[29]

Chemical weapons cause damage within minutes or hours. Some chemical agents, such as sarin gas, disperse relatively fast, whereas others, such as sulfur, mustard, and VX nerve agent, continue to be highly toxic for days or weeks. Contrary to general assumptions about the ease with which chemical weapons can be used by terrorist organizations and countries, most chemical agents are extremely difficult and dangerous to work with and relatively hard to weaponize. Nevertheless, chemical weapons have been used and several countries have them or are attempting to acquire them.

Although countries have attempted to use chemicals in conflicts throughout history, chemical weapons were introduced into modern warfare on a massive scale by Germany during World War I. The Germans used chlorine gas against the allies in 1915 and mustard gas later on. But both sides soon realized that the consequences of these chemical weapons were extremely difficult to control. Wind speeds and wind direction determined the dispersal of chemicals on the battlefields, rendering it virtually impossible to predict which side would suffer greater casualties from their usage. Experiences with chemical weapons during World War I restrained Europeans from using them in World War II, despite large stockpiles that were developed by both sides. In Asia, however, Japan employed chemical weapons against China. As part of the arms race between the superpowers, chemical weapons were produced on a massive scale by the Soviet Union, the United States, and other countries. Contemporary debates about weapons of mass destruction often obscure the role of the superpowers in accelerating the proliferation of nuclear, biological, and chemical weapons. The United States used **Agent Orange**, an extremely toxic chemical spray, to defoliate forests in Vietnam in its war against the Vietcong forces. As we will discuss in Chapter 11, the United States routinely uses chemicals in Colombia and elsewhere in South America to destroy coca crops as part of its war on drugs. Usage of these chemicals that poison the environment and threaten public health is strongly opposed by many groups and members of the European Union.

Agent Orange ■ Extremely toxic chemical spray; used to defoliate forests in Vietnam in its war against the Vietcong forces

Far more controversial is America's role in enabling Iraq to acquire chemical weapons. During the Iraq-Iran war (1980–1988), the United States and pro-American countries such as Saudi Arabia, Kuwait, and Jordan viewed Iraq as a bulwark against the spread of radical and militant Shiite fundamentalism from Iran. Consequently, the administrations of Presidents Ronald Reagan and George H. W. Bush authorized the sale of toxic chemicals to Iraq that were weaponized to strengthen Iraq's defenses against "human wave" attacks by suicidal Iranian troops. It was widely known that Iraq, under Saddam Hussein, routinely used chemical weapons against the Iranians, the Kurds, and others.[30] In the context of instability in the Middle East, the United States perceived Iraq as a valuable ally and ignored Hussein's chemical warfare until Iraq invaded Kuwait in 1990. Donald H. Rumsfeld, who became U.S. Secretary of Defense in 2001 and was a leading architect of America's invasion and occupation of Iraq in 2003, traveled to Baghdad in 1983 and met with Hussein when Iraq was using chemical weapons. America's principal justification for the invasion and occupation of Iraq was, ironically, to destroy that country's weapons of mass destruction.

As we mentioned earlier in this chapter, using biological weapons in conflicts has deep historical roots. **Biological weapons** are composed of living microorganisms and toxins that are capable of causing fatal diseases such as smallpox, plague, and hemorrhagic fever. Anthrax spores delivered to U.S. government offices through the U.S. postal service shortly after the terrorist attack in 2001 underscored the threat posed by biological weapons. In response to threats posed by anthrax, the U.S. government passed legislation in 2004, known as **Project Bioshield,** to provide funding for American drug companies to enable them to develop a vaccine against anthrax. Although biological agents such as anthrax cannot be transmitted from an infected person to others, smallpox, as we discussed earlier, is highly contagious and could be easily spread around the world, thereby creating a pandemic. Although biological weapons agents can be developed by a country or nonstate organization that produces vaccines, antibiotics, feed supplements, and fermented beverages, there are only two significant cases in which they were used in the twentieth century. These are the German efforts during World War I to infect livestock and contaminate animal feed to be exported from neutral countries to Allied forces and Japan's deployment of biological weapons against China during World War II.[31] The globalization of biotechnology and endemic military conflicts combine to influence countries to acquire biological weapons. Russia, North Korea, Iran, Egypt, Israel, and Syria are among the countries suspected of having such weapons. Until the 1991 Persian Gulf War, companies in the United States and France were instrumental in enabling Iraq to develop tons of biological weapons. Specifically, the American Type Culture of Manassas, Virginia, and the Pasteur Institute in Paris provided germ samples to Iraq.[32]

NONPROLIFERATION REGIMES

Preventing the spread of weapons of mass destruction emerged as the dominant priority in the United States following the terrorist attacks in 2001. President George W. Bush, stressing the need to prevent terrorists from acquiring chemical, nuclear, and biological weapons, decided to invade and occupy Iraq, as we discussed earlier, and designated Iraq, North Korea, and Iran as an **Axis of Evil** due to their efforts to obtain weapons of mass destruction. The United States also persuaded the UN Security Council in April 2004 to unanimously approve a resolution that obligated states to enact legislation and strengthen existing laws to prevent terrorists and other nonstate actors from manufacturing, acquiring, possessing, developing, transporting, or using nuclear, chemical, or biological weapons and their means of delivery.[33]

For more than fifty years, the global community has cooperated to construct a nonproliferation regime, which is defined as an interlocking network of treaties, agreements, and organizations designed to prevent the spread or use of weapons of mass destruction.[34] Although building the nonproliferation regime is clearly a global effort, the United States, as a dominant power after World War II, provided indispensable leadership. However, inconsistent and outright contradictory American foreign policies often undermine attempts to strengthen the nonproliferation regime. For example, the United States has largely ignored nuclear ambitions of allies such as Israel and Pakistan. Furthermore, American embrace of unilateralism

Biological Weapons ■ Weapons composed of living microorganisms and toxins capable of causing fatal diseases

Project Bioshield ■ U.S. legislation provided funding for American drug companies to develop a vaccine against anthrax

Axis of Evil ■ Label given to Iraq, North Korea, and Iran due to their efforts to obtain weapons of mass destruction has weakened its commitment to supporting international arms control agreements, even as it places a greater emphasis on developing new weapons and a missile defense system. Nevertheless, counterproliferation remains a cornerstone of U.S. foreign policy. During the Clinton administration, the U.S. Department of Defense stressed what it called the "8 D's" of the nonproliferation regime: dissuasion, disarmament, diplomacy, denial, defusing, deterrence, defenses, and destruction.[35]

Dissuasion is an attempt to convince countries to refrain from acquiring unconventional weapons in exchange for security guarantees.

Disarmament involves agreements to prevent proliferation, such as the NPT.

Diplomacy is instrumental in convincing countries to terminate their weapons programs. Diplomacy has been successful in many cases, including Belarus, Ukraine, Brazil, Argentina, South Africa, and Libya.

Denial deals with enforcing stricter international controls on exports of sensitive technologies and materials.

Defusing concentrates on preventing hair-trigger alert postures and securing weapons.

Deterrence is based on the threat of retaliation.

Defenses range from providing chemical suits, inhalation masks, and vaccines for the population to missile defense.

Destruction of weapons facilities and weapons is a preemptive act.

Nuclear Nonproliferation

Realizing the destructiveness of the bombs dropped on Japan in World War II and aware of the military and strategic stalemate engendered by the proliferation of nuclear weapons, the United States and the Soviet Union, the dominant nuclear powers, collaborated with Britain, France, and China (the other nuclear powers) to develop a nuclear nonproliferation regime. An underlying assumption of this regime was that risks of nuclear war would be diminished by limiting the acquisition of nuclear weapons to this small group of countries that already possessed them. However, given the competitive nature of nations, this nuclear monopoly would be challenged. As George Perkovich observed, to persuade the rest of the world to relinquish its prerogative to acquire nuclear weapons, the nuclear weapons possessors had to do the following:

1. Promise to abandon their nuclear weapons eventually.
2. Pledge not to use their weapons to threaten countries that did not possess nuclear weapons.
3. Help countries that renounced nuclear weapons and accepted international monitoring to acquire and use nuclear technology for civilian and peaceful purposes.
4. Enhance global security by ensuring non-nuclear states that their neighbors would be prevented from becoming nuclear powers.[36]

These objectives are clearly reflected in the nonproliferation agreements signed by American presidents. For example, President Dwight D. Eisenhower proposed creating the IAEA to promote the peaceful uses of atomic energy. President John F. Kennedy signed the Limited Test Ban Treaty to terminate nuclear tests in the atmosphere, in outer space, and under water. President Lyndon B. Johnson negotiated the nuclear NPT, designed to limit the transfer of nuclear weapons, nuclear technology, and nuclear materials to other countries, and Presidents Richard M. Nixon, Jimmy Carter, and Ronald Reagan concluded various agreements to reduce the number of nuclear weapons possessed by the superpowers. The end of the Cold War and the disintegration of the Soviet Union in 1991 enabled Presidents George H. W. Bush and Bill Clinton to continue to pursue negotiations with Russia and parts of the former Soviet Union to dismantle more of their nuclear weapons. Under the Nunn-Lugar-Domenici Cooperative Threat Reduction Programs, named after Senators Sam Nunn, Richard Lugar, and Pete Domenici, the United States provided financial incentives and technical assistance to Ukraine, Belarus, Kazakhstan, and other states of the former Soviet Union to denuclearize. South Africa, one of the world's major suppliers of uranium, unilaterally and voluntarily relinquished nuclear weapons, partly as a consequence of the end of the Cold War and the dismantling of apartheid. [37] As we have seen, despite progress on nonproliferation between the United States and Russia, countries such as India, Pakistan, Israel, and North Korea became nuclear powers. Furthermore, in a significant departure from the traditional approach that embraced the eventual elimination of nuclear weapons, U.S. President George W. Bush concentrated on preventing enemy nations from acquiring nuclear weapons while ignoring nuclear ambitions of friendly nations. In December 2001, Bush announced that America would withdraw from the **Antiballistic Missile Treaty**, which prohibits the development, testing, or deployment of antiballistic missile systems capable of defending entire territories from intercontinental ballistic missile (ICBM) attacks in order to enable the United States to build a missile defense system. Table 6.1 shows significant nuclear weapons agreements. As we discussed earlier, Bush advocated developing and preemptively using small nuclear weapons, known as bunker-busters. A nuclear arms agreement signed by President Bush and Russia's President Vladimir Putin in May 2002 essentially provided the United States and Russia flexibility to retain as many nuclear weapons as they want. The only significant restraint on them was that they had to reduce their nuclear warheads to between 1,700 and 2,200 by the end of 2012. At that point the treaty would have expired, enabling both sides to increase their nuclear weapons. In July 2009, the United States and Russia signed an agreement to create a new treaty to reduce their strategic nuclear arsenals by one-third. The new treaty must be ratified by the U.S. Senate. Robert S. McNamara, who was the U.S. Secretary of Defense from 1961 to 1968 and who helped President John F. Kennedy avoid a nuclear war with the Soviet Union during the Cuban Missile Crisis in 1962, stated that U.S. nuclear weapons policy is "immoral, illegal, militarily unnecessary, and dreadfully dangerous."[38]

Antiballistic Missile Treaty ■ International treaty prohibiting the development, testing, or deployment of antiballistic missile systems

Curbing Chemical and Biological Weapons

1925 Geneva Protocol ■ International treaty that prohibited the use of biological and chemical weapons in war

An important component of the nonproliferation regime in relation to chemical weapons was the **1925 Geneva Protocol**, which prohibited the use of biological and chemical weapons in war. Due partly to the leadership of President Nixon, the United States eventually ratified the Geneva Protocol in 1975

TABLE 6.1

MAJOR NUCLEAR WEAPONS AGREEMENTS

Date Signed	Agreement
August 1963	**Limited Test Ban Treaty.** Prohibits nuclear explosions in the atmosphere, in outer space, and under water.
July 1968	**Nuclear Non-Proliferation Treaty.** Prohibits countries from transferring nuclear weapons or helping other countries acquire them.
May 1972	**Strategic Arms Limitation Treaty (SALT1).** Limited strategic nuclear missile launchers and missile firing submarines.
July 1974	**Threshold Test Ban Treaty.** Limited U.S. and Soviet Union underground nuclear weapons tests.
December 1987	**Intermediate-Range Nuclear Forces Treaty.** Dismantled all Soviet and American medium- and short-range land-based missiles.
July 1991	**Strategic Arms Reduction Treaty (STARTI).** Reduces the number of U.S. and Soviet long-range nuclear warheads from 11,000 to 6,000.
January 1993	**Strategic Arms Reduction Treaty (STARTII).** Requires U.S. and Russia to reduce nuclear warheads and bombs to 3,500 by 2007.
September 1996	**Comprehensive Test Ban Treaty.** Prohibits all nuclear weapons test explosions. (Not ratified by the U.S. Senate.)
May 2002	**U.S.-Russian Nuclear Arms Treaty.** Commits each country to reduce nuclear warheads to between 1,700 and 2,200 by the end of 2012.

Sources: U.S. State Department, U.S. Congressional Research Services, and *New York Times.*

YOU DECIDE

U.S. Missile Defense System

Although the idea of a missile defense system was initially proposed by President Dwight D. Eisenhower, it was President Ronald Reagan who clearly articulated a proposal for placing weapons in space as part of a national missile shield. Research on missile defense continued under Presidents George H. W. Bush and Bill Clinton, but both of them downplayed the need to implement a missile defense system, partly because of technological difficulties and the implications of developing such a system for the functioning of the nonproliferation regime. During the 2000 presidential campaign, George W. Bush strongly supported employing a missile defense system. Following the terrorist attack on the United States in 2001, President Bush stressed the threats posed by terrorists and rogue states that seek weapons of mass destruction. He emphasized the urgency of developing effective defenses against attacks. Concluding that the Antiballistic Missile Treaty hindered the U.S. government's ability to protect Americans from terrorist or rogue-state missile attacks, Bush withdrew the United States from the ABM treaty. In 2007, the Bush administration advocated building a missile defense system in Poland to protect U.S. allies from nuclear attacks by Iran, which does not have nuclear weapons. This plan was strongly opposed by Russia, which viewed it as a threat to its security. The United States abandoned the project in 2009.

Do you think that the U.S. Missile Defense system enhances or undermines the nonproliferation regime and global security? ■

(during the Ford administration). In 1933, the Chemical Weapons Convention (CWC), which prohibits the development, acquisition, transfer, stockpiling, or use of chemical weapons, was signed and ratified by more than 125 countries, including Russia and the United States. The CWC also mandated the internationally monitored destruction of all chemical stockpiles by 2007. Apart from the fact that several countries refused to sign the agreement and continued to produce chemical weapons, most of Russia's massive arsenal of chemical weapons remain in storage, partly because Russia lacks adequate resources to destroy them.

The international regime concerning the nonproliferation of biological weapons began with the 1925 Geneva Protocol. Although the Protocol abolished the use of biological weapons in warfare, it enabled many countries to make reservations, attachments to treaties that allow states to be excluded from the legal effects of certain provisions of the agreement.[39] The Protocol also made compliance with the ban on biological weapons conditional on reciprocity. President Nixon laid the foundation for strengthening the nonproliferation regime when he announced in 1969 that the United States would unilaterally and unconditionally renounce biological weapons and subsequently ordered the destruction of U.S. weapons stockpiles. Nixon negotiated the **Biological Weapons Convention** (BWC), an agreement prohibiting the development, manufacture, and stockpiling of biological weapons.[40] The treaty was signed in 1972.

BWC ■ 1972 agreement negotiated by President Nixon prohibiting the development, manufacture, and stockpiling of biological weapons

SUMMARY AND REVIEW

This chapter addressed the dangers of the proliferation of conventional weapons and weapons of mass destruction. It focused on recent developments in the proliferation of conventional weapons and weapons of mass destruction. First, we looked at the dangers involved in the proliferation of specific conventional weapons. We identified many reasons for the proliferation of conventional weapons, such as superpower rivalry during the Cold War; government concern with political, military, and economic influence over other states; the growth of ethnic and national conflicts throughout the world; and the growth in authoritarian, repressive regimes. Next, we elaborated on the development of various unconventional weapons, including biological, chemical, and nuclear weapons. In this debate over nuclear weapons, we identified emerging nuclear powers, such as Israel, North Korea, and Iran. We also identified many of the efforts made to control the spread and development of all forms of unconventional weapons (biological, chemical, and nuclear), including the Limited Test Ban Treaty, the nuclear NPT, the Antiballistic Missile Treaty, the Geneva Protocol, and the Biological and Chemical Weapons Conventions. A major factor influencing other countries, such as Iran and Korea, to acquire nuclear weapons is America's reluctance to reduce its own nuclear weapons. Furthermore, many analysts believe that the United States pursues a selective policy on nuclear proliferation, ignoring its friends with nuclear weapons and punishing its enemies who are attempting to acquire weapons. A major concern is the availability of nuclear weapons materials in parts of the former Soviet Union.

KEY TERMS

DISCUSSION QUESTIONS

1. Why did the Bush administration label Iran, Iraq, and North Korea the Axis of Evil? Do you think they should or should not have been labeled collectively as such? Why or why not?
2. What did the Limited Test Ban Treaty and the Nuclear Non-Proliferation Treaty seek to accomplish?
3. Discuss the significance of the 1925 Geneva Protocol.
4. Discuss the logic behind developing national missile defense systems. Do you think such efforts will help increase or decrease the level of nuclear proliferation? Why or why not?
5. Discuss global efforts to control chemical and biological weapons.

SUGGESTED READINGS

Blix, Hans. *Disarming Iraq*. New York: Pantheon, 2004.
Chubin, Shahram. *Iran's Nuclear Ambitions*. Washington, DC: Carnegie Endowment, 2006.
Kapur, S. Paul. *Dangerous Deterrent: Nuclear Weapons Proliferation and Conflict in South Asia*. Stanford, CA: Stanford University Press, 2007.
Nasr, Vali and Ray Takeyh. "Why Containing Iran Won't Work," *Foreign Affairs* 87, No. 1 (January/February 2008): 85–94.
Paul, T. V. *The Tradition of Non-Use of Nuclear Weapons*. Stanford, CA: Stanford University Press, 2009.
Wit, Joel S. *Going Critical: The First North Korean Nuclear Crisis*. Washington, DC: Brookings Institution Press, 2004.

END NOTES

1. John Noble Wilford, "How Catapults Married Science, Politics, and War," *New York Times*, 24 February 2004, D3.
2. Tina Rosenberg, "When Smallpox Struck During the Revolutionary War," *New York Times*, 23 December 2001, D8.
3. Gina Kolata, "New York Was Bioterrorism Target, in 1864," *New York Times*, 13 November 2001, D7.

4. David Held et al., *Global Transformations* (Stanford, CA: Stanford University Press, 1999), 103.

5. William Hartung and Rachel Stohl, "Hired Guns," *Foreign Policy* 142 (May/June 2004), 29.

6. James C. McKinley, "U.S. Stymied as Guns Flow to Mexican Cartels," *New York Times*, 15 April 2009, A1.

7. John F. Burns, "Britain Joins a Draft Treaty to Ban Cluster Munitions," *New York Times*, 29 May 2008, A13.

8. Jeffrey Boutwell and Michael T. Klare, "Introduction," in *Light Weapons and Civil Conflict*, eds. Jeffrey Boutwell and Michael T. Klare (Lanham, MD: Rowman and Littlefield, 1999), 2.

9. Michael T. Klare, "International Trade in Light Weapons," in *Light Weapons and Civil Conflict*, 21.

10. William W. Keller and Jane E. Nolan, "The Arms Trade: Business as Usual," *Foreign Policy* 109 (Winter 1997/1998), 114.

11. Peter R. Beckman et al., *The Nuclear Predicament* (Upper Saddle River, NJ: Prentice Hall, 2000), 2.

12. Paul Kennedy, *The Rise and Fall of the Great Powers* (New York: Random House, 1987), 388.

13. Graham Allison, "How to Stop Nuclear Terror," *Foreign Affairs* 83, No. 1 (January/February 2004), 66.

14. Brad Roberts et al., "China: The Forgotten Nuclear Power," *Foreign Affairs* 79, No. 4 (July/August 2000), 57; and Evan S. Medeiros, *Reluctant Restraint: The Evolution of China's Nonproliferation Policies and Practices* (Stanford, CA: Stanford University Press, 2007).

15. Howard W. French, "Taboo Against Nuclear Arms Is Being Challenged in Japan," *New York Times*, 9 June 2002, A1.

16. Paul Bracken, "The Second Nuclear Age," *Foreign Affairs* 79, No. 1 (January/February 2000), 149.

17. Jaswant Singh, "Against Nuclear Apartheid," *Foreign Affairs* 77, No. 5 (September/October 1998), 41.

18. Craig S. Smith, "Roots of Pakistan Atomic Scandal Traced to Europe," *New York Times*, 19 February 2004, A3; and S. Paul Kapur, *Dangerous Deterrent: Nuclear Weapons Proliferation and Conflict in South Asia* (Stanford, CA: Stanford University Press, 2007).

19. Jonathan Schell, "The Folly of Arms Control," *Foreign Affairs* 79, No. 5 (September/October 2000), 33.

20. James Bennet, "Vanunu Says Israel's Atom Reactor Should Be Destroyed," *New York Times*, 20 April 2004, A9; and Andy Newman, "Ex-Engineer for Army Charged with Leaks to Israel in 1980s," *New York Times*, 23 April 2008, A21.

21. Schell, "The Folly of Arms Control," 33.

22. Joby Warrick and Glenn Kessler, "Elsewhere on the Axis of Evil," *Washington Post National Weekly Edition*, 17–23 March 2003, 15; Steven Lee Myers, "An Assessment Jars a Foreign Policy Debate," *New York Times*, 4 December 2007, A1; and Vali Nasr and Ray Takeyh, "The Costs of Containing Iran," *Foreign Affairs* 87, No. 1 (January/February 2008), 85.

23. "Closing Pandora's Box," *The Economist*, 4 January 2003, 30.

24. David Sanger, "U.S. to Offer Incentives to Sway North Korea in Nuclear Talks," *New York Times*, 23 June 2004, A3; and Michael J. Mazaar, "The Long Road to Pyongyang," *Foreign Affairs* 86, No. 5 (September/October 2007), 75.

25. William J. Broad, "Facing a Second Nuclear Age," *New York Times*, 3 August 2003, Sect. 4, 1; and Wolfgang K. H. Panofsky, "Nuclear Insecurity," *Foreign Affairs* 86, No. 5 (September/October 2007), 109–110.

26. John Deutch, "A Nuclear Posture for Today," *Foreign Affairs* 84, No. 1 (January/February 2005), 56.

27. Robert S. McNamara, "Apocalypse Soon," *Foreign Policy* 148 (May/June 2005), 31; and Mark Silver, "U.S., India Embrace Nuclear Deal," *Chicago Tribute*, 3 March 2006, Sect. 1, 1.

28. Jonathan B. Tucker, "Introduction," in *Toxic Terror: Assessing Terrorist Use of Chemical and Biological Weapons*, ed. Jonathan B. Tucker (Cambridge, MA: MIT Press, 2000), 3.

29. Tucker, "Introduction," in *Toxic Terror*, 3.

30. Michael Dobbs, "When an Ally Becomes the Enemy," *Washington Post National Weekly Edition*, 6–12 January 2003, 9.

31. David P. Fidler, *International Law and Infectious Diseases* (Oxford: Clarendon Press, 1999), 225.

32. Philip Shenon, "Iraq Links Germs for Weapons to U.S. and France," *New York Times*, 16 March 2003, A16.

33. Warren Hoge, "Ban on Weapons of Doom Is Extended to Quaeda-Style Groups," *New York Times*, 29 April 2004, A3.

34. Joseph Cirincione, "Historical Overview and Introduction," in *Repairing the Regime*, ed. Joseph Cirincione (New York: Routledge, 2000), 3.

35. Ashton B. Carter, "How to Counter WMD," *Foreign Affairs* 83, No. 5 (September/October 2004), 73.

36. George Perkovich, "Bush's Nuclear Revolution," *Foreign Affairs* 82, No. 2 (March/April 2003), 3.

37. J. W. de Villiers et al., "Why South Africa Gave Up the Bomb," *Foreign Affairs* 72, No. 5 (November/December 1993), 98.

38. Michael R. Gordon, "Treaty Offers Pentagon New Flexibility for New Set of Nuclear Priorities," *New York Times*, 14 May 2002, A8; and McNamara, "Apocalypse Soon," 29.

39. Louis Henkin et al., *International Law* (St. Paul, MN: West Publishing Co., 1980), 605.

40. Cirincione, "Historical Overview," 7.

CHAPTER

7

The Global
Financial Crisis

INTRODUCTION

Financial crises and accompanying economic recessions have occurred throughout history. Periodic crises appear to be part of financial systems of dominant or global powers. The United States is the epicenter of the current financial crisis. Enjoying a unipolar moment following the collapse of the Soviet Union and the failure of Communism, the United States was confident that economic liberalization and the proliferation of computer and communications technologies would contribute to ever-increasing global economic growth and prosperity.

As we discussed in Chapter 1, **finance** is usually the leading force in the growth of globalization. The rise of great powers is inextricably linked to access to investments and their ability to function as leading financial centers, as we saw in Chapter 2. Their decline is also closely linked to financial problems. Finance enables entrepreneurs to start various enterprises and to become competitors of established companies. It is also essential to innovation and scientific discoveries. Finance also facilitates risk sharing and provides insurance for risk-takers. Countries that have large financial sectors tend to grow faster, their inhabitants are generally richer, and there are more opportunities. Financial globalization contributed to the unprecedented growth and prosperity around the world. China and India became significant economic powers and the industrialized countries grew even richer.[1] Closely integrated into the financial system are banks and investment firms. When the financial system is in crisis, banks reduce lending, companies often face bankruptcy, and unemployment rises. Ultimately, as we saw in the financial crisis of 2008–2009, many banks fail.

The financial crisis triggered a global economic recession that resulted in more than $4.1 trillion in losses, unemployment rates that climbed to more than 10 percent in the United States and higher elsewhere, and increased poverty. Stock markets around the world crashed in 2008. American investors lost roughly 40 percent of the value of their savings. Housing prices plummeted from their record highs in 2006. Consumers reduced their spending, manufacturing declined, global trade diminished, and countries adopted protectionist measures, many turning their attention inward to focus on problems caused by the financial crisis. Given the central importance of finance to virtually all aspects of globalization, issues such as trade, the environment, crime, disease, inequality, migration, ethnic conflicts, human rights, and promoting democracy are affected. Furthermore, the financial crisis weakened some countries more than others, thereby engendering significant shifts of power among countries, especially between the United States and China. This chapter examines the causes of the financial crisis, its impact, and responses to it.

CAUSES OF THE GLOBAL FINANCIAL CRISIS

Finance ■ The major catalyst in the growth of globalization and national power

The causes of financial crises are as complex as many of the crises themselves and the human beings responsible for them. There have been at least sixty recorded crises since the early seventeenth century. Human beings seem to have always been obsessed with money, and greed drives them to obtain increasing amounts of it. And humans generally spend more than they have, thereby creating huge debts that undermine the stability of the financial system. As early as 33 A.D., Emperor Tiberius of Rome had to inject public funds into the financial system to prevent it from collapsing.[2] Euphoria and excessive optimism, which often accompany financial bubbles, are usually followed by fear and panic when crisis arrives. Generally, people claim to not know how the crisis happened or that they could not see it coming. The **Asian Financial Crisis** in 1997 was a precursor to the financial crisis of 2008–2009. It started in Indonesia and spread to Malaysia, South Korea, other parts of Asia, and the rest of the world. Once prosperous economies were now in deep recession, with stock markets crashing and capital flowing out of the various countries at unprecedented rates. The Asian crisis was largely caused by "hasty and imprudent financial liberalization, almost always under foreign pressure, allowing free international flows of short-term capital without adequate attention to the potentially potent downside of such globalization."[3]

Asian Financial Crisis ■ Started in Indonesia and caused stock markets to crash and reversed economic growth

But the Asian crisis was part of larger global developments, many of which were driven by the United States. The end of the Cold War left America standing as the world's sole superpower with unprecedented power and unlimited options, or so it seemed. Affected by hubris, and made overly confident by the exponential growth of computer and telecommunications technologies, the United States believed, in the words of Thomas Paine, that it could build a brand-new world characterized by unlimited success. However, terrorist attacks on September 11, 2001, fundamentally altered America's sense of security and plunged the country into a recession.

An integral component of the struggle against terrorism was the restoration of domestic and global confidence in America's economic system in general and its financial system in particular. President George W. Bush launched a perpetual war against terrorism. To accomplish this, the U.S. defense budget was rapidly increased, a department of Homeland Security was created, and two wars, one in Afghanistan and the other in Iraq, were launched. Furthermore, part of the new security strategy was a comprehensive globalization agenda, in which American companies operating in foreign countries would be free from restraints imposed by those countries.[4] This meant increasing government debt and encouraging consumers to spend even more to strengthen both the economy and national security. With easy access to capital created by economic globalization, consumers and the U.S. government relied on other people's money. In addition to concentrating on fighting a perpetual war against nonstate actors, an atmosphere was created in which questioning was discouraged and taking excessive financial risks and getting rich quickly were lauded. From John C. Bogle's perspective, at the root of the problem was a societal change. America valued form over substance, prestige over virtue, money over achievement, charisma over character, and the ephemeral over the enduring.[5] While it is almost impossible to disentangle the causes of the global financial crisis, we will concentrate on those that are most often discussed. They include (1) deregulation of financial markets; (2) sophisticated financial innovations linked to rapid changes in computer technologies; (3) excessive executive compensation; (4) low interest rates; (5) subprime loans, especially for mortgages; and (6) speculation in general, with an emphasis on speculation in housing.

Deregulation of Financial Markets

Just as the current financial crisis has engendered demands for reforms, the Great Depression of the 1930s led to the implementation of financial regulations to stabilize the economy and to give American savers confidence in banks. Banks were widely perceived as boring but safe. Although interest rates were low, inflation was also low. Furthermore, deposits were protected by the **Federal Deposit Insurance Corporation (FDIC)**. An outgrowth of the Great Depression, rising inflation, that also occurred following rapid and dramatic increases in oil prices in 1973–1974, contributed to the erosion of confidence in regulations designed during the Great Depression. Rising inflation in the United States prompted foreigners to lose confidence in the U.S. dollar as the leading currency and to seek security by purchasing gold. In response, President Richard Nixon unlinked the dollar from gold and adopted a regimen of floating interest rates. This created greater volatility in the financial system as well as increased opportunities to earn higher interest rates.[6]

Significant societal changes and developments in technology combined to serve as a catalyst to propel deregulation. Although large banks and financial institutions initiated efforts to eliminate or modify regulations that restrained them, individuals were also more assertive in gaining control over their savings pension funds and investments in the stock market. Between 1974 and 1980, many regulations were removed. For example, in 1980, commercial banks and savings and loans institutions were permitted to determine their own interest rates on deposits and loans, thereby spurring greater competition. Many smaller banks were acquired by larger, more distant banks. The local bank was fast becoming an outdated institution.[7]

Just as financial globalization drives economic globalization, the rapid growth of trade was now facilitating **global financial liberalization**. Globalization in general enabled American banks to argue that they were disadvantaged in competition with British, German, Japanese, and other foreign banks that were free of

FDIC ■ Insures individual bank deposits for up to $250,000

Global Financial Liberalization ■ Opening banks around the world to competition restrictions faced by American banks. Moreover, American banks adopted a global outlook that freed them from limiting their operations to the United States. Many were moving their activities offshore to places such as the Cayman Islands, Bermuda, and the Bahamas. President Ronald Reagan, elected on a platform of limiting the role of government, pressured other countries to open their financial systems to American firms. Financial deregulation in the United States was now inseparable from the globalization of trade and financial services. However, impeding global competition in banking was the **Glass-Steagall Act of 1933**, which prohibited commercial banks from underwriting or marketing securities.[8] The rapid growth of capital flows across national borders and the increasing power of investment bankers eventually led to the demise of the Glass-Steagall Act in 1999.

Glass-Steagall Act of 1933 ■ Prohibited commercial banks from underwriting or marketing securities

The phenomenal proliferation of sophisticated computer technologies and an almost unquestioning faith in the wisdom of markets contributed to escalating demands for and acceptance of less regulation. In essence, federal agencies designed to regulate banking became less effective. There was a general loss of control at all levels, which led to exponential risk taking at many companies, largely hidden from public scrutiny. Violations of financial regulations went largely unpunished.[9] Simon Johnson argues that from the confluence of campaign finance, personal connections, and ideology flowed a river of deregulatory policies. These included:

1. Insistence on free movement of capital across borders.
2. The repeal of Depression-era regulations separating commercial and investment banking.
3. Decreased regulatory enforcement by the Securities and Exchange Commission.
4. Allowing banks to measure their own riskiness.
5. Failure to update regulations to keep up with the tremendous pace of financial innovations.[10]

Financial Innovations

As the global financial crisis unfolded, it was obvious that many of those in the banking and investment communities did not fully comprehend how the financial system they created functioned, or the scope and severity of the crisis. The financial wizards, the best and the brightest from leading business schools, could not really explain what was happening on Wall Street and in global financial markets. Ironically, **financial innovations**, designed by brilliant computer experts to manage risk and make capital less expensive and more available, ultimately led to the global financial crisis. Financial innovations, with instantaneous global impacts due to technologies that made electronic transactions faster and less expensive, raced ahead of regulations. Complex financial products created in one financial center involved assets in another and were sold to investors in a third financial market. As we saw in Chapter 1, governments are increasingly challenged to operate effectively in a globalized world. Whereas governments are restrained by issues of sovereignty, global financial firms enjoy relatively greater flexibility. Furthermore, many different agencies in the United States have regulatory authority, a situation that

Financial Innovations ■ Sophisticated financial engineering, an outgrowth of revolutions in computer and telecommunications technologies creates confusion and ineffectiveness.[11] Among the numerous financial innovations that led to the global financial crisis were securitization and hedge funds.

Prior to the widespread use of securitization, banks, many of them local, provided loans to customers they often knew and the banks were responsible for the risks involved in making loans. This meant that bankers gave loans only to individuals and companies they believed could repay the loans. With securitization, risks inherent in granting loans were passed from the bank giving the loans to others who had no direct interest in the customers' ability to repay the loans. Subprime mortgages, student loans, car loans, and credit card debts were securitized. **Securitization** is a sophisticated process of financial engineering that allows global investment to be spread out and separated into multiple income streams to reduce risk.[12] It involves bundling loans into securities and selling them to investors. In 2009, an estimated $8.7 trillion of assets globally were funded by securitization.[13] This innovation made vast sums of money available to borrowers. For example, securitization increased the amount of money available to individuals purchasing homes. This led to unprecedented growth in house prices. It also resulted in high default rates and the housing crisis. As we will discuss, applicants for mortgages were not carefully examined and were encouraged to obtain subprime loans.

Securitization ■ Financial engineering designed to reduce risk

Another financial innovation was credit **derivatives**, which were bets on the creditworthiness of a particular company, like insurance on a loan. There were two types of credit derivatives: credit default swaps and collateralized debt obligations.[14] **Credit default swaps** were widely used, especially by insurance companies such as the American International Group (AIG). Life insurance companies invested in credit default swaps as assets. Parties involved in a credit default swap agreed that one would pay the other if a particular borrower, a third party, could not repay its loans. Credit default swaps were used to transfer credit risks away from banks. A major problem with credit default swaps was the lack of transparency. They were also unregulated. Ultimately, credit default swaps created confusion and encouraged excessive risk taking. It was difficult to determine where the risk ended up. Designed to pass on risks, loans were packaged as securities. **Collateralized debt obligations** were linked to mortgage companies, which passed on the risk. Mortgages, instead of being held by banks and mortgage companies, were sold to investors shortly after the loans closed, and investors packaged them as securities.

Derivatives ■ Bets on the creditworthiness of a particular company, like insurance on a loan

Credit Default Swaps ■ Financial innovation used to transfer credit risks away from banks

Collateralized Debt Obligations ■ Linked to mortgage companies

Similar to securitization, hedge funds grew rapidly, accounting for more than $1.3 trillion in assets globally before the financial crisis of 2008–2009. The name **hedge funds** implies investment funds with a particular sort of hedging strategy. Created by the Investment Company Act of 1940, hedge funds allowed wealthy investors to avoid many financial regulations, and hedge funds were early participants in financial globalization.[15] Essentially, hedge fund managers created portfolios reflecting an assessment of the performance of diverse global markets. As long as the number of participants was relatively small, hedge funds avoided great systemic risks. This changed with revolutions in computer technology that allowed split-second timing on huge volumes of trades. An integral component of the hedge fund strategy is a technique known as **arbitrage**. This involves simultaneously buying at a lower price in one market and selling at a higher price in another market to make a profit on the spread between the two prices.[16]

Hedge Funds ■ Created by the Investment Company Act of 1940

Arbitrage ■ Simultaneously buying at a lower price in one market and selling at a higher price in another market to make a profit

Executive Compensation

Excessive executive compensation is widely perceived as playing a pivotal role in creating the global financial crisis. Wall Street became a magnet for the brightest Americans who wanted to make a large amount of money very quickly. Most companies rewarded short-term performance without much regard for market fundamentals and long-term earnings. Executives were given stock options, which they could manipulate to earn more money. The more an executive could drive up his or her company's stock price or its earnings per share, the more money he or she would get. Frank Partnoy argues that a mercenary culture developed among corporate executives. They merged with or acquired higher-growth companies and, in many cases, committed accounting fraud.[17] This fraud led to the bankruptcy of companies such as Enron, Global Crossing, and WorldCom. Many executives received long prison sentences. Table 7.1 shows the highest-earning American executives.

Low Interest Rates

A fundamental cause of the global financial crisis was the easy availability of too much money globally. An oversupply of money created unprecedented levels of liquidity and historically low interest rates. As we mentioned earlier, the terrorist attacks on the United States on September 11, 2001, triggered a national embrace of increased government spending as well as consumer spending. To accomplish this, the U.S. Federal Reserve, led by **Alan Greenspan**, lowered interest rates to around 1 percent in late 2001. The European Central Bank and the Bank of Japan also reduced interest rates to record lows. The U.S. government encouraged Americans to purchase homes and to refinance or borrow against the value of homes they owned. As consumers and the government lived beyond their means, they were able to borrow from developing countries that were accumulating huge reserves from

Alan Greenspan ■ Chairman of the U.S. Federal Reserve who kept interest rates low

TABLE 7.1

EXECUTIVE PAY: THE TOP TEN (2008)

Name	Company	Compensation ($ millions)
1. Sanjay K. Jha	Motorola	104.4
2. Lawrence J. Ellison	Oracle	84.6
3. Robert A. Iger	Walt Disney	51.1
4. Kenneth I. Chenault	American Express	42.8
5. Vikram S. Pandit	Citigroup	38.2
6. Mark V. Hurd	Hewlett-Packard	34.0
7. Jack A. Fusco	Calpine	32.7
8. Rupert Murdoch	News Corp	30.1
9. David M. Cote	Honeywell	28.7
10. Alan G. Lafley	Proctor and Gamble	25.6

Source: "Executive Pay: A Special Report," New York Times, 5 April 2009, B12.

YOU DECIDE

Limiting Executive Compensation

Contrary to general assumptions about equality in the United States, executives of leading companies often make more than three hundred times the wages earned by the average worker in those companies. Although some shareholders had voiced concerns about executive pay prior to the financial crisis, most Americans believed that executives should be rewarded for their responsibilities. As the financial crisis deepened, the global economy weakened, unemployment rose, and household wealth declined; as individuals became more financially insecure, they began to focus more on income inequality, especially on the gap between the super rich and the middle class. When General Motors, AIG, and several Wall Street banks were deemed too big to fail because of their impact on the global economy in general and the U.S. economy in particular, the U.S. government created a stimulus package to prevent them from failing. Ultimately, the American taxpayers owned roughly 80 percent of AIG and 70 percent of General Motors. As the global recession deepened, popular demands for limiting executive pay in companies supported by taxpayers became more vociferous and widespread. Senator Charles Grassley, a senior Republican, said that senior AIG executives should apologize Japanese-style and then perhaps commit suicide. Government officials demanded that bonuses be returned or taxed at 100 percent. There were demonstrations outside executives' homes. The U.S. government and governments around the world struggled with the idea of imposing limits on executive compensation.

1. Should governments impose limits on executive pay? Make arguments for and against limiting executive compensation.
2. What are some implications of public ownership of private companies? ■

the phenomenal growth of global trade. Much of the surplus of money in the global system also came from declining investment in the Asian economies following the 1997 financial crisis. Rising oil prices in the Middle East, Russia, and elsewhere enabled many countries to earn more money than they could spend rationally. By the end of 2008, central banks in emerging economies held $5 trillion in reserves.[18]

The money supply increased rapidly in China, India, Russia, and the Persian Gulf states. Whereas it was generally assumed that global monetary policies were set by central banks in the United States, Europe, and Japan, the reality was that three-fifths of the world's money supply growth flowed from emerging economies.[19] Based on their experiences with financial problems, many developing countries decided to save for a rainy day, as it were. They believed that high oil prices or trade surpluses would not last forever. As Table 7.2 indicates, many of these countries created **sovereign wealth funds** to recycle their financial surpluses. It is estimated that by 2012 these funds will be worth roughly $10 trillion, or 3 percent of global traded securities. Several Wall Street firms, such as Merrill Lynch and Citigroup, had to borrow from sovereign wealth funds in 2008.[20]

Sovereign Wealth Funds ■ Created by countries to save and recycle surplus revenues

Subprime Loans ■ High-risk credit given to individuals who fail to meet rigorous standards

Subprime Loans

Another major cause of the financial crisis was the availability of subprime loans, which were directly an outgrowth of easy credit. **Subprime loans** generally refer to credit given to individuals who fail to meet rigorous standards usually expected by

TABLE 7.2

SOVEREIGN WEALTH FUNDS (2008)

Country: Name	Assets ($ Billions)	Inception Year
UAE: Abu Dhabi Investment Authority	875.0	1976
Norway: Government Pension Fund—Global	380.0	1996
Singapore: GIC	330.0	1981
Saudi Arabia: various	300.0	Na
Kuwait: Reserve Fund for Future Generations	250.0	1953
China: China Investment Corporation	200.0	2007
Singapore: Temasek Holdings	159.2	1974
Libya: Oil Reserve Fund	50.0	2005
Qatar: Qatar Inv. Auth.	50.0	2005
Algeria: Fond de Régulation des Recettes	42.6	2000
U.S.: Alaska Permanent Fund Corporation	38.0	1976
Brunei: Brunei Inv. Auth.	30.0	1983
Other	171.4	–
Total	**2876.2**	–

Source: "Asset-backed Insecurity," *Economist*, 19 January 2008, 78.

lending institutions. These individuals could not really afford their loans because of inadequate income and poor credit histories. In most cases, borrowers were not required to have a down payment. With excess liquidity globally, interest rates remained low. People with weak financial histories are generally more vulnerable to being charged higher interest rates. For example, poor people pay exorbitant rates for payday loans. A basic reality of finance is that yields on loans are inversely proportional to credit quality: the stronger the borrower, the lower the yield, and vice versa.[21] Driving the demand for subprime loans was the development of a culture of entitlement and a false egalitarianism that appealed to people's egos. Home ownership was pushed by the U.S. government as an inalienable right, despite borrowers' inability to repay loans. **Fannie Mae** (Federal National Mortgage Association) **and Freddie Mac** (Federal Home Loan Mortgage Corporation), both U.S. government corporations, made more money available to lenders and borrowers by purchasing loans from the lenders and selling them to investors in the secondary markets. Huge amounts of money gravitated to subprime mortgages in the United States and Europe and, ultimately, to weak borrowers globally. Given the complex interdependence that characterizes financial globalization, problems emanating from subprime loans in the United States rapidly spread around the world. Governments were largely unaware of the risks associated with new forms of financing and were unable to prevent the global financial crisis.[22]

Fannie Mae and Freddie Mac ■ U.S. government corporations involved in real estate

As the unprecedented sums of money flowed into commercial and residential real estate, housing prices escalated. For thirty years before the housing boom, the average American house appreciated at an average of 1.4 percent a year. This low return of prime loans discouraged homeowners from viewing their houses as cash machines. Home-equity lines of credit were not available until recently. Things changed dramatically after 2000. Appreciation rates climbed to 7.6 percent between 2000 and 2006, reaching 11 percent before the market crashed between 2006 and 2007. Real estate prices in California, Arizona, Nevada, Florida, and other areas grew even faster.

There was a wide variety of subprime mortgages. These included adjustable-rate mortgages, balloon mortgages, piggyback loans, and interest-only loans. An **adjustable-rate mortgage** is a long-term loan that does not have a fixed interest rate. The interest can be changed, with low rates at the beginning and high rates at the end. It is also possible, but highly unlikely, that rates could decline. Adjustable-rate mortgages were attractive to homebuyers who moved frequently. They were less expensive, or so it seemed, than fixed-rate mortgages, which offered more protection. A variation of the adjustable-rate mortgage is a balloon mortgage. Under this arrangement, lower payments are made on a loan for five to ten years, with a final installment, or balloon payment, that is significantly larger than earlier payments. Most borrowers could not afford to pay the balloon payment. The piggyback loan allows the homeowner to take out a second mortgage that is piggybacked onto the first mortgage. This is a high-risk loan because it clearly indicates that the borrower cannot afford the down payment to purchase real estate.[23] In an environment that encourages consumption over savings, easy credit fueled the housing crisis. Interest-only loans required borrowers to pay the interest on a loan without reducing the principal balance. This enabled weak borrowers to obtain larger loans.

Adjustable-Rate Mortgage ■ A long-term loan that has varying interest rates

Speculation

A combination of low interest rates, unprecedented liquidity, and a belief that the Internet and various computer technologies virtually guaranteed unending and ever-increasing prosperity facilitated the growth of speculative financial forces. Excessive risk taking replaced caution, which was often equated with a lack of optimism. **Speculation**, a deeply ingrained human characteristic, fosters the development of a herd mentality. As prices continued to rise, even the most cautious individuals get caught up in speculation. Ultimately, a speculative bubble is created. *Speculative bubbles generally go through four stages:*

Speculation ■ Involves excessive risk taking, excessive optimism, and the development of a herd mentality

1. A new technology or invention changes people's expectations and those who are well informed try to profit from it.
2. Prices or profits continue to rise, which draws more people into the market.
3. The boom passes into euphoria and rational decision-making is suspended.
4. The bust is almost inevitable. Prices and profits fall, companies and individuals go bankrupt, and the economy plunges into a recession.[24]

Taxpayer Relief Act of 1997 ■ Exempted profits from taxes gained from selling one's home

Many homeowners became speculators. In addition to low-interest loans and financial innovations in the housing market, political pressures to reduce taxes, including real estate taxes, contributed to the housing boom. Congress passed the **Taxpayer Relief Act of 1997**, which, among other things, exempted profits realized from the sale of a home if the home was owned and used as a principal residence for two of the last five years before it was sold. This new provision enabled home-owners to exclude up to $500,000 for couples and $250,000 for singles from capital gains tax. In many cases, removal of the capital gains tax encouraged home buyers to engage in a form of speculation known as **flipping**. The buyer would own the house for a short period with the sole intention of selling it very quickly for a higher price, thereby gaining a significant profit without much effort and by using very little of his or her own money as an investment. When the stock market crashed in 2000, real estate became more attractive to investors. Furthermore, the shock of the terrorist attacks on September 11, 2001, influenced more Americans to seek security in their homes. Consequently, they concentrated their investments in real estate. Because of the huge amounts of money that went into real estate globally and the preponderance of subprime loans and excessive risk taken in home mortgages, the housing crisis was at the epicenter of the global financial crisis.

Flipping ■ A form of speculation

THE IMPACT OF THE GLOBAL FINANCIAL CRISIS

As we mentioned earlier, the global financial crisis affected virtually all areas, including the process of globalization. Housing prices crashed; foreclosures became commonplace; unemployment reached 10 percent in the United States and higher levels in Europe and elsewhere; manufacturing declined sharply, especially in the automotive industry; students were faced with higher costs as colleges suffered financial losses; finding jobs after college became more challenging; and a global recession created widespread hardships. On the other hand, many developing countries that took a prudent approach to finance and

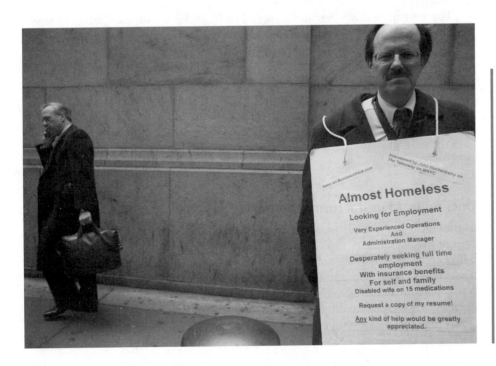

Paul Nawrocki, a former operations manager for a toy manufacturer, commutes to mid-town Manhattan wearing a sign saying "almost homeless" and handing out his resume in search of a decent job with health care benefits for his wife.

saved money were not as badly damaged. In fact, countries that did not fully embrace financial liberalization were less affected than those that gave in to American pressure to fully engage in financial globalization. We also saw a global power shift, with the United States losing ground to China, India, Brazil, and other developing countries.

Foreclosures

Plunging real estate prices affected virtually all areas of the economy. People could no longer afford to purchase homes, which meant that homebuilders were forced to abandon construction projects. Think of all the products that are used in building and furnishing a home; all of the industries that produced these products generally experienced declining sales. Because houses became primary sources of wealth or perceptions of wealth, falling real estate prices made homeowners feel less economically secure. In a vicious circle, the economic recession, fueled by declining real estate markets, further eroded demand for real estate. But, mortgages must be repaid or the consequences can be severe. Despite decreasing home values, homeowners must continue to pay real estate taxes and spend money on maintenance. Many homes were bought at prices much higher than their actual worth just two or three years later. For example, a house purchased in Phoenix in 2006 for $225,000 sold for $110,000 in 2008. Housing prices in parts of California, Arizona, Nevada, and Florida declined by 60 percent or more. Banks also suffer financial losses when homeowners can no longer afford to repay loans. It is estimated that each foreclosure costs lenders $50,000.[25] Rising levels of unemployment also pushed homeowners with strong credit into foreclosure.

The mortgage crisis inevitably spread to financial institutions, causing reputable Wall Street firms such as Lehman Brothers to collapse overnight. Because of Lehman's pivotal role in finance, its demise in September 2008 is generally perceived as the most tangible evidence of the financial crisis on Wall Street. Iceland, which had a very successful banking system, saw its economy and currency collapse along with the banking system. Ireland, widely regarded as the Celtic tiger for its rapid economic growth, experienced a deep recession. American consumers, the backbone of the United States and, to some extent, the global economy, had exhausted their resources and had a savings rate that was close to zero.

Decline in Manufacturing and Trade

Manufacturing, already in decline, fell dramatically. This especially was the case in the automotive industry, with General Motors and Chrysler declaring bankruptcy after closing many factories and dealerships, despite unprecedented financial support from the U.S. government. Industrial production was down by 12 percent in Europe, 11 percent in the United States, and 43 percent in Taiwan. Tightening credit and consumer fear ultimately created a downward spiral that significantly diminished global trade. Germany saw its exports drop by 20 percent. China's exports fell by more than 25 percent and U.S. exports fell by almost 24 percent in 2008.[26]

Global Power Shift

Another major impact of the global financial crisis is a global power shift. Although most countries were negatively affected by the financial crisis and global recession, some emerged stronger than others. Brazil, Russia, India, and China, also known as the **BRIC countries**, enhanced their power vis-à-vis the United States, Western Europe, and Japan. In sharp contrast to the policies adopted by the U.S. Federal Reserve under Chairman Alan Greenspan, the Reserve Bank of India, led by **Yaga Venugobal Reddy**, rejected many financial innovations and limited the participation of foreign investors in India's financial system. Instead of believing that markets are self-regulating, as many Americans do, the Indian government favored regulations and was quick to recognize financial bubbles. Reddy restricted bank lending to real estate developers, increased the amount of money banks had to set aside as reserves, and blocked the use of some derivatives. This conservative approach enabled India to largely avoid the global financial crisis.[27] Given America's role in pressuring the world to adopt a financial system that failed, BRIC countries perceive the financial crisis as a serious economic and political setback for the United States and free-market capitalism. All of these countries, sensing America's vulnerabilities, are becoming more politically and financially assertive. From their perspective, America is declining. It has escalating budget deficits, it is extremely dependent on foreign creditors such as China, and the dollar's status as the main global reserve currency has eroded. As we saw in Chapter 2, America's economic power following World War II enabled it to shape global financial institutions such as the International Monetary Fund (IMF) and the World Bank. As Table 7.3 shows,

BRIC Countries ■ Brazil, Russia, India, and China; emerging global powers

Yaga Venugobal Reddy ■ Governor of the Reserve Bank of India; credited with helping India avoid the financial crisis

TABLE 7.3

VOTING POWER IN THE IMF

Country	Existing Share (%)	Proposed Share (%)
United States	16.77	16.73
Japan	6.02	6.23
Britain	4.86	4.29
France	4.86	4.29
China	3.66	3.81
Russia	2.69	2.39
Belgium	2.09	1.86
India	1.89	2.34
South Korea	1.38	1.36
Brazil	1.38	1.72

Source: Economist, 11 April 2009, 72.

TABLE 7.4

GROWTH OF FOREIGN BANKS IN THE UNITED STATES

Leading Banks (1999)	Share of Market (%)	Leading Banks (2009)	Share of Market (%)
1. Citi (U.S.)	13.9	J.P. Morgan (U.S.)	14.8
2. Merrill Lynch (U.S.)	13.7	Citi (U.S.)	14.7
3. Goldman Sachs (U.S.)	10.4	Bank of America Merrill Lynch (U.S.)	12.9
4. Morgan Stanley (U.S.)	10.4	Morgan Stanley (U.S.)	10.4
5. Lehman Brothers (U.S.)	8.2	Goldman Sachs (U.S.)	8.8
6. Chase Manhattan (U.S.)	7.3	Barclays Capital (British)	7.1
7. Credit Suisse First Boston (Swiss)	6.0	HSBC (British)	4.5
8. J.P. Morgan (U.S.)	6.2	Deutsche Bank (German)	4.2
9. Donaldson Lufkin Jenrette (U.S.)	4.9	Credit Suisse (Swiss)	4.1
10. Bear Stearns (U.S.)	4.6	RBS (Scotland)	3.7

Source: Graham Bowley, "Stalking a Weaker Wall Street," *New York Times*, 17 June 2009, B1.

the BRIC countries are now challenging America's leadership.[28] Another indication of a power shift is the growing role of foreign banks in America's financial system, as indicated in Table 7.4.

GLOBAL RESPONSES TO THE FINANCIAL CRISIS
America's Response

Responses to the global financial crisis varied from country to country, with the strongest actions occurring in the United States. Being largely responsible for the crisis, the United States was not only the most severely affected, but also the most shell shocked and anxious to find solutions. In a sharp reversal of its strong commitment to economic and financial liberalization and free-market capitalism, the United States has led efforts to nationalize its financial and some aspects of its manufacturing sectors to an unprecedented degree. There was general consensus among Republicans and Democrats that a massive financial and economic stimulus package, engineered primarily by Secretary of the Treasury **Henry Paulson**, was essential not just to rescue America's financial institutions but to reassure Americans that their savings and investments were secure. A $787 billion **stimulus package** was passed by Congress. Because the financial crisis was reminiscent of the Great Depression, with its high levels of unemployment and massive withdrawals from banks, the U.S. government responded to avoid repeating the mistakes of the 1930s. Despite various protections implemented to insure the safety of deposits, such as the FDIC, Americans withdrew $150 billion from money market funds over a two-day period in September 2008, compared to average weekly outflows of roughly $5 billion.[29] The huge amount of money

Henry Paulson ■
U.S. Secretary of the Treasury who initiated the stimulus package to rescue banks on Wall Street

Stimulus Package ■
Money allocated by governments to financial institutions and selected industries to prevent their collapse and reinvigorate economic growth

poured into credit markets and banks was designed to restore confidence in financial institutions and to expand credit.

European Responses

Although other countries also implemented stimulus packages, their concerns differed to a significant degree from those of the United States. Germany, for example, resisted American pressure to adopt a more comprehensive, coordinated global stimulus package, partly because many Germans believe that the crisis was primarily an outgrowth of American financial policies and would have to be solved domestically. Germans worry about the possibility of hyperinflation, which the country experienced in the 1920s. Germans are also more frugal than Americans and are reluctant to impose huge deficits on future generations, especially in light of Germany's shrinking population. Europeans in general took a less-frantic approach to the financial crisis because in normal times their governments had created numerous **safety nets**. European governments provide national health insurance and generous pensions, and they have implemented programs to reduce unemployment and lost wages. Although Europeans are negatively affected by the financial crisis, their safety nets have diminished their fears. Because they save a greater percentage of their income, at reduced levels, they have avoided losing their homes on such a massive scale as is the case in the United States.[30]

safety nets ■ The health insurance, pensions and other programs European governments provide citizens that lessen losses in economic hard times

China's Response

China's response involved taking measures to strengthen its power vis-à-vis the United States. Unlike the United States, China regulates its financial institutions, has more than $2 trillion in reserves, and continues to have economic growth rates in excess of 7 percent, and the Chinese save more than 40 percent of their income. Despite rising unemployment and declining exports, China emerged from the financial crisis in a strong position and is taking advantage of new opportunities created by the crisis. China is using its $600 billion economic stimulus package to improve its infrastructure, to help its companies to become more competitive domestically and globally, and to enhance research and development. It is also gaining greater access to resources and augmenting its relations in Latin America, Africa, the Middle East, and elsewhere, even as the United States is preoccupied with its financial and economic crises as well as with fighting wars in Iraq and Afghanistan. China is also acquiring European and American companies in the automotive, textile, food, energy, machinery, electronics, and environmental protection sectors.[31] One of the most visible acquisitions is the Hummer from General Motors.

Financial Regulations

In light of the general consensus among experts that deregulation and the lax enforcement of regulations in the financial sector contributed significantly to the global financial crisis, an immediate response to the crash was to try to strengthen and update regulations. The chairman of the U.S. Federal Reserve, **Ben S. Bernanke,** was particularly aware of the need for new regulations. As a professor at Princeton

Ben S. Bernanke ■ Chairman of the U.S. Federal Reserve

Bank for International Settlements ■ Based in Basel, Switzerland; created to regulate banking and harmonize banking standards

University, Bernanke focused his research on the Great Depression. The American government was now determined to avoid mistakes made during that financial and economic crisis. Efforts to enact international banking regulations began with the creation of the **Bank for International Settlements**, based in Basel, Switzerland. In 1988, the banking community signed the Basel Capital Accord, which attempted to harmonize banking standards, especially those requiring banks to set aside capital to cover the level of risk they faced. However, due to the dominant influence of bankers, the Bank for International Settlements was not very focused on regulations.[32] Since 1999, there has been a greater effort to develop a stronger regulatory framework, known as Basel 2. The new accord gives credit-rating agencies an explicit role in determining how much capital is enough to cover certain risks.[33] But, the failures of financial institutions in the United States, Europe, and elsewhere demonstrate that individual countries' unwillingness or inability to supervise their financial sectors was at the heart of the problem. Consequently, domestic regulatory reforms are likely to be more effective than global regulations. Financial innovations such as derivatives and executive compensation are the primary targets for greater supervision. However, the complex nature of the global financial system and strong reservations in the United States about the government's role in the economy will most likely diminish the effectiveness of regulations.

SUMMARY AND REVIEW

The global financial crisis of 2008–2009 ushered in the most severe global recession since the Great Depression of the 1930s. Given the central role played by finances in globalization, the crisis has serious implications for virtually all global issues and for globalization itself. Although this chapter argues that financial crises seem to be an integral component of capitalism, human beings are ultimately responsible for creating them. Revolutions in computer and telecommunications technologies fostered the development of complex financial engineering that radically altered the global financial system. An emphasis on government deregulation, the growth of a culture that encouraged quick profits and excessive executive compensation, and the availability of low interest rates played significant roles in creating the financial crisis. But a crisis presents both dangers and opportunities. While the United States has suffered severe setbacks, China has gained, thereby shifting global power. The financial crisis has significantly reduced global trade and caused unprecedented home foreclosures and high levels of unemployment. The global response has centered around regulating some of the financial innovations, paying greater attention to risk management, and monitoring executive compensation. Overall, the financial crisis has diminished support for financial liberalization and strengthened the role of governments around the world in economic affairs.

KEY TERMS

finance 149
Asian financial crisis 149
Federal Deposit Insurance
  Corporation (FDIC) 150

global financial
  liberalization 150
Glass-Steagall Act of
  1933 151

financial innovations 151
securitization 152
derivatives 152
credit default swaps 152

DISCUSSION QUESTIONS

1. Discuss how deregulation of financial markets and low interest rates contributed to creating the financial crisis.
2. Discuss the implications of the stimulus package for the United States. In light of the benefits derived from Europe's safety net, discuss the pros and cons of America's adoption of European policies, such as universal health care and job protection.
3. Discuss the role of subprime loans in real estate in the financial crisis.
4. In your view, has the financial crisis weakened the United States globally and strengthened China? Discuss.
5. Evaluate the global responses to the financial crisis.

SUGGESTED READINGS

Ahamed, Liaquat. *Lords of Finance.* New York: Penguin Press, 2009.
Altman, Roger C. "The Great Crash, 2008," *Foreign Affairs* 88, No. 1 (January/February 2009): 2–14.
Helleiner, Eric, and Jonathan Kirshner, eds. *The Future of the Dollar.* Ithaca, NY: Cornell University Press, 2009.
Kuttner, Robert. *The Squandering of America.* New York: Alfred A. Knopf, 2007.
Partnoy, Frank. *Infectious Greed.* New York: Times Books, 2003.
Smick, David M. *The World Is Curved.* New York: Portfolio, 2008.
Wolf, Martin. *Fixing Global Finance.* Baltimore: Johns Hopkins University Press, 2009.

END NOTES

1. "The Financial Crisis," *Economist*, 17 January 2009, 81.
2. Liaquat Ahamed, *Lords of Finance* (New York: Penguin Press, 2009), 14.
3. Jadish Bhagwati, *In Defense of Globalization* (New York: Oxford University Press, 2004), 199.
4. Antonia Juhasz, *The Bush Agenda* (New York: Regan Books, 2006), 47.
5. John C. Bogle, *The Battle for the Soul of Capitalism* (New Haven, CT: Yale University Press, 2005), 3.
6. Robert Kuttner, *The Squandering of America* (New York: Alfred A. Knopf, 2007), 68.
7. Robert B. Reich, *Supercapitalism* (New York: Alfred A. Knopf, 2007), 96.
8. Kuttner, *The Squandering of America*, 250.
9. Frank Partnoy, *Infectious Greed* (New York: Times Books, 2003), 3.
10. Simon Johnson, "The Quiet Coup," *The Atlantic*, May 2009, 52.
11. "The Rules of the Game," *Economist*, 15 September 2007, 16.
12. David M. Smick, *The World Is Curved* (New York: Portfolio, 2008), 44.

13. "Too Big to Swallow," *Economist*, 16 May 2009, 11.

14. Partnoy, *Infectious Greed*, 374.

15. Kuttner, *The Squandering of America*, 106.

16. Virginia B. Morris and Kenneth A. Morris, *Dictionary of Financial Terms* (New York: Lightbulb Press, 2008), 12.

17. Partnoy, *Infectious Greed*, 157.

18. "A Monetary Malaise," *Economist*, 11 October 2008, 22.

19. "Central Banks in the Rich World No Longer Determine Global Monetary Conditions," *Economist*, 11 August 2007, 70.

20. "Asset-Backed Insecurity," *Economist*, 19 January 2008, 79.

21. Roger C. Altman, "The Great Crash, 2008," *Foreign Affairs* 88, No. 1 (January/February 2009), 4.

22. Altman, "The Great Crash, 2008," 4.

23. Blanche Evans, *Bubbles, Booms, and Busts* (New York: McGraw-Hill, 2007), 19.

24. John Cassidy, *dot.con: The Greatest Story Ever Sold* (New York: HarperCollins, 2002), 5; and Charles P. Kindleberger and Robert Aliber, *Manias, Panics, and Crashes: A History of Financial Crises* (New York: Wiley, 2005), 29.

25. Peter S. Goodman and Jack Healy, "Job Losses Push Safer Mortgages to Foreclosure," *New York Times*, 25 May 2009, A1.

26. Nelson D. Schwartz, "Rapid Declines in Manufacturing Spread Global Anxiety," *New York Times*, 20 March 2009, B1.

27. Vikas Bajaj, "In India, Central Banker Played It Safe," *New York Times*, 26 June 2009, B4.

28. Clifford J. Levy, "Seeking Greater Financial Clout, Emerging Powers Prepare to Meet in Russia," *New York Times*, 16 June 2009, A5.

29. Altman, "The Great Crash, 2008," 5.

30. Nicholas Kulish, "Europe, Aided by Safety Nets, Resists U.S. Push on Stimulus," *New York Times*, 27 March 2009, A1.

31. Keith Bradsher, "In Downturn, China Exploits Path to Growth," *New York Times*, 17 March 2009, A1.

32. Kuttner, *The Squandering of America*, 251.

33. "Bank Regulation: Uphill Work," *Economist*, 8 September 2007, 76.

Global Trade

INTRODUCTION

The origins of global trade are as old as human society. Lacking complete self-sufficiency, human beings traded goods and services within their communities and gradually expanded trade with people in distant areas. Global trade clearly shows the political, economic, and cultural aspects of globalization. Global trade is so integral to our daily lives that we are generally oblivious to how it links us to the rest of the world. Some of our most important agricultural crops are not native to North America. In fact, it is difficult to think of a country that has not been affected by the transfer of food crops from some distant area. The global economic crisis of 2008–2009 reinforced concerns and debates about global trade.

The story of *sugarcane* vividly illustrates this point, as Figure 8.1 shows. More than eight thousand years ago, inhabitants of New Guinea, located north of Australia, discovered that grass, similar to bamboo, not only was sweet but could be easily cultivated by planting segments of it. This was the beginning of the global sugar trade, a development that would profoundly affect most of the world. Human craving for sweet foods facilitated the spread of sugarcane from New Guinea across Southeast Asia to India, which began producing crystal sugar around 500 B.C. Traders soon took sugarcane from India to China and Persia (now Iran). The spread of Islam from Saudi Arabia to Egypt, across North Africa, and into the Mediterranean and Spain was accompanied by the spread of sugar cultivation.

Spanish and Portuguese colonization of the Americas marked a turning point in the cultivation, production, and consumption of sugar. Widely regarded by Europeans as a luxury product, sugarcane was soon cultivated on a massive scale throughout the Caribbean and Latin America. Requiring intensive labor, sugarcane cultivation fueled the trans-Atlantic slave trade and numerous conflicts among European countries for control of the sugar-producing Caribbean islands. For example, France gave its territory in Canada

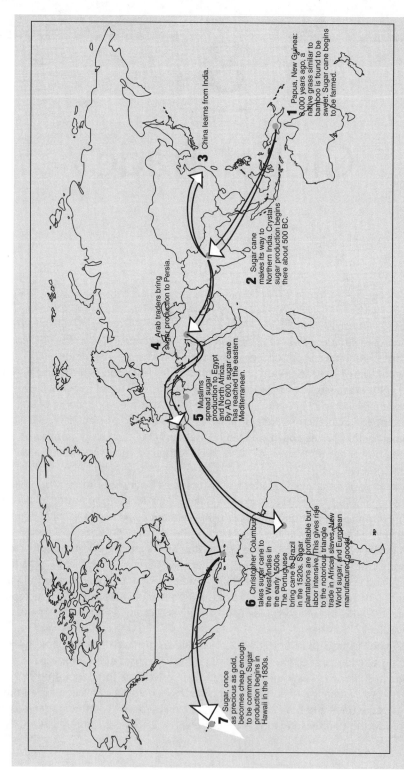

FIGURE 8.1

The Global Spread of Sugar

Sources: Kenneth Kiple and Kriemhild Omelas, eds., *The Cambridge World History of Food* (Cambridge: Cambridge University Press, 2000); and *Christian Science Monitor*, 5 August 2003, 18.

to Britain partly in exchange for the two sugar-growing islands of Martinique and Guadeloupe under the **Treaty of Paris of 1763**, which ended the Seven Years' War between the two European powers. By the 1830s, sugar cultivation spread to Hawaii, thereby completing its journey around the world and becoming a significant part of our diet. Our lives are increasingly affected by the webs of global interdependence that are integral parts of global trade. What's more, the ability of countries to control their economic activities is steadily being eroded by economic globalization.[1]

Many scholars have concluded that global trade and other aspects of globalization are transforming the functions of states. They see a shift in power away from countries to global companies and point to taxing power, an essential component of national sovereignty, to illustrate their point. Many countries attract foreign investments by offering numerous concessions. As Lester Thurow put it, "High profile multinational companies no longer pay taxes to governments. Governments pay taxes to them."[2] Even more important is the weakening of traditional bonds between citizens and governments, a development that is partly due to the state's retreat from providing essential services and the growing trend toward the privatization of even national security functions, such as housing and feeding military forces. One scholar, Kenichi Ohmae, contends that "the nation-state has become an unnatural, even dysfunctional, unit for organizing human activity and managing economic endeavor in a borderless world."[3] Instead of traditional states based on Westphalian sovereignty, Ohmae sees the development of *region states*. The boundaries of the region state are not determined by geopolitical considerations. Instead, they are drawn by "the deft but invisible hand of the global market for goods and services and follow real flows of human activity. Region states are natural economic zones." However, the global economic crisis of 2008–2009 diminished global trade and enhanced the role of the state in virtually all aspects of economic life.[4]

This chapter examines the growth of free trade, concerns about trade deficits and surpluses among countries, and how budget deficits and the relative value of currencies affect global trade. We will discuss various trade disputes and how those disputes are resolved by emerging global institutions. Finally, we will discuss the impact of trade on the environment and the global spread of diseases and their implications for global trade and trade blocs. There is growing recognition that the global marketplace, left to itself, will not automatically produce wealth and prosperity for developing countries and poorer regions within developed countries unless there is rule-making and new structures diminish the potential for destructiveness.[5]

THE GLOBALIZATION OF FREE TRADE

Although discussions of free trade generally start with the repeal of the Corn Laws in Britain in 1846, trade among different groups and countries started much earlier. As early as the third century B.C., various nomadic groups and Chinese merchants established a trading route known as the **Silk Road**. Linking China with the West, the Silk Road served as a commercial and cultural bridge between the two regions. The spread of Islam from Saudi Arabia to North Africa and the Middle East and across Asia and reaching as far as Indonesia (the most populous

Treaty of Paris of 1763 ■ Ended the Seven Years' War between France and Britain

Silk Road ■ Trade route linking China with the West

Mercantilist Model ■ Trade model stressing the role of government in trade and empha- sizing the impor- tance of balance-of- payment surpluses

Autarky ■ Ideology promoting economic national self-suffi- ciency and an end to economic interaction with other countries

Comparative Advantage ■ Theory that each country specializes in produc- ing specific products in order to better trade with other states

Competitive Advan- tage ■ Shift toward the production of goods and services based on cost con- siderations, arbitrary specialization, and government and corporate policies

Strategic Trade Theory ■ Supports government subsi- dies of private industry

Muslim country) was accompanied by trade. But trade in Europe, Asia, and else-where was often restricted by protectionist measures imposed by governments. Many governments adopted the **mercantilist model** of trade. It stressed the role of government in trade and emphasized the importance of balance-of-payment sur-pluses in trade with other countries. At the extreme is **autarky**, which promotes economic national self-sufficiency.

Removing impediments to the free flow of goods and services among countries is the foundation of *free trade* or *trade liberalization*. The consensus among advo-cates of free trade is that it reduces prices, raises the standard of living for more people, makes a wider variety of products available, and contributes to improve-ments in the quality of goods and services. Adam Smith, David Ricardo, and other economists believed that by removing barriers to the free movement of goods among countries, as well as within them, countries would be encouraged to spe-cialize in producing certain products, thereby contributing to the optimum utiliza-tion of resources such as land, labor, capital, and entrepreneurial ability. If countries focused on what they do best and freely trade their goods with each other, all of them would benefit. David Ricardo (1772–1823), a British economist, best articulated this concept, known as **comparative advantage**. Ricardo explained, for example, how it was more economically advantageous for Britain to produce cloth and for Portugal to produce wine, as long as they engaged in free trade.

The theory of comparative advantage has been undermined by the current wave of economic globalization. The growth of transnational or multinational corporations (MNCs) complicates global trading. The production of goods and services is strongly influenced by costs, arbitrary specialization, and government and corporate policies. These developments mark a shift from the conventional theory of comparative advantage to what is known as **competitive advantage**.[6] Despite global acceptance of the concept of free trade, governments continue to engage in protectionism. For example, the European Union (EU) and the United States each support their own commercial aircraft industries so that those indus-tries can compete more effectively in a market dominated by a few companies. The idea of assisting such industries, which represents a departure from free trade, is known as the **strategic trade theory**.[7]

Movement toward free trade occurs because of a consensus that free trade is more beneficial to more countries and individuals than its alternatives. This is demonstrated by Britain's repeal of its Corn Laws and the United States' retreat from protectionism. In 1815, the British Parliament passed the *Corn Laws* to pro-tect the wealthy producers of grain from foreign competition, thereby ensuring that the landed upper classes would receive high prices for their crops. Simultane-ously, Britain promoted exports of its manufactured products to Europe, the United States, and its colonies. However, it became increasingly apparent that Britain could not produce sufficient food to feed its population and that the United States and European countries were adopting their own protectionist poli-cies to safeguard their infant industries from British manufactured products. The Irish potato blight and the accompanying famine highlighted the dangerous and deadly consequences of Britain's policy of keeping food prices artificially high to protect upper-class interests. Outraged by widespread starvation, Britain's trade liberals, inspired by Ricardo's theory of comparative advantage, formed the

Anti-Corn Law League to influence Britain to repeal the Corn Laws and to unilaterally adopt free-trade policies, regardless of whether other countries reciprocated. To a large extent, Britain's global leadership enabled it to induce other countries to adopt free-trade practices by setting the example. Britain's repeal of the Corn Laws and the *Navigation Acts* in 1846, which restricted the transport of goods to British ships, brought about the first period of relatively free trade among Western countries.

Trade protectionism did not retreat completely, however. By the end of the nineteenth century, many countries engaged in trade protectionism. The outbreak of World War I radically altered the global economic system and led to increased international economic instability. Widespread international economic problems that came with the onset of the *Great Depression* in 1929 influenced many countries to pursue autarky and protectionism. The enactment of the *Smoot-Hawley Tariff Act* in the United States in 1930, designed to protect American industries and trade, ultimately influenced other countries to increase their own tariffs. This development worsened global economic conditions. Attempting to diminish the negative economic consequences, the United States moved away from its protectionist policies by enacting the **Reciprocal Trade Agreement Act** of 1934, which authorized the president to negotiate substantial tariff reductions on a reciprocal and *bilateral* (i.e., between two countries) basis with other countries.[8] The rapid decline in global trade between World War I and World War II strongly influenced the United States and Western Europe to embrace freer trade. This realization restrained states from embracing protectionism on a large scale during the 2008–2009 global economic recession.

At the *Bretton Woods Conference* in New Hampshire in 1944, the United States and its allies created (1) the **International Monetary Fund (IMF)** to manage exchange rates and payment imbalances among nations and (2) the **International Bank for Reconstruction and Development (World Bank)** to supplement private capital for international investment, with an emphasis on the reconstruction of Western Europe. American and European concerns about the negative consequences of protectionism and their strong desire to promote free trade led to the establishment of the **General Agreement on Tariffs and Trade (GATT)** in 1947 to serve as a negotiating forum for the reduction of tariffs and other barriers to trade. The original goal was to establish the International Trade Organization (ITO). However, American dissatisfaction with restrictions the ITO placed primarily on the United States led the U.S. Senate to reject it. GATT was then established as a second-choice organization that did not require the same degree of Senate support as did the treaty establishing the ITO. GATT was not a treaty.

There were several *premises*, or assumptions, of *GATT*. These included

1. Multilateral negotiations (involving many countries) are preferable to bilateral negotiations (between two nations) on trade issues.
2. Private economic actors are preferable to governments for conducting and managing international trade.
3. Free trade ultimately benefits the global society.
4. Governments distort the operation of the free market and should minimize their involvement.

Reciprocal Trade Agreement Act ■ Authorized the president to negotiate tariff reductions on a bilateral basis

IMF ■ Created to manage exchange rates and payment imbalances among nations

World Bank ■ Created to supplement private capital for international investment, originally with the intent of reconstructing Europe

GATT ■ Created in 1947 to promote free trade and to reduce tariffs and other trade barriers

Between 1947 and 1992, various meetings of GATT (known as rounds) resulted in significant reductions in tariffs and freer trade. However, GATT covered manufactured products but excluded trade in agriculture and services. The **Uruguay Round** (meetings of GATT held in Uruguay from 1986 to 1992) added services and agriculture to the global trade framework and replaced GATT with the World Trade Organization (WTO) in 1993.

Uruguay Round ■ Meetings that replaced the GATT with the WTO

Although the premises of GATT continue to be the foundations of global trade liberalization, the *WTO differs significantly from GATT*. To a much greater extent than GATT, the WTO directly challenges fundamental aspects of national sovereignty by diminishing both the national barriers to global trade and governments' economic activities. For example, when China joined the WTO in 2001, it was required to make its domestic market more accessible to foreign competition and to privatize its state-owned industries. On the other hand, China benefited from provisions of the Most-Favored Nation Clause that was a key component of GATT. This clause reduces trade discrimination among members. WTO rules apply to activities generally regarded as domestic policies and beyond the reach of international regulations. Compared with GATT, the WTO is much more powerful in terms of governing global commerce and is empowered to settle trade disputes among countries. For example, tariffs imposed by President George W. Bush on steel imports in 2002 were judged by the WTO to violate global trade rules. Agreements establishing the WTO extended GATT rules to cover agriculture, consumer services (restaurants, hotels, travel agencies, and so on), producer services (investment, banking, insurance, **intellectual property rights**, or the control people have over their artistic, creative, scientific, industrial, and educational inventions, and data processing), textiles, clothing, telecommunications, labor standards, and the environment. They also call for greater transparency in writing product standards and testing procedures and in soliciting bids on government contracts.[9] For example, when the United States decided to limit bids on contracts for rebuilding Iraq in 2003 to countries that supported the war, countries that opposed the war, such as Germany and France, complained that America was violating WTO rules. WTO regulations also reduced or eliminated many import quotas and subsidies. For example, the *Multifiber Agreement*, an international arrangement concluded in 1974, used import quotas to regulate the more than $350 billion world trade in garments to benefit many developing countries and to protect domestic industries. Because such arrangements violate WTO rules, the Multifiber Agreement was allowed to expire in 2004.

Intellectual Property Rights ■ Control that people and corporations have over artistic, creative, scientific, industrial, and educational inventions

The 142 member countries of the WTO met in Doha, Qatar, in 2001 to further reduce barriers to trade. The **Doha Agreement**, which reflected the growing power of developing countries regarding trade issues, relaxed patent protection for brand-name drugs by giving poor countries the right to make inexpensive generic medicines patented by global pharmaceutical corporations. Brazil, India, and many other developing countries, especially those ravaged by AIDS, viewed this concession as an important victory.[10] However, resistance to certain aspects of trade globalization in the developing world led to the collapse of the 2003 WTO meeting in Cancun, Mexico. At the heart of the controversy was the extent to which domestic industries should be protected from foreign competition. In 2008, the Doha Round of WTO negotiations ended in failure. The global economic recession of 2008–2009, which sharply reduced global trade, put these issues on the back burner.

Doha Agreement ■ Relaxed patent protection for brand-name drugs by allowing poor countries to manufacture generic medicines

Exchange Rates, Budget Deficits, and Trade

The **exchange rate** for a currency is how much of one country's money can be bought with a specified amount of another country's money.[11] The business section of major newspapers show that the values of currencies fluctuate constantly as a result of trading in foreign exchange markets, just as the values of stocks fluctuate on stock markets. The strength or weakness of currencies is determined by supply and demand, as is the case with commodities. Supply and demand can often be influenced by deliberate actions of governments and their central banks to buy or sell currencies, thereby affecting the price of currencies.

The relative values of currencies directly affect global trade and domestic economies. A weak dollar (weak relative to other currencies) increases prices for imports in the United States. But a weak dollar also makes American exports less expensive in foreign markets, which stimulates economic productivity in the United States. More jobs are created and trade deficits with other countries decline. It allows American manufacturers to more effectively compete with less expensive imported manufactured products. But not all countries allow their currencies to fluctuate, which complicates the positive effects of a weak American dollar. China, for example, is likely to continue to have a trade surplus with the United States as long as its currency, which is somewhat pegged to the U.S. dollar, remains cheap compared with the dollar. Countries can also buy more dollars to increase the dollar's value relative to their own currencies, thereby protecting their exports to both the United States and Europe. A weak U.S. dollar can have substantial negative implications for America. Because the United States is so dependent on imported products—such as electronics, clothing, cars, and petroleum—a weaker dollar ultimately leads to higher consumer prices. Furthermore, huge U.S. budget deficits are funded by a *net inflow of capital* from abroad, meaning that the United States gets more money from other countries than it sends to them. A weak dollar increases demands from China, for example, to replace the dollar as the leading global reserve currency.[12]

Exchange Rate ■
How much of one country's money can be bought with a specified amount of another country's money

Barriers to Free Trade

Even though most countries embrace *trade liberalization* (i.e., the movement toward unrestrained free trade), many governments engage in protectionist practices that impede the global free flow of goods and services. Many contemporary opponents to free trade essentially embrace *neomercantilism* (i.e., a new and more modern version of mercantilism). They argue that protectionism is essential to protect national security. Difficult economic conditions often fuel demands for protectionism, as was the case in 2008–2009. Similarly, many developing countries argue that their need to achieve economic development, which includes economic diversification, justifies implementing protectionist policies. Finally, many antiglobalization activists view free trade as a threat to both the environment and respect for human rights. However, increasing violence against the Roma in Hungary and elsewhere in 2009 underscores that rising unemployment and economic hardships that resulted from a decline in global trade can intensify human rights violations.[13]

For more than forty years, the United States has maintained a trade embargo against Cuba to end the Castro regime and promote democracy that has effectively impeded free trade between the two countries. Furthermore, the United States attempted to pressure other countries, such as Canada and members of the EU, to refrain from engaging in commercial relations with Cuba. These efforts have largely failed. By 2001, domestic pressure influenced the U.S. government to permit the export of surplus American grain and meat to Cuba.[14] Another barrier to free trade is the formation of natural resource cartels, such as the *Organization of Petroleum Exporting Countries (OPEC)*, which deliberately limit supplies to increase prices or impose sanctions on importers to influence their political decisions or to punish them for particular actions.

Do Trade Deficits Matter?

Like millions of Americans who work in the manufacturing sector, Sharon and Michael grew up in families that had a long history of securing reliable jobs that provided enough income to keep them out of poverty. By the time they were eighteen years old, both Sharon and Michael were employed by the local textile company, *Pillowtex*, in Kannapolis, North Carolina. They spent more than twenty years producing sheets and towels with the household names of Cannon and Fieldcrest. Similar to other manufacturing businesses, from electronics to furniture, the textile industry is moving much of its production to China, Mexico, and other developing countries. When Pillowtex decided to join the exodus, more than five thousand employees lost their jobs.[15]

Huge American trade deficits, especially with China, have linked the loss of manufacturing jobs to trade deficits in the minds of many Americans. The persistent rise in the U.S. trade deficit has arisen as a potent social and political issue. The **trade deficit** is the difference between the value of goods and services that a country buys from overseas and the value of goods and services it sells to other countries. The global economic recession led to significant declines in both exports and imports in 2009.[16]

Apart from the loss of manufacturing and service jobs in the United States, trade deficits have other significant consequences. Higher levels of unemployment mean less revenue for the government and higher government expenditures on social services and other benefits for the unemployed. Trade deficits are closely related to budget deficits, although many other factors contribute to the large U.S. budget deficit, which climbed to $1.4 trillion in 2009. To pay for its trade and budget deficits, the United States borrows money from foreign investors, such as China and Japan, and global financial institutions. This reliance on foreign capital to pay for debt makes America vulnerable to pressure from abroad.[17] Having a trade deficit in the United States means that other countries have a **trade surplus**; that is, the value of the goods and services they export is greater than the value of goods and services they import. From a neomercantilist viewpoint, trade deficits and surpluses directly affect a country's economic and military power. Countries with a trade surplus produce more engineers and scientists, attract more talent, and accumulate more financial resources to continue having high levels of productivity and innovation. This means that they acquire greater manufacturing capacity, higher levels of employment, and improvements in the development of intellectual property. For example, China's unprecedented economic

Trade Deficit ■
Difference between the value of goods and services that a country buys overseas and the value of goods and services it sells to other countries

Trade Surplus ■
Occurs when the value of exported goods and services is larger than the value of imported goods and services

growth attracts investments from around the world. Although China is best known for its factories that produce low-tech manufactured goods, foreign direct investment is rapidly flowing into high-technology industries. By 2000, China had emerged as the world's third largest producer of information technology hardware, after the United States and Japan.[18] What a country imports or exports helps to determine if trade deficits or trade surpluses really matter. Also important is the extent to which these imports or exports can be substituted with suitable alternatives. With only 5 percent of the global population, America consumes more than 25 percent of the world's crude oil, much of which is imported.

Contrary to the view that trade surpluses are positive and trade deficits are negative, some scholars, such as Joseph Quinlan and Marc Chandler, argue that this thinking is outdated and does not reflect contemporary global trade realities.[19] A fixation on imports and exports ignores how global companies operate. Many American companies pioneered the practice of establishing foreign affiliates and subsidiaries through which they sell goods and services instead of exporting them from the United States. Most global companies follow the rule of "make where you sell" because of growing competition for global markets. While most Americans think of trade in national terms, American companies focus less on national ties and more on global market considerations. Consequently, they decide to compete not just through trade but also by moving production overseas. Furthermore, what are regarded as imports from other countries are actually transfers from American companies operating abroad. For example, American factories in China produce goods for export to the United States. Almost two-thirds of U.S. imports from Mexico are counted as *related-party trade* (i.e., trade between U.S. companies and their affiliates). In other words, slamming the door on imports from Mexico means slamming the door on corporate America.[20] Many foreign companies establish subsidiaries in the United States to gain access to U.S. markets.

GLOBAL COMPANIES AND GLOBAL FACTORIES

At the heart of trade globalization is the emergence of global companies. Some companies, such as the British East India Company and the Dutch West India Company, collaborated with European countries to expand their power into distant areas, thereby creating an early period of globalization that continues to influence the contemporary period of globalization. These companies were predecessors to modern MNCs. MNCs are closely associated with what some scholars call *Fordism* (i.e., the manufacturing system that stressed mass production of standardized products, and the centralization and vertical integration of production processes). Initially, these companies' factories were located in a major industrial city in Europe or the United States. Between World War II and the early 1970s, many of these companies expanded their operations into industrialized countries but remained characterized by large-scale fixed investments and large structures. They were relatively immobile and vulnerable to sudden interruptions of production due to material shortages or strikes by workers.[21] *Post-Fordism* refers to the period after the mid-1970s when companies became more decentralized in virtually all aspects of production. Corporations became more transnational, or more global, in both their outlook and their operations.

Revolutions in communications and computer technologies and transportation radically altered the way companies organize and conduct business. Communication within corporations occurs almost effortlessly, regardless of where various operations of the corporation are located. Financial globalization also contributes to the growth of global companies because it enables them to gain access to investment capital from around the world. Increasingly, most of America's corporations derive most of their revenues from abroad. Despite the recession in the United States in 2008 and 2009, companies such as Caterpillar, Coca Cola, and McDonald's made money because of their foreign operations. McDonald's corporation is perhaps the most obvious example of a global company. Based in Oak Brook, Illinois, it operates in more than a hundred countries and continues to expand daily. McDonald's is highly decentralized. In India, for example, where cows are sacred to the Hindu majority, McDonald's does not serve beef.[22]

Global companies establish global factories that produce a wide range of goods. Most likely the labels on our clothes indicate that they were made in Mexico, China, Malaysia, Bangladesh, Singapore, Indonesia, or Fiji. Eddie Bauer, Kmart, Sears, Target, Mervyn's, Wal-Mart, and many other companies have their clothing manufactured in global factories. Most consumers are not overly concerned about where these products are made. Distance is less of a factor in determining where factories are located. The fact that transportation by water is so much less expensive than by land encourages global trade and gives certain countries a definite advantage. The invention of the container ship in 1956 by *Malcolm P. McLean* revolutionized the shipping industry. The sealed cargo containers are unloaded in about a tenth of the time it took to unload conventional ships and at a fraction of the cost.[23] These containers are easily transferred from ships to trucks and trains.

GLOBAL TRADE AND LOW WAGES

Founded in 1887, Rawlings Sporting Goods has had an exclusive contract to supply the major leagues with baseballs since 1977. All of the baseballs used in the major leagues are made in Turrialba, Costa Rica, by workers who earn roughly thirty cents for each ball. The average worker produces four balls an hour. The work is hard, often causing carpal tunnel syndrome. But Rawlings is the major source of employment in a town that has few economic opportunities. Rawlings moved to Costa Rica from Haiti in 1986 due to Haiti's political instability, alleged human rights abuses, and criticisms of Rawlings's working conditions. Workers in Haiti earned even less than the Costa Rican workers: approximately $15 to $25 a week.[24] The relentless search for lower production costs in politically stable countries has led to what is known as a *race to the bottom*. The constant loss of manufacturing jobs in the United States, Japan, and Europe as companies move production to countries with low wages and competent workers has motivated coalitions of labor union members, consumers, and environmentalists to try to slow this race to the bottom. However, from the perspective of many developing countries, these efforts are thinly disguised protectionist measures aimed at safeguarding jobs in the developed countries. This is a common theme in the outsourcing debate.

YOU DECIDE

Does Globalization Improve Lives?

Free trade is generally viewed as beneficial. However, many opponents of globalization argue that benefits from free trade are often derived at the expense of poorly paid workers in developing countries such as China, Indonesia, and Thailand. Those supporting globalization point out that the countries that have narrowed the economic gap with the industrial countries embraced free trade and globalization. They argue that globalization is not the evil force that street protestors claim it is, that the idea that American workers or workers in foreign countries will gain from reducing trade is irrational, and that globalization has created opportunities that raised hundreds of millions of people from poverty. The global financial crisis and economic recession in 2008–2009 rekindled debates about globalization. As manufacturing jobs declined and unemployment continued to rise, many rich countries believed that they were negatively affected by globalization and that overall globalization was threatening their economic security. Although many poor countries also suffered from the global recession and poverty continued to grow, they were more supportive of globalization because they were relatively better off economically.

1. Do you think that globalization, overall, contributes to improved standards of living around the world?
2. How does globalization undermine world living standards?
3. In your view, how will the financial crisis affect living standards and lifestyles in the United States? How is the crisis affecting you? ■

Consequently, at the 1999 WTO meeting in Seattle, developing countries rejected a proposal to include a social clause in the global trade agreement. The *social clause* covers freedom of association; freedom to organize and bargain collectively; and freedom from forced labor, child labor, and job discrimination.[25]

China has an almost inexhaustible supply of skilled workers who are willing to work for low wages. In many ways, China is rapidly becoming a factory to the world. Japanese apparel companies, such as Fast Retailing, have built factories in China to avoid paying high wages in Japan. Japanese electronic companies—such as Toshiba Corporation, Sony, Matsushita Electric Industrial Company, and Canon—are expanding operations in China. Like many American workers, Japanese workers accuse these companies of exporting jobs to China.[26] China is also taking jobs away from developing countries, such as Mexico.

LABOR UNIONS AND GLOBAL TRADE

In this section, we will discuss some of the reasons for the relative decline of the power of unions, as well as strategies unions use to enhance their bargaining power as trade becomes increasingly globalized. *Several factors contribute to labor unions' decline.* These include

1. *Public Perceptions of Unions:* Prior to the 1980s, unions throughout the industrialized world exerted great pressure on industries to obtain better wages and benefits. Often, they became forces of conservatism, resisting

much-needed changes. Consequently, they were perceived by many citizens as being responsible for the economic problems that resulted from this rigidity.

2. *Political Change:* During the 1980s, many European countries, the United States, and Canada elected leaders who were strongly committed to free trade, including the operation of free-labor markets. Combined with a wave of privatization and the declining role of government in the economy, the embrace of economic neoliberalism undermined unions' power.[27]

3. *The Shift from Manufacturing to a Knowledge-Based Economy:* Most unions are in the manufacturing and public sectors. The rise of information technology and a knowledge-based economy radically shifted power away from manufacturing to industries that rely on highly educated employees.

4. *The Globalization of Individualism:* A growing sense of individual autonomy and the weakening of loyalties to organizations and institutions worldwide helped to undermine the power of unions, which depend on group solidarity.

5. *Global Competition for Employment:* Workers in developing countries realize that their low wages give them an advantage in their competition with workers in rich countries.

Facing these formidable obstacles, labor unions have attempted to demonstrate that globalization is detrimental to too many people and beneficial to too few. Labor leaders view globalization as a leading cause of both domestic and global inequality and environmental degradation. Consequently, they have formed alliances with environmentalists, consumer advocates, students, and human rights groups to counteract global trade's negative impact on them. Another strategy widely used by labor unions is to organize workers in developing countries to establish acceptable labor conditions. By getting workers in other countries to work toward establishing an internationally recognized set of labor standards, union leaders from developed countries hope to create a *win-win* situation for workers in both rich and poor nations. However, competition among countries for employment diminishes the chances that this strategy will be successful. Linking labor standards to global trade agreements would, in the view of poor countries, effectively undermine their competitive advantage, which is essential for them to achieve their own economic development.[28] Unions are also forming global links to counteract global companies' power. In this regard, they are more successful in Europe and Canada than in developing countries.[29]

The globalization of production clearly reduces labor unions' power. However, the movement of goods on container ships from where they are produced to where they are consumed and the widespread practice of *just-in-time production* (which avoids maintaining an inventory and gets products only when they are needed) strengthen the power of a few labor unions. For example, global trade is very beneficial to dockworkers who unload and load ships in major ports. Compared with most workers, they occupy a very strategic position. Management is reluctant to use inexperienced people to operate cranes that move containers. The just-in-time delivery system used by factories means that delays can be extremely costly. Furthermore, many products are perishable and must be unloaded or loaded quickly. Above all, dockworkers control the chokepoints that can impede the flow of goods that consumers and businesses need. Compared with many union workers who have seen their wages decline in the face of global competition, dockworkers earn about $100,000 a year and have benefit packages averaging $42,000 a year. To consolidate their control over these chokepoints, American dockworkers have created alliances with dockworkers in Canada, Europe, Japan, and elsewhere. For example, Japanese dockworkers refused to unload fruit shipped from a nonunion port in Florida at the request of American dockworkers who are unionized. Similarly, in 2008, the United Steelworkers union, which represented roughly 850,000 workers in the United States and Canada prior to massive layoffs due to the global economic recession, merged with Unite the Union of Britain and Ireland.[30]

GLOBAL TRADE DISPUTES

Controversy is an inevitable part of life. Global trade is no exception. Each country tries to influence other countries to abide by free-trade rules while simultaneously trying to find ways to avoid following free-trade rules that undermine their own economic interests. Although Europeans and Americans steadfastly provide subsidies for their farmers, they routinely accuse each other of engaging in unfair trade because of those subsidies. Trade disputes are often complicated by divergent interests within countries. For example, although Japanese companies are protected from foreign competition by the Ministry of International Trade and Industry (MITI), Japanese consumers pay extremely high prices for food. Inexpensive imports from China benefit many Americans who are raising families on tight budgets but deprive others of their jobs and thus their ability to provide for themselves and their families. Imposing higher tariffs on steel imports benefits steelworkers but hurts autoworkers and others whose jobs depend on imports of relatively inexpensive steel. Trade disputes are intertwined with domestic politics in virtually all countries and with cultural preferences. For example, disputes between Europeans and Americans about genetically modified foods are political, economic, and cultural. European political leaders are constrained by the reluctance of European consumers to eat such foods, whereas American political leaders are pressured to secure export markets by industries producing genetically modified food and are supported by most Americans who are more receptive to scientific advances and less concerned about consuming genetically modified food.

Global trade is sometimes controversial because it directly affects national security. During the Cold War, the United States and its allies restricted trade in products with *dual use*; that is, products that could be used for both civilian and military purposes. Computers, for example, could help students but could also be used by the military. Trade with China is generally perceived in this broader context. The United States has deliberately tried to keep China behind technologically by adopting export controls that restrict the sale of computer chip-making technologies. But China—with the world's largest cellular telephone market and the second largest personal computer market—is determined to achieve greater self-sufficiency in the manufacturing of computer chips. From a military viewpoint, China's access to the most sophisticated chip-making technologies gives it many military advantages and limits America's ability to maintain its military superiority over China in the long run. Competition inherent in global trade means that, despite U.S. efforts, other technologically advanced countries willingly sell to China what it needs to expand its semiconductor industry.[31]

Tariffs

It is generally believed that many tariffs stifle trade. For example, Ghana sells cocoa beans to Europe without having to pay customs tariffs. However, when Ghana processes cocoa beans to make chocolate and other products, which are far more profitable and beneficial to that country's economy than exporting beans is, its exports of processed cocoa are subject to a 50 percent tariff. Despite their emphasis on both global free trade and economic development, the United States, Europe, and Japan impose very high tariffs on basic exports—such as sugar, textiles, and fruits and vegetables—in which developing countries enjoy a comparative advantage because of their low labor costs. The United States imposes a 244 percent tariff on sugar imports and 174 percent tariff on peanuts. The EU has a 213 percent tariff on wheat. Canada restricts imports of butter by charging a 360 percent tax.[32] Confronted with a severe economic recession and high levels of unemployment in 2009, President Barack Obama responded to domestic demands for protectionism by imposing tariffs on imported Chinese tires.[33]

Quotas

A trans-Atlantic banana war raged between Europe and the United States for eight years following Europe's decision to erect barriers against imports of bananas grown by Chiquita and Dole (American companies) in Latin America in an effort to protect banana imports from its former colonies in the Caribbean and Africa. Beginning in 1993, when Europe formed a single agricultural market, banana quotas were imposed. The United States challenged Europe's preferential system in the WTO. The WTO concluded that the European banana quota violated trade rules and authorized the United States to impose retaliatory sanctions on $191 million worth of EU exports. The United States targeted high-end European imports such as Louis Vuitton plastic handbags, Palais Royale bed linens, and pecorino cheese. It imposed 100 percent tariffs on them to make them so costly that consumers would not purchase them. However, Americans continued to purchase Louis Vuitton handbags, which normally sold for around $400 before the tariffs, at twice their usual price after the tariffs went into effect. Exhausted by this relatively insignificant trade dispute that was negatively affecting far more important aspects of their relationship, Europeans and Americans decided to compromise. The Europeans agreed to a transition period of modified quotas and tariffs that lasted until 2006. The United States, which had originally demanded an immediate end to all quotas, agreed to remove its punitive tariffs.[34] The banana war was over.

Now that China has emerged as the country with which America has the largest trade deficit, Chinese exports are becoming a source of dispute between the two countries. In 2003, the United States imposed import quotas on selected

Chinese textiles and clothing, largely in response to pressure from elected officials, businesses, and workers in North Carolina. While China claimed that such quotas violate free trade, the United States invoked a *safeguard clause*, which allows countries facing a sharp increase in textile or apparel imports, combined with job losses, to limit such imports.[35] However, industrialized countries agreed to eliminate all quotas and tariffs on textile and apparel imports from developing countries by 2005. China's apparel exports to Europe, the United States, and other countries increased dramatically in 2005.

Subsidies

In March 2002, about sixty impoverished Haitian rice farmers and their families, unable to compete with rice imports from the United States that are heavily subsidized by the U.S. government, decided to make a dangerous journey to the United States in search of better economic opportunities. They pooled the little money they had managed to save to purchase an unseaworthy boat and headed north toward the Turks and Caicos Islands, their first scheduled stop on their perilous trip to America. Halfway into the first leg of their voyage, their boat capsized, killing all of them.[36] Although government subsidies to various industries create trade disputes among nations, nothing evokes more controversy and conflict than agricultural subsidies in Europe, the United Sates, Japan, and other rich countries. Even as these rich countries prohibit governments in the developing world from subsidizing farming—an occupation that provides a livelihood for roughly two-thirds of the population in poor countries—they continue to spend more than $300 billion to subsidize their own farmers and to give them an unfair advantage in the global market.

Agricultural subsidies in developed countries originated largely to assist farmers and to provide more food security. In Europe and the United States, these subsidies contribute to overproduction and waste. In both Europe and the United Sates, huge amounts of grain, butter, cheese, wine, and other agricultural products are in storage. This overproduction problem is solved partly by encouraging Americans and Europeans to consume more food and by dumping agricultural products in developing countries' markets, selling them for below-cost prices. The EU provides subsidies to agriculture under the **common agricultural policy (CAP)**. The original objectives of CAP included (1) improving agricultural productivity, (2) improving living standards for those engaged in agriculture, (3) stabilizing markets, (4) guaranteeing regular food supplies, and (5) providing food at reasonable prices to consumers.[37] However, agriculture has changed significantly since CAP was established in 1968. Only about 5 percent of Europeans are engaged in agriculture, and agricultural science has contributed to dramatic increases in productivity.

CAP ■ Supports agricultural subsidies to EU member countries

Influenced by the devastating impact of the Great Depression on farmers, the United States enacted *agricultural legislation in 1933* as part of the New Deal in order to stabilize farm prices and to save family farming. At that time roughly 21 percent of the American population engaged in farming, compared with less than 2 percent today. Improved seeds, better farm machinery, and general advances in agricultural science and technology have raised the productivity of an expand their acreage and to overproduce. As is the case in Europe, American agricultural subsidies are maintained through what is known as the *iron triangle*; that is, the political relationship among members of congressional committees who are affected by farm issues, interest groups, and government agencies whose existence is closely linked to farming interests.[38]

Agricultural subsidies in Europe and the United States encountered strong resistance from developing countries during the 2003 WTO meeting in Cancun, Mexico. Opposition to subsidies was strongly supported by some antiglobalization groups and various nongovernmental organizations (NGOs), such as Oxfam. The World Bank also stressed the negative economic implications of agricultural subsidies for developing counties. Pressured by their powerful domestic constituencies, the United States and the EU attempted to avoid addressing the issue of subsidies. But the developing countries effectively blocked discussion of issues important to the United States and Europe. Developed countries' resistance to reducing or eliminating agricultural subsidies and tariffs that block agricultural exports from the developing world contributed to the failure of WTO talks in Cancun in 2003 and again in Geneva in 2006. In 2007, the WTO ruled against America's policy of providing subsidies for its cotton industry. However, the United States continues to subsidize American farmers.

Genetically Modified Food

As global trade facilitates transferring food from one country to another and as consumers become more aware of health risks associated with food, trade disputes based on real and perceived health problems are proliferating. Unlike the other trade disputes we have discussed so far, food disputes are more about cultural (or more precisely, culinary) differences than they are about protecting jobs and financial gains. We are aware of the growing emphasis on consuming organic foods, ranging from milk to eggs. The outbreak of mad cow disease in Washington State in 2003 reinforced the reluctance among consumers to have full confidence in the safety of food supplies. In general, Europeans tend to be more concerned than Americans are about consuming genetically modified foods, partly because they are more skeptical of science. Their confidence in scientists has been undermined by outbreaks of mad cow disease, during which scientists initially assured consumers that they faced no health risks. Also, knowledge of dioxin-infested chickens in Belgium was not reassuring.

An example of a dispute relating to food safety is Europe's decision in 1996 to ban imports of American beef produced from cattle that had been fed growth hormones. These hormones, used to accelerate beef production, are generally accepted by American consumers. However, Europeans, especially the extremely food-conscious French and Italians, prefer beef that has not been fed hormones. These cultural differences became the source for a trade dispute between Europe and the United States. Under global trade agreements, countries are allowed to ban imports of foods if there is scientific evidence to support concerns about safety. Americans argued that scientific evidence showed that beef hormones did not endanger human health. The WTO agreed with the United States and authorized the imposition of punitive tariffs of $117 million a year against European exports. Despite high tariffs on Danish ham, Italian tomatoes, and other European products, Europe refused to lift the ban, citing its own scientific findings that showed that high doses of hormones cause cancer.[39]

Far more controversial than the beef hormone issue is the dispute concerning genetically modified foods. Although human beings have engaged in genetic modifications for centuries, experiments conducted by *Gregor Mendel* with pea plants in his monastery garden in 1866 represented a breakthrough in this area and set the stage for more advanced genetic research. While advances in agricultural science have been embraced globally, the ability to transfer isolated genes into the DNA of another organism is widely viewed as a threat. The idea that a trait for cold resistance can be transferred from a fish to a plant has encountered resistance from environmentalists, consumers, and farmers in Europe and elsewhere. From the other perspective, genetically modified crops, developed by *Monsanto,* solve many problems that plague farmers, such as pest control, soil preservation, and weed control. Most American farmers embraced genetically modified crops, such as "Roundup Ready" soybeans, that required fewer chemicals. Commercial use of genetically modified seeds was made available to farmers in 1996. By 1999, about half of the U.S. soybean crop and about one-third of the corn crop were grown from genetically modified seeds.[40]

In a world awash in grain, there was no sense of urgency in Europe to consume genetically modified crops. Environmental groups, such as Greenpeace, launched a global campaign against them, stressing not only the dangers they posed to consumers but also the dangers they posed to the natural environment. This campaign and others reinforced Europeans' concerns about eating genetically modified foods. Public pressure influenced the European Parliament to enact a food labeling law requiring merchants to clearly indicate if packaged foods contain any amount of genetically modified ingredients. Major food-importing countries, such as Japan and South Korea, also resisted consuming genetically modified crops. American grain exporters and various food companies—such as Gerber, H. J. Heinz, and Frito-Lay—decided to abandon genetically modified crops to maintain their sales in Europe, Japan, and other countries. Many supermarkets in Europe removed genetically modified products from their shelves. The United States, on the other hand, viewed Europe as using the genetically modified food issue to exclude American exports.[41] Attitudes toward genetically modified crops began to change in 2008 due to rapidly increasing food prices and growing food shortages around the world.

GLOBAL TRADE AND THE ENVIRONMENT

The growing link between global trade and the environment can be seen daily and in fundamental ways. The notebooks and textbooks you use are likely to be made from recycled paper. The Chiquita banana and the coffee you had for breakfast were probably produced under conditions that met environmental standards determined by environmental NGOs, such as the Better Banana Project and the Rainforest Alliance. The Body Shop, the British cosmetics producer and retailer that has stores in most American shopping centers, makes protecting the environment an integral component of its global business. Many global companies—such as the Ford Motor Company, BP Amoco, Royal Dutch Shell, Dow Chemical, Sunoco, DuPont, Boeing, and United Technologies—are involved in global efforts to reduce emissions of greenhouse gases in order to diminish global warming and climate change. Home Depot, the world's largest home improvement business, requires its wood suppliers to meet international environmental standards. Many environmentalists, trade analysts, and antiglobalization activists believe that relentless competition in global trade inevitably leads to a disregard for environmental standards. Global trade advocates, on the other hand, tend to believe that economic globalization is instrumental in improving and safeguarding the global environment.[42]

Environmental protection is sometimes used as a barrier to free trade. A coalition of environmental, labor, and consumer groups mounted strong opposition to changing the U.S. policy of excluding Mexican trucks from operating in the United States. Their basic argument was that Mexican trucks were unable to comply with the higher American environmental standards and that they posed a serious threat to public health.[43] Given the interest of labor groups in limiting competition from Mexican trucks, these environmental concerns could not be entirely separated from tangible economic interests. Growing competition from shrimp producers in developing countries was also a factor in the U.S. decision to use environmental laws—requiring shrimp nets to have turtle extruder devices to protect endangered turtles that are often caught in fishing nets—against shrimp exporters. The WTO ruled against the United States, viewing the application of the environmental laws as an illegal barrier to free trade.

Global trade creates many environmental problems. The sharp increase in the number of global factories has contributed to higher levels of pollution in many countries. The maquiladoras along the U.S.-Mexican border have increased pollution. *China's phenomenal economic growth is closely linked to widespread pollution.* It is apparent to anyone visiting China that economic progress has contributed to the country's environmental problems. The air and water in many of China's major cities rank among the dirtiest and most dangerous in the world. China is the world's largest consumer of coal as well as the world's fastest-growing importer of petroleum. As an expanding middle class demands more energy for appliances, cars, and air conditioners, pollution will increase. The International Energy Agency predicts that between 2000 and 2030 China alone will produce the same amount of greenhouse gas emissions as the rest of the world combined.[44] Another aspect of trade that contributes to environmental degradation is the growing demand for inexpensive food and the view in many developing countries that agricultural development is essential to achieving economic growth. Brazil, for example, continues to clear large areas of the Amazon for soybean cultivation and for cattle ranches. There is a direct connection between the rising global demand for soybeans, especially in China, and deforestation in Brazil.[45]

Diseases and Global Trade

The rapid global response to swine flu (H1N1) in 2009 by limiting pork imports underscored the link between diseases and global trade. The spread of diseases is as old as human civilization. As people and products cross national boundaries more

frequently in an increasingly global society, diseases that were once generally confined to a particular country or region now often spread to many other countries.
The speed of international travel and the expansion of free trade make diseases in
almost any part of the world an immediate threat to other places, as was made evident in 2002 when a previously unknown deadly respiratory disease, severe acute
respiratory syndrome (SARS), emerged in China's Guangdong Province. Many
workers fled the major cities to return to rural areas where the transmission of
SARS was less rapid and devastating. Afraid of contracting the disease, customs
officials in Europe and elsewhere delayed entry to ships coming from Asia. There
was a similar response to swine flu in 2009 in Mexico and elsewhere.[46]

Many products purchased at the grocery store are imported. Economic globalization and global migration help to create global cities that are characterized
by great ethnic diversity. Demographic changes in the United States, Canada,
Western Europe, and Australia have been accompanied by the proliferation of
agricultural products available in grocery stores. At the same time, however, the
relentless march toward reducing governments' involvement in the economy has
resulted in a smaller number of food inspectors. Furthermore, the globalization of
many aspects of the food industry means that there is much mixing of products
from different countries, which facilitates the spread of food-related diseases. An
outbreak of foot-and-mouth disease in Britain in early 2001 illustrates the impact
of diseases on global trade. The United States and Canada quickly banned
imports of animals and animal products from the EU.[47] Similarly, an outbreak of
bovine spongiform encephalopathy (BSE), commonly known as mad cow disease,
in Britain in the same year demonstrates how global trade spreads diseases. The
problem was soon discovered in countries that imported British cattle, beef, and
animal feed. Because animal feed is globally traded like any other commodity, and
mixed in with other feed, it is difficult to identify the source of many food-related
diseases. In the case of mad cow disease, Belgium, France, and the Netherlands
imported infected animal feed from Britain and shipped it to the Middle East and
North Africa. In late December 2003, mad cow disease was discovered on a farm
in Washington State. The impact on global markets was immediate. Japan, South
Korea, Venezuela, and many other countries banned imports of beef and beef
by-products from the United States. Japan's refusal to lift the ban became a
major issue for the United States in 2005. Although Japan eventually lifted the
ban in late 2005, it decided to reimpose the ban in 2006 due to concerns over
the safety of U.S. beef. Japan lifted the ban, once again, later in 2006. On the
other hand, Brazil, which has the most beef cattle in the world and is the main
competitor of the United States, viewed America's problems as presenting an
opportunity for its own beef industry to increase exports. In 2007, contaminated
pet food from China brought the problem of unsafe products to America's
attention. Furthermore, widespread use of lead paint on children's toys made in
China forced the Bush administration to take action to inspect imported goods
to a much greater extent. These examples show how globalization creates
greater interdependence as well as greater vulnerability to problems that originate in distant places. Rapid transportation, global travel, migration, and the
integration of markets increase our risk of being infected with diseases that
develop anywhere in the world.

REGIONAL TRADE BLOCS

There are several *reasons for the formation of regional trade blocs*, which vary from one trade group to another.[48] These reasons include

1. *Economic Development:* Many countries pool their resources and create larger markets by integrating their economies.
2. *Managing Trade Regionally:* Many countries regarded global trade institutions as too bureaucratic and slow in responding to both trade opportunities and trade problems.
3. *Economic Competition:* Countries can become far more economically prosperous and enhance their ability to compete in the global market by forming trade blocs.
4. *Political and Strategic Considerations:* Many countries form trade blocs for political and security reasons. The EU, for example, originated because of concerns about Germany's aggression in both World Wars.

Trade organizations range from free-trade areas to economic unions. We will briefly discuss the *main types of regional trade groups*, going from the most basic to the most complex. **Free-trade areas** are characterized by the removal of trade barriers among members. However, each country in the free-trade area maintains its own trade policies toward other countries, which often include significant trade barriers. *Customs unions* are free-trade areas that have a common external commercial and trade policy. Imports to the customs union are treated the same regardless of where they enter. This requires more cooperation and centralization of administrative tasks than in free-trade areas. The **Southern African Customs Union**—formed in 1910 and composed of South Africa, Botswana, Lesotho, Swaziland, and Namibia—is the world's oldest customs union. *Common markets* embrace the characteristics of free-trade areas and customs unions. They go further by providing for the free movement of people and capital, more harmonization of taxation and domestic policies, and more extensive administration. Finally, *economic unions*, which encompass all the features of common markets, represent the highest form of political and economic integration of sovereign countries. Besides the harmonization of government spending and taxation (*fiscal policy*), they have a central bank, a common currency, and numerous political institutions to achieve greater cohesion in foreign as well as internal affairs.[49] The most powerful and recognized trade bloc is the EU.

Free-Trade Areas ■ Characterized by the removal of trade barriers among members

Southern African Customs Union ■ World's oldest customs union, formed in 1910

The European Union

As you travel through Europe, you see that the euro is the common currency (with the notable exceptions of Sweden, Denmark, and Britain) and that passports are not required to cross national boundaries. In fact, common administrative regulations, the free movement of people across national boundaries, and the creation of numerous political, economic, and legal institutions are creating a stronger European identity. Stretching from Ireland and Britain in the west to Poland in the east and from Finland in the north to Cyprus in the south, the EU is the most advanced trade bloc in the world. Beginning with the European Coal and Steel Community (a treaty signed in 1951 that came into effect in 1952), European integration evolved into the European Economic Community (EEC) or Common Market in 1957 with the signing of the Treaty of Rome. Two steps toward transforming the EEC into the EU in 1993 under the **Maastricht Treaty** of 1991 were, first, the establishment of the *European Monetary System (EMS)* in 1979 to stabilize monetary affairs in Western Europe and to safeguard against fluctuations in the value of the U.S. dollar. The second was the signing of the **Single European Act** in 1986, which set the objective of building a unified European trade system by 1992.[50] As we discussed in Chapter 2, European integration focused primarily on political objectives, despite the emphasis on trade. In mid-2002, in an effort to create a union that would resemble the United States, European leaders completed a draft constitution. The proposed constitution provides for EU citizenship for nationals of member states, stresses the supremacy of EU law over those of member states, and designates certain areas (e.g., trade and foreign policy) over which the EU will have full authority and other areas (e.g., justice, transportation, and economic and social policy) over which authority is to be shared between the EU and the countries that belong to it.[51] In an attempt to counter the power of the EU, the United States, Canada, and Mexico formed the North American Free Trade Agreement (NAFTA).

Maastricht Treaty ■ Established the European Monetary System to stabilize monetary affairs in Western Europe

Single European Act ■ Set the objective of building a unified European trading system

The North American Free Trade Agreement

Unlike the EU, which was formed primarily in response to the consequences of war, NAFTA is predominantly concerned with economic issues. Signed on November 18, 1993, NAFTA entered into force on January 1, 1994. It brought together three different economies, with the United States the dominant power, Canada in the middle, and Mexico on the bottom. These divergent levels of economic development motivated the United States, Canada, and Mexico to form the agreement. Mexico, burdened with debt, regarded a trade agreement with the United States as essential to achieving economic development. The United States desired to maintain stability in Mexico and saw abundant and inexpensive Mexican labor as beneficial to U.S. companies that were anxious to gain a competitive advantage over the Japanese and Europeans. Canada, wanting to retain its favorable trading relationship with the United States, viewed economic integration in North America as a way of countering U.S. dominance of the Americas.[52]

The level of integration among the United States, Canada, and Mexico differs significantly from that achieved by the EU. NAFTA, unlike the EU, does not provide for the free movement of people across borders. NAFTA countries pursue their own independent trade, foreign, domestic, and defense policies. Compared with the Europeans, who have given up some aspects of national sovereignty in exchange for European political and economic unification, NAFTA members jealously guard their sovereignty. Consequently, there are few institutions in NAFTA that are comparable to those in the EU (e.g., the European Court of Justice, the Council of Ministers, the European Parliament, and the European Commission) that would diminish the autonomy of the United States, Canada, and Mexico. However, NAFTA has a significant supranational institution, the *Free Trade Commission*, which consists of cabinet-level officials or their designated representatives and is responsible for formulating policies dealing with trade.[53] As the economic recession spread in the United States in 2008 and 2009, many leaders and ordinary citizens viewed NAFTA as a threat to American jobs and increased their opposition to the agreement.

The Association of Southeast Asian Nations

ASEAN ■ Formed in 1967, purpose changed from security to trade interests of non-leading-power nations.

China's rapid economic growth has helped to focus increased attention on the **Association of Southeast Asian Nations (ASEAN)**. Although we generally perceive Asia primarily in terms of its pivotal role in global trade and think of organizations such as ASEAN as trade blocs like the EU, ASEAN's origins were more strongly influenced by political and strategic considerations than by trade competition. The establishment of ASEAN in 1967 resulted primarily from the political and military concerns of Indonesia, Thailand, the Philippines, Malaysia, and Singapore. Southeast Asia had become ground zero in the Cold War. The United States, perceiving nationalist movements in Vietnam as part of the Soviet Union's strategy to expand communism throughout Asia, inexorably militarized the conflict in Vietnam. But while America's policies in Vietnam are now regarded as having been seriously flawed, the threat of communism was real to ASEAN. Only a united front against communism could effectively counteract this threat.

Despite their obvious preoccupation with defeating communism, ASEAN members emphasized that their organization's purpose was to promote economic, cultural, and technological cooperation.[54] As the Vietnam conflict receded, ASEAN membership expanded to include Brunei, Vietnam, Cambodia, Laos, and Burma. In 2003, China and India joined ASEAN's *Treaty of Amity and Cooperation*, a nonaggression agreement designed to promote regional stability. They also agreed to collaborate in the fight against regional terrorism. But the focus has clearly shifted from traditional security issues to trade. ASEAN members believe that only through economic cooperation can they attract foreign investment and effectively compete with China. Apart from their reluctance to make the political compromises essential for forming an economic community similar to the EU, ASEAN countries face other serious obstacles in establishing a trade bloc. China, India, and Japan—the region's leading powers—are determined to participate in ASEAN. China, for example, is interested in creating, by 2010, a free-trade area that would combine its huge market with that of ASEAN, making it the world's most populous market.[55]

Asia-Pacific Economic Cooperation

APEC ■ The primary trade bloc for Asia

Formed in 1989, the **Asia-Pacific Economic Cooperation (APEC)** is primarily a trade bloc composed of the leading trading countries in the region. These include the United States, Japan, Canada, China, Australia, the Republic of Korea, New Zealand, Taiwan, Indonesia, Singapore, Thailand, Malaysia, and the Philippines. APEC's administrative offices are in Singapore, and leaders from the member countries meet once a year. Most of the work is done by specialized groups that focus on the main trade issues such as trade liberalization, energy, investment regulations, technology transfers, and telecommunications. APEC collaborates with the **Pacific Economic Cooperation Council (PECC)**, which was founded in 1980 to serve as a forum for Asia-Pacific countries to share information and ideas on investment, regulation, trade, technology, intellectual property rights, and nontariff barriers to global trade. In addition to APEC members, Mexico, Chile, and Peru participate in PECC.[56] The formation of both APEC and PECC emanated from the rapid economic growth of the Asia-Pacific region in the 1980s. Japan's economic power, widely perceived as a challenge to the United States, contributed to the growing regionalization of trade and investment. The economic success of the *Asian Tigers* (Singapore, Taiwan, Hong Kong, and South Korea) created stronger regional economic ties. The western coasts of the United States and Canada are economically integrated with Asia, a reality that makes the United States and Canada leading members of APEC. Another factor that influenced the formation of APEC was obvious competition with the EU and the United States.

PECC ■ Forum for Asia-Pacific countries to share information on investment, regulation, and other trade issues

The South American Common Market

Latin Americans have made numerous attempts to integrate their economies to achieve economic development and to balance the economic and political power of the United States in the region. The formation of the **South American Common Market (Mercosur)** in 1991 represents a culmination of these efforts. Economic problems plaguing Latin America and economic, political, and border disputes impeded integration efforts. Furthermore, authoritarianism and military dictatorships throughout the region created such antagonism, competition, and distrust among the countries, especially Brazil and Argentina, that economic cooperation was virtually impossible. Not until these countries had resolved their economic and border disputes and had abandoned dictatorship and started to democratize were they able to begin integrating their economies.

Mercosur ■ Trade group created to integrate Latin American economies and foster stronger trading ties with the United States

Brazil and Argentina, the dominant countries in the region, were cognizant of growing economic regionalization and competition for investments and markets among trade blocs. They initiated the development of closer economic and political ties by signing the **Program for Integration and Economic Cooperation (PIEC)** in 1986. Given the economic competition between them, they decided to negotiate integrating specific sectors such as capital goods, food, iron and steel, and the automotive industry. This allowed them to diminish business losses in both countries and to consolidate industrial processes.[57] This effort to open trade between Brazil and Argentina was consolidated by the signing of the *Treaty of Integration, Cooperation, and Development* in 1988. In 1991, Brazil, Argentina, Paraguay, and Uruguay signed the *Treaty of Asunción*, creating Mercosur. Bolivia, Peru, Chile, and Venezuela later joined the trade group as associate members. Barriers to trade among the members were removed; common external tariffs (against nonmembers) were adopted; and a commitment was made to coordinate trade, agricultural, industrial, fiscal, and monetary policies. In addition, they agreed to work toward harmonizing their domestic legislation to facilitate economic integration. Despite initial success, economic problems in

PIEC ■ Agreement to develop closer economic and political ties between Brazil and Argentina

Argentina and Brazil have undermined Mercosur's effectiveness. Furthermore, the United States has aggressively pursued bilateral trade agreements with Chile and other Latin American countries to create the **Free Trade Area of the Americas (FTAA)**, which would essentially engulf Mercosur.[58] Brazil supported the free-trade area to diminish the U.S. influence on trade in the region and to minimize damage to its own economic interests. By 2009, China had surpassed the United States as Brazil's main trading partner. As several Latin American countries elected more leftist leaders, Mercosur became increasingly politicized. President Hugo Chavez of Venezuela, for example, envisioned Mercosur as a powerful rival of the United States.

FTAA ■ Attempt to unify North and South America under one free-trade agreement

SUMMARY AND REVIEW

This chapter focused on the growth of and challenges to global trade and free trade as a way of increasing each country's economic prosperity. It shows how trade is intricately linked to politics, economics, and culture. In an era of global trade and interdependence, we are seeing the power to formulate trade policies shift away from countries and national sovereignty toward MNCs. Accompanying this shift is another: a shift toward increased privatization of national industries and services and a smaller role for the state in providing social services and social welfare programs. Lower prices provided by companies such as Wal-Mart, however, have been accompanied by an increase in corporate reliance on sweatshops that demand employees work long hours for relatively low pay. Such a "race to the bottom," where corporations disregard labor protections and rights in pursuit of the cheapest bottom line, has been a main factor in the backlash against corporate globalization and free trade.

In this chapter, we also looked at the history of the globalization of free trade. As global trade became more important, we saw the development of various trade models distinguishing between the benefits of comparative and competitive advantage. In recent years, we have seen a trend toward increased liberalization in the transition toward free trade and global capitalism. In this transition, we witnessed the conflict between protectionist policies and state socialism and increasingly popular notions of free trade and corporate globalization. With the emergence of the Bretton Woods System after World War II, we saw a strengthening of free trade as promoted by organizations such as the World Bank, the IMF, GATT, and most recently, the WTO. Under the WTO, we have seen the growing importance of reducing trade barriers and protecting intellectual property rights as valuable components of global capitalism.

There is widespread debate about the virtues and drawbacks of corporate globalization and global capitalism. This debate is likely to turn to conflict, as it did in the 1999 Seattle WTO protests. Whatever happens in the future, issues relating to free trade and globalization are likely to incite passion and disagreement between supporters and opponents of global capitalism for years to come.

KEY TERMS

Treaty of Paris of 1763 167
Silk Road 167
mercantilist model 168
autarky 168
comparative advantage 168
competitive advantage 168
strategic trade theory 168
Reciprocal Trade Agreement Act 169
International Monetary Fund (IMF) 169
International Bank for Reconstruction and Development (World Bank) 169

General Agreement on Tariffs and Trade (GATT) 169
Uruguay Round 170
intellectual property rights 170
Doha Agreement 170
exchange rate 171
trade deficit 172
trade surplus 172
common agricultural policy (CAP) 179
free-trade areas 184
Southern African Customs Union 184
Maastricht Treaty 185
Single European Act 185

Association of Southeast Asian Nations (ASEAN) 186
Asia-Pacific Economic Cooperation (APEC) 186
Pacific Economic Cooperation Council (PECC) 187
South American Common Market (Mercosur) 187
Program for Integration and Economic Cooperation (PIEC) 187
Free Trade Area of the Americas (FTAA) 188

DISCUSSION QUESTIONS

1. What exactly is the mercantilist model?
2. Can you distinguish between the global roles of the IMF and the World Bank?
3. What are the premises and principles of GATT addressed in this chapter?
4. What are intellectual property rights? Do intellectual property rights potentially violate principles of free trade? Please explain.
5. What factors discussed in this chapter have helped environmental issues become a concern in global trade?

SUGGESTED READINGS

Barton, John, et al. *The Evolution of the Trade Regime.* Princeton, NJ: Princeton University Press, 2006.
Bernstein, William J. *A Splendid Exchange: How Trade Shaped the World.* New York: Atlantic Monthly, 2008.
Bremmer, Ian. "State Capitalism Comes of Age," *Foreign Affairs* 88, No. 3 (May/June 2009): 40–55.
Elliott, Kimberly. *Delivering on Doha: Farm Trade and the Poor.* Washington, DC: Institute for International Economics, 2006.
Frost, Ellen. *Asia's New Regionalism.* Boulder, CO: Lynne Rienner, 2008.
Lanoszka, Anna. *The World Trade Organization.* Boulder, CO: Lynne Rienner, 2009.
Schwab, Klaus. "Global Corporate Citizenship," *Foreign Affairs* 87, No. 1 (January/February 2008): 107–118.
Steil, Benn. "The End of National Currency," *Foreign Affairs* 86, No. 3 (May/June 2007): 83–96.

END NOTES

1. Richard Devetak and Richard Higgott, "Justice Unbound? Globalization, States, and the Transformation of the Social Bond," *International Affairs* 99, No. 3 (July 1999), 486.
2. Lester Thurow, "Globalization: The Product of a Knowledge-Based Economy," *Annals of the American Academy of Political and Social Science* 542 (July 2000), 20.
3. Kenichi Ohmae, "The Rise of the Region State," *Foreign Affairs* 72, No. 2 (Spring 1993), 78.
4. Ohmae, "The Rise of the Region State," 78; and Ian Bremmer, "State Capitalism Comes of Age," *Foreign Affairs* 88, No. 3 (May/June 2009), 40–55.
5. Louis Uchitelle, "Globalization Marches On, as U.S. Eases Up on the Reins," *New York Times*, 17 December 2001, C12.
6. Robert Gilpin, *The Challenge of Global Capitalism* (Princeton, NJ: Princeton University Press, 2000), 95.
7. Gilpin, *The Challenge*, 96.
8. Thomas D. Lairson and David Skidmore, *International Political Economy* (Forth Worth, TX: Holt, Rinehart, and Winston, 1993), 57.
9. Peter Morici, "Export Our Way to Prosperity," *Foreign Policy* 101 (Winter 1995–1996), 12.
10. Celia W. Dugger, "A Catch-22 on Drugs for the World's Poor," *New York Times*, 16 November 2001, W1.
11. Lairson and Skidmore, *International Political Economy*, 24.
12. Jack Healy, "As Dollars Pile Up, Uneasy Traders Lower the Currency's Value," *New York Times*, 23 May 2009, B1.
13. W. Raymond Duncan et al., *World Politics in the 21st Century* (New York: Longman, 2002), 501; Gilpin, *The Challenge*, 92; and Nicholas Kulish, "As Economic Turmoil Mounts, So Do Deadly Attacks on Hungary's Gypsies," *New York Times*, 27 April 2009, A1.
14. David Gonzalez, "Cuba Receives U.S. Shipment, First Purchase Since Embargo," *New York Times*, 17 December 2001, A10.
15. Ron Scherer and Patrik Jonsson, "Beginning China Trade Rankles U.S.," *Christian Science Monitor*, 5 August 2003, 1.
16. Steven R. Weisman, "China Agrees to Remove Certain Export Subsidies," *New York Times*, 30 November 2007, C4.
17. Mark Landler, "IMF Puts Bank Losses from Global Financial Crisis at $4.1 Trillion," *New York Times*, 13 May 2009, B1.
18. Nicholas R. Lardy, "Sweet and Sour Deal," *Foreign Policy* 129 (March/April 2002), 21.
19. Joseph Quinlan and Marc Chandler, "The U.S. Trade Deficit: A Dangerous Obsession," *Foreign Affairs* 80, No. 3 (May/June 2001), 87–97.
20. Quinlan and Chandler, "The U.S. Trade Deficit," 97.
21. Alessandro Bonanno and Douglas Constance, *Caught in the Net: The Global Tuna Industry, Environmentalism, and the State* (Lawrence: University Press of Kansas, 1996), 3–4.
22. James L. Watson, "Introduction," in *Golden Arches East*, ed. James L. Watson (Stanford, CA: Stanford University Press, 1997), 19.
23. Don Phillips, "The Modern Merchant Mariner," *Washington Post National Weekly Edition*, 3–9 September 2001, 18.
24. Tim Weiner, "Low-Wage Costa Ricans Make Baseballs for Millionaires," *New York Times*, 25 January 2004, A3.

25. Robert J. S. Ross and Anita Chan, "From North-South to South-South," *Foreign Affairs* 81, No. 5 (September/October 2002), 8; and Daniel W. Drezner, "Bottom Feeders," *Foreign Policy* 121 (November/December 2000), 64.

26. Clay Chandler, "Workers of the World," *Washington Post National Weekly Edition*, 10–16 December 2001, 17.

27. Kathleen Newland, "Workers of the World, Now What?" *Foreign Policy* 114 (Spring 1999), 53.

28. Wayne Arnold, "Translating Union into Khmer," *New York Times*, 12 July 2001, C1.

29. Jay Mazur, "Labor's New Internationalism," *Foreign Affairs* 79, No. 1 (January/February 2000), 86.

30. Steven Greenhouse, "A Union Wins the Global Game," *New York Times*, 6 October 2002, Sect. 4, 1; and Steven Greenhouse, "Steelworkers Merge with British Union," *New York Times*, 3 July 2008, A15.

31. Craig S. Smith, "China Finds Way to Beat Chip Limits," *New York Times*, 6 May 2002, C4.

32. William Drozdiak, "Protectionism in a Golden Age," *Washington Post National Weekly Edition*, 21–27 May 2001, 17.

33. "The Tire Wars," *Economist*, 19 September 2009, 37.

34. Anthony DePalma, "U.S. and Europeans Agree on Deal to End Banana Trade War," *New York Times*, 12 April 2001, C1.

35. Keith Bradsner, "China Protests U.S. Limit on Textiles," *New York Times*, 20 November 2003, A1.

36. Michael Dobbs, "The Price of Global Reforms," *Washington Post National Weekly Edition*, 23 April–1 May 2002, 8.

37. John S. Marsh and Pamela J. Swanney, "The Common Agricultural Policy," in *Institutions and Policies of the European Community*, ed. Juliet Lodge (New York: St. Martin's Press, 1983), 57.

38. Robert Samuelson, "Paying Off America's Farmers," *Chicago Tribune*, 10 May 2002, Sect. 1, 13.

39. Edmund L. Andrews, "Europe Refuses to Drop Ban on Hormone-Fed U.S. Beef," *New York Times*, 25 May 2000, C4.

40. Robert Paarlbert, "The Global Food Fight," *Foreign Affairs* 79, No. 3 (May/June 2000), 26.

41. Lizette Alvarez, "Consumers in Europe Resist Gene-Altered Foods," *New York Times*, 11 February 2003, A3; and Andrew Pollack, "In Lean Times, Biotech Grains Are Less Taboo," *New York Times*, 21 April 2008, A1.

42. Elizabeth Dowdeswell and Steven Charnovitz, "Globalization, Trade, and Interdependence," in *Thinking Ecologically*, eds. Marian R. Chertow and Daniel C. Esty (New Haven, CT: Yale University Press, 1997), 92.

43. Steven Greenhouse, "Suit Seeks to Halt Bush Plan on Entry of Mexican Trucks," *New York Times*, 2 May 2002, A19.

44. Keith Bradsher, "China's Boom Adds to Global Warming Problem," *New York Times*, 22 October 2003, A1; and Elizabeth Economy, "The Great Leap Backwards? The Costs of China's Environmental Crisis," *Foreign Affairs* 86, No. 5 (September/October 2007), 38.

45. Larry Rohter, "Relentless Foe of the Amazon Jungle: Soybeans," *New York Times*, 17 September 2003, A1.

46. Keith Bradsher, "Economies Sickened by a Virus, and Fear," *New York Times*, 21 April 2003, A1; and Marc Lacey, "Mexican Tourism Bears Blow of a Health Scare," *New York Times*, 27 April 2009, A10.

47. Christopher Marquis, "Meat from Europe Is Banned as Illness Spreads," *New York Times*, 14 March 2001, A1.

48. May T. Yeung et al., *Regional Trading Blocs in the Global Economy* (Cheltenham, UK: Edward Elgar, 1999), 3–5.

49. Yeung et al., *Regional Trading*, 18–19.

50. Gilpin, *The Challenge*, 195.

51. Elaine Sciolino, "Seeking Unity, Europe Drafts a Constitution," *New York Times*, 15 June 2003, A1.

52. Gustavo Vega-Canovas, "NAFTA and the EU: Toward Convergence?" in *Regional Trading Blocs in the Global Economy*, 230.

53. Lloyd Gruber, *Ruling the World: Power Politics and the Rise of Supranational Institutions* (Princeton, NJ: Princeton University Press, 2000), 96.

54. Andrew Mack and John Ravenhill, *Pacific Cooperation* (Boulder, CO: Westview Press, 1995), 3.

55. Jane Perlez, "Southeast Asian Nations Meet to Tighten Economic Bonds," *New York Times*, 6 October 2003, A4.

56. Frank B. Gibney, "Creating a Pacific Community," *Foreign Affairs* 72, No. 5 (November/December 1993), 22.

57. Lia Valls Pereira, "Toward the Common Market of the South," in *Mercosur: Regional Integration, World Markets*, ed. Riordan Roett (Boulder, CO: Lynne Rienner, 1999), 9.

58. Larry Rohter, "South American Trade Bloc Under Siege," *New York Times*, 24 March 2001, B2.

CHAPTER

9

Global Inequality

INTRODUCTION

Discussions about wealth and poverty and how to achieve greater equality are as old as human society. They demonstrate a perennial concern about the implications of inequality for the security and well-being of communities. Given the persistence of inequality among individuals, groups, and nations over centuries, this debate is interminable. Struggles to achieve equality are also endless. Issues pertaining to global inequality permeate almost every significant global problem, from trade to the environment, from terrorism and criminal activities to democratization and human rights, and from ethnic conflicts to the proliferation of weapons of mass destruction. Consequently, as our discussion shows, inequality is closely connected to politics, economics, and culture.

This chapter examines the controversial issue of global and domestic inequalities. One temptation that students encounter in studying this problem is trying to find a dominant cause for such economic disparities. Similar to other global issues, inequality is the result of a combination of complex causes, many of which cannot be measured accurately. For example, many scholars argue that colonialism and its legacies contribute to the growing gap between rich and poor countries. However, several countries that were colonized in Asia and Latin America are much better off than most countries in Africa. Some causes of inequality are comparatively concrete, but many are nebulous. For example, values and attitudes are extremely important in determining success in life. Ways of thinking have direct and far-reaching consequences for the global distribution of wealth. But we also know that location and social, economic, and political connections are crucial determinants of success.

A central question addressed in this chapter is whether inequality matters. Human societies are inherently unequal due to variations of abilities, opportunities, geographic location, luck, personal characteristics, and so on. Empirical evidence shows that inequality is a constant feature of human societies. But why is it important to address issues of inequality, something that societies have struggled with historically? Globalization is widely perceived as the major cause of global inequality. Yet, as we have noted, unequal distributions of wealth existed independent of the current wave of globalization and are present in societies little affected by it. This chapter analyzes the globalization and inequality debate, and the current state of global inequality. In addition to focusing on inequality between rich and poor countries and inequality within both developed and developing societies, we will examine the issue of gender inequality. Finally, this chapter discusses the enduring issues of global poverty, hunger, and malnutrition and concludes with an analysis of various efforts to close the gap between rich and poor and reduce the negative effects of global and domestic inequality.

DOES INEQUALITY MATTER?

The existence of inequality is not automatically a major problem, especially when the economy is growing and there are many opportunities for upward mobility. As long as the standard of living is improving for those on the bottom of the economic ladder, concerns about inequality tend to diminish. The last two decades of the twentieth century were characterized by a widening gap between rich and poor and the proliferation of millionaires and billionaires. While economic disparities remained a serious problem in developing countries, the forces of globalization created conditions that helped widen the gap between rich and poor in industrialized societies. When the economy deteriorates, the gap between rich and poor tends to be narrower but concerns about inequality are heightened. During the global economic recession of 2008–2009, the wealthy lost money but the poor lost their jobs, houses, and health insurance. In the United States, the poverty rate climbed to 13.2 percent in 2008.[1] Widespread demonstrations in the United States in 2009 against excessive executive compensation, especially those in companies that received financial assistance from the government, underscores the dangers of economic inequality. The perception that economic inequality is essentially transitory when opportunities for economic advancement are widely available mitigates negative effects of actual inequality.

However, persistent inequality and enduring poverty challenge beliefs in the equality of opportunity and the possibility of upward mobility. Eventually, the legitimacy of the economic system and political and social institutions are challenged. The legitimacy of the global economic system is likely to be strengthened if a larger number of countries and individuals are benefiting from it. Extreme inequality perpetuates poverty and the concentration of economic and political power and reduces economic efficiency. It strengthens inequality-perpetuating institutions in *three ways*:

1. Inequality discourages the political participation of poor people, which, in turn, diminishes their access to education, health care, and other services that contribute to economic growth and development.
2. Inequality often prevents the building and proper functioning of impartial institutions and observance of the rule of law.

3. Inequality enables the wealthy to refuse to compromise politically or economically, which further weakens poor societies in a global society that requires relatively fast responses to economic developments.[2]

These consequences of inequality combine to ensure that poor societies will remain poor and unequal, trapping most of their inhabitants in a destructive cycle of poverty. Growing inequality among as well as within nations has direct and indirect implications for globalization. Inequality could undermine globalization by influencing countries to adopt protectionist policies and disengage, to the extent possible, from the global economy. But the ramifications extend beyond economic issues to problems such as terrorism, the environment, and the spread of infectious diseases. As Joseph S. Nye observed, "It would be ironic if current protests curtailed the positive aspects of globalization while leaving the negative dimensions untouched."[3]

As Chapter 4 shows, the democratization process and the effective functioning of consolidated democracy depend largely on a significant degree of economic and social equality. The legitimacy of any democratic system is contingent upon the voters' belief that they have a vested interest in its preservation. Their allegiance to the democracy is influenced partly by the benefits they derive from the economic system. Widespread protests in Thailand in 2009 against the government underscore this point. The unequal distribution of wealth is often mitigated by government redistributive policies. Extreme inequality sometimes results in the voters pressuring governments to enact trade protection legislation to safeguard their employment and livelihoods. In this case, voters exercising their democratic rights could inadvertently undermine the economic system that supports democracy. The erosion of democracy also has implications for national, regional, and global security. Although democracies are not always peaceful, they are less likely than nondemocratic societies to engage in conflicts.

Global and domestic inequalities often directly affect many areas. The 2001 terrorist attacks in the United States were widely linked to poverty within developing nations, especially Afghanistan. Huge inequalities often fuel resentment, which finds expression in global crime and a general disregard for the rules and norms of global society. Those who are extremely poor are often excluded from participation in decisions that negatively impact their lives. They become vulnerable to being influenced by radical minorities who are committed to violent change. For example, the Taliban in both Pakistan and Afghanistan was strongly supported in 2009 by landless peasants who were frustrated by the great power of wealthy landlords as well as by widespread government corruption. This seriously undermined U.S. military efforts in both countries. Poverty contributes to global and regional problems by fueling ethnic and regional conflicts, creating large numbers of refugees, and inhibiting access to resources, such as petroleum. Finally, global and domestic inequality is perceived as stimulating the global drug trade. For example, poor farmers in Bolivia regard the cultivation of coca as essential to their survival. In 2006, Evo Morales, a former coca farmer, a socialist protest leader, and an Indian, became Bolivia's first indigenous president. More than three-quarters of the heroin sold in Europe is refined from opium grown in Afghanistan by poor farmers. The costs of fighting the war against drugs in poor countries, such as

Colombia and Afghanistan, are extremely high. Global criminal activities, including terrorism, are often intertwined with the production and global distribution of drugs.

THE GLOBALIZATION AND INEQUALITY DEBATE

The impact of globalization on income distribution and living standards is a controversial topic. Studies by the World Bank, the United Nations (UN), and other international organizations also concentrate on this issue. Various analyses by academics and nongovernmental organizations (NGOs) are similarly divided into contending camps about the effects of globalization on wealth and poverty. Such preoccupation with globalization to the exclusion of other factors often muddles the debate about globalization and inequality. Would less globalization produce more equality and would more equality among and within nations result in an improved quality of life for the poor? There are two dominant, but sometimes overlapping, viewpoints on this issue. The globalists argue that globalization has increased economic growth and decreased global inequality and poverty. The antiglobalists generally perceive globalization as a negative and destructive force that is responsible for the increasing global inequality and poverty and the declining levels of human welfare.[4]

Globalists Make Their Case

From the globalists' perspective, the basic cause of inequality and poverty is the relatively low level of globalization in some countries. In other words, the poorest societies are the least integrated into the global economy. Openness to foreign trade, investments, and technology—combined with reforms such as the privatization of the domestic economy—will ultimately accelerate economic growth. The **Organization for Economic Cooperation and Development (OECD)** calculated that countries that are relatively open to trade grew about twice as fast as those that are relatively closed to trade.[5] China's rapid economic growth is an obvious example. But Ireland is also a country that became relatively prosperous due to its participation in the global economy, particularly in the European Union (EU). In 1985, significant poverty in Ireland was, in many ways, comparable to poverty in the developing world. Ireland today is one of the wealthiest and most globalized countries. Spain, Portugal, South Korea, Taiwan, and India are other beneficiaries of globalization. On the other hand, North Korea, Myanmar (formerly Burma), and Kenya are on the margins of globalization and remain impoverished.

Globalists also argue that globalization has contributed to the decline of inequality. Furthermore, poverty can be reduced even as inequality increases. David Dollar and Aart Kraay found that "a long-term global trend toward greater inequality prevailed for at least 200 years; it peaked around 1975. But since then, it has stabilized and possibly even reversed."[6] The accelerated economic growth of China and India, the world's two most populous countries, which is seen as directly linked to globalization, is given as the principal reason for the change. Much of the inequality that persists within countries is due less to

OECD ■ Organization focusing on global economic development globalization and more to policies dealing with education, taxation, and social problems. Moreover, more inequality in China, for example, has been accompanied by a spectacular reduction in poverty.[7]

Globalists emphasize that the number of people moving out of poverty has increased. The World Bank calculated that 800 million people abandoned the ranks of absolute poverty in the last decade of the twentieth century. The number of people living on less than one U.S. dollar a day remains high—around 1.2 billion. But given rapid population growth rates in the poorest countries, the decline in global poverty is impressive. The world's poor are seen as getting to be less poor in both absolute and relative terms. The more globalized poor nations become, the better off their populations are in both absolute and relative terms.[8] Globalization has generally helped the poor by contributing to reductions in the cost of numerous consumer products. Wal-Mart, for example, is so competitive and growing so fast that it is forcing other companies to reduce their prices. Lower labor costs, increased global competition for markets, low transportation costs, the overproduction of goods, and less government regulation of economies have benefited the poor. Less money has higher purchasing power in a globalized economy. Finally, by facilitating migration, establishing small businesses that rely on the Internet, and improving access to jobs in telecommunications and computer technologies in countries such as India and China, globalization improves the quality of life for the poor. Migration, for example, is a major factor in the development of Mexico, as remittances from migrants account for that country's second largest source of income. However, strong antimigrant sentiment in the United States and increased security along the U.S.-Mexico border in 2007 and 2008 reduced the flow of migrants as well as remittances. This trend was reinforced by the financial crisis and recession that emanated from problems in the housing sector. Many migrants were employed in construction and other areas related to housing.

Antiglobalists Make Their Case

Antiglobalists believe that globalization is widening the gap between the haves and the have-nots. Concerned with making global capitalism more equitable, they view globalization as primarily benefiting the rich while making life more difficult for the poor. Antiglobalists argue that globalization is a *zero-sum* game, meaning that the rich are winning at the expense of the poor. Antiglobalists also argue that globalization benefits rich countries, such as the United States. China is one of the few developing countries that is generally regarded as profiting from free trade and open markets. The United States, the locomotive of globalization, benefits the most from open markets worldwide. **George Soros**—a leading financier, philanthropist, and critic of globalization, though not an antiglobalist—believes that globalization drains surplus capital from periphery or developing countries to the United States, thereby allowing Americans to spend more than they save and import more than they export.[9] Similarly, Jack Beatty contends that the foundation of inequality resulting from globalization is that rich countries do not play by the rules that they made to govern the global economic system. Basically, the United States and other Western countries require developing countries to open their

George Soros ■
Leading financier, philanthropist, and critic of corporate globalization

markets without reciprocating commensurably. To support this argument, Beatty points out that although global rules on trade discourage governments from subsidizing industries, rich countries continue to provide more than $245 billion in subsidies to agriculture. He calculates that developing countries lose about $100 billion a year due to Western countries' export subsidies and trade barriers.[10]

Critics also argue that globalization is like an "economic temptress," promising riches but not delivering.[11] Global communications have heightened awareness of the vast disparities between rich and poor within the same society and especially between rich and poor countries. Simultaneously, global communications spawn aspirations of escaping poverty and enjoying the good life. Unfortunately, globalization is unable to make these dreams real. Countries integrated into the global economic system are the most severely affected by downturns in the economy. For example, Southeast Asia, which depends on exports of steel, textiles, and electronic components, suffers significantly in global economic crises and is unable to generate enough jobs and sufficient wages for a population with aspirations nurtured by television programs that depict prosperity.[12] Although conceding that globalization is not entirely responsible for global poverty, antiglobalists generally view globalization as a tide that lifts a few boats while leaving the majority mired to the bottom. For example, 50 percent of Mexico's population lived in poverty in 1980; today 50 percent of all Mexicans are still in poverty. Even when global companies create jobs within societies, the race to the bottom in labor standards and wages inevitably results in the poor in developing countries being unable to escape poverty while, at the same time, reducing the wages for workers in rich countries or depriving them of employment.

Antiglobalists contend that globalization compounds existing inequalities and creates more inequality. By giving priority to privatization, globalization weakens governments' commitment to the public sector.[13] As Vito Tanzi states, "Even as the forces of globalization boost the demand for strong social safety nets to protect the poor, these forces also erode the ability of governments to finance and implement large-scale social welfare policies."[14] The emphasis on integrating poor nations into the global economy diverts resources from more urgent development needs, such as education, public health, industrial capacity, and social cohesion. Many trade agreements impose tight prerequisites on developing countries in exchange for crumbs of enhanced market access. The **African Growth and Opportunity Act**, signed by U.S. President Clinton in May 2000, is an example. It provides increased access to the U.S. market only if African apparel manufacturers use fabric and yarns produced in the United States, instead of using their own or supplies from less expensive sources. In other words, the antiglobalists perceive globalization as perpetuating inequality by impeding development.[15] Furthermore, they argue, countries such as South Korea and Taiwan, frequently held up as models for the benefits of globalization by the globalists, developed under radically different conditions. These countries were not required to pay the costs that are now an integral component of integration into global markets. During the 1960s and 1970s when they were rapidly growing, Taiwan and South Korea did not face contemporary globalization's pressures to privatize their economies and open their borders to capital flows. The demands of globalization undermine efforts essential for a comprehensive development agenda.[16] These demands were

African Growth and Opportunity Act ■ Trade agreement to strengthen apparel trade between the U.S. and African states weakened by both the financial crisis and the global economic recession of 2008–2009, as more governments focused on internal affairs.

GLOBAL INEQUALITY

The UN estimated that *the world's richest 1 percent* receives as much income as the poorest 57 percent. The richest 10 percent of Americans have incomes equal to the combined incomes of the poorest 43 percent of the world's population. In other words, the 23 million richest Americans have as much money as 2 billion people, a third of the world's population. The richest 5 percent of the world's people have incomes that are roughly 114 times those of the poorest 5 percent.[17] These inequalities are reflected in many areas. For example, a girl born in Japan in 2005 has a 50 percent chance of living into the twenty-second century, whereas a girl born in Afghanistan the same year has a one in four chance of dying before she is five years old. On the other hand, global inequalities are not permanent or irreversible. For example, the proportion of the world's population living in extreme poverty declined between 1990 and 2005. The number of individuals living above the poverty line in the developing world increased from 1.4 billion to 2.6 billion. In China, the number of people living on $2–13 a day rose from 174 million to 806 million. Similarly, during that period, primary school enrollments grew from 80 percent to 84 percent, an additional 800 million people had clean water, and about 750 million had improved sanitation.[18] The general tendency among scholars, global NGOs, and officials connected with international organizations is to focus principally on the gap between rich and poor countries. However, disparities within countries, as we will discuss, are large, and in many cases, growing even wider. Tables 9.1 and 9.2 show some of these disparities in greater detail.

Discussions of global inequality remind us of many of the reasons some societies created powerful and prosperous civilizations while others did not. Western Europe emerged as the most prosperous region of the world. Areas that are now the United States, Canada, Australia, and New Zealand were conquered and settled by Europeans, many of whom embodied the characteristics that contributed to Europe's rise to global prominence and economic prosperity. The advantages Europeans enjoyed have been consolidated. This, in turn, contributes to global inequality today. Several factors combined to produce Europe's economic success and profound global economic inequality. A major factor is *freedom of expression*. Societies that encouraged people to have their own ideas, to be innovative, and to interact with each other eventually surpassed societies that were totalitarian or authoritarian. The latter generally stifled innovation because of their preoccupation with traditions, conformity, and respect for authority. Initiative was often equated with heresy. Another factor encompasses *social values*. Chief among these is an emphasis on economic opportunity and social equality. In his *Wealth and Poverty of Nations*, David S. Landes stresses that China's restrictions on women hampered its growth, whereas women in Europe, who were less confined to the home and were free to find employment in certain occupations, were instrumental in that region's industrial development and expansion.[19]

TABLE 9.1

INCOME INEQUALITY AMONG COUNTRIES

	GDP Per Capita (US$)	
Rich Countries	**(2004)**	**(2005)**
Luxembourg	69,961	60,228
United States	**39,676**	**41,890**
Ireland	38,827	38,505
Norway	38,454	41,420
Iceland	33,051	36,510
Switzerland	33,040	35,633
Austria	32,276	33,700
Denmark	31,914	33,973
Netherlands	31,789	32,684
Canada	31,263	33,375
Belgium	31,096	32,119
Australia	30,331	31,794
Japan	29,251	31,267
Poor Countries		
China	5,896	6,757
Egypt	4,211	4,337
India	3,139	3,452
Pakistan	2,225	2,370
Haiti	1,892	1,663
Bangladesh	1,870	2,053
Nigeria	1,154	1,128
Zambia	943	1,023
Ethiopia	756	1,055
Sierra Leone	561	806
High-Income Countries	31,331	33,082
Middle-Income Countries	6,756	7,416
Low-Income Countries	2,297	2,531
World	8,833	9,543

Sources: United Nations Development Program, *Human Development Report 2006* (New York: Oxford University Press, 2006), 331–334; and United Nations Development Program, *Human Development Report 2007/2008* (New York: Oxford University Press, 2007), 277–280.

Free Market and Institutionalized Property Rights ■ Rights to private property protected under the market system

A third factor is the functioning of a **free market and institutionalized property rights.** Chinese authorities became antagonistic toward free enterprise and eventually regulated it out of existence. Muslim countries failed to develop institutions that would have enabled businesses to expand. Islamic partnership law and inheritance law worked against the growth of large corporations. In Europe, a partner in a business could designate heirs, thereby providing continuity in the business

TABLE 9.2

HEALTH INEQUALITIES

Country	Physicians (per 100,000 people) 2000–2004	Life Expectancy at Birth (years) 2000	Life Expectancy at Birth (years) 2006	Under Age 5 Mortality Rate (per 1,000 live births) 2002	Under Age 5 Mortality Rate (per 1,000 live births) 2005
High Human Development					
Norway	313	79	79.9	4	4
Sweden	328	80	80.7	3	4
Canada	214	79	80.4	7	6
United States	**256**	**77**	**78.0**	**8**	**7**
Netherlands	315	78	79.4	5	5
Japan	198	81	82.4	5	4
France	337	79	80.4	4	5
United Kingdom	230	77	79.2	7	6
Germany	337	77	79.3	4	5
Italy	420	79	80.4	6	4
Spain	330	78	80.7	6	5
Israel	382	78	80.5	6	6
Greece	438	78	79.1	5	5
Mexico	198	73	75.8	29	27
Cuba	591	76	77.9	9	7
Russian Federation	425	65	65.2	21	18
Saudi Arabia	137	73	72.4	28	26
Brazil	115	68	72.0	36	33
Medium Human Development					
Colombia	135	72	72.5	23	21
Venezuela	194	73	73.4	22	21
Thailand	37	69	70.0	28	21
Philippines	58	69	71.3	38	33
Turkey	135	70	71.6	42	29
Jamaica	85	79	72.3	20	20
India	60	63	64.1	93	74
Pakistan	74	63	64.9	107	99
Sudan	22	55	57.8	94	90
Low Human Development					
Sierra Leone	3	61	42.1	77	282
Zambia	12	53	41.2	123	182
Nigeria	25	47	46.6	183	194
Chad	4	48	50.4	200	208

Sources: United Nations Development Program, *Human Development Report 2007/2008* (New York: Oxford University Press, 2007), 229–232; 247–250; 261–264; and United Nations Development Program, *Human Development Report 2004* (New York: Oxford University Press, 2007), 139–142; 156–159.

after the partner's death. Islamic law did not provide mechanisms for partnerships to be easily reconstituted following a partner's death. Similarly, Islamic law prescribed in rigid detail both immediate and extended family members who had to inherit property. Europe, on the other hand, allowed property to be inherited by one person, thereby minimizing the chances that a business would disintegrate and be prevented from getting larger. Virginia Postrel points out that "the fragmentation produced by inheritance law, combined with the structures of partnership law, kept Middle Eastern enterprises small. That, in turn, limited the pressure to evolve new economic forms."[20] However, increasing wealth from petroleum has significantly strengthened many companies in the Persian Gulf area, especially those involved in finance.

A final factor undergirding Europe's economic success and setting the foundation for global inequality is the *separation of the secular from the religious*. Whereas Islam became inseparable from the state, the origins of Christianity and its spread to Rome forced it to compromise with secular authority, a compromise encapsulated in the warning that Christians should give to Caesar what belongs to him and give God what is God's. However, Muslim societies prospered when religion was less restrictive. Muslims, commanded by the Koran to seek knowledge, became leading scientists, physicians, artists, mathematicians, philosophers, architects, and builders. For more than five hundred years, Arabic was the language of scholars and scientists. The Muslims transmitted Chinese scientific inventions, Greek and Persian texts, and their own impressive scientific discoveries and inventions to Europe. From the tenth to the thirteenth century, Europeans translated Arabic works into Hebrew and Latin, thereby giving impetus to a rebirth of learning that ultimately transformed Western civilization.[21]

Inequality Between Developed and Developing Countries

Despite rising living standards throughout most of the world in the last century, the gap between rich and poor countries has steadily widened. Historic trends suggest that most of the richest countries will maintain their lead over most of the poorest countries. The gap between the richest country and the poorest country was 3 to 1 in 1820, 11 to 1 in 1913, 35 to 1 in 1950, 44 to 1 in 1973, and 72 to 1 in 1992. By the end of the twentieth century, the richest 20 percent of the world's population had eighty-six times as much income as the poorest 20 percent. At the beginning of the twenty-first century, the average income in the richest twenty countries was thirty-seven times that in the poorest twenty countries.[22] As Table 9.1 indicates, income disparities between developed and developing countries are very wide. Economic development, while dramatically improving the standard of living in most countries, has not significantly closed the gap because of differential growth rates between rich and poor countries. Rich countries have experienced higher economic growth rates than poor countries. Furthermore, per capita income actually declined in more than one hundred of the world's poorest countries, many of them in Africa. Even developing countries that have enjoyed unprecedented economic growth, such as China and India, have failed to close the gap between themselves and rich countries. It is estimated that it would take China and India a hundred years of constant growth rates higher than those now experienced by industrialized countries just to reach current American income levels.[23] However, given the extraordinarily high standard of living in the United States, both China and India would be relatively prosperous if they achieved half the income level of Americans. Furthermore, globalization is profoundly altering many old assumptions. Because the income gap between rich and poor countries has widened historically, it does not necessarily follow that this will always be the case. Singapore and Kuwait, two high-income countries, illustrate that poor countries can become prosperous by implementing astute political, social, and economic policies (in the case of Singapore) or by having valuable natural resources (in the case of Kuwait). Economic disparities between the developed and the developing world have focused on the **global digital divide.** But access to the Internet and improved telecommunications are not automatic panaceas for solving the problems of developing societies.

Global Digital Divide ■ Contrast between those who have and those who don't have access to the Internet and other forms of digital communication

Causes of Inequality Between Rich and Poor Countries

In this section, we will briefly discuss some causes of the widening gap between rich and poor countries. It is important to remember that *several factors combine to contribute to inequality*: (1) geography, (2) colonialism and its legacies, (3) the structure of the global economy, (4) population growth, (5) government policies, (6) political instability, and (7) natural disasters.

GEOGRAPHY   Countries that are poor, some argue, have certain geographic characteristics that contribute to their economic problems. For example, they are in tropical regions or face high transportation costs in accessing global markets because of their location. Apart from the prevalence of tropical diseases, which have been controlled to a large extent by modern medicines and practices, countries in the Southern Hemisphere also tend to suffer from being landlocked. Countries with extensive coastlines and good harbors tend to be better off economically than landlocked countries that lack the physical **infrastructure** (i.e., a system of roads and railroads) essential for gaining access to navigable rivers and the sea. Landlocked countries or countries located far from global markets are disadvantaged by high transportation costs.[24]

Infrastructure ■ Essential systems, such as education, roads, and hospitals, needed by nation-states in order to provide necessary public services

COLONIALISM   Many argue that European colonization of Africa, Asia, and Latin America laid the foundation for economic disparities between rich and poor nations. Inequality breeds inequality. Just as wealth tends to perpetuate wealth, poverty tends to perpetuate poverty. Countries that grew rich two hundred years ago, partly because of their colonization of the developing world, are generally still rich today. European groups that migrated to Australia, Canada, the United States, South Africa, New Zealand, and throughout Latin America continue to enjoy significant advantages over indigenous populations. However, it is also argued that colonization is not the main reason for ongoing global inequality. Some states, such as Singapore, South Korea, and Taiwan, that were colonized are now relatively rich.

STRUCTURE OF THE GLOBAL ECONOMY   Colonialism and historical experiences, as well as contemporary economic practices, are widely perceived as creating an unfair global economy that keeps poor countries poor and rich countries rich. The Scottish economist **Adam Smith**, who wrote *An Inquiry into the Nature and Causes of the Wealth of Nations*, believed that governments should not interfere with the functioning of markets and that business persons would be led by an invisible hand to do the best for society. However, many leaders of poor countries argue that governments and multinational corporations in rich countries cooperate to maintain an unfair global economy. They generally subscribe to the **dependency theory**, which holds that poor countries' reliance on exports of primary commodities, many of which were started during colonization for the benefit of Europeans, puts them at a severe economic disadvantage. The prices obtained from their exports decline relative to the prices of manufactured imports from industrialized countries.

Adam Smith ▪ Scottish economist and historic proponent of the capitalist system

Dependency Theory ▪ Concept that poor countries' over-reliance on exports puts them at an economic disadvantage

POPULATION GROWTH   Rapid population growth in most developing countries plays a central role in perpetuating the economic chasm between rich and poor countries. Population growth decreased in the industrialized countries as the economic gap was widening. Since 1950, the population in rich countries grew by about 50 percent. In sharp contrast, the population in poor countries grew by 250 percent. Large families perpetuate poverty in most cases. Lester C. Thurow argues that "people who are poor in poor countries with rapid rates of population growth are going to die in poor countries. Whatever one believes about the world's ability to provide enough food, huge income gaps will emerge not just with the first world but within those parts of the third world that have their populations under control and those that do not."[25]

GOVERNMENT POLICIES   Discussing causes of poverty in the Arab world, Alan Schwartz observed that many of these countries are poor because of the policies they pursue. For example, Saudi Arabia tolerates monopolies that help to sustain an elite clan that all too often opposes technological, economic, and social change. Many Arab countries use import duties to discourage trade and impede the flow of investment by disregarding the rule of law. Furthermore, many of these governments emphasize religion instead of science and technology and therefore do not adequately develop human capital. Perhaps the most serious policy failure is the lack of adequate investment in women's education and opposition to allowing women to have equal employment opportunities.[26] When Korea was divided in 1948, South Korea adopted capitalist policies that fostered economic success, whereas North Korea isolated itself from the global community and adopted a communist system of government. Today, South Korea is prosperous and North Korea routinely faces starvation. The People's Republic of China, India, Malaysia, and Singapore, for example, implemented policies that have a positive impact on their economies. Latin America, on the other hand, allocates resources disproportionately to the wealthy. The poor there remain trapped in the cycle of poverty.[27]

POLITICAL INSTABILITY   Angola, a country twice the size of Texas, has abundant supplies of petroleum, diamonds, fish, and fresh water. However, life expectancy there is forty-five years, infant mortality is among the highest in the world, and Angolans are extremely poor. For twenty-seven years, the country was devastated by ethnic conflicts. Political instability directly contributes to economic disparities between developed and developing countries. Conflict not only discourages foreign investment, it also influences the best educated, most talented, and most financially successful citizens to flee or to invest their money outside the country.

NATURAL DISASTERS   At the beginning of this section, we discussed how geographic location directly affects the wealth and poverty of countries. Drought, earthquakes, volcanic eruptions, hurricanes, and other natural disasters are closely linked to geography. The tsunamis that caused widespread destruction in Asia in late 2004 and in July 2006, hurricanes Katrina and Rita in the United States in 2005, the earthquakes in Pakistan in 2005 and in China in 2008, the cyclone in Myanmar (Burma), and the frequent flooding in Bangladesh are the most obvious examples. These natural disasters routinely destroy important economic sectors, increase severe infrastructure problems, force the relocation of a large number of people, and lead to greater impoverishment.

INEQUALITY WITHIN RICH COUNTRIES

History and literature are replete with examples of the difficulties endured by the poverty-stricken citizens of Britain and the United States and how the lives of the poor sharply contrasted with those of the wealthy. Theories of socialism and communism, articulated by **Karl Marx** who was living in Britain, underscore the durability of inequality within rich countries. Great economic disparities have existed in the United States throughout its history, with the *Gilded Age* of the nineteenth century, the *Roaring Twenties*, and the *Roaring Nineties* bringing unprecedented levels of both prosperity and economic inequality. The stock market crash of 1929, the Great Depression of the 1930s, the implementation of the **New Deal** programs designed to help the poor, and the outbreak of World War II combined to redistribute wealth in the United States. The concentration of income declined dramatically, and the middle class grew rapidly. Income distribution remained relatively equal until the 1970s. In virtually all industrial countries, income inequality grew between the 1970s and the early twenty-first century. Globalization, new technologies, and other factors contributed to this development.

> **Karl Marx** ■ German thinker who pioneered the theories of socialism and communism

> **New Deal** ■ Social welfare system created in the 1930s to help the poor and restore trust in capitalism and government

The United States

The United States has the greatest degree of income inequality among industrialized countries. The richest country on earth also has pockets of poverty that are similar to many parts of the developing world. Out of a population of 300 million, 37 million Americans lived below the **poverty line**, which was defined as an income of roughly $20,050 a year for a family of four in 2009. The poorest 10 percent of Americans receive 1.8 percent of the total income, whereas the richest 10 percent gets almost a third. The average for rich countries is 2.9 percent of the

> **Poverty Line** ■ The income level under which people cannot adequately sustain themselves; a measure of need

total income going to the poorest 10 percent of the population. Economic statistics support the general perception of unprecedented inequality in the United States, with most of the income concentrated at the very top of society. The top 20 percent of households earned 56 percent of the nation's income and controlled 83 percent of the nation's wealth, which includes stocks, bonds, real estate, businesses, savings, insurance, and other assets. In 2003, the *top 1 percent* owned about 57 percent of the country's wealth. Incomes in the top 1 percent of households ranged from $237,000 to several billion dollars.[28] According to the **Center for Budget and Policy Priorities**—a nonprofit research organization in Washington, DC, that advocates tax and federal spending policies to benefit the poor—the richest 2.8 million Americans had $950 billion after taxes, or 15.5 percent of the $6.2 trillion economic pie in 2000. In contrast, the poorest 110 million Americans, or roughly 39 percent of the population, received 14.4 percent of all after-tax money.[29]

The tax cuts passed in 2001 and 2003 were widely regarded as creating an even wider gap between the rich and poor in the United States. While most Americans received modest increases between 1979 and 2000, averaging 10 percent, compensation for the nation's top one hundred chief executive officers (CEOs) climbed from $1.3 million, or thirty-nine times the pay of an average worker, to $37.5 million, or more than one thousand times the pay of ordinary workers. For example, Lee R. Raymond, chairman and chief executive of Exxon, got $144,573 for each day he led the company between 1993 and 2005. Various corporate scandals and the financial crisis of 2008–2009 influenced U.S. leaders to more closely examine these disparities. Although the median pay for chief executives fell in 2008, many of them received more than three hundred times the pay of the average American worker. For example, Sanjay K. Jha of Motorola was paid $104 million. E. Stanley O. Neal received $131 million when he left Merrill Lynch, a failed company.[30] Think of the salaries of major athletes compared with what the average American makes. In 1998, the top 0.01 percent of Americans received more than 3 percent of all income in the United States. In other words, the richest thirteen thousand families had almost as much income as the 20 million poorest households and roughly three hundred times the incomes of average American families.[31] The devastation caused by Hurricane Katrina in August 2005 and the economic recession of 2008–2009 underscored the gap between rich and poor in the United States.

Perhaps one of the most overlooked aspects of inequality is the growing income gap between urban areas and rural America. As one drives through the numerous small towns in Illinois, Iowa, North Dakota, Alabama, and elsewhere, these income disparities become obvious. Homes, businesses, barns, and grain elevators have been abandoned and are decaying, creating what are referred to as **rural ghettos**. Two New York academics, Frank and Debra Popper, have suggested that, given the relentless decay of rural towns, the federal government should accelerate the depopulation of the entire Great Plains region and turn it into a vast **"Buffalo Commons,"** a refuge for large mammals, hikers, and a reviving Native American population. As we saw in Chapter 7, the global financial and economic crises of 2008–2009 forced factories to close and people to abandon their homes. Cities dependent on the automobile industry were devastated.

Center for Budget and Policy Priorities ■ A non-profit research organization advocating tax spending to benefit the poor

Rural Ghettos ■ Poverty-stricken rural areas

Buffalo Commons ■ Proposed refuge for wildlife and Native American populations

YOU DECIDE

Inequality and Democracy

Income inequality in the United States is likely to be perpetuated for reasons discussed earlier in this chapter. Wealth, as opposed to income, can be passed on to future generations. One of the most controversial issues in the United States is the influence that those with large amounts of money have on the political process, especially on democracy. Politicians generally concentrate on raising money from wealthy constituents, while largely ignoring the poor. Inequality of incomes often translates into inequality in politics. Americans at the lower economic strata have been most adversely affected by the global economic recession. Many have lost their jobs and their homes and have expressed outrage at excess corporate executive compensation. Overall, many poor Americans are preoccupied with their economic problems.

1. Do you think that economic inequality in the United States threatens democracy?
2. What are some implications of inequality in America for U.S. foreign policy, especially in relation to promoting democracy? ■

Detroit, for example, lost roughly half its population. Arizona, California, Nevada, and Florida suffered from widespread foreclosures.[32]

Income disparity between men and women in the United States is an integral component of economic inequality in the country. (We will discuss global gender inequality later in this chapter.) The gender gap continues to be a contentious issue. Data gathered by the U.S. Internal Revenue Service showed that although women are earning more money than a generation ago, men continue to earn higher salaries than women. Men outnumbered women in the $1 million-plus category by more than 13 to 1. Men also outnumbered women 10 to 1 in the $500,000 to $1 million category. As Table 9.3 indicates, women earn as much as men only in the $25,000 to $30,000 salary range.

Other Industrialized Countries

Britain, Japan, and Ireland are also experiencing high levels of income inequality. Britain's rural areas have higher poverty rates than urban areas, and schools, railroad stations, and post offices are closing, just as they are in rural parts of the United States. The gap between the prosperous Southeast and the poorer North has steadily expanded. Londoners enjoy a higher share of the country's income than people living in the northern part of England, Wales, and Scotland.[33] Japan's long economic recession has heightened the problem of inequality. Unlike the United States, which is more tolerant of huge economic gaps among different groups, Japan emphasizes the oneness of its society. Although about 90 percent of Japan's citizens regard themselves as middle class, the economic recession that began in the early 1990s has weakened the middle class and sharpened distinctions between rich and poor. Income disparities grew by nearly 50 percent between 1995 and 2000, and more Japanese were homeless.[34] Improvements in Japan's economy have helped to diminish some of this inequality.

Rapid economic growth in Ireland, fueled largely by an influx of investments in technology and the country's increased globalization, had contributed to significant

TABLE 9.3

GENDER INEQUALITY IN AMERICA

Annual Salary	People in Each Range, Millions	Share That Are Women (%)
Under $5,000	19.81	59.8
$5,000–$10,000	15.22	58.8
$10,000–$15,000	14.43	58.9
$15,000–$20,000	13.75	57.1
$20,000–$25,000	12.65	51.9
$25,000–$30,000	11.01	48.0
$30,000–$40,000	16.45	41.6
$40,000–$50,000	10.05	34.4
$50,000–$75,000	10.06	34.4
$75,000–$100,000	13.23	24.9
$100,000–$200,000	2.27	17.4
$200,000–$500,000	0.67	9.9
$500,000–$1 million	0.11	9.2
Over $1 million	0.05	6.9

Source: David Cay Johnston, "As Salary Grows, So Does a Gender Gap," *New York Times*, 12 May 2002, Sect. 3, 8.

income inequality. The global financial crisis severely eroded Ireland's economy, thereby diminishing some of the income inequality. Wage inequality grew in the late 1980s, the gap widening between the middle and the top of the income distribution. Those at the bottom of society, the poorest 40 percent, have seen their incomes remain essentially unchanged.

Causes of Inequality

Globalization ■ The worldwide spread of ideas, values, markets, technology, and other developments

Globalization is generally seen as a major cause of the rapid rise in inequality in the last two decades of the twentieth century. Integral to globalization is the proliferation of new telecommunications and computer technologies. Individuals with technical skills have outperformed those who have few or no technical skills. The globalization of trade also contributed to shifting employment patterns, with low-wage workers in industrial countries losing out to workers in the developing world. Closely related to globalization and technology is *education*. The knowledge-based economies of rich countries give educated individuals an advantage over those who are less educated, less skilled, and less entrepreneurial. The interdependence of economies enables educated people to be more mobile and marketable. This disparity in income between those with a high school education on the one hand and those with a college education on the other became obvious between 1979 and the early 1990s. In 1979, the average American male college graduate earned 49 percent more than a male high school graduate. By 1993, the gap had grown to 89 percent. By 2008, the forces of globalization had widened this gap. Individuals with doctorates and professional graduate degrees experienced significant income growth.[35] The *weakening of labor unions* also contributed to rising inequality. Compared with most European countries, where unions remain relatively strong and where governments influence wage regulations, the United States has weak unions and relies on market forces to a much greater extent to determine wages. Significant job cuts and plant closings by Ford Motor Company, Chrysler, and General Motors between 2006 and 2009 only underscored the weakness of unions in a competitive global economy as well as the wider impact of the financial crisis and global recession.[36]

INEQUALITY WITHIN POOR COUNTRIES

Although leaders of the developing world consistently stress the inequality between rich and poor countries, very little emphasis is put on the gulf that separates rich and poor in developing countries. One persistent characteristic of the developing world is the lack of a large enough middle class to bridge the extremes of wealth and poverty. In most poor countries, there are basically two distinct worlds: one inhabited by the middle and upper classes that comprise a small percentage of the population and the other by the poor majority. Traveling in the developing world, one observes high walls around the homes of the wealthy people to protect them from the poor. One also notices that the lifestyles of the rich are virtually identical to those of rich individuals in the developed countries.

The zabaleen or "garbage people" of Egypt live and scavenge among the city's garbage dumps, recycling items when possible. The scavenged garbage is usually carried out of the dumps by children with donkey carts.

NAFTA ■ Trade agreement signed by Canada, the United States, and Mexico aiming at economic integration under the capitalist system

Apartheid Laws ■ Laws that legally and forcibly separate people of different ethnic and racial backgrounds

Black Empowerment Initiative ■ South African government effort to encourage the expansion of black-owned businesses

Caste System ■ Religiously driven ideology and social system that promotes hierarchy and inequality

Brahmans ■ Priests and scholars at the top of the caste system

Ksatriyas ■ The second highest group in the caste system includes those in the military, lawmakers, and rulers

Vaisyas ■ The third highest group in the caste system includes merchants, landowners, industrialists, and artisans

Sudras ■ Laborers and farm workers at the bottom of the caste system

Untouchables ■ Outcasts excluded from the caste system

Some of the world's most unequal countries are in Latin America. In Brazil, for example, the richest 20 percent of the population receives 64.1 percent of the wealth, and the poorest 20 percent gets 2.2 percent. As is the case in rich countries, the gap between rich and poor in Brazil is widening. In 1960, the poorest 50 percent of the population received 18 percent of the national income; their share dropped to 11.6 percent by 1995. Regional inequalities are large and growing. In the Northeast region, only 50 percent of the children are enrolled in school, compared with 98 percent of the children in the Central-West region.[37] The distribution of income in Mexico is similar to that of Brazil. Whereas the richest 20 percent of the population gets 57.4 percent of the income, the poorest 20 percent receives 1.3 percent of the income. Despite significant economic progress made under the **North American Free Trade Agreement (NAFTA)**, formed in 1994 to integrate trade among the United States, Canada, and Mexico, more than 54 million Mexicans are mired in poverty. About 24 million Mexicans are extremely poor and unable to afford adequate food. Many of them earn less than $1.40 a day. By contrast, the richest 10 percent controls about half of the country's financial and real estate assets.[38]

In some developing societies, inequality is institutionalized. During the period when South Africa was ruled by **apartheid laws**—which rigidly segregated blacks, whites, Asians, and mixed-race people and distributed resources according to a racial hierarchy—whites enjoyed a privileged position and blacks faced widespread and persistent discrimination. The economic chasm between whites and blacks still exists. However, since apartheid was abolished in 1991, an economic gap within the black group has grown as more opportunities have opened up for blacks. The number of black households earning as much as or more than the average white household income of $20,708 has risen from fewer than 1,000 to more than 1.2 million. But the average income of the poorest 40 percent of black South Africans has declined from $601 to $510. The government's **Black Empowerment Initiative**, which uses lucrative government contracts as leverage to encourage the expansion of black-owned businesses, has created black millionaires in a relatively short period of time, further widening inequality among blacks.[39]

India's **caste system** is the most obvious and pervasive example of structured inequality. The caste system is a rigid hierarchical system of social classes in *Hinduism*, which determines the status, rights, privileges, occupations, and social interactions of each person from birth. One inherits one's caste or social standing in the community. Each child is born into one of four main castes: Brahmans, Ksatriyas, Vaisyas, and Sudras. Even though the caste system has been outlawed and is constantly challenged, it is widely adhered to in Indian society. **Brahmans** (the priests and scholars) stand at the top, the **Ksatriyas** (the military, lawmakers, and rulers) are second, the **Vaisyas** (merchants, landowners, industrialists, and artisans) are third, and the **Sudras** (laborers and farm workers) are at the bottom of the caste system. The lowest group in India is the **untouchables**, who are literally regarded as outcasts. This means that they do not belong to a caste or class. The poorest 10 percent of India's population controlled 3.5 percent of the country's wealth compared with 33.5 percent controlled by the richest 10 percent. The richest 20 percent of Indians received 46 percent of the country's income, compared with 8.1 percent for the poorest 20 percent.[40]

The same set of factors that have contributed to the widening gap between rich and poor in the developed world are also present in developing countries. China is an example of this phenomenon. Economic benefits of China's rapid growth are most concentrated in urban coastal areas. Small towns, rural areas, and the interior experience much slower growth rates and are poorer than coastal industrial centers. About 84 percent of foreign investment is in the eastern coastal cities, 9 percent in the central region, and 4.6 percent in the western part of China. Similarly, 57 percent of the country's income is generated on the east coast, compared with 17 percent in the west. Finding ways to diminish economic disparities became a major priority of the Chinese government. By 2007, China had approximately 100 billionaires, making it second only to the United States, which had roughly 415 billionaires.[41]

Gender Inequality

Women worldwide experience various degrees of inequality. In all countries, the poorest of the poor are women, the majority of those at the bottom of society. Perceptions of women and the reality of inequality are mutually reinforcing, creating a vicious cycle of inequality. Clearly, women are not a monolithic group. Some enjoy great wealth, power, and high positions in society. More women, especially in the industrialized countries, are gaining equality with men of similar educational achievement. Table 9.4 shows income inequality between men and women. Based on our previous discussion about the economic advantages college-educated people enjoy over those who do not attend college, women are beginning to surpass men in terms of income. Observing gender composition of college classes, it is obvious that women outnumber men by a significant margin. The economic recession of 2008–2009 created higher unemployment rates for men than for women, thereby giving women a relative economic advantage. Leadership roles in society twenty years from now are likely to be dominated by women.

The beliefs, values, perceptions, and ideas about the roles of men and women and power relations between them is referred to as **gender ideology**. Gender ideology is based on the assumption that women are naturally suited for particular jobs. In Afghanistan, for example, cultural beliefs and practices make family planning very difficult, and many women have ten or more children. Women's role as child bearers reinforces their unequal status, trapping them and their children, especially girls, in a cycle of poverty. In many parts of the world, women are perceived as being naturally suited for factory jobs that are part of globalization. In Mexico, China, Thailand, and elsewhere women are concentrated in low-wage employment.

Gender Ideology ■
Beliefs, values, perceptions, and ideas about the roles of men and women and power relations between them

Globalization and other developments have also contributed to greater gender equality globally. Countries that are the least globalized tend to have higher levels of inequality. For example, the gender gap in education is concentrated largely in the developing world, particularly in Africa, which is the least globalized continent. Women in the United States, by contrast, are experiencing increased equality with men. For decades following World War II, income inequality remained relatively unchanged. Women received about three-fifths of what men

TABLE 9.4

INCOME INEQUALITY BETWEEN MEN AND WOMEN

Country	Estimated Earned Income (US$) 2005		Ratio of Female to Male Earned Income
	Female	Male	
High Human Development			
Norway	30,749	40,000	0.77
Sweden	29,044	36,059	0.81
Canada	25,448	40,000	0.64
Australia	26,311	37,414	0.70
United States	**25,005**	**40,000**	**0.63**
Netherlands	25,625	39,845	0.64
Japan	17,802	40,000	0.45
France	23,945	37,169	0.64
United Kingdom	26,242	40,000	0.66
Germany	21,823	37,461	0.58
Ireland	21,076	40,000	0.53
Italy	18,501	39,136	0.47
Spain	18,335	36,324	0.50
Greece	16,738	30,184	0.55
Chile	6,871	17,293	0.40
Bahamas	14,656	20,803	0.70
Costa Rica	6,983	13,271	0.53
Mexico	6,039	15,680	0.39
Russian Federation	8,476	13,581	0.62
Medium Human Development			
Colombia	5,680	8,966	0.63
Venezuela	4,560	8,683	0.53
Thailand	6,695	10,732	0.62
Haiti	1,146	2,195	0.52

Source: United Nations Development Program, *Human Development Program 2007/2008* (New York: Oxford University Press, 2007), 326–329.

received for similar work. However, as we mentioned previously, the gap is closing as more women attend college and abandon lower-paying professions (such as teaching) for more lucrative employment in business, engineering, and the sciences. Generational change and the enactment of civil rights legislation in the 1960s facilitated women's access to employment outside the home and equalized pay for men and women to a greater degree than previously. Nevertheless, women's pay still lags behind men's in almost every sector of the economy. Full-time female workers earned 77.5 percent of what men earned in 2002.[42] In 2006, the gap narrowed, with women making 81 percent of what men were paid. Globalization, particularly the Internet, created new ways of conducting business as well as new opportunities for women, who are increasingly able to integrate family responsibilities and business endeavors. Trends toward gender equality are being consolidated in every field, including the military. For example, in 2002, Kathleen McGrath, a mother of two, became the first woman to command a U.S. Navy warship, the USS *Jarrett*.[43] Gender equality is increasing across the developed world. For example, in 2001, the London Stock Exchange appointed Clara Furse as the first female chief executive in its two hundred-year history.[44] There are also many examples of women gaining greater equality with men in the news media.

Global Poverty

Poverty, the most obvious indicator of global and domestic inequality, is an enduring reality for more than two-thirds of the world's population. Although poverty in developing countries is readily apparent, poverty is a growing reality in the richest countries, including the United States. Poverty persists despite improvements in living standards. But improvements—such as increases in per capita income, declining infant mortality rates, increased access to clean water, and decreases in illiteracy—are often counteracted by rapid population growth rates in the developing world. Nonetheless, the percentage of people living in **extreme poverty**, defined as living on less than $1 a day, has declined. Even the absolute number of very poor people declined between 1980 and 1998 by at least 200 million, to almost 1.2 billion in 1998. Economic growth in China and India contributed to this decrease in extreme poverty.[45] In 2000, the UN adopted the Millennium Declaration, which aimed at reducing extreme poverty by half and child mortality by two-thirds by 2015. But the struggle to further reduce poverty must take into consideration some powerful realities. These include

Extreme Poverty ■
The very poorest of the poor, or those living on less than $1 a day

1. *Weak political support for foreign assistance* in most rich countries, including the United States;
2. *Uncertainty of commitment* from the World Bank, the International Monetary Fund (IMF), the WTO, and other multilateral agencies; and
3. *Ongoing armed conflicts* that impede efforts to help the poor in many parts of the developing world.[46]

These realities are compounded by the diminished role of governments worldwide in efforts to alleviate poverty.

Defining poverty is to some extent subjective. There are basically two aspects to poverty: **absolute poverty** (i.e., the absolute number of poor people below the defined poverty line) and **relative poverty** (which reflects the distribution of income in society). For example, in relative terms, many Americans are poor. However, a much smaller number of Americans are poor in absolute terms. Although poverty is not always easily defined, an important aspect of poverty is a subjective feeling of being poor either absolutely or relative to others.[47] The concept of the poverty line is not always a reliable indicator of poverty. The poverty line in the United States was developed in 1963–1964 by the Social Security Administration on the basis of a 1955 household food consumption survey by the

Absolute Poverty ■
The absolute number of poor people below the defined poverty line

Relative Poverty ■
Level of poverty based on the society in question

U.S. Department of Agriculture. The poverty line is adjusted each year to reflect changes in the **Consumer Price Index (CPI)**. The CPI measures changes over time in the cost of purchasing the "market basket" of goods and services used by a typical family. But the poverty line does not adequately reflect higher costs for transportation, child care, health care, and other costs associated with employment. Unlike the 1960s, when many mothers stayed home, both parents now work, thereby incurring expenses that were not taken into consideration when the poverty line was developed. Furthermore, the poverty level measurement assumes that costs are the same across the United States, with the exception of Alaska and Hawaii, where the poverty level is higher.[48] Global measurements of poverty are in reality estimates, despite the certainty conveyed by statistics.

Regardless of where poor people live, there are at least *six dimensions of poverty*:[49]

1. *Hunger.* Poverty throughout the world is about inadequate food supplies.
2. *Psychological Dimensions.* Poverty is usually characterized by a sense of powerlessness, dependency, humiliation, and shame.
3. *Inadequate Infrastructure.* Poor people generally lack access to roads, electricity, clean water, and transportation.
4. *Low Levels of Literacy.* Educational opportunities are often unavailable.
5. *Health Problems.* Poor people everywhere generally suffer from illness, which further impoverishes them.
6. *Inadequate Income.* Poor people stress managing physical, human, social, and environmental assets to cope with their vulnerability. Incomes receive less emphasis.

Hunger and Malnutrition

Table 9.5 shows the percentage of the population in selected countries living on $2 or less a day. Hunger and malnutrition are at the foundation of global inequality. **Malnutrition** causes impaired vision, an inability to concentrate and to learn, greater vulnerability to disease and poor health, and a shorter life expectancy. In its report on the state of food insecurity in the world in 2003, the UN Food and Agriculture Organization set a goal of reducing world hunger by half by 2015. There is evidence to suggest that this goal, set in 1996, is unlikely to be achieved. Between 1999 and 2001, the number of hungry people globally climbed, especially in Africa. More than 840 million people, or one-seventh of humanity, experienced hunger. Between 1995 and 2001, the number of malnourished people grew by an average of 4.5 million a year.[50] China and Mozambique reduced hunger and malnutrition, whereas India, Nigeria, Zimbabwe, North Korea, Ethiopia, and Eritrea faced growing starvation. Violence, AIDS, and natural disasters contribute to increased hunger in many parts of Africa, the continent most seriously affected by food shortages. For example, a civil war in the Democratic Republic of the Congo left more than 75 percent of the population undernourished. Similarly, violence in Afghanistan and Burundi contributed to the malnutrition of roughly 70 percent of their populations. Malnutrition also spread across Central America's drought corridor, which has experienced declining rainfall during the crucial planting and

TABLE 9.5

PERCENTAGE OF POPULATION LIVING ON $2 OR LESS A DAY

Country	Population Below $1 a Day (%)	Population Below $2 a Day (%)
Medium Human Development		
Colombia	7.0	17.8
Venezuela	18.5	40.1
Peru	10.5	30.6
Jamaica	<2	14.4
Sri Lanka	5.6	41.6
Paraguay	13.6	29.8
Ecuador	17.7	40.8
China	9.9	34.9
Indonesia	7.5	52.4
Egypt	3.1	43.9
India	34.3	80.4
Zimbabwe	56.1	83.0
Ghana	44.8	78.5
Kenya	22.8	58.3
Pakistan	17.0	73.6
Low Human Development		
Nigeria	70.8	92.4
Zambia	63.8	87.2
Mali	36.1	72.1
Central African Rep.	66.6	84.0
Ethiopia	23.0	77.8
Sierra Leone	57.0	74.5

Source: United Nations Development Program, *Human Development Report 2007/2008* (New York: Oxford University Press, 2007), 238–240.

growing periods. The **World Food Program**, the UN agency and the world's largest food distribution organization, estimated that 1.5 million people were threatened with malnutrition in Honduras, Nicaragua, El Salvador, and Guatemala in 2002. The emphasis on using corn to produce ethanol in the United States and Western Europe contributed to a major food crisis in 2008, thereby increasing inequality. Despite strong economic growth and rising incomes in India, approximately 42.5 percent of the children under age five are malnourished. In many cases, money allocated for child nutrition programs remains unspent.[51]

World Food Program ■ UN agency that is also the world's largest food distribution organization

Closing the Gap

Speaking at the UN conference in Monterrey, Mexico, in March 2002, President George W. Bush stressed that while poverty does not cause terrorism, "persistent poverty and oppression can lead to hopelessness and despair. And when governments fail to meet the most basic needs of their people, these failed states can become havens for terror."[52] At their meeting in the United States in 2005, the Group of Eight (G–8) industrial countries also emphasized the urgent need to reduce poverty. In 2008, the director of the World Food Program, Josette Sheeran, called for urgent action by the global community to prevent another 100 million people from becoming poor and hungry due to the food crisis influenced by using corn for biofuel. Globalization not only makes national borders less significant, it also links the fates of rich and poor nations in an unprecedented web of interdependence. This section offers some suggestions for diminishing inequality.

EDUCATION AND FAMILY PLANNING   Education and family planning are essential for diminishing inequality. Societies that make education available to as many people as possible, such as the United States, are also the most prosperous societies. Because education affects ways of thinking, perceptions, and creativity, it is at the foundation of any effort to alleviate poverty. Education, especially for women, has a direct impact on the number of children women have, their level of education, and their quality of life. Countries that make education and family planning priorities usually have healthier, more productive, and more economically and technologically competitive populations.

DEMOCRACY MAY HELP   India, the world's largest democracy, is also one of the world's poorest and most unequal societies. Nevertheless, democratic societies offer poor people an opportunity to improve their lives through their voting power. Democratic governments may be pressured to reduce economic inequalities by interest groups and political parties. Zimbabwe, once a major food producer, experienced both dictatorship and extreme poverty in 2008.

GOVERNMENT POLICIES AND FREE TRADE COULD MAKE A DIFFERENCE   Decisions made by governments have profound implications for inequality within and among nations. Government priorities, reflected in the allocation of resources in national budgets, directly affect chances of reducing inequality. For example, Brazil's government suspended a $760 million purchase of twelve jet fighters for its air force to use the money to alleviate hunger. This choice of spending money on guns or butter confronts most governments, and most of them place military expenditures ahead of poverty-reduction programs. Brazil has launched an anti-poverty program, Bolsa Familia, or Family Fund, that is a model for many countries. Poor families receive financial assistance and are encouraged to send their children to school and give them medical care. By increasing economic growth, the program also decreases inequality. China's government has tried to diminish regional inequalities by investing more money in economically depressed areas. Brazil decided to address inequality by "democratizing" land titles and expanding poor people's access to credit. Granting formal property rights to millions of slum dwellers is viewed as a way of creating greater economic opportunities for the poor.[53] Korea, Brazil, and India have implemented various forms of affirmative action programs to diminish regional, racial, or caste inequalities.

REDUCE CORRUPTION   The poorest countries in the world are invariably the most corrupt countries. Corruption drains scarce resources away from vital public services and infrastructural projects, rewards incompetence and stifles innovation and change, and discourages foreign investment. At a more fundamental level, corruption infuses society with cynicism, which is detrimental to efforts to achieve economic development and greater equality. Much of the illegally obtained money is invested abroad, instead of being invested at home.

PAY ATTENTION TO WOMEN   Societies that reward women for their participation in economic, political, and social life benefit from the talents of more than half of their population. Because women play a crucial role in raising, educating, and encouraging children to achieve, their treatment directly influences economic development and equality issues. The UN, the World Bank, and other international organizations recognize that women must be included in the decision-making process. Governments are paying attention to **gender budgeting**, which is essentially an analysis of national budgets to determine how spending priorities affect women. Gender-responsive budgets were developed to hold public officials accountable for promoting gender equity.[54]

Gender Budgeting ■ Analysis of national budgets to determine how spending priorities affect women

IMPROVE AGRICULTURE IN POOR COUNTRIES   Poverty and inequality are reinforced by the inability of the poor to produce sufficient food. The poorest countries routinely suffer from food shortages and malnutrition. Many of the world's poorest people live in societies where land is concentrated in the hands of a relatively small number of powerful families. Land redistribution in places such as Brazil and Venezuela is regarded as a major step toward reducing hunger and creating greater equality of opportunity. Large subsidies to farmers in North America, Europe, and Japan are widely believed to be detrimental to the efforts of poor countries to develop agriculture and become self-sufficient in food production. The **Green Revolution**—which dramatically increased agricultural production through the development of high-yielding hybrids and faster-growing plants and the application of large amounts of fertilizers and insecticides—enabled countries such as Mexico and India to produce more food and reduce starvation. In 2006, the Bill and Melinda Gates Foundation and the Rockefeller Foundation allocated $150 million to increase agricultural productivity in Africa.

Green Revolution ■ Dramatic increase in agricultural production involving hybrids, fast-growing plants, and the use of fertilizer and insecticides

THINK SMALL   Personal choices that reinforce poverty within families will eventually reinforce national poverty and global inequality. Many college students are involved in volunteer efforts, and some think that joining the Peace Corps can help improve living conditions in an African or Latin American village. Similarly, poor people in Brazil have decided to help people even poorer than themselves by volunteering. Volunteers work in soup kitchens, homeless shelters, legal-aid clinics, and antiviolence organizations.[55] Another example of how thinking small can help to close the gap between rich and poor is **microlending**, or the granting of small loans to help the smallest entrepreneurs, who do not have access to conventional financial services, expand their businesses, and climb out of poverty. Started in Bangladesh by **Muhammad Yunus**, founder of the Grameen Bank, microcredit is now a global phenomenon. Both Yunus and the Grameen Bank won the Nobel Peace Prize in 2006.

Microlending ■ Practice of granting small loans to help those who do not have access to conventional financial loan services

Muhammad Yunus ■ Founder of the Grameen Bank microlending institution

FOREIGN AID HELPS   During the 1980s, the prevailing view in industrialized countries was that economic globalization offered greater benefits to poor countries than official development assistance did. Consequently, foreign aid declined sharply. However, in the aftermath of the 2001 terrorist attacks in the United States, a global consensus emerged around the need to increase economic assistance to the poorest countries, especially those that are democratizing and have relatively low levels of official corruption. In their *Global Monitoring Report 2005*, the IMF and the World Bank proposed doubling foreign aid to poor countries to reduce global poverty and inequality. Increasingly, individuals are providing significant aid to poor countries. For example, in 2006, George Soros gave $50 million to assist efforts to alleviate poverty in Africa.

Although it is difficult to determine how much money NGOs provide, it is estimated that they give $35 billion each year, a figure that is more than three and a half times the amount of official development assistance given by the U.S. government. U.S. foundations, such as the Bill and Melinda Gates Foundation, the David and Lucille Packard Foundation, and the UN Foundation, which is funded by Ted Turner, provide more than $3 billion in economic assistance to poor countries.[56] Equally important is the growth of global remittances to developing countries. Worldwide, remittances grew from $30 billion to $80 billion between 1990 and 2003. Mexico and India were among the major recipients. In 2006, the Inter-American Development Bank estimated that remittances from the United States to Latin America totaled more than $45 billion. Here again, small amounts sent to Mexico or India by immigrants make a difference in efforts to achieve greater equality. Carol C. Adelman argues that "remittances have an equal or greater impact on the quality of life in developing countries than official aid, trade, and investment."[57]

SUMMARY AND REVIEW

This chapter examined global and domestic inequality in an attempt to identify some of the causes of poverty. It discussed the linkages between inequality and politics, economics, and culture. It shows that global concerns about inequality are durable. We addressed colonialism, gender inequality, malnutrition, global poverty, and globalization in order to identify their roles in exacerbating or reducing global and domestic inequality. We focused on the inequality gap between rich and poor countries, as well as the inequality gaps within both developed and developing societies. We also addressed a central question in the debate over inequality: Does inequality matter? Since human societies are inherently unequal due to variations in individual abilities, opportunities, and geographic locations, it seems that inequality will always be a feature in society. As a result, we focused less on the existence of social inequality within countries and more on the importance of the degree of opportunity for upward mobility available to each individual within given societies. We examined a number of concepts and developments, such as extreme poverty, malnutrition, and relative and absolute poverty. We elaborated on the views of globalists and antiglobalists, who take contending views on the importance and effects of globalization. We identified factors that contribute to global inequality, including geography, colonialism, global economic structures, population growth, government policies, political instability, and natural disasters. Next, we examined conditions contributing to inequality at the national level. Women are disproportionately represented among the poorest of the poor throughout all countries today. As we discussed, various reasons help explain such a trend, including prevalence of religious ideology and patriarchal morals and values; traditional repression of women; and lower levels of education, pay, and job opportunities for women. Finally, we looked at possible solutions for reducing global and national poverty and inequality.

KEY TERMS

Organization for Economic Cooperation and Development (OECD) 196
George Soros 197
African Growth and Opportunity Act 198
free market and institutionalized property rights 200
global digital divide 203
infrastructure 203
Adam Smith 204
dependency theory 204
Karl Marx 205
New Deal 205

poverty line 205
Center for Budget and Policy Priorities 206
rural ghettos 206
Buffalo Commons 206
globalization 208
North American Free Trade Agreement (NAFTA) 210
apartheid laws 210
Black Empowerment Initiative 210
caste system 210
Brahmans 210
Ksatriyas 210
Vaisyas 210
Sudras 210

untouchables 210
gender ideology 211
extreme poverty 213
absolute poverty 213
relative poverty 213
Consumer Price Index (CPI) 214
malnutrition 214
World Food Program 215
gender budgeting 217
Green Revolution 217
microlending 217
Muhammad Yunus 217

DISCUSSION QUESTIONS

1. What role do government redistributive programs have on either increasing or decreasing inequality? Can you think of specific examples of such programs implemented in the United States?
2. Do you think globalization increases or reduces global and domestic inequality?
3. What effect does domestic or global inequality have in promoting or hindering democratization? Is there an inverse relationship between increasing inequality and lower prospects for democratization?
4. What are some of the main factors contributing to increasing global and domestic inequality discussed in this chapter?
5. How can microlending, as practiced by groups like the Grameen Bank, help to alleviate poverty and to decrease inequality?

SUGGESTED READINGS

Collier, Paul. *The Bottom Billion*. New York: Oxford University Press, 2007.
Fisman, Raymond, and Edward Miguel. *Economic Gangsters: Corruption, Violence, and the Poverty of Nations*. Princeton, NJ: Princeton University Press, 2009.
Krugman, Paul. *Development, Geography, and Economic Theory*. Cambridge, MA: MIT Press, 1995.

Landes, David S. *The Wealth and Poverty of Nations: Why Some Are So Rich and Some So Poor.* New York: W. W. Norton, 1997.

Lawrence, Robert. *Blue Collar Blues: Is Trade to Blame for Rising U.S. Income Inequality?* Washington, DC: Peterson Institute, 2008.

Powell, Benjamin. *Making Poor Nations Rich.* Stanford, CA: Stanford University Press, 2007.

Runge, C. Ford, and Benjamin Senauer. "How Biofuels Could Starve the Poor," *Foreign Affairs* 86, No. 3 (May/June 2007): 41–54.

Sachs, Jeffrey D. *The End of Poverty.* New York: Penguin, 2006.

END NOTES

1. Eric Eckholm, "Last Year's Poverty Rate Was Highest in 12 Years," *New York Times*, 11 September 2009, A12.

2. World Bank, *World Development Report 2003* (New York: Oxford University Press, 2003), 89.

3. Joseph S. Nye, "Globalization's Democratic Deficit," *Foreign Affairs* 80, No. 4 (July/August 2001), 2.

4. Nancy Birdsall, "That Silly Inequality Debate," *Foreign Policy* 130 (May/June 2002), 92; Nancy Birdsall et al., "How to Help Poor Countries," *Foreign Affairs* 84, No. 4 (July/August 2005), 136–152; and Robert Lawrence, *Blue Collar Blues: Is Trade to Blame for Rising U.S. Income Inequality* (Washington, DC: Peterson Institute, 2008).

5. John Micklethwait and Adrian Wooldridge, "The Globalization Backlash," *Foreign Policy* 126 (September/October 2001), 22.

6. David Dollar and Aart Kraay, "Spreading the Wealth," *Foreign Affairs* 81, No. 1 (January/February 2002), 120.

7. Dollar and Kraay, "Spreading the Wealth," 121.

8. Robert Wright, "Will Globalization Make You Happy?" *Foreign Policy* 120 (September/October 2000), 58.

9. Joseph Kahn, "Losing Faith: Globalization Proves Disappointing," *New York Times*, 21 March 2002, 24.

10. Jack Beatty, "Do as We Say, Not as We Do," *The Atlantic Monthly*, February 2002, 24.

11. Kahn, "Losing Faith," A6.

12. Wayne Arnold, "Globalization Stirs Asian Dreams, but Rural Poverty Grows Endemic," *New York Times*, 17 December 2001, C14.

13. Caroline Thomas, "Globalization and the South," in *Globalization and the South*, eds. Caroline Thomas and Peter Wilkin (London: Macmillan Press, 1997), 6.

14. Vito Tanzi, "Globalization Without a Net," *Foreign Policy* 125 (July/August 2001), 78.

15. Dani Rodrik, "Trading in Illusions," *Foreign Policy* 123 (March/April 2001), 78.

16. Rodrik, "Trading in Illusions," 59.

17. UN Development Program, *Human Development Report 2002* (New York: Oxford University Press, 2002), 19.

18. "Who Is in the Middle?" *Economist*, 14 February 2009, 4.

19. David S. Landes, *The Wealth and Poverty of Nations* (New York: W. W. Norton, 1998), 56.

20. Virginia Postrel, "Economic Scene: The Decline of the Muslim Middle East," *New York Times*, 8 November 2001, C2.

21. Dennis Overbye, "How Islam Won, and Lost, the Lead in Science," *New York Times*, 30 October 2001, D1.

22. UN Development Program, *Human Development Report 1999* (New York: Oxford University Press, 1999), 38; and World Bank, *World Development Report 2003*, 2.

23. Nancy Birdsall, "Life Is Unfair: Inequality in the World," *Foreign Policy* 111 (Summer 1998), 76.

24. Ricardo Hausmann, "Prisoners of Geography," *Foreign Policy* 122 (January/February 2001), 46–47.

25. Lester C. Thurow, *The Future of Capitalism* (New York: William Morrow, 1996), 91.

26. Alan Schwartz, "Getting at the Roots of Arab Poverty," *New York Times*, 1 December 2001, A27.

27. Kwan S. Kim, "Income Distribution and Poverty: An Interregional Comparison," *World Development* 25, No. 11 (1997), 1916; and Nancy Birdsall and Juan Luis Londono, "No Tradeoff: Efficient Growth Via More Equal Human Capital Accumulation," in *Beyond Tradeoffs*, eds. Nancy Birdsall et al. (Washington, DC: Inter-American Development Bank, 1998), 1.

28. Ray Boshara, "The $6,000 Solution," *The Atlantic Monthly*, January/February 2003, 94; and David Cay Johnston, "Corporate Wealth Share Rises for Top-Income Americans," *New York Times*, 29 January 2006, A21.

29. Lynnley Browning, "U.S. Income Gap Widening," *New York Times*, 25 September 2003, C2.

30. Jad Mouawad, "For Leading Exxon to Its Riches, $144,573 a Day," *New York Times*, 15 April 2006, A1; and Kathryn Jones, "Executive Pay: A Special Report," *New York Times*, 5 April 2009, B1.

31. Paul Krugman, "For Richer: How the Permissive Capitalism of the Boom Destroyed American Equality," *New York Times Magazine*, 20 October 2002, 65.

32. Joel Kotkin, "The Withering of Rural America," *Washington Post Weekly National Edition*, 29 July–4 August 2002, 22; and "Blue-Collar America," *Economist*, 6 June 2009, 34.

33. "Getting Wider," *Economist*, 2 December 2000, 57; and Sarah Lyall, "Grumbles Grow Louder in Quiet Rural Britain," *New York Times*, 2 October 2002, A3.

34. Doug Struck and Kathryn Tolbert, "Economic Gap in Japan," *Chicago Tribune*, 6 January 2002, Sect. 1, 6.

35. "Winners and Losers," *Economist*, 28 September 1996, 24; and Kenneth F. Scheve and Matthew Slaughter, "A New Deal for Globalization," *Foreign Affairs* 86, No. 4 (July/August 2007), 34.

36. Louis Uchitelle, "Once a Key to Recovery, Detroit Adds to the Pain," *New York Times*, 1 June 2009, B1.

37. UN Development Program, *Human Development Report 1998* (New York: Oxford University Press, 1998), 29.

38. Mary Jordan and Kevin Sullivan, "Very Little Trickles Down," *Washington Post National Weekly Edition*, 31 March–6 April 2003, 15.

39. John Jeter, "In South Africa, a New Apartheid," *Washington Post National Weekly Edition*, 10 July 2000, 15.

40. UN Development Program, *Human Development Report 2002*, 196.

41. David Hale and Lyric Hughes Hale, "China Takes Off," *Foreign Affairs* 82, No. 6 (November/December 2003), 41; and David Barboza, "Little-Known Entrepreneurs Putting China Near Top of Billionaires' List," *New York Times*, 7 November 2007, C1.

42. David Leonhardt, "Wage Gap Between Men and Women Closes to Narrowest," *New York Times*, 17 February 2003, A1.

43. Justin Brown, "A Crack Appears in the Navy's Brass Ceiling," *Christian Science Monitor*, 31 March 2000, 1.

44. Bruce Stanley, "New Leader for London Exchange," *Chicago Tribune*, 25 January 2001, Sect. 3, 5.

45. World Bank, *World Development Report 2003*, 2.

46. Moises Naim, "Missing in Monterrey," *Foreign Policy* 130 (May/June 2003), 104.
47. A. M. Khusro, *The Poverty of Nations* (New York: St. Martin's Press, 1999), 5.
48. Deepak Bhargava and Joan Kuriansky, "Drawing the Line on Poverty," *Washington Post National Weekly Edition*, 23–29 September 2002, 23.
49. Deepa Narayan et al., *Can Anyone Hear Us: Voices of the Poor* (New York: Oxford University Press, 2000), 5.
50. Somini Sengupta, "Hunger Worsens in Many Lands," *New York Times*, 26 November 2003, A3.
51. C. Ford Runge and Benjamin Senauer, "How Biofuels Could Starve the Poor," *Foreign Affairs* 86, No. 3 (May/June 2007), 41; and Somini Sengupta, "As Indian Growth Soars, Child Hunger Persists," *New York Times*, 13 March 2009, A1.
52. Tim Weiner, "More Entreaties in Monterrey for More Aid to the Poor," *New York Times*, 22 March 2002, A10; and "World Food Crisis a Silent Tsunami," *New York Times*, 23 April 2008, A9.
53. Larry Rohter, "Brazil to Let Squatters Own Homes," *New York Times*, 19 April 2003, A7; and "Happy Families," *Economist*, 9 February 2008, 39.
54. UN Development Program, *Human Development Report 2002*, 80.
55. Stephen Buckley, "In Brazil, the Poor Help the Poorer," *Washington Post National Weekly Edition*, 15–21 January 2001, 17.
56. Carol C. Adelman, "The Privatization of Foreign Aid," *Foreign Affairs* 82, No. 6 (November/December 2003), 9; and Neil MacFarquhar, "Haiti's Woes Are Top Test for Aid Effort," *New York Times*, 31 March 2009, A5.
57. Adelman, "The Privatization of Foreign Aid," 12; and Eduardo Porter, "Flow of Immigrants' Money to Latin America Surges," *New York Times*, 19 October 2006, A23.

Environmental Issues

INTRODUCTION

In 2009, the Global Humanitarian Forum concluded that each year global warming is causing more than 300,000 deaths and roughly $125 billion in economic losses. China's impressive industrial growth, improved agricultural productivity, and rapidly growing Gobi desert are creating growing environmental problems for China and the neighboring countries. It was estimated that China built a coal-fired power plant each week in 2009. However, about 60 percent of these plants are highly efficient. In fact, China leads the world in the construction of more efficient, less polluting coal power plants. But pollution from China is also creating problems in the United States and Canada. In fact, in an unusually severe dust storm in the spring of 1998, pollution levels in Oregon, Washington, and British Columbia were unprecedented. Air quality control officials in Seattle were astonished to see measurements showing that 75 percent of the pollution came from China.[1] Poor Africans, Asians, and Latin Americans clear forests for farmland and firewood, thereby contributing to an already serious problem of deforestation. Many burn coal to cook their food and to keep warm. Economic growth in the developing world fuels greater consumption of energy and is a major cause of environmental problems. Despite the global economic recession of 2008–2009, greater awareness of environmental issues and a global search for renewable energy sources, wealthy Americans, Europeans, and an increasing number of people in the developing world continued to drive gas-guzzling sports utility vehicles, air condition their homes and offices in the summer and heat them in the winter, maintain perfect lawns, rely on numerous labor-saving appliances, and discard industrial and household wastes. In many ways, both affluence and poverty have devastating environmental consequences. Environmental problems underscore global interdependence and illustrate connections among political, economic, and cultural aspects of globalization.

Environmental issues remind us that the earth is a single biosphere and that problems in one country are other countries' problems as well. Imagine that you are a resident of Boston in 1676 and that your cows are grazing the **commons**, which is land used by the entire community. Overgrazing would eventually destroy the commons and the cattle. But overgrazing is a problem that cannot be solved by restraining only a few members of the community. It is only through the cooperation of all members that overgrazing can be avoided. On a larger scale, environmental problems underscore the reality of global interdependence. Where these problems originate is less important than their global impact. A Soviet nuclear power plant in **Chernobyl** that exploded in 1986 illustrates this point. The power plant explosion released extensive radioactive material that spread to Europe, killing thirty people, damaging crops and animals, and polluting the environment for thousands of miles from the explosion.

Increasingly, scholars, politicians, leaders of international organizations and nongovernmental organizations (NGOs), and ordinary citizens worldwide are linking environmental security to human security (i.e., the challenges ordinary people face every day) and to traditional concerns about national security. The **environmental security** approach to international relations emphasizes that the ecological crisis we face is also a threat to national security. Environmental degradation is perceived to be as serious a threat to human societies as the traditional military threat. For the Carteret Islands, Tuvalu, Kiribati, Palau, the Maldives, and Bangladesh, climate change is a direct and growing threat to their survival; the leader of the Maldives, for example, is attempting to relocate 300,000 islanders to a safe haven.[2] Influenced by this reality, the Nobel Prize Committee awarded former U.S. Vice President Al Gore the Nobel Peace Prize for his work on global warming in 2007.

Throughout history, environmental factors have had serious implications for all aspects of human existence, including the rise and fall of great civilizations, the spread of infectious diseases, war and peace, economic prosperity and hunger, migration and resettlement, population growth, and global inequality. The destruction of Mayan civilization on the Yucatan peninsula in southern Mexico in the tenth century shows how climate change and population pressures can dramatically alter human societies. This chapter discusses how environmental problems became central concerns of the global community.

Commons ■ Land designated for use by the entire community

Chernobyl ■ Soviet nuclear power plant that suffered a meltdown in 1986

Environmental Security ■ A concept placing protection of the environment on equal ground with national security

THE GLOBALIZATION OF ENVIRONMENTAL PROBLEMS

Ancient civilizations confronted some of the environmental challenges that are familiar to modern societies. For example, almost 3,700 years ago, Sumerian cities in the southern part of **Mesopotamia** (now modern Iraq) prospered because high levels of agricultural productivity supported permanent human resettlements. But these agricultural surpluses that helped develop the cradle of civilization came at a cost: extensive irrigation, which ultimately resulted in fields that were saline and waterlogged. Environmental decay forced people to abandon the Sumerian cities. Similarly, roughly 2,400 years ago, Plato was concerned about the impact of deforestation and overgrazing on soil erosion in the hills of Attica. Shipbuilding by the ancient Italian maritime states contributed to deforestation along the Mediterranean coasts. And air pollution from burning coal in medieval

Earth as Seen from
Apollo Space Craft.
(NASA)

England was so bad that by 1661 the naturalist **John Evelyn** compared London with the "Court of Vulcan or the Suburbs of Hell."[3] Despite obvious environmental problems, the environmental movements did not germinate until 1865, when a private group called the Commons, Footpaths, and Spaces Preservation Society was founded in Britain. By the late 1890s and the turn of the century, groups in the United States that were committed to wilderness preservation and resource conservation emerged, strongly supported by President Theodore Roosevelt.

Contemporary ecological challenges differ significantly from those of earlier periods in *four main ways*:

1. Contemporary environmental problems are predominantly global in their cumulative consequences.
2. Whereas our current environmental problems represent biodegenerative products of humanity—such as air and water pollution, deforestation, overfishing, and soil erosion—our ancestors faced environmental constraints that were primarily related to the biophysical parameters of nature, such as access to water, soil fertility, and temperature.
3. Natural forces created environmental problems for our ancestors. Today, however, some populations are more vulnerable to environmental crises principally because of human activities and government policies.
4. Ancient societies had more time and space to deal with environmental threats than we do today.[4]

Globalizing environmental issues is always a gradual, controversial, and complex process. In the past, most attempts to diminish environmental damage were primarily at the local and national levels. Before World War II, concerns about endangered wildlife and growing threats of ocean oil pollution led to bilateral and limited international environmental agreements. The globalization of environmental

Mesopotamia ■ An ancient civilization between the Tigris and Euphrates rivers, now known as Iraq

John Evelyn ■ Naturalist who criticized London for its high levels of pollution issues reflects the growth of global interdependence after World War II and the emergence of the United States as a superpower. The global environmental movement emerged principally in Western Europe, the United States, and Canada. A catalyst for growing concerns about how we are destroying our environment, and ultimately ourselves, was the publication of Rachel Carson's book *Silent Spring* in 1962. The book focused on how the widespread use of pesticides was devastating birds and other wildlife. Furthermore, space exploration reinforced perceptions of the oneness of the earth as well as its fragility. Exploding population growth and rapid industrialization, often with reckless disregard for environmental ramifications, focused more attention on resource scarcity, deforestation, and deteriorating health standards. Nuclear weapons proliferation, especially by the United States and the Soviet Union, also helped to reinforce our vulnerability to environmental threats resulting from our activities.

Silent Spring ■ A book that focused on the negative effects of pesticides

Images of "spaceship earth" facilitated a deeper understanding of global interdependence of environmental issues by illustrating that national boundaries are artificial and national issues are ultimately global issues. Like our example of the Boston common, the world was increasingly being perceived as a global common. Oil pollution, because of its immediate and drastic impact on coastal areas, clearly showed the dangers of environmental disasters. When the oil tanker *Torrey Canyon* was wrecked on the coast of England and spilled about 875,000 barrels of crude oil in 1967, public opinion worldwide generated support for globalizing environmental issues. Globalization of the economy further reinforced environmental globalization by stimulating trade in endangered species, tropical hardwoods, and various metals. The production and distribution of chlorofluorocarbons (CFCs) around the world for use as a propellant in spray cans, as a refrigerant, and as cleaning solvents caused significant damage to the protective ozone layer in the earth's upper atmosphere.[5] European integration, a component of globalization, enabled animal rights groups in Europe to pressure the European Union (EU) to ban inhumane treatment of animals as well as international trade that contributed to the destruction of endangered species.

Torrey Canyon ■ Oil tanker that crashed off the coast of England in 1967

International agreements were made in response to specific environmental problems. The earliest ones concentrated on protecting wildlife in Africa and in the Western Hemisphere, Pacific fur seals, and whaling. Ocean oil pollution and the proliferation of nuclear weapons became major priorities of the environmental movement after 1945. The **Biosphere Conference**, held in Paris in 1968, focused on how human activities—such as air and water pollution, deforestation, the drainage of wetlands, and overgrazing—affected the biosphere. The **UN Conference on the Human Environment** (also known as Stockholm Conference), held in Stockholm in 1972, is often viewed as the beginning of serious global cooperation on the environment. Developed countries in particular acknowledged that multilateral efforts were essential in order to adequately address transboundary environmental problems.[6] The Stockholm Conference created the United Nations Environmental Program (UNEP), an institutional framework to address the issues discussed in the conference. The 1992 UN Conference on Environment and Development (also known as the Rio Summit or the Earth Summit) and the 2002 **World Summit on Sustainable Development** (also known as the Johannesburg Action Plan) emphasized priorities of developing countries.

Biosphere Conference ■ Held in 1968; focused on the degradation of the environment from human activities

UN Conference on the Human Environment ■ Held in 1972; aimed at international cooperation in environmental protections

World Summit on Sustainable Development ■ Focused simultaneously on economic growth and environmental protections

States may join international agreements as a way of pressuring neighboring states into doing the same, thereby enhancing chances of widespread cooperation to protect the environment. Domestic political and economic considerations also play a role. Governments often respond to pressure from environmental activists. Industries that must comply with environmental laws in their home countries often support international agreements to prevent companies in other countries from gaining a competitive advantage.[7] Even though states recognize the need to cooperate, *political and economic considerations often weaken the effectiveness of environmental agreements*. These include disagreements between rich and poor countries about the economic implications of environmental agreements and efforts by economic interests and governments to avoid compliance.[8]

The implementation of and compliance with environmental agreements are influenced by at least four factors.[9] *One is the nature of the substances or activities that are regulated.* At the heart of many environmental debates is how international agreements will affect economic activities and the costs and benefits of complying with the agreements. *Two is the characteristics of the agreement.* This relates to the process of reaching the agreement. Who initiates the treaty? What is required of the countries that sign it? Is the agreement vague or does it spell out clearly the conditions for compliance? *Three is the global environment.* How major countries, international organizations—such as the World Bank, the United Nations, the World Trade Organization (WTO), and environmental NGOs—view the agreement will impact its implementation. *Fourth is domestic factors.* Ultimately, the effectiveness of an environmental agreement depends on the nature of the society in which it is being implemented.

Nongovernmental Organizations and the Environment

Older environmental groups, such as the National Wildlife Federation and the National Audubon Society, were joined by numerous other environmental organizations, many having originated on college and university campuses in the 1960s and 1970s. The Environmental Defense Fund, the Natural Resources Defense Council, Greenpeace, Environmental Action, and Friends of the Earth were among them. Scientific groups, such as the Union of Concerned Scientists and Physicians for Social Responsibility, strengthened and broadened the environmental movement.[10] While most environmental groups operate on a local or national level and concentrate on specific problems facing particular communities, many of them have a global reach. For example, many NGOs participate in global conferences on behalf of small, ecologically vulnerable islands of the Pacific. There are also NGOs—such as the Global Climate Coalition and the Alliance for Responsible CFC Policy—that represent industries and attempt to limit the effectiveness of other environmental organizations.[11]

Women and the Environment

The connection between women and environmental issues is acknowledged by UNEP, which has held conferences on women and the environment and established a committee of senior women advisers on sustainable development. The general emphasis on the gendered nature of environmental issues arises from the

Green Belt Movement ■ Kenyan movement focusing on preventing further deforestation

leading roles women have in environmental NGOs and numerous grassroots movements worldwide. Women in Kenya organized the **Green Belt Movement** to prevent further deforestation and to restore the land through reforestation. In 2004, Wangari Maathai, an environmentalist involved in the planting of more than 30 million trees, was awarded the Nobel Peace Prize for her work. Women's participation in environmental NGOs and at the grassroots level has resulted in *three main arguments about the connection between women and the environment*: (1) women are disproportionately disadvantaged by environmental problems, (2) gender bias is an impediment to achieving sustainable development, and (3) women's participation is vital to efforts to achieve sustainable development.[12]

Strategies Used by Nongovernmental Organizations

Regimes ■ Rules for governing state and nonstate actors

At the global level, NGOs must spend considerable resources to develop **regimes**; that is, the rules, codes of conduct, principles, and norms necessary to govern the behavior of both states and nonstate actors. Environmental NGOs that operate primarily on the global level encounter *three major impediments*. First, there is no common authority or power that can effectively force members of the global community to comply with rules. Second, the decentralized nature of international bureaucracies and their dependence on states make it difficult for NGOs to get international rules implemented. Third, global agreements and organizations are primarily produced by governments. Environmental NGOs are required in many cases to work though those governments to influence agreements and global institutions.[13] There are *several major strategies* that environmental NGOs use to accomplish their objectives:

1. Get media coverage and publicity for their issues. Generating domestic and global public awareness and support is crucial to NGOs' efforts to persuade policymakers to take action.
2. Share information among groups in order to educate each other on the issues, coordinate strategies and activities, and provide each other with needed support.
3. Lobby government officials and intergovernmental organizations, such as the World Bank.
4. Acquire and manage property to protect the environment.
5. Pressure companies to protect the environment.[14]

BIODIVERSITY

Biodiversity ■ The large number and diversity of organisms on earth

Biodiversity is defined as the number and the variety of living organisms on earth. It includes genetic diversity, species diversity, and ecosystem diversity. Crucial to biodiversity is the interdependence of species and ecosystems and how their complex relationships affect the environment. Biodiversity is concentrated in the forests of developing countries, especially Brazil, China, Colombia, Ecuador, India, Indonesia, Madagascar, Zaire, Peru, Mexico, Costa Rica, and Malaysia. Australia is the only developed country that has a large variety of species. The United States, Canada, and Europe are relatively poor in biodiversity. Biodiversity is at the heart of environmental globalization because it affects so many groups and individuals, including those interested in deforestation, agriculture, biotechnology, anthropology, pharmaceuticals, sustainable development, global trade, and ethics.[15]

Biodiversity provides many benefits. Ecosystem functions—such as carbon exchange, watershed flows of surface and ground water, the protection and fertility of soils, and the regulation of surface temperatures and local climates—are influenced by biodiversity. Diversity lessens the vulnerability of agricultural crops to diseases and pests. This is increasingly important for large-scale specialized agriculture. Through crossbreeding of diverse genetic stock, crops become more resistant to disease and pests. Biodiversity is especially important for medicinal and pharmaceutical product development. Preserving biodiversity is regarded as an ethical obligation. The basis of the ethical argument is that biodiversity is an intrinsic value and people should avoid destroying other species.[16] The destruction of rain forests in Brazil, for example, directly affects biodiversity, especially since Brazil alone contains almost 25 percent of the world's plant species. Perhaps the most widespread cause of damage to biodiversity is pollution and global environmental change.[17] Because the economic benefits derived from biodiversity, especially involving pharmaceuticals, are significant and potential benefits are even greater, governments are imposing strict controls on medicinal plants. In 2002, the Group of Allied Mega-Biodiverse Nations was created to certify the legal possession of biological material and to negotiate terms to transfer it.

Developed countries attempted to reduce the destruction of the world's biodiversity by calling for the establishment of an international regime. Negotiations for such a regime, known as the **Convention on Biological Diversity**, began in 1991. Whereas the developed countries viewed genetic resources as belonging to all, as common heritage, developing countries saw these resources as national resources. The rich countries of the **North** wanted unimpeded access to these resources, particularly for their pharmaceutical and agricultural resources. The poor countries of the **South** wanted to control genetic resources to derive economic benefits from them. The Convention on Biological Diversity provides for (1) national identification and monitoring of biological diversity, (2) the development of national strategies and programs for conserving biological diversity, (3) environmental assessment procedures to take into account the effects of projects on biological diversity, (4) sharing of research findings in a fair and equitable way, (5) the provision of technology for the conservation and use of genetic resources by the industrial countries, and (6) the facilitation of participation in biotechnology research by countries that provide genetic resources.[18]

Convention on Biological Diversity ■ Designed to establish an international regime to protect biodiversity

North/South Divide ■ Refers to the large economic divide between many Northern and Southern states

Endangered Species and Wildlife Protection

At Taruichi restaurant in Tokyo's trendy Shinjuku district, business executives, domestic workers, and ordinary Japanese gather to dine on whale meat. Among the thirty-six choices on the menu are fried whale, raw whale, whale bacon, whale heart, whale testicle, whale kidney, and ice cream made from whale fat.[19] Many governments, environmental NGOs, and most Americans oppose whale hunting and eating whales—especially after Greenpeace's successful campaign,

"Save the Whales." In Japan, however, eating whales is viewed as part of the national culture, especially by older Japanese who survived on whale meat provided by the government after World War II.

Whales have received widespread attention partly because of the popularity of *Moby-Dick*, a book by Herman Melville about the whaling industry in the first half of the nineteenth century. At that time, Americans sailed the Pacific for up to four years at a time searching for whales. They returned to America with great wealth, since whales provided oil for lubricating industrial machinery and for making soap and margarine, baleen for manufacturing corsets and umbrellas, and food. Whaling was also important for making glycerin, which was an essential component in nitroglycerin that was used in manufacturing dynamite. Military competition among European countries and the outbreak of World War I created a great demand for glycerin. This, in turn, led to an expansion and intensification of whaling. The development of the harpoon cannon between 1864 and 1868 and the invention of factory ships that could process whales at sea hastened the depletion of whales.[20]

One of the earliest attempts by the international community to prevent the decline and extinction of whales, especially the widely hunted blue whale, came in 1935 when the League of Nations tried to regulate their exploitation. By 1946, the International Convention for the Regulation of Whaling, called for by nations involved in the whaling industry, established the **International Whaling Commission (IWC)** to protect the price of whale oil. For the most part, whales remained unprotected until 1964, when the IWC specifically advocated for the preservation of humpback whales. Blue whales were designated as a protected species a year later. The 1975 **Convention on International Trade in Endangered Species of Wild Fauna and Flora (CITES)** effectively prohibited trade in whale products. By 1982, the IWC had agreed to a moratorium on whaling, except whaling done by the Inuit of Alaska and Canada, whose diet and culture depended on hunting whales. An exception was also made for catching whales for scientific purposes, a provision that provides a loophole for Japan to continue harvesting a limited number of whales for consumption. In 1986, the moratorium came into effect, and in 1994, the IWC created a whaling sanctuary in the Southern Atlantic and Antarctica.[21] However, in 2006, Japan was able to secure a majority on the IWC, a development that facilitated Japan's resumption of commercial whaling. Japan escalated its whaling activities between 2007 and 2009. Another major threat to whales that is receiving more attention is ships and boats. Many whales are killed or wounded in collisions with oceangoing vessels.

Dolphins, considered an endangered species, especially by the United States, are widely regarded as having human-like qualities. Environmental campaigns, movies and other media, and aquariums have strengthened the perception of dolphins as friendly creatures that must be protected. Threats to dolphins were a by-product of fishing with purse-seine nets for tuna that schooled beneath the dolphins. Many dolphins drowned or were severely injured in the nets. Global environmental NGOs pressured consumers to boycott tuna that was caught in such nets. Because the United States is the world's largest market for tuna, environmentalists in America used the power of consumers to force tuna producers to adopt dolphin-safe measures for catching tuna. The **Inter-American Tropical Tuna Commission (IATTC)**,

IWC ■ Established to protect the price of whale oil

CITES ■ Convention prohibiting trade in whale products

IATTC ■ Commission devoted to protecting dolphins, among other things under American leadership, adopted regulations to prevent the endangerment of dolphins, a development that has helped to protect dolphins globally.[22]

Sea turtles are also listed as an endangered or threatened species under the U.S. Endangered Species Act. While overfishing of turtles and harvesting their eggs continue to be serious concerns, one major threat to turtles comes from shrimp trawlers. Turtles caught in shrimp nets usually drown. To eliminate this problem, the U.S. government required shrimp trawlers to use turtle extruder devices (TEDs) on their nets. Essentially, these devices are trap doors through which turtles can escape if caught in the net. Apart from arguing that TEDs were a financial burden and that they were losing almost half of the shrimp they caught, shrimp fishers pointed out that foreign fleets did not face similar restrictions, a fact that put U.S. shrimpers at a competitive disadvantage.[23] American environmentalists ultimately succeeded in getting foreign shrimpers to comply with U.S. laws protecting turtles by agreeing with domestic shrimpers that all shrimpers should play by the same rules to ensure fair competition. Another threat to endangered turtles—especially the leatherback turtle, which can weigh up to 1,400 pounds and grow to a length of seven feet—comes from long-line fishing. Long-line fishing involves a main line that can be as long as thirty miles. The line has branch lines that are roughly two hundred feet apart and are equipped with baited hooks. Some turtles swallow the hooks or become entangled in the lines.[24]

The African elephant, hunted mostly for ivory tusks for export, is also an endangered species, a designation that drew opposition from some countries, such as Botswana, Malawi, Mozambique, South African Zambia, and Zimbabwe. These countries had carefully managed their elephant herds and believed that restrictions on ivory exports would unfairly penalize them economically. Compared with African states that depleted their elephant herds, Botswana and the other countries had too many elephants. In 1997, Botswana, Namibia, and Zimbabwe were granted permission to sell stockpiled ivory tusks to Japan. Other animals in peril are gorillas and chimpanzees. Roughly 80 percent of the world's gorillas and most of its chimpanzees inhabit Gabon and the Republic of Congo. These great apes, our closest relatives, face severe threats from hunting, deforestation, and infectious diseases. The ongoing violence and endemic poverty in Congo continue to contribute to the destruction of wildlife. It is estimated that the gorilla and chimpanzee populations declined by more than 50 percent between 1983 and 2000 and that they are likely to drop by an additional 80 percent in the next thirty years.[25] Worldwide, rare and exotic animals are threatened with extinction because of escalating exotic animal trade in them, aided by the Internet and a global network of traffickers. In fact, sales of exotic animals comprise the third largest global illegal trade—behind illegal drugs and weapons—and generate between $5 billion and $20 billion a year.[26]

DEFORESTATION

One of the principal threats to biodiversity is the accelerating rate of global deforestation. The Amazon rainforest is estimated to be disappearing at the rate of 3 million acres a year. The **Congo basin**—comprised of Cameroon, Gabon, the

Congo Basin ■
Tropical area in central Africa

Central African Republic, Republic of Congo, the Democratic Republic of Congo (former Zaire), and Equatorial Guinea, which had the second largest tropical forests in the world—is losing about 8.9 million acres a year to deforestation. Similarly, Russia, which has roughly 22 percent of the world's forests, is depleting its natural forests. Deforestation is also a major concern in many parts of Asia, especially in light of China's rapid economic growth and its demand for forest products. Forests are essential in biodiversity and to preserve the quality of life, and life itself, for human beings. Forests, especially large rain forests such as the Amazon, have an impact on the global climate. Air quality, water supplies, climate stability, agricultural productivity, and countless human communities are affected by deforestation. It is widely believed that protecting existing forests and planting more trees are essential to diminishing some environmental problems, such as global warming and climate change, because forests soak up between 10 and 20 percent of the heat-trapping carbon dioxide released by industrial smokestacks and automobiles. On the positive side, slower population growth, increasing urbanization, and the abandonment of marginal agricultural land are contributing to the growth of secondary forests.[27]

Causes of Deforestation

The most pervasive cause of deforestation is the combination of *population pressures and poverty*. Throughout most of the world, poor people rely on forests for fuel, shelter, agricultural land, and grazing for their animals. The relationship between population pressure, poverty, and deforestation is demonstrated by developments in **Chiapas**, the poorest state in Mexico. Destitute villagers in hundreds of communities in Chiapas cut down trees and burn the undergrowth to create fields for cultivation and grazing cattle. Soon after, the thin layer of topsoil is planted with corn, and the land is left to return to pasture, which is often overgrazed. The exposed soil becomes vulnerable to erosion during heavy tropical rains. Somalia, on the Horn of Africa, provides another example of how poverty accelerates deforestation. Somalia, which lacks an effective central governmental authority to protect the environment, exports tons of charcoal to Middle Eastern countries.

Deforestation is also caused by the *deliberate setting of fires* by small farmers, commercial farmers, cattle ranchers, logging companies, and governments. **Selective logging** involves cutting down large and particular types of trees in an effort to manage exploitation of forest resources and to promote sustainability. Selective logging contributes to forest fires because, as forests are thinned out, humidity decreases and drier conditions in the forest facilitate the spread of both natural and human-made fires. The forces of *economic development* play a significant role in global deforestation. Development involves building an extensive **infrastructure**, which includes roads, highways, electrical plants, airports, harbors, railways, large reservoirs, and dams. Another cause of deforestation is the **commercial logging** practices that disregard sustainable development of forest resources. The demand for tropical hardwoods, such as mahogany and teak, is

Chiapas ■ The poorest state in Mexico

Selective Logging ■ Cutting specific trees in order to promote forest sustainability

Infrastructure ■ Necessary elements of a stable society

Commercial Logging ■ Process disrupting sustainable development contributing to deforestation in Southeast Asia, Central America, Africa, and elsewhere in the developing world. *Government policies* have aggressively promoted deforestation in an effort to relocate people to less crowded areas in order to diminish population pressures and encourage economic development. Brazil has used this strategy. Opening up the Amazon was viewed in Brazil as important for national economic growth as well as a way to strengthen the country's strategic position in South America. Environmental protection was not a priority of the military governments that ruled Brazil. Consequently, between 1970 and 1974, the government implemented its **Plan for National Integration**. This plan included the construction of the Trans-Amazon Highway and offered incentives to agribusiness enterprises and landless peasants, especially from the northeast, to encourage them to settle in the Amazon and to clear the land for cultivation, cattle grazing, and industrialization.[28]

Plan for National Integration ■ Brazil's efforts to encourage the development of the Amazon

Efforts to Prevent Deforestation

Efforts to slow down the rapid pace of global deforestation appear to be largely ineffective. Nonetheless, governments, NGOs, and grassroots organizations are making some progress. In Brazil, the transition from military rule to democracy has been accompanied by government programs aimed at halting deforestation. Since the 1990s, the Brazilian government's perception of the environment has shifted from frontier development toward environmental protection. This change is partly due to growing global awareness of the Amazon's importance to environmental health and increased global and domestic pressures for change. In 1989, the Brazilian government announced the development of its **Nossa Natureza (Our Nature) Program** to reduce the destruction of the Amazon rain forests. The program included (1) suspending fiscal incentives for developing forest resources, (2) limiting log exports, (3) creating national parks, and (4) increasing the emphasis on environmental protection and research. An important component of this effort was the formation of **IBAMA**, the federal environmental protection agency, to monitor environment problems and to enforce environmental laws.[29] But loggers, ranchers, and farmers continue to destroy the forests and wildlife and to threaten the livelihoods of the indigenous inhabitants. The murder of Sister Dorothy Stang, an American nun opposed to deforestation, in February 2005 and more aggressive steps by the Brazilian government in 2008 to protect the Amazon underscore the ongoing conflict in the Amazon. Another example of government involvement in efforts to diminish deforestation is the agreement reached in 2000 by logging companies, the government of Gabon, and several environmental NGOs to preserve 1,900 square miles of forests that comprise **Gabon's Lope Reserve**. This area contains very valuable trees and the highest density of large animals, including elephants and gorillas, ever recorded in a tropical rain forest.[30]

Nossa Natureza Program ■ Designed to reduce the destruction of the Amazon

IBAMA ■ Brazilian environmental protection agency

Gabon's Lope Reserve ■ Area in Gabon containing rich biodiversity

One of the most successful grassroots reforestation efforts is by the Green Belt Movement of Kenya. Its objectives include (1) *raising awareness* of the connection between the environment and poverty; (2) *promoting the planting of multi-use trees* to meet fuel needs, provide employment, protect the environment, and provide food for the community; and (3) *disseminating information* on environmental protection through research, seminars, and workshops.[31]

Another approach to addressing the problem of deforestation is **forest certification.** The basic idea is to inform consumers about the origin of wood products and how their production affects the environment. This approach, which aims to promote eco-friendly lumber, has been championed by the **Forest Stewardship Council**, a coalition of environmentalists and lumber executives. The guidelines for gaining certification include complying with national laws aimed at (1) protecting forests, (2) protecting the rights of indigenous peoples, and (3) promoting economic development.[32]

Ocean Resources—Fishing

Concerned about proper nutrition, more people around the world—especially in Europe, Canada, and the United States—are eating more seafood. The modernization of fishing fleets has made more fish available to global markets. This modernization involves using technology such as electronic fish locators, satellite navigation, temperature-depth gauges, purse-seine nets, and long-line fishing gear. More than any other food commodity, seafood crosses national boundaries daily. Most fish are exported from Africa and Southeast Asia to Europe and the United States, making it very likely that the fish you had for dinner came from another country. In fact, it is estimated that the United States exports $2 billion but imports $9 billion in seafood each year.[33]

Fish remained abundant throughout much of the world until relatively recently. John Cabot, the fifteenth-century explorer, claimed that cod were so abundant off the coast of Newfoundland, Canada, that he caught them simply by putting a bucket over the side of his ship. The cod fishing grounds in that area supported the fishing fleets of the United States and Canada for hundreds of years after John Cabot was there. By 1992, however, the cod had essentially disappeared. A ban on cod fishing, imposed to rejuvenate the stock, appeared to be futile. There are numerous examples of overfishing and the eventual collapse of fisheries. California's sardine industry, popularized by John Steinbeck, declined rapidly in the early 1940s and died out three decades later. In 1996, the UN **Food and Agriculture Organization (FAO)** estimated that more than half of global fisheries were overexploited and were facing a collapse.[34]

Apart from the growing awareness of the health benefits derived from consuming seafood, *there are several reasons for overfishing*. At the heart of the problem is that there are so many fishing fleets operating that fish stocks are not harvested in a way that is environmentally sustainable. For example, many fish are caught before they are old enough to reproduce and replenish fish supplies. The most important cause of overfishing is government subsidies.[35]

Faced with declining catches of fish, communities have historically attempted to regulate fishing. Countries that share North Sea fisheries have been very aware of the dangers of overfishing and have tried to adopt measures to limit the problem. Coastal states with rich fishing grounds often clash with countries that support long-distance fishing fleets. To protect their resources, coastal states successfully pushed for the establishment of **exclusive economic zones,** which extend to two hundred miles and over which coastal states exercise jurisdiction. These sovereign rights of coastal areas are recognized by the **Law of the Sea Treaty**, which came into effect in 1994. In early 1999, the FAO's Committee on Fisheries attempted to mobilize global support for reducing overcapacity in the fishing industry by adopting the **International Plan for the Management of Fishing Capacity (IPMFC)**. But this is a nonbinding agreement. Most states have few incentives to comply with it. Another approach to protecting global fisheries is boycotting restaurants that serve fish that are being severely depleted. Environmentalists and scientists believe that by educating consumers about fisheries and by monitoring the global market for seafood, they can save endangered species such as swordfish and Chilean sea bass. An important group supporting this effort, which demonstrates collaboration between environmentalists and businesses, is the National Chefs Collaborative. This organization is composed of more than fifteen hundred environmentally conscious restaurant owners throughout the United States who refuse to serve endangered species of fish.[36] Although controversial, because of environmental concerns and its impact on wild fish, the most promising approach to slowing the depletion of wild fisheries is aquaculture, or fish farming.

Law of the Sea Treaty ■ Recognizes state rights over territorial coastal waters

IPMFC ■ FAO plan to reduce overcapacity in the fishing industry

INVASIVE SPECIES

Fascinated by William Shakespeare, Eugene Schieffelin imported sixty starlings from Europe and released them in Central Park in 1890 in order to give the birds mentioned in Shakespeare's plays an American home. As starlings blacken the summer skies and invade once quiet and pristine neighborhoods in the Midwest and elsewhere, it is difficult to believe that the original sixty starlings claim more than a billion descendants. When the population of imported European zebra mussels exploded in the Great Lakes in the 1980s and clogged industrial intake pipes, the issue of invasive species gained national attention. Imported Burmese pythons and other species of giant constricting snakes are proliferating in Florida. Although invasive species are as old as human migrations, the rapid growth of economic and cultural globalization has made this issue extremely important. Invasive species, often referred to as exotic aliens, are generally perceived as dangerous, threatening, and unacceptable. These exotics are more aggressive, prolific, competitive, and predatory than the indigenous species. They often threaten the survival of native species listed as endangered or threatened under the Endangered Species Act. Ecologists generally define an **invasive, or alien, species** as one that people inadvertently or deliberately carried to its new location. European contacts with the Americas in 1492 marked a major shift in the spread of species, including crops and animals. Think of the beneficial invasive species that we now consider American: corn, wheat, rice, potatoes, cattle, and poultry. Although exotics received a lot of negative attention, only a small percentage of invasive species create problems in their new habitats.[37]

Many species now regarded as detrimental to the environment were initially perceived as solutions to problems or as providing economic opportunities. Millions of kudzu seedlings were planted by the **Civilian Conservation Corps** during

Invasive/Alien Species ■ A species that invades other ecosystems

Civilian Conservation Corps ■ Created in the United States during the Great Depression to protect the environment and provide employment the Great Depression to prevent erosion and to provide employment. Kudzu is now a serious threat to the environment in parts of the American South. The multicolored Asian ladybugs—which many people now regard as pests, especially as they migrate indoors for winter—were brought from China to control aphids and other agricultural pests. The population of the Asian longhorn beetle, native to China, exploded in fields of poplar planted to reverse deforestation in China. Wood from trees, infested with Asian longhorns, was used for packaging products being exported to the United States. But America also exports invasive species. A tiny beetle, known as the western corn rootworm, is native to the United States. After boarding a plane at Chicago's O'Hare International Airport, the beetle landed in Belgrade and began to invade cornfields across Europe, with devastating consequences.[38] Since most global trade relies on shipping, invasive species often arrive at distant places in ballast water releases, in containers, in used tires, and on the ships themselves. The Leidy's comb jellyfish, native to the East Coast of the Americas, made its way to the Black Sea in ballast water and began eating zooplankton. Facing no natural competition, the jellyfish represents one of the most significant massive invasions in history and has caused severe damage to the Black Sea ecosystem.[39] The Asian tiger mosquito, which was largely confined to the Indian and Pacific regions, arrived in the United States and elsewhere in containers of used tires. This mosquito—which transmits dengue fever, yellow fever, and various forms of encephalitis—is now established in Brazil, Southern Europe, South Africa, Nigeria, New Zealand, and Australia.[40] Invasive species, those exotic aliens, are fast becoming natives.

OCEAN POLLUTION

Exxon Valdez ■ Oil tanker that spilled off the coast of Alaska

Long perceived as an almost bottomless sink, the seas have been used as dumping grounds for centuries. Major oil spills, rapid development of coastal areas, increased use of petroleum products, the dramatic increase in shipping to meet demands for global trade, and economic globalization and the rise of leisure travel on cruise ships, among other factors, have contributed to significant increases in the pollution of the oceans by oil. Oil spills by tankers, such as the one caused by the *Exxon Valdez* in 1989 off the Alaskan Coast, often generate a sense of urgency about actions to prevent ocean pollution.

Charles Darwin ■ The leading proponent of evolution theory

Natural Selection ■ A prevalent theory regarding the evolution of plant and animal species

The toxic and carcinogenic properties of petroleum and the damage it causes to sea life, most of which is immobilized when soaked with oil, are the most obvious negative effects of oil spills. But the longer oil remains on the surface of the oceans, the more it blocks sunrays and oxygen essential for the health and survival of marine life. When an Ecuadorian tanker spilled 243,000 gallons of diesel and bunker fuel in the Galapagos Islands, located about six hundred miles off the Pacific Coast of South America, there was global concern about the impact of the spill on the environment. Apart from the economic consequences, environmentalists, scientists, and others worried about the effects of oil pollution on the species of marine iguanas, giant tortoises, and penguins that are found nowhere else.[41] The unusual diversity of wildlife in the Galapagos Islands was popularized by **Charles Darwin,** who visited the area in 1835 and developed his theory of **natural selection.**

Although major oil spills receive global attention, these accidents account for around 20 percent of global oil pollution at sea. Far more damaging is pollution caused by the deliberate dumping of oil used in shipping operations in the oceans. Oil tankers, container ships, and cruise ships, for example, use ballast water, which is sea water that is pumped into the bottom of the ship to keep it stable when it is not loaded with cargo. Because cargo serves as ballast, ballast water is pumped out when a ship is being loaded. Large ships carry thousands of cubic meters of ballast water, which is often contaminated by oil. Much of the 400 million pounds of waste generated annually by cruise ships is dumped into the oceans, according to the **Ocean Conservancy**, an organization that focuses on protecting the oceans from pollution.[42]

The most important source of marine oil pollution is from land-based activities in which most of us engage. As your car drips oil onto the driveway, the streets, and the parking lot, you are likely to think of it as a minor inconvenience. Small amounts of oil from your outboard motorboat and jet skis are responsible for roughly 70 percent of marine pollution. These tiny amounts of oil are washed into lakes, streams, and rivers and eventually make their way to the sea, where they damage coastal ecosystems and marine life far beyond the coasts. A study by the **National Research Council**—the branch of the National Academy of Sciences in Washington, DC, that conducts independent studies for the U.S. government—concluded that, globally, people release about 210 million gallons of petroleum a year into the sea.[43] Oil spills have influenced the development of international law on environmental pollution. The first significant international agreement aimed at reducing ocean pollution was the **International Convention for the Prevention of Pollution of the Sea (ICPS)** by Oil in 1954. The 1973 **International Convention for the Prevention of Pollution by Ships (ICPPS)** limited the amount of discharges from both land and sea for specific pollutants, including oil.

Ocean Conservancy ■ Focus on protecting the oceans from pollution

National Research Council ■ Conducts environmental studies for the U.S. government

ICPS ■ First international agreement aimed at reducing ocean pollution

ICPPS ■ Limited the discharge amounts of land and sea pollutants

GLOBAL WARMING AND CLIMATE CHANGE

There is a consensus among scientists that greenhouse gases are altering the atmosphere in ways that ultimately contribute to climate change and higher temperatures. The basic assumption is that human activities are the main causes of these climatic developments. But determining human influence on global warming and climate change is complicated by a relative lack of accurate information about climate change over past centuries. Historically, climate has varied significantly. Natural forces such as volcanic eruptions can create climate changes, as was evidenced by the eruption of **Mount Pinatubo** in the Philippines in 1991. Ocean currents also change temperatures. Apart from greenhouse gases, factors such as deforestation, urbanization, and agricultural activities also affect the climate.[44]

When our ancestors discovered how to make fire and how to use it, they set into motion a chain of events that would ultimately alter their environment and ours. However, it was the Industrial Revolution that marked a radical step toward the current problems of global warming and climate change because of its use of massive amounts of fossil fuels—coal, oil, and natural gas. More than a hundred years ago, Svante Arrhenius, a Swedish chemist and T. C. Chamberlain,

Mount Pinatubo ■ Erupted in the Philippines in 1991

Pollution in
China. (Ng Han
Guan/AP
Images)

**Greenhouse
Effect** ■ Rise in
Earth's temperature
from greenhouse
gases

an American geologist, independently discovered that industrialization could lead
to increasing levels of carbon dioxide in the atmosphere. This could ultimately
raise the atmosphere's temperature by trapping solar radiation that would otherwise be reflected back into space, creating a **greenhouse effect**.[45] The U.S. government issued a report in 1965 that raised concerns about global warming and
climate change. However, national security during the Cold War took precedence
over more distant threats such as environmental problems. Congress, under the
leadership of Representative Al Gore, held hearings in the early 1980s on global
warming. In 1988, after National Aeronautics and Space Administration (NASA)
scientist James Hansen told Congress that he was 99 percent certain that the
greenhouse effect had been detected and that it was already changing our climate,

USGCRP ■ Establis-
hed to study ozone
depletion and the
greenhouse effect

Congress established the **U.S. Global Change Research Program (USGCRP)** to
study human-induced climate change and stratospheric ozone depletion from
industrial emissions.[46] Tables 10.1 and 10.2 show the implications of global
warming and regional climate change, respectively.

Acid rain and ozone depletion preceded global awareness and concern about
global warming. Air pollution from Europe's industrial societies, especially
Britain and Germany, was identified by Svante Oden, a Swedish scientist, as a
leading cause of the increasing acidification of precipitation, known as acid rain,
in the Scandinavian countries in the late 1960s. Acid rain caused by industrial
activities in the United States was also a major concern for Canada, where more

Acid Rain ■ Toxic
rain caused by indus-
trial activities

than sixteen thousand lakes were affected. **Acid rain**, composed of sulfur dioxide,
nitrogen oxide, and volatile organic compounds, is caused primarily by burning
coal. By increasing the acidity of lakes, rivers, and streams, acid rain damages
animal and plant life. It has also destroyed buildings in Greece, Italy, and other

TABLE 10.1

GLOBAL WARMING

Effects of Global Warming	Implications	Areas Most Affected
Floods	• Rising sea levels and heavy rains could displace millions of people and leave many areas under water • More refugees	Coastal U.S., Australia, Pacific Islands, Holland, Philippines, Bangladesh, China, Mozambique, Nigeria
Heat Waves	• Increase in deaths from heatstroke, forest fires, and skin cancer	Southern Europe, U.S., China, Brazil, Indonesia, Russia
Diseases	• Warmer, wetter weather could increase insect-transmitted and water-borne illnesses	U.S., Central, and South America, Africa, Asia
Coral Bleaching	• Depleting fisheries	Caribbean, Australia, Philippines, India
Pollution	• Coastal flooding	
Drought	• Decline of tourism	
	• More respiratory problems, cancer, lung and heart diseases	U.S., Mexico, India, China, Egypt, Russia
	• Crop failure	U.S., Mexico, Brazil, China, India, Africa, Middle East, Spain
	• Malnutrition	
	• Forest fires	
	• Water-related conflicts	

Sources: U.S. News and World Report, 5 February 2001; and Elizabeth Rosenthal, "Water Is a New Battleground in a Drying Spain," New York Times, 3 June 2008, A1.

parts of Europe. Ozone depletion was also identified as a serious environmental problem resulting from air pollution. The **ozone layer** of our atmosphere protects us from ultraviolet (UV) radiation that causes skin cancers, genetic changes in animals and plants, eye disorders, and suppression of our immune systems. Agricultural productivity and fisheries are also affected. Ozone depletion is most severe in Antarctica and the Northern Hemisphere. The major cause of ozone depletion was discovered to be **CFCs**, synthetic products developed by DuPont and used in a wide range of products, including air conditioning, refrigeration, foam packaging, and aerosols. CFCs, when released into the atmosphere, react with UV light to form chlorine. It is this chlorine that destroys the ozone.

Reductions in the production of greenhouse gases are widely perceived to be the solution to diminishing global warming and climate change and their effects. The Kyoto Protocol to the UN Framework Convention on Climate Change, generally known as the **Kyoto Protocol**, is clearly the most important global environmental agreement and reflects an increasing awareness of environmental globalization. But economic, scientific, and ideological disagreements have weakened the Kyoto Protocol's effectiveness. The United States, the leading producer

Ozone Layer ■ Layer of atmosphere blocking UV radiation

CFCs ■ Synthetic products causing ozone depletion

Kyoto Protocol ■ International agreement on reducing carbon dioxide emissions

---

TABLE 10.2

REGIONAL CLIMATE CHANGE IN THE UNITED STATES

Region	Likely Climate Changes
Northeast	Decline in winter weather extremes; more flooding; hotter summers; changes in forest species
Southeast	Rising sea levels; disappearance of some coastal wetlands, barrier islands, and beaches; increase in water quality problems
Great Lakes	Declining water levels due to increased evaporation; increased transportation and shoreline problems due to lower water levels; warmer weather will keep shipping lanes open longer
Midwest—Great Plains	Extreme summer heat; milder winters; longer growing season; heavier rainfall; flash flooding; more droughts
Mountain West	Warmer winters; less snow; water problems; drier mountain regions; loss of mountain ecosystems
Southwest	Increased moisture; increased crop diversity; more flooding and fire risks; changes in desert ecosystem
Northwest—Alaska	Warmer water temperatures in the Pacific could cause salmon to migrate northward; more rain in summer; rising sea levels; warmer weather in Alaska will increase permafrost thawing and damage roads and buildings; warmer weather will keep shipping lanes open longer

Sources: "Temperature Increase to Change American Life," *Pantagraph,* 9 June 2000, A17; and Andrew C. Revkin, "Report Forecasts Warming's Effects," *New York Times,* 12 June 2000, A1.

---

of greenhouse gases, opposed the agreement on the grounds that the imposition of emission controls would be detrimental to the American economy. India and China are also responsible for significant shares of global carbon dioxide emissions. Developing countries that are energy exporters give *four main reasons* for opposing global efforts to reduce emissions: (1) emission controls will reduce their revenues by decreasing energy consumption, (2) imports from industrialized countries would be more expensive because of measures taken to reduce carbon dioxide emissions, (3) the development of new fuels to help cut down emissions is likely to reduce demand for their exports, and (4) oil, gas, and coal resources are part of their heritage. In 2003, following the ratification of the Kyoto Protocol by more than ninety-six countries, many developing countries supported the Delhi Ministerial Declaration on Climate Change and Sustainable Development, which supports the right of poor countries to develop their own appropriate strategies to reduce carbon dioxide emissions. This position was endorsed by the United States. In December 2007, the global community held a two-week conference in Bali, Indonesia, to begin negotiations on a new climate change treaty to replace the Kyoto Agreement by 2009. In June 2009, delegates from one hundred countries met in Bonn, Germany, to conclude discussions to actually produce the new treaty in Copenhagen in December 2009.[47]

Table 10.3 shows carbon dioxide emissions for selected countries. The Kyoto Protocol allows countries to use market forces to reduce carbon dioxide

TABLE 10.3

Top Twenty Countries in Carbon Dioxide Emissions (2006)

Country	Total Emissions (in million metric tons of carbon dioxide)	Per Capita Emissions (in tons/capita)
China	6017.69	4.58
United States	**5902.75**	**19.78**
Russia	1704.36	12.00
India	1293.17	1.16
Japan	1246.76	9.78
Germany	857.60	10.40
Canada	614.33	18.81
United Kingdom	585.71	9.66
South Korea	514.53	10.53
Iran	471.48	7.25
Italy	468.19	8.05
South Africa	443.58	10.04
Mexico	435.60	4.05
Saudi Arabia	424.08	15.70
France	417.75	6.60
Australia	417.06	20.58
Brazil	377.24	2.01
Spain	372.61	9.22
Ukraine	328.72	7.05
Poland	303.42	7.87

Source: Union of Concerned Scientists, "Global Warming: Each Country's Share of CO_2 Emissions," http://www.ucsusa.org/global_warming/science_and_impacts/science/each-countrys-share-of-co2.html (accessed 22 October 2009).

emissions. Targets are determined for lower levels of emissions and then permits are issued for that set level. Companies that exceed their target by not producing so much pollution can sell extra permits to companies that need to meet their targets. This approach is referred to as **emissions trading**. Many European countries use this approach. Britain and Denmark, for example, trade greenhouse gases to reduce climate change. The **Chicago Climate Exchange** is the first attempt to decrease greenhouse gases through a market approach. Participants in this effort include DuPont, Motorola, Ford Motor Company, American Electric Power, and the City of Chicago. However, high oil prices in 2008 influenced many countries in Europe to increase their reliance on less expensive coal, thereby increasing carbon emissions. Another approach, favored by the United States, is to rely primarily on forests to reduce the effects of emissions from industries and automobiles. But the long-term effectiveness of using forests instead of taking other major steps to reduce greenhouse gases is debatable. Research conducted at Duke University concluded that forests are likely to be a modest, if not disappointing, sink for carbon dioxide.[48]

Emissions Trading ■ Trading of greenhouse gases to reduce climate change

Chicago Climate Exchange ■ Attempts to decrease greenhouse gases through a market approach

HAZARDOUS WASTES

International concern about transporting toxic wastes across national boundaries was heightened in the early 1980s and continued to grow as more people, governments, and environmental NGOs became more aware of the extent of the problem and the dangers involved. Greenpeace played a leading role in focusing global attention on deliberate efforts to export very dangerous chemicals to poor countries. Several notorious cases galvanized support in the global community to address the problem of hazardous wastes. In one case, called the Seveso Affair, forty-one missing drums of topsoil contaminated with highly toxic dioxin were found in a barn in France. The toxic material came from the Seveso chemical plant in Italy that had exploded in 1976. Another case that received global attention was the discovery of 150 tons of **polychlorinated biphenyl (PCBs)**, a highly toxic and radioactive waste, on a farm in Koko, Nigeria.[49] Finally, the disintegration of Soviet Union in 1991 drew global attention to the large amount of radioactive materials and toxic wastes that were produced by the Soviet military. In 2006, a tanker ship owned by a Dutch firm dumped several tons of toxic wastes in the Ivory Coast. Despite Europe's strict laws against exporting waste, shipping garbage to developing countries continues. Shipbreaking in countries such as Bangladesh and India results in significant amounts of toxic wastes. Although many leaders and groups in developing countries facilitated the transfer of hazardous wastes, the general perception was that the rich countries were circumventing their own costly regulations regarding toxic wastes by simply dumping these toxic materials in economically vulnerable developing societies. Poor countries endorsed a comprehensive global approach to dealing with the problem for three main reasons: (1) they were unable to monitor and enforce their own policies restricting imports of hazardous wastes, (2) they lacked the technical and scientific expertise to deal with hazardous wastes, and (3) they believed that the global community had an ethical obligation to prevent the rich countries from using poor countries as toxic dumps. In May 2009, an international agreement, the International Convention for the Safe and Environmentally Sound Recycling of Skips, was signed to diminish these problems.[50]

The first concrete action to address the problem was taken by the UNEP committee in 1985, which developed the **Cairo Guidelines**. These guidelines included the following: (1) prior notification of the state receiving any export of hazardous wastes, (2) consent by the receiving state prior to export, and (3) verification by the sending country that the receiving state's disposal requirements were as stringent as those of the state exporting hazardous wastes. These guidelines were strengthened by the **Basel Convention on the Control of Transboundary Movements of Hazardous Wastes and Their Disposal**, concluded in Basel, Switzerland, in 1989.[51]

Developing countries signed several regional agreements to combat the transfer of hazardous wastes. The African, Caribbean, and Pacific (ACP) states included a clause in the **Fourth Lome Convention** of 1989 that requires the EU to ban exports of hazardous wastes to ACP countries. It also prohibits ACP states from receiving hazardous wastes. In 1992, the Central American Regional Agreement on the Transboundary Movement of Hazardous Wastes prohibits member states from importing dangerous wastes. Similarly, members of the

PCBs ■ A highly toxic, radioactive, industrial waste

Cairo Guidelines ■ Developed to ensure the regulation of hazardous waste

Basel Convention ■ Strengthened the Cairo Guidelines on hazardous waste

Fourth Lome Convention ■ Prohibited the export of hazardous wastes to ACP states

YOU DECIDE

Exporting E-waste to China

In the Chinese city of Guiyu, entire communities, including children, try to earn a living by scavenging for metals, glass, and plastics from dumps, disregarding the harm to the environment and to themselves. At the heart of the problem is an unwillingness of wealthy societies to bear the expense of recycling computers to keep them out of landfills. In the United States, where more than 40 million computers become obsolete each year, the general approach to solving environmental problems associated with the disposal of computers is to sell them to China. Because the United States has not ratified the Basel Convention (i.e., an international agreement that limits the export of hazardous wastes), the practice of shipping used computers to China is legal.

1. Should the United States ratify the Basel Convention and prevent the export of e-waste?
2. What can individuals do to reduce environmental problems caused by e-waste? What can you do? ■

South Pacific Forum signed an agreement in 1995, the Waigani Treaty on Hazardous and Toxic Wastes (WTHTW), to control the movement of wastes generated within the Pacific region and to ban hazardous wastes imports by Pacific states. Finally, African countries, dissatisfied with the Basel Convention's decision to not impose a total ban on exporting toxic and radioactive wastes, concluded the **Bamako Convention** in 1996. This agreement prohibits the import of all hazardous wastes.[52]

Bamako Convention ■ Prohibits the import of hazardous wastes in many African states

WATER SCARCITY

At the foundation of human existence and life on earth is water. The most common and abundant liquid in the world, water is at the heart of global environmental issues. Water, particularly potable water, is fueling conflicts globally. Increasing demands for water by the world's growing and increasingly more affluent populations threaten to create widespread shortages of freshwater. Water, in many ways, defines how we live and determines the limit of sustainable development. Imagine life without adequate water. Think of all the adjustments you would have to make just to survive. Water usage has grown by 600 percent over the past seventy years. Worldwide, an estimated 54 percent of the annual available freshwater is being used. Based solely on population growth, the UN Population Fund estimated that by 2025, we would use 70 percent of available freshwater.[53] Rivers throughout the world are drying up or no longer reach the sea year round. Parts of the United States—especially Arizona, Colorado, Utah, Nevada, and Wyoming—experience severe water shortages as they continue to be some of the fastest growing areas of the country. Tensions routinely flare up between the United States and Mexico over water rights to the Rio Grande and the Colorado rivers. Water is becoming a serious source of conflict in the Middle East, an area that already endures sustained violence. Increasing urbanization, industrialization, and the environmental problems we have discussed are likely to accelerate these problems. Southern Europe, Australia, South Korea, China, and parts of Africa are experiencing severe water shortages. India faces severe water problems that seriously threaten to undermine its economic growth and public health.

Water Scarcity ■ A lack of secure, uninterrupted, long-term availability of adequate clean freshwater

Water scarcity—defined as a lack of secure, uninterrupted, and long-term availability of adequate amounts of freshwater of required quality[54]—is becoming an important component of the broader issues of environmental and global security. As we saw in Chapter 1, security issues go beyond traditional military threats. Water scarcity is likely to lead to direct military confrontation. Unlike oil, which can be replaced by several substitutes, there is no viable substitute for water at reasonable prices. When a country that is extremely dependent on water coming from rivers or streams in another country perceives that its supplies are threatened, it could use military force to resolve the problem. For example, when Lebanon decided to begin pumping water from the Wazzani Springs in late 2002, tensions with Israel intensified. The Wazzani Springs supply the Hasbani River, which is a tributary of the Jordan River. Israel depends on the Jordan River for water. Concerned about tensions over water erupting into war, the United States dispatched a water expert from the U.S. Department of State to try to resolve the conflict. The struggle to control water supplies is an important component of the Palestinian-Israeli conflict. While Israel controls water supplies in Palestinian lands and Israeli settlers in Palestinian territories have water for sprinklers and swimming pools, Palestinian water supplies are controlled by Israel and are severely restricted and polluted. In coastal areas and on islands worldwide, rising seawater, due in part to global warming, is likely to contaminate freshwater supplies. In Indonesia, Vietnam, and other parts of Southeast Asia, rising seawater is creating numerous problems, including reduced rice harvests and the relocation of millions of people.[55]

MILITARY ACTIVITIES AND THE ENVIRONMENT

From the beginning of civilization, our ancestors have enlisted the environment in their conflicts, with destruction of the environment being the inevitable outcome. The Romans sowed salt on Carthaginian farms during the Third Punic War (149–146 B.C.), thereby destroying the land's agricultural productivity. Water supplies have been contaminated, infectious diseases inflicted on the enemy, and forests destroyed to make war and as a consequence of war. Bombs remain unexploded in fields around the world. The preoccupation with the survival of the state, to be achieved by developing lethal military weapons, relegated environmental concerns to the back burner. But growing environmental awareness and increased activism have heightened concerns about the impact of military activities on the ecosystems. Environmental damage caused by war and training for war is increasingly being taken into consideration by the U.S. military, among others.[56]

Agent Orange ■ Highly toxic defoliant used by the United States in the Vietnam War

Links between military activities and the environment became a prominent issue during the Vietnam War. During the Vietnam War, many Americans were directly affected by exposure to America's use of millions of gallons of **Agent Orange**, a herbicide that defoliated the forests as part of a strategy designed to deprive Vietcong forces of forest cover. Decaying ordnance, nuclear wastes, chemicals, and other toxic pollutants created long-term environmental problems. The Pentagon allocates about $5 billion a year to its **environmental security program,** designed to protect and rehabilitate the environment. Environmentalists have launched campaigns to get the military to protect endangered species that inhabit military bases. They also succeeded in getting the U.S. Navy to abandon the Puerto Rican island of Vieques, which was used for a firing range and various military exercises. The Pacific islanders linked nuclear testing directly to environmental issues, partly because radiation on some islands forced their inhabitants to abandon them. After many years of U.S., British, and French nuclear testing in the Pacific, the islanders, together with New Zealand and Australia, created the **South Pacific Nuclear Weapon Free Zone** in 1985 to reduce the risk of nuclear contamination.

Numerous conflicts have created major environmental problems. During the first Persian Gulf War in 1991, retreating Iraqi soldiers ignited Kuwaiti oil fields, causing 3 to 6 million barrels of oil a day to burn and contaminate Kuwait and surrounding countries. Similarly, Russian soldiers deliberately ignited oil wells in Chechnya, making a large part of that area an ecological disaster zone. When North Atlantic Treaty Organization (NATO) forces bombed oil refineries, industrial plants, electrical transformers, and other parts of the Serbian infrastructure in 1999, toxins—such as PCBs, liquid mercury, and vinyl chloride monomer (VCM)—were released into the Danube River, the air, and the soil. The environmental consequences are significant and will last for a long time.[57]

A more common and devastating environmental problem related to war is the proliferation of landmines in conflicts around the world. Landmines continue to kill long after wars end. Vietnam, Angola, Afghanistan, Mozambique, and other developing countries have abandoned forests and agricultural areas because of the dangers posed by landmines. While it is easy to plant mines, removing them is very difficult, time consuming, and dangerous. Numerous civilians are killed or injured daily in many countries by landmines laid in wars that are largely forgotten in countries not affected by them. Environmentalists have focused their attention not only on removing landmines but also on banning their production and use in wars. Their efforts resulted in the signing of the **Ottawa Treaty** in 1999. Israel's use of cluster bombs during its invasion of Lebanon in 2006 shows how difficult it is to prevent countries from using weapons that kill innocent civilians indiscriminately.

ECO-TERRORISTS

There is a small group of environmentalists who are extremists and anarchists. This fringe radical group believes that violence, the destruction of property, and arson are legitimate instruments of political protest. Because their goal is to effectuate change by creating a climate of fear and intimidation, radical environmentalists are indistinguishable from terrorists and are widely regarded as **eco-terrorists.** Many threw paint on fur coats to demonstrate their opposition to slaughtering animals. Others drove metal spikes into trees in the American Northwest to impede logging by lumber companies. But the eco-terrorists are much more radical and operate in small cells that are not part of a hierarchical organization. These

Environmental Security Program ■ Pentagon environmental program

South Pacific Nuclear Weapon Free Zone ■ Created in 1985 to reduce the risk of nuclear contamination

Ottawa Treaty ■ Addressed the danger of land mines

Eco-terrorists ■ Extremist wing of the environmental movement groups include the Earth Liberation Front (E.L.F.), the Strawberry Liberation Front, Seeds of Resistance, Cropatistas, Reclaim the Seeds, and the Anarchist Golfing Association.

Eco-terrorists are also responding to the significant loss of farmland, wetlands, and forests to urban sprawl and to what they view as excessive energy consumption. Experimental agricultural crops have been destroyed, and research centers involved in genetic engineering have been vandalized and burned. For example, arsonists destroyed a genetic-research faculty at Michigan State University in 2000. Lumber companies, such as Boise Cascade Corporation, have also suffered from arson. Eco-terrorists burned large homes and resorts that they believed contributed to environmental degradation. Despite the fact that builders were more environmentally sensitive, eco-terrorists burned five luxury homes near Seattle, Washington, in March 2008. They have also firebombed sport utility vehicles (SUVs) because of their high energy consumption. Many eco-terrorists are convinced that governments are unwilling or unable to protect the environment. Ironically, high oil prices between 2005 and 2008 effectively reduced the sales of SUVs and declining real estate prices slowed the building of large homes in particular and new construction in general. Several eco-terrorists were arrested and convicted in 2006 and 2007.

SUMMARY AND REVIEW

Environmental problems illustrate how much developments in other parts of the world can impact our lives. Environmental problems cannot be contained by arbitrary national boundaries. Environmental factors have played an important historical role in the rise and fall of great civilizations, the spread of infectious diseases, war, economic prosperity, and many other international issues. Environmental problems are intertwined with politics, economics, and culture. Despite the importance of the environment in our lives, however, movements to protect the environment are relatively new. The global environmental movement emerged principally in Western Europe, the United States, and Canada. Attention to the environment was spurred, in large part, by a tremendous population growth and rapid industrialization that took place with little regard for the serious environmental ramifications, such as deforestation and deteriorating health standards. Nuclear weapons proliferation in the United States and Soviet Union also increased concern for environmental issues.

Biodiversity is a fundamental preoccupation of environmentalists and NGOs. This is such an important issue because the destruction of some species could upset the balance of the ecosystem, resulting in the loss of other species and the alteration of the ecosystem. Biodiversity affects many groups and individuals, such as those interested in deforestation, agriculture, biotechnology, anthropology, pharmaceuticals, sustainable development, global trade, and ethics. Another major concern of environmentalists is water, the foundation for human existence. The planet's increasing population is threatening to create widespread shortages of freshwater. Roughly two-thirds of freshwater consumed each year goes to irrigate farms. Compared with other environmental problems, global warming is sometimes perceived as being a less immediate issue. While there is evidence that human activities cause most climate changes, determining how much human activity influences global warming and climate change continues to be debated, partly because there is little information about climate change over past centuries. However, global warming is generally viewed as contributing to rising oceans and more destructive hurricanes, such as Katrina and Rita in 2005. The relative calm hurricane season of 2007–2008 did not significantly alter this view.

KEY TERMS

commons 224
Chernobyl 224
environmental security 224
Mesopotamia 225
John Evelyn 225
Silent Spring 226
Torrey Canyon 226
Biosphere Conference 226
UN Conference on the Human Environment 226
World Summit on Sustainable Development 226
Green Belt Movement 228
regimes 228
biodiversity 228
Convention on Biological Diversity 229
North/South Divide 229
International Whaling Commission (IWC) 230
Convention on International Trade in Endangered Species of Wild Fauna and Flora (CITES) 230
Inter-American Tropical Tuna Commission (IATTC) 230
Congo basin 231
Chiapas 232
selective logging 232

infrastructure 232
commercial logging 232
Plan for National Integration 233
Nossa Natureza Program 233
IBAMA 233
Gabon's Lope Reserve 233
forest certification 234
Forest Stewardship Council 234
Food and Agriculture Organization (FAO) 234
exclusive economic zones 234
Law of the Sea Treaty 235
International Plan for the Management of Fishing Capacity (IPMFC) 235
invasive/alien species 235
Civilian Conservation Corps 235
Exxon Valdez 236
Charles Darwin 236
natural selection 236
Ocean Conservancy 237
National Research Council 237
International Convention for the Prevention of Pollution of the Sea (ICPS) 237

International Convention for the Prevention of Pollution by Ships (ICPPS) 237
Mount Pinatubo 237
greenhouse effect 238
U.S. Global Change Research Program (USGCRP) 238
acid rain 238
ozone layer 239
CFCs 239
Kyoto Protocol 239
emissions trading 241
Chicago Climate Exchange 241
polychlorinated biphenyl (PCBs) 242
Cairo Guidelines 242
Basel Convention 242
Fourth Lome Convention 242
Bamako Convention 243
water scarcity 244
Agent Orange 244
environmental security program 245
South Pacific Nuclear Weapon Free Zone 245
Ottawa Treaty 245
eco-terrorists 245

DISCUSSION QUESTIONS

1. The global environmental movement emerged primarily in Western Europe and North America. What were some of the issues that led to the creation of this movement?
2. Because of the global nature of environmental problems, international agreements are often used to address environmental issues. What are some factors that influence these agreements?
3. What are some of the domestic factors that influence a country's effectiveness in enforcing strong environmental standards?

4. As discussed in previous chapters, revolutions in technologies have played an important role in a number of global issues. How have these developments both helped and hindered the current environmental movement?

5. What are some examples of how environmental problems more negatively affect women than men?

6. What are some of the strategies that environmental NGOs use to achieve their objectives?

SUGGESTED READINGS

Brainerd, Lael, et al. *Climate Change and Global Poverty*. Washington, DC: Brookings Institution Press, 2009.

Cline, William R. *Global Warming and Agriculture*. Washington, DC: Peterson Institute, 2007.

Diamond, Jared. *Guns, Germs, and Steel*. New York: W. W. Norton, 1999.

Economy, Elizabeth. "A Great Leap Backward?" *Foreign Affairs* 86, No. 5 (September/October 2007): 38–60.

McNeill, J. R. *Something New Under the Sun: An Environmental History of the Twentieth-Century World*. New York: W. W. Norton, 2000.

Stern, Nicholas. *The Global Deal*. New York: Public Affairs, 2009.

END NOTES

1. Andrew C. Revkin, "Forum Says Climate Shift Brings Deaths," *New York Times*, 29 May 2009, A5; and Keith Bradsher, "China Far Outpaces U.S. in Building Cleaner Coal-Fired Plants," *New York Times*, 11 May 2009, A1.

2. Neil MacFarquhar, "Islanders Fearing Climate Change Press a U.N. Debate," *New York Times*, 29 May 2009, A4.

3. John McCormick, *Reclaiming Paradise: The Global Environmental Movement* (Bloomington: Indiana University Press, 1989), vii.

4. Barbara Johnson, *Life and Death Matters: Human Rights and the Environment at the End of the Millennium* (Walnut Creek, CA: Alta Mira Press, 1997), 13–14.

5. Elizabeth Economy and Miranda A. Schreurs, "Domestic and International Linkages in Environmental Politics," in *The Internationalization of Environmental Protection*, eds. Miranda A. Schreurs and Elizabeth Economy (Cambridge: Cambridge University Press, 1997), 6.

6. Lorraine Elliott, *The Global Politics of the Environment* (New York: New York University Press, 1998), 7.

7. Jacqueline Vaughn Switzer and Gary Bryner, *Environmental Politics* (New York: St. Martin's Press, 1998), 201; and Scott Barrett, *Environment and Statecraft* (New York: Oxford University Press, 2006), 1–3.

8. Elliott, *The Global Politics of the Environment*, 28.

9. Harold K. Jacobson and Edith Brown Weiss, "A Framework for Analysis," in *Engaging Countries: Strengthening Compliance with the International Environmental Accords*, eds. Edith Brown Weiss and Harold K. Jacobson (Cambridge, MA: MIT Press, 1998).

10. Philip Shabecoff, *Earth Rising: American Environmentalism in the 21st Century* (Washington, DC: Island Press, 2000), 7.

11. Paul Wapner, "The Transnational Politics of Environmental NGOs," in *The Global Environment in the Twenty-First Century*, ed. Pamela S. Chasek (Tokyo: United Nations University Press, 2000), 93.

12. Elliott, *The Global Politics of the Environment*, 148.
13. John McCormick, "The Role of Environmental NGOs in International Regimes," in *The Global Environment*, eds. Norman J. Vig and Regina S. Axelrod (Washington, DC: Congressional Quarterly Press, 1999), 69.
14. McCormick, "The Role of Environmental NGOs," 67–68; and Wapner, "The Transnational Politics of Environmental NGOs," 100.
15. Marian A. L. Miller, *The Third World in Global Environmental Politics* (Buckingham: Open University Press, 1995), 109.
16. OECD, *Trade Measures in Multilateral Environmental Politics* (Paris: OECD, 1999), 11; and Elliott, *The Global Politics of the Environment*, 75.
17. "Preventing Pillage in the Rainforest," *Economist*, 28 February 2009, 39.
18. Miller, *The Third World*, 115; and Elliott, *The Global Politics of the Environment*, 78.
19. Calvin Sims, "Japan, Feasting on Whale, Sniffs at Culinary Imperialism of U.S.," *New York Times,* 10 August 2000, A1; and Bruce Wallace and Corol J. Williams, "Japan Gains Support on Whaling, Sparking Fears of New Slaughter," *Chicago Tribune*, 18 June 2006, Sect. 1, 14.
20. J. R. McNeill, *Something New Under the Sun: An Environmental History the Twentieth-Century World* (New York: W. W. Norton, 2000), 241.
21. McNeill, *Something New*, 242; and Elliott, *The Global Politics of the Environment*, 135.
22. Elizabeth R. DeSombre, *Domestic Sources of International Environmental Policy* (Cambridge, MA: MIT Press, 2000), 1.
23. DeSombre, *Domestic Sources*, 64.
24. Judith Graham, "Fear for Turtles' Fate Prompts Proposed Hawaii Fishing Ban," *Chicago Tribune*, 16 July 2000, Sect. 1, 6.
25. Severine Austesserre, "The Trouble with Congo," *Foreign Affairs* 87, No. 3 (May/June 2008), 97–99.
26. Patrice M. Jones, "Brazil Grapples with Animal Trade," *Chicago Tribune*, 20 August 2001, Sect. 1, 1.
27. "Deforestation and Extinction," *Economist*, 17 January 2009, 79.
28. Anthony Hall, *Sustaining Amazonia* (Manchester: Manchester University Press, 1997), 47; and Jane Perlez, "Forests in Southeast Asia Fall to Prosperity's Ax," *New York Times*, 29 April 2006, A1.
29. Hall, *Sustaining Amazonia*, 56.
30. Andrew C. Revin, "Pact Is Reached to Save a Rich Tropical Forest," *New York Times*, 1 August 2000, D3.
31. The Greenbelt Movement, Nairobi, Kenya.
32. Dan Murphy, "The Quest for Certifiably Eco-friendly Lumber," *Christian Science Monitor*, 23 August 2001, 13.
33. William Mullen, "Popularity Tips Scales Against Fish," *Chicago Tribune*, 27 August 2000, Sect. 1, 1.
34. David K. Schorr, "Fisheries Subsidies and the WTO," in *Trade, Environment, and the Millennium*, eds. Gary P. Sampson and W. Bradnee Chambers (New York: UN University Press, 1999), 144.
35. Schorr, "Fisheries Subsidies," in *Trade, Environment, and the Millennium*, 145.
36. Mullen, "Popularity Tips Scales Against Fish," 11.
37. Mark Derr, "Alien Species Often Fit in Fine," *New York Times*, 4 September 2001, D4.
38. Tom Hundley, "Midwestern Pest Is Eating up Europe," *Chicago Tribune*, 26 August 2001, Sect. 1, 3.
39. Christopher Bright, *Life Out of Bounds: Bioinvasion in a Borderless World* (New York: W. W. Norton, 1998), 157.

40. Bright, *Life Out of Bounds*, 169.

41. Larry Rohter, "Oil Spills Shift in Course Aids Galapagos Mop-up," *New York Times*, 24 January 2001, A3.

42. Edwin McDowell, "For Cruise Ships, a History of Pollution," *New York Times*, 16 June 2002, Sect. 5, 3.

43. Andrew C. Revkin, "Offshore Oil Pollution Comes Mostly as Runoff," *New York Times*, 24 May 2002, A14.

44. Daniel Sarewitz and Roger Pielke, "Breaking the Global Warming Gridlock," *Atlantic Monthly*, July 2000, 61; and Ernesto Zedillo, ed., *Global Warming: Looking Beyond Kyoto* (Washington, DC: Brookings Institution Press, 2008).

45. Sarewitz and Pielke, "Breaking the Global Warming Gridlock," 56.

46. National Research Council, *Global Environmental Change* (Washington, DC: National Academy Press, 1999), 2.

47. Elizabeth Rosenthal, "Climate Change Treaty, to Go Beyond the Kyoto Protocol, Is Expected by the Year's End," *New York Times*, 13 June 2009, A5.

48. OECD, *Trade Measures*, 98; and Ruth Greenspan Bell, "What to Do About Climate Change," *Foreign Affairs* 85, No. 3 (May/June 2006), 105.

49. OECD, *Trade Measures*, 102.

50. Keith Bradsher, "International Pact on Ship Recycling Wins Wide Support," *New York Times*, 15 May 2009, A12.

51. OECD, *Trade Measures*, 103.

52. OECD, *Trade Measures*, 102–103.

53. "Report: Too Many People, Too Little Freshwater," *Pantagraph*, 11 November 2001, A6.

54. Arun P. Elhance, *Hydropolitics in the Third World* (Washington, DC: U.S. Institute of Peace Press, 1999), 4.

55. Thomas Fuller, "Study Says Warming Poses Peril to Asia," *New York Times*, 27 April 2009, A4.

56. Joshua W. Busby, *Climate Change and National Security* (New York: Council on Foreign Relations, 2008).

57. Joan McQueeney Mitric, "The War Is Over, but the Damage Is Spreading," *Washington Post National Weekly Edition*, 11–17 July 2000, 21.

Population and Migration

INTRODUCTION

Population and migration issues, perhaps more than any other global problem, demonstrate the reality of globalization. Hunger, inequality, ethnic conflicts, environmental degradation, sustainable development, the treatment of women, global security, economic development, trade, poverty, democratization, human rights concerns—all aspects of globalization are intertwined with population. To a large extent, population factors will determine the future of humanity and the world. Rapid population growth is a silent threat to both human and global security, making it as grave a concern as the proliferation of weapons of mass destruction.

Demographic disparities among countries generally influence the distribution of economic, military, and political power among states. For example, France dominated continental Europe for a long time partly because of its relatively large population, although Britain used its geographic location and its navy to counter French power. America's growing population is likely to consolidate its power, whereas Europe's aging and declining population is likely to diminish its power in the global system. Russia's population decline has contributed to its loss of power globally. High population growth rates continue to be a significant impediment to economic growth in developing countries, a reality recognized by China and India.

Migration makes population issues an even more pressing global concern. Each wave of globalization has been accompanied by migration. The movement of capital, technology, and products across national boundaries is inseparable from the migration of people. The current period of globalization is marked by an unprecedented movement of people around the world. The creation of global institutions and the globalization of human rights and democracy have facilitated migration as well as given rise to a global human rights regime that protects migrants, independent of their nationality.[1] This chapter focuses on population growth and its global implications. The different kinds of migrants and migrations are discussed. The role of gender in migration, rural-to-urban migration, transcontinental migration, forced migration, refugees, reform migration, and the global smuggling of immigrants are all examined. The causes of migration are as old as human civilization. After analyzing them, we will look at case studies that illustrate the dynamics of global—as opposed to regional and internal—migration.

POPULATION

Overpopulation ■ Excessive population within an area that lacks enough resources for long-term sustainment

At the heart of population as a global issue is the extent to which population growth threatens the earth's carrying capacity. **Overpopulation** (i.e., too many people living in an area that has inadequate resources to support them) has been a global preoccupation for centuries. Population problems must be seen in the context of consumption. In this context, the population of the developed world, which consumes much, is seen as a bigger problem for the world's resources than the population of the developing world, which consumes little. Often, population problems can be avoided if population growth remains stable, assuming that resources are also carefully managed. The rate at which the population remains relatively stable is referred to as the **replacement rate**. To achieve this, fertility rates must average 2.1 children per couple. Migration influences the replacement rate, population growth, and population decline.

Replacement Rate ■ Rate at which a population remains stable

Thomas Malthus (1766–1834), an English economist, sociologist, and pioneer in demographics, wrote *An Essay on the Principle of Population* in 1798. In it, he argued that because population increases by a geometrical ratio and food supplies increase by an arithmetical ratio, the world would have high rates of population growth and suffer from poverty and starvation. The widespread practice of family planning and technological and scientific revolutions in food production, transportation, and storage essentially rendered these dire predictions false. The invention of genetically modified crops and other agricultural scientific breakthroughs further challenge Malthus's argument. However, food shortages and higher prices in 2008, due partly to the use of corn to produce biofuels, complicate the discussion on food and population. High population growth remains a serious threat to most developing countries and, as we discussed in Chapter 8, frustrates efforts to reduce global poverty and economic inequality. Malthus was concerned about the earth's carrying capacity. **Carrying capacity** refers to the maximum number of humans or animals a given area can support without creating irreversible destruction of the environment and, eventually, humans and animals themselves.

Carrying Capacity ■ The maximum number of humans or animals that can survive within a given area

Combined with fervent nationalism and a perception that survival itself is at stake, population pressures often result in military conflict. The Palestinian-Israeli struggle is an example of how demographic changes are perceived as determining destiny. Jews now comprise roughly 50.5 percent of the population in Israel and the Palestinian territories. By 2020, the proportion of Jews will decline to 42.1 percent, whereas the Palestinians, who now make up 44.3 percent of the population, will see their share of the population grow to 52 percent. The birthrate for Palestinians in the West Bank and Gaza is forty for every one thousand people.

The birthrate for Palestinians in Israel is thirty-six per one thousand people. Compare this with a birthrate for Jews of 18.3 per 1,000, and you will see why demographic changes are perceived as threats to Israel's security.[2] These demographic realities influenced Israel's decision to dismantle Jewish settlements in Gaza in 2005. This process was reversed in 2006 when conflicts escalated between Palestinians and Israelis and after Israel invaded Lebanon to fight Hezbollah following Hezbollah's seizure of two Israeli soldiers. Israel continued to build settlements on Palestinian land.

Population Issues in Developing Countries

Most developing countries have high population growth rates and suffer from vast differences in income. Inadequate education, low rates of contraception usage, cultural norms that value large families and male virility, the need for labor in subsistence economies, and the need to have children to support parents are some of the reasons population growth is higher in poorer countries. Most of the countries with the largest populations and the highest growth rates are in the developing world. Roughly 97 percent of the increase in the global population is occurring in Africa, Asia, the Middle East, and Latin America, with the more prosperous countries in these regions experiencing declining growth rates. Industrialized countries, on the other hand, are experiencing declining growth rates and even depopulation in some cases. Poverty is clearly a major cause of high population growth rates.

TABLE 11.1

DEMOGRAPHIC CONTRASTS BETWEEN RICH AND POOR COUNTRIES

Country	% of population 15 and under (2005)	% of population 65 and older (2005)	Population annual growth rate % (1975–2005)
Rich Countries			
Japan	13.9	19.7	0.5
France	18.4	16.3	0.5
United States	20.8	12.3	1
Italy	14	19.7	0.2
Germany	14.4	18.8	0.2
Poor Countries			
Bangladesh	35.2	3.5	2.2
Haiti	38	4.1	2
Nigeria	44.3	2.9	2.8
Zambia	45.7	2.9	2.7
Sierra Leone	42.8	3.3	2.1

Source: United Nations Development Program, *Human Development Report 2007/2008* (New York: Oxford University Press, 2007).

In India, more than 360 million people—roughly the combined populations of the United States and Britain—live in dire poverty. In addition, an estimated 400 million Indian people are illiterate. Nonetheless, the population in India grows by about three people a minute, or two thousand an hour, or forty-eight thousand per day. In other words, the growth of India's population each day is equivalent to that of a medium-sized American city. By 2025, India is projected to surpass China as the world's most populous country, with about 1.5 billion people, compared with China's 1.4 billion people. China and India alone account for one out of every three children added to the global population.[3]

Problems arising from rapid population growth have influenced governments, nongovernmental organizations (NGOs), and women to take action to limit population growth. It is generally agreed that *women's level of education strongly influences fertility rates*. Education helps to determine factors that affect population growth rates, such as contraceptive usage, the age of marriage and childbearing, social status and self-perception, and employment opportunities outside of the home and residence.

An interesting development is the declining birthrates in Brazil, Mexico, Bangladesh, India, the Philippines, Iran, Vietnam, Indonesia, and Egypt, where poverty and illiteracy remain serious and pervasive problems. Even women who are less educated have become more assertive about their reproductive choices. Factors influencing this change include economic and cultural globalization, greater access to education, increasing urbanization, the declining influence of religion on women's reproductive lives, greater access to medical technologies, and the cumulative effects of satellite television and other media that stress the advantages of having fewer children. In Brazil, for example, the fertility rate dropped from 6.15 to 2.27 in the last half-century.[4]

Sexism ■ Discrimination against an individual or group based on sex or gender classifications

Son Complex ■ Preference for male children

Sexism strongly influences population decisions in developing countries. In many societies, tradition supports having large families by praising the fertility of women and the virility of men. The **son complex**—the preference for having boys instead of girls—influences many parents worldwide to continue having children until a boy is born. For example, a Chinese farmer dreamed of having a son. After seven daughters, he finally had a son and stopped having children. As one woman put it, "A woman without a son will be cursed by her mother-in-law and laughed at by the village. Everybody thinks it is the duty of a woman to bear a boy."[5] Parents, especially mothers, are demeaned in many societies if they do not produce boys. In many traditional South Asian families, a boy is expected to live with his parents, be employed, inherit property, provide financial security for aging parents, and light their funeral pyres. A daughter, by contrast, is widely perceived as a financial and social liability. When she marries, her family is required, by tradition, to provide the bridegroom's family with a substantial **dowry**, which can be money, property, or both. Parents often incur significant debt to provide dowries. Sexism also conspires with advanced medical technology to reduce the number of girls in some countries such as India and China. With the use of ultrasound machines to determine the sex of the fetus, many parents often decide to abort female fetuses. Combined with the practice of female infanticide, ultrasound technology has contributed to a widening divergence in the ratio of females to males in many parts of India and China.[6]

Dowry ■ Financial gift given to the husband's family by the wife's family at marriage in many traditional societies

Confronted with the challenges of rapid population growth, most countries rely on educational programs that emphasize family planning. During the 1970s, **Indira Gandhi,** prime minister of India, implemented policies that allowed forced mass sterilization, an approach that Indians violently rejected. Although these coercive policies were quickly abandoned, Indians are now experimenting with aggressive approaches to limit population growth. Some states in India encourage civil servants to choose sterilization after having one or two children by providing incentives such as salary increases or access to land or housing.[7]

Indira Gandhi ■
Prime minister of India in the 1970s

China's **one-child policy,** initiated in 1979 by Deng Xiao Ping, China's leader, to reduce its population growth is the most controversial approach to dealing with rapid population growth. China established the state family planning bureau to formulate policies and procedures for enforcing the one-child policy. Family planning committees at the local level, a part of the Communist Party, are responsible for rewarding those who comply with the policy and punishing those who violate the one-child policy. Those who comply with receive a monthly stipend until the child is fourteen years old and get preferential treatment when applying for housing, education, and health benefits for the child; they are also granted a pension when they are old. Those who fail to comply with the one-child policy risk the loss of benefits for the first child, jeopardize their employment with the government, and risk having their property seized. Women are often forced to be sterilized, especially after the birth of a second child. *Exceptions to the one-child policy* include the following cases: (1) if the first child has a defect; (2) in the case of a remarriage, if one partner does not have a child; (3) if couples are involved in certain jobs, such as mining; or (4) if both partners come from families with one child. Economic and political developments combined to pressure the Chinese government to consider changing this policy in 2008. The policy was relaxed in areas devastated by the 2008 earthquakes.

One-Child Policy ■
Imposed on families in China to limit population growth

Population Issues in Developed Countries

Compared with the developing world, Europe has always had a smaller population. Among the *reasons for this disparity* are:

1. Europe was settled by humans who migrated from Africa into Asia. In other words, it started out with a smaller population.
2. Geography and climate discouraged large numbers of people from settling in Europe.
3. Confronted with overpopulation, Europe was able to conquer, colonize, and settle in North America, South America, parts of Africa, parts of Asia, Australia, and New Zealand.

The Industrial Revolution and scientific advances in agriculture made Europeans prosperous and diminished the need to have large families.

Europe is faced with the spread of **subreplacement fertility regimes**; that is, patterns of childbearing that would eventually result in indefinite population decline.[8] The sharpest dip in population is in Russia. Communicable diseases, widespread environmental problems, alcohol poisoning, sexually transmitted diseases, and an abortion rate that is twice as high as live births have combined to

Subreplacement Fertility Regimes ■
Patterns of child-bearing resulting in population decline

decrease Russia's population by roughly 700,000 each year. If current demographic trends continue, Russia will see its current population of 142.7 million drop precipitously to 100 million in forty to fifty years.[9] Such long-range predictions are often highly speculative and turn out to be inaccurate. Nevertheless, it is clear that Russia is going through a population implosion. Though immigration has slowed the decline of Western Europe's populations, immigration levels are not high enough to alter the demographic realities. The United States, Canada, and Australia are actually gaining population largely due to increased immigration and rising fertility rates.

It is estimated that by 2050, the median age in the United States will be 35.4, compared with 52.3 in Europe, due to the rapid growth in the number of the elderly and the subreplacement problem. For example, in 1950, about 30 percent of Germany's population was under twenty years and only 2 percent exceeded eighty years. By 2050, however, it is estimated that only 16 percent will be under twenty years, whereas those who are eighty years and older will constitute 12 percent of Germany's population.[10] Three major reasons account for Europe's aging societies:

1. Life expectancy has climbed due to medical advancements, a healthier environment, improved nutrition, and greater concerns about safety and public health.
2. The huge baby boom generation of the 1940s and 1950s is now entering middle-age and moving into the old-age category.
3. Declining fertility rates, below the replacement rate, increase the proportion of the population that is old.[11]

America's aging population, while growing, will comprise a smaller percentage of the overall population because of the number of young immigrants and higher fertility rates. Japan faces not only an aging population but also subreplacement fertility rates.

Developed countries face many challenges that require the implementation of difficult and controversial strategies.[12] These strategies include

1. Substantially increasing immigration to offset declining fertility rates,
2. Postponing or abandoning retirement,
3. Encouraging higher fertility rates,
4. Investing more in the education of workers to increase productivity,
5. Strengthening intergenerational responsibilities within families,
6. Targeting government-paid benefits to those who need them most, and
7. Requiring workers to invest for their own retirements.

The implications of these changes are far-reaching. Significant tensions within rich countries over such strategies are already evident in many European countries.

GLOBAL MIGRATION

Migration ■ Movement of people from one place to another

Migration—the movement of people from one place to another—is an integral component of human behavior. Our ancestors moved out of curiosity and a sense of adventure to find food; to search for better grazing and agricultural lands; to seek protection from adversaries; to conquer land for new settlements; and to obtain religious, political, social, and economic freedoms. Contemporary migration is rooted in the earlier periods of political, military, economic, and financial globalization that we discussed in Chapter 1. Migration includes the movement of people within a country's geographical boundaries as well as movement across national boundaries. People who migrate fall into several categories. A **migrant** is a person who moves from one country or area to another country or location. Migrants often move from one part of a country to another location within that country. The broad category of migrant is subdivided into refugees, displaced persons, and immigrants. **Refugees** are essentially migrants who live outside their country and are unable or unwilling to return because of documented cases of persecution or a well-founded fear of persecution. Historically and today, conflicts, famine, natural disasters, and political, religious, and economic oppression have been dominant factors contributing to the creation of refugees. Refugees who attempt to obtain permanent residence in the country to which they fled are referred to as **asylum-seekers**. The immigration laws of most countries distinguish asylum-seekers from other categories of migrants and generally grant them preferential treatment, in accordance with international law. A **displaced person** is someone who has been forced to leave his or her home because of violence, conflict, persecution, or natural disaster but has not crossed an international border. Many displaced people eventually cross national boundaries, thereby becoming refugees. An **immigrant** is someone who goes to a foreign country to become a permanent resident. Most migration occurs in a relatively limited geographical area, despite growing **transcontinental migration** (i.e., the movement of people from one continent to another).

Migrant ■ A person who moves from one country or area to another country or location

Refugees ■ Migrants living outside their country of origin who are unwilling or unable to return

Asylum-Seekers ■ Refugees attempting to obtain permanent residence in the country to which they fled

Displaced Person ■ One who has fled his or her home but has not left the home country

Immigrant ■ One who travels to a foreign country, often to become a permanent resident

Transcontinental Migration ■ Movement of people from one continent to another

Gender and Migration

Men are more likely than women to migrate under ordinary circumstances. There are several reasons for this. Who migrates is determined to a large extent by the requirements imposed by countries, companies, or individuals who need labor. Much of the work to be done is culturally defined as work for men. Large numbers of men from Turkey, North Africa, and the Caribbean migrated to Germany, France, and Britain, respectively, after World War II to help rebuild these countries. Men throughout the world have been recruited to work in industry, construction, and mining. Cultural norms and sex roles within sending countries also determine whether men are more likely than women to migrate. Gender roles also influence men to migrate in search of employment. Men are generally perceived as breadwinners in most countries, whereas women are viewed as being responsible for taking care of the home. Economic development and greater access to education for women change cultural views of gender roles and provide more employment opportunities for women. Demographic changes and greater employment opportunities for women in developed countries are transforming gender migration. Women migrate to rich societies to work in factories, tourism, education, hospitals, businesses, and private homes. As more women work outside the home in rich countries, more women from poor countries are hired to do domestic work.

Types of Migration

Although migration, as a contemporary global issue, is often thought of primarily as movement from developing countries to rich countries, far more common is the movement of people within countries and from one country to another within a particular geographical or cultural region. **Regional migration** is fueled by increasing economic opportunities in a country or group of neighboring countries. For example, people in North Africa move to Spain, France, and Italy to find employment, and people from Zimbabwe, Mozambique, Botswana, and Lesotho have migrated to South Africa to work in mining and other industries. Rural-to-urban migration is the dominant pattern of migration in both rich and poor countries. Many rural areas across the United States are losing population as residents seek better opportunities in urban areas. Much of the migration in the developing world is from rural areas to cities. Rural-to-rural migration (i.e., the movement of people from one rural area to another) is common in many parts of the world, despite the relatively limited economic opportunities found in most small towns or agricultural areas. Many migrants follow the planting, cultivation, and harvesting of various crops. Urban-to-urban migration is common in most countries. Families and individuals move from one city to another *to find employment, to pursue a college degree, or to be in a culturally dynamic area.* Urban-to-rural migration is usually designed to encourage the economic development of the countryside and to relieve population pressures on urban centers. Brazil, China, Indonesia, and Nigeria are countries that have used this strategy. Another type of migration is **seasonal migration**. People often move from one area to another because of the seasonal demand for labor. Agricultural industries often demand more labor at certain times of the year than at others. Harvesting fruit, sugarcane, coffee, and other crops requires intensive labor for a short period of time. Seasonal migration is also driven by other industries such as tourism.

Another type of migration is **transit migration**. In this case, those seeking to enter a specific country pass through another country or stay there temporarily. For example, migrants use Mexico as a transit point for illegal entry into the United States. Visiting Mexico's main immigration detention center, you see migrants from Ecuador, India, Cuba, China, Albania, Russia, Ukraine, Tanzania, Sierra Leone, Sri Lanka, Bangladesh, and other countries.[13] Similarly, migrants attempting to enter Western Europe use countries such as Bosnia, Croatia, Serbia, Bulgaria, Hungary, Poland, and the Czech Republic as transit points. Many migrants also stop temporarily in Europe on their way to the United States and Canada. Within Europe, France is used as a transit point for migrants attempting to enter Britain in order to take advantage of its asylum policies.

Forced and induced migration is an integral component of human history. Various minorities have been routinely expelled from countries because of political, social, ethnic, and religious differences. The Spanish crown forced Jews to leave Spain in 1492; Africans were forcibly removed from their homeland and enslaved in the Americas, the Middle East, and other parts of the world; and the Cuban and Chinese governments have used forced migration to achieve various political and economic objectives. Another type of migration—one that is becoming common in an age of globalization—is **return migration**. For example, many

Regional Migration ■ Movement of people within a specified region

Seasonal Migration ■ Movement of people based on seasonal demand for labor

Transit Migration ■ Movement of people to one country on the way to another

Forced and Induced Migration ■ Involuntary movement of people, often due to a government initiative

Return Migration ■ Movement of people back to the country from which they originally emigrated

YOU DECIDE

Return Migration

Debates about immigration problems in the United States generally focus on how to prevent illegal immigrants from entering the country. Given the historical reality of migration, many of the policies designed to keep illegal immigrants out have the opposite effect. Even when it was dangerous to cross the Atlantic Ocean in ships, many migrants, estimates range from 25 percent to 30 percent, returned home eventually. Revolutions in transportation and communications clearly make it much easier for people to cross national boundaries quickly and frequently. It is argued that when migrants are free to come and go as they wish, not as many of them migrate. Tougher border controls and restrictive immigration policies deter illegal migrants from returning home. When Mexicans were free to migrate to the United States to work in agriculture under the Bracero Program, many of them returned to Mexico. Ending the Bracero Program in the early 1960s actually contributed to a sharp increase of illegal immigrants from Mexico. The high costs involved in entering the United States illegally and the low probability of an illegal immigrant being caught once in the United States encouraged migrants to remain in the country. However, the global economic recession of 2008–2009, which had a devastating impact on construction and other low-wage industries that employed many Mexicans, led to a sharp reduction in the number of Mexican migrants in the United States.

1. Do you think that relaxing immigration controls would encourage return migration?
2. How can the United States help Mexico discourage migration? What should Mexico do? ∎

American citizens retain meaningful ties with another country. Throughout history, some migrants have returned to the places they left. In the late nineteenth century, roughly a third of European migrants to the United States were returning after a few years. Immigrants from Southern Europe, particularly Italy, were most likely to return after saving enough money to build homes, start small businesses, or buy farms. This trend of migration was strengthened by the relative newness of migration from Southern Europe and by declining transportation costs and faster and more reliable means of transportation.[14] The global economic recession in 2008–2009 forced migrants to return from the United States to Mexico and from Western Europe to Eastern Europe.

Economic success in the new country also motivates people to return to their country of origin. India and China, for example, encourage return migration to assist economic development. India offers incentives to Indians living in the United States, Britain, Australia, Canada, Singapore, and elsewhere to return. Similarly, China, which received about $60 billion in investments from roughly 55 million overseas Chinese, perceives return migration as an essential component of its development strategy.[15] Growing economic opportunities in China, India, and other countries, combined with the forces of globalization, facilitate the trend toward return migration.

Causes of Migration

Although the causes of migration are diverse and vary from one individual to another, demographers generally divide them into two categories: namely, push

Push Factors ■
Negative developments leading many people to leave their homes

Pull Factors ■
Positive developments inducing people to move from their homes

factors and pull factors.[16] **Push factors** are negative developments and circumstances that motivate or force people to leave their homes. These include widespread abuses of fundamental human rights, political oppression, forced resettlement programs and expulsion, high levels of violence and endemic political instability, rapid population growth, high rates of unemployment, poverty, natural and environmental disasters, the relative lack of educational and cultural opportunities, globalization, and discrimination that excludes specific groups and individuals from competition for resources and power. **Pull factors** are positive developments and circumstances in other areas or countries that attract people away from their homes. These include economic opportunities, higher wages, political and cultural freedom and stability, a comparatively healthy environment, educational and cultural opportunities, and family reunification. Push and pull factors are strongly influenced by geographic proximity; individual initiative; technology; transportation; and social, political, and economic beliefs.

PUSH FACTORS

Widespread *abuses of fundamental human rights*, discussed in Chapter 3, have traditionally pushed people from their homes. The United States was settled by many individuals who were deprived of basic human rights. Many Jews, political dissidents, homosexuals, and others fled Nazi Germany because of the government's systematic and profound violations of the most basic human rights, including the right to life. During the Cold War, many Central and Eastern Europeans fled oppression in the communist countries. Cubans migrated in large numbers when Fidel Castro came to power and imposed severe restrictions on fundamental freedom. Dictatorships worldwide, despite their efforts to regulate and control the movement of people within their own countries, are generally so odious and disrespectful of human rights that many individuals take extreme risks to leave their country.

Forced resettlement programs and expulsion are significant push factors. Governments have both forced and encouraged people to migrate for several reasons. These include

Huguenots ■
French Protestants expelled from France in the sixteenth century

Han Chinese ■
China's dominant ethnic group

Cultural Revolution ■
Zedong's forced implementation of communist economy, politics, and culture in China

Mao Zedong ■
China's repressive, former communist leader

1. *To achieve cultural homogeneity.* This is particularly the case in newly independent countries that were faced with incompatible ethnic groups living in their artificially constructed boundaries. Yet the practice of achieving cultural homogeneity by expelling people perceived as different has deep historical roots. Catholic Spain expelled the Jews in the fifteenth century, and Catholic France expelled the **Huguenots** (i.e., French Protestants and followers of John Calvin) in the sixteenth century.
2. *To subdue a region or a people.* China's occupation of Tibet in 1950 was followed by the mass migration of **Han Chinese** settlers. During the **Cultural Revolution** (1966–1976), **Mao Zedong**, China's leader, sent his Red Guard storm troopers to subdue Tibet. They destroyed temples, imprisoned Tibetan monks, desecrated Buddhist sacred objects and scriptures, and punished those who practiced Buddhism. These issues were stressed in 2008 as China prepared to host the 2008 Olympic Games and took the Olympic torch around the world.

3. *To evict dissidents and opponents of the government.* Fidel Castro, determined to build a communist society, influenced and coerced almost a million people to leave Cuba. **Saddam Hussein**, who ruled Iraq from 1979 until he was overthrown and captured by American military forces in 2003, pushed more than a million Kurds out of Iraq into the hills of neighboring Turkey following his country's defeat in the 1991 Gulf War.

Saddam Hussein ■ Iraq's former dictator

4. *To achieve foreign policy objectives.* Forced emigration is sometimes implemented as a component of broader foreign policy objectives. Governments use forced emigration to exert pressure on neighboring countries.[17] For example, Castro has used emigration as an instrument of his foreign policy toward the United States.

5. *To achieve economic and national security objectives.* Several governments have forcibly removed people from one area of the country to another as part of an overall economic development or national security strategy.

High levels of violence and political instability are factors that push people away from home. Another push factor is rapid population growth, as we have seen in our previous discussion. Declining population growth rates in rich countries facilitate migration that is driven by high population growth rates in the developing world. High rates of unemployment and poverty are widely regarded as dominant and constant push factors that are strongly connected to population problems. *Natural disasters, environmental problems, and famines* push people away from their homelands or force them to relocate within their countries.

Globalization and discrimination are also push factors. Globalization has contributed to the creation of strong economic regions within, as well as among, countries. Globalization's emphasis on economic liberalization, free trade, and diminished government involvement in the economy has resulted in the displacement of millions of small farmers in the developing world. Thousands of farmers in Mexico, unable to compete with subsidized agriculture in the United States and Europe, move to urban areas in Mexico or make the dangerous journey to the United States. Migration is often induced by governments that fail to provide adequate support for rural communities or alternative sources of employment. Many Haitians drown attempting to illegally enter the United States. There are approximately 30,000 Haitians facing deportation from the United States.[18] These problems are compounded by **competitive exclusion,** which occurs when governments allow more land to be taken by large agro-export companies to create megafarms. This generally drives up land prices and decreases the amount of land available to small subsistence farmers. Discrimination also contributed to emigration. Successful ethnic minority groups have historically been scapegoated for problems within societies, the most obvious being the Jews in Nazi Germany. Idi Amin forced Ugandans of Asian descent to leave Uganda because of their economic success. Ethnic Chinese in Indonesia and other Asian countries have had similar experiences.[19]

Competitive Exclusion ■ Process by which government allows agro-corporations to monopolize productive land

United Nations Geneva Convention ■ Stressed the importance of granting asylum to refugees who have been persecuted

Refugees

In 2001, the European Union (EU) decided to recognize as refugees women and homosexuals fleeing violence or sexual abuse.[20] The 1951 **United Nations Geneva Convention** stressed that individuals or groups persecuted on the grounds of race, religion, nationality, membership in a particular social group, and holding certain political opinions would be recognized as refugees and granted asylum. However, these categories have been expanded to reflect a growing awareness of other forms of persecution. In many ways, the interaction of economic problems, political instability, and violence makes it difficult to separate economically motivated migrants from refugees.

Refugees are individuals who leave their homes because of violence, death threats, and well-founded fears of persecution and move across national boundaries to seek safety. They believe that their government is unable or unwilling to protect them from violence or that their government is directly responsible for the violence against them. Complicating the refugee problem is the growing number of internally displaced people, who are differentiated from refugees only by the fact that they remain within the boundaries of their country. Displaced persons do not enjoy the same international legal safeguards and protections as those accorded to refugees. Most governments are reluctant to accept large numbers of refugees and generally prefer to provide humanitarian assistance to displaced persons to stem the flow of refugees. Widespread refugee problems in Europe and elsewhere during and after World War II influenced the United States, Western Europe, the Soviet Union, and China to develop institutions, such as the office of the United Nations High Commissioner for Refugees (UNHCR), to help with refugees. Established in 1950, the UNHCR is funded primarily by governments, NGOs, and individuals. Because the proliferation of ethnic conflicts and natural disasters has severely restrained UNHCR's resources, other UN agencies, the **International Committee of the Red Cross**, and various NGOs are involved in helping refugees globally. Their task is often made even more difficult by the inability or unwillingness of some countries to separate fighters from innocent civilians in refugee camps, despite international legal guidelines for doing so. Increasingly, the UN is pressured to take measures to prevent the outbreak and escalation of ethnic conflicts, which are a major cause of the refugee problem. More countries, including the United States, favor selective **humanitarian intervention** (i.e., the military invasion of a country) to prevent or diminish human rights abuses that drive people away from their homes.

Numerous ethnic conflicts and civil wars in Africa have left that continent with more than 4 million refugees. In the Middle East, violence against the Kurds has not only led to the growth of Kurdish refugees in the region but also influenced many Kurds to seek refuge in Europe and North America. There are more than 500,000 Kurds in Western Europe, with Germany and France receiving most of them. Germany has about 400,000 and France has 60,000. America's invasion of Iraq in 2003 led to more than 2 million refugees and internally displaced persons by 2008. The conflict in Pakistan and Afghanistan created millions of refugees. For example, fighting in the Swat Valley in Pakistan between the Taliban and Pakistan forced nearly 3 million people to leave their homes in 2009. The Vietnam War produced a mass exodus of Vietnamese, with most of the refugees settling in the United States. As economic conditions deteriorated, and as the communist government consolidated its power, many Vietnamese also sought refuge in neighboring countries. More than 200,000 ethnic Chinese who lived in Vietnam fled to China when conflict erupted between China and Vietnam in 1978

International Committee of the Red Cross ■ Organization involved in humanitarian operations worldwide

Humanitarian Intervention ■ Use of military force in defense of human rights and 1979. Another 70,000 Vietnamese arrived in Hong Kong in small boats or were rescued from small boats by oceangoing ships on their way to Hong Kong.[21]

Palestinian Refugees

The Palestinian refugee problem is one of the oldest, most serious, and most intractable global refugee cases. Resolving this problem remains a central challenge to efforts to secure peace between the Israelis and Palestinians. The creation of the state of Israel in 1948 as well as wars and low-intensity conflicts between the Israelis and Arabs led to the creation of roughly 3.5 million Palestinian refugees. Many Palestinians have lived in refugee camps throughout the Arab World for more than half a century. Many of them were born and raised in these camps, and many have also died in these camps. Between 1947 and 1948, approximately 800,000 Palestinians became refugees. The 1967 war, during which all of Palestine was occupied by Israel, created a second wave of Palestinian refugees. Roughly 400,000 Palestinians, out of a population of 2.5 million, left Palestine to seek refuge in Jordan, Lebanon, Kuwait, Syria, and other Arab countries. The civil war in Lebanon in the 1970s and 1980s and Israel's invasion of Lebanon in 1982 forced more Palestinians to become refugees again. Roughly 5.1 million Palestinians live abroad, mostly in Jordan, which has 3 million of them. Some of them left for Europe, the United States, and Canada. There are more than 200,000 Palestinians living in the United States and Canada and roughly 200,000 in Europe.[22] Many Palestinian refugees migrated to oil-producing Arab countries that needed both skilled and unskilled labor. However, when Iraq invaded Kuwait in

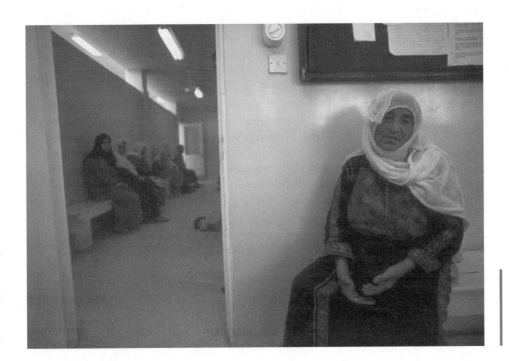

Palestinian Refugee Hoping to Return Home.

(Barry Iverson/Time Life Pictures/Getty Images)

1990, many Palestinians supported Saddam Hussein. The Gulf War in 1991 contributed to the expulsion of about 350,000 Palestinians from Kuwait alone. Palestinians also left Iraq and Saudi Arabia. Although many Palestinians hope to return to their homes in Israel and the Palestinian territories, the Palestinian refugee problem is at the heart of the Palestinian-Israeli conflict and is likely to remain unresolved in the near future. The **United Nations Relief Works Agency for Palestinian Refugees in the Near East (UNRWA)** was established in 1949 to provide relief, education, and welfare services to Palestinian refugees.

UNRWA ■ UN agency established to aid in relief, education, and welfare services for Palestinian refugees

PULL FACTORS

Pull factors are developments and circumstances that attract people to specific areas or countries. Freedom has always been a significant pull factor, both within countries and across international boundaries. Freedom, associated with cities, enticed many individuals to leave the countryside with its relative lack of freedom. *Freedom* in Britain, Holland, and the United States has served as a magnet for European migrants and, more recently, for migrants from the developing world. Religious, artistic, economic, political, and scientific freedoms remain almost irresistible pull factors, which, in turn, usually enhance the degree of freedom that existed. New York, London, Paris, Sydney, Toronto, Los Angeles, Seattle, Chicago, Miami, and Boston are vibrant and dynamic because of the freedom that characterizes them and attracts talent and financial resources from around the world.

Economic opportunities are one of the most powerful pull factors. People have historically migrated to industrial areas that offered employment and financial and entrepreneurial opportunities. Income inequality between rural and urban areas or between developing and developed countries generally induces people to migrate to seek higher income. Economic opportunities of an earlier period of globalization, between 1870 and 1910, influenced roughly 10 percent of the world's population to immigrate. Millions of Europeans migrated from poor countries to industrialized societies on the continent and to the United States, Canada, Australia, Argentina, Brazil, and other Latin American countries. It is estimated that 12 million Chinese emigrated between 1815 and 1914, many of them from the south of China.[23] Mexicans are motivated to migrate to the United States partly because many of them can earn much more money doing similar jobs in the United States. This is a global phenomenon. Higher wages in Britain, France, and Germany, combined with labor shortages in those countries following World War II, attracted immigrants from the Caribbean, India, Africa, and Turkey. Similarly, higher wages in the mining industry in South Africa induced people from neighboring countries to migrate to South Africa. Oil wealth and jobs in the Persian Gulf countries pulled more than 3.5 million Asians to the region.[24] Demand for inexpensive and reliable labor contributed to the development of an Indian diaspora that covers sixty-three countries and has more than 20 million people. A **diaspora** is a community of people living outside their original or ancestral country.

Diaspora ■ A community of people living outside their original or ancestral country

Colonization and financial globalization combined to create a very powerful pull factor between 1820 and 1920. European colonization of the Americas, Asia, and Africa was accompanied by massive flows of capital. Industrialization in Europe generated a significant supply of capital, which stimulated an expansion of industrialization overseas. Colonization enticed millions of Europeans and others to emigrate. Many of these areas had been settled long before the arrival of Europeans, a reality that often resulted in the forceful removal and even death of native populations. More than 60 million Europeans migrated to the Americas, Asia, and Eastern and Southern Africa.[25] Demand for inexpensive labor in the European colonies led to the migration of roughly 12 million Chinese and 30 million Indians to areas conquered and colonized by Europeans. The British, who colonized India, encouraged Indians to migrate to British colonies, including Burma, Malaysia, Singapore, Australia, Fiji, Trinidad and Tobago, British Guyana, Kenya, South Africa, and Uganda. Many Indians returned to India eventually, but a significant number, estimated to be 6 million, remained abroad.[26]

Globalization is widely viewed as one of the most significant pull factors in relation to migration. Globalization erodes national boundaries, weakens the ability of governments to control many aspects of national life, and strengthens the interdependence of countries, nonstate actors, and individuals. Globalization, especially economic and cultural globalization, enables poor people to see prosperity in rich countries. Movies, magazines, television, and tourism contribute to promoting glamorous and desirable lifestyles in developed countries. Globalization shrinks the world, thereby making it easier for people to compare themselves not only with their immediate neighbors but also with people around the world.[27] Globalization creates dreams that many individuals in poor countries find irresistible. **Global cities** enable immigrants to blend into the population and become low-wage workers in hotels, restaurants, sweatshops, homes of American families, manufacturing and retail companies, and agro-business.

Family reunification and **cultural ties** are major pull factors. In many parts of the world, people migrate to places where they know someone, which gives rise to a concentration of immigrants from a particular country or a region of a country in certain areas. For example, many early Scandinavian immigrants went primarily to the United States and settled in Midwestern agricultural states, including Minnesota, Wisconsin, Nebraska, Illinois, and Iowa.

These preferences were often reinforced by actions of the receiving countries that encouraged or discouraged the immigration of different groups.[28] Many immigrants live in particular parts of the countries they settle. For example, many Polish immigrants settled in Chicago, making it the city with the largest number of people of Polish ancestry in the United States and second only to Warsaw, Poland. The largest group of migrants is composed of relatives of individuals who are already living in a specific country. Family reunification is a leading objective of immigration policies in several countries. Roughly 75 percent of legal immigrants in the United States have relatives in that country, and about 80 percent of legal immigrants in Sweden have family members in Sweden. In many cases, one family member will immigrate to a particular country and, once relatively economically secure, will encourage family members to join him or her. This phenomenon is known as **chain migration**.

Sparsely populated areas, as we have seen, provide a significant pull factor. As we mentioned earlier, European conquest and colonization of the Americas,

Global Cities ◼
Cities that contain enough migrants to make them international in scope and appeal

Family Reunification ◼ Major pull factor encouraging global migration

Cultural Ties ◼
Major pull factor in promoting global migration

Chain Migration ◼
Process by which one family member immigrates to a country and then encourages other family members to join him or her

Asia, and Africa provided opportunities for certain parts of Europe to relieve their population pressures. North America and Australia attracted millions of European emigrants. However, anthropological evidence supports the view that the Americas had vast human populations when the Europeans arrived. Today, many European countries have declining population growth, a development that is inducing the growth of both legal and illegal migration to that region. Many countries have large areas that have few inhabitants. In Brazil, for example, the vast and sparsely settled Amazon region continues to attract settlers from other parts of Brazil and other countries. Earlier we pointed out how many states in the American Midwest have been losing population. To ease this population decline, Iowa, for example, has responded by creating an **immigration enterprise zone**. Iowa hopes to become a priority destination for refugees and foreigners who are willing to migrate in search of economic opportunities. Low population growth or decline is widely perceived as a serious threat to Iowa's economy.[29]

Immigration Enterprise Zone ■ Areas created to attract immigrants due to underpopulation problems

Closely related to freedom and economic opportunities as pull factors is the *availability of educational and cultural opportunities*. Western Europe, Canada, and the United States have long been magnets for students, artists, and professionals from many countries. Globalization has facilitated educational and cultural exchanges to an unprecedented degree and, in the process, is creating a global community of individuals who are connected by common educational and cultural experiences. Many foreign-born students and professionals achieve great success in the United States, which encourages more students and professionals to immigrate to that country. For example, the unpopularity of careers in science among American students reinforces the demand for foreign students to study science and engineering and to become part of the science and engineering workforce in the United States. From 1990 to 2000, the percentage of foreign-born workers in science and engineering with doctoral degrees rose from 24 percent to 38 percent, reflecting the country's growing dependence on immigration to sustain its technologically advanced economy.[30] On the other hand, it is argued that the United States remains the leader in training highly educated engineers and scientists and that there are many Americans who can replace foreign-born workers. However, due to global competition, many American companies employ foreigners at lower salaries than they pay Americans.

CASE STUDIES

The following case studies provide examples of how specific countries are affected by global migration. The case studies show that both developed and developing societies are being transformed, to varying degrees, by the influx of people from different countries and that governments and nonstate actors regard migration and population issues as extremely important components of human, national, and global security.

The United States

More than any country in the world, the United States is known as an immigrant country. Consequently, most Americans—with the exception of Native Americans and Americans of English and African descent—are descendents of people who migrated to the United States less than three hundred years ago. The demand for labor in the United States, together with poverty, conflict, and oppression in Europe, led to the migration of millions of Europeans to America. Rapid westward expansion and the need for a growing population to develop agriculture as well as industry attracted emigrants primarily from Western and Northern Europe until the early 1900s. Agricultural problems in Scandinavia, for example, prompted Swedes, Danes, Norwegians, and Finns to emigrate and settle in agricultural states in the Midwest.[31] By 1901, most emigrants came from Southern and Eastern Europe. Chinese and Japanese immigrants came to California in the 1850s to work in the gold mines, on the railroads, and in agriculture.

The United States adopted policies that excluded Asians and restricted immigrants from non-European countries. Growing fears about America's changing ethnic composition and about competition from new arrivals among "old stock" Americans led to the passage of legislation in 1921 that initiated the national quota system, which remained in place until 1965. The **national quota system** was designed to preserve the ethnic or national composition of the United States as of 1920. Quotas for emigrants from any one country were calculated in terms of 1/16 of 1 percent of persons of that national origin already in the United States. There was an absolute ceiling of two thousand emigrants from the Asia-Pacific region.[32] Improved economic conditions in Europe and the abolishment of the national quota system in 1965 changed the pattern of U.S. immigration. Most of the new arrivals are from the developing world, with various groups dominating particular parts of the country. For example, Mexicans comprise the majority of new immigrants in California, Texas, and Illinois; Dominicans, Chinese, and Indians are prominent in New York; and Cubans are the leading group in Florida. Immigrants make up a large proportion of America's population, and demographic projections indicate that they will be largely responsible for the country's population growth.

Mexico's geographic proximity to the United States and historical factors combine to make the growing number of Mexican migrants in the United States a contentious issue. Many Mexicans were already living in Texas, California, Arizona, New Mexico, Utah, Nevada, and Colorado when these areas were taken by the United States from Mexico during the **Mexican-American War**, which lasted from 1846 to 1848. The annexation of these territories by the United States did not significantly alter migration across the newly established borders. Economic and political problems in Mexico have traditionally served as push factors, and the demand for labor and economic opportunities in the United States functioned as pull factors. For example, the demand for labor in the United States during World War II brought Mexicans to America under the **Bracero Program**. The Bracero Program was a set of agreements between the United States and Mexico that facilitated the migration of Mexican workers, on a temporary basis, to work principally in agriculture. The increase in legal migration under the program was accompanied by the growth of illegal immigration. From 1942 to 1952, roughly 900,000 Mexican workers entered the United States under the Bracero Program, compared with more than 2 million illegal workers during the same period. In response to economic competition as well as fears about communists entering the country through Mexico, the United States launched **Operation Wetback** (from

National Quota System ■ System to limit immigration into the United States

Mexican-American War ■ (1846–1848); war in which the United States seized half of Mexico's territory, which is now Texas, California, Arizona, New Mexico, Utah, Nevada, and Colorado

Bracero Program ■ Agreements between the United States and Mexico to promote the migration of Mexican workers to the United States on a temporary basis (ended in 1964)

Operation Wetback ■ U.S. operation that deported hundreds of thousands of Mexican migrants

1954 to 1959) in which hundreds of thousands of Mexicans were arrested and deported. However, by the time the Bracero Program had ended in 1964, the relationship between Mexican workers and American employers was so well established that controlling the flow of migrants across the U.S.-Mexican border was almost impossible. Emigration from Mexico, both legal and illegal, became a reality of American life. Mexican emigrants throughout the United States are employed in all sectors of the economy. More than a million emigrants boycotted work and classes to demonstrate in favor of immigration reform in 2006. These protests, however, engendered popular opposition to illegal immigration. Apart from stationing the National Guard along the U.S.-Mexican border, the U S. government decided to build a fence along its borders with Mexico.[33] Politics in the United States between 2007 and 2009 essentially stifled discussions of immigration reform. Significantly fewer immigrants demonstrated on May 1, 2008. The economic recession in the United States and strong anti-immigrant attitudes combined to influence many migrants to return to Mexico, Brazil, and elsewhere.

Western Europe

The growing unification of Europe, manifested in the creation and strengthening of the EU, also enables illegal immigrants to move from one country to another once they enter a member country of the EU. Italy's extensive coastline provides many entry points for migrants desperate to settle in Western Europe. Despite numerous tragic accidents involving migrants on unseaworthy and overcrowded vessels, migrants continue to enter Italy. Europe has surpassed the United States as a magnet for refugees and asylum-seekers. Illegal immigrants come from North Africa, Eastern and Central Europe, the Middle East, Latin America and the Caribbean, China, sub-Saharan Africa, India, Russia, the former Soviet Republics, and elsewhere. Variations in immigration policies among EU members make some countries more attractive than others to migrants. For example, thousands of refugees gather in France at the entrance of the English Channel tunnel waiting for an opportunity, often fatal, to hide in trains and trucks going to Britain, which has more generous refugee policies than France.

FRANCE   The influx of large numbers of immigrants from developing countries into France must be seen in the broader context of French colonialism and the demand for labor. France, like the United States, views its revolution as having universal significance and has developed a tradition of respecting the civil and human rights of foreigners. Its self-perception as a champion of the developing world reinforced its policy of accepting migrants from poor countries. France adopted a **policy of assimilation** toward its colonies in Africa, Asia, the Caribbean, and the Pacific, under which many residents of French colonies gained French citizenship and were free to migrate in France. Many Africans, Asians, and people from the Caribbean found employment in France, especially following World War I, which had such a devastating impact on the French population that the country had to import labor for its industries. World War II also created demand for labor from the colonies. Algeria's struggle for independence from France (1954–1962) resulted in hundreds of thousands of Algerians gaining

Policy of Assimilation ■ French policy allowing many people from its colonies to become residents and citizens of France asylum in France because of their support for France. More migrants from France's former colonies arrived in the 1960s to meet the labor needs of France's growing economy. The largest number of migrants came from Muslim countries—such as Algeria, Tunisia, Morocco, and Senegal—a development, as we have seen, that resulted in the large number of Muslims in France today.[34]

As in other parts of Europe, rising immigration is fueling political and social extremism in France. **Jean-Marie Le Pen**, leader of the National Front party, has consistently advocated ending legal immigration and deporting illegal immigrants. There was strong popular support for Le Pen in French presidential elections in 2002. In those elections, he received the second highest percentage of votes in the preliminary and runoff elections and qualified to run against President Jacques Chirac in the runoff elections. This popular support for Le Pen demonstrated widespread French opposition to immigration. On the other hand, strong French opposition and strong negative reactions from other European countries to Le Pen following his unexpected political success led to his defeat in the runoff elections.[35] However, in 2006, France began deporting illegal immigrants. Economic problems, especially high oil prices and food prices and rising unemployment in 2008 and 2009, reinforced anti-immigrant attitudes in France.

Jean-Marie Le Pen ■ Anti-immigration leader

GERMANY Unlike the United States, Canada, and Australia, Germany is not traditionally an immigrant country. Instead, Germany encouraged its citizens to immigrate to North America, Eastern Europe, Latin America, and elsewhere in order to diminish population pressures and economic problems at home. Between 1920 and 1950, almost 7 million Germans settled in the United States, many of them in the midwestern agricultural states. This pattern of migration was radically altered by Germany's initiation of World War II and the devastation it experienced in that conflict. Similar to Britain and France, Germany lost so many of its citizens in the war that it was forced to import labor to help in its economic reconstruction. This was especially so after the construction of the **Berlin Wall**, built by the Soviet Union to divide East Germany from West Germany. The Berlin Wall effectively reduced to a trickle the flow of migrants from communist East Germany to the more prosperous capitalist West Germany.

Berlin Wall ■ Cold War barrier between Soviet-occupied Germany and democratic West Germany, in place 1961–1989

The growing domestic and global market for West Germany's cars, machine tools, appliances, and other manufactured products influenced the government to recruit foreign workers, primarily from Spain, Greece, Turkey, and Portugal. The government and trade unions agreed that Germans and foreigners would receive equal wages. Under the **Gastarbeiter rotation system**, foreign workers were regarded as guest workers who would remain in Germany for one to three years and then return to their home countries.[36]

Gastarbeiter Rotation System ■ West German plan for foreign workers to stay one to three years then return home

Today, almost 3 million Turks live in Germany. The fall of the Berlin Wall in 1989 and the reunification of Germany complicated immigration issues as millions of East Germans migrated to West Germany for economic opportunities and as Germany struggled to develop the former East Germany. Unemployment became a major issue as Germany's economy weakened. Faced with the influx of migrants from Eastern Europe, the former Yugoslavia, and other countries, Germans began to perceive immigrants as economic competitors and threats to their country's cultural values. These developments have been compounded by what Ralph Rotte calls "a permanent latent potential of culturally and ethnically oriented xenophobia"[37] or Germany's reluctance to include people who are not of German ancestry. Terrorist activities by Muslims in Europe, the United States, and elsewhere after September 11, 2001, reinforced this tendency.

THE IMPACT OF MIGRATION ON SENDING COUNTRIES

The movement of people within countries and across national boundaries tells various stories that underscore the growing interdependence of nation-states, NGOs, and individuals. Because globalization is a manifestation of complex relationships among states and nonstate actors, migration as a central component of this process is also complicated. Both gains and losses result when large numbers of people migrate, especially since those who leave are usually the best educated, the most ambitious, and enterprising individuals. However, by leaving, these individuals also position themselves to make significant contributions to their original homes.

Brain Drain ■ Migration of highly educated, skilled, and trained people from one country to another

Brain drain (i.e., the migration of highly educated and trained people) is widely regarded as a serious problem and a major impediment to development in poor countries. Many doctors, nurses, teachers, and university professors leave poorer countries and rural areas for higher paying jobs and better opportunities in neighboring countries as well as in rich industrial countries. As many as 70,000 educated and skilled Africans migrate to Western Europe, Canada, the United States, and elsewhere each year. This brain drain has significant implications for poor countries. Many medical problems in poor countries are negatively impacted by a shortage of medical personnel. For example, countries such as Tanzania, Malawi, and Sierra Leone had three or fewer doctors per 100,000 people, compared to 256 doctors per 100,000 people in the United States. Many European countries, especially following World War II, were concerned about losing talented individuals who were attracted to better opportunities in the United States. Canada faces brain drain to the United States, a problem that is solved partly by encouraging brain drain from developing countries. Many small towns in the United States suffer from the loss of their most talented residents to urban areas.

It is estimated that half of the recent graduates from the prestigious Indian Institute of Technology migrate to the United States. They are driven out by push factors such as overregulation, higher taxes, stagnant career paths, and numerous impediments to entrepreneurship. Many are attracted to the United States by better economic opportunities and a dynamic environment conducive to economic success and personal growth.[38] The fact that most Indian immigrants speak English enables them to easily integrate into American society. It is estimated that one-third of the engineers in Silicon Valley are of Indian origin. About 7 percent of Silicon Valley's high-tech firms are managed by Indians. Sabeer Bhatia, for example, founded Hotmail and sold it to Microsoft, and Vinod Khosla is a co-founder of Sun Microsystems.[39] But the migration of talented individuals is seen as detrimental to India's economic development. On the other hand, many countries have a problem of **brain overflow**, which is

Brain Overflow ■ When countries retain an oversupply of skilled individuals essentially an oversupply of skilled individuals. Many poor countries, such as the Philippines, India, and Egypt, have become exporters of highly educated people because of their inability to utilize their talents. **Remittances** (i.e., money earned abroad that is sent by migrants to their home countries) play a crucial role in the economic development of poor societies. Given the fact that remittances are transferred by millions of migrants in various ways, it is extremely difficult to know how much money migrants send to their families or invest in their home countries. Remittances clearly create networks of interdependence among countries, NGOs, and individuals. The growing number of migrants challenges traditional international relations theories of citizenship. It also forces many poorer countries to embrace dual citizenship, which enables their citizens to find better jobs abroad and to send even more money home.[40] Some organizations—such as the Inter-American Development Bank (IDB) and the U.S. Agency for International Development (USAID)—have developed strategies to assist migrants to transmit remittances more economically. This development reflects the growing economic impact of remittances on developing countries. For example, it is estimated that Mexican migrants and Mexican-Americans sent approximately 24.7 billion in 2007 to Mexico, which was twice the value of Mexico's agricultural exports and over a third more than Mexico's tourist revenues. However, the global economic recession and the decline of Mexicans migrating to the United States led to a significant reduction in remittances. Migrants sent $1.8 billion in April 2009, which was 18 percent less than in April 2008.[41] The complexity of migration in an increasingly global age makes it difficult to assess its costs and benefits for sending countries.

Remittances ■
Money earned abroad sent by migrants to their home countries

SUMMARY AND REVIEW

Migration is an important issue throughout many countries and regions of the world today. It has greatly contributed to globalization and to an increased interdependence among many countries and peoples. This chapter illustrates how population and migration issues are essentially about politics, economics, and culture. Population issues are an increasing problem in the developed and developing countries as they hinder economic growth and place great pressures on already strained populations. Underpopulation has become a major problem due to a rapid increase in aging populations throughout developed countries. In an attempt to rectify this problem, some states have attempted to increase fertility rates domestically and encourage immigration from abroad. High rates of population growth have had devastating consequences in the developed world as well. In an effort to ease overpopulation, many developing countries have resorted to strict population controls; an example is China's one-child policy. Other countries have encouraged their citizens to migrate to other states.

Migration has various forms. It can be forced or induced. Sometimes it is temporary, as when workers return to their countries of origin. Migration can be regional or transcontinental, and it can be seasonal or permanent. Many factors have contributed to increased migration. Push factors—such as environmental disasters, high unemployment, high population growth rates, state repression, and discrimination—have encouraged many to look for safer homes where they can pursue prosperous futures. Pull factors have also enticed many to migrate, seeking economic and political freedoms, a safer environment for themselves and their families, educational opportunities, and a chance to earn higher wages.

KEY TERMS

overpopulation 252
replacement rate 252
carrying capacity 252
sexism 254
Son Complex 254
dowry 254
Indira Gandhi 255
one-child policy 255
subreplacement fertility
  regimes 255
migration 256
migrant 257
refugees 257
asylum-seekers 257
displaced person 257
immigrant 257
transcontinental migration
  257
regional migration
  258
seasonal migration 258
transit migration 258

forced and induced
  migration 258
return migration 258
push factors 260
pull factors 260
Huguenots 260
Han Chinese 260
Cultural Revolution 260
Mao Zedong 260
Saddam Hussein 261
competitive exclusion 261
United Nations Geneva
  Convention 261
International Committee of
  the Red Cross 262
humanitarian intervention
  262
United Nations Relief Works
  Agency for Palestinian
  Refugees in the Near East
  (UNRWA) 264
diaspora 264

global cities 265
family reunification 265
cultural ties 265
chain migration 265
immigration enterprise
  zone 266
national quota system
  267
Mexican-American War
  267
Bracero Program 267
Operation Wetback 267
policy of assimilation 268
Jean-Marie Le Pen 269
Berlin Wall, 269
Gasterbeiter rotation
  system, 269
Brain drain 270
brain overflow 270
remittances 271

DISCUSSION QUESTIONS

1. How has migration challenged the traditional divisions between nation-states?
2. What are some of the causes, as well as negative consequences, of high and low population growth rates?
3. In what way do remittances help strengthen the ties between economies and people? Do you think remittances are a positive thing?
4. Can you identify some of the push and pull factors that traditionally lead to increased regional and global migration?

SUGGESTED READINGS

Bhagwati, Jagdish. "Borders Beyond Control," *Foreign Affairs* 82, No. 1 (January/February 2003): 98–104.

Connelly, Matthew. *Fatal Misconception: The Struggle to Control World Population.* Cambridge, MA: Harvard University Press, 2008.

Giry, Stephanie. "France and Its Muslims," *Foreign Affairs* 85, No. 5 (September/October 2006): 87–104.

Hanson, Gordon. *Why Does Immigration Divide America?* Washington, DC: Institute for International Economics, 2005.

Kirkegaard, Jacob. *The Accelerating Decline in America's High-Skilled Workforce.* Washington, DC: Peterson Institute, 2008.

Schiff, Maurice, and Caglar Ozden, eds. *International Migration, Economic Development and Policy.* Washington, DC: World Bank, 2007.

Skerry, Peter. "How Not to Build a Fence," *Foreign Policy* 156 (September/October 2006): 64–67.

UN High Commissioner for Refugees. *The State of the World's Refugees.* New York: Oxford University Press, 2006.

END NOTES

1. Christian Joppke, "Why Liberal States Accept Unwanted Immigration," *World Politics* 50, No. 2 (1998), 268.
2. Tom Hundley, "Foes' Births Alarm Israel," *Chicago Tribune*, 23 April 2002, Sect. 1, 1.
3. Gurcharan Das, "The India Model," *Foreign Affairs* 85, No. 4 (July/August 2006), 16.
4. Barbra Crossette, "Population Estimates Fall as Poor Women Assert Control," *New York Times*, 10 March 2002, A3.
5. "More Girls Being Abandoned in China's Countryside," *Pantagraph*, 23 November 2001, A11.
6. David Rohde, "India Steps Up Effort to Halt Abortions of Female Fetuses," *New York Times*, 26 October 2003, A3.
7. Amy Waldman, "States in India Take New Steps to Limit Births," *New York Times*, 7 November 2003, A1.
8. Nicholas Eberstadt, "The Population Implosion," *Foreign Policy*, 123 (March/April 2001), 44.
9. Sara Rhodin, "A Holiday and a Park Bench from Russia with Love," *New York Times*, 9 July 2008, A12.
10. Richard Bernstein, "Aging Europe Finds Its Pension Is Running Out," *New York Times*, 29 June 2003, A3.
11. Peter G. Peterson, *Gray Dawn* (New York: Random House, 1999), 5.
12. Peter G. Peterson, "The Global Aging Crisis," *Foreign Affairs* 78, No. 1 (January/February 1999), 53.
13. Kevin Sullivan and Mary Jordan, "World's Refugees Deluge Mexico on Way to U.S." *Chicago Tribune*, 8 June 2001, Sect. 1, 4.
14. Tim Hatton, "The Age of Mass Migration," in *Migration and Mobility*, eds. Subrata Ghatak and Anne Showstack Sassoon (New York: Palgrave, 2001), 25.
15. Amy Waldman, "India Harvests Fruits of a Diaspora," *New York Times*, 12 January 2003, A4.
16. Kimberly A. Hamilton and Kate Holder, "International Migration and Foreign Policy," *Washington Quarterly* (Spring 1996), 196.
17. Myron Weiner, "Security, Stability, and Migration," in *Conflict After the Cold War*, ed. Richard K. Betts (New York: Longman, 2002), 470.
18. Damien Cave, "10 Die as Haitian Immigrants' Boat Sinks," *New York Times*, 14 May 2009, A-18.
19. Myron Weiner, *The Global Migration Crisis* (New York: HarperCollins, 1995), 30.
20. "Europe Urges Wider Definition of Refugees," *New York Times*, 12 September 2001, B4.
21. Sabrina Tavernise, "Invisible Refugees Push Pakistani Cities' and Families' Hospitality to Brink," *New York Times*, 18 June 2009, A6.
22. Samih K. Farsoun and Christina E. Zacharia, *Palestine and the Palestinians* (Boulder, CO: Westview Press, 1997), 138–139; and Michael Fischbach, *The Peace Process and Palestinian Refugee Claims* (Washington, DC: U.S. Institute of Peace Press, 2006).

23. David Held et al., *Global Transformations* (Stanford, CA: Stanford University Press, 1999), 294.

24. Cameron W. Barr, "Kuwait Shifts Welfare Costs to Immigrants," *Christian Science Monitor*, 18 April 2001, 7.

25. Martin Wolf, "Will the Nation-State Survive Globalization?" *Foreign Affairs* 80, No. 1 (January/February 2001), 181.

26. Held et al., *Global Transformation*, 294; and Steve Raymer, *Images of a Journey: India in Diaspora* (Bloomington: Indiana University Press, 2008).

27. Peter Stalker, *Workers Without Frontiers* (Boulder, CO: Lynne Rienner, 2000), 100.

28. Hatton, "The Age of Mass Migration," in *Migration and Mobility*, 24–25.

29. Pam Belluck, "Short of People, Iowa Seeks to Be Ellis Island of Midwest," *New York Times*, 20 November 2003, A24.

30. James Glanz, "Study Warns of Lack of Scientists as Visa Applications Drop," *New York Times*, 20 November 2003, A24; and Fareed Zakaria, "The Future of American Power," *Foreign Affairs* 87, No. 3 (May/June 2008), 31.

31. Hans Norman, "Swedes in North America," in *From Sweden to America*, eds. Harald Runblom and Hans Norman (Minneapolis: University of Minnesota Press, 1976), 246.

32. Henry J. Steiner and Detlev F. Vagts, *Transnational Legal Problems* (Mineola, NY: Foundation Press, 1976), 19; and Gordon H. Hanson, *Why Does Immigration Divide America?* (Washington, DC: Institute for International Economics, 2005).

33. Kitty Calavita, "U.S. Immigration and Policy Responses," in *Controlling Immigration: A Global Perspective*, eds. Wayne Cornelius et al. (Stanford, CA: Stanford University Press, 1994), 59; Michael Martinez; "Rallies Draw Over 1 Million," *Chicago Tribune*, 2 May 2006, Sect. 1, 7; and Peter Skerry, "How Not to Build a Fence," *Foreign Policy* 156 (September/October 2006), 64.

34. Milton Viorst, "The Muslims of France," *Foreign Affairs* 75, No. 5 (September/October 1996), 78; James F. Hollifield, "Immigration and Republican France," in *Controlling Immigration*, 153; Stephanie Giry, "France and Its Muslims," *Foreign Affairs* 85, No. 5 (September/October 2006), 89–91; and Jytte Klausen, *The Islamic Challenge* (New York: Oxford University Press, 2008).

35. Suzanne Daley, "French Political Leaders Rally Around Chirac," *New York Times*, 23 April 2002, A1.

36. Herman Kurthen, "Germany at the Crossroads," *International Migration Review* 29, No. 4 (Winter 1995), 922.

37. Ralph Rotte, "Immigration Control in United Germany," *International Migration Review* 34, No. 2 (Summer 2000), 358.

38. Stephan-Gotz Richter, "The Immigration Safety Valve," *Foreign Affairs* 79, No. 2 (March/April 2000), 15.

39. Anthony Spaeth, "The Golden Diaspora," *Time*, 19 June 2000, B28.

40. Devesh Kapur and John McHale, "Migration's New Payoff," *Foreign Policy* 139 (November/December 2003), 50; and Maurice Schiff and Caglar Ozden, eds., *International Migration: Economic Development and Policy* (Washington, DC: World Bank, 2007).

41. Elizabeth Malkin, "Money Sent Home by Mexican Workers in U.S. Falls Sharply," *New York Times*, 2 June 2009, A5.

12

Global Crime

INTRODUCTION

Global crime is intricately intertwined with revolutionary technological, financial, communications, economic, cultural, and political changes that characterize globalization, and it is increasingly difficult to separate criminal activities from legitimate global transactions. As national boundaries become more porous and as different legal and political systems are more closely integrated, uncertainties about the legality of various activities abound. What some countries regard as serious problems are often viewed as lower priorities for others. Furthermore, different countries—influenced by divergent cultural attitudes and beliefs—adopt different approaches to solving problems.

The disintegration of the Soviet Union contributed to the strengthening and unleashing of criminal organizations that have constructed global networks involved in drug trafficking, human trafficking, money laundering, illegal arms sales, and other criminal activities. Global crime is also linked to global poverty and inequality, failed states, global migration, growth of global cities, the expansion of free trade, rapid communications and computer technologies, and easy global financial transactions. This chapter examines the globalization of crime, the perpetual global drug problem, the global smuggling of migrants, contemporary slavery and human trafficking, criminal gangs and kidnapping, money laundering, illegal trade in exotic animals and plants, illegal trade in human organs, cybercrimes and piracy, and stolen art and antiquities. It concludes with a discussion of various global responses to crime.

THE GLOBALIZATION OF CRIME

Global crime has existed with legal commerce for centuries. In fact, crime has been an integral component of human society. By diminishing the significance of geographic distance, globalization enables criminal networks to grow alongside legal global activities and to establish connections within many different countries. As we will discuss, alliances are common among criminal organizations involved in trafficking in humans, drugs, weapons, and various illicit products. Moises Naim observed that criminal networks have benefited more than nation-states from the information revolution, economic links, and other aspects of globalization.[1]

Although globalization has contributed to increased economic equality among and within nations, as Thomas Friedman argues in *The World Is Flat*, it is widely perceived as contributing to more inequality. To an unprecedented degree of poignancy, globalization heightens the awareness of the economic and social disparities between the rich and the poor within nations and between rich and poor countries. Not only do poor people perceive themselves as losers in the process of globalization, they have little incentive to adhere to rules that they perceive to be adverse to their interests. For example, convincing coca farmers in Peru, Colombia, and Bolivia that they should not participate in illegal drug production has been difficult. Similarly, small farmers in Afghanistan continue to produce poppies used to make heroin. Although organized crime imposes excessive burdens on society, particularly the poor, many criminal groups, in order to gain political influence and legitimacy, invest in social services, athletic facilities, housing, and medical services. These areas have been largely neglected by many governments as part of the privatization process required by economic globalization. Ultimately, global crime is integrated into the fabric of these societies and enjoys significant official and unofficial protection. In some cases, weak institutional capabilities have prevented governments from reducing global crime. Consequently, there has been an unprecedented escalation in crimes such as trade in pirated goods, illegal arms, human trafficking, stolen art, and illegal drugs.[2]

The disintegration of the Soviet Union in 1991 was one of the most important developments contributing to the emergence and growth of global crime. Rapid political and economic changes in Eastern and Central European countries further enhanced opportunities for widespread criminal activities. Exploiting weakness of the Russian government, organized criminal groups consolidated their power domestically and built strategic alliances with global criminal organizations in Latin America and the Caribbean. Russian criminal groups proliferated throughout Central Europe, in countries such as the Czech Republic, as successful revolutions against communism ushered in social disorganization, poorly guarded national borders, free-market economies, and a willingness of young people to experiment with drugs. Furthermore, as we discussed in Chapter 1, the expansion of the European Union (EU) into Central and Eastern Europe and the removal of many national barriers to the movement of people and products facilitated the growth of criminal activities.[3]

THE GLOBAL DRUG PROBLEM

From Shanghai to San Francisco, from London to Buenos Aires, in Christian, Jewish, Islamic, Hindu, and Buddhist societies, in small towns and big cities, and in rich and poor countries, the use of illegal drugs is a serious problem. Norway—which generally ranks first in the world in terms of income, health care, life expectancy, and education—is widely regarded as having one of Europe's worst drug problems. For many years, Oslo has been ranked as Europe's drug overdose capital.[4] Illegal drug use is one of the most important global issues. No society has managed to escape the consequences of the global drug trade, largely because the global drug problem is so closely intertwined with other areas of globalization. The foundations of the contemporary global drug problem were laid during an earlier period of globalization that was marked by European expansion, colonization, and trade.

The discoveries of tobacco in the Caribbean, chocolate in South America, coffee in the Middle East and Africa, and tea in Asia marked the beginning of a global trade that eventually included opium. The growth of the opium trade was influenced partly by China's huge trade advantage with Portugal, Holland, and Britain. Whereas China had silk, teas, pottery, and other items that Europeans wanted, Europe had little to trade with China, thereby creating a trade deficit in China's favor. Europeans, who had trafficked in opium in parts of Asia, decided to sell it to China in order to reduce the trade imbalances.[5] The **British East India Company**, for example, paid Asian farmers to produce opium, which was then sold to independent wholesalers. Opium cultivation in India grew steadily, and the British pressured China to import it. Chinese resistance to the importation and consumption of opium ultimately led to the **Opium Wars** with Britain in 1839 and 1842, in which Britain forced China to import opium, despite an already horrendous drug addiction problem in China. British military power was instrumental in the legalization of opium in China in 1858. The Portuguese, French, Spanish, and Dutch also participated in the trade, creating opium addicts in their colonies as well as in Europe. The Spanish, for example, promoted the use of coca leaves to enable enslaved Indians to endure harsh physical labor. Toward the end of the nineteenth century, *the demand for opium in Europe and America was on the rise due to several factors.* These included

British East India Company ■ British company that dominated Indian trade

Opium Wars ■ Fought so that the British could force the opium trade onto the Chinese people

1. *The advancement in medical practices,* especially the discovery of morphine and heroin (both obtained from opium) and the invention of the hypodermic needle to administer them;
2. *Significant cultural and economic changes* that resulted from the Industrial Revolution, particularly the consumption of natural stimulants;
3. *The migration of Chinese,* many of whom used opium, to America and elsewhere;
4. *The growth of global trade;*
5. *The rise of mass-consumption habits,* influenced by marketing and mass communication;[6] and
6. *Military conflicts,* including the U.S. Civil War, which increased the demand for drugs to diminish pain.

Globalization combined with major cultural changes worldwide—especially in the United States, Canada, and Europe—is driving the global drug trade. Most experts agree that widespread use of illegal drugs in Western societies during the 1960s and 1970s created a global demand for drugs, which in turn stimulated worldwide illegal drug production. Heroin was smuggled in from areas that cultivated opium poppies, primarily the **Golden Triangle** countries (Burma/Myanmar,

Golden Triangle ■ Countries that cultivate opium poppies (Burma/Myanmar, Thailand, and Laos)

Thailand, and Laos) and the Golden Crescent countries (Afghanistan, Pakistan, and Iran). Cocaine came primarily from Colombia, Peru, Bolivia, and other South American countries. Marijuana, now increasingly grown within consuming countries, came primarily from Mexico, Jamaica, Colombia, and Thailand. Global trafficking networks quickly developed or were expanded to produce, distribute, and sell illegal drugs. Global commerce and migration have helped to consolidate the global drug trade. For example, Mexican drug traffickers took advantage of the growing number of Mexican immigrants in Dalton, Georgia, to turn that area into a distribution center for methamphetamine and other drugs.[7] Industrial countries are now themselves major sources of illegal drugs. Nightclub crowds worldwide routinely use Ecstasy, a euphoria-producing psychedelic drug that was initially used in Europe around 1912 as an appetite suppressant. What's more, distinctions between legal and illegal drugs are diminishing as more people abuse prescription medications.

Efforts to Control the Drug Problem

War on Drugs ■
Stresses supply-side control and harsh treatment of drug users

The reality of the global drug trade and the inability of governments to prevent drugs from entering countries have spawned essentially two different approaches to dealing with the drug problem. The first approach, the **war on drugs**, stresses supply-side control and harsh treatment of drug users. The second approach, *drug prevention and harm reduction*, emphasizes the need to keep drugs out of society and to treat drug abuse as a disease. The first approach is strongly embraced by the United States; the second approach is widely practiced in

Colombia's President Destroying Coca Plants.

(Fernando Vergara/ AP/Wide World Photos)

Europe. Before discussing these two strategies, we will briefly examine historical efforts to control the use of illegal drugs. Drug-exporting countries usually become major drug-consuming societies. As we saw earlier, European countries openly and aggressively built a global drug trade. By the beginning of the twentieth century, the widespread use of cocaine-based tonics, heroin, opium, and other narcotics in Europe, the United States, Japan, and China raised concerns about their negative impact on public morals. Religious groups, temperance societies, and others in Britain and the United States advocated ending the opium trade. As the United States expanded its power into Asia, especially after the Spanish-American War in 1898 (which resulted in the end of Spain's empire and America's acquisition of the Philippines), Americans became more concerned about drug abuse. The Philippines had many drug addicts.

Partly because of its interest in gaining greater influence in China, the United States collaborated with China to persuade other countries to participate in an international conference designed to convince drug-exporting countries to reduce their production of drugs. The conference, held in Shanghai in 1909, created the International Opium Commission. Although the twelve countries involved agreed to gradually suppress opium smoking in their territories, very little progress on controlling drugs was made. The **Hague Convention** of 1911 broadened the drug-fighting effort by including morphine and cocaine and committed the signatories to reducing their production and distribution of drugs. However, the Hague Convention was ineffective, partly because some countries—such as Germany, which at the time was the world's largest cocaine producer—insisted that the implementation of the treaty be made conditional on its worldwide acceptance.[8] Given the lucrativeness of drugs, few countries were willing to comply with the restrictive agreements. A turning point in the effort to control the drug trade was America's enactment of the **Harrison Act** in 1914, which required distributors and medical prescribers of specified drugs to be registered and pay taxes. Britain and other European countries enacted similar legislation. The League of Nations (1919) helped to consolidate drug-control efforts by stressing the development of mandatory international controls to be supervised by international organizations. The **Opium Control Board** was established by the League of Nations to monitor countries' compliance with international agreements on controlling drugs. The rapid spread of drug usage in the 1960s and 1970s influenced the United Nations (UN) to sponsor the International Conference on Drug Abuse and Illicit Traffic in 1987 to discuss strategies for dealing with the problem. In 1988, strongly influenced by America's emphasis on the war-on-drugs approach, the global community signed the UN Convention Against Illicit Traffic in Narcotic Drugs and Psychotropic Substances. This convention stressed sharing law enforcement evidence, providing mutual legal assistance, controlling the sale of chemicals used in producing drugs, and escalating the eradication of drug crops.[9] Founded in 1990, the UN International Drug Control Program (UNDCP) stressed the need for both demand reduction and alternative development. In 1998, the UN General Assembly Special Session on Drugs had advocated the goal of a drug-free world by 2008. Obviously, achieving this goal continues to be elusive.

Confronted with the rapid rise in drug abuse, the United States mobilized financial, law enforcement, and military resources to combat the problem. The

Hague Convention ■ Broadened the international drug-fighting effort by cracking down on morphine and cocaine

Harrison Act ■ U.S. act requiring distributors and prescribers of drugs to be registered and pay taxes

Opium Control Board ■ Established under the League of Nations to monitor countries' compliance with international drug agreements war on drugs concentrates primarily on reducing global drug trafficking and drug use by eliminating supplies and implementing punitive drug laws. It is estimated that between 50 and 80 percent of Americans who are imprisoned have committed a drug-related offense. The United States has cooperated with governments throughout Latin America to eradicate drug crops, implement crop-substitution programs, and destroy trafficking networks. In 2000, for example, the United States and Colombia launched **Plan Colombia**, an antidrug program that had the goal of reducing Colombia's coca crop in half by 2005. The plan involved aerial spraying, promoting crop substitution, destroying cocaine labs, and disrupting transportation routes. The United States allocated $1.3 billion to Plan Colombia.[10] Given how lucrative the drug business is, the war on drugs has not significantly reduced the drug trade. Poverty and tradition motivate many small farmers in Latin America and Asia to grow drug crops. The money they earn from crop substitution is only a fraction of what they can earn from drug crops. Ironically, success in removing drugs from the market increases the demand for declining supplies, thereby driving up prices. This, in turn, influences people to cultivate drug crops. Corrupt law enforcement officials worldwide also undermine the war on drugs. Most importantly, the war on drugs largely ignores the demand for drugs within the United States, Europe, and elsewhere. Coca production in Colombia was not significantly reduced, despite the more than $6 billion pumped into that effort by the United States. Homicides escalated at the U.S.-Mexico border in 2009 as drug cartels fought to dominate the illegal drug trade. The drug war and weapons sales became a major issue in U.S.-Mexican relations.

Plan Colombia ■
U.S.-sponsored antidrug campaign implemented to eradicate Colombia's cocaine production

YOU DECIDE

Strategies to Reduce Global Drug Use

Whereas the United States stresses eliminating the growth of drug crops, cutting off supplies, and punishing drug abusers, the Europeans treat drug addiction as a medical problem, do not arrest people for possessing or using small amounts of drugs, and generally believe that focusing primarily on the supply of drugs and declining to acknowledge that demand for drugs is a major part of the problem will not reduce global drug usage. Most Americans, however, view Europe's permissive drug policies as promoting drug abuse. The number of drug users in Europe has grown. Overall, Europe now accounts for 17 percent of cocaine seizures, compared to 3 percent in 1980. But America continues to have serious drug problems, and drug supplies have not been significantly reduced. Methamphetamine labs can be found across the United States, and prescription drugs are widely abused. America has the largest prison population in the world, due primarily to the large number of Americans who are imprisoned for violating drug laws. In 2009, U.S. Secretary of State Hillary Rodham Clinton made a direct connection between what she called Americans' insatiable demand for illegal drugs fueling the trade and America's inability to stop weapons from being smuggled into Mexico feeding the violence. Many Americans, however, argue that their right to keep and bear arms must be protected. The drug violence on the U.S.-Mexican border has led some observers to refer to Mexico as being on the verge of becoming a failed state.

1. Evaluate the effectiveness of the European and American approaches to drugs.
2. Do you think the war on drugs is counterproductive?
3. Does the right to bear arms contribute to drug use in America? ■

By contrast, Europeans concentrate on treating drug addiction more as a medical problem while supporting efforts to reduce drug supplies. **Harm-reduction approaches** acknowledge the weaknesses of the war-on-drugs approach. Holland became a pioneer in implementing the harm-reduction approach. It decriminalizes possession and use of small amounts of "soft" drugs (such as marijuana), provides "safe injection rooms" so that addicts can avoid public places, distributes sterile syringes to reduce the spread of HIV and AIDS, and supports medical treatment for drug addicts.[11] Europeans strongly oppose Plan Colombia and the U.S. war on drugs. The EU voted 474 to 1 to oppose the large-scale use of chemical herbicides and biological agents to eradicate coca plants because of the consequences for human health and the environment.

Harm-Reduction Approaches ■ Aim at drug prevention and drug treatment

GLOBAL SMUGGLING OF MIGRANTS

The global/economic recession of 2008–2009 significantly diminished the demand for migrant workers. In fact, as we have seen, return migration is now the global trend. However, desperate people continue to be smuggled to areas where they perceive economic and social opportunities. In June 2000, British customs officials discovered the bodies of fifty-eight illegal Chinese immigrants in a sealed compartment of a Dutch-registered tomato truck. They had been smuggled into Dover after a five-hour journey across the English Channel from the Belgian port of Zeebrugge. France is also a transit point for illegal immigrants who pay global smuggling operations to get them into Britain and, in many cases, eventually to the United States and Canada. Despite general antimigrant attitudes and actions in Europe in 2008, migrants waited on the French coast to be smuggled across the English Channel into Britain. The extensive U.S.-Mexican border provided smugglers with a relatively easy way to get migrants to the most popular destination, especially prior to 2007. Increased U.S. border-control activities have contributed to reduced illegal immigration. Immigrant communities along the border, the existence of criminal organizations that operate between the countries, the well-established drug trade, and the flow of people and products across the U.S.-Mexican border facilitate the successful smuggling of migrants from around the world. It is estimated that more than a million migrants are smuggled across this border each year. But the tragic deaths of nineteen migrants who were being smuggled across the border in May 2003 refocused national attention on the illegal and brutal nature of global smuggling. At least seventy-seven migrants were packed into an unconventional tractor-trailer without water for a 325-mile journey across the scorching desert. Some who survived had body temperatures as high as 105 degrees. The person in charge of the smuggling operation had been smuggled across the border about ten years before this deadly tragedy. In April 2008, fifty-four migrant workers from Myanmar (formerly Burma) died in a sealed truck in which they were being smuggled into Thailand.[12]

Chinese global smuggling organizations are generally regarded as the most sophisticated and most brutal. Many migrants come from the Fujian province in Southern China and take advantage of connections with family members and friends already established in the United States, Canada, and European countries.

Chinese communities worldwide, especially those in large cities, provide extensive networks of connections that enable global smuggling operations to be efficient and lucrative. Chinese migrants pay smugglers between $30,000 and $60,000 to be transported to Europe, the United States, and Canada. They travel across many countries or across nine thousand miles of the Pacific Ocean for five weeks in unsanitary, unseaworthy ships. Many of them land in Central America and make a long and perilous journey across Mexico and into the United States, where they find employment in Chinese communities to repay their debt for being smuggled. Often, they pay an initial 10 percent of the smuggling cost, and relatives pay the rest once the migrants arrive at their destinations. One of the most famous smuggling cases involved Cheng Chui-Ping, known affectionately in New York City's Chinatown as Sister Ping. She sold clothes and operated a restaurant that served dishes from her native Fujian province. She also used her entrepreneurial skills to build a global smuggling network that brought Chinese migrants to Mexico, Belize, and other Central American countries and eventually to the United States. She was able to bribe immigration officials and obtain false documents for migrants. Once migrants arrived in the United States, they usually found employment in restaurants and garment factories, which enabled them to repay her. By the time she was arrested by an undercover U.S. police officer, she had built a global smuggling network from which she received more than $40 million, making her a major player in the roughly $7 billion to $12 billion global smuggling business.[13]

CONTEMPORARY SLAVERY AND HUMAN TRAFFICKING

Human trafficking ■ Forced movement of people within or between countries

Contemporary Slavery ■ Transporting people from one area to another, where they are subjugated to forced labor or prostitution

Human trafficking (i.e., the forced or coerced movement of people across national borders as well as within countries) is probably as old as human civilization. Throughout history, human beings have enslaved each other and forced each other to work under the most inhumane conditions, justifying this exploitation in many ways. From ancient Egypt to the present-day United States, slavery was and is an integral component of economic life. **Contemporary slavery** is the transporting of victims under false pretenses from one nation, or province, to another, where they are subjugated to forced labor or prostitution.[14] Compared with the global drug trade, human trafficking receives much less attention. Nonetheless, it is a growing problem, partly because it combines high profits, increasing demand, abundant supply, relatively low risks of punishment, increasing sexual tolerance worldwide, and varying perceptions of the problem in the global community. Although the U.S. Central Intelligence Agency estimates that almost a million people worldwide are enslaved each year, including twenty thousand in the United States, it is impossible to know how many people are actually trafficked.[15]

The exponential growth in contemporary slavery and human trafficking is inseparable from increasing levels of economic and cultural globalization. As we discussed in Chapter 10, global migration is extremely difficult to manage. The porousness of borders that are inadequately monitored facilitates human trafficking. Because much of the trafficking is conducted by individuals and small groups, often in cooperation with large criminal organizations, it is difficult to detect and control. Global inequality and demographic factors contribute to the

rapid growth of labor migration, a development in which most countries participate. Migrants are employed to do the most strenuous and undesirable jobs in
most countries, including the United States. Globalization and changing attitudes
about women have led to a dramatic increase in women migrants. Many women
are employed as domestic helpers in service industries and as dancers, strippers,
and sex workers in the entertainment industry. This **feminization of migration**
(i.e., the increasing percentage of women in the migrant population) complicates
the human trafficking problem.[16]

Despite the global emphasis on women and girls being trafficked for sexual
exploitation, labor trafficking of males as well as females is more prevalent. The
International Labor Organization (ILO) found that of the estimated 9.5 million
victims of forced labor in Asia, less than 10 percent were trafficked for commercial sexual exploitation. Globally, less than half of all trafficking victims are
involved in the sex trade.[17] Forced labor exists worldwide. The deaths of twelve
workers who had been trafficked from Nepal to Iraq demonstrated the pervasive-
ness of human trafficking. The workers became entangled in a trail of deceit,
fraud, coercion, and negligence. Contractors and subcontractors, employed
directly or indirectly by the U.S. government at American facilities in Iraq, put the
workers in the war zone. All twelve workers were kidnapped on their way to
work on a U.S. military base and were subsequently executed by militants.[18]

Women and girls are generally perceived as replaceable commodities by
human traffickers. Although virtually all societies have experienced human trafficking for sexual purposes, this practice seems to be more prevalent in several
Asian countries. Prior to the Russian Revolution in 1917, Russian and Eastern
European women were trafficked into China and Argentina. Between the 1970s
and today, there have been *four distinct waves of sexual human trafficking*, all of
which are manifestations of increasing globalization. The *first wave* began in the
1970s and was primarily composed of trafficked women from Southeast Asia,
particularly Thailand and the Philippines. The *second wave* started in the early
1980s and involved trafficked women mostly from Africa, especially Ghana and
Nigeria. The *third wave*, from the 1980s to the 1990s, was made up of Latin
Americans, with most of the women coming from Colombia, Brazil, and the
Dominican Republic. The *fourth wave*, which mirrors the rapid expansion and
growing complexity of globalization, is closely connected to the demise of the
Soviet Union. The women are coming from Eastern and Central Europe.[19]

Although women are trafficked globally, the Netherlands, Germany, Japan,
the United Arab Emirates, Israel, Greece, South Korea, Turkey, Austria, Belgium,
Bosnia, the United States, and Canada are the principal destinations. Criminals
collaborate to maximize their profits from human trafficking. Groups in the
Russian Far East cooperate with Japanese and Korean organized crime to transport women to China, Japan, Korea, Thailand, and other countries of the Pacific
Rim. Groups in the Caucasus collaborate with human traffickers in Turkey to
transport women to brothels in Turkey, Cyprus, and countries in the Middle East.
Women from Kazakhstan are trafficked to Bahrain, where the Muslim links of
the traffickers provide women for this free-trade zone.[20]

Most trafficked women are forced into prostitution. Many young women
worldwide are seduced by romantic images of the West to take risks that often

**Feminization of
Migration** ■ The
increasing percent-
age of women in the
migrant population

result in their sexual exploitation. Poverty has usually been a major factor influencing human trafficking. Radical economic changes that accompanied the fall of communism in the Soviet Union and the transition from a centralized economy to a market-based economy undermined economic security for many women, even as these changes provided the impetus for increased globalization. Women became more vulnerable to trafficking as they attempted to find employment in other countries to support their families.

Economic deprivation also facilitates trafficking of orphans throughout Eastern Europe and elsewhere. Forced to leave orphanages at age sixteen or seventeen, many of them become homeless. Other children, abandoned by impoverished families, are unable to even find places in overcrowded orphanages in some countries such as Russia, the Ukraine, and Romania. Furthermore, as the role of the state shrinks and privatization becomes dominant, financial support for social services has diminished globally, thereby rendering the poor even more vulnerable to global crime. Finally, revolutions in communications and transportation facilitate the proliferation of matchmaking services, many of which are owned and operated by organized crime.[21]

Although trafficking across national boundaries for sexual exploitation is a significant component of global crime, most trafficked women and girls remain within their countries or regions. In India alone, for example, more than half a million girls are in brothels, more than any other country in the world. The rapid growth of sex tourism in Asia and elsewhere reinforces the sexual exploitation of women and girls within their own societies. What's more, the AIDS pandemic is influencing human traffickers to find younger women and girls, especially virgins, because customers believe they are less likely to be infected with HIV and AIDS.[22] The global response to human trafficking has largely been ineffective. Several efforts to address this problem have been made at both national and global levels. In 1989, the European Parliament adopted a resolution that called for tough measures to eradicate human trafficking. Meeting in Beijing at the **Fourth World Conference on Women** and declaring that women's rights are human rights, delegates from 189 countries unanimously adopted a platform for action, which called on governments to dismantle criminal networks engaged in trafficking women. In response to the unprecedented growth in human trafficking, the **UN Protocol Against the Trafficking in Women and Children** was adopted along with the UN Convention on Transnational Crime in 2000. At a world summit on organized crime in 2000 in Palermo, Italy, leaders from eighty countries signed the UN protocol. Also in 2000, a coalition of Democrats, Republicans, feminists, and evangelical Christians pressured the U.S. Congress to enact the **Victims of Trafficking and Violence Protection Act** to prosecute traffickers in the United States and to take action abroad against this global crime. This law recognized human trafficking as a federal crime and requires the U.S. Department of State to publish an annual report on the state of human trafficking globally.[23]

While the global community was responding to the problem of human trafficking, several countries were legalizing the sex trade, which consists predominantly of foreign women in most European countries. For example, roughly half a million women are trafficked as prostitutes in Europe every year. In Germany, three out of four sex workers are foreigners, and in the Netherlands, one out of

Fourth World Conference on Women ■ Called on governments to prevent trafficking in women

UN Protocol Against the Trafficking in Women and Children ■ Global effort in 2000 to address growing trafficking problem

Victims of Trafficking and Violence Protection Act ■ Requires the United States to prosecute human traffickers and to publish an annual report on global trafficking

YOU DECIDE

Does Legalizing Prostitution Reduce Global Crime?

Legalizing prostitution in the Netherlands, Germany, and elsewhere was widely believed to be a solution to numerous global crimes including human trafficking, money laundering, slavery, drug abuse, and violence. Contrary to expectations that by regulating the sex industry, the government could collect taxes, allow adults to engage freely in sexual transactions, and enable the police and the courts to concentrate on criminals. Sweden, on the other hand, decided to penalize people who patronized prostitutes while treating prostitutes as victims. The Swedish approach has also been implemented in England and Wales. The link between prostitution and crime remains strong in the Netherlands.

Sweden, on the other hand, has experienced a reduction in the number of both prostitutes and crimes associated with the sex trade. However, countries that have legalized prostitution attract people from other countries who want to engage in prostitution. Many Europeans, for example, visit Thailand and other developing countries as sex tourists. Globalization is rendering many efforts by countries to control crime extremely difficult. Global sex rings are increasingly common and the Internet facilitates the growth of prostitution.

1. Does legalizing prostitution contribute to global crime?
2. How should the global community respond to prostitution? ■

two sex workers comes from another country. In 2000, the Netherlands legalized prostitution, which is a $1 billion-a-year industry and represents roughly 5 percent of that country's economy. Germany legalized prostitution in 2001. The sex trade contributes approximately $4.5 billion to Germany's economy.[24] Very few traffickers are prosecuted and convicted. Furthermore, the illegal immigration status of trafficked women becomes an impediment to punishing criminals involved in trafficking. Some success in efforts to reduce human trafficking came in 2006 when John R. Miller, a senior adviser to U.S. Secretary of State Condoleezza Rice, persuaded Japan to reduce the number of entertainment visas for women from the Philippines from eighty thousand to five thousand a year.[25]

CRIMINAL GANGS AND KIDNAPPING

Carmen Toro stops by the morgue in Guatemala City on her way to work to see if her son's body is there. A member of the extremely violent Maria 18 street gang, he disappeared after being abducted by three masked gunmen who forced him into an unmarked car. Such experiences are increasingly common in Central America and around the world as violent gangs proliferate to create an upsurge in global crime. The same communications and technological revolutions that drive globalization also help gangs to grow. The Internet enables them to form alliances, to learn from each other, and to terrorize.[26] Repeated exposure to cultural globalization—especially violent television programs, movies, video games, and magazines—reinforces their violent behavior. Ethnic conflicts and civil wars, combined with easy access to guns, provide fertile ground for gang violence to

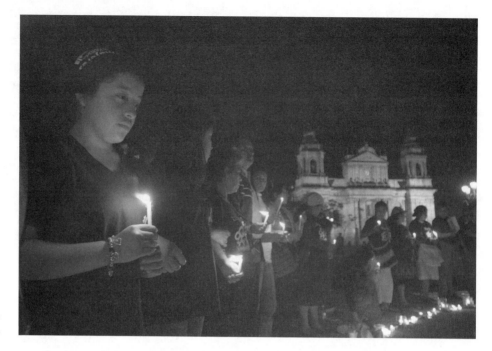

Vigil for Victims
of Gang
Violence in
Guatemala.

(Moises Castillo/AP/
Wide World Photos)

flourish. Aspects of globalization—especially global migration, global inequality, and fewer government-provided public services due to privatization and trade liberalization—contribute to the growth of gangs. Demographic factors also play an important role. Young people between the ages of sixteen and twenty-four tend to commit most of the crimes, especially in densely populated areas. As we discussed earlier in this chapter, poverty and the decline of social services often combine to influence parents to abandon their children, making them vulnerable to gangs. Gang violence increases political instability, weakens democratic institutions, increases human rights violations, and impedes economic development. Kidnapping is often an integral component of gang violence. Gang violence usually generates counterviolence by vigilante groups, the military, and police officers.

Foundations for rising gang violence in Central America were laid during the civil wars that devastated the region in the 1980s, driven partly by military and political rivalry between the United States and the Soviet Union. The Cold War in Central America was accompanied by widespread human rights abuses, rape, torture, extrajudicial executions, kidnappings, and drug production and trafficking. In Guatemala alone, more than 200,000 people were killed or missing (out of a population of 14 million) during these conflicts. Civil wars also bring with them the proliferation of weapons. As we discussed in Chapter 11, violence is a factor that pushes people to migrate. Many Central Americans came to the United States and settled in the ghettos of Los Angeles and other major American cities. Many young migrants soon became involved in street gangs, committed violent crimes, including murder, and participated in drug trafficking. When the U.S. Congress decided to enact very punitive immigration laws in 1996, noncitizens who were sentenced to a year or more in prison could be repatriated to their country of origin. Foreign-born U.S. citizens who committed felonies could lose their American citizenship and be expelled from the country after serving their sentences. Consequently, roughly twenty thousand young Central American criminals were deported to El Salvador, Guatemala, Honduras, Nicaragua, and elsewhere.[27] Gang members recreated their violent lifestyles in Central America, drug trafficking escalated, "crack babies" became more common, and murder rates rose sharply. Gang members routinely force residents of poor neighborhoods to pay what they call protection fees, demand war taxes from businesses, and often murder individuals who refuse to or cannot pay them. Rapes of young women have increased, homes are robbed, schoolchildren are turned into drug addicts, and kidnappings occur frequently.

Kidnappings in Iraq heightened global awareness of a very old criminal activity. Previously, most victims of kidnappings were wealthy individuals who could arrange to pay large ransoms. Today, however, ordinary individuals are being kidnapped for a variety of reasons. Terrorists have used kidnappings as bargaining chips and to create widespread fear. Islamic terrorists in the Philippines routinely kidnap foreigners, especially Westerners, to extract money to finance terrorism. Kidnappings are an integral component of violence and drug trafficking in Colombia. Colombia is by far the world's leader in kidnappings, despite an increase in kidnappings in China. In Mexico, Brazil, Kenya, and other places, most kidnappings are fueled by glaring economic inequalities and poverty. These crimes are very lucrative, generating hundreds of millions of dollars each year in ransoms.[28] Economic inequality and poverty also motivate Nigerians in the Niger Delta region to kidnap petroleum workers employed by Royal Dutch Shell.[29]

MONEY LAUNDERING

When you open a bank account, you are usually required to show some identification. However, many criminals open bank accounts without having to face any financial scrutiny. The globalization of financial services, the growth of "megabyte money," the proliferation of small states with corrupt officials and weak economies, and the ease with which money is transferred electronically have facilitated the practice of money laundering.[30] **Money laundering** is the concealment of money obtained from illegal activities and finding ways to make the money appear as though it was derived from legitimate sources. Many banks in the Bahamas, Bermuda, Cayman Islands, Nauru, Liechtenstein, Panama, and elsewhere have strict secrecy laws designed to conceal money and allow it to be easily transferred and invested in legal activities. As the scandal involving affluent Germans with bank accounts in Liechtenstein in 2008 demonstrated, even money from legal sources is often concealed. Among the islands that promote offshore banking, Grand Cayman stands out. With a population of approximately thirty-six thousand, Grand Cayman is one of the largest financial centers in the world. Although generally perceived as a tourist destination, Grand Cayman is dominated by banking and financial industries. It is estimated that more than 2,200 mutual funds, 500 insurance companies, 60,000 businesses, and 600 banks and trust companies with almost $800 billion in assets are located in Grand Cayman.[31]

Money Laundering ■ The act of concealing money obtained from illegal activities

As Grand Cayman illustrates, many legitimate businesses routinely incorporate themselves in countries that are also used by money launderers to reduce their tax burdens and avoid regulations in rich countries. For many years, the United States expressed little interest in preventing money laundering, partly because it viewed such efforts as impediments to free markets and financial globalization. Many American banks sheltered money from dictators and others from around the world. For example, Riggs Bank in Washington, DC, was caught in a scandal in 2005 that involved sheltering funds from Augusto Pinochet, the former dictator of Chile. The ease with which terrorists could launder money became a major U.S. preoccupation only after the 2001 terrorist attacks in the United States.

The issue of money laundering is complicated by the very nature of financial globalization and the speed and complexity of financial transactions in a global economy. Technological revolutions facilitate concealing both legitimate income from taxation authorities and financial gains from drug trafficking and other global criminal activities. Furthermore, the proliferation of financial institutions globally makes government regulation of them extremely difficult. In most countries, less government regulation is regarded to be an important component of economic globalization. Many societies have always found informal ways to hide money received from illegal activities and to invest it in legitimate businesses.[32] Divergent interests and values among countries complicate dealing with money laundering. Many small countries in the Caribbean, Latin America, and the Pacific, which have fragile economies and very little manufacturing, often perceive their sovereignty as an asset that can assist in their economic development. Consequently, their financial institutions actively promote both the legal and illicit sheltering of financial assets. However, America's actions against tax evasion in 2009 have undermined efforts by U.S. residents to shelter money abroad.

ILLEGAL TRADE IN ENDANGERED ANIMALS AND PLANTS

Endangered Species ■ Animals and plants vulnerable to extinction

The illegal trade in **endangered species** coexists with legal transactions, thereby making it difficult to ascertain the magnitude of the problem. Nevertheless, there is general agreement that many of the factors we discussed earlier about the globalization of crime combine to sustain and expand both the legal and illicit aspects of this trade. Local and individual decisions directly affect trade in endangered animals and plants. These decisions have significant global consequences. For many individuals, the trade liberalization that characterizes globalization augments perceptions that almost anything can be traded, regardless of long-term consequences for the environment. Economic inequality between conservationists in rich countries and poor people in the developing world, where most animals and plants are located, often gives rise to divergent perceptions of and approaches to illegal trade. For example, elephants are generally regarded as exotic by many residents in rich countries, but many Africans view them as threats to their safety and their crops. On the other hand, carefully managed animals and plants can play a major role in ecotourism and other aspects of economic development. It is estimated that one elephant in Kenya generates $1 million in tourist revenue over its lifetime. Political instability and ethnic conflicts in many countries often facilitate both trade in and the destruction of many endangered animals and plants. Illicit trade fuels many conflicts. Illegal wildlife trade also raises issues such as sustainability and biological diversity. Also, imports of animals and plants sometimes contribute to problems associated with invasive species that threaten native species.

Given the global reach of traffickers in endangered animals and plants and the numerous small illegal transactions that occur daily by individuals worldwide, ascertaining the financial gains from this global crime is extremely difficult, if not impossible. However, estimates of illegal trade revenues range from $5 billion to $20 billion annually and are usually ranked in the same category as illegal drugs, weapons, and human trafficking in terms of revenue.[33] While global attention was drawn to illicit trade in endangered animals by large sales of African elephant tusks to Japan and elsewhere, the expansion of legal trade and the Internet have significantly broadened this criminal activity. The most endangered species—such as tigers, Asian bears, rhinoceros, hyacinth macaws from the Amazon, Australian palm cockatoos, Saiga antelopes, and hawksbill turtles—command high prices. For example, the gall bladder of a bear can be sold for as much as $15,000, the palm cockatoo for $10,000, and the hyacinth macaw for $8,000. Many of the highly valued illegally traded species are believed to have medicinal properties and are usually in great demand in several Asian countries. Many traditional Chinese medicines contain ingredients composed of tiger bone, bear bile, deer musk glands, and shark fins. Many animals are sold for food and to pet shops worldwide. Products derived from endangered wildlife include exotic leather goods, ornaments, and tourist souvenirs. Increasing wealth, engendered by economic globalization, has also led to a growth in demand for expensive products such as caviar. As countries around the Caspian Sea attempt to conserve the sturgeon population, illegal trade in caviar has escalated. Global trade in plants and forest products is accompanied by illegal logging operations and lumber sales, especially in Southeast Asia, Central Africa, the Amazonian countries, and Russia. Millions of plants are sold illegally, and medicinal plants that are in great demand due to a global preoccupation with finding easy solutions to health problems are threatened with extinction. These include hoodia (which is used in diet pills), cistanche (a natural tonic), and the Chinese yew tree (which is believed to have cancer-fighting properties).

Concerned about animal and plant extinction, the global community responded by signing the Convention on International Trade in Endangered Species of Wild Flora and Fauna (CITES) in 1973. This convention provides a framework within which countries adopt domestic legislation to ensure that CITES is implemented at the national level. Combating illegal trade in endangered animals and plants is an integral component of efforts to strengthen wildlife management, promote sustainability, and diminish deforestation. Several nongovernmental organizations (NGOs) participate in efforts to protect endangered species, including the World Conservation Union, World Wide Fund for Nature, Fauna and Flora International, Trade Records Analysis of Flora and Fauna in Commerce, and the World Conservation Monitoring Center. CITES accords varying degrees of protection to roughly five thousand animal species and twenty-five thousand plant species. The global community has achieved significant success in its effort to protect elephants. A worldwide ban on ivory in 1989 essentially eliminated elephant poaching and led to a sharp decline in the price of ivory. Similarly, in 1992, the United States, a leading importer of parrots for pets, enacted the **Wild Bird Conservation Act**, which bans imports of all wild-caught threatened parrots listed in CITES. Consequently, parrot imports dropped sharply. The global community collaborates with various countries to regulate hunting certain animals in ways that promote both conservation and economic benefits.

Wild Bird Conservation Act ■ Bans imports of all wild-caught threatened parrots listed in CITES

ILLEGAL TRADE IN HUMAN ORGANS

Global trade in human organs has been rapidly expanding. Although the majority of these transactions are legal, illicit trade in organs is a growing global issue. Globalization has contributed to trading in human organs in several ways. Countries purchasing organs are wealthy, and countries supplying organs are generally poor. Global inequality is a major factor: the rich demand organs and the poor sell their organs to obtain money. This gap between the rich and the poor provides many opportunities for global criminals to get involved in this lucrative trade, especially in light of an ever-expanding list of patients urgently waiting for organ transplants. For example, kidney donations from deceased donors in the United States increased by 33 percent between 1990 and 2003. Demand, on the other hand, grew by 236 percent.[34] In many cases, diseases associated with both affluence and overconsumption by the less affluent, such as type 2 diabetes, are influencing the growth of the global trade in organs. The typical donor, generally male, has an annual family income of roughly $480, whereas the average recipient has an annual family income of $53,000. Demographic factors also play a crucial role in the organs trade. People in rich countries are living longer and are older on average than people in the developing world. As people worldwide age, demand for human organs is increasing. Demographic disparities facilitate these transactions. For example, the average seller is around twenty-nine years old, whereas the average buyer is roughly forty-eight years old.[35] Rapid communications and transportation also play a role in the global trade in organs. In many cases, both organ sellers and organ recipients travel abroad for the operation. South Africa was a common meeting ground until 2003, when South African authorities broke up an organ trafficking ring involving South Africans, Israelis, and Brazilians. The globalization of medical technology makes removing and transplanting organs relatively routine procedures worldwide.

Many organs are obtained from nonconsenting donors who are forced to undergo operations. This practice is increasingly prevalent in impoverished neighborhoods in the world's poorest countries where human life is viewed as being less valuable, where human rights abuses abound, and where weak political institutions and endemic corruption exist. For example, in 2008, Indian criminal groups came under closer scrutiny for forcibly obtaining kidneys from poor Indians to supply transplants for rich Indians and foreigners. Organs are also illegally obtained from morgues, both in the developed and in the developing world, a ghoulish practice that often leaves relatives of the deceased traumatized. Medical centers in Germany, for example, used human heart valves obtained illegally from cadavers of poor South Africans. But the rich and famous are not exempt from organ theft. **Alistair Cooke**, the popular host of *Masterpiece Theater* and author of a weekly radio commentary, *Letter from America*, died at the age of ninety-five in 2004. Investigators found that Cooke's bones were stolen and sold for $7,000 by organ traffickers in the United States.[36] In early 2006, U.S. government officials ordered Biomedical Tissue Services, a New Jersey company linked to a national organ looting scandal, to refrain from recovering and distributing organs. Biomedical Tissue Services produced inauthentic death certificates that indicated the wrong ages and causes of death for several organ donors. Many patients in Chicago received organs that were believed to have come from donors with communicable diseases. The globalization of illegal organ trading spread the problem from the United States to Germany, the Netherlands, and China.[37]

Alistair Cooke ■ Popular host of *Masterpiece Theater* and author of *Letter from America*

CYBERCRIMES AND PIRACY

Just as individuals use the Internet to conduct legal business, organized crime as well as individuals take advantage of this technology to commit crimes. In fact, a national survey commissioned by IBM Corporation in 2006 found that most Internet users believe that they are more likely to be victims of cybercrime than a physical crime. In 2008, the U.S. government discovered that roughly 41 million credit and debit card numbers were stolen by criminals from the United States, Estonia, China, Belarus, and Estonia.[38] **Cybercrimes** are standard crimes committed online or harmful behavior that is connected to computers. Examples of cybercrimes are fraud, pornography, smuggling, copyright and software piracy, identity theft, and extortion.[39] The proliferation of online shopping has been a boon for cybercriminals. **eBay**, the biggest online marketplace, has roughly 180 million members worldwide, who are connected to the Internet, and more than 60 million items for sale at any particular moment. Both distance and anonymity conspire to render these global online shopping centers perfect places for fraudulent activities. As a marketplace that links buyers and sellers, eBay has very little control over transactions.[40]

Cybercrimes ■ Standard crimes committed online

eBay ■ The biggest online marketplace

The essential role of computer software in global computer operations makes it a prime target for cybercriminals. So pervasive is software piracy that many ordinary individuals do not perceive stealing software as a crime, thereby further blurring the boundaries between legal and illegal behavior. Like other global crimes we have discussed, it is impossible to determine the exact value of pirated software. However, it is estimated that the global market for pirated computer software is around $30 billion. This crime is concentrated in Western countries, where computer technologies are most prevalent. China, with its rapid industrialization and technological growth, is also involved to a significant degree in software piracy. The estimated market for software piracy in the United States is twice as large as the market in China.

The global expansion of the Internet, the widespread use of credit cards, and the growth of electronic banking combine to facilitate a wide array of fraudulent activities. From Mattoon, a small town in central Illinois, Clyde Hood ran an investment scam that brought in roughly $12.5 million from people worldwide by promising that each dollar invested would generate $50 in profit. The **Nigerian scam** is one of the most common cyberspace crimes and one of the most persistent.

Nigerian Scam ■ One of the most common cybercrimes

A Nigerian sends an e-mail asking prospective victims to assist him or her to transfer millions of recently acquired dollars out of Nigeria in exchange for a substantial part of the money. Prospective victims are instructed to deposit their own money into a specified bank account to demonstrate their honesty and willingness to cooperate. If these instructions are followed, the money and the Nigerian e-mail sender simply vanish. Credit card fraud on the Internet involves the use of stolen credit card numbers and information, such as the date of expiration and delivery address, to purchase products from virtual shopping malls and auction sites. Often, highly organized global criminal networks are involved in cybercrimes

Despite increasingly sophisticated computer security measures, criminals are becoming adept at crashing computer systems and impeding their operation. A growing concern among governments, including the U.S. government, is that cybercriminals could be successful at penetrating security organizations and threaten vital national interests. Extortion schemes by organized criminal groups based primarily in Russia and Eastern European countries have been implemented in Australia, Britain, Canada, Thailand, the United States, and elsewhere. In 2004, VIP Management Services, an online betting and gambling company based in Curacao in the Caribbean, received an e-mail from criminals who had hacked into its computer system. The criminals demanded $30,000 in ransom. To avoid having its computer systems disabled, VIP paid the ransom.[41]

Kama Sutra ■ The venerable Indian guide to eroticism

Criminals employ sophisticated viruses to disable computer systems. In 2006, an Internet virus named **Kama Sutra**—after the venerable Indian guide to eroticism— was programmed to overwrite documents, images, and compressed computer files. Aimed principally at home computers, the virus infected computers through an e-mail that promised racy pictures. In 2008, a Russian criminal gang used software tools to infect thousands of personal computers in corporate and government networks with programs that stole passwords and other information.[42]

Global Piracy ■ Includes online music piracy and counterfeiting

Intellectual Property Rights ■ Control that people and corporations have over artistic, creative, scientific, industrial, and educational inventions

Global trade, computer technologies, and the globalization of American and European cultures have contributed to the growth of **global piracy**, which includes online music piracy, counterfeiting, and old-fashioned piracy on the high seas. Online music piracy and counterfeiting deal with **intellectual property rights**, copyrights, and patent laws. Downloading music is generally regarded as a harmless activity by those engaged in it. However, the music industry views online music piracy as theft. In April 2009, a Swedish court convicted four men linked to an Internet file-sharing service, *The Pirate Bay*, of violating copyright law. Each was sentenced to a year in prison and fined $3.6 million in damages. Throughout China, one can purchase inexpensive counterfeit DVDs of the most recent American movies, as well as counterfeit shoes, clothes, computer software, books, and many other products. It is estimated that the piracy industry in China employs between 3 million and 5 million people and generates $40 billion to $80 billion in revenues.[43]

Piracy on the high seas has reemerged as a significant threat to global shipping. It also demonstrates new threats from nonstate actors to global military powers such as the United States. Modern piracy ranges from desperately impoverished people committing petty larcenies at sea to highly organized syndicates slaughtering ships' crews to steal not only the valuable cargo but also the multi-million-dollar ships.[44] More than two-thirds of piracy attacks occur in Asian waters. The Horn of Africa and the Gulf of Aden experienced a significant increase in piracy between 2007 and 2009, along with greater American involvement in efforts to reduce it. The failure of the Somali state, the withdrawal of the Soviet and American military forces from the area with the end of the Cold War, the widespread poverty and violence in Somalia, and the ease with which cargo ships can be seized and large ransoms can be collected by small groups of men in small speed boats that are armed with grappling hooks, assault rifles, rock-propelled grenades, knives, and satellite telephones have contributed to escalating pirate attacks. When pirates seized the U.S.-flagged cargo ship, the *Maersk Alabama*, and held the captain for ransom, a U.S. Navy–guided destroyer and other warships were sent to the Somali coast. U.S. Navy Seals on the destroyer *Bainbridge* were experienced snipers. They killed the three pirates and rescued the captain, Richard Phillips, of the *Maersk Alabama*. Other countries such as France and the Netherlands have been involved in rescue efforts along the Somali coast.

STOLEN ART AND ANTIQUITIES

Trade in stolen art is usually ranked as a leading global crime, behind only illegal drugs, money laundering, and weapons. Although it is difficult to ascertain the profits associated with most global criminal activities, the value of stolen art is comparatively easier to determine. The current period of globalization, dominated by computer technologies and financial transactions, has generated unprecedented wealth. Historically, wealthy individuals have invested in art. Demand for art contributed to the escalation of prices for rare artworks, and criminals began to meet this demand. But the issue of stolen art goes beyond ordinary criminals to governments and prestigious art museums. During World War II, the Nazis looted art from prominent Jewish families. For many centuries, European colonial powers as well as individual American explorers and archaeologists removed highly prized artifacts and antiquities from countries around the world. Many countries are now reinvigorating their efforts to have what they regard as part of their national heritage returned to them.

Global communications and computer technologies have aided art criminals, but they have also enabled law enforcement officials to catch them. For example, Robert Mang, a fifty-year-old specialist in security-alarm systems, managed to steal the **Saliera** (or saltcellar), a rare gold-plated sculpture by Benvenuto Cellini, valued at $60 million, from the Kunsthistorisches Museum in Vienna, Austria. The sculpture was made by Cellini between 1540 and 1543 on commission from Francis I of France. For three years, Mang attempted to collect $12 million in ransom for the Saliera. He used several different cell phones (to avoid being detected) to send instructions during what Austrian police called a scavenger hunt. He had purchased the cell phones months in advance. Irritated by what he perceived to be police in an unmarked car flouting his instructions, Mang used a recently purchased cell phone to call off

Saliera ■ A rare gold-plated sculpture made by Benvenuto Cellini between 1540 and 1543

arrangements to pick up the ransom money. The cell phone was traced to a store in Vienna, which uses a hidden video camera to record all purchases. This enabled the police to obtain Mang's picture, which was made public. Mang immediately contacted the police to identify himself as the man in the picture but denied that he had stolen the sculpture. He was so upset about the publication of his picture that he asked the police to refrain from further publication of it. Naturally, the police were even more convinced that Mang was the thief. Searching his apartment, police found notes about the scavenger hunt Mang had conducted with them. That was how they caught him.[45] The sculpture was recovered. But not all art thieves appreciate sculpture to that extent. More than twenty large bronze sculptures were taken from museums, sculpture gardens, and private collections in and around London in late 2005. Art thieves simply put them in trucks and drove away. These criminals are believed to have melted down the sculptures and sold the bronze for scrap. It is estimated that a two-ton sculpture by Henry Moore, Reclining Figure, valued at $18 million as a work of art, was worth about $9,000 as scrap metal. In 2008, three men stole four paintings—a Cezanne, a Degas, a Van Gogh, and a Monet—valued at $163 million from the Zurich Museum.[46]

Partly influenced by increased sales in art during the 1980s and 1990s, many Jewish families and organizations renewed their efforts to have numerous artworks that were stolen by the Nazis in World War II or acquired by art museums under dubious circumstances returned to their legitimate owners. In 2006, in one of the largest restitutions of art seized by the Nazis, the Dutch government announced that it would return more than two hundred Old Masters paintings to the heir of **Jacques Goudstikker**, a wealthy Dutch Jewish dealer and collector who fled Amsterdam ahead of advancing German troops in May 1940. Due partly to an eight-year campaign led by Marei von Saher of Greenwich, Connecticut, the widow of Goudstikker's son, the Dutch government formed a restitution commission to investigate the provenance of all of the art in its museums. The restitution committee eventually recommended returning the art to its rightful owners.[47]

Similarly, various governments have reinvigorated their efforts to have art and antiquities returned to them. In early 2006, the Metropolitan Museum of Art in New York decided to relinquish claims to ownership of a 2,500-year-old Greek vase, regarded as one of the finest artworks in the world. The vase, known as the Euphronios Krater, had long been claimed by the Italian government, which contended that the vase had been stolen from an Etruscan tomb near Rome and smuggled from Italy.[48] University museums are also confronted with charges that they have stolen art and antiquities. Yale University's exhibition about **Machu Picchu** attracted more than a million visitors while traveling to six cities in the United States. The exhibition returned to Yale's Peabody Museum of Natural History in 2005, only to be mired in a dispute with the government of Peru. Peru argued that the artifacts excavated at Machu Picchu in 1912 by a Yale University professor and explorer, Hiram Bingham III, were loaned to the University, which has failed to return them. Yale University contended that it was the rightful owner of the artifacts.[49] In 2007, Yale agreed to return many of the artifacts to Peru.

Jacques Goudstikker ■ A wealthy Dutch Jewish art dealer and collector

Machu Picchu ■ Fortress city of the Incas in Peru, site of valuable artifacts and antiquities

GLOBAL RESPONSES TO CRIME

Countries are ill equipped to effectively respond to global criminal activities. As we pointed out earlier in this chapter, globalization has been far more beneficial to nonstate actors, including smugglers, drug traffickers, and other global criminal networks, than it has been to nation-states. The hierarchical structure of countries is a liability in an increasingly decentralized, global society. Furthermore, globalization has diminished the ability of states to exercise effective jurisdiction over their territories and to regulate trade and other activities. The nature of globalization makes it difficult to determine where the crimes occurred and which country or countries have jurisdiction over them. Few governments have the resources to effectively control global crime, especially in light of reduced government budgets for public services. Furthermore, divergent views among countries about crime and different priorities render effective collaboration among states difficult to achieve.

The International Criminal Police Organization, commonly known as **Interpol**, is a global clearinghouse for police information. Based in France, Interpol had a minuscule budget of roughly $25 million in 2001.[50] Compared to the resources available to Interpol, global criminal organizations make more than $1.5 trillion a year. The global drug trade alone generates in excess of $320 billion a year. As we have seen, global crime is proliferating so rapidly and on such a vast scale at a time when cultural attitudes are generally much more tolerant of many global criminal activities that global efforts to reduce the crimes we have discussed are significantly undermined. Nevertheless, Interpol's role in combating drug trafficking and other global crimes is important. Interpol collects and analyzes data, supports global crime investigations, organizes operational working meetings among countries, and organizes regional and global conferences on a wide range of criminal activities. Despite support from Interpol, fighting crime is essentially a local activity, and states themselves are ultimately responsible for reducing global crime. But as with many domestic crimes, states confront many serious obstacles in fighting global crime.

> **Interpol** ■ Global clearinghouse for police information that assists countries in criminal cases

Attempting to be more effective in countering global crime, 178 countries have joined Interpol. In 2000, most of these countries signed the **UN Convention Against Transnational Organized Crime**, a global agreement that outlaws bank secrecy, keeps prosecutors worldwide in contact by e-mail, allows international arrest warrants to be sent by e-mail, provides for videoconferences to allow witnesses to testify without having to travel around the world, and creates international witness protection programs.[51] The challenge confronting the global community is the ability to implement these provisions. The forces of globalization are likely to give global criminals the advantage in the worldwide struggle to reduce global crime.

> **UN Convention Against Transnational Organized Crime** ■ Global agreement aimed at reducing crime through global cooperation

SUMMARY AND REVIEW

Global criminal activities have proliferated with the rapid growth of economic, financial, technological, cultural, and other forms of globalization. Increased global migration, global inequality, the growth of global cities, the explosion of global trade, inexpensive communications, revolutions in computer technologies, and the disintegration of the Soviet Union have contributed to the spread and intensification of global crime. As we saw, global crime is intricately intertwined with politics, economics, and culture. This chapter shows how illegal activities occur alongside legal activities and how difficult they sometimes are to separate. Furthermore, there are divergent perceptions about global crimes as well as different approaches to dealing with them. Globalization has weakened states in ways that prevent them from effectively combating many global crimes. We discussed major global crimes such as drug trafficking, human trafficking, illegal trade in endangered species, money laundering, cybercrimes, and trade in human organs. Throughout history, the world has experienced an increase in the global drug trade, accompanied by growing drug use and addiction. This global crime commands the attention of the global community, although countries adopt divergent approaches to dealing with illegal drugs. There are global responses to all of the crimes discussed. Organizations such as Interpol provide information on criminal activities and cooperate with countries in an effort to reduce global crime.

KEY TERMS

British East India Company 277
Opium Wars 277
Golden Triangle 277
war on drugs 278
Hague Convention 279
Harrison Act 279
Opium Control Board 279
Plan Colombia 280
harm-reduction approaches 281
human trafficking 282
contemporary slavery 282
feminization of migration 283

Fourth World Conference on Women 284
UN Protocol Against the Trafficking in Women and Children 284
Victims of Trafficking and Violence Protection Act 284
money laundering 287
endangered species 288
Wild Bird Conservation Act 290
Alistair Cooke 291
cybercrimes 291
eBay 291

Nigerian scam 291
Kama Sutra 292
global piracy 292
intellectual property rights 292
Saliera 293
Jacques Goudstikker 294
Machu Picchu 294
Interpol 295
UN Convention Against Transnational Organized Crime 295

DISCUSSION QUESTIONS

1. Discuss ways in which globalization facilitates the growth of global crime.
2. How and what extent has globalization affected the ability of states to diminish global criminal activities?
3. Compare European and American approaches to dealing with illegal drugs.
4. What is Plan Colombia? Is America losing the war on drugs?
5. Discuss the growth of criminal gangs, the causes, and possible ways to reduce violence.
6. What can individuals do to reduce the growth of cybercrime?

SUGGESTED READINGS

Andreas, Peter, and **Ethan Nadelman.** *Policing the Globe.* New York: Oxford University Press, 2006.

Arana, Ana. "How the Street Gangs Took Central America," *Foreign Affairs* 84, No. 3 (May/June 2005): 98–110

Bales, Kevin. *Ending Slavery*. Berkeley: University of California Press, 2007

Kapstein, Ethan. "The New Global Slave Trade," *Foreign Affairs* 85, No. 6 (November/December 2006): 103–116

Murphy, Martin. *Small Boats, Weak States, Dirty Money: The Challenge of Piracy*. New York: Columbia University Press, 2009.

Naim, Moises. *How Drug Smugglers, Traffickers, and Copycats Are Hijacking the Global Economy*. Washington, DC: Carnegie Endowment, 2005.

Van Schendel, Willem, and Itty Abraham. *Illicit Flows and Criminal Things*. Bloomington: Indiana University Press, 2006

END NOTES

1. Moises Naim, "Five Waves of Globalization," *Foreign Policy* 134 (January/February 2003), 29.
2. Moises Naim, "It's the Illicit Economy, Stupid," *Foreign Policy* 151 (November/December 2005), 96.
3. Bruce Michael Bagley, "Globalization and Transnational Organized Crime," in *The Political Economy of the Drug Industry*, ed. Menno Vellinga (Gainesville: University Press of Florida, 2004), 261; and Miroslav Nozina, "Crossroads of Crime: The Czech Republic Case," in *Transnational Organized Crime*, eds. Emilio C. Viano et al. (Durham: Carolina Academic Press, 2003), 147.
4. Warren Hoge, "In Scenic Norway, a Death Scene of Addictions," *New York Times*, 8 August 2002, A3.
5. William B. McAllister, *Drug Diplomacy in the Twentieth Century* (London: Routledge, 2000), 11.
6. Paul B. Stares, *Global Habit: The Drug Problem in a Borderless World* (Washington, DC: Brookings Institution Press, 1996), 16.
7. Tim Golden, "Mexican Drug Dealers Turning U.S. Towns into Major Depots," *New York Times*, 16 November 2002, A1; and James C. McKinley, "Drug War Causes Wild Blood Bath, Killing 210 in a Mexican Border Town," *New York Times*, 16 April 2008, A10.
8. Stares, *Global Habit*, 17.
9. Stares, *Global Habit*, 36.
10. Juan Forero, "No Crops Spared in Colombia's Coca War," *New York Times*, 31 January 2001, A1.
11. Ethan A. Nadelmann, "Commonsense Drug Policy," *Foreign Affairs* 77, No. 1 (January/February 1998), 114.
12. Kate Zernike and Ginger Thompson, "Deaths of Immigrants Uncover Makeshift World of Smuggling," *New York Times*, 29 June 2003, A1; and Seth Mydans, "54 Who Suffocated in Thailand Were Smuggled Workers," *New York Times*, 11 April 2008, A12.
13. Edward Barnes, "Two-Faced Woman," *Time*, 31 July 2000, 48; and Jeffrey Bartholet, "The New People Trade," *Newsweek*, 3 July 2000, 32–33.
14. Joel Brinkley, "A Modern-Day Abolitionist Battles Slavery Worldwide," *New York Times*, 4 February 2006, A4; and Kevin Bales and Zoe Trodd, eds., *To Plead Our Own Cause: Personal Stories by Today's Slaves* (Ithaca, NY: Cornell University Press, 2008).
15. Brinkley, "A Modern-Day Abolitionist," A4.
16. Elena Tiuriukanova, "Female Labor Migration Trends and Human Trafficking," in *Human Traffic and Transnational Crime*, eds. Sally Stoecker and Louise Shelley (Lanham, MD: Rowman and Littlefield, 2005), 98.

17. David A. Feingold, "Human Trafficking," *Foreign Policy* 150 (September/October 2005), 26.
18. Cam Simpson, "U.S. to Probe Claims of Human Trafficking," *Chicago Tribune*, 19 January 2006, Sect. 1, 1.
19. Victor Malarek, *The Natashas: Inside the Global Sex Trade* (New York: Arcade Publishing, 2004), 6; and H. Richard Friman and Simon Reich, eds., *Human Trafficking, Human Security, and the Balkans* (Pittsburgh, PA: University of Pittsburgh Press, 2008).
20. Louise Shelley, "Russian and Chinese Trafficking," in *Human Traffic and Transnational Crime*, 70.
21. Malarek, *The Natashas*, 14.
22. Nicholas D. Kristof, "Slavery in Our Time," *New York Times*, 22 January 2006, A17.
23. Feingold, "Human Trafficking," 30.
24. Malarek, *The Natashas*, 255.
25. Brinkley, "A Modern-Day Abolitionist," A4.
26. Andrew V. Papachristos, "Gang World," *Foreign Policy* 147 (March/April 2005), 51.
27. Ginger Thompson, "Guatemala Bleeds in Vise of Gangs and Vengeance," *New York Times*, 1 January 2006, A4; and Ana Arana, "How Street Gangs Took Central America," *Foreign Affairs* 84, No. 3 (May/June 2005), 100.
28. Jeffrey Gettleman, "Kenya's Criminals Tap a Growth Industry," *New York Times*, 12 October 2009, A4.
29. Lydia Polgreen, "Poor Nigerian Villages Become Oil Battleground," *New York Times*, 1 January 2006, A1; and "Delta Villages Fear Troops in Nigeria," *New York Times*, 26 January 2006, A10.
30. William F. Wechsler, "Follow the Money," *Foreign Affairs* 80, No. 4 (July/August 2001), 43.
31. Naim, "Five Waves of Globalization," 34.
32. Peter Grabosky and Russell Smith, "Telecommunications Fraud in the Digital Age," in *Crime and the Internet*, ed. David S. Wall (London: Routledge, 2001), 32.
33. Patrice M. Jones, "Brazil Grapples with Animal Trade," *Chicago Tribune*, 20 August 2001, Sect. 1, 1.
34. Nancy Scheper-Hughes, "Organs Without Borders," *Foreign Policy* 146 (January/February 2005), 26; and Amelia Gentleman, "Kidney Theft Ring Preys on India's Poorest Laborers," *New York Times*, 30 January 2008, A3.
35. Scheper-Hughes, "Organs Without Borders," 27.
36. Jeremy Manier and Tonya Maxwell, "Tissue Fraud Fears Spread," *Chicago Tribune*, 3 February 2006, Sect. 1, 1.
37. Jeremy Manier, "FDA Orders Firm to Stop Tissue Recovery," *Chicago Tribune*, 4 February 2006, Sect. 1, 3.
38. Jon Van, "Computer Crimes Seen as More Likely Than Physical Ones," *Chicago Tribune,* 28 January 2006, Sect. 2, 3; and Brad Stone, "U.S. Reveals a Ring That Stole 41 Million Card Numbers," *New York Times,* 6 August 2008, C6.
39. David S. Wall, "Cybercrimes and the Internet," in *Crime and the Internet*, ed. David S. Wall (London: Routledge, 2001), 3.
40. Katie Hafner, "Seeing Fakes, Angry Traders Confront eBay," *New York Times*, 29 January 2006, A1.
41. Nir Kshetri, "Hacking the Odds," *Foreign Policy* 148 (May/June 2005), 93.
42. Robert Manor, "Primitive Computer Virus Hits Few So Far," *Chicago Tribune*, 4 February 2006, Sect. 2, 1; and John Markoff, "Russian Gang Hijacking PCs in Vast Scheme," *New York Times*, 6 August 2008, C1.

43. Robert Marquand, "China's Pirate Industry Thriving," *Christian Science Monitor*, 9 January 2002, 6; and Eric Pfanner, "Four Convicted in Internet Piracy Case," *New York Times*, 18 April 2009, B1.

44. Jack Hitt, "Bandits in the Global Shipping Lanes," *New York Times Magazine*, 20 August 2000, 37; and "Somalia: Hostages on French Ship Freed, and Six Pirates and Loot Are Seized," *New York Times*, 12 April 2008, A9.

45. Richard Bernstein, "For Stolen Saltcellar, a Cellphone Is Golden," *New York Times*, 26 January 2006, B1.

46. Sarah Lyall, "Thieves Fond of Heavy Lifting Are Making Off with England's Bronze Sculptures," *New York Times*, 26 January 2006, B7; and Uta Harnischfeger and Nicholas Kulish, "At Zurich Museum, a Daylight Theft of 4 Masterworks," *New York Times*, 12 February 2008, A6.

47. Alan Riding, "Dutch to Return Art Seized by Nazis," *New York Times*, 7 February 2006, B1.

48. Randy Kennedy and Hugh Eakin, "The Met, Ending 30-Year Stance, Is Set to Yield Prized Vase to Italy," *New York Times*, 3 February 2006, A1.

49. Hugh Eakin, "Inca Show Pits Yale Against Peru," *New York Times*, 1 February 2006, B1.

50. "Meet the World's Top Cop," *Foreign Policy* 122 (January/February 2001), 32.

51. Peter Ford, "A Treaty to Counter Global Crime," *Christian Science Monitor*, 13 December 2000, 1.

CHAPTER

13

The Globalization of Disease

INTRODUCTION

Globally, infectious diseases remain the leading killers of human beings. More than a quarter of all deaths today are linked to infectious diseases, with the developing world facing the brunt of the problem. As discussed in Chapter 9, the poorest countries are the most vulnerable to infectious diseases because of widespread malnutrition, unsanitary conditions, inadequate medical care, and poverty. More than 40 million people live with HIV (the virus that causes AIDS), and more than 3 million die of AIDS each year. Infectious diseases—such as malaria, influenza, tuberculosis, dengue, and yellow fever—claim millions of lives in the developing world each year, with the very young and the very old being the primary victims. In the case of AIDS, more women are becoming victims due to violence and **survival sex** (i.e., having sex to feed their families and to protect themselves from physical abuse and economic deprivation). Diseased populations are vulnerable to contracting other diseases due to compromised immune systems. For example, many individuals who suffer from HIV/AIDS die from tuberculosis.

Infectious diseases are intertwined with numerous global issues and are inseparable from political, economic, and cultural components of globalization. Ethnic conflicts make populations vulnerable to infectious diseases. Fighting contributes to the collapse of public services, which means that many people die from what would ordinarily be treatable diseases, such as diarrhea and respiratory infections. Conflicts also create refugees, overcrowding, and unsanitary conditions, thereby creating environments conducive to the spread of infectious diseases.

Environmental degradation and deforestation expose humans to a variety of infectious diseases. They also contribute to global warming and flooding, which facilitate the emergence of infectious diseases. Rising temperatures in winter enable germs to survive in large numbers, and flooded areas become potent breeding grounds for mosquito-related diseases and cholera. Rapid population growth and urbanization bring more people closer together and into contact with infectious diseases.

Illegal drug use, especially intravenous drug use, spreads diseases such as HIV/AIDS. As we will discuss, AIDS contributes to a growing number of orphans; many of them become street children who are vulnerable to human trafficking and recruitment into criminal gangs. Finally, trade has long been a major facilitator of the spread of infectious diseases. Consequently, trade suffers greatly when outbreaks occur, as we saw with the spread of severe acute respiratory syndrome (SARS) in 2003 and swine flu in 2009. In many ways, trade liberalization contributes to the spread of infectious diseases by reducing the role of many governments in providing essential basic health care and other services. Infectious diseases have far-reaching social, economic, demographic, security, and political consequences.

This chapter first examines the globalization of infectious diseases, the concept of human security, and the nature and spread of infectious diseases. Given the global significance and far-reaching consequences of HIV/AIDS, this chapter focuses on AIDS, particularly in Africa. Africa is the epicenter of the AIDS pandemic. Within Africa, South Africa is the most adversely affected country. This chapter concludes with a discussion of global responses to the growth, persistence, and transmission of infectious diseases.

GLOBALIZATION OF INFECTIOUS DISEASES

Survival Sex ■ Having sex to feed families and for self-protection

Although infectious diseases dominated the daily existence of almost all human societies throughout history, the ability of rich countries to eliminate many leading diseases diminished global concern and the sense of urgency about eradicating the diseases that were concentrated in the developing world. The rapid spread of globalization, especially starting in the 1980s, underscored links between infectious diseases in poor countries and outbreaks of these diseases in rich countries. The most dramatic development was the discovery of HIV/AIDS in the United States, Western Europe, and other rich countries. Although perceived initially as a disease limited primarily to homosexuals, HIV/AIDS began to spread to the general population through blood transfusions, intravenous drug usage, and heterosexual practices. Furthermore, prominent people who were suffering from the disease fought to put it on both domestic and global agendas. By the 1990s, there was a definite shift toward recognizing the globalization of infectious diseases. Many of the diseases that were believed to have been eradicated in rich countries reemerged and were placed on the global agenda. Two factors explain this reemergence: (1) *growing resistance to common antibiotics* and (2) *the devastating impact of new epidemics*. The new epidemics included cholera in Latin America, particularly in Peru; plague in India; the Ebola virus in Africa; dengue fever in Asia; West Nile virus in the United States; and bovine spongiform encephalitis (mad cow disease) in Europe.[1]

Global Travel and Communications

Human beings are the most efficient transmitters of diseases. In the past, large proportions of populations were killed by plagues as people traveled to distant places.

The Plague of Justinian, which occurred around 541 A.D., devastated Europe. In the twelfth and thirteenth centuries, the bubonic plague, known as the Black Death, killed 25 million (or one of every three) Europeans. The decimation of Native American populations by European diseases is another example of how travelers spread infectious diseases. More recently, China and other Asian countries have spawned deadly infectious diseases, which have spread quickly to the rest of the world because of travel and excellent global links. In 1968, the Hong Kong flu, originating in South China, spread from Hong Kong to other countries. About 700,000 people died worldwide. In 1997, the avian flu (bird flu) was transmitted by chickens imported by Hong Kong from South China. The global spread of **SARS** originated in South China in November 2002.[2] Consider, too, how the West Nile virus outbreak started in the United States. Most European airlines linking the developing world with rich countries routinely use insecticides to destroy mosquitoes. Airlines from the United States, by contrast, hesitate to use sprays to control mosquitoes, partly due to fears about lawsuits by passengers. The West Nile virus was transported to the United States on airplanes. It is believed that African mosquitoes that transmit yellow fever and dengue fever arrived in South America and other parts of the New World aboard ships engaged in the trans-Atlantic slave trade. Since then, the speed of air transportation and communications have combined to rapidly spread infectious diseases and information about them worldwide.

SARS ■ Deadly viral disease that originated in South China in 2002

Trade

Trade has also been a major facilitator in the globalization of infectious diseases. The bubonic plague (Black Death) was transmitted to Europe through trade with Asia. Today, the rapid expansion of trade with China exposes the world to many diseases. The global trade in agricultural products has also escalated the risk of the global transmission of diseases. Mad cow disease has become a contentious issue between the United States and Japan, for example, because of fears among the Japanese of being infected by imports of American beef.[3]

Environmental Factors

As we saw in Chapter 10, human activities have profoundly affected the natural environment. People have migrated to areas that bring them into contact with animals and soils that play a role in the spread of infectious diseases. Furthermore, gradual increases in the earth's temperature (i.e., global warming) are conducive to the global spread of diseases.

Ethnic Conflicts and Wars

Ethnic conflicts, widespread violence, and wars have always contributed to the outbreak of disease and often the spread of infectious diseases. Combatants are often more likely to die from infectious diseases than from actual fighting. It is estimated that more than two-thirds of the roughly 600,000 deaths in the American Civil War were caused by infectious diseases. Furthermore, the movement of troops and mass migrations of civilians as a consequence of war contributed to the wider transmission of infectious diseases.[4] During the Spanish flu pandemic of 1918–1920, many American soldiers who were transported on trains and troop ships perished. On the battlefields of Vietnam and Iraq, American troops have suffered from infectious diseases, many of which are drug resistant. Endemic ethnic conflicts in Africa play a leading role in that continent's struggle with infectious diseases.

Refugees and Migration

Conditions that influence people to leave one area to settle in another initiate the downward spiral leading to infectious diseases. The deterioration of health services, the destruction of infrastructure, food shortages, and the lack of proper sanitation make refugees susceptible to communicable diseases. For example, following the Gulf War in 1991, roughly 400,000 Kurdish refugees fled Iraq and ended up in squalid camps in adverse weather conditions on the border with Turkey. More than 70 percent of the deaths there were attributed to diarrhea and cholera. Malaria has also been a killer of refugees in the border regions of Thailand, Cambodia, Ethiopia, and Sudan. As we will discuss, migrants are primarily responsible for transmitting diseases, such as tuberculosis, in the United States and Western European countries.

Poverty

The poorest countries, like poor individuals, are generally more vulnerable to contracting infectious diseases. Poverty is usually a reliable incubator of disease. Overcrowding, malnutrition, inadequate medical care, and unsanitary conditions facilitate the growth and transmission of infectious diseases.

Modern Medical Practices

A growing problem that assists the spread of infectious diseases is overuse and misuse of antibiotics. The increasing use of antibiotics in agricultural products has contributed to a process of pathogenic natural selection, which promotes the emergence of more virulent, resilient, resistant, and powerful disease strains.[5]

Changing Social and Behavioral Patterns

Globalization, especially cultural globalization, profoundly affects behavioral patterns worldwide. Pervasive and instant communications, television programs, movies, and the Internet facilitate the global spread of information about social practices that were once limited to smaller groups within societies. The global sex industry is an example of how changing behavior contributes to the globalization of infectious diseases such as HIV/AIDS. The spread of infectious diseases has focused attention on human security.

HUMAN SECURITY AND INFECTIOUS DISEASES

As we discussed in Chapter 1, the forces of globalization have strengthened the concept and reality of **global security**, which stresses a common and comprehensive security. The concept of global security moves us beyond the narrow traditional

Global Security ■
Stresses a common and comprehensive security worldwide

view of national security with its emphasis on military force and war to emphasize the global dimensions of emerging threats and problems and the need to achieve security with others.[6] Within the broader context of global security is the concept of **human security,** derived from the globalist school of thought. Human security focuses on the individual as the primary object of security. It embraces a people-centered approach of anticipating and coping with the multiple threats ordinary individuals face in an increasingly globalized society.[7] The emergence of the concept of human security during the 1990s is attributed to *three developments*: (1) *the end of the Cold War*, which radically altered the global political and security environment; (2) *a better understanding of the everyday insecurities* experienced by the world's poor, the vast majority of the world's population; and (3) the process of globalization, which ushered in *unprecedented changes and uncertainty*, thereby influencing a reevaluation of traditional views of security.

Human Security ■ Focuses on the individual as the primary object of security

Links between human security and human health were reinforced by anthrax bioterrorism in the United States shortly after the 2001 terrorist attacks and the unrelenting spread of the HIV/AIDS pandemic. These developments are augmented by links between health and economic development on the global agenda, especially the **UN Millennium Development Goals.** In fact, four of the eight Millennium Goals concentrate on health-related issues. The *globalization of infectious diseases threatens human security in several ways. First*, diseases kill far more people than wars. *Second*, disease undermines public confidence in the state, thereby eroding its legitimacy. *Third*, disease weakens the economic foundations of human security. *Fourth*, disease profoundly affects social order and stability. *Fifth*, the spread of infectious diseases contributes to regional instability. *Sixth*, disease can be used in biowarfare and bioterrorism.[8]

UN Millennium Development Goals ■ Four of the goals concentrate on health-related issues

INFECTIOUS DISEASES

The microbes (such as bacteria), viruses, parasites, and fungi that are the agents of infectious diseases are integral components of the natural and human environments. Throughout recorded history, our ancestors have been extremely vulnerable to, and mostly defenseless against, infectious diseases. **Pathogens** (i.e., organisms capable of causing disease) have routinely demolished societies. In many cases, there are outbreaks of diseases; that is, essentially localized, endemic occurrences. When infectious diseases spread to a relatively large number of people, they are classified as **epidemics.** Although epidemics generally impact populations worldwide, **pandemics** are long lasting, catastrophic, and truly global in their consequences. Two factors that have always been at the root of infectious disease threats to human populations are (1) social, economic, and environmental conditions that enable infectious diseases to exist among human hosts and (2) various means of transmission to new populations. As our ancestors developed agriculture and moved from isolated villages to more densely populated areas, they were exposed to more diseases.[9] Altering the natural environment enables microbes to infect humans. Humans are infected when they come into contact with natural **hosts** (i.e., organisms that carry diseases). The hosts are not negatively affected by the disease. Transmission of infectious diseases can occur within a single species or from one species to another. Humans often infect other humans. But host animals

Pathogens ■ Organisms capable of causing disease

Epidemics ■ When infectious diseases spread to a large number of people

Pandemics ■ Long-lasting, catastrophic global epidemics

Hosts ■ Organisms that carry diseases

also infect humans, a transmission known as **zoonosis**. Infectious diseases are transmitted through air, water, direct contact with the host's bodily fluids, and sexual activity, as well as through vectors such as mosquitoes and other insects.

To better understand contemporary concerns about infectious diseases, we will discuss the problem within the framework of epidemiologic transition theory. Each transition is characterized by "a unique pattern of diseases that is ultimately related to modes of subsistence and social structure."[10] There are basically *three distinct epidemiologic transitions*. The **first epidemiologic transition**, as we mentioned earlier, occurred when our ancestors established agricultural communities. Think about sanitation problems in permanently settled areas and the close interaction of humans and their domesticated animals. Both of these situations provided favorable environments for the dispersal of infectious diseases. Cattle, goats, sheep, pigs, and fowl transmitted tuberculosis, anthrax, and other diseases. Large proportions of populations were routinely killed by plagues, especially as trade among communities increased and people traveled to distant places. An example of an early pandemic is the **Plague of Justinian**, named after the Roman emperor, which devastated Europe around 541 A.D. Increased trade and migration between Asia and Europe and the Medieval Warm Period of the twelfth and thirteenth centuries contributed to the proliferation of rats and fleas that transmitted bubonic plague. Believing that cats were witches, Europeans inadvertently helped to spread the plague by killing cats. Known as the **Black Death**, the bubonic plague killed roughly 25 million people, or one of every three Europeans.[11] Individuals who manage to survive infectious diseases acquire immunity to them but transmit them to others. For example, most Europeans survived diseases such as tuberculosis and smallpox. West Africans lived with malaria and yellow fever. However, groups that lived in isolation from Europeans or Africans became quickly infected with their diseases. Millions of Native Americans were killed by diseases brought to the Americas by Europeans.[12] Many Europeans died of malaria and yellow fever in Africa, Asia, and the Americas.

The **second epidemiologic transition** coincided with the Industrial Revolution in Europe. Various inventions that accompanied the Industrial Revolution contributed to declining rates of infectious diseases. But overcrowding, environmental degradation, and unsanitary conditions led to the rebounding of cholera, smallpox, and tuberculosis. Developments in medical science and technology diminished epidemics, not only in Europe but also in places affected by European migration, colonization, and commercial relations. We are now experiencing the **third epidemiologic transition**. Just in the past three decades we have seen an unprecedented emergence of new diseases and a reemergence of infectious diseases that were thought to have been eliminated. Another characteristic of this third transition is growing antimicrobial resistance, due primarily to the frequent use and misuse of antibiotics and other antimicrobials. Incomplete drug treatment for various diseases also contributes to antimicrobial resistance.

Zoonosis ■ Transmission of diseases from host animals to humans

First Epidemiologic Transition ■ Related to the establishment of agricultural communities

Plague of Justinian ■ Named after the Roman emperor, it devastated Europe around 541 A.D.

Black Death ■ Bubonic plague that killed roughly 25 million people throughout Europe

Second Epidemiologic Transition ■ Coincided with the Industrial Revolution

Third Epidemiologic Transition ■ The current wave of infectious diseases

INFLUENZA AND AVIAN FLU

The spread of H5N1 avian flu (bird flu) in 2006 to areas beyond Asia galvanized global efforts to prevent or diminish the impact of an influenza pandemic. Of all the major infectious diseases, influenza demands the unique and urgent attention of the global community because of its lethality and the speed with which it is transmitted. Of the more than fifteen hundred microbes known to cause disease in humans, influenza continues to dominate in terms of overall mortality. Every year, 5 percent to 10 percent of the American population gets the flu and about thirty-six thousand of them die. Even in normal times, an estimated 1.5 million people worldwide die from influenza infections or related complications each year.[13] **Influenza**, which is a viral infection of the respiratory tract, is very contagious and poses serious threats to children, the elderly, and individuals with compromised immune systems. It is estimated that three influenza pandemics in the twentieth century killed more than 50 million people. The **Spanish flu** pandemic of 1918–1920 is generally regarded as the most lethal plague in history, causing roughly 50 million deaths worldwide. Pandemics in 1957 and 1968, which originated in China and Hong Kong, together killed more than 2.5 million people.[14] Given the efficiency with which flu is transmitted through air, close contact is not required for people to become infected. Furthermore, it is very difficult to identify and quarantine infected people who are spreading the disease.

Throughout the world, large commercial poultry farms, as well as the *proliferation of chickens kept by families, have provided ideal conditions for the avian flu to spread*. Furthermore, rapid population growth, especially in Asia, has given rise to densely populated urban areas. For example, during the 1968–1969 influenza pandemic, China had 790 million people and 12.3 million chickens and other poultry. China now has 1.3 billion people and 13 billion chickens.[15] Poultry, pigs, and people living together or in close proximity enhances the transmission of avian flu from animals to humans. Although the avian flu had caused 88 deaths out of a total of 165 cases globally by early 2006, transmission from human to human had not occurred. The global community feared that the virus would undergo changes enabling it to **reassort** (i.e., mix genes with other human influenza viruses that are also present). This process can produce an entirely new viral strain, capable of sustained human-to-human transmission. If such a virus has never existed, humans will lack immunity and the global population will be vulnerable to contracting the disease. The new strain would be easily transmitted from person to person, thereby causing a new pandemic. Approximately 1.7 million Americans would die, and there would be roughly 180 million to 360 million deaths globally.[16]

By 2006, humans had been infected in several countries outside Asia, such as Turkey, Iraq, India, and Iran. Dead birds infected with the H5N1 virus have been discovered in Russia, Romania, France, Croatia, Austria, Greece, Germany, and Nigeria. Migratory birds are believed to be primarily responsible for spreading the disease to other birds. The migratory route over East Asia overlaps with the Central Asian flyway, which overlaps with flyways to Africa and Europe. The deadly form of the H5N1 strain in Asia had not been found in North and South America, where migratory patterns are separate from those in Europe, Africa, and Asia.[17] However, when the H5N1 virus was detected in Nigeria in early 2006, the global community became increasingly concerned about the ability of the virus to spread from human to human, given Africa's widespread poverty and the inability of the governments to deal with any health crisis.

Responding to the threat of a pandemic, governments, international organizations, and nongovernmental organizations (NGOs) have concentrated on quarantine

Influenza ■ A contagious viral infection of the respiratory tract

Spanish Flu ■ Most lethal influenza pandemic

Reassort ■ Mutation of viruses that enhance chances of human-to-human transmission of disease

YOU DECIDE

Pharmaceutical Companies' Role in Fighting Infectious Diseases

The increasing globalization of infectious diseases has contributed to a growing awareness of the connectedness among the rich and poor countries and the need for increased cooperation between them to deal with these problems. Diseases are closely linked to a variety of global concerns, including malnutrition, inadequate education, poverty, and inequality. Roughly 460 million people are affected by HIV/AIDS, tuberculosis, and malaria, which together are responsible for an estimated 5.6 million deaths each year. Although there is an abundance of expensive drugs available in wealthy societies, more than a third of the world's population lacks adequate access to essential medications. Pharmaceutical companies are primarily concerned with developing drugs that are profitable. This means that most medical research focuses overwhelmingly on diseases in rich countries. In 2006, Bill Gates, chairman of Microsoft, decided to concentrate less on leading his company and more on working with the Bill and Melinda Gates Foundation to find ways to reduce the spread of infectious diseases. Between 1999 and 2006, the Bill and Melinda Gates Foundation gave $908.5 million to the Global Alliance for Vaccines and Immunization to fight infectious diseases. During the same period, governments worldwide contributed a total of $791.5 million. In 2009, Glaxo Smith Kline, Pfizer, and Novartis decided to waive patent restrictions to allow generic drug companies to produce HIV drugs for sale in poor countries. However, pharmaceutical companies have largely resisted providing inexpensive drugs that would cure those suffering from infectious diseases in developing countries.

1. What policies do you think the global community could develop and implement to influence more pharmaceutical companies to produce medicines for poor countries?
2. To what extent are individuals and government responsible for preventing the spread of HIV/AIDS?

Sources: Erika Check, "Quest for the Cure," *Foreign Policy* 155 (July/August 2006): 28–37; and "Drug Companies and Poor Countries," *Economist*, 18 July 2009, 60. ■

and the extensive culling of birds in affected areas. European countries were advised by the Animal Production and Health Division of the UN Food and Agriculture Organization to require travelers to fill out forms detailing their travel history and the agricultural products in their possession, which is the practice in the United States. Increased checks of airline passengers and their belongings are also regarded as effective countermeasures.[18] A major obstacle to an effective global response is the weakness of governments and poverty, which will eventually undermine global cooperation. As we will see, poor countries lack adequate resources to deal with routine health problems, and fighting avian flu is not their principal priority. Within rich countries, governments have allocated resources to develop vaccines, primarily **Tamiflu**, to deal with a pandemic. However, even in rich countries, there is insufficient medication for all of their inhabitants.

Tamiflu ■ Medicine used to treat patients infected with the avian flu

MALARIA, DENGUE, AND YELLOW FEVER

Malaria, dengue, and yellow fever are found primarily in the Tropics and are transmitted by mosquitoes. These are the most common vector-borne diseases. The spread of human settlements and various activities in forested areas have led to increased contact with mosquitoes that carry the viruses that cause these diseases. Global transportation and global warming have enabled these diseases to spread and grow outside tropical areas. Discarded tires, bottles, cans, and other containers that collect water become fertile breeding grounds for mosquitoes. Humans contract *malaria* when bitten by female mosquitoes. Malarial parasites infect red blood cells, causing chills, fever, and often death. Of the estimated 300 million to 500 million people infected with malaria each year, roughly 1.5 million die from the disease.[19] *Dengue*, a viral disease, is transmitted by mosquitoes that acquire the virus when they suck blood from an infected person, replicate the virus in their system, and transmit it to the next person they bite. Dengue is marked by fever, severe headaches, muscle and bone pain, shock, and fatal hemorrhaging. There are roughly 50 million cases of dengue infection worldwide each year.[20] *Yellow fever* is endemic in Africa, Asia, Latin America, and several Caribbean islands. It is estimated that thirty thousand people die each year of yellow fever. Symptoms include fever, muscle pain, backaches, headaches, shivering, loss of appetite, nausea, and vomiting. After a few days, most people who are infected improve and their symptoms disappear. However, approximately 15 percent of infected individuals experience a toxic phase, in which they develop jaundice, abdominal pains, bleeding, and kidney failure. Roughly half of those who enter the toxic phase die within ten to fourteen days.[21] Malaria is by far the most pervasive and deadly of these three diseases.

Malaria

Globally, Africa suffers the most from malaria. More than 90 percent of malaria deaths occur there, despite the relative ease with which the disease can be prevented and cured. In many ways, the prevalence of malaria in Africa is a manifestation of that continent's endemic poverty. Malaria was once believed to be caused by swamp air. The role that mosquitoes play in transmitting the disease was not discovered until 1898. Several factors have contributed to the increase of malaria in different parts of the world. As *population pressures* have influenced farmers to cultivate areas bordering on swamps and as agroforestry has grown, mosquitoes have multiplied and have more opportunities to infect humans. The *construction of dams and irrigation systems* for agriculture has radically altered the natural environment and provided breeding places for mosquitoes. Natural disasters, such as earthquakes, often destroy sanitation facilities, cause severe flooding, and allow standing water to accumulate in which mosquitoes breed. Finally, global warming is widely believed to be responsible for increased rainfall and higher temperatures, which can result in flooding. These environmental conditions facilitate the spread of malaria.[22]

Pregnant women and children bear the heaviest burdens. Malaria during pregnancy threatens the child's development, both in the uterus and as an infant. Mothers who have had limited exposure to malaria parasites and therefore less immunity are extremely vulnerable during pregnancy when their immunity is generally lower. Often, malaria infections cause anemia, which often results in maternal mortality. Malaria usually causes low-birth-weight babies, brain damage, and cognitive impairment.[23]

Efforts to eradicate malaria began in 1898, when the connection between mosquitoes and the disease was discovered. In addition to draining swamps and removing standing water from around homes, insecticides and larvicides were used. Quinine was also used to treat infections. A major breakthrough in fighting malaria came after World War II when DDT was applied. DDT was first used in 1939 as an agricultural insecticide in Switzerland. However, it was during the war that its public health applications were discovered. The allies had used DDT to control typhus epidemics. Complete eradication of malaria was achieved in places such as the United States, Southern Europe, Sri Lanka, and much of Brazil by massive DDT spraying.[24] Success in reducing malaria problems influenced the World Health Organization (WHO) to initiate its **Global Malaria Campaign** in 1955 to intensify the use of DDT to control malaria. However, by the 1960s malaria began to reemerge in countries that had made significant progress in eliminating it because many countries were unable to continue the highly organized and costly spray program essential for success. Furthermore, widespread use of DDT engendered resistance to it at a time when more people were becoming aware of its danger to human health and the environment. As we discussed in Chapter 10, the toxicity of pesticides was stressed by Rachel Carson in her influential book, *Silent Spring*. The WHO adopted a more comprehensive approach that included strengthening basic health services, focusing on the unique social and economic conditions in each region, and concentrating on treating malaria patients. Known as the **horizontal approach**, this new strategy emphasized control and containment, as opposed to complete eradication.[25] This change was due partly to limited supplies of DDT and escalating costs, as efforts to ban the use of DDT were increasingly successful. Both interest in and funding for malaria control declined during the 1970s, which enabled the disease to spread.

> **Global Malaria Campaign** ■ Intensified the use of DDT to control malaria

> **Horizontal Approach** ■ Strategy that emphasized the control and containment, as opposed to the eradication, of malaria

Concerned about the proliferation of infectious diseases, the U.S. Agency for International Development (USAID) in 1997 cooperated with the World Bank, the WHO, and other international agencies to form the Africa Initiative for Malaria Control (AIM). AIM was expanded to become a more comprehensive global initiative known as Roll Back Malaria (RBM) in 1998. A major objective of the RBM campaign was to reduce malaria-related mortality by half by 2012.

The globalization of infectious diseases has contributed to increased global awareness of malaria and has engendered renewed efforts to eradicate it. Furthermore, many individuals and NGOs are involved in these efforts. Rotarians worldwide have made eradicating malaria a major goal. In 1993, Drake Zimmerman of the Rotary Club of Normal, Illinois, played a leading role in distributing bed nets treated with safe insecticides to reduce malaria problems. The emphasis on bed nets was influenced by the growing ineffectiveness and health hazards of other approaches, such as indoor spraying and the use of chloroquine. Other organizations, such as the United Nations Children's Fund (UNICEF), play a leading role in providing bed nets. An insecticide-treated bed net costs around $3. However, even at that price many poor families cannot afford to purchase them. Based on recommendations of Jeffrey Sachs, the UN Secretary General's special adviser on the Millennium Development Goals, these bed nets are heavily subsidized or given away. A special initiative to eradicate malaria in Zambia was launched in 2006. Using $35 million donated by the **Bill and Melinda Gates Foundation**,

> **Bill and Melinda Gates Foundation** ■ Provides bed nets to Zambia to control the spread of malaria

Zambia's objective is to provide bed nets to 80 percent of its population by 2009. An additional $82 million was donated by international organizations and governments to supply the most effective malaria drugs to every public clinic and to pay for coordinated spraying programs across Zambia.[26] Death rates from malaria have declined significantly due to increased use of mosquito nets and artemisinin, a new medicine.

TUBERCULOSIS

Links between tuberculosis and the HIV/AIDS pandemic reinvigorated global interest in diminishing the spread of tuberculosis. The combination of tuberculosis and AIDS is lethal, with each disease contributing to the rapid progress of the other. HIV weakens the immune system, making it easier for an HIV-positive person to contract tuberculosis. In Africa, the epicenter of the HIV/AIDS pandemic, HIV is the single most important factor determining the increased incidence of tuberculosis.[27] The resurgence of tuberculosis underscores how globalization is instrumental in the transmission of infectious diseases and how increasing numbers of societies are unable to avoid the consequences. Migration from poor countries is a significant cause of the reemergence of tuberculosis in rich countries. In the United States, Sweden, Norway, Canada, Australia, Denmark, France, and other European countries, a large proportion of new cases of tuberculosis, as high as half in some countries, is found in immigrants. In fact, Mexico, the Philippines, China, India, and Vietnam—countries that are major sources of migrants to the United States—have some of the highest rates of tuberculosis in the world. High rates of illegal immigration reduce the ability of governments to screen and exclude infectious migrants. Tuberculosis is also rampant in refugee camps. For example, during the **Balkan conflict** (between 1992 and 1995), tuberculosis cases quadrupled. Similarly, famine and civil war throughout Africa have spawned significant growth in tuberculosis cases. Overcrowding in urban areas, rapid growth of prison populations (particularly in the United States), the rapid growth in global travel on airplanes with limited air circulation, and the global trend toward privatizing public health care systems (which generally deprives the poor of adequate medical treatment) have contributed to the reemergence of tuberculosis in affluent countries.

Balkan Conflict ■
Occurred from 1992 to 1995 and contributed to the quadrupling of tuberculosis in the Balkans

The WHO estimates that someone in the world is newly infected with tuberculosis bacilli every second and that one-third of the world's population is infected with tuberculosis.[28] More than 1.7 million die from tuberculosis each year, with the highest number of deaths in Southeast Asia. However, the highest mortality rate per capita is in Africa, due primarily to the prevalence of HIV/AIDS. In the mid-nineteenth century, tuberculosis was the leading cause of death in Europe and North America. It was a terrifying disease because it could not be prevented from spreading and it was incurable. Being transmitted through air, changing one's behavior provided no protection. As social, economic, and sanitary conditions improved in Europe and North America, tuberculosis began to recede. Furthermore, survivors of the disease developed greater immunity to it. The discovery of effective medicines starting in 1944 to control tuberculosis diminished the epidemic, with wealthier countries experiencing steady declines in tuberculosis-related deaths.[29] By 1991, pharmaceutical companies had abandoned manufacturing streptomycin, a drug commonly used to treat tuberculosis, and many developed countries sharply reduced spending on programs designed to combat the disease. Sanitariums, which had proliferated to treat tuberculosis patients, were closed, giving the perception that tuberculosis was no longer a major public concern. Although many poor areas within rich countries continue to experience cases of tuberculosis, the gap between the rich and the poor had created a general sense of indifference to the disease. *Four factors have contributed to tuberculosis as a global disease:*

1. Whereas tuberculosis declined in rich countries, it increased in the developing world.
2. Many policymakers and the general population in wealthy countries underestimated the degree to which their health was intertwined with that of people in other parts of the world.
3. The emergence of the HIV/AIDS pandemic rejuvenated tuberculosis, creating new concerns for wealthy countries.
4. The world was unprepared for an increase in outbreaks of multi-drug-resistant tuberculosis.[30]

Faced with the global spread of tuberculosis, various governmental organizations and NGOs rejuvenated efforts to diminish the transmission of the disease.

In 1991, the WHO introduced the **DOTS strategy** to control tuberculosis. This *strategy is composed of five elements*: (1) government's commitment to sustained tuberculosis control, (2) detection of tuberculosis cases through sputum-smear microscopy among people with symptoms, (3) regular and uninterrupted supply of high-quality antituberculosis drugs, (4) six to eight months of regularly supervised treatment, and (5) reporting systems to monitor treatment progress and program performance.[31] The DOTS strategy has achieved treatment success rates as high as 90 percent in some countries, a decline in the incidence of tuberculosis infections, and the prevention of an estimated 70 percent of deaths among infectious cases between 1991 and 2000. Nonetheless, the 2004 WHO report on global TB control concluded that governments must do more to meet global targets in order to eradicate and control tuberculosis. It recommends that governments and national tuberculosis control programs must adopt a more strategic approach to planning, match budgets more closely to plans, and match fundraising activities to realistic budgets.[32]

DOTS Strategy ■ Introduced in 1991 by the WHO to control tuberculosis

HIV/AIDS

When AIDS was first recognized in 1981, the general assumption was that this deadly disease was essentially limited to homosexuals and West Africans. Today, however, **HIV and AIDS** have become a pandemic. By 2007, more than 33 million people worldwide, 60 percent of them women, had been infected. Roughly 3 million people die every year from AIDS. Although Africa remains the epicenter of the AIDS pandemic, the disease is rapidly growing in China, India, Russia,

HIV/AIDS ■ Evolved from SIV found in chimpanzees in southwestern Africa

Latin America and the Caribbean, Eastern and Central Europe, and elsewhere. India, with more than 2.5 million cases of HIV, ranks second in the world, behind South Africa. Homosexuals, heterosexuals, bisexuals, intravenous drug users, recipients of infected blood transfusions, and children are victims of AIDS.

Simian Immunodeficiency Virus ■
Believed to be the source of HIV/AIDS

HIV (human immunodeficiency virus) is probably as old as human society. It is generally accepted that HIV evolved from the **simian immunodeficiency virus** (SIV) found in chimpanzees in southwestern Africa. It is believed that individuals acquired the disease from exposure to blood in the process of handling the meat of a chimpanzee that carried the virus. Compared with other infectious diseases, HIV/AIDS—while devastating—is transmitted in very specific ways and is thus more controllable. The virus is passed from one individual to another through the exchange of bodily fluids during sexual intercourse, through blood transfusions, from mother to fetus, through intravenous drug use, and through other activities in which infected blood is transmitted from one person to another. Early symptoms of HIV infection include chronic fatigue or weakness, noticeable and sustained weight loss, extensive and persistent swelling of the lymph glands, routine diarrhea, and sustained deterioration of the central nervous system. These conditions make HIV-positive patients vulnerable to contracting many other infectious diseases, especially tuberculosis.

Sex Tourism ■
Traveling to countries to participate in the sex industry

Globalization is a major factor contributing to the spread of HIV/AIDS. As global tourism continues to grow and people venture to all corners of the world, they increase their risk of contracting infectious diseases. **Sex tourism**, which is traveling to specific countries to participate in the local sex industry, is a potent source of infectious diseases, especially HIV/AIDS. Furthermore, as we discussed in Chapter 12, the growth in human trafficking and the sex trade in many parts of the world helps to spread HIV/AIDS. Poverty, ethnic conflicts, and wars facilitate the transmission of HIV/AIDS. And, as we will see in the case of South Africa, traditional values and perceptions of women are also important factors that assist the transmission of HIV/AIDS.

The HIV/AIDS pandemic has disastrous consequences. Eurasia, home to five out of every eight people on the planet, is an area with substantial economic power. It is also the location of countries that have nuclear weapons. Rapid increases in AIDS are likely to have profound global demographic, economic, political, and military strategic implications.[33] Compounding the problem is widespread poverty and the unwillingness or inability of governments to adequately address the AIDS crisis. The South African government was strongly criticized at the 16th International AIDS Conference in Toronto in 2006 for its refusal to take a more serious approach to the problem and to use available antiretroviral drugs. Nowhere are the devastating consequences of HIV/AIDS more prominent than in Africa, a continent estimated to have 70 percent of the people infected with the disease globally. Just as previous plagues radically altered European and Asian societies, AIDS is currently reshaping Africa. In some southern African countries, such as South Africa, Botswana, and Zambia, more than a third of the adults are infected with HIV. The AIDS epidemic in Africa deepens the continent's economic and health care problems and facilitates the spread of other diseases, including tuberculosis, that severely strain medical resources. Because AIDS kills more women than men, and because women are primarily responsible for farming and child care, starvation increases. Economic life is severely affected as employees become more disabled and die of AIDS.[34] Perhaps one of the most severe economic and social aspects of HIV/AIDS is the nature of the disease itself. Unlike previous pandemics, HIV/AIDS is a slow and deliberate killer. The Black Death and Spanish flu were devastating but quick. HIV/AIDS, by contrast, is long term and consequently more destructive in many ways. Since its discovery in 1981, the HIV/AIDS pandemic has been characterized by waves of infection, followed years later by waves of debilitating illness, and followed years after that by waves of death and family disruption.[35]

Africa

Africa bears the burden of the HIV/AIDS pandemic. Because of its poverty, which is exacerbated by debilitating infectious diseases. Africa is marginalized in the process of globalization. Within the continent, southern Africa, especially **South Africa**, has become the epicenter of HIV/AIDS. More than 5.3 million South Africans, out of a population of 45 million, are living with the virus, making the country with the largest number of HIV/AIDS cases in the world. All aspects of South African life are affected by the pandemic. By examining South Africa, we can get a deeper understanding of the gravity of this global issue for South Africa and other developing countries. South Africa is experiencing only the first phase of the pandemic.

> **South Africa** ■ The epicenter of the global HIV/AIDS crisis

Apart from the fact that HIV/AIDS originated in Africa, several other factors have contributed to its rapid growth in South Africa. Economic, cultural, and political factors combine to make South Africa a special case. Settled by Europeans, primarily from Holland and Britain, South Africa experienced racial conflicts and endured forced racial segregation under the system of **apartheid**. The political and social components of apartheid provided the breeding ground for the HIV/AIDS problem. Apartheid laws required men who worked in the gold, diamond, and other mines; the factories; and all sectors of the economy to leave their families. **Rural-to-urban migration** occurs throughout Africa, as we discussed in Chapter 11. Under various colonial administrations, Africans were forced to leave rural areas in search of employment in urban centers, in mining, and in agriculture. The majority of these migrant workers returned home periodically. This pattern of migration was firmly rooted in South Africa and it continues. As in other parts of Africa, HIV/AIDS cases were initially concentrated along major trading routes and areas frequented by long-distance truck drivers. Bars and hotels along these routes became centers for the sex trade. HIV prevalence is often extremely high among the women, with documented rates up to 76 percent prevalence in Uganda.[36] The men transmit the virus to women in rural areas, making HIV/AIDS a predominantly heterosexual disease in Africa. Another factor that facilitates the spread of HIV/AIDS in South Africa is the casual, unsafe, and abusive nature of sexual relationships. Cultural attitudes and behaviors influence many South Africans to accept having multiple partners and engage in unprotected sex, rejecting the use of condoms. Traditional sexual practices (such as **dry sex**, which involves the use of powders and herbs to prevent vaginal lubrication) result in increased friction and greatly elevate the risk of viral transmission through internal

> **Apartheid** ■ South Africa's system of rigid, legal, racial segregation that was violently enforced

> **Rural-to-Urban Migration** ■ Facilitates the spread of HIV/AIDS in South Africa

> **Dry Sex** ■ A practice that facilitates the transmission of AIDS

abrasion and lesions.[37] In a predominantly patriarchal society, women are generally perceived as being inferior to men. Women are expected to meet the sexual demands of men and are relatively passive, if not powerless, in insisting on safer practices, such as using condoms.

Social values and practices that are associated with the spread of HIV/AIDS are partly rooted in the violent and the abusive culture spawned by several decades of apartheid. A culture of sexual abuse and violence is now firmly established in South Africa. South Africa has one of the highest rates of rape in the world. Many HIV-infected men believe that they can be cured by having sex with a virgin, and the incidence of sex between older men and younger women is growing. Apartheid also contributed to the development of a risk-taking culture. Many South Africans have experienced a general disregard for life and have adopted attitudes that promote living for the moment and being fatalistic. Under these circumstances, unsafe sexual practices are perceived as normal behavior.[38]

The costs associated with HIV/AIDS are extremely high. The virus is most prevalent among South Africans who range in age from eighteen to forty-four; it essentially destroys the most productive citizens. Education suffers as teachers die or are too sick to work. Extended families, already struggling to survive, face additional responsibility for raising orphans of relatives. More than a million children under the age of fifteen have already lost their mothers to the disease. This huge group is likely to fuel crime and other social problems. The economic implications are profound. Not only are more resources being allocated to treat and prevent HIV/AIDS, those infected with the virus are unproductive. Valuable skills are lost, and businesses often bear additional costs and inefficiencies resulting from HIV infections among employees. Agriculture also suffers, as women, who do most of the agricultural work, are unable to concentrate on providing food for their families. Finally, because HIV/AIDS is prevalent among the age groups involved in the military, South Africa's national security is undermined and its ability to effectively participate in solving many conflicts in Africa is severely weakened. Unit cohesiveness, discipline, morale, and combat readiness are all adversely affected by the prevalence of HIV/AIDS in the military.[39]

Global Responses to AIDS

Condom usage is a relatively inexpensive and effective approach to reducing the risk of infection and transmission of HIV. Governments, NGOs, and international organizations support condom distribution programs, although this practice remains controversial for some groups that stress abstinence. Given the reality of increased human sexuality, using condoms will undoubtedly be the dominant and practical approach to fighting HIV/AIDS. Thailand provides an example of how governments have integrated condom usage into an overall strategy to impede the spread of the disease. In 1989, Thailand began mandatory HIV testing of high-risk individuals, such as homosexuals, commercial sex workers, and intravenous drug users. It also implemented "the **100 Percent Condom Program.**" The principal objectives of the program are to protect 100 percent of commercial sex acts through mandatory condom usage in brothels and to diminish the commercial sex trade through sustained educational efforts. Free condoms are distributed to the

100 Percent Condom Program ■ Thailand's program to protect commercial sex acts through mandatory condom usage

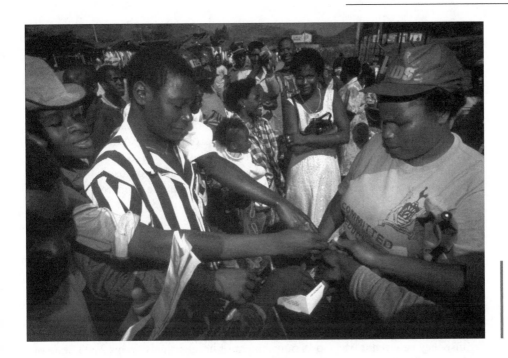

AIDS Worker
Distributing Free
Condoms in
Zimbabwe.

(UN/DPI/Michel
Szulc-Kryzanowoski)

sex workers, who are instructed to use them or face several penalties. The commercial sex business is closely monitored by the government to ensure compliance. It is estimated that Thailand's 100 Percent Condom Program increased condom usage in the sex trade from 14 percent in 1989 to around 94 percent in 1993.[40] This program has been so successful that Thailand is mainly concerned about growing discrimination against those with AIDS.

When confronted with outbreaks of infectious diseases, most governments respond by erecting barriers to international travel and immigration and quarantining those carrying the disease. As HIV/AIDS became a major national concern, especially in the United States and Western Europe, governments imposed border restrictions on foreigners with HIV.[41] Africans, Haitians, and others from countries with high HIV/AIDS rates came under special scrutiny. However, as we have discussed in Chapter 11, global migration has weakened the ability of governments to exercise meaningful control over their borders in order to prevent the spread of infectious diseases.

Medical advances and a deeper understanding of HIV/AIDS—in addition to the fact that the disease was concentrated among high-risk groups—enabled rich countries to make significant progress in decreasing the transmission of the virus. Antiretroviral drug therapies, though expensive, allowed many HIV/AIDS patients to continue living relatively normal lives. Deaths from the disease have declined in most developed countries, although both HIV/AIDS and mortality rates have increased among the poor in these societies, especially among African Americans. Despite opposition by pharmaceutical companies concerned about intellectual property rights, Brazil, Argentina, Costa Rica, Cuba, and Uruguay took the unprecedented approach of providing government-subsidized antiretroviral medications to HIV/AIDS patients, thereby setting global precedents for widespread access to AIDS medications. Brazil, in particular, has made it legal for government laboratories to ignore drug patents in order to produce low-cost generic drugs to stop the spread of the disease. Brazil's aggressive strategy to control HIV infections and transmission stands in sharp contrast to the approach adopted by South Africa. Despite its massive problems with the disease, South African officials attempted to ignore them. Faced with unrelenting domestic and global pressure to confront the seriousness of its HIV/AIDS problem, the South African government eventually implemented the Comprehensive HIV/AIDS Care, Management, and Treatment Plan in 2004. This program focuses on using antiretroviral medicines to treat people, voluntary counseling, testing, and increasing the distribution of free condoms.

Although the United States has been involved in the global efforts to reduce HIV infections, a significant change in the U.S. policy was initiated by Franklin Graham, the son of evangelist Billy Graham and founder of **Samaritan's Purse,** an evangelical charity based in South Carolina. Bringing together evangelical Protestants and Catholic leaders, as well as overseas missionaries who worked in countries devastated by HIV/AIDS, Graham focused national attention on the problem. Perceptions of the disease as affecting primarily heterosexuals, as opposed to only homosexuals, enabled many conservatives to take action instead of disregarding the pandemic because they believed it was God's punishment of homosexuals. In his 2003 State of the Union address, President George W. Bush, influenced by Graham and the evangelicals, announced the Emergency Plan for AIDS Relief and committed $15 billion over five years to preventing HIV infections and treating patients.[42] However, political pressure from conservatives influenced the U.S. government to allocate a third of the money to abstinence-promoting programs and to avoid spending money on sterile syringes and needles for intravenous drug users. Essentially, the U.S. government adopted Uganda's **ABC (Abstinence, Be Faithful, and Use Condoms) program,** which helped to significantly reduce the prevalence of HIV/AIDS in that country. In 2003, the William J. Clinton Presidential Foundation HIV/AIDS Initiative concluded an agreement with generic drug manufacturers to lower the price of triple combination antiretroviral drug regimens to less than $140 per patient per year. The Clinton Foundation has concentrated its efforts against HIV/AIDS in Mozambique, Rwanda, Tanzania, South Africa, and several Caribbean states.

Confronted with the emergence of HIV/AIDS, the global community responded. The WHO and U.S. government agencies—including the U.S. Food and Drug Administration (FDA) and the Alcohol, Drug Abuse, and Mental Health Administration—convened the First International AIDS Conference in Atlanta, Georgia, in 1984. This was followed by the initiation of WHO's Special Program on HIV/AIDS in 1985, which set the objective of reducing the growth of HIV/AIDS globally and to lessen the disease's impact on the countries most seriously affected. Concerned about HIV/AIDS patients' inability to afford drugs to treat the disease, members of the World Trade Organization (WTO) ratified the **Agreement on Trade-Related Aspects of Intellectual Property Rights (TRIPS)** in 1994. TRIPS included a provision to allow states to waive patent protections without authorization from the patent holder in national emergencies for noncommercial use.[43] This provision facilitated the ability of governments, such as Brazil's, to manufacture

Samaritan's Purse ■ An evangelical charity involved in fighting the spread of HIV/AIDS

ABC Program ■ Developed in Uganda to fight HIV/AIDS, stresses abstinence, fidelity, and using condoms

TRIPS ■ Allowed states to waive patent protections unilaterally to deal with national emergencies generic drugs used to treat HIV/AIDS patients. A major breakthrough in the fight against the pandemic came in 1996 when the **Joint United Nations Program on AIDS (UNAIDS)** was founded. UNAIDS's main objective is to be the leading advocate for global action against HIV/AIDS. Several organizations, reflecting UNAIDS's comprehensive approach to the problem, participate in the program. These include UNICEF; the UN Development Program; the UN Population Fund; the UN Educational, Scientific, and Cultural Organization (UNESCO); the World Bank; the UN Office on Drugs and Crime; and the International Labor Organization. These organizations have been joined by the eight leading industrial countries (known as the G-8), various NGOs, and pharmaceutical companies (such as Boehringer Ingelheim, Bristol-Myers Squibb, GlaxoSmithKline, Merck, and F. Hoffmann-LaRoche). Giving in to global pressure to lower drug prices to make them accessible to the poor, pharmaceutical companies responded by discounting their antiretroviral medications in poor countries. In 2006, Bristol-Myers reached an agreement with India and South Africa that allowed these countries to manufacture drugs inexpensively for patients in poor countries.[44]

UNAIDS ■ The leading advocate for global action against HIV/AIDS

SARS

SARS emerged in China's Guangdong Province in late 2002. The virus that caused SARS was transmitted from the civet cat to individuals handling and consuming the animal's meat. This highly contagious disease is spread when individuals come into contact with droplets from an infected person's coughing or sneezing. The symptoms of SARS are high fever, chills, muscle aches, and a dry cough. The vast majority of individuals infected with SARS improve without having to undergo extensive medical treatment. However, between 10 and 20 percent of those contracting the disease require breathing assistance with a mechanical ventilator for an extensive period of time. Many of them eventually die.

The transmission of the disease globally began when twelve guests in the Metropole Hotel in Hong Kong contracted it from an infected physician from Zhongshan University. Unaware of being infected, these guests carried the disease to Singapore, Vietnam, Canada, Ireland, and the United States. More than eight hundred cases of SARS worldwide are believed to have been originated with this one **superspreader**.[45] Global communications helped to spread the most recent information about SARS, thereby heightening global awareness of the deadly virus and generating pressure on governments, especially that of China, to take action to prevent its spread globally. Global communications also enabled the scientific community to engage in unprecedented cooperation to control the virus.

Superspreader ■ Person responsible for spreading disease to a large number of individuals

Governments responded quickly. Vietnam—which had the first documented case of SARS even though SARS originated in southern China—implemented *detection-and-prevention measures* immediately. These included (1) prompt identification of people with SARS, their movements, and their contacts; (2) appropriate protection of medical personnel treating these patients; (3) isolation of suspected SARS cases; (4) exit screening of international travelers; and (5) timely and accurate reporting and sharing information with others.[46] Canada, the United States, and other countries took similar actions. President Bush, for example, signed an executive order allowing U.S. officials to quarantine victims of SARS to prevent its transmission into the United States. The WHO also responded promptly by sending investigation teams to Guangdong, the first Chinese city that experienced SARS. The WHO also visited Beijing and pressured government officials to give an accurate assessment of the SARS problem and to improve its reporting system. Roughly sixty teams of public health officials and experts were recruited from the United States, Britain, Germany, France, and other countries to assist with efforts to control the spread of infections in areas affected by SARS. *Several factors contributed to this rapid global response*:

1. *Fear and Uncertainty.* The rapid spread of the disease and its lethality created a sense of urgency to respond.
2. *Stronger Leadership.* The WHO was proactive in raising global awareness and mobilizing the global response.
3. *Scientific Advances.* New scientific knowledge and techniques enabled researchers to find solutions quickly.
4. *Heightened Awareness of Biological Weapons Threat.* Concerns with terrorism and the threat of biological weapons influenced countries to act quickly to identify new infectious diseases.
5. *Concerns About Missing Another AIDS Problem.* Public health officials reacted swiftly to SARS, believing that the slow global response to HIV/AIDS allowed that disease to build up devastating momentum.[47]

The global response to SARS marks a radical departure from earlier responses to infectious diseases and has become a model for dealing with potential pandemics, including the avian flu.

SWINE FLU

By June 2009, swine flu (H1N1) had reached seventy-four countries spreading from Mexico and the United States to Japan and Australia. Although only thirty thousand cases had been reported globally, infectious disease experts believed that hundreds of thousands or millions of people had actually been infected. There was no scientific measurement of the spread of swine flu. However, in June 2009, the WHO declared that swine flu was a pandemic. Experiences with SARS and avian flu prompted a quick global response to swine flu. Perhaps more importantly, the swine flu reminded experts of the 1918 Spanish flu pandemic. Countries reacted quickly. The United States declared a public health emergency, and Mexico closed schools, museums, movie theaters, nightclubs, and sports stadiums. Mexico City was essentially shut down for five days. China quarantined seventy-one Mexican citizens and allowed the Mexican government to fly them home on a chartered plane. The global economy, already in a recession, was negatively affected by swine flu. Consumers were reluctant to purchase pork. Some countries, such as China and Russia, banned imports from Mexico. Mexico, the epicenter of the swine flu pandemic, suffered major economic losses, especially in the tourist industry. Several airlines terminated flights to the country, and consumers, burdened by the global financial crisis and recession, canceled travel plans.[48]

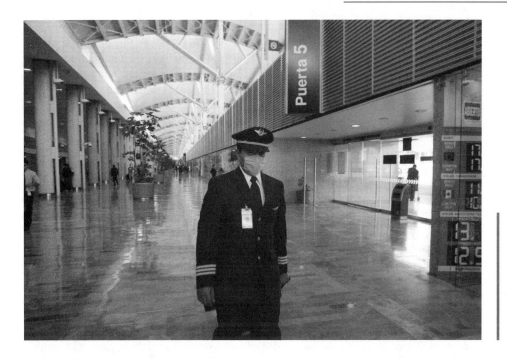

Mexico City Airport Official Wearing a Mask in an Empty Airport.

(Adriana Zehbrauskas/The New York Times/Redux Pictures)

GLOBAL RESPONSES TO INFECTIOUS DISEASES

The global community has long recognized that preventing, treating, and controlling the spread of infectious diseases can be accomplished only through cooperation among individuals, NGOs, governments, and international organizations. As early as 1851, European countries convened the **International Sanitation Conference** in an effort to prevent the spread of infectious diseases from developing countries to Europe, primarily through travel and trade. Significant improvements in sanitation, nutrition, and medical technology in Europe have reduced outbreaks of infectious diseases. But Europe remained vulnerable to the importation of diseases. Shortly after the United Nations was founded, the WHO was created as a specialized agency to develop international rules concerning infectious disease control. Under the International Health Regulations developed by the WHO, countries are required to report outbreaks of yellow fever, cholera, plague, and other diseases. This information is disseminated to other countries, and surveillance strategies are implemented to help prevent transmission. Countries are also required to provide safe drinking water, food, and disposal of refuse, wastewater, and other things dangerous to health at their airports and ports. International Health Regulations also require counties to provide health services, equipment, and services for isolating infected persons and for disinfecting, disinsecting, and deratting ships and aircraft.[49] The U.S. **Centers for Disease Control and Prevention (CDC)**, based in Atlanta, Georgia, also plays a leading role in preventing and controlling the transmission of infectious diseases into the United States. Both the CDC and the WHO emphasize the importance of research and the development

International Sanitation Conference ■ Effort to prevent the spread of infectious diseases from developing countries to Europe

CDC ■ U.S. organization devoted to preventing and controlling the transmission of infectious diseases into the United States of medicines to prevent the emergence and spread of infectious diseases. One major problem relating to health issues in the developing world is access to medical information. The WHO persuaded six major publishers of medical journals to reduce their prices so that doctors and researchers in poor societies could have increased access to information to improve health care systems and develop new treatments.[50]

As we have seen, an important component of the global response to the emergence and reemergence of infectious diseases is stressing preventive measures. These include protecting and chlorinating water supplies, disposing of human feces in a sanitary manner and maintaining fly-proof latrines, paying special attention to cleanliness in food preparation and food handling, stressing the importance of frequent hand washing, and eliminating potential mosquito breeding sites. Routine preventive immunization programs have effectively reduced outbreaks of many infectious diseases. The WHO launched the 3 by 5 anti-AIDS initiative, which aimed to provide anti-AIDS drugs to 3 million people in poor countries by the end of 2005. Of the roughly 42 million people infected with AIDS in 2004, only 400,000 of them received the necessary drugs.[51] In 2006, WHO launched the *universal access initiative* to bring an even greater sense of urgency and commitment to HIV prevention and treatment. The United States made a commitment to spend $15 billion on efforts to prevent and control the spread of AIDS. In 2006, the Bill and Melinda Gates Foundation gave $287 million to researchers to develop an HIV vaccine. A basic challenge was persuading pharmaceutical companies to lower drug prices and to permit developing countries, such as India and Brazil, to be exempt from patent restrictions so that they could produce relatively inexpensive anti-AIDS drugs. By 2006, as we have seen, many major pharmaceutical companies had agreed to arrangements allowing poor countries to have access to relatively inexpensive drugs. The SARS virus, the growing concern about terrorists using biological weapons, and the emergence of avian flu contributed to a greater awareness of the globalization of infectious diseases and the need to act promptly and decisively to prevent both infections and transmission.

SUMMARY AND REVIEW

This chapter discussed the globalization of infectious diseases; rapid increases in global travel, trade, and migration; growing use of illegal drugs; human trafficking for sexual purposes; rapid population growth; environmental changes; widespread poverty; and inadequate medical resources—all factors that have facilitated the global spread of infectious diseases. These diseases pose significant threats to humans as well as to global security. By discussing infectious diseases—such as influenza, avian flu, malaria, tuberculosis, HIV/AIDS, and SARS—we were able to see the social, economic, and political challenges these diseases pose and the ease with which they are spread globally. Special emphasis was given to HIV/AIDS because of its grave threats to the global society. We discussed various responses to the globalization of infectious diseases. The case of SARS demonstrates that rapid transportation and instantaneous communications have raised global awareness of how quickly infectious diseases are transmitted worldwide.

The global response to SARS is widely regarded as a model for how to deal with emerging as well as current infectious diseases. Some organizations, such as the WHO, play a pivotal role in reducing the expansion of infectious diseases. NGOs as well as individuals are also actively involved in fighting pandemics. However, many governments have inadequate resources to deal with multiple infectious diseases. Furthermore, countries have different priorities. Cultural values and practices also complicate global efforts to prevent the emergence and spread of infectious diseases.

KEY TERMS

survival sex 301
SARS 302
global security 303
human security 304
UN Millennium
  Development Goals 304
pathogens 304
epidemics 304
pandemics 304
hosts 304
zoonosis 305
first epidemiologic
  transition 305
Plague of Justinian 305
Black Death 305
second epidemiologic
  transition 305
third epidemiologic
  transition 305

influenza 306
Spanish flu 306
reassort 306
Tamiflu 307
Global Malaria Campaign
  309
horizontal approach 309
Bill and Melinda Gates
  Foundation 309
Balkan conflict 310
DOTS strategy 311
HIV/AIDS 311
simian immunodeficiency
  virus 312
sex tourism 312
South Africa 313
apartheid 313
rural-to-urban migration
  313

dry sex 313
100 Percent Condom
  Program 314
Samaritan's Purse 316
ABC program 316
Trade-Related Aspects of
  Intellectual Property
  Rights (TRIPS) 316
Joint United Nations
  Program on AIDS
  (UNAIDS) 317
superspreader 317
International Sanitation
  conference 319
Centers for Disease Control
  and Prevention (CDC)
  319

DISCUSSION QUESTIONS

1. Discuss the emergence of SARS and the global response to it.
2. Discuss the role of the WHO in preventing the spread of infectious diseases.
3. Discuss the factors that facilitate the spread of HIV/AIDS and various efforts to deal with this pandemic.
4. Compare domestic and global approaches to malaria and tuberculosis.
5. Discuss how conflicts, global warming, and poverty contribute to the emergence and spread of infectious diseases.

SUGGESTED READINGS

Brower, Jennifer, and Peter Chalk. *The Global Threat of New and Reemerging Infectious Diseases*. Santa Monica, CA: Rand, 2003.
Garrett, Laurie. "The Lessons of HIV/AIDS," *Foreign Affairs* 84, No. 2 (July/August 2005): 51–64.
Garrett, Laurie. "The Challenge of Global Health," *Foreign Affairs* 86, No. 1 (January/February 2007): 14–38.

Greenfeld, Karl. "The Virus Hunters," *Foreign Policy* 153 (March/April 2006): 42–55.

Knobler, Stacey, et al. *Learning from SARS*. Washington, DC: National Academies Press, 2004.

Price-Smith, Andrew. *Contagion and Chaos*. Cambridge, MA: MIT Press, 2009.

Stillwagon, Eileen. *AIDS and the Ecology of Poverty*. New York: Oxford University Press, 2005.

END NOTES

1. Lincoln Chen and Vasant Narasimhan, "A Human Security Agenda for Global Health," in *Global Health Challenges for Human Security*, eds. Lincoln Chen et al. (Cambridge, MA: Global Equity Initiative, 2003), 8.
2. Tommy Koh, "The New Global Threat," in *The New Global Threat*, eds. Tommy Koh et al. (London: World Scientific, 2003), 147.
3. Vikas Bajaj, "Japan Again Suspends Shipments of Beef from U.S.," *New York Times*, 21 January 2006, B3.
4. Michael J. Toole, "Refugees and Migrants," in *The Politics of Emerging and Resurgent Infectious Diseases*, ed. Jim Whitman (New York: St. Martin's Press, 2000), 110.
5. Jennifer Brower and Peter Chalk, *The Global Threat of New and Reemerging Infectious Diseases* (Santa Monica, CA: Rand, 2003), 17.
6. Brower and Chalk, *The Global Threat*, 4.
7. Chen and Narasimhan, "A Human Security Agenda," in *Global Health Challenges*, 3.
8. Brower and Chalk, *The Global Threat*, 10.
9. David P. Fidler, *International Law and Infectious Diseases* (Oxford: Clarendon Press, 1999), 9.
10. Ronald Barrettt et al., "Emerging and Reemerging Infectious Diseases: The Third Epidemiologic Transition," *Annual Review of Anthropology* 27 (1998), 247.
11. Paul R. Epstein, "Climate, Ecology, and Human Health," in *Plagues and Politics*, ed. Andrew T. Price-Smith (New York: Palgrave, 2001), 49.
12. Alfred W. Cosby, *The Columbian Exchange: Biological and Cultural Consequences of 1492* (Westport, CT: Greenwood Press, 1972), 37.
13. Michael T. Osterbolm, "Preparing for the Next Pandemic," *Foreign Affairs* 84, No. 2 (July/August 2005), 26.
14. National Research Council, *Under the Weather: Climate, Ecosystems, and Infectious Disease* (Washington, DC: National Academies Press, 2001), 54.
15. Osterbolm, "Preparing for the Next Pandemic," 37.
16. Osterbolm, "Preparing for the Next Pandemic," 26.
17. Howard Markel, "If the Avian Flu Hasn't Hit, Here's Why, Maybe," *New York Times,* 1 January 2006, A10; and Seth Mydans, "Indonesian Chickens, and People, Hard Hit by Bird Flu," *New York Times,* 1 February 2008, A3.
18. Elizabeth Rosenthal, "Europe Urged to Check Travelers to Prevent Spread of Bird Flu," *New York Times,* 17 January 2006, A3.
19. National Research Council, *Under the Weather*, 48.
20. National Research Council, *Under the Weather*, 47.
21. World Health Organization, *Yellow Fever: Fact Sheet No. 100*, December 2001, 1.
22. Lisa Sattenspiel, "The Evolution, Transmission, and Geographic Spread of Infectious Diseases," in *The Changing Face of Disease*, eds. Nick Mascie-Taylor et al. (London: CRC Press, 2004), 44.
23. S. W. Lindsay et al., "Protecting Pregnant Women from Malaria," in *The Changing Face of Disease*, 104.

24. Roger Bate, "Testimony on Fighting Malaria," *Congressional Quarterly*, 13 May 2005, 3.
25. Bate, "Testimony on Fighting Malaria," 3.
26. Laurie Goering, "Zambia Expands Effort to Control Its Biggest Killer," *Chicago Tribune*, 14 February 2006, Sect. 1, 5; and Laurie Garrett, "The Challenge of Global Health," *Foreign Affairs* 86, No. 1 (January/February 2007), 14–15.
27. World Health Organization, *Tuberculosis*, April 2005, 2.
28. World Health Organization, *Tuberculosis*, 1.
29. Kraig Klaudt, "The Political Causes and Solutions of the Current Tuberculosis Epidemic," in *The Politics of Emerging*, 87.
30. Klaudt, "The Political Causes," in *The Politics of Emerging*, 89.
31. World Health Organization, *Tuberculosis*, 2.
32. World Health Organization, *Tuberculosis*, 4.
33. Nicholas Eberstadt, "The Future of AIDS," *Foreign Affairs* 81, No. 6 (November/December 2002), 23.
34. "The Cost of AIDS: An Imprecise Catastrophe," *Economist*, 22 May 2004, 68.
35. Laurie Garrett, "The Lessons of HIV/AIDS," *Foreign Affairs* 84, No. 2 (July/August 2005), 52.
36. Richard G. Marlink and Alison G. Kotin, *Global AIDS Crisis* (Santa Barbara, CA: ABC-CLIO, 2004), 28.
37. Brower and Chalk, *The Global Threat*, 39.
38. Brower and Chalk, *The Global Threat*, 42.
39. Brower and Chalk, *The Global Threat*, 50.
40. Marlink and Kotin, *Global AIDS Crisis*, 79.
41. Lawrence O. Gostin, *The AIDS Pandemic* (Chapel Hill: University of North Carolina Press, 2004) 279.
42. Holly Burkhalter, "The Politics of AIDS," *Foreign Affairs* 83, No. 1 (January/February 2004), 10.
43. Marlink and Kotin, *Global AIDS Crisis*, 123.
44. Donald G. McNeil, "Bristol-Myers Allows Two Major AIDS Drugs to Be Sold Cheaply," *New York Times*, 15 February 2006, A6.
45. Stacey Knobler et al., *Learning from SARS* (Washington, DC: National Academies Press, 2004), 6.
46. Aileen J. Plant, "SARS and Public Health," in *The New Global Threat*, 4.
47. Knobler et al., *Learning from SARS*, 260.
48. Donald G. McNeil and Denise Grady, "To Flu Experts, Pandemic Label Confirms the Obvious," *New York Times*, 12 June 2009, A12; and Marc Lacey, "Mexican Tourism Bears Blow of a Health Scare," *New York Times*, 27 April 2009, A10.
49. Fidler, *International Law and Infectious Diseases*, 62.
50. Melody Peterson, "Medical Journals Plan to Offer Far Lower Rates in Poor Nation," *New York Times*, 9 July 2001, A3.
51. "The Global Effort Against AIDS Is Changing Gear," *Economist*, 15 May 2004, 78.

14

Cultural Clashes and Conflict Resolution

INTRODUCTION

Some groups and individuals promote globalization as a positive force to advance their own interests, whereas others perceive globalization as threatening. Global integration is increasing while, simultaneously, national cohesion is weakening as smaller groups seek increased political and cultural autonomy. As we have seen, globalization is widely equated with Americanization. The dual forces of globalization and antiglobalization are reflected in the contradictory trends of Americanization and anti-Americanism. Progress toward global order and security is accompanied by persistent outbreaks of violent conflicts and insecurity. Most cultural clashes, as this chapter shows, are inseparable from politics and economics.

Globalization challenges traditional certainties, conservative values, and parochialism; it also erodes identities based on nationality, geographic location, religion, social status, and ethnicity. Global financial markets, a borderless world, the growth of transnational elites, and weakening national institutions fuel insecurity. Insecurity gives rise to global, international, and domestic conflicts. That these clashes occur at different levels (global, international, regional, national, and local) and often operate interdependently manifests the complexity of global society. Benjamin R. Barber, for example, envisions two possible global futures, both of them negative: (1) the McDonaldization or interdependence of the world and (2) a **jihad** (or struggle) in the name of a hundred narrowly conceived faiths against every kind of interdependence, every kind of artificial social cooperation and civic mutuality.[1] Barber's view of a jihad is essentially synonymous with ethnic conflicts. Another perspective, best articulated by Samuel P. Huntington, is that the world is divided into distinct civilizations that inevitably clash.[2]

This chapter examines the role of culture in global conflicts, focusing on civilization clashes, international conflicts, and ethnic conflicts. Dividing the world into distinct and mutually exclusive civilizations and races is deeply rooted in the academic world, which facilitates a general acceptance of the clash-of-civilizations perspective. The **hybridization** theory emphasizes cultural mixing due to complex global interdependence. Jan Nederveen Pieterse argues that "hybridization has been taking place all along but has been concealed by religious, national, imperial, and civilization chauvinisms."[3] Think about the most violent conflicts in recent history. Most of these clashes have occurred among countries belonging to the same civilizations. In fact, many wars have been civil wars. The conflict in Iraq between Sunnis and Shiites represented the larger and growing conflict within Islam. Sharp distinctions between religions, especially Islam on the one hand and Christianity and Judaism on the other, are stressed by proponents of the clash-of-civilizations theory. This view holds that civilizations are separate and distinct—like billiard balls—and that conflicts between them are almost inevitable. The rise of Islamic fundamentalism and terrorism by Islamic groups, such as al-Qaeda, are marshaled to buttress this view. Pope Benedict's quotation in 2006 of a fourteenth-century scholar who linked Islam to violence reinforced the perceptions of clashing civilizations. However, these three monotheistic religions are closely related.[4] Cultural influences on international conflicts are generally analyzed as one component of a complex set of factors that motivate countries to go to war.[5]

The end of the Cold War brought a renewed focus on **ethnic conflicts**, generally understood as violent clashes between or among groups within a particular country. As we mentioned earlier, while some analysts view clashes between civilizations as the dominant feature of global politics, others see increased fragmentation of the world into violent ethnic groups. Both perspectives share the common assumption that world conflicts are fueled by ancient hatreds and irreconcilable cultural differences. Another assumption is that ethnic identities motivate people to persecute and kill. A third assumption is that ethnic diversity, enhanced by globalization, inevitably leads to ethnic conflicts.[6] We will frame our discussion at three levels of analysis: civilizations, nations, and ethnic groups.

CULTURAL INFLUENCES ON CONFLICTS

Culture and nationalism have generally been closely intertwined. In fact, culture has been synonymous with nations, races, and ethnic groups. Nations have traditionally been defined in terms of their common identity, values, customs, languages, and geographic boundaries. How nations and nonstate actors, such as ethnic groups, interact and resolve disagreements is determined largely by the cultural reservoirs created among them or the lack of them. A **cultural reservoir** may be defined as an accumulation of goodwill and understanding that emanates from a common set of values, beliefs, attitudes, historical experiences, and racial and ethnic links. Similarities are augmented by international exchanges, military alliances, interpersonal connections, and economic interdependence. When disputes between countries or ethnic groups occur, cultural reservoirs, or the lack of them, play a pivotal role in how differences are resolved. Leaders usually draw upon cultural similarities to diminish tensions and, conversely, upon cultural differences and hatreds to promote conflict. Cultural reservoirs strengthen the perception that friendly relations between culturally similar countries or groups are the norm and that a particular disagreement is a deviation from an otherwise

Jihad ■ Arabic word symbolizing a religiously based inner struggle between "good" and "evil" that exists within all people

Hybridization ■ Stresses cultural mixing due to increasing globalization

Ethnic Conflicts ■ Generally understood as violent clashes between or among groups within a particular country

Cultural Reservoir ■
An accumulation
of goodwill and
understanding that
emanates from a
common set of val-
ues, beliefs, attitudes,
experiences, and
racial and ethnic links

Material Culture ■
Tangible products of
human society

**Nonmaterial Cul-
ture** ■ Intangible
products of society,
such as values and
rules of right and
wrong behavior

Culture ■ A set of
shared learned
values, beliefs, per-
ceptions, attitudes,
modes of living, cus-
toms, and symbols

Subculture ■ A
subgroup that exists
within a larger cul-
tural group

Ethnocentrism ■
Practice of societies
promoting their
values as positive
and desirable while
simultaneously
devaluing those of
other societies

peaceful and amicable relationship. On the other hand, absence of strong cultural links and of significant economic interaction between states often facilitates indifference or hostility.[7] Yet culturally similar countries have clashed militarily, and culturally distant countries have been allies when significant interests were perceived to be at stake. For example, Russia cooperated with the United States during the Napoleonic Wars, in an effort to keep an emerging America from formally joining France, and again during both World Wars. On the other hand, Britain and the United States fought each other in the American Revolution and in the War of 1812, with Russia acting as a mediator in the latter.[8]

Anthropologists, sociologists, and political scientists define culture in different ways. A distinction can be made between **material culture** (i.e., the tangible products of human society) and **nonmaterial culture** (i.e., the intangible products of society, such as values and rules of right and wrong behavior). Nonmaterial culture is the learned ideational aspects of human society.[9] In most countries, culture is generally equated with civilization. The clash-of-civilizations theory adopts this definition of culture. **Culture** is generally defined as a set of shared learned values, beliefs, perceptions, attitudes, modes of living, customs, and symbols. According to Clifford Geertz, "The concept of culture denotes an historically transmitted pattern of meanings embodied in symbols, a system of inherited conception expressed in symbolic form by means of which men communicate, perpetuate, and develop their knowledge about and attitudes toward life."[10] The concept of culture is understood in a pluralist sense as differentiation within a collectivity. Subcultures are the bedrock of a pluralist view of culture. A **subculture** "is the way of defining and honoring the particular specification and demarcation of different interests of a group of people within a larger collectivity."[11] Emile Durkheim, in *Division of Labor*, articulated the view that as societies become more complex, cultural consensus is weakened. Divergent attitudes and values develop, and beliefs and attitudes are modified in ways that are significantly different from those prescribed or proscribed by the collective conscience or a strongly defined moral consensus.[12]

One of the first questions we tend to ask someone who appears to be different is, Where are you from? This question, though routine, goes to the heart of identity and belonging. Do you belong to this society? Are you foreign? All societies, directly and indirectly, promote their values as positive and desirable while, simultaneously, devaluing those of other societies. This behavior is referred to as **ethnocentrism**. Positive images of one's society are developed and reinforced by rewards for conformity. Ken Booth, for example, contends that each society views itself as the center of the world, perceives and interprets other societies within its peculiar frame of reference, and invariably judges them to be inferior.[13] The more culturally distinct the other society is perceived to be, the more inferior it is often deemed to be and thus suitable for negative treatment.

Cultural beliefs, attitudes, and values of ordinary people help to shape decisions to engage in conflicts, the objectives of conflicts, how wars are fought, how they are terminated, and postconflict relations among combatants. Leaders often tap into their cultures to find ways to dehumanize and demonize those designated as enemies. The greater the distance between cultures in conflict, the easier it is for leaders to mobilize public support for war and to dehumanize others. Dehumanization of others is designed not only to destroy the humanity of others but also to reassure those who dehumanize of their own presumed goodness. Dehumanization facilitates the justification of the inhumane treatment of those regarded as enemies by diminishing empathetic faculties.[14] Empathy, viewed as the emotional cornerstone of moral judgment, enables us to feel with other human beings, to cognitively and effectively put ourselves in their place, and to become more aware of others' needs and concerns.[15] Personalizing the injurious effects experienced by others makes their suffering much more noticeable and troubling. It is therefore difficult to kill people we do not dehumanize without risking personal distress and self-censure.[16] Dehumanization is closely related to moral exclusion, a practice that is intertwined with cultural values. Those who are morally excluded are perceived as being outside the boundary within which moral values, rules, and considerations of fairness apply. Because those who are morally excluded are regarded as expendable, subhuman, threatening, and undeserving, harming them often appears acceptable, appropriate, and just.[17]

CLASHING CIVILIZATIONS

According to the clash-of-civilizations perspective, global conflicts occur due to cultural differences. Although nationstates will continue to be the most powerful actors in global affairs, civilizations will be the dividing lines. A civilization is broadly defined as a cultural entity that, despite variations within it, is distinct from another civilization. For example, despite differences between Spain and Britain, they belong to the same Western civilization and are distinguished from Arab or Chinese civilizations. Huntington states that "a civilization is the highest cultural grouping of people and the broadest level of cultural identity people have short of that which distinguished humans from other species. It is defined by common objective elements, such as language, history, religion, customs, institutions, and by the subjective self-identification of people."[18] From Huntington's perspective, *there are eight major civilizations:* Western, Confucian, Japanese, Islamic, Hindu, Slavic-Orthodox, Latin American, and African.[19] The clash-of-civilizations theory stresses conflict instead of cooperation among civilizations.[20]

Many scholars have criticized the clash-of-civilizations perspective. For example, Fouad Ajami argues that "Huntington has found his civilization whole and intact, watertight under an eternal sky. Buried alive, as it were, during the Cold War, these civilizations rose as soon as the stone was rolled off, dusted themselves off, and proceeded to claim the loyalty of their adherents."[21] Similarly, Stanley Hoffmann criticized Huntington's concept of what constitutes a civilization as being hazy. From Hoffmann's perspective, Huntington "failed to take into account sufficiently conflicts within each so-called civilization, and he overestimated the importance of religion in the behavior of non-Western elites, who are often secularized and westernized. Hence he could not clearly define the link between a civilization and the foreign policies of its member states."[22] Civilizational bonds have not restrained countries from competing with each other for power. Furthermore, civilizations are products of cultural cross-fertilization. Their members are complex, and the lines separating civilizations are often blurred and messy. For example, music by Haydn, Mozart, and Beethoven have Turkish origins. The Ottomans used giant war drums and cannons to frighten their enemies on the battlefield and to terrify the population in places like Vienna, Austria. Eventually, West Europeans adopted many Turkish cultural practices, including its military music for its marching bands. Haydn wrote his *Military Symphony,* and Mozart composed the piano sonata *Rondo Alla Turca* under the influence of Turkish music.[23]

Religion, a foundation of civilizations, is regarded by Huntington as essentially pure and unaffected by other religions. The mixing of religions is as old as human civilization. As Susanne Rudolph observes, "Religious communities are among the oldest of the transnationals. Sufi orders, Catholic missionaries, and Buddhist monks carried word and practice across vast spaces before those places became nationstates. Religious communities have become vigorous creators of an emergent transnational civil society."[24] The forces of globalization are contributing to the spread of religions across national and civilizational boundaries. As you look around any major metropolitan area, you will see Protestant and Catholic churches, Muslim mosques, Hindu temples, Sikh gurdwaras, Jewish synagogues, and Buddhist temples. More than 60 percent of Christians are found in Africa, Asia, and Latin America. The Republic of Korea has four times as many Presbyterians as America. While Christianity is growing rapidly in China, it is shrinking in Europe. Missionaries from Africa reinvigorate Christianity in the United States. Muslims, including some Latin American immigrants, are an integral component of American culture and society.

The West and the Muslim World

At the heart of the theory of the inevitability of cultural clashes between the West and the Muslim world is the assumption that the two civilizations are inherently incompatible and hostile. But Western perceptions of Islam, like perceptions in general, are rooted in selective historical memories. Cooperation and similarities between these cultures are overlooked or downplayed while historical conflicts are stressed. Despite the Muslim conquest of part of Spain in the eighth century, Muslims were largely tolerant of Jews and Christians, regarding them as **Dhimmis** (i.e., people of the Book who also believed in one God, the God of Abraham). The advent of the Crusades in 1096 aided the foundation for the clashes between the West and Islam. The Crusades became a potent experience that continues to influence many Muslims' perceptions of the West and their own self-perceptions. The Crusaders' brutality symbolized Western hatred not only of Muslims but also of Islam.

A small number of European Christians regularly made pilgrimages to the Holy Land (then Palestine) since the fourth century without encountering systematic or widespread violence. However, in 1009, the Egyptian caliph (religious ruler) Hakim ordered the destruction of the Holy Sepulcher in Jerusalem (where Christians believed that Jesus was buried). This action engendered increased conflicts between Christian pilgrims and Muslims in Syria and Palestine. Hoping to unite European Christians, who were engaged in incessant feudal warfare against each other, and to terminate attacks on pilgrims, **Pope Urban II** (in 1095) called on European Christians to proclaim their faith by taking military action to force the infidels (primarily Muslims) out of Jerusalem. The First Crusade (1096–1099)

Dhimmis ■ People of the Book who also believe in the God of Abraham

Pope Urban II ■ Initiated the Crusades

represented unprecedented European cooperation as well as Europe's emergence from the Dark Ages. There were nine Crusades. The final Crusade (1271–1272) was followed by the Muslim reconquest of the last Christian stronghold in the Islamic world in 1291. Armstrong states, "The Christianity of the Angles, the Saxons, and the Franks was rudimentary. They were aggressive and martial people and they wanted an aggressive religion."[25] Crusaders, believing that Jews had killed Christ, slaughtered Jews in communities along the Rhine Valley and elsewhere on their three-thousand-mile journey to fight Muslims, about whom they were largely unaware. Believing that they were "God's Chosen People," the Crusaders were unrestrained in their cruelty. When they conquered Jerusalem in 1099, "they fell on the Jewish and Muslim inhabitants with the zeal of Joshua and massacred them with a brutality that shocked even their contemporaries."[26] The ability of the less culturally sophisticated European Christians to plunder and defile Islam's holy sites, including the **Dome of the Rock** in Jerusalem, has been interpreted by many Muslims as a consequence of their religious shortcomings. Contemporary Muslim grievances are often linked to the Crusades. Believing that Islam continues to be attacked by the West, many Muslims feel an obligation to engage in jihad (or holy war) against unbelievers. The establishment of the state of Israel in 1948 and the Palestinian-Israeli conflict combine to reignite clashes between the West and Islam.

Dome of the Rock ■ One of Islam's holy sites in Jerusalem

The Palestinian-Israeli Conflict

The Palestinian-Israeli conflict is rooted in rampant anti-Semitism throughout most of Europe, culminating in the Holocaust in Nazi Germany. But Jewish interest in a homeland cannot be divorced from the destruction of Jerusalem by the Romans and the exile of the Jewish people. The tragedy of European Jews led ultimately to the Palestinian tragedy. In a very real sense, both Jews and Palestinians became victims of Hitler's hatred of the Jews. Contrary to popular assumptions, the Palestinian-Israeli problem and the wider Arab-Israeli conflict are not rooted in ancient hatreds between Jews and Muslims, as is evident from our discussion of the Muslims in Spain and the Crusades. Circumstances in Europe influenced the emergence of Zionism and **Theodor Herzl's** determination to establish a Jewish state. Arab revolts against the Ottoman Empire in 1916, the capture of Jerusalem by the British from the Turks in 1917, and the subsequent British control over Palestine under the League of Nations mandate system paved the way for establishing a Jewish homeland in Palestine. As a Class A mandate, Palestine was technically an independent state under British supervision. The United States played a minor role in the critical events that became the roots of the Palestinian-Israeli conflict. U.S. President Woodrow Wilson endorsed the Balfour Declaration, issued by British Foreign Secretary Lord Balfour in 1917 in a letter to Lord Rothschild, an advocate of a Jewish homeland. The **Balfour Declaration** called for a Jewish homeland in Palestine that would not replace the Palestinian state. But British actions as well as clarifications of the Balfour Declaration added to confusion and angst among both Arabs and Jews. The **Churchill White Paper**, issued by Britain's Prime Minister Winston Churchill to clarify the Balfour Declaration, reaffirmed that Palestine was not to be converted into a "Jewish National Home." It further

Theodor Herzl ■ Early Zionist proponent of the creation of a Jewish homeland and state

Balfour Declaration ■ British statement calling for a Jewish homeland in Palestine

Churchill White Paper ■ Stated that the British were committed to Palestinian and Jewish coexistence in Palestine

FIGURE 14.1

Israel and the Palestinian Territories

emphasized that the British government would not contemplate the disappear-
ance or subordination of the Arab population, language, or culture in Palestine.[27]
Compounding the misunderstanding and feelings of betrayal among Arabs was
the rapidly increasing Jewish immigration to Palestine between 1922 and 1939 due
to horrifying events in Nazi Germany and many countries' refusal to allow the
immigration of Jewish refugees seeking to escape from the impending Holocaust.

   Frustrated by their inability to move the British more decisively toward establishing a Jewish state in Palestine, Zionists shifted their lobbying efforts to the
United States. They organized the **Biltmore Conference** in New York in May
1942 to articulate their objectives and to pressure the United States to persuade
Britain to act in their favor. But strategic considerations during the war forced
U.S. President Franklin Delano Roosevelt to balance his sympathies toward Zionist
aspirations against Allied military strategy. With German forces in North Africa
and the eastern Mediterranean, the United States concluded that Arab support
was essential to defending the Middle East.[28] American and Soviet opposition
to British imperial designs in the Middle East led to a tacit alliance between
Washington and Moscow in favor of the Jews at the end of World War II. Weakened

**Biltmore Confer-
ence** ■ Zionist lob-
bying effort to
pressure the United
States to persuade
Britain to act in favor
of a Jewish home-
land in Palestine

by war and a terrorist campaign by the Irgun and other groups, Britain became more vulnerable to American pressure. Britain relinquished control of Palestine, turning over the Palestinian problem to the fledgling United Nations (UN). While the United States supported the UN vote on the creation of Israel and recognized the new state literally minutes after it came into existence on May 14, 1948, Britain abstained on the UN vote and did not recognize Israel until a year later. Attempting to maintain Arab support, the United States embargoed arms sales to the Middle East in 1947 and did not play a major role in the first Arab-Israeli war of 1948–1949.[29]

Many of Israel's policies directly conflicted with America's new global responsibilities, including its efforts to prevent Communist expansion into the oil-rich and strategically important Middle East. Alienating the Arab states was contrary to America's strategy of **containment**, a policy of establishing a strategic alliance between North Atlantic Treaty Organization (NATO) and Middle Eastern countries to frustrate Soviet ambitions in the region. Consequently, the United States opposed the attack by Israel, Britain, and France on Egypt in 1956. By the Six-Day War in 1967, however, the United States had moved away from its position of impartial friendship and neutrality in the Arab-Israeli conflict to overt support for Israel. The 1967 war resulted in the defeat of the Arab armies and Israel's occupation of Palestinian, Syrian, and Egyptian territories. The city of Jerusalem and other holy places of great significance to Jews, Muslims, and Christians came under Israel's control. When Egypt and Syria launched a surprise attack against Israel on Yom Kippur in 1973, the United States responded by organizing a massive airlift of military supplies to Israel and by engaging in unprecedented diplomatic efforts to end hostilities. The Arabs responded with an oil embargo against Israel's supporters, including the United States.[30] By 1979, the United States, led by President Jimmy Carter, had managed to persuade Egypt and Israel to sign the **Camp David Peace Accords**, which ended hostilities between the two countries, returned Egyptian territory, and promised Palestinian autonomy by May 26, 1980. Despite much effort to reach a negotiated settlement of the Palestinian-Israeli conflict, violence escalated. In 1987, the Palestinians launched an **intifada** (i.e., uprising) to improve their living conditions and gain a homeland.

Following the first Gulf War in 1991, President George H. W. Bush initiated a peace conference on the Palestinian-Israeli conflict that culminated in the Oslo Accord in 1993. This agreement called for Israel's gradual withdrawal from Palestinian territory in the West Bank and Gaza. Failure of the Oslo peace process was accompanied by violence throughout the 1990s, a development that influenced President Bill Clinton to persuade Ehud Barak (Israel's prime minister) and Yasser Arafat (head of the Palestine Liberation Organization and chairman of the Palestinian Authority) to attempt to resolve all of the major issues in the conflict at Camp David in 2000. This failed endeavor eventually contributed to the outbreak of a second intifada between 2000 and 2005, during which more than three thousand Palestinians and one thousand Israelis were killed. This upsurge in violence was also characterized by the widespread use of suicide bombers against Israelis by Hamas and other Palestinian groups as well as by increased Israeli military action against Palestinians, targeted assassinations of Palestinian militants, the

Containment ■ U.S. policy of establishing strategic alliances with other countries to contain Soviet ambitions throughout the world

Camp David Peace Accords ■ 1979 peace agreement between Egypt and Israel

Intifada ■ Palestinian uprising against Israeli occupation of the West Bank and the Gaza Strip intensification of economic hardships for Palestinians, the expansion of Jewish settlements in the West Bank and Gaza, and the construction of a barrier or wall that balkanized Palestinian territory and brought Palestinian land under Israel's control. Following the U.S. invasion and occupation of Iraq in 2003, President George W. Bush linked the overthrow of Saddam Hussein to a "road map for peace" between Israel and the Palestinians. An essential component of the road map was the establishment of a Palestinian state. Arafat's death in late 2004 and the election of Mahmoud Abbas, also known as Abu Mazen, as president of the Palestinian Authority facilitated negotiations between the Palestinians and Israelis. Both Israel's Prime Minister Ariel Sharon and President Bush, viewing Arafat as corrupt, an impediment to peace, and a supporter of terrorism against Israel, refused to work with him to resolve the conflict. Encouraged by the United States and Egypt, Sharon and Abbas held a summit at the **Sharm el-Sheikh** resort in Egypt in February 2005, during which they pledged to "stop all violence against all Israelis and Palestinians everywhere." However, Abbas's inability to exercise effective control over Palestinian militants and Israel's unilateral determination of the borders of a Palestinian state, together with issues such as the status of Jerusalem, Jewish settlements in Palestinian territory, and the return of and compensation for Palestinian refugees complicated the road map to peace. In August 2005, Israel dismantled all of its settlements in Gaza and four in the West Bank. Palestinians demonstrated their frustrations with Fatah by giving Hamas, the radical Islamic party, a commanding majority of the legislative seats in elections held in January 2006. Hamas won 76 out of 132 seats, compared with 43 seats won by Fatah. This victory by Hamas, widely viewed as a terrorist group and strongly opposed to Israel, created new challenges for the Palestinian-Israeli conflict. In addition to the refusal of the international community to provide financial assistance to Hamas, Palestinians faced renewed Israeli military action in 2006. Israel's invasion of Lebanon, following Hezbollah's kidnapping of two Israeli soldiers, was accompanied by Israel's capture of Hamas officials, thereby negatively affecting efforts to negotiate an end to the conflict. In 2007, Hamas seized control of Gaza and fought Fatah. Israel maintained dialogue only with Fatah leaders. In November 2007, the United States arranged an international peace conference at Annapolis, Maryland, to encourage the Israelis and the Palestinians to reach a peace treaty by the end of 2008. Such an agreement would establish a Palestinian state and help make Israel more secure. However, increased violence and the building of new settlements by Israel on Palestinian land in 2008 and 2009 made both peace and a Palestinian state elusive.

Sharm el-Sheikh ■
Resort in Egypt where Israelis and Palestinians pledged to end violence against each other

The United States and Islam

Deeply shocked by massive terrorist attacks by al-Qaeda in the United States on September 11, 2001, many Americans asked why Muslims hated them. To answer this question, many U.S. politicians, scholars, and commentators retrieved the clash-of-civilizations theory and downplayed analysis of complex causes of terrorism. President Bush declared on September 15, 2001, that "this crusade, this war on terrorism is going to take a while," thereby stunning many Muslims.[31] For Muslims, a crusade evokes a highly emotional historical experience that laid the foundation for their interactions with the West. Furthermore, the clash-of-civilizations theory, with its assumption of a monolithic Islamic civilization, frustrated many Muslims who are aware of the diversity within the Islamic world and who also face terrorist threats from the Islamic extremists. The clash-of-civilization theme was reiterated by Bush in 2006 on the fifth anniversary of the September 11 attack when he asserted that the United States was in a struggle for civilization. Although cultural differences have contributed to conflicts between the United States and particular Muslim countries, specific national interests were by far the most important influences. The first significant clash was between a fledgling United States and the **Barbary States**, or North Africa (Tunisia, Algeria, Morocco, and Libya or Tripolitania). As part of its wars with Spain, the Ottoman Empire, which controlled the Barbary States, encouraged piracy against Spain. Barbary pirates enslaved Europeans and Americans and demanded tribute (payment) from European and American commercial interests. U.S. President Thomas Jefferson eventually tried to end this piracy by sending the U.S. Marines "to the shores of Tripoli" (1801–1805).

> **Barbary States** ■ Practiced piracy against the United States; place where the United States first clashed with Muslims

The United States maintained a neutral approach to the region until the Six-Day War of 1967. As American petroleum companies became more deeply involved in the Middle East and as Britain reduced its role in the region after World War II, the United States developed closer relations with strategically important Islamic countries. Consequently, America was also increasingly perceived by many Muslims as colonial Europe's replacement. Muslims' perceptions of American indifference to Palestinian suffering as well as increasing globalization influence contemporary U.S. relations with the Muslim world. Globalization, especially American culture, both attracts and repels. Ajami observes that "in the burning grounds of the Muslim world and on its periphery, U.S. embassies and their fate in recent years bear witness to a duality of the United States as Satan and redeemer. The embassies targeted by the masters of terror are besieged by visa-seekers dreaming of the golden, seductive country."[32] Globalization reinforces connections between some Muslims and the United States while, simultaneously, undermining traditional society, compounding inequality, and generating feelings of alienation and insecurity.

The rise of militant Islam coincides with the growth of Islamic fundamentalists, whom many believe they are engaged in an apocalyptic struggle with Western infidels. Some Islamic militants believe that by attacking the United States, viewed as a strong supporter of Israel, they will eventually reconquer Jerusalem from Israel or even destroy Israel itself. But Islamic militancy is also linked to U.S. involvement in Muslim countries. For example, American actions in Iran contributed to contemporary conflicts between the West and Islam. When Iranian students discovered America's role in the 1953 overthrow of Iran's Prime Minister Mohammad Mossadeq from declassified U.S. Central Intelligence Agency documents in 1978, they engaged in mass demonstrations against the United States and the Iranian government, led by **Shah Muhammad Reza**. Widespread opposition to the Shah culminated in the Islamic Revolution, which forced the Shah out of Iran in 1979, and facilitated Ayatollah Khomeini's return to Iran from exile in France. American diplomats were taken hostage and demonstrators occupied the American embassy. Although secularists who supported the revolution wanted to develop democracy in Iran, the Ayatollah's followers were able to create an Islamic political system.[33]

> **Shah Muhammad Reza** ■ Iranian leader responsible for high levels of repression committed against the Iranian people

Egyptian Islamic Jihad ■ Islamist group responsible for the 1981 assassination of Egypt's President Anwar Sadat

Mujahedeen ■ Holy warriors who traveled to Afghanistan to fight the Soviet occupation

Ironically, peace between Egypt and Israel also fueled the emergence of extremist Islamic groups in Egypt, such as **Egyptian Islamic Jihad**, which was responsible for the assassination of Egypt's President Anwar Sadat in 1981. Sadat was killed because he signed the Camp David Accords with Israel and because of Egypt's close links with the United States. Egyptian Islamic Jihad was strengthened by Muslims who went to Afghanistan to fight with the **mujahedeen** (i.e., holy warriors) to resist Soviet occupation of that country. When the Soviets invaded Afghanistan in 1979, the United States provided military assistance to the mujahedeen. Osama bin Laden, from Saudi Arabia, also joined the mujahedeen. Assisted by veterans from Afghanistan's war, Egyptian Islamic Jihad carried out a series of bombings against U.S. targets, including American embassies in Kenya and Tanzania in 1998, and cooperated with al-Qaeda, led by bin Laden.[34]

Sources of Muslim hatred of the United States are found within many Islamic countries. Many Arab governments are authoritarian and have used their considerable economic resources from petroleum to preserve the status quo. Barry Rubin argues that Muslim hatred of America is "largely the product of self-interested manipulation by groups that use anti-Americanism as a foil to distract public attention from other, far more serious problems within those societies."[35] It is generally agreed that the spread of Islamic fundamentalism is, to some extent, a product of deteriorating economic conditions, growing economic inequality, rapid population growth, rural-to-urban migration, and declines in social services, health care, and educational opportunities. Furthermore, increasing Westernization of these countries is perceived by traditionalists as undermining Islam, the foundation of their societies. America is viewed as corrupting these countries' elites and humiliating Muslims. America's invasion of Iraq, widely perceived as an effort to consolidate its power in the Middle East, has heightened Arab anti-Americanism. Widely disseminated photographs of Americans abusing Iraqi prisoners at the **Abu Ghraib** prison in Iraq served to confirm Muslim perceptions of the United States. The acts of brutality, sadism, and dehumanization that occurred at Abu Ghraib demonstrated to Muslims that America regarded them as culturally distant and excludable from moral considerations that govern its own society. U.S. sanctions against the Hamas government and the U.S. refusal to pressure Israel to exercise restraint when it invaded Lebanon in 2006 reinforced perceptions throughout the Muslim world that America was indifferent to the plight of both the Palestinians and the Lebanese. In an effort to change these perceptions, President Barack Obama traveled to Turkey, Saudi Arabia, and Egypt in 2009. In a major speech at Cairo University on June 4, 2009, President Obama downplayed differences between Islam and the United States and stressed that he wanted to base American relations with Muslims on mutual respect and mutual interests.[36]

Abu Ghraib ■ Prison in Iraq where Americans abused and tortured prisoners

CLASHES AMONG NATIONS

Clashes among nations within the same civilization are common realities of international relations. For example, France and Britain sharpened their national identities through constant conflict with each other. Linda Colley contends that "Britain was an invention forged above all by war. Time and time again, war with

France brought Britons, whether they hailed from Wales or Scotland or England, into confrontation with an obviously hostile other and encouraged them to define themselves collectively against it."[37] The consolidation of diverse cultural groupings within England, France, Spain, and Germany was an essential component of the rise of national identity and nationalism. Growing nationalism culminated in clashes with the Catholic Church and the Holy Roman Empire. This clash within Western civilization elevated states above civilizations. Following the conclusion of the Peace of Westphalia in 1648, marking the birth of the nationstate, European countries routinely engaged in wars to settle boundary disputes, underscoring not only the territoriality of states but also their preoccupation with who belongs to them.

A combination of cultural distance and threatened national interests makes international conflicts more likely, partly because negotiations with distant others are generally downplayed or rejected. Two wars between the United States and Iraq (in 1991 and 2003) demonstrate this point. Many Americans lack close relationships with Arabs and few are knowledgeable of Arab history and culture. Few believe that they share many common cultural values with Arabs. Instead, Americans generally rely on negative stereotypes when dealing with them. The Arab oil embargo in 1973–1974 etched a negative view of Arabs in American minds, which was reinforced by the terrorist attacks on the United States in 2001. Often Arabs are perceived as dangerous, untrustworthy, immoral, undemocratic, barbaric, and primitive.[38] Iraq's leader, Saddam Hussein, reinforced these stereotypes. But American cultural values also played a significant role in conflicts with Iraq. In both wars, disputes with Iraq were framed in terms of good versus evil. The United States also viewed the wars as transformative: Saddam Hussein's destruction would bring peace and democracy to the Middle East and resolve the Palestinian-Israeli conflict. A major criticism of the United States in both wars was that it hastily embraced action to resolve the problems. Although both wars remain controversial, cultural distance and cultural values on both sides influenced decisions to go to war.[39]

The United States' reliance on force to resolve conflicts and its handling of international relations reinforced negative views held by the global community against it. Minxim Pei states that "today's strident anti-Americanism represents much more than a wimpy reaction to U.S. resolve or generic fears of a hegemon running amok. Rather, the growing unease with the United States should be seen as a powerful global backlash against the spirit of American nationalism that shapes and animates U.S. foreign policy."[40] This anti-Americanism is found among close European allies, in rich and poor countries, and in Christian as well as Islamic countries, a reality that directly challenges the clash-of-civilizations theory. Historically, countries threatened by a hegemonic power usually form alliances to balance that power. Fareed Zakaria argues that "by crudely asserting U.S. power and disregarding international institutions and alliances, the Bush administration pulled the curtain on decades of diplomacy and revealed that the United States' constraints are self-imposed."[41] From the European perspective, American power must be constrained. As Robert Jervis put it, "They fear a world in which their values and interests are served only at Washington's sufferance."[42] But great powers often experience a sense of permanent insecurity. Their quest for the illusive absolute security makes other countries feel less secure, which often engenders conflicts. By strongly supporting the UN and multilateral action to resolve disputes, the United States reduced global opposition to its overwhelming power. Conversely, America's unilateral exercise of military might created fears among Europeans and others who perceive the UN as playing an essential role in promoting global governance. Furthermore, as America grows more nationalistic, Europeans are concentrating on building European political and economic cooperation. In sharp contrast with the United States, which is widely perceived as carrying the mantle of masculine Mars, the Europeans are combining military power and diplomacy and are emerging as "the world's first metrosexual superpower."[43]

International conflicts that are influenced by cultural differences and divergent national interests are also prevalent in Asia. China's rapid economic expansion and growing U.S. dependence on imports from China have engendered both cooperation and conflict between the two countries. China is widely perceived as a rising power that will eventually compete with America for global hegemony. Its strong economy attracts advanced technology from around the world, which enables it to improve its military capabilities. Japan's historical rivalry with China is reinvigorated by Japan's economic problems and the transfer of some of its manufacturing industries to China. Nationalism in both China and Japan is resurging, even as economic cooperation between them strengthens. North Korea's decision to test nuclear devices in 2006 and 2009 further reinforced Japan's nationalism and security concerns.

ETHNIC CONFLICTS

Horrific bloodshed in Rwanda, Bosnia, Sudan, Iraq, Chechnya, and elsewhere is widely publicized by the global media. The proliferation of humanitarian organizations and other nonstate actors has also helped to make the world more aware of ethnic conflicts. As our discussion of global terrorism in Chapter 5 demonstrates, European countries, such as Spain, are challenged by violent groups that claim separate ethnic identities. In fact, as Europe moves toward greater unification, minority groups—such as Catalans, Basques, Corsicans, Scots, and Flemish—are seeking more autonomy. However, most of these ethnic or nationalist groups are not violent.[44] Although the brutality and intractability of many ethnic conflicts tend to reinforce perceptions of escalating ethnic wars, there has actually been a decline in their number. Ted Robert Gurr identifies *four regional and global forces that help to explain the decline in the number of ethnic wars:*

1. The active promotion of democratic institutions and practices that protect minority rights.
2. Engagement by the UN, regional organizations, and nongovernmental organizations (NGOs) on behalf of minority rights.
3. The virtual consensus among the global foreign policy elite in favor of reestablishing and maintaining global and regional order.
4. The costs of ethnic conflicts, which have become evident to both governing elites and rebel leaders.[45]

TABLE 14.1

ETHNIC CONFLICTS

Country	Estimated Deaths	Description of Conflict
Nigeria	1 million (1966–1970)	Ibo region declared independence, calling itself Biafra
Angola	600,000 (1975–2002)	Civil War following independence from Portugal
East Timor	307,000 (1975–2000)	Struggle for independence against Indonesian occupation
Sri Lanka	70,000 (1983–2009)	Tamils fighting the Sinhalese government for a separate state
Iraq	45,000 Kurds and Shiites (1983–1992)	Suppression of rebellion against Saddam Hussein
Sudan (Darfur)	2 million (1983–2009)	Arab/Muslim North fighting Christian and animist South
Turkey	40,000 (1984–2009)	Kurdish groups fighting for autonomy
Sierra Leone	15,000 (1992–2000)	Attempt to overthrow the government
Burundi	250,000 (1993–1999)	Tutsis and Hutus fought after the president, a Hutu, was assassinated
Yugoslavia	400,000 (1994)	Serbs against Muslims and Croats
Rwanda	800,000 (1994)	Hutus slaughtered Tutsis and moderate Hutu
Congo (Zaire)	4 million (1997–2009)	Overthrow of Mobutu Sese Seko

While globalization contributes to cultural clashes, it also restrains them. Ethnic conflicts are much less pervasive or durable in areas that are integrated into the global economy than they are in countries that are relatively unaffected by global interdependence or regional integration.

Ethnicity and Ethnic Identity

Tribalism, ethnicity, and ethnic nationalism are terms that are often used interchangeably. **Tribalism** is usually regarded as an anachronistic term that refers to groups of indigenous people. Most scholars prefer to refer to these groups as ethnic groups. Sometimes ethnic groups are across the artificially created boundaries of several countries. Ethnic groups within states as well as those that straddle national boundaries may aspire to create their own country. To achieve this, they develop a strong sense of nationalism. For example, the **Kurds**, an ethnic group that has nationalistic aspirations, are scattered among Turkey, Iraq, Iran, Syria, and parts of the former Soviet Union. Most ethnic groups attempt to achieve more political and cultural autonomy within the boundaries of existing states.

An ethnic group is composed of individuals who generally have a sense of common identity based on a common set of historical experiences, national sentiments, religious beliefs, geographic location, language and culture, and, in countries such

Tribalism ■ Groups of indigenous people in Africa, Asia, Latin America, and North America

Kurds ■ An ethnic group residing in Turkey, Iraq, Iran, and Syria

Ethnicity ■ A subjective perception of who belongs to a particular ethnic group

Identity ■ A concept of oneself based on physical, psychological, emotional, or social attributes

Ethnic Pluralism ■ Also known as ethnic diversity

as the United States, largely arbitrary racial categories. **Ethnicity** is a subjective perception of who belongs to a particular group. Ethnicity serves as a rallying point for mobilizing ethnic group members to compete for economic resources, positions in government and social and economic organizations, and social and religious status.[46] An essential component of ethnicity is a strong sense of identity. **Identity** may be defined as a concept of the self, a selection of physical, psychological, emotional, or social attributes of particular individuals.[47] Identity provides a framework within which people construct reality and determine their positions on a wide range of issues. Members of different ethnic groups are predisposed to hold certain stereotypes about each other and to act on the basis of these assumptions.

Identity is generally about drawing sharp distinctions among groups and building boundaries that separate one group from another. It contributes to developing a feeling of us versus them, insiders versus outsiders. We treat members of our own group differently from members of another group. Discrimination on the basis of ethnic identity is a common problem worldwide. Instead of seeing discrimination as being inherently wrong and unfair, it becomes the norm. **Ethnic pluralism** (i.e., ethnic diversity) is the presence of many different groups within a specific geographic boundary. *Several factors contribute to ethnic pluralism.* These include

1. Conquest and annexation;
2. The decision by colonial powers to put different ethnic groups together in newly created countries;
3. The deliberate attempts by colonizers and others to divide people in order to control them; and
4. Migration.[48]

The Causes of Ethnic Conflict

Although conflicts between ethnic groups are often perceived as the result of "ancient hatreds," most ethnic conflicts are very complex and have little to do with ancient animosities. In all societies, generational change and economic and social developments generally modify ancient hatreds. Contemporary ethnic conflicts have more immediate causes. Although the Scots and the English fought each other for centuries, these ancient hatreds do not influence them to fight today. *Most ethnic wars occur in poor countries that have weak political institutions.* Paul Collier has found that once a country achieves a per capita income similar to those of rich countries, its risk of ethnic conflict is negligible. The potential for conflict is concentrated in the poorest countries with declining economies and a heavy reliance on natural resources for a large share of national income.[49] Think about the countries that suffer from perennial ethnic wars. These include Sudan, Angola, Rwanda, Sierra Leone, Afghanistan, and Turkey. Although many rich countries experience ethnic tensions, these problems generally do not erupt into sustained or widespread violence.

Another cause of ethnic conflict is *the deliberate manipulation of negative perceptions* by leaders to mobilize group support for their own individual political, economic, and social objectives. Leaders rely on the emotional intensity and loyalty of ethnic group members. They know that distrust can be instrumental in

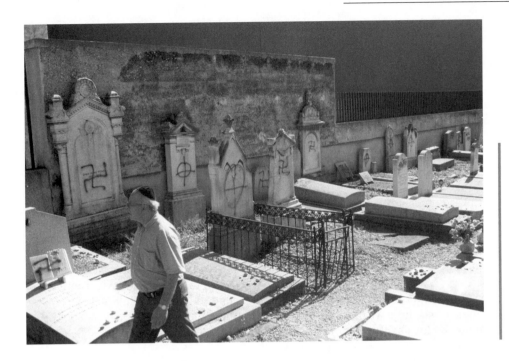

Jewish tomb-stones were scrawled with Nazi symbols and anti-Semitic and anti-Muslim slurs recently in Lyon, as part of a rash of neo-Nazi acts. Taken August 13, 2004.

fueling fears and that fears usually override logical, objective thinking. Consequently, despite misgivings individuals may have about engaging in or condoning violence against another group, these fears and an emotional commitment to their own group generally influence ethnic group members to follow their leaders. The most terrifying example is the violence in Rwanda that claimed as many as 800,000 lives in 1994. Hutus killed more than three-fourths of Rwanda's Tutsi population because Hutu political leaders incited fear and hatred among the Hutus in order to remain in power.

Competition among groups for scarce economic resources is a major cause of ethnic violence. Growing economic disparities, resulting from economic development, may increase the fears and insecurities of those ethnic groups that are disadvantaged. On the other hand, ethnic conflict may emanate from attempts by an ethnic group to monopolize scarce resources. In Nigeria, for example, the **Ibos** fought to create a separate country (called Biafra) partly because of their experience with violence and discrimination and because they did not want to share their wealth from petroleum found in their region of the country. The discovery of oil in the Sudan has contributed to humanitarian crisis in Darfur and the inability of the global community to prevent the deaths of roughly 200,000 people and the displacement of more than 2 million. Even prosperous groups sometimes feel insecure because the same forces of modernization that enrich them also make them vulnerable. Their status could deteriorate in a volatile global economic environment. Ethnic Chinese in Indonesia and elsewhere in Southeast Asia are often victims of ethnic conflicts due primarily to their economic success.

Cultural globalization, evidenced by the Westernization of architecture; the proliferation of fast-food restaurants; the influx of consumer items, automobiles,

Ibos ■ Ethnic group in Nigeria that tried to create a separate state (called Biafra)

television, movies, books, and magazines; and increased access to computers and telecommunications threaten ethnic groups' perception of the uniqueness and purity of their culture.[50] These forces of globalization help to destroy boundaries essential to ethnic group solidarity and identity. Many leaders' power is threatened, a development that often influences them to promote ethnic identity more zealously. *Weak political institutions* contribute to ethnic conflicts, especially when countries are experiencing economic transformation. The inabilities of political institutions to effectively regulate change and provide mechanisms through which differences can be managed frequently contribute to ethnic violence.

Systematic and widespread frustration of human needs may culminate in outbreaks of ethnic violence. Tensions are heightened by perceptions of favoritism toward other groups, compared with disadvantages suffered by the particular ethnic group. Ethnic group members are mobilized to articulate their grievances and to seek solutions to them.[51] In many cases, violence is seen as the most effective instrument to get the government to respond favorably to their demands. This, in turn, influences the government to respond with violence against the ethnic group. Finally, *the proliferation of automatic weapons*, especially AK-47s, is a significant contributor to ethnic conflicts around the world. While it may be argued that these weapons do not cause conflict, their availability increases the potential for deadly clashes among ethnic groups or the use of violence by ethnic groups against governments.

Although ethnic violence is clearly more prevalent in poor countries, developed countries are also experiencing ethnic tensions and renewed ethnic nationalism. Since the end of the Cold War and the fall of the Berlin Wall, there has been a resurgence of anti-Semitism in Europe, especially in France. Mark Strauss states

Kristallnacht ■
Nazi-led pogrom
against German Jews

that "not since **Kristallnacht**, the Nazi-led pogrom [violent campaign] against German Jews in 1938, have so many European synagogues and Jewish schools been desecrated."[52] One of the oldest hatreds in Europe, anti-Semitism is strongest in Alsace, France, a region that has strong cultural ties to Germany. This traditionally German-speaking area was annexed by Germany in 1871, following the Franco-Prussian War, and remained under German control until the French conquered it in World War I. Alsace became a Nazi stronghold in the 1930s, and many Alsatians joined the Nationalist Socialist Party (Nazi Party) when Alsace was annexed by Adolf Hitler in 1940. The worst German atrocity in France against the Jews was the massacre at Oradour in Alsace in 1944. This historical

National Front ■
Conservative French
political movement
led by Jean-Marie
Le Pen

affiliation with Nazism was rekindled by the rise of the **National Front**, an extremely conservative political movement led by Jean-Marie Le Pen. Both Jews and Muslims are targets of violence. There was a surge in 2004 in the number of Jewish and Muslim holy places, including tombstones, desecrated by neo-Nazis.[53] In April 2008, neo-Nazis desecrated 148 Muslim graves in the Notre Dame de Lorette cemetery in northern France.

The growing number of Muslims in countries across Europe is perceived as a threat to cultural institutions. This perception of threat escalated with the rise of Islamic terrorism and the terrorist attacks on the United States, Spain, and Britain between 2001 and 2007. But Germany, Austria, France, Britain, Spain, Italy, and other countries have been concerned about demographic changes brought about largely by Muslim immigrants. Many Europeans define their cultures in terms of

Christianity, but Muslims are making Islam a part of European culture. Religious symbols, especially the Muslim headscarf, have been politicized. France, stressing the separation of church and state, has been the most aggressive European country in terms of banning headscarves in public schools. Most Muslim girls complied with the law banning scarves, which went into effect in September 2004. And when kidnappers in Iraq threatened to kill two French hostages if France did not revoke the ban, most French Muslims, who opposed the law, supported France's refusal to change its laws to appease terrorists.

Canada and the United States, two of the world's most ethnically diverse countries, have managed to reduce ethnic violence by bringing various ethnic minorities into the democratic process and by outlawing discrimination. Canada was confronted with separatist movements in Quebec until recently. Quebec, colonized and settled by the French, was conquered by the British in 1759. The **Treaty of Paris** in 1763 officially transferred Quebec from France to Britain, making it part of British Canada. Many people in Quebec maintained close ties with France and nurtured French culture and language. Generational change, economic interdependence, political reforms, and increased immigration to Quebec combined to lessen nationalistic aspirations.[54] However, the growing numbers of Muslims in Canada, as well as that country's strong commitment to multiculturalism, have created new ethnic tensions. Autonomy granted to various Native American groups has inspired other ethnic groups to seek more cultural autonomy. Muslims, for example, point to Jews and their ability to use Jewish laws to govern their communities and argue that **Shari'a law** (Islamic law) should govern Muslim communities.

The fall of communism and the disintegration of the Soviet Union rekindled ethnic conflicts in Eastern Europe, Central Asia, the Balkans, and elsewhere. Ethnic conflicts in the former Yugoslavia produced widespread military confrontation in which ethnic identity literally became a matter of life and death. These conflicts also underscored how cultural links with various countries influenced both military actions and efforts to terminate the bloodshed. The Croats have historically been the most thoroughly integrated into European civilization, largely as a consequence of their domination by Austria-Hungary and Venice. Serbs identify with Eastern Orthodox countries, such as Greece and Russia, and the Muslims, though they are also Europeans and Slavic, are regarded as remnants of the Ottoman Empire and identify with Turkey and other Islamic countries. Composed of six republics—Bosnia-Herzegovina, Croatia, Macedonia, Montenegro, Serbia, and Slovenia—and the two provinces of Kosovo and Vojvodina, Yugoslavia was an artificial nationstate held together by **Marshall Josip Tito's** domineering personality and the League of Communists of Yugoslavia (LCY) until Tito's death in 1980 and the fall of communism in the late 1980s. As Yugoslavia's disintegration became obvious, the Republic of Serbia intensified its efforts to arrest Yugoslavia's fragmentation and to continue Serbia's dominance. Bosnia's Serbs, led by **Radovan Karadzic**, favored increased centralization, whereas the Muslims and Croats opted for a loose confederation. Acting on their fears of each other and remembering historical experiences, Croats and Serbs began to dismember Bosnia. Muslims, aware that Bosnia had been divided between Croatia and Serbia prior to World War II, resisted reabsorption into those states.[55] Serbia clearly intended to use its superior military might to fashion

Treaty of Paris ■ Transferred Quebec from France to Britain in 1763

Shari'a Law ■ Islamic law used to govern Muslim communities

Marshall Josip Tito ■ Communist leader who ruled Yugoslavia until his death in 1980

Radovan Karadzic ■ Bosnian leader who favored continued Serbian dominance of Yugoslavia

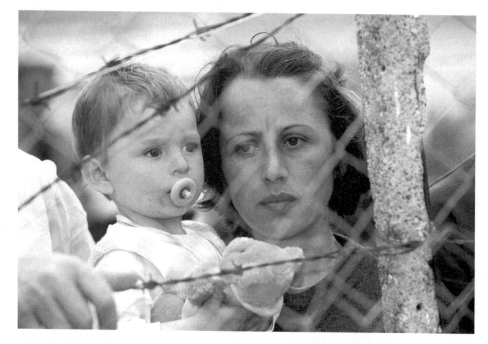

09 Apr 1999—
Kosovo Albanian
refugees being
supervised by
the Albanian
Army

(Jean-Paul Bajard/
Editing Server/New
York Times/Redux)

**Slobodan Milose-
vic** ■ President of
Yugoslavia who was
tried for war crimes
at the International
Criminal Court

Ethnic Cleansing ■
Mass forced reloca-
tion or expulsion of
one ethnic or reli-
gious group by
another ethnic or
religious group

Greater Serbia out of Croatia and Bosnia. **Slobodan Milosevic**, president of Yugoslavia (who was later tried for war crimes at the International Criminal Court at the Hague), boasted that the Serbs were on the threshold of "the final solution."[56] Milosevic died in prison in 2006.

Although Muslims and Croats engaged in their own campaigns of **ethnic cleansing**, the Serbs were primarily responsible for genocide and Muslims were the principal victims. After depriving Muslims of their jobs and property, the Serbs began to destroy their villages and cities and forced them to leave, thereby creating the greatest refugee crisis in Europe since World War II. Many refugees were shipped out of northern Bosnia in sealed freight trains, a practice reminiscent of Nazi Germany's treatment of the Jews. Atrocities included the massacre of villagers; the torture, rape, and killing of prisoners; the use of Muslims as human shields; and the taking of hostages. Many civilians, imprisoned in forty-five concentration camps, were executed. Serbian gunmen raped more than fifty thousand Muslim women and children as part of their program of ethnic cleansing. Echoing Nazi Germany's plan to exterminate the Jews and eliminate all traces of Jewish culture, Serb nationalists attempted to destroy the Muslims' culture. Mosques, central to Muslims' identity and society, were principal targets. Historical monuments and libraries that were depositories for more than five centuries of Muslim culture were reduced to rubble.[57]

Ethnic conflicts in Rwanda also demonstrate how ethnic differences are socially constructed and how deadly the consequences of policies exaggerating and emphasizing small differences can be. Genocide in Rwanda and genocide in Sudan illustrate that the decline in the number of ethnic conflicts globally is largely irrelevant to Africa, the continent most marginalized from globalization. As we discussed earlier, the world's poorest countries, most of which are in Africa, are the most vulnerable to prolonged and widespread ethnic violence. Africa also has a very large number of ethnic groups, many of which live together in artificially created countries. When the Germans conquered what is now Rwanda in 1899, they encountered two main groups: the **Hutus,** who comprised the majority of the population, and the **Tutsis,** a small group of cattle herders who ruled the area. Many smaller groups spoke the same language and shared the same culture. Years of intermarriage made it difficult to neatly separate them into distinct ethnic groups.[58] The Germans relied primarily on the ruling Tutsis to help them control the territory. They designated the Tutsis as the superior group, a perception reinforced by the Belgians who gained control of Rwanda in 1916, following Germany's defeat in World War I. Germany's and Turkey's colonies became mandates under the League of Nations. Finding it difficult to distinguish Hutus from Tutsis, the Belgians issued mandatory identity cards to all Rwandans, placing each person into a fixed ethnic category. Eventually the Tutsis, who received preferential treatment from the Belgians, believed that they were indeed superior to the Hutus.[59] However, Belgian missionaries, believing in equality and social progress, helped disadvantaged Hutus obtain an education. Educated Hutus, facing discrimination, challenged the system that gave Tutsis significant advantages and advocated ethnic separation. In 1959, the Hutus rebelled and killed more than twenty thousand Tutsis. When Rwanda became independent in 1962, the Hutu majority gained political control.

Ethnic rivalries escalated in 1990 when the Hutus' power was challenged by the Rwanda Patriotic Front army, composed of Tutsis. To restore a measure of peace and stability, moderate Hutus agreed to share power with the Tutsis. Hutu extremists responded by killing both Tutsis and moderate Hutus. When a plane carrying Rwanda's President Juvenal Habyarimana, a Hutu, crashed on April 6, 1994, ethnic violence erupted with a force that stunned the global community. Believing that Tutsis were responsible for destroying the plane, the Hutus circulated lists of names of those favoring democracy and national reconciliation. They set up roadblocks and demanded identity cards and systematically killed Tutsis. Students were slaughtered by their teachers, neighbors killed neighbors, and clergymen participated in the genocide. In many cases, husbands killed their families and then committed suicide to avoid a more terrible death.[60] About 800,000 people were slaughtered in thirteen weeks of fighting in Rwanda. In the aftermath of this genocide, Rwandan authorities decided to outlaw ethnic identity.[61]

Hutus ■ Majority group in Rwanda who committed genocide against the minority Tutsi population

Tutsis ■ Small group of cattle herders who had ruled Rwanda under German and Belgian colonization

RESOLVING CULTURAL CONFLICTS

In many ways, globalization was widely perceived as instrumental in creating a more harmonious world. Global markets and the promotion of democracy were believed to diminish violent clashes. Although the realization of Immanuel Kant's vision of perpetual peace seemed distant, many political scientists and others observed that democratic norms that emphasize compromise, persuasion, peaceful competition, the protection of minority rights, and so on would move the global community closer to Kant's vision. In other words, they assert that democracies rarely fight each other.[62] But, as we have seen, democracies fight countries that are not democratic, and poor, marginalized, and undemocratic countries fight each other and are often plagued with ethnic conflicts. Nevertheless, the end of the Cold War and increasing globalization contributed to a stronger global emphasis on peacefully resolving conflicts. UN Secretary General Boutros Boutros-Ghali, in his Agenda for Peace, a 1992 report written at the request of the UN Security Council, emphasized various techniques for resolving conflicts, such as preventive diplomacy, confidence-building measures, fact-finding, and preventive deployment. We will examine *four interrelated approaches to conflict resolution*: (1) negotiation, (2) peacekeeping (which includes humanitarian intervention), (3) peacemaking, and (4) peacebuilding.

Negotiation

Negotiation is back-and-forth communication to reconcile contradictory positions and conflicting interests in order to reach an agreement acceptable to the parties involved. Negotiation is principally concerned with helping your opponent make a particular decision. An important impetus for advancing proposals and making concessions and compromises is that there are common interests that can be secured through cooperation.[63] Each side must be willing to make those adjustments that are essential to reaching a compromise, thereby creating what Roger Fisher and William Ury in *Getting to Yes* call a win-win situation (where both sides gain) instead of taking a zero-sum approach (where one side wins and the other loses). But negotiation is not entirely separated from the use of coercion or violence. Most conflicts cannot be resolved by relying on either negotiation or the threat of force. Negotiations involve both **carrots** (inducements) and **sticks** (punishments).

Carrots and Sticks ■ Practice by which states rely on inducements and punishments in their relations with other states

Raymond Cohen stresses that cultural values directly influence negotiation strategies and the success of negotiations in *Negotiating Across Cultures*. When individuals, countries, and ethnic groups focus primarily on their underlying interests and objectives, they have a better chance of resolving disputes than if they allow their emotions and beliefs to dominate. Learning the other side's real interests necessitates a careful and patient probing of the needs, hopes, fears, perceptions, and cultural values that form their sense of what is threatening or vital to protecting their identity.[64] This requires willingness on the negotiator's part to listen actively to the other side and to put himself or herself in the other side's shoes, as it were. Active listening involves trying to hear and absorb the other side's views of the facts as distinct from one's own, to seek further clarification through questioning, and to process the information received in terms of the larger context of the situation and the issues of the movement.[65] In addition to active listening, negotiators must develop formulas or **trade-offs**. A trade-off is essentially an exchange to address the fears and interests of those involved. An example of a trade-off is the 1967 **UN Security Council Resolution 242**, which attempted to resolve the Middle East conflict by exchanging land for peace. Israel would withdraw its armed forces from territories it conquered and occupied in exchange for the Arabs' termination of belligerency against Israel and recognition of Israel's sovereignty and territorial boundaries.

Trade-offs ■ An exchange designed to address the interests of both groups involved in mediation

UN Security Council Resolution 242 ■ Attempted to resolve the Palestinian-Israeli conflict by exchanging land for peace

Numerous barriers impede successfully negotiating cultural conflicts. Perceptions often complicate negotiations between parties that have very different cultures. Information and facts that contradict our perceptions and images of ourselves and others are usually ignored or overlooked. Stereotypes impede the negotiating process between nations and ethnic groups that are culturally distant by fostering negative interpretations of motives behind actions that could be viewed as positive developments. Public opinion is also important. If citizens or ethnic group members believe that force is an effective and desirable means of dealing with disputes, leaders are likely to consider military action against the opponent. A society or group that perceives compromise as a sign of weakness is likely to produce leaders who devalue negotiations with adversaries.[66] Similarly, leaders and policymakers who perceive the world as hostile and conflict-ridden and who believe that only military force provides real security are generally likely to reject or downplay negotiations.

Peacekeeping and Humanitarian Intervention

Increasingly, the UN and regional organizations intervene militarily to end international and interethnic violence or to prevent it from escalating. This is called **peacekeeping**. A principal objective is to create an environment that is conducive to both humanitarian operations and negotiations. Peacekeeping missions are generally supported by the global community as well as the combatants. Nonstate actors—such as Amnesty International, Catholic Relief Services, Oxfam, and the International Committee of the Red Cross—cooperate with the UN and regional organizations. However, as the cases of Rwanda, Bosnia, Sudan, and East Timor demonstrate, the global community is often slow in responding to ethnic conflicts. Another issue raised in humanitarian intervention is the concept of a **just war**. *A just war must meet certain criteria:*

1. Support a just cause,
2. Be just in intent,
3. Be of last resort,
4. Have limited objectives,
5. Be proportional,
6. Be declared by legitimate authorities, and
7. Not involve noncombatants.

Peacemaking

Peacemaking, which generally occurs after peacekeeping has made significant progress, involves the intervention of neutral third parties. Their objective is to get the combatants to reach a political settlement through negotiations. These intermediaries rely on certain methods such as arbitration, mediation, and facilitation. **Arbitration** refers to "binding, authoritative third-party intervention in which conflict parties agree to hand the determination of a final settlement to outsiders."[67] **Mediation** is a process of facilitating communication between combatants to encourage them to brainstorm, invent options for mutual gains, try to see the other side's perception of reality and legitimate concerns, as well as help them understand difficulties that might prevent the other side from meeting their demands. Mediators generally have some leverage over parties to a conflict and are generally seen as impartial. **Facilitation** is a cooperative, nonhierarchal, and noncoercive approach to conflict resolution. Facilitation attempts to get those involved in conflict to see the problem as a shared problem that requires cooperation to be solved. The third party's objective is to get the adversaries to engage in joint decisionmaking to reach a settlement that is self-sustaining.[68]

Peacekeeping ■ International intervention designed to limit or end state interethnic violence

Just War ■ War fought for noble, humanitarian purposes

Peacemaking ■ Intervention intended to convince combatants to reach a political settlement through peaceful negotiations

Arbitration ■ Negotiations under which a third party determines the final settlement between two conflicting groups

Mediation ■ Process of facilitating communication between combatants in order to reach a peaceful settlement of disputes

Facilitation ■ Cooperative, noncoercive approach to conflict resolution that seeks to get conflicting parties to acknowledge a shared problem that requires cooperation to be solved

Women and Peacemaking

The proliferation of women's peace groups in the 1980s reinvigorated the view that women have historically been leading proponents of nonviolent settlements of disputes. Such groups as the Women's International League for Peace and Freedom challenged World War I and supported the Comprehensive Test Ban Treaty. Swanee Hunt and Cristina Posa argue that women are more collaborative than men and are thus more inclined toward compromise. Furthermore, given their roles as family nurturers, women have a huge investment in the stability of their communities. They believe that allowing men who plan wars to plan peace is a bad habit. They stress the need to include more women, regarded as peace promoting, in efforts to negotiate peaceful solutions to conflicts.

1. Are women better than men at peacemaking?
2. Have women leaders approached issues of war and peace differently than men? Give some examples.

Source: Swanee Hunt and Cristina Posa, "Women Waging Peace," *Foreign Policy* 124 (May/June 2001), 38–41. ■

Peacebuilding

Peacebuilding ■
Long-term process of implementing social change through economic development, political reforms, and territorial compromises

Peacebuilding is a long-term process of implementing peaceful social change through economic development and reforms, political reforms, and territorial compromises. Peacebuilding concentrates on improving conditions for a country's population or an ethnic group's members. By making economic reform, more equal distribution of economic opportunities, and economic development leading priorities, governments of ethnically torn countries can end the cycle of conflict. Ongoing violence in Afghanistan and the civil war in Iraq are widely perceived as partly due to the failure of the United States to provide essential economic change and help people with basic human security needs. Paul Collier observes that the postconflict period is a good time to reform because vested interests are loosened up.[69] Diaspora organizations can play a major role in the economic recovery of their original countries by providing money, skills, and valuable connections. Political reforms, including transitions to democracy, and power-sharing arrangements can be helpful. However, equating holding elections with democracy is a fallacy that is usually counterproductive. Building democracy takes time. This is clearly demonstrated by the failure of U.S. efforts to promote democracy in Iraq by stressing holding elections. **Power-sharing arrangements** divide political power

Power-Sharing Arrangements ■
Division of political power among different ethnic groups

among different ethnic groups. However, unless periodic adjustments are made to reflect changing demographics, these arrangements tend to disintegrate and ethnic conflicts erupt. In Lebanon, for example, government positions and political power were divided between the Maronite Christians and Sunni Muslims. But the power-sharing arrangement was not changed to reflect the rapid growth of the Muslim population. The country was plunged into a brutal civil war from 1975 to 1990. Israel's invasion of Lebanon in 2006 weakened the Lebanese government and exacerbated tensions among the various ethnic and religious groups. Federalism (i.e., the sharing of power between the central government and states, provinces, or regions) helps to solve ethnic conflicts. Ethnic groups can enjoy a degree of autonomy while remaining within the existing country. Finally, **partition** (i.e., the forming of a separate and independent country from an ethnic group) is generally regarded

Partition ■ Forming of separate and independent countries between ethnic groups as a last resort. Many Kurds in Iraq and Turkey have advocated creating separate states to solve ethnic conflicts. As ethnic violence escalated in Iraq, many Shiites advocated dividing the country along ethnic lines. States are extremely reluctant to agree to partition, as America's Civil War clearly demonstrates.

SUMMARY AND REVIEW

Various periods of globalization have contributed to the cross-fertilization of cultures as well as to cultural clashes. This chapter focused on how the contemporary period of globalization is creating cultural homogenization and hybridization even as scholars and others believe that the world is divided into clashing civilizations. As we have seen throughout history, most of the violent conflicts have occurred within civilizations, within regions, and among groups within the same country. We see that culture and nationalism have often been closely intertwined. We discussed the problem of ethnocentrism as a major factor in civilizational, international, and ethnic conflicts. We challenged the dominant perspective that Western states and the Muslim world are inherently incompatible and hostile. However, the political, economic, and cultural forces of globalization heighten insecurities among states, groups, and individuals.

This chapter examined ethnic conflicts, several causes of ethnic conflicts, and some of the reasons for the decline in ethnic wars. The rising costs of ethnic conflicts, active global promotion of democracy, global concerns about human rights, and increased global efforts to find peaceful solutions to conflicts have contributed to the decline or limitation of many ethnic wars. Nevertheless, many leaders continue to manipulate ethnic differences to achieve their various objectives. Finally, we examined global and regional efforts to end conflicts. These include negotiation, peacekeeping, peacemaking, and peacebuilding.

KEY TERMS

jihad 325
hybridization 325
ethnic conflicts 325
cultural reservoir 326
material culture 326
nonmaterial culture 326
culture 326
subculture 326
ethnocentrism 326
Dhimmis 328
Pope Urban II 328
Dome of the Rock 329
Theodor Herzl 329
Balfour Declaration 329
Churchill White Paper 329
Biltmore Conference 330
containment 331
Camp David Peace Accords 331

intifada 331
Sharm el-Sheikh 332
Barbary States 333
Shah Muhammad Reza 333
Egyptian Islamic Jihad 334
mujahedeen 334
Abu Ghraib 334
tribalism 337
Kurds 337
ethnicity 338
identity 338
ethnic pluralism 338
Ibos 339
Kristallnacht 340
National Front 340
Treaty of Paris 341
Shari'a law 341
Marshall Josip Tito 341

Radovan Karadzic 341
Slobodan Milosevic 342
ethnic cleansing 342
Hutus 343
Tutsis 343
carrots and sticks 344
trade-offs 344
UN Security Council Resolution 344
peacekeeping 345
just war 345
peacemaking 345
arbitration 345
mediation 345
facilitation 345
peacebuilding 346
power-sharing arrangements 346
partition 346

DISCUSSION QUESTIONS

1. What is ethnocentrism? How has it contributed to national conflicts?
2. Can you give a short background on the Hutu/Tutsi ethnic conflict that resulted in the Rwandan genocide?
3. What are the four approaches to resolving cultural conflicts discussed in this chapter?
4. What is the difference between peacekeeping, peacemaking, and peacebuilding?

SUGGESTED READINGS

Autesserre, Severine, "The Trouble with Congo," *Foreign Affairs* 87, No. 3 (May/June 2008): 94–110.

Durch, William J., ed. *Twenty-First-Century Peace Operations.* Washington, DC: U.S. Institute of Peace Press, 2006.

Fiscbatch, Michael. *The Peace Process and Palestinian Refugee Claims.* Washington, DC: U.S. Institute of Peace Press, 2006.

Huntington, Samuel P. *The Clash of Civilizations and the Remaking of World Order.* New York: Simon and Schuster, 1996.

Kelsay, John. *Arguing the Just War in Islam.* Cambridge, MA: Harvard University Press, 2008.

Moisi, Dominique. "The Clash of Emotions," *Foreign Affairs* 86, No. 1 (January/February 2007): 8–13.

Power, Samantha. *A Problem from Hell: America and the Age of Genocide.* New York: Basic Books, 2002.

END NOTES

1. Benjamin R. Barber, *Jihad vs. McWorld* (New York: Ballantine Books, 1996), 1.
2. Samuel P. Huntington, *The Clash of Civilizations and the Remaking of World Order* (New York: Simon and Schuster, 1996).
3. Jan Nederveen Pieterse, *Globalization and Culture* (Lanham, MD: Rowman and Littlefield, 2004), 82.
4. Karen Armstrong, *A History of God: The 4,000-Year Quest of Judaism, Christianity, and Islam* (New York: Ballantine Books, 1994).
5. Richard J. Payne, *The Clash with Distant Cultures: Values, Interests, and Force in American Foreign Policy* (Albany: State University of New York Press, 1995).
6. John R. Bowen, "The Myth of Global Ethnic Conflict," *Journal of Democracy* 7, No. 4 (1996), 3.
7. Payne, *The Clash with Distant Cultures*, 5.
8. Eugene V. Rostow, *Toward Managed Peace* (New Haven, CT: Yale University Press, 1993), 104.
9. Chris Jenks, *Culture* (New York: Routledge, 1993), 8.
10. Clifford Geertz, *The Interpretation of Cultures* (New York: Basic Books, 1973), 89.
11. Jenks, *Culture*, 10.
12. Anthony Giddens, ed., *Emile Durkheim: Selected Writings* (Cambridge: Cambridge University Press, 1972), 5.
13. Ken Booth, *Strategy and Ethnocentrism* (New York: Pergamon Press, 1990), 343.
14. Payne, *The Clash with Distant Cultures*, 36–37; and Alexander B. Downes, *Targeting Civilians in War* (Ithaca, NY: Cornell University Press, 2008).
15. Rafael Moses, "Empathy and Dis-empathy in Political Conflict," *Political Psychology* 6, No. 1 (March 1985), 135.

16. Albert Bandura, "Selective Activism and Disengagement of Moral Control," *Journal of Social Issues* 46, No. 1 (1990), 1.

17. Payne, *The Clash with Distant Cultures*, 37.

18. Huntington, *The Clash of Civilizations*, 25.

19. Huntington, *The Clash of Civilizations*, 25.

20. Huntington, *The Clash of Civilizations*, 25–27.

21. Fouad Ajami, "The Summoning," *Foreign Affairs* 72, No. 4 (September/October 1993), 2.

22. Stanley Hoffmann, "Clash of Globalizations," *Foreign Affairs* 81, No. 4 (July/August 2002), 105.

23. "Invading Turks' Music Marched West," *New York Times*, 10 March 2002, A6.

24. Susanne Rudolph, "Introduction," in *Transnational Religion and Fading States*, eds. Susanne Rudolph and James Piscatori (Boulder, CO: Westview Press, 1997), 1.

25. Armstrong, *A History of God*, 197.

26. Armstrong, *A History of God*, 197.

27. Rosemary Hollis, "Great Britain," in *Powers in the Middle East*, ed. Bernard Reich (New York: Praeger, 1987), 186.

28. Dan Tschirgi, *The American Search for Mideast Peace* (New York: Praeger, 1989), 2.

29. Richard J. Payne, *The West European Allies, the Third World, and U.S. Foreign Policy* (New York: Greenwood Press, 1991), 76.

30. Payne, *The West European Allies*, 84; and Oliver Roy, *The Politics of Chaos in the Middle East* (New York: Columbia University Press, 2008).

31. Ken Ringle, "A Thousand Years of Bad Memories," *Washington Post National Weekly Edition*, 29 October–4 November 2001, 8; and Michael Scheuer, *Marching Toward Hell: America and Islam After Iraq* (New York: Free Press, 2008).

32. Fouad Ajami, "The Falseness of Anti-Americanism," *Foreign Policy* 138 (September/October 2003), 53.

33. Richard J. Payne and Jamal R. Nassar, *Politics and Culture in the Developing World* (New York: Longman, 2003), 35.

34. Neil MacFarquhar, "Islamic Jihad, Forged in Egypt, Is Seen as bin Laden's Backbone," *New York Times*, 4 October 2001, B4.

35. Barry Rubin, "The Real Roots of Arab Anti-Americanism," *Foreign Affairs* 81, No. 6 (November/December 2002), 73.

36. "Findings on Abu Ghraib: Sadism, Deviant Behavior, and a Failure of Leadership," *New York Times*, 25 August 2004, A10; and "Excerpts from President Obama's Speech in Cairo," *New York Times*, 5 June 2009, A8.

37. Linda Colley, *Britons: Forging the Nation 1707–1837* (New Haven, CT: Yale University Press, 1992), 5.

38. Michael W. Suleiman, *The Arabs in the Mind of America* (Brattleboro, VT: Amana Books, 1988), 147.

39. Payne, *The Clash with Distant Cultures*, 94–95.

40. Minxim Pei, "The Paradoxes of American Nationalism," *Foreign Policy* 136 (May/June 2003), 31.

41. Fareed Zakaria, "Hating America," *Foreign Policy* 144 (September/October 2004), 48.

42. Robert Jervis, "The Compulsive Empire," *Foreign Policy* 137 (July/August 2003), 85.

43. Parag Khanna, "The Metrosexual Superpower," *Foreign Policy* 143 (July/August 2004), 66.

44. Charles A. Kupchan, "Introduction," in *Nationalism and Nationalities in the New Europe*, ed. Charles A. Kupchan (Ithaca, NY: Cornell University Press, 1995), 1.

45. Ted Robert Gurr, "Ethnic Warfare on the Wane," *Foreign Affairs* 79, No. 3 (May/June 2000), 59.

46. Donald Rothchild, *Managing Ethnic Conflict in Africa* (Washington, DC: Brookings Institution Press, 1997), 4.

47. Virginia R. Dominguez, *White by Definition* (New Brunswick, NJ: Rutgers University Press, 1986), 266.

48. Milton J. Esman, *Ethnic Politics* (Ithaca, NY: Cornell University Press, 1994), 3.

49. Paul Collier, "The Market for Civil War," *Foreign Policy* 136 (May/June 2003), 40.

50. Robin Wright, "Ethnic Conflict: An Overview," in *National and Ethnic Conflict*, ed. Charles P. Cozic (San Diego, CA: Greenhaven Press, 1994), 158.

51. Connie Peck, *Sustainable Peace* (Lanham, MD: Rowman and Littlefield, 1998), 16.

52. Mark Strauss, "Antiglobalism's Jewish Problem," *Foreign Policy* 139 (November/December 2003), 58.

53. Craig S. Smith, "Thwarted in Germany, Neo-Nazis Take Fascism to France," *New York Times*, 13 August 2004, A3.

54. Clifford Krauss, "Quebec Result: Solidly for Canada," *New York Times*, 16 April 2003, A8.

55. Josef Joffe, "The New Europe: Yesterday's Ghosts," *Foreign Affairs* 72, No. 1 (1993), 31.

56. James O. Jackson, "A Lesson in Shame," *Time*, 2 August 1993, 38.

57. Roy Gutman, *A Witness to Genocide* (New York: Macmillan, 1993).

58. Yahya Sadowski, "Ethnic Conflict," *Foreign Policy* 111 (Summer 1998), 13.

59. Alain Destexhe, *Rwanda and Genocide in the Twentieth Century* (New York: New York University Press, 1995), 40; and Michael Ignatieff, *The Warrior's Honor: Ethnic War and the Modern Conscience* (New York: Metropolitan Books, 1997), 62.

60. Destexhe, *Rwanda and Genocide*, 31.

61. Marc Lacey, "A Decade After Massacres, Rwanda Outlaws Ethnicity," *New York Times*, 9 April 2004, A3.

62. Bruce M. Russett, *Controlling the Sword: Democratic Governance of National Security* (Cambridge, MA: Harvard University Press, 1990), 121–124.

63. Roger Fisher and William Ury, *Getting to Yes: Negotiating Agreement Without Giving In* (New York: Penguin, 1983).

64. Harold H. Saunders, "An Historic Challenge to Rethink How Nations Relate," in *Psychodynamics of International Relationships*, eds. Vamik Volkan et al. (Lexington, MA: Lexington Books, 1990), 15.

65. George A. Lopez and Michael S. Stohl, "Diplomacy, Bargaining, and Coercion," in *International Relations*, eds. George A. Lopez and Michael S. Stohl (Washington, DC: Congressional Quarterly Press, 1989), 16.

66. Martin Patchen, *Resolving Disputes Between Nations* (Durham, NC: Duke University Press, 1988), 107.

67. Raymond C. Taras and Rajat Ganguly, *Understanding Ethnic Conflicts* (New York: Longman, 2002), 95.

68. Taras and Ganguly, *Understanding Ethnic Conflicts*, 96.

69. Collier, "The Market for Civil War," 44.

INDEX